THE

PRACTICAL DRAUGHTSMAN'S

BOOK OF INDUSTRIAL DESIGN,

AND

MACHINIST'S AND ENGINEER'S DRAWING COMPANION:

FORMING A COMPLETE COURSE OF

Mechanical, Engineering, and Architectural Drawing.

TRANSLATED FROM THE FRENCH OF

M. ARMENGAUD, THE ELDER,

PROFESSOR OF DESIGN IN THE CONSERVATOIRE OF ARTS AND INDUSTRY, PARIS,

AND

MM. ARMENGAUD, THE YOUNGER, AND AMOUROUX,

CIVIL ENGINEERS.

REWRITTEN AND ARRANGED, WITH ADDITIONAL MATTER AND PLATES, SELECTIONS FROM AND EXAMPLES OF
THE MOST USEFUL AND GENERALLY EMPLOYED MECHANISM OF THE DAY.

BY

WILLIAM JOHNSON, Assoc. Inst., C.E

EDITOR OF "THE PRACTICAL MECHANIC'S JOURNAL."

PHILADELPHIA:
HENRY CAREY BAIRD,
INDUSTRIAL PUBLISHER,
No. 406 WALNUT STREET.
1870.

PREFACE.

INDUSTRIAL DESIGN is destined to become a universal language ; for in our material age of rapid transition from abstract, to applied, Science—in the midst of our extraordinary tendency towards the perfection of the means of conversion, or manufacturing production—it must soon pass current in every land. It is, indeed, the medium between thought and Execution : by it alone can the genius of Conception convey its meaning to the skill which executes—or suggestive ideas become living, practical realities. It is emphatically the exponent of the projected works of the Practical Engineer, the Manufacturer, and the Builder ; and by its aid only, is the Inventor enabled to express his views before he attempts to realise them.

Boyle has remarked, in his early times, that the excellence of manufactures, and the facility of labour, would be much promoted, if the various expedients and contrivances which lie concealed in private hands, were, by reciprocal communications, made generally known ; for there are few operations that are not performed by one or other with some peculiar advantages, which, though singly of little importance, would, by conjunction and concurrence, open new inlets to knowledge, and give new powers to diligence ; and Herschel, in our own days, has told us that, next to the establishment of scientific institutions, nothing has exercised so powerful an influence on the progress of modern science, as the publication of scientific periodicals, in directing the course of general observation, and holding conspicuously forward models for emulative imitation. Yet, without the aid of Drawing, how can this desired reciprocity of information be attained ; or how would our scientific literature fulfil its purpose, if denied the benefit of the graphic labours of the Draughtsman ? Our verbal interchanges would, in truth, be vague and barren details, and our printed knowledge, misty and unconvincing.

Independently of its utility as a precise art, Drawing really interests the student, whilst it instructs him. It instils sound and accurate ideas into his mind, and develops his intellectual powers in compelling him to observe—as if the objects he delineates were really before his eyes. Besides, he always does that the best, which he best understands ; and in this respect, the art of Drawing operates as a powerful stimulant to progress, in continually yielding new and varied results.

A chance sketch—a rude combination of carelessly considered pencillings—the jotted memoranda of a contemplative brain, prying into the corners of contrivance—often form the nucleus of a splendid invention. An idea thus preserved at the moment of its birth, may become of incalculable value, when rescued from the desultory train of fancy, and treated as the sober offspring of reason. In nice gradations, it receives the refining touches of leisure—becoming, first, a finished sketch,—then a drawing by the practised hand—so that many minds may find easy access to it, for their joint counsellings to improvement—until it finally emerges from the workshop, as a practical triumph of mechanical invention—an illustrious example of a happy combination opportunely noticed.   Yet many ingenious men are barely able even to start this train of production, purely from inability to adequately delineate their early conceptions, or furnish that transcript of their minds which might make their thoughts immortal.   If the present Treatise succeeds only in mitigating this evil, it will not entirely fail in its object ; for it will at least add a few steps to the ladder of Intelligence, and form a few more approaches to the goal of Perfection—

> "Thou hast not lost an hour whereof there is a record ;
> A written thought at midnight will redeem the livelong day."

The study of Industrial Design is really as indispensably necessary as the ordinary rudiments of learning. It ought to form an essential feature in the education of young persons for whatever profession or employment they may intend to select, as the great business of their lives ; for without a knowledge of Drawing, no scientific work, whether relating to Mechanics, Agriculture, or Manufactures, can be advantageously studied. This is now beginning to receive acknowledgment, and the routines of study in all varieties of educational establishments are being benefited by the introduction of the art.

The special mission of the *Practical Draughtsman's Book of Industrial Design* may almost be gathered from its title-page.   It is intended to furnish gradually developed lessons in Geometrical Drawing, applied directly to the various branches of the Industrial Arts : comprehending Linear Design proper ; Isometrical Perspective, or the study of Projections ; the Drawing of Toothed Wheels and Eccentrics ; with Shadowing and Colouring ; Oblique Projections ; and the study of parallel and exact Perspective ; each division being accompanied by special applications to the extensive ranges of Mechanics, Architecture, Foundry-Works, Carpentry, Joinery, Metal Manufactures generally, Hydraulics, the construction of Steam Engines, and Mill-Work.   In its compilation, the feeble attraction generally offered to students in elementary form has been carefully considered ; and after every geometrical problem, a practical example of its application has been added, to facilitate its comprehension and increase its value.

The work is comprised within nine divisions, appropriated to the different branches of Industrial Design. The first, which concerns Linear Drawing only, treats particularly of straight lines—of circles—and their application to the delineation of Mouldings, Ceilings, Floors, Balconies, Cuspids, Rosettes, and other forms, to accustom the student to the proper use of the Square, Angle, and Compasses.   In addition to this, it affords examples of different methods of constructing plain curves, such as are of frequent occurrence in the arts, and in mechanical combinations—as the ellipse, the oval, the parabola, and the volute ; and certain figures, accurately shaded, to represent reliefs, exemplifying cases where these curves are employed.

The second division illustrates the geometrical representation of objects, or the study of projections. This forms the basis of all descriptive geometry, practically considered.   It shows that a single figure is insufficient for the determination of all the outlines and dimensions of a given subject ; but that two projections, and one or more sections, are always necessary for the due interpretation of internal forms.

The third division points out the conventional colours and tints for the expression of the sectional details of objects, according to their nature ; furnishing, at the same time, simple and easy examples, which may at once interest the pupil, and familiarise him with the use of the pencil.

In the fourth division are given drawings of various essentially valuable curves, as Helices, and different kinds of Spirals and Serpentines, with the intersection of surfaces and their development, and workshop applications to Pipes, Coppers, Boilers, and Cocks.   This study is obviously of importance in many professions, and clearly so to Ironplate-workers, as Shipbuilders and Boiler-makers, Tinmen and Coppersmiths.

The fifth division is devoted to special classes of curves relating to the teeth of Spur Wheels, Screws and Racks, and the details of the construction of their patterns. The latter branch is of peculiar importance here, inasmuch as it has not been fully treated of in any existing work, whilst it is of the highest value to the pattern maker, who ought to be acquainted with the most workmanlike plan of cutting his wood, and effecting the necessary junctions, as well as the general course to take in executing his pattern, for facilitating the moulding process.

The sixth division is, in effect, a continuation of the fifth. It comprises the theory and practice of drawing Bevil, Conical, or Angular Wheels, with details of the construction of the wood patterns, and notices of peculiar forms of some gearing, as well as the eccentrics employed in mechanical construction.

The seventh division comprises the studies of the shading and shadows of the principal solids—Prisms, Pyramids, Cylinders, and Spheres, together with their applications to mechanical and architectural details, as screws, spur and bevil wheels, coppers and furnaces, columns and entablatures. These studies naturally lead to that of colours—single, as those of China Ink or Sepia, or varied ; also of graduated shades produced by successive flat tints, according to one method, or by the softening manipulation of the brush, according to another.

The pupil may now undertake designs of greater complexity, leading him in the eighth division to various figures representing combined or general elevations, as well as sections and details of various complete machines, to which are added some geometrical drawings, explanatory of the action of the moving parts of machinery.

The ninth completes the study of Industrial Design, with oblique projections and parallels, and exact perspective. In the study of exact perspective, special applications of its rules are made to architecture and machinery by the aid of a perspective elevation of a corn mill supported on columns, and fitted up with all the necessary gearing. A series of Plates, marked A, B, &c., are also interspersed throughout the work, as examples of finished drawings of machinery. The Letterpress relating to these Plates, together with an illustrated chapter on Drawing Instruments, will form an appropriate Appendix to the Volume. The general explanatory text embraces not only a description of the objects and their movements, but also tables and practical rules; more particularly those relating to the dimensions of the principal details of machinery, as facilitating actual construction.

Such is the scope, and such are the objects, of the PRACTICAL DRAUGHTSMAN'S BOOK OF INDUSTRIAL DESIGN.

Such is the course now submitted to the consideration of all who are in the slightest degree connected with the Constructive Arts. It aims at the dissemination of those fundamental teachings which are so essentially necessary at every stage in the application of the forces lent to us by Nature for the conversion of her materials. For " man can only act upon Nature, and appropriate her forces to his use, by comprehending her laws, and knowing those forces in relative value and measure." All art is the true application of knowledge to a practical end. We have outlived the times of random construction, and the mere heaping together of natural substances. We must now design carefully and delineate accurately before we proceed to execute—and the quick pencil of the ready draughtsman is a proud possession for our purpose. Let the youthful student think on this ; and whether in the workshop of the Engineer, the studio of the Architect, or the factory of the Manufacturer, let him remember that, to spare the blighting of his fondest hopes, and the marring of his fairest prospects—to achieve, indeed, his higher aspirations, and verify his loftier thoughts, which point to eminence—he must give his days and nights, his business and his leisure, to the study of

Industrial Design.

ABBREVIATIONS AND CONVENTIONAL SIGNS.

In order to simplify the language or expression of arithmetical and geometrical operations, the following conventional signs are used:—

The sign $+$ signifies *plus* or *more*, and is placed between two or more terms to indicate addition.

EXAMPLE: $4 + 3$, is 4 *plus* 3, that is, 4 added to 3, or 7.

The sign $-$ signifies *minus* or *less*, and indicates subtraction.

Ex.: $4 - 3$, is 4 minus 3, that is, 3 taken from 4, or 1.

The sign $\times$ signifies *multiplied by*, and, placed between two terms, indicates multiplication.

Ex.: 5×3, is 5 multiplied by 3, or 15.

When quantities are expressed by letters, the sign may be suppressed. Thus we write, indifferently—

$$a \times b, \text{ or } ab.$$

The sign $:$ or (as it is more commonly used) $\div$, signifies *divided by*, and, placed between two quantities, indicates division.

Ex.: $12 : 4$, or $12 \div 4$, or $\dfrac{12}{4}$, is 12 divided by 4.

The sign $=$ signifies *equals* or *equal to*, and is placed between two expressions to indicate their equality.

Ex.: $6 + 2 = 8$, meaning, that 6 plus 2 is equal to 8.

The union of these signs, $\because :: :$ indicates geometrical proportion.

Ex.: $2 : 3 :: 4 : 6$, meaning, that 2 is to 3 as 4 is to 6.

The sign $\sqrt{}$ indicates the extraction of a root; as,

$$\sqrt{9} = 3, \text{ meaning, that the square root of 9 is equal to 3.}$$

The interposition of a numeral between the opening of this sign, $\sqrt{}$, indicates the degree of the root. Thus—

$$\sqrt[3]{27} = 3, \text{ expresses that the cube root of 27 is equal to 3.}$$

The signs $\angle$ and $\diagup$ indicate respectively, *smaller than* and *greater than*.

Ex.: $3 \angle 4$, $= 3$ smaller than 4, and, reciprocally, $4 \diagup 3$, $= 4$ greater than 3.

Fig. signifies figure; and pl., plate.

FRENCH AND ENGLISH LINEAR MEASURES COMPARED.

French.		English		English.		French.
	1 Millimètre	=	·0394 Inches.		1 Inch.	= { 25·400 Millimètres. 2·540 Centimètres.
10 Millimètres	= 1 Centimètre	=	·3937 "			
10 Centimètres	= 1 Decimètre	=	3·9371 "	12 Inches	= 1 Foot	= 3·048 Decimètres.
10 Decimètres	= 1 Mètre	= { 3·2809 Feet. 1·0936 Yards.	3 Feet	= 1 Yard	= 9·144
10 Mètres	= 1 Decamètre	=	1·9884 Poles or Rods.	5½ Yards	= 1 Pole or Rod	= 5·029 Mètres.
10 Decamètres	= 1 Hectomètre	=	19·8844 "	40 Poles	= 1 Furlong	12 Decamètres.
10 Hectomètres	= 1 Kilomètre	= { 49·7109 Furlongs. 6·2139 Miles.	8 Furlongs } 1760 Yards }	= 1 Mile	= 1·610 Hectomètres
10 Kilomètres	= 1 Myriamètre	=	62·1386 "			

CONTENTS.

————◆◆◆————

INDEX TO THE TABLES.

PRACTICAL DRAUGHTSMAN'S

BOOK OF INDUSTRIAL DESIGN.

CHAPTER I.
LINEAR DRAWING.

In Drawing, as applied to Mechanics and Architecture, and to the Industrial Arts in general, it is necessary to consider not only the mere representation of objects, but also the relative principles of action of their several parts.

The principles and methods concerned in that division of the art which is termed *linear drawing*, and which is the foundation of all drawing, whether industrial or artistic, are, for the most part, derived from elementary geometry. This branch of drawing has for its object the accurate delineation of surfaces and the construction of figures, obtainable by the studied combinations of lines; and, with a view to render it easier, and at the same time more attractive and intelligible to the student, the present work has been arranged to treat successively of definitions, principles, and problems, and of the various applications of which these are capable.

Many treatises on linear drawing already exist, but all these, considered apart from their several objects, seem to fail in the due development of the subject, and do not manifest that general advancement and increased precision in details which are called for at the present day. It has therefore been deemed necessary to begin with these rudimentary exercises, and such exemplifications have been selected as, with their varieties, are most frequently met with in practice.

Many of the methods of construction will be necessarily such as are already known; but they will be limited to those which are absolutely indispensable to the development of the principles and their applications.

DEFINITIONS.
OF LINES AND SURFACES.
PLATE I.

In Geometry, *space* is described in the terms of its three dimensions—length, breadth or thickness, and height or depth.

The combination of two of these dimensions represents *surface*, and one dimension takes the form of a *line*.

Lines.—There are several kinds of lines used in drawing— *straight* or *right lines*, *curved lines*, and *irregular* or *broken lines*.

Right lines are *vertical*, *horizontal*, or *inclined*. Curved lines are *circular*, *elliptic*, *parabolic*, &c.

Surfaces.—Surfaces, which are always bounded by lines, are *plane*, *concave*, or *convex*. A surface is plane when a straight-edge is in contact in every point, in whatever position it is applied to it. If the surface is hollow so that the straight-edge only touches at each extremity, it is called concave; and if it swells out so that the straight-edge only touches in one point, it is called convex.

Vertical lines.—By a vertical line is meant one in the position which is assumed by a thread freely suspended from its upper extremity, and having a weight attached at the other; such is the line A B represented in fig. Ⓐ. This line is always straight, and the shortest that can be drawn between its extreme points.

Plumb-line.—The instrument indicated in fig. Ⓐ is called a plumb-line. It is much employed in building and the erection of machinery, as a guide to the construction of vertical lines and surfaces.

Horizontal line.—When a liquid is at rest in an open vessel, its upper surface forms a horizontal plane, and all lines drawn upon such surface are called horizontal lines.

Levels.—It is on this principle that what are called fluid levels are constructed. One description of fluid level consists of two upright glass tubes, connected by a pipe communicating with the bottom of each. When the instrument is partly filled with water, the water will stand at the same height in both tubes, and thereby indicate the true level. Another form, and one more generally used, denominated a spirit level—spirit being usually employed— consists of a glass tube (fig. Ⓑ) enclosed in a metal case, *a*, attached by two supports, *b*, to a plate, *c*. The tube is almost filled with liquid, and the bubble of air, *d*, which remains, is always exactly in the centre of the tube when any surface, C D, on which the instrument is placed, is perfectly level.

Masons, carpenters, joiners, and other mechanics, are in the habit of using the instrument represented in fig. Ⓒ, consisting simply of a plumb line attached to the point of junction of the two inclined side pieces, *a b*, *b c*, of equal length, and connected near their free ends by the cross-piece, A B, which has a mark at its centre. When the plumb line coincides with this mark, the object, c D, on which the instrument is placed, is exactly horizontal.

Perpendiculars.—If the vertical line, A B, fig. 1, be placed on the horizontal line, c D, the two lines will be perpendicular to, and form right angles with, each other. If now we suppose these lines to be turned round on the point of intersection as a centre, always preserving the same relative position, they will in every position be perpendicular to, and at right angles with, each other. Thus the line, I O, fig. 5, is at right angles to the line, E F, although neither of them is horizontal or vertical.

Broken lines.—It is usual to call those lines broken, which consist of a series of right lines lying in different directions—such as the lines B, A, E, H, F, N, fig. 14.

Circular lines—Circumference.—The continuous line, E F G H, fig. 5, drawn with one of the points of a pair of compasses—of which the other is fixed—is called the circumference : it is evidently equally distant at all points from the fixed *centre*, o.

Radius.—The extent of opening of the compasses, or the distance between the two points, o, F, is called a radius, and consequently all lines, as O E, O F, O G, drawn from the centre to the circumference are equal radii.

Diameter.—Any right line, L H, passing through the centre o, and limited each way by the circumference, is a *diameter*. The diameter is therefore double the length of the radius.

Circle.—The space contained within the circumference is a *plane surface*, and is called a circle : any part of the circumference, E I F, or F L G, is called an *arc*.

Chords.—Right lines, E F, F G, connecting the extremities of arcs, are *chords ;* these lines extended beyond the circumference become *secants*.

Tangent.—A right line, A B, fig. 4, which touches the circumference in a single point, is a *tangent.* Tangents are always at right angles to the radius which meets them at the point of contact, B.

Sector.—Any portion, as B O H C, fig. 4, of the surface of a circle, comprised within two radii and the arc which connects their outer extremities, is called a *sector*.

Segment.—A segment is any portion, as E F I, fig. 5, of the surface of a circle, comprised within an arc and the chord which subtends it.

Right, continuous, and broken lines, are drawn by the aid of the square and angle ; circular lines are delineated with compasses.

Angles.—We have already seen that, when right lines are perpendicular to each other, they form right angles at their intersections : when, however, they cross each other without being perpendicular, they form *acute* or *obtuse* angles. An acute angle is one which is less than a right angle, as F C D, fig. 2 ; and an *obtuse* angle is greater than a right angle, as G C D. By *angle* is generally understood the extent of opening of two intersecting lines, the point of intersection being called the *apex*. An angle is *rectilinear* when formed by two right lines, *mixtilinear* when formed by a right and a curved line, and *curvilinear* when formed by two curved lines.

Measurement of angles.—If, with the apex of an angle as the centre, we describe an arc, the angle may be measured by the portion of the arc cut off by the lines forming the angle, with reference to the whole circle ; and it is customary to divide an entire circle

into 360 or 400* equal parts, called degrees, and instruments called protractors, and represented in figs. D, E, are constructed, whereby the number of degrees contained in any angle are ascertainable. The first, fig. D, which is to be found in almost every set of mathematical instruments, being that most in use, consists of a semicircle divided into 180 or 200 parts. In making use of it, its centre, b, must be placed on the apex of the angle in such a manner that its diameter coincides with one side, a b, of the angle, when the measure of the angle will be indicated by the division intersected by the other side of the angle. Thus the angle, a b c, is one of 50 degrees (abbreviated 50°), and it will always have this measure, whatever be the length of radius of the arc, and consequently whatever be the length of the sides, for the measuring arc must always be the same fraction of the entire circumference. The degree is divided into 60 minutes, and the minute (or 1') into 60 seconds (or 60″) ; or when the circle is divided into 400 degrees, each degree is subdivided into 100 minutes, and each minute into 100 seconds, and so on.

The other protractor, fig. E, of modern invention, possesses the advantage of not requiring access to the apex of the angle. It consists of a complete circle, each half being divided on the inner side into 180 degrees, but externally the instrument is square. It is placed against a rule, R, made to coincide with one side, c e, of the angle—the other side, d c, crosses two opposite divisions on the circle indicating the number of degrees contained in the angle. It will be seen that the angle, d c e, is one of 50°.

Oblique lines.—Right lines, which do not form right angles with those they intersect, are said to be oblique, or inclined to each other. The right lines, G C and F G, fig. 2, are oblique, as referred to the vertical line, K C, or the horizontal line, C J.

Parallel lines.—Two right lines are said to be parallel with each other when they are an equal distance apart throughout their length ; the lines, I K, A B, and L M, fig. 1, are parallel.

Triangles.—The space enclosed by three intersecting lines is called a triangle ; when the three sides, as D E, E F, and F D, fig. 12, are equal, the triangle is *equilateral* ; if two sides only, as G H, and G I, fig. 9, are equal, it is *isosceles ;* and it is *scalene*, or irregular, when the three sides are unequal, as in fig. 6. The triangle is called *rectangular* when any two of its sides, as D L and L K, fig. 10, form a right angle ; and in this case the side, as D K, opposite to, or subtending the right angle, is called the *hypothenuse*. An instrument constantly used in drawing is the set-square, more commonly called *angle* ; it is in the shape of a rectangular triangle, and is constructed of various proportions ; having an angle of 45°, as fig. G, of 60° as fig. H, or as fig. I, having one of the sides which form the right angle at least double the length of the other.

Polygon.—A space enclosed by several lines lying at any angle to each other is a *polygon*. It is plane when all the lines lie in one and the same plane ; and its outline is called its *perimeter*. A polygon is *triangular, quadrangular, pentagonal, hexagonal, heptagonal, octagonal, &c.*, according as it has 3, 4, 5, 6, 7, or 8 sides. A square is a *quadrilateral*, the sides of which, as A B, B C, C D,

---

* As another step towards a decimal notation, it was proposed, in 1790, to divide the circle into 400 parts. The suggestion was again revived in 1840, and actually adopted by several distinguished individuals. The facility afforded to calculators by the many submultiples possessed by the number 360, however, accounts for the still very general use of the ancient system of division.

and D A, fig. 10, are equal and perpendicular to one another, the angles consequently also being equal, and all right angles.

A *rectangle* is a quadrilateral, having two sides equal, as A B and F N, fig. 14, and perpendicular to two other equal and parallel sides, as A F and B N.

A *parallelogram* is a quadrilateral, of which the opposite sides and angles are equal; and a *lozenge* is a quadrilateral with all the sides, but only the opposite angles equal.

A *trapezium* is a quadrilateral, of which only two sides, as H I and M L, fig. 9, are parallel.

Polygons are *regular* when all their sides and angles are equal, and are otherwise *irregular*. All regular polygons are capable of being inscribed in a circle, hence the great facility with which they may be accurately delineated.

OBSERVATIONS.

We have deemed it necessary to give these definitions, in order to make our descriptions more readily understood, and we propose now to proceed to the solution of those elementary problems with which, from their frequent occurrence in practice, it is important that the student should be well acquainted. The first step, however, to be taken, is to prepare the paper to be drawn upon, so that it shall be well stretched on the board. To effect this, it must be slightly but equally moistened on one side with a sponge; the moistened side is then applied to the board, and the edges of the paper glued or pasted down, commencing with the middle of the sides, and then securing the corners. When the sheet is dry, it will be uniformly stretched, and the drawing may be executed, being first made in faint pencil lines, and afterwards redelineated with ink by means of a drawing pen. To distinguish those lines which may be termed working lines, as being but guides to the formation of the actual outlines of the drawing, we have in the plates represented the former by dotted lines, and the latter by full continuous lines.

PROBLEMS.

1. *To erect a perpendicular on the centre of a given right line, as* C D, *fig.* 1.—From the extreme points, C, D, as centres, and with a radius greater than half the line, describe the arcs which cross each other in A and B, on either side of the line to be divided. A line, A B, joining these points, will be a perpendicular bisecting the line, C D, in G. Proceeding in the same manner with each half of the line, C G and G D, we obtain the perpendiculars, I K and L M, dividing the line into four equal parts, and we can thus divide any given right line into 2, 4, 8, 16, &c., equal parts. This problem is of constant application in drawing. For instance, in order to obtain the principal lines, V X and Y Z, which divide the sheet of paper into four equal parts; with the points, r s t u, taken as near the edge of the paper as possible, as centres, we describe the arcs which intersect each other in P and Q; and with these last as centres, describe also the arcs which cut each other in y, z. The right lines, V X and Y Z, drawn through the points, P, Q, and y, z, respectively, are perpendicular to each other, and serve as guides in drawing on different parts of the paper, and are merely pencilled in, to be afterwards effaced.

2. *To erect a perpendicular on any given point, as* H, *in the line* C D,

fig. 1—Mark off on the line, on each side of the point, two equal distances, as C H and H G, and with the centres C and G describe the arcs crossing at I or K, and the line drawn through them, and through the point H, will be the line required.

3. *To let fall a perpendicular from a point, as* L, *apart from the right line,* C D.—With the point L, as a centre, describe an arc which cuts the line, C D, in G and D, and with these points as centres, describe two other arcs cutting each other in M, and the right line joining L and M will be the perpendicular required. In practice, such perpendiculars are generally drawn by means of an angle and a *square*, or T-square, such as fig. F.

4. *To draw parallels to any given lines, as* V X *and* Y Z.—For regularity's sake, it is well to construct a rectangle, such as R S T U, on the paper that is being drawn upon, which is thus done:—From the points V and X, describe the arcs R, S, T, U, and applying the rule tangentially to the two first, draw the line R S, and then in the same manner the line T U. The lines R T and S U are also obtained in a similar manner. In general, however, such parallels are more quickly drawn by means of the T-square, which may be slid along the edge of the board. Short parallel lines may be drawn with the angle and rule.

5. *To divide a given right line, as* A B, *fig.* 3, *into several equal parts.*—We have already shown how a line may be divided into 2 or 4 equal parts. We shall now give a simple method for dividing a line into *any* number of equal parts. From the point A, draw the line A C, making any convenient angle with A B; mark off on A C as many equal distances as it is wished to divide the line A B into; in the present instance seven. Join C B, and from the several points marked off on A C, draw parallels to C B, using the rule and angle for this purpose. The line A B will be divided into seven equal parts by the intersections of the parallel lines just drawn. Any line making any angle with A B, as A J, may be employed instead of A C, with exactly the same results. This is a very useful problem, especially applicable to the formation of scales for the reduction of drawings.

6. A *scale* is a straight line divided and subdivided into feet, inches, and parts of inches, according to English measures; or into mètres, décimètres, centimètres, and millimètres, according to French measures; these divisions bearing the same proportion to each other, as in the system of measurement from which they are derived. The object of the scale is to indicate the proportion the drawing bears to the object represented.

7. *To construct a scale.*—The French scale being the one adopted in this work, it will be necessary to state that the *mètre* (=39·371 English inches) is the unit of measurement, and is divided into 10 decimètres, 100 centimètres, and 1000 millimètres. If it is intended to execute the drawing to a scale of $\frac{1}{4}$ or $\frac{1}{5}$; the mètre is divided by 4 or 5, one of the divisions being the length of a mètre on the reduced scale. A line of this length is drawn on the paper, and is divided into reduced decimètres, &c., just as the mètre is itself. Fig. 7 is part of a scale for reducing a drawing to one-fifth. In this scale an extra division is placed to the left of zero, which is subdivided, to facilitate the obtainment of any required measure. For example, if we want a length corresponding to 32 centimètres, we place one point of the compasses on the division marked 3 to the right of zero, and the other on the second

division to the left, and the length comprised between these points will be 3 decimètres, 2 centimètres, = 32 centimètres.

The *diagonal scale.*—When very minute measurements are required, greater precision is obtained with a diagonal scale, such as fig. 8. It is thus constructed:—Having drawn a line and divided it, as in fig. 7, draw, parallel and equal to it, ten other lines, as *c, d, e, f,* &c., at equal distances apart, crossing these with perpendiculars at the decimètre divisions. From one of the smaller divisions to the left of zero, draw the diagonal, *b i,* and draw parallels to it from the remaining centimètre divisions, 1′, 2′, 3′, &c. From the division corresponding to 1 decimètre, draw a diagonal to the point on the extreme parallel, *i* 4, cut by the zero perpendicular, and draw also the parallel diagonals, 1—2, 2—3, and 3—4. It will be evident, that as in the space of the ten horizontal lines, the diagonal extends one division to the left, it will intersect each intermediate line, as the 1st, 2d, 3d, &c., at the distance of 1, 2, 3, &c., tenths of such division, in the same direction, so that the diagonal line, 2′, will cut the 5th line at a point $2\frac{5}{10}$ of a division distant from zero. Thus, one point of the compasses being placed on the point *l*, and the other on the intersection of the same horizontal line with the perpendicular of the decimètre division 3, the measure comprised between them will be 3 decimètres, 2 centimètres, and $\frac{5}{10}$, or 5 millimètres = 325 millimètres.

8. *To divide a given angle, as* F C D, *fig.* 2, *into two equal angles.*—With the apex, c, as a centre, describe the arc, H I, and with the two points of intersection, H, I, as centres, describe the arcs cutting each other in J; join J C, and the right line, J C, will divide the angle, F C D, into two equal angles, H C J and J C I. These may be subdivided in the same manner, as shown in the figure. An angle may also be divided by means of either of the protractors, D, E.

9. *To draw a tangent to a given circle,* O B D H, *fig.* 4.—If it is required to draw the tangent through a given point, as D, in the circle, a radius, C D, must be drawn meeting the point, and be produced beyond it, say to E. Then, by the method already given, draw a line, F G, perpendicular to C E, cutting it in D, and it will be the tangent required. If, however, it is required to draw the tangent through a given point, as A, outside the circle, a straight line must be drawn joining the point, A, and the centre, c, of the circle. After bisecting this line in the point, O, with this point as a centre, describe a circle passing through A and C, and cutting the given circle in B and H; right lines joining A B and A H will both be tangents to the given circle, and the radii C B and C H will be perpendiculars to A B and A H respectively.

10. *To find the centre of a given circle, or that with which a given arc, as* E F G, *fig.* 5, *is drawn.*—With any three points, E, F, G, as centres, describe arcs of equal circles, cutting each other, and through the points of intersection draw right lines, I O and L O; C, the point of intersection of these two lines, is the required **centre.**

11. *To describe a circle through any three points not in a right line.*—Since only one circle can pass through the same three points, and since any circle may be described when the centre is found and a point in the circumference given—this problem is solved in exactly the same manner as the preceding.

12. *To inscribe a circle in a given triangle, as* A B C, *fig.* 6.—

A circle is said to be *inscribed* in a figure, when all the sides of the latter are tangents to it. Bisect any two of the angles by right lines, as A O, B O, or C O; and from the point of intersection, O, let fall perpendiculars to the sides, as O E, O F, and O G. These perpendiculars will be equal, and radii of the required circle, O being the centre.

13. *To divide a triangle, as* G K I, *fig.* 9, *into two equal parts.*—If the parts are not required to be similar, bisect one side, as G I, in the point, O, with which, as a centre, describe the semicircle, G K I, of which G I is the diameter. This semicircle will be cut in the point, K, by the perpendicular, K O; mark off on G I a distance, G L, equal to G K, and draw the line, L M, parallel to H I. The triangle, G L M, and the trapezium, H I L M, will be equal to each other, and each equal to half the triangle, G H I. If the given triangle were G N I, it would also be divided into two equal parts by the line, L M.

14. *To draw a square double the size of a given square,* A B C D, *fig.* 10.—After producing from different corners any two sides which are at right angles to each other, as D A and D C, to H and L, with the centre, D, and radius, D B, describe the *quadrant* or quarter of a circle, F B E; and through the points of intersection, F and E, with the lines, D A and D L, draw parallels to D L and D A respectively, or tangents to the quadrant, F B E; the square, F G E D, will be double the area of the given square, A B C D; and in the same manner a square, H K L D, may be drawn double the area of the square, F G E D. It is evident that the diagonal of one square is equal to one side of a square twice the size.

15. *To describe a circle half the size of a given circle, as* A C B D, *fig.* 11.—Draw two diameters, A B and C D, at right angles to each other; join an extremity of each, as A, C, by the chord, A C. Bisect this chord by the perpendicular, E F. The radius of the required circle will be equal to E G. It follows that the annular space shaded in the figure is equal to the smaller circle within it.

16. *To inscribe in given circles, as in fig.* 12, *an equilateral triangle and a regular hexagon.*—Draw any diameter, G F, and with G, as a centre, describe the arc, D O E, its radius being equal to that of the given circle; join D E, E F, and E D, and D E F will be the triangle required. The side of a regular hexagon is equal to the radius of the circumscribing circle, and, therefore, in order to inscribe it in a circle, all that is necessary is to mark off on the circumference the length of the radius, and, joining the points of intersection, as K I L H M J, the resulting figure will be the hexagon required. To inscribe figures of 12 or 24 sides, it is merely necessary to divide or subdivide the arcs subtended by the sides obtained as above, and to join the points of intersection. It is frequently necessary to draw very minute hexagons, such as screw-nuts and bolt-heads. This is done more quickly by means of the angle of 60°, H, which is placed against a rule, R, or the square, in different positions, as indicated in fig. 12.

17. *To inscribe a square in a given circle, as* A C B D, *fig.* 13.—Draw two diameters, as A B, C D, perpendicular to one another, and join the points of intersection with the circle, and A C B D will be the square required.

18. *To describe a regular octagon about a circle having a given radius, as* O E, *fig.* 13.—Having, as in the last case, drawn two diameters, as E F, G H, draw other two, I J, K L, bisecting the angles formed by the former; through the eight points of intersec-

tion with the circle draw the tangents, E, K, G, J, F, L, I—these tangents will cut each other and form the regular octagon required. This figure may also be drawn by means of the square, and angle of 45°, ⓒ.

19. *To construct a regular octagon of which one side is given, as* A B, *fig.* 14.—Draw the perpendicular, O D, bisecting A B; draw A F parallel to O D, produce A B to C, and bisect the angle, C A F, by the line E A, making E A equal to A B. Draw the line O G, perpendicular to, and bisecting E A. O G will cut the vertical, O D, in O, which will be the centre of the circle circumscribing the required octagon. This may, therefore, at once be drawn by simply marking off arcs, as E H, H F, &c., equal to A B, and joining the points, E, H, F, &c. By dividing and subdividing the arcs thus obtained we can draw regular figures of 16 or 32 sides. The octagon is a figure of frequent application, as for drawing bosses, bearing brasses, &c.

·20. *To construct a regular pentagon in a given circle, as* A B C D F, *also a decagon in a given circle, as* E R M, *fig.* 15.—The pentagon is thus obtained; draw the diameters, A I, E J, perpendicular to each other; bisecting O E in K, with K as a centre, and K A as radius, describe the arc, A L; the chord, A L, will be equal to a side of the pentagon, which may accordingly be drawn by making the chords which form its sides, as A E, F D, D C, C B, and B A, equal to A L. By bisecting these arcs, the sides of a decagon may be at once obtained. A decagon may also be constructed thus:—Draw two radii perpendicular to each other, as O M and O R; next, the tangents, N M and N R. Describe a circle having N M for its diameter; join R, and P the centre of this circle, the line, R P, cutting the circle in *a*; R *a* is the length of a side of the decagon, and applying it to the circle, as R *b*, &c., the required figure will be obtained. The distance, R *a* or R *c*, is a *mean proportional* between an entire radius, as R N, and the difference, *c* N, between it and the radius. A *mean proportional* between two lines is one having such relation to them that the square, of which it is the one side, is equal to the rectangle, of which the other two are the dimensions.

21. *To construct a rectangle of which the sides shall be mean proportionals between a given line, as* A C, *fig.* 16, *and one a third or two-thirds of it.*—A C, the given line, will be the diagonal of the required rectangle; with it as a diameter describe the circle A B C D. Divide A C into three equal parts in the points, *m, n*, and from these points draw the perpendiculars, *m* D and *n* B; the lines which join the points of intersection of these lines with the circle, as A B, A D, C B, C D, will form the required rectangle, the side of which, C D, is a mean proportional between C *m* and C A, or—

$$C\,m : C\,D :: C\,D : C\,A\,;$$

that is to say, the square of which C D is a side, is equal to a rectangle of which C A is the length, and C *m* the height, because

$$C\,D \times C\,D = C\,m \times C\,A*$$

In like manner, A D is a mean proportional between C A and *m* A. This problem often occurs in practice, in measuring timber. Thus the rectangle inscribed in the circle, fig. 16, which may be considered as representing the section of a tree, is the form of the beam of the greatest strength which can be obtained from the tree.

---

* See the notes and rules given at the end of this chapter

APPLICATIONS.

DESIGNS FOR INLAID PAVEMENTS, CEILINGS, AND BALCONIES.

PLATE II.

The problems just considered are capable of a great variety of applications, and in Plate II. will be found a collection of some of those more frequently met with in mechanical and architectural constructions and erections. In order, however, that the student may perfectly understand the different operations, we would recommend him to draw the various designs on a much larger scale than that we have adopted, and to which we are necessarily limited by space. The figures distinguished by numbers, and showing the method of forming the outlines, are drawn to a larger scale than the figures distinguished by letters, and representing the complete designs.

22. *To draw a pavement consisting of equal squares, figs.* Ⓐ *and* 1.—Taking the length, *a b*, equal to half the diagonal of the required squares, mark it off a number of times on a horizontal line, as from A to B, B to C, &c. At A erect the perpendicular I H, and draw parallels to it, as D E, G F, &c., through the several points of division. On the perpendicular, I H, mark off a number of distances equal to A B, and draw parallels to A B, through the points of division, as H G, I F, &c. A series of small squares will thus be formed, and the larger ones are obtained simply by drawing the diagonals to these, as shown.

23. *To draw a pavement composed of squares and interlaced rectangles, figs.* Ⓑ *and* 2.—Let the side, as *c d*, of the square be given, and describe the circle, L M Q B, the radius of which is equal to half the given side. With the same centre, O, describe also the larger circle, K N P I, the radius of which is equal to half the side of the square, plus the breadth of the rectangle, *a b*. Draw the diameters, A C, E D, perpendicular to each other; draw tangents through the points, A, D, C, E, forming the square, J H F G; draw the diagonals J F, G, H, cutting the two circles in the points, I, B, K, L, M, N, P, Q, through which draw parallels to the diagonals. It will be perceived that the lines, A E, E C, C D, and D A, are exactly in the centre of the rectangles, and consequently serve to verify their correctness. The operation just described is repeated, as far as it is wished to extend the pattern or design, many of the lines being obtained by simply prolonging those already drawn. In inking this in, the student must be very careful not to cross the lines. This design, though analogous to the first, is somewhat different in appearance, and is applicable to the construction of trellis-work, and other devices.

24. *To draw a Grecian border or frieze, figs.* ⓒ *and* 3.—On two straight lines, as A B, A C, perpendicular to each other, mark off, as often as necessary, a distance, A *i*, representing the width, *ef*, of the ribbon forming the pattern. Through all the points of division, draw parallels to A B, A C—thus forming a series of small squares, guided by which the pattern may be at once inked in, equal distances being maintained between the sets of lines, as in fig. ⓒ. This ornament is frequently met with in architecture, being used for ceilings, cornices, railings, and balconies; also in cabinet work and machinery for borders, and for wood and iron gratings.

25. *To draw a pavement composed of squares and regular octa-*

gons, *figs.* Ⓓ *and* 4.—With a radius, E O, equal to half the width, E F, of the octagon, describe a circle, E G F H, and, as was shown in reference to fig. 13, Plate I., draw the octagon circumscribing it—the square, A B C D, being first obtained, and its diagonals, A C, B D, drawn cutting the circle in the points, I, J, K, L, tangents being then drawn through these points. The octagon may also be formed by marking off from each corner of the square, A, B, C, D, a distance equal to A O, or half its diagonal—and thereby will be obtained the points of junction of the sides of the octagon. The pattern is extended simply by repeating the above operation, the squares being formed by the sides of four contiguous octagons, which are inclined at an angle of 45° to the horizontal lines. This pattern is generally produced in black and white marble, or in stones of different colours, whereby the effect is distinctly brought out.

26. *To draw a pavement composed of regular hexagons, figs.* Ⓔ *and* 5.—With a radius, A O, equal to a side, *a b*, of the hexagon, describe a circle, in which inscribe the regular hexagon, A B C D E F. The remaining hexagons will readily be obtained by producing, in different directions, the sides and diagonals of this one. In fig. Ⓔ, the hexagons are plain and shaded alternately, to show their arrangement; but in practice they are generally all of one colour.

27. *To draw a pavement composed of trapeziums, combined in squares, figs.* Ⓕ *and* 6.—Draw the square, A B C D; also its diagonals, A C, B D; construct the smaller square, *a b c d*, concentric with the first. On the diagonal, B D, mark the equal distances, *o e*, *e f*, and through *e* and *f* draw parallels to the diagonal, A C; join the points of intersection of these with the smaller squares by the lines, *k l*, *m n*, which will give all the lines required to form the pattern, requiring merely to be produced and repeated to the desired extent. Very beautiful combinations may thus be formed in different kinds of wood for furniture and panels.

28. *To draw a panel design composed of lozenges, figs.* Ⓖ *and* 7.—On a straight line, A B, mark off the length of a side of the lozenge twice; construct the equilateral triangle, A B C; draw the line C D, perpendicular to A B; and draw A E and B F parallel to D C, and E F parallel to A B. Construct the equilateral triangle, E D F, cutting the triangle, A B C, in G and H, and join G H. In this manner are obtained the lozenges, A G H D and E G H C, and by continuing the lines and drawing parallels at regular distances apart, the remainder of the pattern will be readily constructed—this being repeated to any desired extent.

29. *To draw a panel pattern composed of isosceles triangles, figs.* Ⓛ *and* 12.—If in the last-mentioned fig. Ⓖ, we draw the longitudinal diagonal of each lozenge, we shall obtain the type of the pattern Ⓛ. We will, however, suppose that the base, *a b*, of the triangle is given, instead of the side of the lozenge. Mark off this length twice on the line, A B, and construct the equilateral triangle, A C D, just as in the preceding case; also the second similar triangle, D E F, thus obtaining the points G and H. Join A H, G B, E H, and G F, &c., and each point of intersection, as I, L, &c., will be the apex of three of the isosceles triangles. The pattern, Ⓛ, is produced by giving these triangles various tints.

The patterns we have so far given are a few of the common arrangements of various regular polygons. An endless variety of patterns may be produced by combining these different figures,

and these are of great use in many arts, particularly for cabinet inlaid mosaic work, as well as for pavements and other ornamental constructions.

30. *To draw an open-work casting, consisting of lozenges and rosettes, figs.* Ⓗ *and* 8.—The lozenge, *a b c d*, being given, the points, *a, b, c, d*, being each the centre of a rosette, draw and indefinitely produce the diagonals, *a c*, *b d*, which must always be perpendicular to each other. Through the points, *a, b, c, d*, draw parallels to these diagonals, also an indefinite number of such parallels at equal distances apart. The intersections of these lines will be the centres of rosettes and lozenges alternately, and the former may accordingly be drawn, consisting merely of circles with given radii. The centres of the rosettes are joined by straight lines, and to right and left of these, at the given distances, *f g*, *f h*, parallels to them are drawn, thereby producing the concentric lozenges completing the pattern.

31. *To draw a pattern for a ceiling, composed of small squares or lozenges, and irregular but symmetrical octagons, figs.* Ⓘ *and* 9.—The rectangle, A B C D, being given, its corners forming the centres of four of the small lozenges, draw the lines, E F, G H, dividing the rectangle into four equal parts; next mark off the semi-diagonals of the lozenges, as A I, A O, and join I and O. The centre lines of the pattern being thus obtained, the half-breadths, *f g*, *f h*, are marked on each side of these, and the appropriate parallels to them drawn. In extending the pattern by repetition, the points corresponding to I and O will be readily obtained by drawing a series of parallel lines, as I I and O O. By varying the proportions between the lozenges and the octagons, as also those between the different dimensions of each, a number of patterns may be produced of very varied appearance, although formed of these simple elements.

32. *To draw a stone balustrade of an open-work pattern, composed of circular and straight ribbons interlaced, figs.* Ⓙ *and* 10.—Construct the rectangle, A B C D, its corners being the centres of some of the required circles, which may accordingly be drawn, with given radii, as A *b*, *c d*; after bisecting A B in E, and drawing the vertical E G, make E F equal to E A, and with F as a centre, draw the circle having the radius, F *g*, equal to A *b*, drawing also the equal circles at C, B, E, &c. Draw verticals, such as *g h*, tangents to each of the circles, which will complete the lines required for the part of the pattern, Ⓙ, to the left. The rosettes to the right are formed by concentric circles of given radii, as E *e*, E *f*. The duplex, fig. Ⓙ, may be supposed to represent the pattern on the opposite sides of a stone balustrade. Where straight lines are run into parts of circles, the student must be careful to make them join well, as the beauty of the drawing depends greatly on this point. It is better to ink in the circles first, as it is practically easier to draw a straight line up to a circle than to draw a circle to suit a straight line.

33. *To draw a pattern for an embossed plate or casting, composed of regular figures combined in squares, figs.* Ⓚ *and* 11.—Two squares being given, as A B C D and F G H I, concentric, but with the diagonals of one parallel to the sides of the other, draw first the square, *a b c d*, and next the inner and concentric one, *e f g h*. The sides of the latter being cut by the diagonals, A C and B D, in the points, *i, j, k, l*, through these draw parallels to the sides of the square, A B C D, and finally, with the centre, O, describe a small

circle, the diameter of which is equal to the width of the indented crosses, the sides of these being drawn tangent to this circle. Thus are obtained all the lines necessary to delineate this pattern; the relievo and intaglio portions are contrasted by the latter being shaded.

In the foregoing problems, we have shown a few of the many varieties of patterns producible by the combination of simple regular figures, lines, and circles. There is no limit to the multiplication of these designs; the processes of construction, however, being analogous to those just treated of, the student will be able to produce them with every facility.

SWEEPS, SECTIONS, AND MOULDINGS.

PLATE III.

34. *To draw in a square a series of arcs, relieved by semicircular mouldings, figs. Ⓐ and 1.*—Let A B be a side of the square; draw the diagonals cutting each other in the point, c, through which draw parallels, D E, C F, to the sides; with the corners of the square as centres, and with a given radius, A G, describe the four quadrants, and with the points, D, F, E, describe the small semicircles of the given radius, D *a*, which must be less than the distance, D *b*. This completes the figure, the symmetry of which may be verified by drawing circles of the radii, C G, C H, which should touch, the former the larger quadrants, and the latter the smaller semicircles. If, instead of the smaller semicircles, larger ones had been drawn with the radius, D *b*, the outline would have formed a perfect *sweep*, being free from angles. This figure is often met with in machinery, for instance, as representing the section of a beam, connecting-rod, or frame standard.

35. *To draw an arc tangent to two straight lines.*—First, let the radius, *a b*, fig. 2, be given; with the centre, A, being the point of intersection of the two lines, A B, A C, and a radius equal to *a b*, describe arcs cutting these lines, and through the points of intersection draw parallels to them, B O, C O, cutting each other in O, which will be the centre of the required arc. Draw perpendiculars from it to the straight lines, A B, A C, meeting them in D and E, which will be the points of contact of the required arc. Secondly, if a point of contact be given, as B, fig. 3, the lines being A B, A C, making any angle with each other, bisect the angle by the straight line, A D; draw B O perpendicular to A B, from the point, B, and the point, O, of its intersection with A D, will be the centre of the required arc. If, as in figs. 2 and 3, we draw arcs, of radii somewhat less than O B, we shall form *congés*, which stand out from, instead of being tangents to, the given straight lines. This problem meets with an application in drawing fig. Ⓑ, which represents a section of various descriptions of castings.

36. *To draw a circle tangent to three given straight lines, which make any angles with each other, fig. 4.*—Bisect the angle of the lines, A B and A C, by the straight line, A E, and the angle formed by C D and C A, by the line, C F. A E and C F will cut each other in the point, O, which is at an equal distance from each side, and is consequently the centre of the required circle, which may be drawn with a radius, equal to a line from the point, O, perpendicular to any of the sides. This problem is necessary for the completion of fig. Ⓑ.

37. *To draw the section of a stair rail, fig. Ⓒ.*—This gives rise to the problems considered in figs. 5 and 6. First, let it be required to draw an arc tangent to a given arc, as A B, and to the given straight line, C D, fig. 6—D being the point of contact with the latter. Through D draw E F perpendicular to C D; make F D equal to O B, the radius of the given arc, and join O F, through the centre of which draw the perpendicular, G E, and the point, E, of its intersection with E F, will be the centre of the required arc, and E D the radius. Further, join O E, and the point of intersection, B, with the arc, A B, will be the point of junction of the two arcs. Secondly, let it be required to draw an arc tangential to a given arc, as A B, and to two straight lines, as B C, C D, fig. 5. Bisect the angle, B C D, by the straight line, C E; with the centre, C, and the radius, C H, equal to that of the given arc, O A, describe the arc, O G; parallel to B C draw I H J, cutting E C in J. Join O J, the line, O J, cutting the arc, H G, in G; join C G, and draw O K parallel to C G; the point, K, of its intersection with E J, will be the centre of the required arc, and a line, K L or K M, perpendicular to either of the given straight lines, will be the radius.

38. *To draw the section of an acorn, fig. Ⓓ.*—This figure calls for the solution of the two problems considered in figs. 9 and 10. First, it is required to draw an arc, passing through a given point, A, fig. 9, in a line, A B, in which also is to be the centre of the arc, this arc at the same time being a tangent to the given arc, C. Make A D equal to O C, the radius of the given arc; join O D, and draw the perpendicular, F B, bisecting it. B, the point of intersection of the latter line, with A B, is the centre of the required arc, A E C, A B being the radius. Secondly, it is required to draw an arc passing through a given point, A, fig. 10, tangential to a given arc, B C D, and having a radius equal to *a*. With the centre, O, of the given arc, and with a radius, O E, equal to O C, plus the given radius, *a*, draw the arc E; and with the given point, A, as a centre, and with a radius equal to *a*, describe an arc cutting the former in E —E will be the centre of the required arc, and its point of contact with the given arc will be in C, on the line, O E. It will be seen that in fig. Ⓓ, these problems arise in drawing either side of the object. The two sides are precisely the same, but reversed, and the outline of each is equidistant from the centre line, which should always be pencilled in when drawing similar figures, it being difficult to make them symmetrical without such a guide. This is an ornament frequently met with in machinery, and in articles of various materials and uses.

39. *To draw a wave curve, formed by arcs, equal and tangent to each other, and passing through given points, A, B, their radius being equal to half the distance, A B, figs. Ⓔ and 7.*—Join A B, and draw the perpendicular, E F, bisecting it in c. With the centres, A and c, and radius, A c, describe arcs cutting each other in G, and with the centres, B and c, other two cutting each other in H; G and H will be the centres of the required arcs, forming the curve or sweep, A C B. This curve is very common in architecture, and is styled the *cyma recta*.

40. *To draw a similar curve to the preceding, but formed by arcs of a given radius, as A I, figs. Ⓕ and 11.*—Divide the straight line into four equal parts by the perpendiculars, E F, G H, and C D; then, with the centre, A, and given radius, A I, which must always be greater than the quarter of A B, describe the arc

cutting c ᴅ in c; also with the centre, ʙ, a similar arc cutting ɢ ʜ in ʜ; c and ʜ will be the centres of the arcs forming the required curve. Whatever be the given radius, provided it is not too small, the centres of the arcs will always be in the lines, c ᴅ and ɢ ʜ. It will be seen that the arcs, c ɪ and ʜ ʟ, cut the straight lines, c ᴅ and ɢ ʜ, in two points respectively. If we take the second points, ᴋ ʟ, as centres, we shall form a similar curve to the last, but with the concavity and convexity transposed, and called the *cyma reversa.* The two will be found in fig. F, the first at *a,* and the second at *b.* This figure represents the section of a door, or window frame—it is one well known to carpenters and masons.

The little instrument known as the "Cymameter," affords a convenient means of obtaining rough measurements of contours of various classes, as mouldings and bas-reliefs. It is simply a light adjustable frame, acting as a species of holding socket for a mass of parallel slips of wood or metal—a bundle of straight wires, for example. Previous to applying this for taking an impression of measurement, the whole aggregation of pieces is dressed up on a flat surface, so that their ends form a perfect plane, like the ends of the bristles in a square cut brush; and these component pieces are held in close parallel contact, with just enough of stiff friction to keep them from slipping and falling away. The ends of the pieces are then applied well up to the moulding or surface whose cavities and projections are to be measured, and the frame is then screwed up to retain the slips in the position thus assumed. The surface thus moulds its sectional contour upon the needle ends, as if the surface made up of these ends was of a plastic material, and a perfect impression is therefore carried away on the instrument. The nicety of delineation is obviously bounded by the relative fineness of the measuring ends.

41. *To draw a baluster of a duplex contour, figs.* G *and* 8.—It is here necessary to draw an arc tangent to, or sweeping into two known arcs, *a i* and c ᴅ, and having its centre in a given horizontal, *e i.* Extend *e i* to ʜ, making *i* ʜ equal to ɢ ᴅ, the radius of the arc, c ᴅ. Join ɢ ʜ, bisecting ɢ ʜ by a perpendicular; this will cut *e* ʜ in the point, *e,* which is the centre of the required arc— *e i* being its radius. A line joining *e* ɢ cuts c ᴅ in c, the point of contact of the two arcs. The arc, ᴅ ꜰ, which is required to be a tangent to c ᴅ, and to pass through the point, ꜰ, is drawn with the centre, o, obtained by bisecting the chord, ᴅ ꜰ, by a perpendicular which cuts the radius of the arc, c ᴅ. This curve has, in fig. G, to be repeated both on each side of the vertical line, *m n,* and of the horizontal line, *f g.*

42. *To draw the section of a baluster of simple outline, as fig.* H. —We have here to draw an arc passing through two points, ᴀ, ʙ, fig. 12, its centre being in a straight line, ʙ c; this arc, moreover, requiring to join at ᴅ, and form a sweep with another, ᴅ ᴇ, having its centre in a line, ꜰ ᴅ, parallel to ʙ c. Joining ʙ ᴀ, a perpendicular bisecting ʙ ᴀ, will cut ʙ c in o, which will be the centre of the first arc, and that of the second may now be obtained, as in problem 37, fig. 6.

43. The base of the baluster, fig. H, is in the form of a curve, termed a *scotia.* It may be drawn by various methods. The following are two of the simplest—according to the first, the curve may be formed by arcs sweeping into each other, and tan-

gents at ᴀ and c to two given parallels, ᴀ, ʙ, c ᴅ, fig. 13. Through ᴀ and c draw the perpendiculars, c o and ᴀ ᴇ, and divide the latter into three equal parts. With one division, ꜰ ᴀ, as a radius, describe the first arc, ᴀ ɢ ʜ; make c ɪ equal to ꜰ ᴀ, join ɪ ꜰ, and bisect ɪ ꜰ by the perpendicular, o ᴋ, which cuts c o in o. o will be the centre of the other arc required. The line, o ʜ, passing through the centres, o and ꜰ, will cut the arcs in the point of junction, ʜ. It is in this manner that the curve in fig. H is obtained. The second method is to form the curve by two arcs sweeping into each other and passing through the given points, ᴀ ʙ, fig. 14, their centres, however, being in the same horizontal line, c ᴅ, parallel to two straight lines, ᴇ ꜰ and ʙ c, passing through the given points. Through ᴀ, draw the perpendicular, ᴀ ɪ. ɪ, its point of intersection with c ᴅ, is the centre of one arc, ᴀ ᴅ. Next draw the chord, ʙ ᴅ, the perpendicular bisecting which, will cut c ᴅ in o, the centre of the other arc, the radius being o ᴅ or o ʙ. This curve is more particularly met with in the construction of bases of the Ionic, Corinthian, and Composite orders of architecture.

With a view to accustom the student to proportion his designs to the rules adopted in practice in the more obvious applications, we have indicated on each of the figs. A, B, C, &c., and on the corresponding outlines, the measurements of the various parts, in millimètres. It must, however, at the same time be understood, that the various problems are equally capable of solution with other data; and, indeed, the number of applications of which the forms considered are susceptible, will give rise to a considerable variety of these.

ELEMENTARY GOTHIC FORMS AND ROSETTES.

PLATE IV.

44. Having solved the foregoing problems, the student may now attempt the delineation of more complex objects. He need not, however, as yet, anticipate much difficulty, merely giving his chief attention to the accurate determination of the principal lines, which serve as guides to the minor details of the drawing.

It is in Gothic architecture that we meet with the more numerous applications of outlines formed by smoothly joined circles and straight lines, and we give a few examples of this order in Plate IV. Fig. 5 represents the upper portion of a window, composed of a series of arcs, combined so as to form what are denominated *cuspid* arches. The width or span, ᴀ ʙ, being given, and the apex, c, joining ᴀ c, c ʙ, draw the bisecting perpendiculars, cutting ᴀ ʙ in ᴅ and ᴇ. These latter are the centres of the sundry concentric arcs, which, severally cutting each other on the vertical, c ꜰ, form the arch of the window. The small interior cuspids are drawn in the same manner, as indicated in the figure; the horizontal, ɢ ʜ, being given, also the span and apexes. These interior arches are sometimes surmounted by the ornament, ᴍ, termed an *œil-de-bœuf,* consisting simply of concentric circles.

45. Fig. 1 represents a rosette, formed by concentric circles, the outer interstices containing a series of smaller circles, forming an interlaced fillet or ribbon. The radius, ᴀ o, of the circle, containing the centres of all the small circles, is supposed to be given. Divide it into a given number of equal parts. With the points of division, 1, 2, 3, &c., as centres, describe the circles tangential to

each other, forming the fillet, making the radii of the alternate ones in any proportion to each other. Then, with the centre, o, describe concentric circles, tangential to the larger of the fillet circles of the radius, A b. The central ornament is formed by arcs of circles, tangential to the radii, drawn to the centres of the fillet circles, their convexities being towards the centre, o; and the arcs, joining the extremities of the radii, are drawn with the actual centres of the fillet circles.

46. Fig. 6 represents a quadrant of a Gothic rosette, distinguished as *radiating*. It is formed by a series of cuspid arches and radiating *mullions*. In the figure are indicated the centre lines of the several arches and mullions, and in fig. 6ᵈ, the capital, connecting the mullion to the arch, is represented drawn to double the scale. With the given radii, A B, A C, A D, A E, describe the different quadrants, and divide each into eight equal parts, thus obtaining the centres for the *trefoil* and *quadrefoil* ornaments in and between the different arches. We have drawn these ornaments to a larger scale, in figs. 6ᵃ, 6ᵇ, and 6ᶜ, in which are indicated the several operations required.

47. Fig. 4 also represents a rosette, composed of cuspid arches and trefoil and quadrefoil ornaments, but disposed in a different manner. The operations are so similar to those just considered, that it is unnecessary to enter into further details.

48. Fig. 7 represents a cast-iron grating, ornamented with Gothic devices. Fig. 7ᵃ is a portion of the details on a larger scale, from which it will be seen that the entire pattern is made up simply of arcs, straight lines, and sweeps formed of these two, the problems arising comprehending the division of lines and angles, and the obtainment of the various centres.

49. Figs. 2 and 3 are sections of *tail-pieces*, such as are suspended, as it were, from the centres of Gothic vaults. They also represent sections of certain Gothic columns, met with in the architecture of the twelfth and thirteenth centuries. In order to draw them, it is merely necessary to determine the radii and centres of the various arcs composing them.

Several of the figures in Plate IV. are partially shaded, to indicate the degree of relief of the various portions. We have in this plate endeavoured to collect a few of the minor difficulties, our object being to familiarize the student to the use of his instruments, especially the compasses. These exercises will, at the same time, qualify him for the representation of a vast number of forms met with in machinery and architecture.

OVALS, ELLIPSES, PARABOLAS, VOLUTES, &c.

PLATE V.

50. The *ove* is an ornament of the shape of an egg, and is formed of arcs of circles. It is frequently employed in architecture, and is thus drawn :—The axes, A B and C D, fig. 1, being given, perpendicular to each other ; with the point of intersection, o, as a centre, first describe the circle, C A D E, half of which forms the upper portion of the ove. Joining B C, make C F equal to B E, the difference between the radii, o C, o B. Bisect F B by the perpendicular, G H, cutting C D in H. H will be the centre, and H C the radius of the arc, C J ; and I, the point of intersection of H C with A B, will be the centre, and I B the radius of the smaller arc,

I B K, which, together with the arc, H K, described with the centre, L, and radius, L D, equal to H C, form the lower portion of the required figure ; the lines, G H, L K, which pass through the respective centres, also cut the arcs in the points of junction, J and K. This ove will be found in the fragment of a cornice, fig. A. A more accurate and beautiful ove may be drawn by means of the instrument represented in elevation and plan in the annexed engraving.

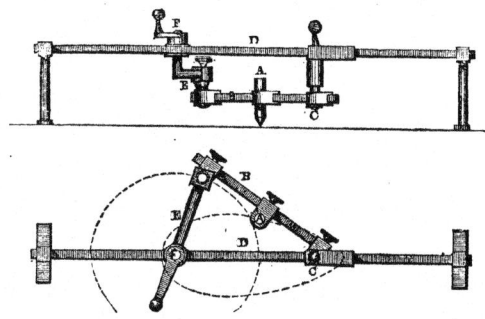

The pencil is at A, in an adjustable holder, capable of sliding along the connecting-rod, B, one end of which is jointed at C, to a slider on the horizontal bar, D, whilst the opposite end is similarly jointed to the crank arm, E, revolving on the fixed centre, F, on the bar. By altering the length of the crank, and the position of the pencil on the connecting-rod, the shape and size of the ove may be varied as required.

51. The *oval* differs from the ove in having the upper portion symmetrical with the lower ; and to draw it, it is only necessary to repeat the operations gone through in obtaining the curve, L B F, fig. 1.

52. The *ellipse* is a figure which possesses the following property :—The sum of the distances from any point, A, fig. 2, in the circumference, to two constant points, B, C, in the longer axis, is always equal to that axis, D E. The two points, B, C, are termed *foci*. The curve forming the ellipse is symmetric with reference both to the horizontal line or axis, D E, and to the vertical line, F G, bisecting the former in o, the centre of the ellipse. Lines, as B A, C A, B F, C F, &c., joining any point in the circumference with the foci, B and C, are called *vectors*, and any pair proceeding from one point are together equal to the longer axis, D E, which is called the *transverse*, F G being the *conjugate* axis. There are different methods of drawing this curve, which we will proceed to indicate.

53. *First Method.*—This is based on the definition given above, and requires that the two axes be given, as D E and F G, fig. 2. The foci, B and C, are first obtained by describing an arc, with the extremity, G or F, of the conjugate axis as a centre, and with a radius, F C, equal to half the transverse axis ; the arc will cut the latter in the points, B and C, the foci. If now we divide D E unequally in H, and with the radii, D H, E H, and the foci as centres, we describe arcs severally cutting each other in I, J, K, A ; these four points will lie in the circumference. If, further, we again unequally divide D E, say in L, we can similarly obtain four other

points in the circumference, and we can, in like manner, obtain any number of points, when the ellipse may be traced through them by hand. The large ellipses which are sometimes required in constructions, are generally drawn with a *trammel* instead of compasses, the trammel being a rigid rule with adjustable points.—The *gardener's ellipse:* To obtain this, place a rod in each of the foci of the required ellipse; round these place an endless cord, which, when stretched by a tracer, will form the vectors; and the ellipse will be drawn by carrying the tracer round, keeping the cord always stretched.

54. *Second Method.*—Take a strip of paper, having one edge straight, as *d b*, and on this edge mark a length, *a b*, equal to half the transverse axis, and another length, *b c*, equal to half the conjugate axis. Place the strip of paper so that the point, *a*, of the longer measurement, lies on the conjugate, F G, and the other point, *c*, on the transverse axis, D E. If the strip be now caused to rotate, always keeping the two points, *a* and *c*, on the respective axes—the other point, *b*, will, in every position, indicate a point in the circumference which may be marked with a pencil, the ellipse being afterwards traced through the points thus obtained.

55. *Third Method, fig. 3.*—It is demonstrated, in that branch of geometry which treats of solids, as we shall see later on, that if a cone, or cylinder, be cut by a plane inclined to its axis, the resulting section will be an ellipse. It is on this property that the present method is based. The transverse and conjugate axes being given, as A B and C D, cutting each other in the centre, O, draw any line, A E, equal in length to the conjugate axis, C D, and on A E, as a diameter, describe the semicircle, E G A. Join E B, and through any number of points, taken at random, on E A, as 1, 2, 3, &c., draw parallels to E B. Then, at each point of division, on B A, erect perpendiculars, 1 *a*, 2 *b*, 3 *c*, &c., cutting the semicircle, and, at the corresponding divisions obtained on A B, erect perpendiculars, as 1′ *a*′, 2′ *b*′, 3′ *c*, &c., and make them equal to the corresponding perpendiculars on E A. A line traced through the various points thus obtained, that is, the extremities, *a*′, *b*′, *c*′, &c., of the lines, will form the required ellipse.

56. *Fourth Method.*—On the transverse axis, A B, and with the centre, O, describe the semicircle, A F B, the axis forming its diameter; and with the diameter, H I, equal to the conjugate axis, describe the smaller semicircle, H D I. Draw radii, cutting the two semicircles, the larger in the points, *i, j, k, l*, &c., and the smaller in the points, *i′, j′, k′, l′*, &c. It is not necessary that the radii should be at equiangular distances apart, though they are drawn so in the plate for regularity's sake. Through the latter points draw parallels to the transverse axis, A B, and through the former, parallels to the conjugate axis, C D, the points of intersection of these lines, as *q, r, s, t*, &c., will be so many points in the required ellipse, which may, accordingly, be traced through them. It follows from this, that, in order to draw an ellipse, it is sufficient to know either of the axes, and a point in the circumference. Let the axis, A B, be given, and a point, *r*, in the circumference, which must always lie within perpendiculars passing through the extremities of the given axis. Through *r* draw a line, *r j′*, parallel to A B, and a line, *r j*, perpendicular to it; with the centre, O, and radius, O A, equal half the given axis, describe the arc, cutting *r* in *j*; join *j* O, and the line, *j* O, will cut *r j′* in *j′*: O *j′* will be

equal to half the conjugate axis, C D. If the conjugate axis, C D, be given, proceed as before; the arc, however, in this case, having the smaller radius, O D, and cutting *r j′* in *j′*; then join O *j′*, producing the line till it cuts *r j*, which will be in *j*, and O *j* will equal half the transverse axis, A B. It has already been shown how to describe an ellipse, when the two axes are given.

We may here give a method invented a short time back by Mr. Crane of Birmingham, for constructing an ellipse with the compasses. This method applies to all proportions, and produces as near an approximation to a true ellipse, as it is possible to obtain by means of four arcs of circles.

By applying compasses to any true ellipse, it will be seen that certain parts of the curve approach very near to arcs of circles, and that these parts are about the vertices of its true axes; and by the nature of an ellipse, the curve on each side of either axis is equal and similar; consequently, if arcs of circles be drawn through all the vertices, meeting one another in four points, the opposite arcs being equal and similar, the resulting figure will be indefinitely near an ellipse. Four circles, described from four different points, but with only two different radii, are then required. These four points may be all within the figure; the centres of the two greater circles may either be within or without, but the centres of the two circles at the extremities of the major axis must always be within, and, consequently, the whole four points can never be without the figure. Again, the proportions of the major and minor axes may vary infinitely, but they can never be equal; therefore, any rule for describing ellipses must suit all possible proportions, or it does not possess the necessary requirements. Moreover, if any rule apply to one certain proportion and not to another, it is evident that the more the proportions differ from that one—whether *crescendo* or *diminuendo*—the greater will be the difference of the result from the true one. From this it follows, that if a rule applies not to all, it can only apply to one proportion; and also, that if it apply to a certain proportion and not to another, it can only be correct in that one case.

Let A B be any major axis, and C D any minor axis; produce them both in either direction, say towards F and H, and make A F equal to C G; then join C A, and through F draw F H parallel to C A.

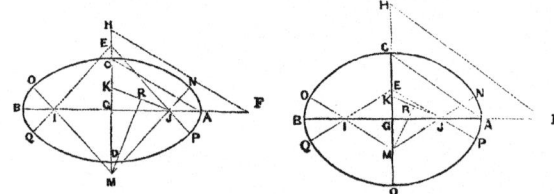

Set off B I, A J, and C K, equal to H C; join J K, and bisect it in R, and at R erect a perpendicular, cutting C D, or C D produced, at M; then make G E equal to G M; J, E, I, M, will be the centres of the four circles required. Through the points, J and I, draw M N, M O, E P, E Q, each equal to M C; then M N and E P will be the radii of the greater circles, and J N, I O, of the less: the points of contact will therefore be at N, O, P, Q, and the figure drawn through A, N, C, O, B, Q, D, P, will be the required ellipse.

Several instruments have been invented for drawing ellipses, many of them very ingeniously contrived. The best known of these contrivances, are those of Farey, Wilson, and Hick—the last of which we present in the annexed engraving. It is shown

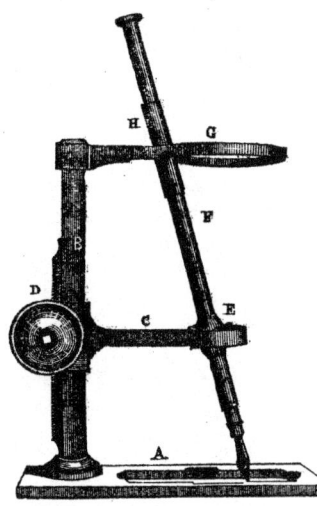

as in working order, with a pen for drawing ellipses in ink. It consists of a rectangular base plate, A, having sharp countersunk points on its lower surface, to hold the instrument steady, and cut out to leave a sufficient area of the paper uncovered for the traverse of the pen. It is adjusted in position by four index lines, setting out the transverse and conjugate axes of the intended ellipse — these lines being cut on the inner edges of the base. Near

one end of the latter, a vertical pillar, B, is screwed down, for the purpose of carrying the traversing slide-arm, C, adjustable at any height, by a milled head, D, the spindle of which carries a pinion in gear with a rack on the outside of the pillar. The outer end of the arm, C, terminates in a ring, with a universal joint, E, through which the pen or pencil-holder, F, is passed. The pillar, B, also carries at its upper end a fixed arm, G, formed as an elliptical guide-frame, being accurately cut out to an elliptical figure, as the nucleus of all the varieties of ellipse to be drawn. The centre of this ellipse is, of course, set directly over the centre of the universal joint, E, and the pen-holder is passed through the guide and through the joint, the flat-sided sliding-piece, H, being kept in contact with the guide, in traversing the pen over the paper. The pen thus turns upon its joint, E, as a centre, and is always held in its proper line of motion by the action of the slider, H. The distance between the guide ellipse and the universal joint determines the size of the ellipse, which, in the instrument here delineated, ranges from $2\frac{7}{8}$ inches by $1\frac{3}{8}$, to $\frac{7}{16}$ by $\frac{1}{4}$ inch. In general, however, these instruments do not appear to be sufficiently simple, or convenient, to be used with advantage in geometrical drawing.

57. *Tangents to ellipses.*—It is frequently necessary to determine the position and inclination of a straight line which shall be a tangent to an elliptic curve. Three cases of this nature occur: when a point in the ellipse is given; when some external point is given apart from the ellipse; and when a straight line is given, to which it is necessary that the tangent should be parallel.

First, then, let the point, A, in the ellipse, fig. 2, be given; draw the two vectors, C A, B A, and produce the latter to M; bisect the angle, M A C, by the straight line, N P; this line, N P, will be the tangent required; that is, it will touch the curve in the point, A, and in that point alone.

Secondly, let the point, L, be given, apart from the ellipse, fig 3. Join L with I, the nearest focus to it, and with L as a centre, and a radius equal to L I, describe an arc, M I N. Next, with the more distant focus, H, as a centre, and with a radius equal to the transverse axis, A B, describe a second arc, cutting the first in M and N. Join M H and N H, and the ellipse will be cut in the points v and x; a straight line drawn through either of these points from the given point, L, will be a tangent to the ellipse.

58. Thirdly, let the straight line, Q R, fig. 2, be given, parallel to which it is required to draw a tangent to the ellipse. From the nearest focus, B, let fall on Q R the perpendicular, S B; then with the further focus, C, as a centre, and with a radius equal to the transverse axis, D E, describe an arc cutting B s in s; join C s, and the straight line, C s, will cut the ellipse in the point, T, of contact of the required tangent. All that is then necessary is, to draw through that point a line parallel to the given line, Q R, the accuracy of which may be verified by observing whether it bisects the line, S B, which it should.

59.—*The oval of five centres, fig. 4.*—As in previous cases, the transverse and conjugate axes are given, and we commence by obtaining a mean proportional between their halves; for this purpose, with the centre, O, and the semi-conjugate axis, O C, as radius, we describe the arc, C I K, and then the semi-circle, A L K, of which A K is the diameter, and further prolong O C to L, O L being the mean proportional required. Next construct the parallelogram, A G C O, the semi-axes constituting its dimensions; joining C A, let fall from the point, G, on the diagonal, C A, the perpendicular, G H D—which, being prolonged, cuts the conjugate axis or its continuation in D. Having made C M equal to the mean proportional, O L, with the centre, D, and radius, D M, describe an arc, a M b; and having also made A N equal to the mean proportional, O L, with the centre, H, and radius, H N, describe the arc, N a, cutting the former in a. The points, H, a, on one side, and H', b, obtained in a similar manner on the other, together with the point, D, will be the five centres of the oval; and straight lines, R H a, S H' b, and P a D, Q b D, passing through the respective centres, will meet the curve in the points of junction of the various component arcs, as at R, P, Q, S.

This beautiful curve is adopted in the construction of many kinds of arches, bridges, and vaults; an example of its use is given in fig. 6.

60. The *parabola*, fig. 5, is an open curve, that is, one which does not return to any assumed starting point, to however great a length it may be extended; and which, consequently, can never enclose a space. It is so constituted, that any point in it, D, is at an equal distance from a constant point, C, termed the *focus*, and in a perpendicular direction, from a straight line, A B, called the *directrix*. The straight line, F G, perpendicular to the directrix, A B, and passing through the focus, C, is the *axis* of the curve, which it divides into two symmetrical portions. The point, A, midway between F and C, is the apex of the curve. There are several methods of drawing this curve.

61. First method:—This is based on the definition just given and requires that the focus and directrix be known, as C, and A B Take any points on the directrix, A B, as A, E, H, I, and through them draw parallels to the axis, F G, as also the straight lines

C

A C, E C, H C, I C, joining them with the focus. Draw perpendiculars bisecting these latter lines, and produce them until they cut the corresponding parallels, and the points of intersection, b, c, D, e, will be in the required curve, which may be traced through them.

62. The straight lines which were just drawn, cutting the parallels in different points of the curve, are tangents to the curve at the several points. If, then, it is required to draw a tangent through a given point, c, it is obtained simply by joining c c, making H c equal to c c, and bisecting the angle, H c c, by the straight line, c d, which will be the required tangent. If the point given be apart from the curve, the procedure will be the same, but the line corresponding to H c will not be parallel to the axis.

63. Second method:—We have here given the axis, a G, the apex, a, and any point, l, in the curve. From the point, l, let fall on the axis the perpendicular, l G, and prolong this to e, making c e equal to l G. Divide l G into any number of equal parts, as in the points, i, j, k, through which draw parallels to the axis; divide also the axis, a G, into the same number of equal parts, as in the points, f, g, h; through these draw lines radiating from the point, e, and they will intersect the parallels in the points, m, n, o, which are so many points in the curve.

64. If it is required to draw a line tangent to a given parabola, and parallel to a given line, J K, we let fall a perpendicular, c L, on this last; this perpendicular will cut the directrix in p, and p n drawn parallel to the axis will cut the curve in the point of contact, n.

We find frequent applications of this curve in constructions and machinery, on account of the peculiar properties it possesses, which the student will find discussed as he proceeds.

65. The objects represented in figs. D, D', are an example of the application of this curve. They are called *Parabolic Mirrors*, and are employed in philosophical researches. The angles of incidence of the vectors, a b, a c, a d, are equal to the angles of reflection of the parallels, b b', c c', d d'. It follows from this property, that if in the focus, a, of one mirror, b f, the flame of a lamp, or some incandescent body be placed, and in the focus, a', of the opposite mirror, b' f', a piece of charcoal or tinder, the latter will be ignited, though the two foci may be at a considerable distance apart; for all the rays of caloric falling on the mirror, b f, are reflected from it in parallel lines, and are again collected by the other mirror, b' f', and concentrated at its focus, a'.

66. *To draw an Ionic volute, fig. 6.*—The vertical, A o, being given, and being the length from the summit to the centre of the volute, divide it into nine equal parts, and with the centre, o, and a radius equal to one of these parts, describe the circle, a b c d, which forms what is termed the *eye* of the volute. In this circle (represented on a larger scale in fig. 7) inscribe a square, its diagonals being vertical and horizontal; through the centre, o, draw the lines, 1—3, and 4—2, parallel to the sides, and divide the half of each into three equal parts. With the point, 1, as a centre, and the radius, 1 A (fig. 6), draw the arc, A e, extending to the horizontal line, 1 e, which passes through the point, 2. With this latter point as a centre, and a radius equal to 2 e, draw the next arc, extending to the vertical line, 2 f, which passes through the point, 3, the next centre. The points, 4, 5, 6, &c., form the sub-

sequent centres; the arcs in all cases joining each other on a line passing through their respective centres. The internal curve is drawn in the same way; the points, 1', 2', 3', &c., fig. 7 bis, being the centres of the component arcs. The first arc is drawn with a radius, 1' A', a ninth less than 1 A, and the others are consequently proportionately reduced, as manifest in fig. 6. The application of the volute will be found in fig. B.

67. *To draw a curve tangentially joining two straight lines, A B and B C, fig. 8, the points A and C being the points of junction.*—Join A C, and bisecting A C in D, join D with B, the point of intersection of the lines, A B, B C. Bisect B D in E', which will be a point in the curve. Join E C, E A, and bisect the lines, E C, E A, by the perpendiculars, a b, c d; make e f and e' f' equal to a fourth part of E D; f and f' will be other two points in the curve. Proceed in the same way to obtain the points, g h and g' h', or more if desirable, and then trace the curve through these several points. This method is generally adopted by engineers and constructors, and will be met with in railways, bridges, and embankments, and wherever it is necessary to connect two straight lines by as regular and perfect a curve as possible. It is also particularly applicable where the scale is large.

RULES AND PRACTICAL DATA.

LINES AND SURFACES.

68. The *square mètre* is the unit of surface measurement, just as the linear mètre is that of length. The square mètre is subdivided into the *square décimètre*, the *square centimètre*, and the *square millimètre*. Whilst the linear decimètre is a tenth part of the mètre, the square decimètre is the hundredth part of the square mètre. In fact, since the square is the product of a number multiplied into itself,

$$0 \cdot 1 \text{m.} \times 0 \cdot 1 \text{m.} = 0 \cdot 01 \text{ square mètres.}$$

In the same manner the square centimètre is the ten-thousandth part of the square mètre; for

$$0 \cdot 01 \text{ m.} \times 0 \cdot 01 \text{ m.} = 0.0001 \text{ square mètres.}$$

And the square millimètre is the millionth part of the square mètre; for,

$$0 \cdot 001 \text{ m.} \times 0 \cdot 001 \text{ m.} = 0 \cdot 000001 \text{ square mètres.}$$

It is in this way that a relation is at once determined between the units of linear and surface measurement.

Similarly in English measures, a square foot is the ninth part of a square yard; for

$$1 \text{ foot} \times 1 \text{ foot} = \tfrac{1}{3} \text{ yard} \times \tfrac{1}{3} \text{ yard} = \tfrac{1}{9} \text{ square yard.}$$

A square inch is the 144th part of a square foot, and the 1296th part of a square yard; for

$$1 \text{ inch} \times 1 \text{ inch} = \tfrac{1}{12} \text{ foot} \times \tfrac{1}{12} \text{ foot} = \tfrac{1}{144} \text{ square foot,}$$

and

$$1 \text{ inch} \times 1 \text{ inch} = \tfrac{1}{36} \text{ yard} \times \tfrac{1}{36} \text{ yard} = \tfrac{1}{1296} \text{ square yard.}$$

This illustration places the simplicity and adaptability of the decimal system of measures, in strong contrast with the complexity of other methods.

69. *Measurement of surfaces.*—The surface or area of a square, as well as of all rectangles and parallelograms, is expressed by the product of the base or length, and height or breadth measured

perpendicularly from the base. Thus the area of a rectangle, the base of which measures 1·25 mètres, and the height ·75, is equal to

$$1\cdot 25 \times \cdot 75 = \cdot 9375 \text{ square mètres.}$$

The area of a rectangle being known, and one of its dimensions, the other may be obtained by dividing the area by the given dimension.

Example.—The area of a rectangle being ·9375 sq. m., and the base 1·25 m., the height is

$$\frac{\cdot 9375}{1\cdot 25} = \cdot 75 \text{ m.}$$

This operation is constantly needed in actual construction; as, for instance, when it is necessary to make a rectangular aperture of a certain area, one of the dimensions being predetermined.

The area of a *trapezium* is equal to the product of half the sum of the parallel sides into the perpendicular breadth.

Example.—The parallel sides of a trapezium being respectively 1·3 m., and 1·5 m., and the breadth ·8 m., the area will be

$$\frac{1\cdot 3 + 1\cdot 5}{2} \times \cdot 8 = 1\cdot 12 \text{ sq. m.}$$

The area of a *triangle* is obtained by multiplying the base by half the perpendicular height.

Example.—The base of a triangle being 2·3 m., and the perpendicular height 1·15 m., the area will be

$$2\cdot 3 \times \frac{1\cdot 15}{2} = 1\cdot 3225 \text{ sq. m.}$$

The area of a triangle being known, and one of the dimensions given—that is, the base or the perpendicular height—the other dimension can be ascertained by dividing double the area by the given dimension. Thus, in the above example, the division of (1·3225 sq. m. × 2) by the height 1·15 m. gives for quotient the base 2·3 m., and its division by the base 2·3 m. gives the height 1·15 m.

70. It is demonstrated in geometry, that the square of the hypothenuse, or longest side of a right-angled triangle, is equal to the sum of the squares of the two sides forming the right angle. It follows from this property, that if any two of the sides of a right-angled triangle be given, the third may be at once ascertained.

First, If the sides forming the right angle be given, the hypothenuse is determined by adding together their squares, and extracting the square root.

Example.—The side, A B, of the triangle, A B C, fig. 16, Pl. I., being 3 m., the side B C, 4 m., the hypothenuse, A C, will be

$$\text{A C} = \sqrt{3^2 + 4^2} = \sqrt{9 + 16} = \sqrt{25} = 5 \text{ m.}$$

Secondly, If the hypothenuse, as A C, be known, and one of the other sides, as A B, the third side, B C, will be equal to the square root of the difference between the squares of A C and A B.

Thus assuming the above measures—

$$\text{B C} = \sqrt{25 - 9} = \sqrt{16} = 4 \text{ m.}$$

The diagonal of a square is always equal to one of the sides multiplied by $\sqrt{2}$; therefore, as $\sqrt{2} = 1\cdot 414$ nearly, the diagonal is obtained by multiplying a side by 1·414.

Example.—The side of a square being 6 mètres, its diagonal

$$= 6 \times 1\cdot 414 = 8\cdot 484 \text{ m.}$$

The sum of the squares of the four sides of a parallelogram is equal to the sum of the squares of its diagonals.

71. *Regular polygons.*—The area of a regular polygon is obtained by multiplying its perimeter by half the *apothegm* or perpendicular, let fall from the centre to one of the sides.

A regular polygon of 5 sides, one of which is 9·8 m., and the perpendicular distance from the centre to one of the sides 5·6 m., will have for area—

$$9\cdot 8 \times 5 \times \frac{5\cdot 6}{2} = 137\cdot 2 \text{ sq. m.}$$

The area of an irregular polygon will be obtained by dividing it into triangles, rectangles, or trapeziums, and then adding together the areas of the various component figures.

TABLE OF MULTIPLIERS FOR REGULAR POLYGONS OF FROM 3 TO 12 SIDES.

NAMES.	Sides.	MULTIPLIERS.			D Area 1 side = 1.	E Internal Angle.	F Apothegm or Perpendicular.
		A	B	C			
Triangle,	3	2·000	1·730	·579	·433	60° 0′	·2886751
Square,	4	1·414	1·412	·705	1·000	90° 0′	·5000000
Pentagon,	5	1·238	1·174	·852	1·720	108° 0′	·6881910
Hexagon,	6	1·156	radius.	side.	2·598	120° 0′	·8660254
Heptagon,	7	1.111	·867	1·160	3·634	128° 34′$\frac{2}{7}$	1·0382607
Octagon,	8	1·080	·765	1·307	4·828	135° 0′	1·2071069
Enneagon,	9	1·062	·681	1·470	6·182	140° 0′	1·3737387
Decagon,	10	1·050	·616	1·625	7·694	144° 0′	1·5388418
Undecagon,	11	1·040	·561	1·777	9·365	147° 16′$\frac{4}{11}$	1·7028436
Duodecagon,	12	1·037	·516	1·940	11·196	150° 0′	1·8660254

By means of this table, we can easily solve many interesting problems connected with regular polygons, from the triangle up to the duodecagon. Such are the following :—

First, *The width of a polygon being given, to find the radius of the circumscribing circle.*—When the number of sides is even, the width is understood as the perpendicular distance between two opposite and parallel sides; when the number is uneven, it is twice the perpendicular distance from the centre to one side.

Rule.—Multiply half the width of the polygon by the factor in column A, corresponding to the number of sides, and the product will be the required radius.

Example.—Let 18·5 m. be the width of an octagon; then,

$$\frac{18\cdot 5}{2} \times 1\cdot 08 = 9\cdot 99 \text{ m.;}$$

or say 10 mètres, the radius of the circumscribing circle.

Second, *The radius of a circle being given, to find the length of the side of an inscribed polygon.*

Rule.—Multiply the radius by the factor in column B, corresponding to the number of sides of the required polygon.

Example.—The radius being 10 m., the side of an inscribed octagon will be—

$$10 \times \cdot 765 = 7 \cdot 65 \text{ m.}$$

Third, *The side of a polygon being given, to find the radius of the circumscribing circle.*

Rule.—Multiply the side by the factor in column C, corresponding to the number of sides.

Example.—Let 7·65 m. be the side of an octagon; then

$$7 \cdot 65 \times 1 \cdot 307 = 10 \text{ m., nearly.}$$

Fourth, *The side of a polygon being given, to find the area.*

Rule.—Multiply the given side by the factor in column D, corresponding to the number of sides.

Example.—The side of an octagon being 7·65 m., the area will be—

$$7 \cdot 65 \times 4 \cdot 828 = 36 \cdot 93 \text{ sq. m.}$$

THE CIRCUMFERENCE AND AREA OF A CIRCLE.

72. If the circumference of any circle be divided by its diameter, the quotient will be a number which is called, *the ratio of the circumference to the diameter.* The ratio is found to be (approximately)—

$$3 \cdot 1416, \text{ or } 22 : 7;$$

that is, the circumference equals 3·1416 times the length of the diameter. It is expressed, in algebraic formulas, by the Greek letter π (*pi*). Thus, if C represents the circumference of a circle, and D its diameter, the following formula,

$$C = \pi D, \text{ or } C = 3 \cdot 1416 \times D,$$

expresses the development of the circumference. Thus, if the diameter of a circle, or D, = 2·7 m., or the radius R = 1·35 m., the circumference will be equal to—

$$3 \cdot 1416 \times 2 \cdot 7, \text{ or } 3 \cdot 1416 \times 1 \cdot 35 \times 2 = 8 \cdot 482 \text{ m.}$$

The circumference of a circle being known, its diameter, or radius, is found by dividing this circumference by 3·1416 for the former, or 6·2832 for the latter. Thus, the diameter, D, of a circle, the circumference of which is 8·482 m., is—

$$\frac{8 \cdot 482}{3 \cdot 1416} = 2 \cdot 7 \text{ m.};$$

and the radius, R, is—

$$\frac{8 \cdot 482}{6 \cdot 2832} = 1 \cdot 35 \text{ m.}$$

The area of a circle is found by multiplying the circumference by half the radius.—This rule is expressed in the following formula:—

$$\text{The area of a circle} = 2 \pi R \times \frac{R}{2} = \pi R^2.$$

This term, πR^2, is merely the simplification of the formula. The number 2 being both multiplier and divisor, may be cancelled, and the product of R into R is expressed by R^2, or the square of the radius. It follows, then, that the area of a circle is equal to the square of the radius multiplied by the circumference, or 3·1416.

Example.—The radius of a circle being 1·05 m., the area will be—

$$3 \cdot 1416 \times 1 \cdot 05 \times 1 \cdot 05 = 3 \cdot 4635 \text{ sq. m.}$$

The area of a circle being known, the radius is determined by dividing the area by 3·1416, and extracting the square root of the quotient.

Example.—The area of a circle being 3·4635 sq. m., the radius is—

$$\sqrt{\frac{3 \cdot 4635}{3 \cdot 1416}} = 1 \cdot 05 \text{ m.}$$

The area of a circle is derived from the diameter; thus—

$$\text{Area} = \frac{\pi D \times D}{4}, \text{ or } \frac{\pi D^2}{4};$$

then, since $\frac{\pi}{4}$ or $\frac{3 \cdot 1416}{4} = \cdot 7854,$

the formula resolves itself into

$$\text{Area} = \cdot 7854 \times D^2.$$

That is to say, if we multiply the fraction, ·7854, by the square of the diameter, the product will be the area.

Example.—The area of a circle, the diameter of which measures 2·1 m., is—

$$\cdot 7854 \times 2 \cdot 1 \times 2 \cdot 1 = 3 \cdot 4635 \text{ sq. m.}$$

It follows from this, that if the area of a square is known, that of an inscribed circle is obtainable, by multiplying by ·7854; that is, the area of a square is to the area of the inscribed circle, as,

$$4 : 3 \cdot 1416, \text{ or } 1 : \cdot 7854.$$

TABLE OF APPROXIMATE RATIOS BETWEEN CIRCLES AND SQUARES.

1. The diameter of a circle,	×	·8862 }	= the side of a square of equal area.
2. The circumference of a circle,	×	·2821 }	
3. The diameter,	×	·7071 }	= the side of the inscribed square.
4. The circumference,	×	·2251 }	
5. The area of a circle,	×	·6366	= the area of the inscribed square.
6. The side of an inscribed square,	×	1·4142	= the diameter of the circumscribing circle.
7. " " "	×	4·4430	= the circumference of the circumscribing circle.
8. The side of a square,	×	1·1280	= the diameter of an equal circle.
9. " "	×	3·5450	= the circumference of an equal circle.

This table affords a ready solution of the following amongst other problems:—

First, The diameter of a circle being ·125 m. or 125 $^m/_m$ (millimètres), the side of a square of equal area is

$$125 \times \cdot 8862 = 110 \cdot 775^m/_m.$$

Second, The circumference of a circle being 860 $^m/_m$, the side of the inscribed square is

$$860 \times \cdot 2251 = 193 \cdot 586^m/_m.$$

Third, The side of a square being 215·86 $^m/_m$, the diameter of the circumscribing circle is

$$215 \cdot 86 \times 1 \cdot 4142 = 305 \cdot 27^m/_m.$$

The radii and diameters of circles are to each other as the circumferences, and *vice versâ*. The areas, therefore, of circles are to each other as the squares of their respective radii or diameters.

It follows, hence, that if the radius or diameter be doubled, the circumference will only be doubled, but the area will be quadrupled; thus, a drawing reduced to one-half the length, and half the breadth, only occupies a quarter of the area of that from which it is reduced.

73. *Sectors—Segments.*—In order to obtain the area of a sector or segment, it is necessary to know the length of the arc subtending it. This is found by multiplying the whole circumference by the number of degrees contained in the arc, and dividing by 360°.

Example.—The circumference of a circle being 3·5 m., an arc of 45° will be

$$\frac{3·5 \times 45}{360} = ·4375 \text{ m.}$$

The length of an arc may be obtained approximately when the chord is known, and the chord of half the arc, by subtracting the chord of the whole arc from eight times the chord of the semi-arc, and taking a third of the remainder.

Example.—The chord of an arc being ·344 m., and that of half the arc ·198, the length of the arc is

$$\frac{·198 \times 8 - ·344}{3} = ·4133 \text{ m.}$$

The area of a sector is equal to the length of the arc multiplied into half the radius.

Example.—The radius being ·169 m., and the arc ·266;

$$\frac{·266 \times ·169}{2} = ·0225 \text{ sq. m., the area of the sector.}$$

The area of a segment is obtained by multiplying the width; that is, the perpendicular between the centre of the chord, and the centre of the arc, by ·626, then adding to the square of the product the square of half the chord, and multiplying twice the square root of the sum by two-thirds of the width.

Example.—Let 48 m. be the length of the chord of the arc, and 18 m. the width of the arc, then we have

$$18 \times ·626 = 11·268, \text{ and } (11·268)^2 = 126·9678; \text{ whilst}$$

$$\left(\frac{48}{2}\right)^2 = 576; \text{ therefore, } 2 \times \sqrt{126·9678 + 576} \times \frac{2 \times 18}{3} = 636·24$$

sq. m., the area of the segment.

The area of a segment may also be obtained very approximately by dividing the cube of the width by twice the length of the chord, and adding to the quotient the product of the width into two thirds of the chord. Thus, with the foregoing data, we have

$$\frac{18^3}{48 \times 2} = 60·7$$

$$\text{and, } \frac{48 \times 2 \times 18}{3} = \underline{576·0}$$

$$\text{Total, } 636·7 \text{ sq. m.}$$

A still simpler method, is to obtain the area of the sector of which the segment is a part, and then subtract the area of the

---

COMPARISON OF CONTINENTAL MEASURES, WITH FRENCH MILLIMÈTRES AND ENGLISH FEET.

COUNTRY.	DESIGNATION OF MEASURE.	Value in Millimètres.	Value in Feet.	COUNTRY.	DESIGNATION OF MEASURE.	Value in Millimètres.	Value in Feet.
Austria,.....	(Vienna) Foot or Fuss = 12 inches = 144 lines,........	316·103	1·037	Holland,.....	(Amsterdam) Foot = 3 spans = 11 inches,.............	283·056	·928
	(Bohemia) Foot,.............	296·416	·970		(Rhine) Foot,......·.......	313·854	1·030
	(Venice) Foot,.............	435·185	1·469	Lubeck, ...,...	(Lubeck) Foot,.............	291·002	·954
	" Foot (Palmo),........	347·398	1·140	Mecklenburg, ..	Foot,....................	291·002	·954
	" Foot (Architect's Meas.)	396·500	1·301	Modena,.....	(Modena) Foot,............	523·048	1·716
Baden,........	(Carlsruhe) Foot (new) = 10 inches = 100 lines,........	300·000	·984		(Reggio),................	530·898	1·742
Bavaria, ...	(Munich) Foot = 12 inches = 144 lines,............	291·859	·958	Ottoman Empire	(Constantinople) Grand pie,....	669·079	2·195
	(Augsburg) Foot,..........	296·168	·972	Parma,.......	Arms-length = 12 inches = 1728 atomi,................	544·670	1·787
Belgium, ...	(Brussels) Ell or Aune = 1 mètre,	1,000·000	3·281	Poland, ...	(Varsovie) Foot = 12 inches = 144 lines,............	297·769	·977
	" Foot,...........	285·588	·937	Portugal,.....	(Lisbon) Ft. (Architect's Measure)	338·600	1·111
Bremen,.......	(Bremen) Foot = 12 inches = 144 lines,............	289·197	·949	"	" Vara = 40 inches,....	1,008·363	3·636
Brunswick, ...	(Brunswick) Foot = 12 inches = 144 lines,.............	285·362	·936	Prussia,......	(Berlin) Foot = 12 inches,....	309·726	1·016
Cracovia,.....	(Cracow) Foot,.............	356·421	1·169	Russia,.....	(St. Petersburg) Russian Foot,	538·151	1·765
Denmark,.....	(Copenhagen) Foot,.........	313·821	1·029		" Archine,.....	711·480	2·334
Spain,.....	(Madrid) Foot (according to Lohman,..................	282·655	·927	Sardinia,.....	(Cagliari) Span,.........	202·573	·664
	Castilian Vara (" Liscar),	835·906	2·742	Saxe,........	(Weimar) Foot,...........	281·972	·925
	(Havana) Vara = 3 Madrid feet,	847·965	2·782	Sicilies,......	Span = 12 inches (ounces = 60 minuti),..............	263·670	·865
Papal States,.	(Rome) Foot,.............	297·896	·977	Sweden,......	(Stockholm) Foot,.......	296·838	·974
	Architect's Span = ¼ foot,.....	223·422	·733		(Bâle and Zurich) Foot,....	304·537	·999
	Ancient Foot,.............	294·246	·965		(Berne and Neufchatel) Foot = 12 inches,............	293·258	·962
Frankfort, ...	Foot,.................	284·610	·933	Switzerland, .	(Geneva) Foot,...........	487·900	1·600
Hamburg,....	Foot = 3 spans = 12 inches = 96 parts,.............	286·490	·940		(Lausanne) Foot = 10 inches = 100 lines,............	300·000	·984
Hanover,......	(Hanover) Foot = 12 inches = 144 lines,............	291·995	·958		(Lucerne and other Cantons) Ft.,	313·854	1·030
Hesse,........	(Darmstadt) Foot = 10 inches = 100 lines,.............	300·000	·984	Tuscany,.....	Foot,..................	548·167	1·798
				Wurtemburg,....	Foot = 10 inches = 100 lines..	286·490	·940

triangle constituting the difference between the sector and segment.

To find the area of an annular space contained between two concentric circles, multiply the sum of the diameters by their difference, and by the fraction ·7854.

Example.—Let 100 m. and 60 m. be the respective diameters; then, $(100 + 60) \times (100 - 60) \times \cdot 7854 = 5026 \cdot 56$ sq. m. the area of the annular space.

The area of a fragment of such annular space will be found by multiplying its radial breadth by half the sum of the arcs, or, more correctly, by the arc which is a mean proportional to them.

CIRCUMFERENCE AND AREA OF AN ELLIPSE.

74. The circumference of an ellipse is equal to that of a circle, of which the diameter is a mean proportional between the two axes;

therefore, it will be obtained by multiplying such mean propor tional by 3·1416, the ratio between the diameter and circumference of a circle.

Example.—Let 10 m. and 6·4 m. be the lengths of the respective axes; then,

$$\sqrt{10 \times 6 \cdot 4} \times 3 \cdot 1416 = 25 \cdot 1328 \text{ m.}$$

The area of the ellipse is obtained by multiplying the product of the two axes by ·7854, the ratio between the diameter and the area of the circle.

Example.—$10 \times 6 \cdot 4 \times \cdot 7854 = —50 \cdot 2656$ sq. m.

These rules meet with numerous applications in the indus trial arts, and particularly in mechanics, as will be seen further on. The examples given will enable the student to understand the various operations, as well as to solve other analogous problems.

CHAPTER II.

THE STUDY OF PROJECTIONS.

75. To indicate all the dimensions of an object by pictorial deli neation, it is necessary to represent it under several different aspects. These various views are comprehended under the general denomination of *Projections*, and usually consist of *elevations*, *plans*, and *sections*. The object, then, of the study of projections, or *descriptive geometry*, is the reproduction on paper of the appear ances of all bodies of many dimensions as viewed from different positions.

It is customary to determine the projections of a body on two principal planes, one of which is distinguished as the *horizontal plane*, and the other as the *vertical plane*, or *elevation*. These two planes are also called *geometric* projections or plans. They are annexed to each other, the horizontal plan being the lower; the line intersecting them is called the *base line*, and is always parallel to one of the sides of the drawing.

It is of great importance to have a thorough knowledge of the elementary principles of descriptive geometry, in order to be able to represent, in precise and determinate forms, the contours of all kinds of objects; and we shall now enter upon such explanatory details as are necessary, commencing primarily with the projections of a point and of a line.

ELEMENTARY PRINCIPLES.

THE PROJECTIONS OF A POINT.

PLATE VI.

76. Let A B C D, figs. 1 and 1ª, be a horizontal plane—repre senting, for example, the board on which the drawing is being made, or perhaps the surface of a pavement. Also, let A B E F be a vertical plane, such as a wall at one side of the piece of pave ment; the straight line, which is the intersection of these two

planes, is the *base line*. Finally, let o be any point in space, the representation of which it is desired to effect. If, from this point, o, we suppose a perpendicular, o o, to be let fall on the horizontal plane, the point of contact, o, or the foot of this perpendicular, will be what is understood as the horizontal projection of the given point. Similarly, if from the point, o, we suppose a per pendicular, o ó, to be let fall on the vertical plane, A B E F, the point of contact, ó, or foot of this perpendicular, will be the vertical projection of the same point. These perpendiculars are reproduced in the vertical and horizontal planes, by drawing lines, ó n and n o, respectively parallel and equal to o ó and o o.

77. It follows from this construction, that, when the two pro jections of any point are given, the position in space of the point itself is determinable, it being necessarily the point of intersection of perpendiculars erected on the respective projections of the point.

As in drawing, only one surface is employed, namely, the sheet of paper, and we are consequently limited to one and the same plane, it is customary to suppose the vertical plane, A B E F, fig. 1, as forming a continuation of the horizontal plane, A B C D, being turned on the base line, A B, as a hinge, so as to coincide with it— just as a book, half open, is fully opened flat on a table. We thus obtain the figure, D C E F, fig. 1ª, representing on the paper the two planes of projection, separated by the base line, A B, and the points, o, ó, fig. 1ª, represent the horizontal and vertical pro jections of the given point.

It will be remarked, that these points lie in one line, perpen dicular to the base line, A B; this is because, in the turning down of the previously vertical plane, the line, n ó, becomes a prolonga tion of the line, n o. It is necessary to observe, that the line, n ó, measures the distance of the point from the horizontal plane, whilst n o measures its distance from the vertical plane. In other words, if on o we erect a perpendicular to the plane, and measure the distance, n o', on this perpendicular, we shall obtain the exact position of the point in space. It is thus obvious, that the position of a point in space is fully determinable by means of two projections, these being in planes at right angles to each other.

THE PROJECTIONS OF A STRAIGHT LINE.

78. In general, if, from several points in the given line, perpendiculars be let fall on to each of the planes of projection, and their points of contact with these planes be joined, the resulting lines will be the respective projections of the given line.

When the line is straight, it will be sufficient to find the projections of its extreme points, and then join these respectively by straight lines.

79. Let M O, fig. 2, represent a given straight line in space, which we shall suppose to be, in this instance, perpendicular to the horizontal, and, consequently, parallel to the vertical plane of projection. To obtain its projection on the latter, perpendiculars, M m', O o', must be let fall from its extremities, M, O; the straight line, m' o', joining the extremities of these perpendiculars, will be the required projection in the vertical plane, and in the present case it will be equal to the given line.

The horizontal projection of the given line, M O, is a mere point, m, because the line lies wholly in a perpendicular, M m, to the plane, and it is the point of contact of this line which constitutes the projection. In drawing, when the two planes are converted into one, as indicated in fig. 2ª, the horizontal and vertical projections of the given right lines, M O, are respectively the point, m, and the right line, m' o'.

80. If we suppose that the given straight line, M O, is horizontal, and at the same time perpendicular to the vertical plane, as in figs. 3 and 3ª, the projections will be similar to the last, but transposed; that is, the point, o', will be the vertical, whilst the straight line, m o, will be the horizontal projection.

In both the preceding cases, the projections lie in the same perpendicular line, m m, fig. 2ª, and o' o, fig. 5ª.

81. When the given straight line, M O, is parallel to both the horizontal and the vertical plane, as in figs. 4 and 4ª, its two projections, m o and m' o', will be parallel to the base line, and they will each be equal to the given line.

82. When the given straight line, M O, figs. 5 and 5ª, is parallel to the vertical plane, A B E F, only, the vertical projection, m' o', will be parallel to the given line, whilst the horizontal projection, m o, will be parallel to the base line. Inversely, if the given straight line be parallel to the horizontal plane, its horizontal projection will be parallel to it, whilst its vertical projection will be parallel to the base line.

83. Finally, if the given straight line, M O, figs. 6 and 6ª, is inclined to both planes, the projections of it, m o, m' o', will both be inclined to the base line, A B. These projections are in all cases obtained by letting fall, from each extremity of the line, perpendiculars to each plane.

The projections of a straight line being given, its position in space is determined by erecting perpendiculars to the horizontal plane, from the extremities, m o, of the projected line, and making them equal to the verticals, n m' and p o'. The same result follows, if from the points, m', o', in the vertical plane, we erect

perpendiculars, respectively equal to the horizontal distances m n and p o. The free extremities of these perpendiculars meet each other in the respective extremities of the line in space.

THE PROJECTIONS OF A PLANE SURFACE.

84. Since all plane surfaces are bounded by straight lines, as soon as the student has learned how to obtain the projections of these, he will be able to represent any plane surface in the two planes of projection. It is, in fact, merely necessary to let fall perpendiculars to each of the planes, from the extremities of the various lines bounding the surface to be represented; in other words, from each of the angles or points of junction of these lines, by which means the corresponding points will be obtained in the planes of projection, which, being joined, will complete the representations. It is by such means that are obtained the projections of the square, represented in different positions in figs. 7, 7ª, 8, 8ª, and 9, 9ª. It will be remarked, that, in the two first instances, the projection is in one or other of the planes an exact counterpart of the given square, because it is parallel to one or other of the planes.

85. Thus, in fig. 7. we have supposed the given surface to be parallel to the horizontal plane; consequently, its projection in that plane will be a figure, m o p q, equal and parallel to itself, whilst the vertical projection will be a straight line, p' o', parallel to the base line, A B.

86. Similarly, in fig. 8, the object being supposed to be parallel to the vertical plane, its projection in that plane will be the equal and parallel figure, m' o' p' q', whilst that in the horizontal plane will be the straight line, m o. When the two planes of projection are converted into one, the respective projections will assume the forms and positions represented in figs. 7ª, 8ª.

87. If the given surface is not parallel to either plane, but yet perpendicular to one or the other, its projection in the plane to which it is perpendicular will still be a straight line, as p' o', figs. 9 and 9ª, whilst its projection in the other plane will assume the form, m o p q, being a representation of the object somewhat foreshortened in the direction of the inclination.

The cases just treated of have been those of rectangular surfaces, but the same principles are equally applicable to any polygonal figures, as may be seen in figs. 12 and 12ª, which will be easily understood, the same letters in various characters indicating corresponding points and perpendiculars. Nor does the obtainment of the projections of surfaces bounded by curved lines, as circles, require the consideration of other principles, as we shall proceed to show, in reference to figs. 10 and 11.

88. In the first of these, fig. 10, the circular disc, M O P Q, is supposed to be parallel to the vertical plane, A B E F, and its projection on that plane will be a circle, m' o' p' q', equal and parallel to itself, whilst its projection on the horizontal plane, A B C D, will be a straight line, q m o, equal to its diameter. If, on the other hand, the disc is parallel to the horizontal plane, as in fig. 11, its vertical projection will be the straight line, p' o' m', whilst its horizontal projection will be the circle, o p m q.

If the given circular disc be inclined to either plane, its projection in that plane will be an ellipse; and if it is inclined to both planes, both projections will be ellipses. This will be made evident by obtaining the projections of various points in the circumference.

89. When constructing the projections of regular figures, it facilitates the process considerably if projections of the centres and centre lines be first found, as in figs. 10, 11, and 12.

In general, the projection of all plane surfaces may be found, when it is known how to obtain the projections of points and lines. And, moreover, since solids are but objects bounded by surfaces and lines, the construction of their projections follows the same rules.

PRISMS AND OTHER SOLIDS.

PLATE VII.

90. Before entering upon the principles involved in the representation of solids, the student should make himself acquainted with the descriptive denominations adopted in science and art, with reference to such objects; and we here subjoin such as will be necessary.

DEFINITIONS.—A *solid* is an object having three dimensions; that is, its extent comprises *length*, *width*, and *height*. A solid also possesses magnitude, volume, or capacity.

There are several forms of solids. The *polyhedron* is a solid, bounded by plane surfaces; the *cone*, the *cylinder*, and the *sphere*, are bounded by curved surfaces. Those are termed *solids of revolution*, which may be defined as generated by the revolution of a plane about a fixed straight line, termed the *axis*. Thus, a ring, or annular *torus*, is a solid, generated by the revolution of a circle about a straight line, lying in the plane of the circle, and at right angles to the plane of revolution. A *prism* is a polyhedron, the lateral faces of which are parallelograms, and the ends equal and parallel polygons. A prism is termed *right*, when the lateral faces, or *facets*, are perpendicular to the ends; and it is *regular*, when the ends are regular polygons. A prism is also called a *parallelopiped*, when the ends are rectangles, or parallelograms; and when it is formed of six equal and square facets, it is termed a *cube*, or regular *hexahedron*. This solid is represented in fig. Ⓐ. Other regular polyhedra, besides the cube, are distinguished by appropriate names; as, the *tetrahedron*, the *octahedron*, and the *icosahedron*, which are bounded externally, respectively, by four, eight, and twenty equilateral triangles; and the *duodecahedron*, which is terminated by twelve regular pentagons. A *pyramid* is a polyhedron, of which all the lateral facets are triangles, uniting in one point, the *apex*, and having, as bases, the sides of a polygon, which is the base of the pyramid, as fig. Ⓒ. The prism and pyramid are triangular, quadrangular, pentagonal, hexagonal, &c., according as the polygons forming the bases are triangles, squares, pentagons, hexagons, &c.

By the *height* of a pyramid is meant the length of a perpendicular let fall from the apex on the base; the pyramid is a *right* pyramid when this perpendicular meets the centre of the base.

A *truncated* pyramid, or the *frustum* of a pyramid, is a solid which may be described as a pyramid having the apex cut off by a plane parallel, or inclined to the base.

A *cylinder* is a solid which may be described as generated by a straight line, revolving about, and at any given distance from, a

rectilinear axis to which it is parallel. A cylinder which is generated by a rectangle, revolving about one of its sides as an axis, is said to be a right cylinder; such a one is represented in fig. Ⓔ.

A *cone*, fig. Ⓕ, is a solid generated by a triangle, revolving about one of its sides as an axis. A *truncated* cone is one which is terminated short of the apex by a plane parallel, or inclined to the base. This solid is also called the *frustum* of a cone. A cone is said to be right when its base is a circle, and when a perpendicular let fall from the apex passes through the centre of the base.

A *sphere* is a solid generated by the revolution of a semicircle about its diameter as an axis, as fig. Ⓖ.

A *spheric sector* is a solid generated by the revolution of a plane sector, as o′ L E′, about an axis, *a b*, which is any radius of the sphere of which the sector forms a part. When the axis of revolution is exterior to the generating sector, the spheric sector obtained will be annular or zonic. The *zone* described by the arc, L E′, is the base of the spheric sector. The zone becomes a *spheric arc* when the axis of revolution is one of the radii forming the sector.

A *spheric wedge*, or *ungula*, is any portion, as I H G F, fig. 7*, comprised between two semicircular planes inclined to each other and meeting in a diameter, as I G, of the sphere. That portion of the surface of the sphere which forms the base of the ungula, is termed a *gore*.

A *spheric segment* is any part of a sphere cut off by a plane, and may be considered as a solid of revolution generated by the revolution of a plane segment about its centre line. The plane surface is the base of the segment. When the plane passes through the centre of the sphere, two equal segments are obtained, termed *hemispheres*.

A *segmental annulus* is a solid generated by the revolution of a plane segment, D′ B′ K, fig. 7, about any diameter, *a b*, of the sphere, apart from the segment. D′ K is the chord, and *m n*, its projection on the axis, is the height of the segmental annulus.

A *zonic segment* of a sphere is the part, L N K D′, of a sphere comprised between two parallel planes.

A *spheric pyramid*, or *pyramidal sector*, is a pyramid of which the base is part of the surface of a sphere, of which the apex is the centre; the base may be termed a *spheric polygon*.

THE PROJECTIONS OF A CUBE, FIG. Ⓐ.

91. A cube, of which two sides are respectively parallel to the planes of projection, is represented in these planes by equal squares, A B C D, and A′ B′ E′ F′, figs. 1* and 1.

This is indeed but a combination of some of the simple cases already given. We have seen that when a side, such as A B E F, fig. Ⓐ, is parallel to the vertical plane, its projection on the horizontal plane is reduced to a straight line, A B, fig. 1*, its projection on the vertical plane being a figure, A′ B′ E′ F′, fig. 1, equal to itself.

Similarly, the side, A B C D, which is parallel to the horizontal plane, is projected on the vertical plane in the line, A′ B′, fig. 1, and by the figure, A B C D, fig. 1*, in the horizontal plane. The sides, A D H E and B C G E, fig. Ⓐ, which are perpendicular to both the horizontal and the vertical plane, are represented in both by straight lines, as A D and B C, fig. 1, and A′ F′ and B′ E′, fig. 1, being respectively in the same straight lines perpendicular to the base line, L T. It will also be perceived, that the base, F E G H, fig. A, cannot be represented in the horizontal projection, nor the side, D C G H, in the vertical, since they are respectively immediately behind and hidden by the sides, A B C D and A B E F, represented in the projections by the squares, A B C D, fig. 1*, and A' B' E' F', fig. 1. They are, however, indicated in the planes to which they are perpendicular, by the straight lines, F' E' and D C.

92. It will be evident from these remarks, that in order to design a cube so that a model may be constructed, it is sufficient to know one of the sides, for all the sides are equal to each other.

When the plans are intended to be used in the actual construction of machinery or buildings, the objects should be represented in the projections as having their principal sides parallel or perpendicular to the horizontal and vertical plane respectively, in order to avoid the *foreshortening* occasioned by an oblique or inclined position of the object with reference to these planes, because the actual measurements of the different parts cannot be readily ascertained where there is such foreshortening.

To obtain, then, the projections of the cube, fig. A, a square must be constructed, as A B C D, fig. 1*, having its sides equal to the given side or edge, the sides A B and D C being disposed parallel to the base line; next, the square must be reproduced as at A' B' E' F', fig. 1, on the prolongations of the sides, A D and B C, which are perpendicular to the base line.

THE PROJECTIONS OF A RIGHT SQUARE-BASED PRISM, OR RECTANGULAR PARALLELOPIPED, FIG. B.

93. The representation of this solid is obtained in precisely the same manner as that of the cube, the sides being supposed to be parallel or perpendicular to the respective planes of projection. The base of the prism being square, its horizontal projection is necessarily also a square, A B C D, fig. 2*; but its vertical projection will be the rectangle, A' B' E' F', fig. 2, equal to one of the sides of the prism. For the construction of these projections, the same datum as in the preceding case is required; namely, a side of the base, and in addition, the height of the parallelopiped, or prism.

THE PROJECTIONS OF A QUADRANGULAR PYRAMID, FIG. C.

94. This pyramid is supposed to be inverted, and having its base, A B C D, parallel to the horizontal plane: it follows upon this assumption, that its horizontal projection is represented by the square, A B C D, fig. 3*. The axis, or centre line, O S, which is supposed to be vertical, and consequently passes through the centre of the base, is projected on the horizontal plane as a point, O, fig. ᵃ*, and on the vertical plane as a line, O' S; drawing through the point, O', of this line, the horizontal line, A' B', equal to a side of the base, which is supposed to be parallel to the vertical plane, we shall obtain the vertical projection of the base; and joining A's, B's', that of the whole pyramid, the points A' and B' may be found by prolonging the parallels, A D, B C, fig. 3*. This may be conveniently done with the square, and the operation is usually termed *squaring* over a measurement—that is, from one projection to another. The lateral facets, S B C and S A B, are represented in the vertical projection by the straight lines, A' S, B' S, fig. 1, since they are per-

pendicular to the vertical plane; and the projection of the facet, D S C, is identical with A' S B', that of the front facet, A S B, immediately behind which it is. Since each of the inclined converging facets is hidden by the base, they cannot be drawn in sharp lines in the horizontal projection; we have, however, indicated their positions in faint lines, fig. 3*. Were these lines full, the projection would be that of a pyramid with the apex uppermost, or of a hollow, baseless pyramid, in the same position as fig. C.

THE PROJECTIONS OF A RIGHT PRISM, PARTIALLY HOLLOWED. AS FIG. D.

95. The vertical and horizontal projections of the exterior of this solid, are precisely the same as those of fig. B; they are represented respectively by the square, A B C D, fig. 4*, and the rectangle, A' B' E' F', fig. 4. It will be perceived, that the internal surfaces of this figure are such as may be supposed to form some of the sides of a smaller prism; the sides, G H I J and K L M N, are parallel to the vertical plane, and G K N J and H I M L perpendicular to it, and it follows that the projections of this lesser figure will assume the forms, G' H' I' J', fig. 4, and G H L K, fig. 4*. The lines, K G, L H, are faint dotted lines, instead of being sharp and full, as being hid by the base, A B C D, of the external prism. These lines will be found to be different to the projection lines, or *working* lines. The latter are composed of irregular dots, whilst those which indicate parts of the figure which actually exist, but are hidden behind more prominent portions, are composed of regular dots. This distinction has been adhered to throughout the entire series of Plates.

97. On examining the examples just treated of, it will be observed, from the horizontal projections, that the contour, or outline, is in every case square, whilst, from the vertical projections, it will be seen that each object is different. This demonstrates that one projection is not sufficient for the determination of all the dimensions of an object; and that, even in the simplest cases, two different projections are absolutely necessary. It will, moreover, be seen, as we advance, that in many cases, three, and at times more, projections are required, as well as sections through two or more planes.

THE PROJECTIONS OF A RIGHT CYLINDER, FIG. E.

98. The axis, O M, of this cylinder is supposed to be vertical, and its bases, A B, E F, will consequently be horizontal. Its projections in figs. 5 and 5* are represented by the rectangle, A' B' E' F', on the one hand, and the circle, A C B D, on the other. It is evident, that to draw these figures, it is quite sufficient to know the radius, O A, of the base, and the height, O M; with the given radius, we describe the circle, A C B D, which is the horizontal projection of the whole cylinder; then making the vertical, O' M, equal to the given height, and squaring over by means of the parallels, A A', B B', the diameter of the circle, we draw, through O' and M, the horizontals, A' B', E' F', completing the parallelogram, A' B' E' F', which is the vertical projection of the cylinder.

THE PROJECTIONS OF A RIGHT CONE, FIG. F.

99. The projections of a right cone differ from those of the cylinder solely as far as regards the vertical plane. Thus it will be seen,

D

in figs. 6 and 6ᵃ, that the horizontal projection of the cone, s A B, is exactly the same as that of a cylinder having an equal base; but the vertical projection, s′ A′ B′, in place of being a rectangle, is an isosceles triangle, of which the base is equal to the diameter of the circle, forming the horizontal projection, whilst the height is that of the cone. Similarly to the preceding case, in order to construct these projections, it is sufficient to know the radius of the circular base and the height.

THE PROJECTIONS OF A SPHERE, FIG. Ⓖ.

100. A sphere, in whatever position it may be with reference to the planes of projection, is invariably represented in each by a circle, the diameter of which is equal to its own; consequently, if the two projections, o and o, figs. 7ᵃ and 7, of the centre be given, we have merely to describe circles with these centres, with a radius equal to that, o A, of the given sphere.

It would seem from this, that one projection should be sufficient to indicate that the object represented is a sphere; but on referring to figs. 5ᵃ, and 6ᵃ, and 7ᵃ, it will be seen that a circle is one projection of three very different solids—namely, the cylinder, the cone, and the sphere. This is a further illustration of the inadequacy of one projection to give a faithful representation of any solid form. It is true, that by shading the single projection, we approach nearer to the desired representation; but still, such shaded projection would equally represent that of a cylinder with a hemispherical termination. The same remark applies to the shaded projections of cylinders and cones, and, indeed, to all solid bodies.

OF SHADOW-LINES.

101. To distinguish and relieve those parts of a drawing which are intended to indicate the more prominent portions of the object represented, it is customary to employ fine sharp lines for that part of the outline on which the light strikes in full, and strong and heavy lines for the parts which are at the same time in relief and in the shade; the latter description of lines are called *shadow-lines*.

For the maintenance of uniformity, it is obviously expedient to suppose the light to strike any object in some constant and particular direction. The assumed direction should be inclined, in order that some parts of the object may be thrown into shade, whilst others are more strongly illuminated. Hitherto, a uniform method has not been generally adopted with regard to the assumed direction of the rays of light. Some authors have recommended that it should be, as it were, parallel to that diagonal, A G, of the cube, fig. Ⓐ, of which the projections are A c and A′ E′, figs. 1 and 1ᵃ; others, however, cause the ray of light to take the direction A′ E′ in the vertical, and D B in the horizontal plane of projection, and some have proposed that the ray should strike the object in a direction perpendicular to either of the planes. We have adopted the first mentioned system, and we shall shortly indicate in what points it is superior, and on what account it is preferable, to any other.

The line which we take as the diagonal of the cube, is that which extends from the corner, A, of the front facet of the cube, fig. Ⓐ to the extreme and opposite corner, G, of the posterior facet. The projections of this straight line in the representations of the cube, figs. 1 and 1ᵃ, are respectively the lines, A c and A E′, lying each at an angle of 45° with the base line. Thus, in general, in our drawings the objects are supposed to receive the light in the direction of the arrows, R and R′, in fig. 8, according as the projection is in the vertical or horizontal plane.

102. We must observe, that the actual inclination of the straight line thus adopted, is not that of 45° with respect to either plane of projection; the angle of inclination is in fact somewhat less, and may be determined by means of the diagram, fig. 9. For this purpose, it is necessary to suppose the perpendicular plane in which the ray or line lies, as turned or folded down upon the vertical or horizontal plane, the turning axis being perpendicular to the base line. Let us, in the first place, suppose the two projections, R and R′, of the ray, to meet in the point, o, in the base line, L T; taking any point in this ray, as projected in the horizontal plane at a, and in the vertical at a′, with the point, o, as a centre, and radius, a o, describe the arc, a c a′, cutting the base line in the point, c; through this point draw the perpendicular, b b′, limited each way by the lines, a b, a′ b′, drawn parallel to the base line through the points, a, a. Joining o b and o b′, the lines thus obtained indicate the position and inclination of the ray, when folded down, as it were, on either plane of projection; and on applying a protractor, it will be found that the actual angle of inclination is one of 35° 16′ nearly. Having, then, fixed upon the direction of the rays of light, which are, of course, supposed to be parallel amongst themselves, it will be easy to determine which part of an object is illuminated, and which is in the shade. It will be perceived, for example, in figs. 1 and 1ᵃ, that the illuminated portions are those represented by the lines, A B and A D, on the one hand, and A′ B′ and A′ F′ on the other; and that those in the shade are represented respectively by the lines, B c, c D, and B′ E′, F′ E′. It must be observed, that according to this system, whatever part of the object is represented as illuminated in one projection, is equally so in the other; the shaded parts corresponding in a similar manner. What has just been said with reference to the cube, is equally applicable to all prisms or solids bounded by sharp definite outlines, care being taken to employ heavy shadow-lines only on the outlines of parts which are both prominent and in the shade—such shadow-lines separating the facets which are illuminated, from those which are not.

103. With regard to round bodies, the projections of the lateral portions being bounded by lines which should not indicate prominent and sharply defined edges, so full a shadow-line should not be employed as that forming the outline of a plane and prominent surface. Thus, in figs. 5, 6, and 7, the lines, B′ E′, s′ B′, and c′ B′ D′, are not nearly as strong as the corresponding lines, B′ E′, in figs. 1 to 4. Nevertheless, these lines should not be as fine as those on the illuminated side of the object, but of a medium strength or thickness, to indicate the portion of the object which is in the shade. In other words, a sharp fine line indicates the fully illuminated outline, a fuller line the portion in shade, and a shadow-line still stronger that portion which is both in the shade, and has a prominent sharply defined edge. The straight lines, F′ E′ and A′ B′, figs. 5 and 6, will necessarily be full shadow lines, as representing the edges of planes entirely in the shade.

In the horizontal projection of the cylinder, fig. 5ᵃ, the illuminated portion corresponds to the semi-circle, *a d b*, whilst that in the shade is the other semi-circle, *a c b*; the points, *a*, *b*, of separation of the two halves, are obtained by drawing through the centre, o, a diameter, *a b*, perpendicular to the ray of light, *d* o, or by drawing a couple of tangents to the circle parallel to this ray. The straight line, *a b*, is inclined to the base line at an angle of 45°. Great care is necessary in producing the circular shadow-line, *a c b*, and the nibs of the drawing-pen should be gradually brought closer as the extremities, *a* and *b*, of the shadow-line are approached, so that it may gradually die away into the thickness of the illuminated line. By inclining the drawing-pen, or by pressing it sideways against the paper, the desired effect may be produced; the exact method, however, being obtained rather by practice than by following any particular instructions. A very good effect may also, in some instances, be produced, by first drawing the entire circle with the fine line, and then retracing the part to be shadow-lined with a centre slightly to one side of the first centre, and repeating this until the desired strength of the shadow-line is obtained.

104. In the plan of a cone, fig. 6ᵃ, the part in the shade is always less than the part illuminated; but it requires an especial construction, which will be found in the chapter treating of Shadows, for the determination of the lines of separation, s *e*; and it is seldom that such extreme nicety is observed in outline drawings, the shadow-line of the plan of the cone being generally made the same as that of a cylinder, or perhaps a little less, according to the judgment of the artist. Yet, if the height of the cone be less than the radius of the base, the whole conical surface will be illuminated, and consequently its outline should have no shadow-line.

105. In explanation of the motives which have guided us in the adoption of the diagonal of a cube, as projected in the lines, R, R', fig. 8, as the direction of the rays of light, in preference to the other systems proposed, we shall proceed to point out some of the inconveniences attending the latter.

In the first place it must be observed, that if we adopt, as the direction of the rays of light, the diagonals projected in A' E' and D B, figs. 1 and 1ᵃ, that part of the object which is represented in the plan as illuminated, does not correspond with the part represented as illuminated in the elevation: in such case, the shadow-lines would be A B and B C in the horizontal projection, and F' E', D' E' in the vertical, so that there is no distinction made between the plan and the elevation; whereas, according to the system adopted by us, it is at first sight apparent which is the plan, and which the elevation, from the mere shadow-lines, which are in the latter at the lower parts of the object; whilst, in the former, they are, on the contrary, at the upper parts. It is not natural, moreover, to suppose that in the representation of any object, the light can be made to come as it were from behind the object, for in that case the side nearest the spectator would evidently be in the shade; and yet it is only on such a supposition that the projections of the ray of light can be such as D B and A' E'. Thus a double inconvenience may be urged against this system.

If, on the other hand, the rays of light are supposed to be perpendicular to either plane, such confusion will result as to render it impossible to ascertain, by any reference to the shadow-lines what is, or what is not, illuminated, and thus the object of employing shadow-lines would be lost sight of. Thus let us suppose, for example, that the light is perpendicular to the vertical plane, whence it follows that the whole of the anterior facet, figs. 1 to 4, is fully illuminated; but, at the same time, all the facets perpendicular to the vertical plane are equally in the shade, and it would consequently be necessary to use shadow-lines all round, or else not at all; and whichever plan was adopted, would be quite unintelligible. Besides this, it is unnatural to suppose that the spectator should place himself between the light and the object. Indeed, it is unquestionable that the most appropriate direction to be given to the ray of light is as before stated, that of the diagonal of a cube, of which the facets are respectively parallel to the two planes of projection; and the projections of this diagonal are, consequently, inclined to the base line at an angle of 45°, but proceeding from above in the vertical projection, and from below in the horizontal projection, as shown by the arrows, R and R', fig. 8.

PROJECTIONS OF GROOVED OR FLUTED CYLINDERS AND RATCHET WHEELS.

PLATE VIII.

106. The various diagrams in this plate are designed principally with the view of making the student practically conversant with the construction of the projections of objects; and, besides teaching him how to delineate their external contours, to enable him to represent them in *section*, that their internal structure may also be recorded on the drawing.

Figs. 1 and 1ᵃ are, respectively, the plan and elevation of a right cylinder, which is grooved on its entire external surface. The grooves on one-half of the circumference are supposed to be pointed, being formed by isosceles triangles of regular dimensions, and may represent the rollers used in flax machinery, in apparatus for preparing food for animals, and in many other machines. The other half of the circumference is formed into square or rectangular grooves, the lateral faces of which are either parallel to the centre lines which radiate from the centre, or are themselves radiating.

107. To construct the horizontal projection of this cylinder, that is, as seen from above, we must first ascertain how many grooves are contained in the whole circumference; then drawing a circle with a radius, A O, which should always be greater than that of the given cylinder, divide it into twice as many equal parts as there are grooves. If the student will refer back to the section treating of linear drawing, illustrated in Plate I., he will find simple methods of dividing circles into 2, 3, 4, 6, 8, and 12 equal parts, and, further, of subdividing these. Thus, as the cylinder, fig. 1, contains 24 grooves, its circumference must be divided into 48 equal parts. To obtain these, begin by drawing two diameters, A B, C D, perpendicular to each other; then, from each extremity, mark off the length of the radius, A O, thus obtaining the four points numbered 8 on one side, and the points numbered 4 on the other—making, with the points of intersection of the two diameters with the circumference, in all, 12 points. It remains simply to bisect each space, as A—4, B—4, or 4—8, &c., as well as the lesser spaces

thus found; this will give the 48 divisions required. Through the points of division draw a series of radii, which will divide the inner circle described, with the radius, o f, into the same number of equal parts.. The depth of the grooves is limited by the circle described with the radius, o e, whilst the outside of the intervening ridges is defined by the circle of the radius, o f. All the operations which we have so far indicated, are called for in the construction of both the triangular and rectangular grooves. In proceeding, we must, in the former case, join the points of intersection, a, b, c, d, which are in each circumference alternately; whilst in the latter case we require no fresh lines, but have simply to ink in alternate portions of the two circles, as well as the radial lines joining these.

108. To draw the vertical projection, fig. 1ᵉ, it is necessary that the depth should be given, say m′ n′ = 54. First set out the two horizontals, m′ p′, n′ q′, limiting the depth of the figure; then, to obtain the projection of the grooves and ridges, square over each of the points, e, f, g, h, &c., and draw parallels through the points thus found in fig. 1ᵉ, as e′, f′, g′, h′. This completes the elevation, and represents the whole exterior of that part of the cylinder below the horizontal, m p.

109. It has already been observed, that two projections are not always sufficient to form a complete representation of an object; thus it will be evident, from a consideration of figs. 1 and 1ᵉ, that a third view is necessary to explain the interior of the cylinder. The radius, o g = 42, of the central circular opening, is not apparent in fig. 1ᵉ, it is only to be found in the plan; whereas we have already seen, that, to determine its exact position, it should be represented in two projections. From figs. 1 and 1ᵉ, it is impossible to see if the opening exists throughout the depth of the cylinder, or if its radius be the same down to the bottom; and the same remark applies to the key-way. In consequence of this, it is expedient to draw the object as sectioned—for example, through the centre line, m p—by a plane parallel to the projection. Such a section is represented in fig. 1ᵇ; and from it, it is at once manifest that the central eye or opening, as well as the key-way, extend equally throughout the depth of the cylinder. The outline of these parts is formed by the verticals drawn through the points, g′, m′, n′, h′, obtained by squaring over the corresponding points, g, m, n, h, in the plan. This view also shows that the external grooves are equal throughout their depth, as indicated by the verticals drawn through m′, l′, r′, f′. When the outlines of the interior of an object are few and simple, they may be indicated in an elevation, such as 1ᵉ, by dotted lines. But if the outlines are numerous or complex, too great a confusion would result from this method; and it is far better, in such case, to give a sectional view.

That portion of the solid mass of the cylinder, through which the sectional plane passes, is indicated in fig. 1ᵇ, by a flat-tinted shading, so as to distinguish it from the parts which the plane does not meet: this is the plan generally adopted to show the parts in section; the strength of the shade, or sectioning, is varied according to the nature of the material. Thus, for cast-iron, a darker shade is used, whilst a lighter one indicates wood or stone; and as an example of this distinctive use of various degrees of shade, we have to point out that the sectioning in fig. 1ᵇ, indicates

the object to be made of copper, whilst that in fig. 2ᵇ corresponds to cast-iron, and in fig. 3ᵇ to wood or masonry.

110. It must be observed, that the *section lines*, of whatever description they may be, are always inclined at an angle of 45° with the base line; this is to distinguish the sectioning from flat tints frequently employed in elevations, to show that one surface is less prominent than another: this latter flat-tinting is generally produced by perpendicular or horizontal lines. The line, i′ j′, which indicates the base of the internal cylinder, g m h, should not be a shadow-line equal in strength to the bases of the sectional parts, for the latter are more prominent. This point is seldom attended to as it should be; greater beauty and effect, however, would result if it were. This remark applies equally to all projections of objects, of which one portion is more prominent than another. Thus, in figs. 1ᵉ, 2ᵉ, 3ᵉ, the vertical lines passing through f are considerably more pronounced than those passing through p′ q′ and lying in a posterior plane. It is the more important to observe these distinctions in representations of complex objects, so as to assist as much as possible a comprehension of the drawing. After the preceding consideration of fig. 1 on this plate, figs. 2 and 3, representing ratchet wheels and fluted cylinders, will be quite intelligible to the student; such operations as are additional, being rendered quite obvious by the views themselves.

THE ELEMENTS OF ARCHITECTURE.
PLATE IX.

111. Columns of the different orders of architecture are frequently employed in buildings, and also in mechanical constructions, as supports, where it is desired to combine elegance with strength. The ancient orders of architecture number five;* as,

1. The Tuscan.
2. The Doric.
3. The Ionic.
4. The Corinthian.
5. The Composite.

A sixth order is sometimes met with, denominated the Pœstum-Doric.

112. Each order of architecture comprises three principal parts: the *pedestal*, the *column*, and the *entablature*. In all the orders, the pedestal is a third of the length of the shaft in height, and the depth of the entablature is a fourth of the shaft. The proportion between the diameter and height of the column varies in each order. The height of the Tuscan column is seven times the diameter at the lowest part; the Doric, eight times; the Ionic, nine times; the Corinthian and Composite, ten times. The pedestal is frequently altogether dispensed with. All the different parts, in the various orders, bear some proportion to a *module*, which is half the diameter of the lower part of the column. This module may be termed, the unit of proportion. It is divided

* We have adhered to the classification which, from being of more ancient date, is supported by superior authority; but we do not profess, in this work, to decide which carries more reason with it. Reason frequently runs counter to authority. Modern architects say there are only three orders—the first comprising Ancient, Modern, and Tuscan Doric: the second, Greek, Roman, and Modern Ionic; and the third, Corinthian and Composite.

into 12 parts, in the Tuscan and Doric orders; and into 18 parts, in the Ionic, Corinthian, and Composite. The whole height of the Tuscan order is 22 modules 2 parts, apportioned as follows:— The column is 14 modules; the pedestal, 4 modules 8 parts; and the entablature, 3 modules 6 parts. The whole height of the Doric order is 25 modules 4 parts—the column being 16 modules; the pedestal, 5 modules 4 parts; and the entablature, 4 modules. The whole height of the Ionic order is 28 modules 9 parts—the pedestal, 6 modules; the column, 18 modules; and the entablature, 4 modules 9 parts. The whole height of the Corinthian and Composite orders is 31 modules 12 parts—of which 6 modules 12 parts form the pedestal, 20 modules the column, and 5 modules the entablature.

As we do not propose to treat especially of architecture, we have not given drawings of all the various orders, but have confined ourselves to the Tuscan, as being the simplest, as well as the one more generally adopted in the construction of machinery. At the end of this Chapter, will be found tables of the dimensions of the various components of the Tuscan order, and we also there give a similar table for the Doric order.

OUTLINE OF THE TUSCAN ORDER.

113. The whole height being given, as M N, the proportions of the different parts may always be determined. Let this height be, for example, 4 mètres 272 millimètres, fig. 7. First, divide it into 19 equal parts, then take 4 such parts for the height of the pedestal, 12 for that of the column, and the remaining 3 for the entablature. Then, according to the order which it is intended to follow, the height, $m\,n$, of the column, is divided into 7, 8, 9, or 10 equal parts, and the diameter of the lower part of the column will be equal to one of these divisions: thus, in the Tuscan order, the diameter, $a\,b$, is $\frac{1}{7}$ of the height, $m\,n$; the half of this diameter, or the radius of the shaft, is the unit of proportional measurement, called the module, and with which all the components of the order are measured: it follows then, that in the Tuscan order this module is $\frac{1}{14}$ of the height of the column, in the Doric $\frac{1}{16}$, in the Ionic $\frac{1}{18}$, and $\frac{1}{20}$ in the Corinthian and Composite.

114. The three members of an order are each subdivided into three divisions. Thus the Pedestal is composed of the Socle, or lower Plinth, A; of the Dado, B; and Cornice, C: the column consists of the Base, or Plinth, D; the Shaft, E; and the Capital, F; and in the entablature are the Architrave, G; the Frieze, H; and the Cornice, I.

115. Before proceeding to delineate these different parts, and the mouldings with which they are ornamented, it is expedient to set off a scale of modules, determined in the manner just stated, the module being, of course, subdivided into 12 equal parts.

To make the mouldings and various details more intelligible, we have drawn the various portions of the order, separately, to a larger scale. Thus the socle and pedestal of the column are represented in elevation in fig. 2, and in plan in fig. 3, to a scale $2\frac{1}{2}$ times that of the complete view, fig. 1, and the module will, of course, be proportionately larger. All the numbers indicated on these figures, give the exact measurements of each part and each moulding, so that they may be drawn in perfect accordance with the scale given. It conduces considerably to the symmetry and exactitude of the

drawing, to set off all the measurements from the axis or centre line, $c\,d$. The module being but an arbitrary measurement, it is necessary, in practically carrying out any design, to ascertain the different measures in mètres and parts of mètres; and for this reason we have given additional scales in mètres, to correspond to those in modules; and we have also expressed in millimètres, on each figure, the measurements of the various details, placing the métrical in juxtaposition with the modular ones. And, to give a distinct idea as to the degrees of prominence or relief of the various members, a part of the elevation is shown as sectioned by a plane passing through the axis of the shaft, this part being sufficiently distinguishable from the sectional flat-tinting. In the horizontal projection, fig. 3, are also represented portions of sections in two different planes, one being at the height of the line, 5—6, and the other at that of 7—8. The first shows that the shaft is round, as well as the fillet, f, and the torus, g, whilst the base, h, and cornice, $i\,j$, are square: the second section shows, in a similar manner, that the dado, B, the socle, A, and its fillet, p, are square. The flat-tintings sufficiently indicate the parts in section.

Fig. 4 represents the entablature and the capital of the column in elevation and in section. Fig. 5 is a horizontal section of the column with its capital, as it were inverted, and is supposed to be half through the line, 1—2, and half through 3—4. The whole is what is termed a false section, the parts in section being in parallel, but not identical planes. The different measurements are given in modules and mètres, as in the other figures; they indicate the respective distances from the axis, $c'\,d'$.

116. The execution of this design offers little or no difficulty; but all the operations required, as well as the parts to which the measurements apply, are carefully indicated. It is, therefore, unnecessary to enter into further details, except as far as relates to such parts as involve some peculiarity; the shaft of the column, for example, and one or two of the mouldings.

Referring, in the first place, to the column, it is to be observed that it is customary to make the shaft cylindrical for one third of the height, that is, of equal diameter throughout that extent: above that point, however, it diminishes gradually in diameter up to the capital. This taper is not regular throughout, being scarcely perceptible at the lower part, and becoming more and more convergent towards the top. Its contour is consequently a curve, instead of a straight line. This curvature constitutes what is termed the *entasis*, and is employed to correct the apparent narrowness of a rectilinear column at the middle. Such defective appearance only takes place when the cylindrical piece, or column, is between a pedestal and an entablature having plane surfaces. A cylinder, or sphere, always seems to occupy less space than a plane surface equal to its greatest section. Thus the outline of a cylinder or sphere, appears to grow less when it is shaded. Now, where the column is in contact with the plane surface of the pedestal or entablature, it cannot appear less in proportion, the proximity of the latter correcting such appearance, whilst the influence is less felt at the central part, which is furthest from the pedestal and entablature. A true cylinder, therefore, in such position, appears to be thinner at the middle, and this is corrected by the entasis. or curved contour.

But many authorities consider this a fastidious nicety, and it is frequently disregarded, particularly in designing short thick columns for machinery, and also where the other extreme is reached, and the columns become mere rods.

What may be termed the *mechanical entasis*, is, moreover, employed in beams, levers, and connecting-rods of all descriptions; the object of this convexity, and increased width in the middle part, in such cases, being to obtain strength and rigidity, whilst it undoubtedly adds to the beauty of form.

To determine the amount of the entasis in the Tuscan column, divide the line, *c d*, fig. 6, which represents two-thirds the height of the shaft, into any number of equal parts, say six. With the point, *d*, as centre, and a radius, *d e*, equal to one module, draw an arc of a circle; next, having made *c v* equal to $9\frac{1}{2}$ parts, draw through *v* a line, *v x*, parallel to the axis, *c d¹*, this parallel will cut the arc in the point, *x*; divide the arc, *e x*, into six equal parts, and then through the points, 1, 2, 3, &c., thus obtained, draw parallels to the axis. These parallels will intersect the horizontal lines drawn through the divisions, *q, r, s, t*, of the axis, respectively, in the points, 1′, 2′, 3′, &c., and through these will pass the required curve, forming the contour of the shaft. This curve, being symmetrically reproduced on the opposite side of the axis, *c d*, will complete the outline of the shaft.

In the entablature and pedestal will be found two similar mouldings, termed *cymatia*; they are both examples of the *cyma reversa*, discussed in reference to Plate 3. The slight peculiarities in their construction, will be easily understood from the enlarged view, fig. 8. The *quarter rounds* and accompanying minor mouldings belonging to the capital and entablature, are also represented separately, and on a larger scale, in figs. 9 and 10.

RULES AND PRACTICAL DATA.
THE MEASUREMENT OF SOLIDS.

117. We have already seen that the volume or solidity of a body, is the extent of space embraced by its three dimensions—length, width, and height; the last of these being frequently termed depth, or thickness. The volume of a solid is determined when it is ascertained what relation it bears to, or how many times it contains, any cube which is adopted as the unit of the measurement. Such a unit is the *cubic mètre*, just as a square mètre is employed to measure surface, and a linear mètre length.

The subdivisions of the cubic mètre are the cubic décimètre, the cubic centimètre, and the cubic millimètre. The relations these bear to the linear subdivisions will be obvious from the following comparison.

Whilst 1 mètre = 10 décimètres = 100 centimètres = 1000 millimètres.

1 Cubic mètre = $(10^{d.} \times 10^{d.} \times 10^{d.} =)$ 1000 cubic décimètres = $(100^{c.} \times 100^{c.} \times 100^{c.} =)$ 1,000,000 cubic centimètres = $(1000\ ^{m}/_{m} \times 1000\ ^{m}/_{m} \times 1000^{m}/_{m} =)$ 1,000,000,000, cubic millimètres; consequently, 1 cubic décimètre = ·001 or $\frac{1}{1000}$ cubic mètre, the cubic centimètre = ·0000001 or $\frac{1}{1000000}$ cubic mètre.

Similarly, we measure volume by cubic yards, feet, or inches, just as we measure surface by square, and length by linear yards, feet, and inches. A cubic foot is $\frac{1}{27}$ of a cubic yard, for—

1 cubic foot = $\frac{1}{3}$ yard × $\frac{1}{3}$ yard × $\frac{1}{3}$ yard = $\frac{1}{27}$ yard;

and an inch, or

$\frac{1}{12}$ foot × $\frac{1}{12}$ foot × $\frac{1}{12}$ foot = $\frac{1}{1728}$ foot.

119. *Parallelopipeds.*—The volume of a parallelopiped is equal to the product of its base multiplied into its height.

Example.—Fig. ⒝. Pl. 7. Let A F = 2 feet, F E = 1·4 feet, and F H = 1·4 feet. Then the base = 1·4 × 1·4 = 1·96, and 1·96 × 2 = 3·92 cubic feet; or more simply, 1·4 × 1·4 × 2 = 3·92 c. ft. A *cube* itself, having all its dimensions equal—its volume is expressed by the third *power* of the measure of one of its sides; that is, by the product of one side three times into itself.

Thus the cube, fig. ⒜, of which one side measures, say 1·4 feet, contains 1·4 × 1·4 × 1·4, or 1·4³ = 2·744 cubic feet.

In general, the volume of a right prism, whatever be its base, is equal to the product of the base into the height.

TABLE OF SURFACES, AND VOLUMES OF REGULAR POLYHEDRA.

NUMBER OF SIDES.	NAME	SURFACE.	VOLUME.
4	Tetrahedron,	1·7820508	·1178519
6	Hexahedron, or Cube,	6·0000000	1·0000000
8	Octahedron,	3·4641016	·4714045
12	Dodecahedron,	20·6457788	7·6631189
20	Icosahedron,	8·6602540	2·1816950

120. *Pyramids.*—The volume of a polygonal pyramid is equal to its base multiplied into a third of its height.

Example.—Let S O, fig. ⒞ = 2 inches, A B and A D each = 1·4 inches; the cubic contents of the pyramid are—

$$\frac{1·4 \times 1·4 \times 2}{3} = 1·3066 \text{ cubic inches.}$$

Thus the volume of a pyramid is one-third of that of a right prism, having an equal base, and being of the same height.

The volume of a truncated pyramid, with parallel bases, is equal to the product of a third of the height, into the sum of the two bases added to the square root of their product.

Thus, if V represent the volume of a truncated pyramid, of which the height, H, = 3 feet, the lower base, B, = 6 square feet, the upper, B′, = 4 square feet; we have—

$$V = \frac{H}{3} \times (B + B′ + \sqrt{B\,B′}) =$$

$$\frac{3}{3} \times (6 \text{ s. f.} + 4 \text{ s. f.} + \sqrt{6 \times 4}) = 14·898 \text{ sq. feet.}$$

In practice, when there is little difference between the areas of the bases, a close approximation to the volume is obtained by taking the half of the sum of the bases, multiplied into the height. Thus, with the preceding data, we have

$$V = H \times \left(\frac{B + B'}{2}\right) = 15 \text{ sq. ft.}$$

121. Cylinders.—The cubic contents of any cylinder, as fig. $\boxed{E}$, is equal to the product of the base into the height. Thus, in the case of a cylinder of a circular base, we have $B = \pi R^2$ (72);* consequently, the volume, V, $= \pi R^2 \times H$.

First Example.—What is the volume of a cast-iron cylinder, of which the radius, R, $= 20$ inches, and the length, H, $= 108$ inches ?

$$V = 3 \cdot 1416 \times 20^2 \times 108 = 135,717 \text{ cubic inches.}$$

The volume may also be derived from the diameter of the cylinder, in which case we have—

$$V = \frac{\pi D^2}{4} \times H; \text{ or,}$$

$$V = \cdot 7854 \times 40^2 \times 108 = 135,717 \text{ cubic in.}$$

The convex surface of a right cylinder, when developed, is equal to the area of a rectangle, having for base the rectilinear development of the circumference, and for height that of the cylinder. It is therefore obtained by multiplying the circumference into the height or length. With the data of the preceding case, the convex surface is expressed by the formula—

$$S = 2\pi R \times H, \text{ or } \pi D \times H = 3 \cdot 1416 \times 40 \times 108 =$$
$$13,571 \cdot 7 \text{ cubic inches.}$$

The volume of a hollow cylinder is equal to the difference between that of a solid cylinder of the same external radius, and that of one whose radius is equal to the internal radius of the hollow cylinder. Or, it is equal to the product of the sectional area into the height, such area being equal to the difference between two circles of the external and internal radius, respectively.

Example.—It is required to find the volume, V, and the internal surface, S', of a steam-engine cylinder, including its top and bottom flanges in the volume. Let the following be the dimensions :— External diameter, D, $= 56$ inches ; internal diameter, D', $= 50$ inches ; length or height, H, $= 120$ inches ; external projection of the flanges, F, $= 5$ inches, and their thickness, E, $= 4$ inches. Then, for the internal surface, we have—

$$S' = 3 \cdot 1416 \times 50 \times 120 = 18,850 \text{ sq. in.}$$

For the volume of the body of the cylinder, we have—

$$V' = \frac{\pi 56^2}{4} - \frac{\pi 50^2}{4} \times 120 = (\cdot 7854 \times 56^2) - (\cdot 7854 \times 50^2) \times$$
$$120 = 60,000 \text{ cubic inches.}$$

And for the additional volume of the flanges—

$$V'' = \frac{\pi (56 + 10)^2}{4} - \frac{\pi 56^2}{4} \times 4 \times 2 = (\cdot 7854 \times 66^2) -$$
$$(\cdot 7854 \times 56^2) \times 8 = 7666 \text{ cubic inches.}$$

Whence the whole volume—

$$V' + V'' = 67,666 \text{ cubic inches.}$$

---

* When we wish to refer the student to any rule or principle already given, we do so by means of the number of the paragraph containing such rule or principle. In the present instance, what is referred to will be found at page 20.

122. Cones.—The cubic content of a cone is equal to the product of its base into a third of its height ; or,

$$V = B \times \frac{H}{3}$$

In the right cone, fig. $\boxed{F}$, of which the base is circular—

$$V \pi = R^2 \times \frac{H}{3} = \frac{\pi D^2}{4} \times \frac{H}{3};$$

and as π, or $3 \cdot 1416 \div (4 \times 3) = \cdot 2618$, the formula resolves itself into—

$$V = \cdot 2618 \times D^2 \times H.$$

Example.—What is the volume of a right cone, of which the height, H, $= 24$ inches, and the diameter of the base, or D, $= 17$ inches ?

We have—

$$V = \cdot 2618 \times 17^2 \times 24 = 1816 \text{ cubic inches.}$$

As we shall demonstrate, at a more advanced stage, the development of the convex surface of a right cone is equal to the sector of a circle, of which the radius is the generatrix, and the arc the circumference of the base of the cone—consequently, the conical surface is equal to the product of the circumference of the base into the half of the generatrix : whence is derived the following formula :—

$$S = 2\pi R \times \frac{G}{2} = \pi R \times G.$$

With the data of the foregoing example, and allowing the generatrix to be equal to $25\frac{1}{2}$ inches, we have—

$$S = 3 \cdot 1416 \times 8 \cdot 5 \times 25 \cdot 5 = 681 \text{ cubic inches.}$$

123. Frustum of a cone.—The volume of the frustum of a cone may be obtained in the same manner as that of the truncated pyramid (120). The convex surface of a truncated cone is equal to the product of half the generatrix of the frustum into the sum of the circumferences of the bases, and is expressed in the following formula :

$$S = \frac{L}{2} \times 2\pi (R + R') = L \times \pi (R + R').$$

Example.—Let the length, L, of the generatrix of the cone frustum, $= 14$ inches ; the radius, R, of the lower base, $= 8 \cdot 5$ inches ; the radius, R', of the upper base, $= 3 \cdot 8$ inches ; then the convex surface—

$$S = 14 \times 3 \cdot 1416, \times (8 \cdot 5 + 3 \cdot 8) = 54 \text{ square inches.}$$

124. Sphere.—The volume of a sphere may be ascertained as soon as its radius is known. Its surface is equal to four times that of a circle of equal diameter. This is expressed by the formula—

$$S = 4\pi R^2 = \pi D^2 = 3 \cdot 1416 \times D^2,$$

or the square of the diameter multiplied by $3 \cdot 1416$.

The volume is equal to the product of the surface into one-third of the radius, as in the formula—

$$V = 4\pi R^2 \times \frac{R}{3} = \frac{4}{3} \times \pi R^3, \text{ or } V = 4 \cdot 188 \times R^3 :$$

or, if we employ the diametral ratio—

$$V = \pi D^2 \times \frac{D}{6} = \cdot 5236 \times D^3$$

Example.—We would know what is the surface and the volume of a sphere, of which the diameter measures 25 inches.

The surface—

$$S = 25^2 \times 3 \cdot 1416 = 1963 \cdot 5 \text{ sq. inches}$$

The volume—

$$V = \cdot 5236 \times 25^3 = 8181 \cdot 25 \text{ cubic inches.}$$

To find the radius or diameter of a sphere, of which the volume is known, it is sufficient to invert the preceding operations, the formulas becoming as follows—

$$R^3 = \frac{3V}{4\pi} = \frac{V}{4 \cdot 188};$$

whence,

$$R = \sqrt[3]{\frac{V}{4 \cdot 188}}.$$

Similarly,

$$D^3 = \frac{V}{\cdot 5236};$$

whence,

$$D = \sqrt[3]{\frac{V}{\cdot 5236}};$$

which, with the preceding data, gives R = 12·5 inches, and D = 25 inches.

The radius is derived from the surface by means of the following formula:—

$$R^2 = \frac{S}{4 \times 3 \cdot 1416};$$

whence,

$$R = \sqrt{\frac{S}{12 \cdot 5664}}$$

or,

$$D^2 = \frac{S}{3 \cdot 1416};$$

whence,

$$D = \sqrt{\frac{S}{3 \cdot 1416}}.$$

125. *Spheric sectors, segments, and zones.*—The surface of a zone or spheric segment, is equal to the product of the circumference of a circle of the sphere, into the height of the zone or segment; or,

$$S = 2\pi R \times H.$$

Example.—The height, H, of a spheric segment being 1·5 inches, and the radius, R, of the sphere, 7·5 inches, the surface—

$$S = 2 \times 3 \cdot 1416 \times 7 \cdot 5 \times 1 \cdot 5 = 70 \cdot 686 \text{ sq. inches.}$$

The volume of a spheric sector is equal to the product of the surface of its spherical base, into one-third the radius of the sphere of which it is a portion.

The corresponding formula is therefore—

$$V = 2\pi R \times H \times \frac{R}{3} = \frac{2}{3}\pi \times R^2 H = 2 \cdot 094 \times R^2 \times H.$$

Example.—The volume of the spheric sector, whose spheric base is equal to the surface considered in the previous example, is—

$$V = 2 \cdot 094 \times 7 \cdot 5^2 \times 1 \cdot 5 = 176 \cdot 68 \text{ cubic inches.}$$

The volume of a spheric segment is equal to the product of the arc of the circle of which the chord is radius, into one-sixth of the height of the segment; or,

$$V = \pi r^2 \times \frac{H}{6} = \cdot 5296 \times r^2 \times H.$$

Example.—Let r = 6·5 inches, and H 1·5 inches; the then volume—

$$V = \cdot 5296 \times 6 \cdot 5^2 \times 1 \cdot 5 = 33 \cdot 56 \text{ cubic inches.}$$

The volume of a spheric ungula is equal to the product of the gore, which is its base, into a third of the radius.

The formula is—

$$V = \frac{2}{3} A \times R^2;$$

where A = the area of the gore.

The volume of a zonic segment is equal to half the sum of its bases, multiplied by its height, *plus* the volume of a sphere of which that height is the diameter; whence the formula—

$$V = \left(\frac{\pi R^2 + \pi R'^2}{2}\right) \times H + \frac{\pi H^3}{6}.$$

126. *Observations.*—The volumes of spheres are proportional to the cubes of their radii, or diameters. Let V = 14·137 cubic inches, and v = 4·188 cubic inches. It will be found that the respective radii are—

$$R = \sqrt[3]{\frac{V}{4 \cdot 188}} = \sqrt[3]{\frac{14 \cdot 137}{4 \cdot 188}} = 1 \cdot 5:$$

and

$$r = \sqrt[3]{\frac{v}{4 \cdot 188}} = \sqrt[3]{\frac{4 \cdot 188}{4 \cdot 188}} = 1;$$

and, consequently, D = 3 and d = 2.

The cubes of these numbers, that is, 27 and 8, have the same ratio to each other as the volumes given; that is to say—

$$27 : 8 :: 14 \cdot 137 : 4 \cdot 188.$$

When of equal height, cylinders are to each other, as well as cones, as the squares of the radii of their bases.

When of equal diameter, these solids are to each other as their heights.

First, then, we have—

$$V = \pi R^2 \times H, \text{ and } v = \pi r^2 \times H;$$

whence,

$$V : v :: R^2 : r^2$$

And, secondly,

$$V = \pi R^2 \times H, \text{ and } v = \pi R^2 \times h;$$

whence,

$$V : v :: H : h.$$

The volume of a sphere is to that of the circumscribed cylinder as 2 to 3. A sphere is said to be inscribed in a cylinder, when its diameter is equal to the height and diameter of the cylinder.

The volume of an annular torus, or ring, is equal to the product of its section into the mean circumference. We have pointed out (90) that an annular torus is a solid, generated by the revolution of a circle about an axis, situated in the plane of the circle, and at right angles to the plane of revolution.

Let R be the radius of the generating circle, and r the distance of its centre from the axis, we have—

$$V = \pi R^2 \times 2\pi r = 19 \cdot 72 R^2 \times r.$$

PROPORTIONAL MEASUREMENTS OF THE VARIOUS PARTS OF AN ENTIRE ORDER.

THE (MODERN) DORIC ORDER.

Designations of the Members and Mouldings constituting the Order.			Measurements according to Vignoles, in Modules of 12 Parts. — Amount of Projection from the Axis of the Shaft. M. P.	Heights. M. P.	M. P.	M. P.	Measures in Decimals. The Module = 1. — Amount of Projection from the Axis of the Shaft.	Heights.		
ENTABLATURE.	CORNICE, . .	Reglet,	2 10	1			2·833	·083		
		Cavetto,	2 7	3			2.583	·250		
		Fillet,	2 6½	½			2·542	·042		
		Cymatium,	2 6 2 5	1½			2·500 2·417	·125		
		Corona,	2 4½	4			2·375	·333		
		Fillet,	2 2	½	1 6		2·167	·042	1·500	
		Mutules,	2 1½	½			2·125	·042		
		Guttæ,	1 3	2½			1·250	·209		
		Fillet,	1 1	½		4 0	1·083	·042		4·000
		Cymatium,	1 0½ 11½	2			1·042 ·959	·166		
		Capitals of the Triglyphs,	11	2			·917	·166		
	FRIEZE,		10	1 6	1 6		·833	1·500	1·500	
	ARCHITRAVE,	Tænia,	11½	2	1 0		·959	·167	1·000	
		Facia,	10	10			·833	·833		
COLUMN.	CAPITAL, . .	Reglet,	1 3½	½			1·292	·042		
		Cymatium,	1 3¼ 1 2¼	1			1·271 1·188	·083		
		Abacus,	1 2	2½			1·167	·209		
		Echinus,	1 1¾	2½	1 0		1·146	·209	1·000	
		Three Annulets,	11½ 10½	1½			·959 ·875	·124		
		Necking,	10	4			·833	·333		
	SHAFT, . . .	Beading or Astragal,	1 0	1		16 0	1·000	·083		16·000
		Cincture,	11½	½			·959	·042		
		Shaft Proper,	10 1 0	13 10½	14 0		·833 1·000	13·875	14·000	
	BASE, ...	Fillet,	1 1¼	1			1·104	·083		
		Beading,	1 2	1			1·167	·083		
		Torus,	1 5	4	1 0		1·417	·334	1·000	
		Plinth,	1 5	6			1·417	·500		
PEDESTAL.	CORNICE, . .	Reglet,	1 11	½			1·917	·042		
		Quarter-Round,	1 10⅔	1			1·889	·083		
		Fillet,	1 9⅔	½			1·806	·042		
		Corona,	1 9	2½	6		1·750	·209	·500	
		Cymatium,	1 6½ 1 5½	1½			1·542 1·459	·124		
	DADO,		1 5	4 0	4 0	5 4	1·417	4·000	4·000	16 000
	BASE, ...	Fillet,	1 6	½			1·500	·042		
		Beading,	1 7	1			1·583	·083		
		Cyma Reversa,	1 7 1 8½	2	10		1·583 1·708	·166	8·333	
		Plinth,	1 9	2½			1·750	·209		
		Sub-Plinth or Socle,	1 9½	4			1·792	·333		
Total height of the Order,			. . . . .	. . . .		25 4	. . . . .	. . . .		25·333

PROPORTIONAL MEASUREMENTS OF THE VARIOUS PARTS OF AN ENTIRE ORDER.

THE TUSCAN ORDER.

Designations of the Members and Mouldings constituting the Order.	Measurements according to Vignoles, in Modules of 12 Parts. — Amount of Projection from the Axis of the Shaft (M. P.)	Measurements according to Vignoles — Heights (M. P.)	Measurements in Decimals. The Module = 1. — Amount of Projection from the Axis of the Shaft	Measurements in Decimals — Heights
ENTABLATURE — CORNICE — Quarter-Round	2 3½	4	2·292	·333
Beading	2 0	1	2·000	·083
Fillet	1 11½	½	1·959	·042
Larmier or Corona	1 10½	6 } 1 4	1·875	·500 } 1·333
Fillet	1 7½	½	1·625	·042
Cymatium	*1 1½ / 10	4 } 3 6	1·125 / ·833	·333 } 3·500
FRIEZE	9½	1 2 | 1 2	·792	1·167 | 1·167
ARCHITRAVE — Listel	11½	2 } 1 0	·959	·167 } 1·000
Facia	9½	10	·792	·833
COLUMN — CAPITAL — Listel	1 2½	1	1·209	·083
Abacus	1 1½	3	1·125	·250
Echinus, or Quarter-Round	1 1	3 } 1 0	1·083	·250 } 1·000
Fillet	10½	1	·875	·083
Necking	9½	4	·792	·334
SHAFT — Astragal { Beading	11	1	·917	·083
Astragal { Cincture	10½	½ } 12 0	·875	·042 } 12·000
Shaft Proper	9½ / 1 0	11 10½	·792 / 1·000	11·875
BASE — Fillet	1 1½	1	1·125	·083
Torus	1 4½	5 } 1 0	1·375	·417 } 1·000
Plinth	1 4½	6	1·375	·500
PEDESTAL — CORNICE — Listel	1 8½	2 } 6	1·709	·167 } ·500
Cymatium	1 8 / 1 5	4	1·667 / 1·417	·333
DADO	1 4½	3 8 | 3 8 } 4 8	1·375	3·667 | 3·667 } 4·667
BASE — Listel	1 6½	1 } 6	1·542	·083 } ·500
Socle or Plinth	1 8½	5	1·709	·417
Total height of the Order,	.....	.... 22 2	.....	.... 22·167

COLUMN total: 14 0 ; 14·000

* When two measurements are given, the first applies to the upper portion, the second to the lower.

With the help of these tables we can easily determine the proper measurement for any member or moulding, in feet, inches, or metres, when the height of the whole order is given. For this purpose the given height must be divided by the decimal measurement in the tables for the total given height; the quotient is the measurement of the module proportioned to such height. Then that of any required member is found by multiplying this module into the decimal in the table corresponding to such member.

First Example.—It is required to know what is the diameter of the lower part of the shaft according to the Tuscan order, the height of the entire order being 15 feet.

The height of the entire order being 22·167 when the module $=1$, we have $\frac{22 \cdot 167}{15} = 1 \cdot 4778$ the module, and $1 \cdot 4778 \times 2 = 2 \cdot 9556$ feet, the diameter of the lower part of the shaft.

Second Example.—What is the height of the socle or lower plinth according to the Tuscan order, supposing the module to be 1·4778 feet? We have $1 \cdot 4778 \times \cdot 417 = \cdot 616$.

In like manner the dimensions of all the other details may be easily determined according to the Tuscan or Doric order.

CHAPTER III.
ON COLOURING SECTIONS, WITH APPLICATIONS.

CONVENTIONAL COLOURS.

127. Hitherto we have indicated the sectional portions of objects by means of linear flat-tinting. This is a very tedious process, whilst it demands a large amount of artistic skill—only obtainable by long practice—to enable the draughtsman to produce pleasing and regular effects; and although, by varying the strength or closeness of the lines, as we have already pointed out, it is possible to express approximately the nature of the material, yet the extent of such variation is extremely limited, and the distinction it gives is not sufficiently intelligible for all purposes. If, however, in place of such line sectioning, we substitute colours laid on with a brush, we at once obtain a means of rapidly tinting the sectional parts of an object, and also of distinctly pointing out the nature of the materials of which it is composed, however numerous and varied such materials may be. Such colours are generally adopted in geometrical drawings; they are conventional —that is, certain colours are generally understood to indicate particular materials.

In Plate X. we give examples of the principal materials in use, with their several distinctive colours; such as stone and brick, steel and cast-iron, copper and brass, wood and leather. We propose now to enter into some details of the composition of the various colours given in this plate.

THE COMPOSITION OR MIXTURE OF COLOURS.
PLATE X.

128. *Stone.*—Fig. 1. This material is represented by a light dull yellow, which is obtained from Roman ochre, with a trifling addi- ton of China ink.

129. *Brick.*—Fig. 2. A light red is employed for this material, and may be obtained from vermilion, which may sometimes be brightened by the addition of a little carmine. A pigment found in most colour-boxes, and termed *Light Red*, may also be used when great purity and brightness of tint is not wanted. If it is desired to distinguish firebrick from the ordinary kind, since the former is lighter in colour and inclined to yellow, some gamboge must be mixed with the vermilion, the whole being laid on more faintly. In external views it is customary to indicate the outlines of the individual bricks, but in the section of a mass of brickwork this refinement may be dispensed with, except in cases where it is

intended to show the disposition or method of building up. Thus, in furnaces, as also in other structures, the strength depends greatly on the method of laying the bricks. When vermilion is used in combination with other colours, the colour should be constantly mixed up by the brush—as, from its greater weight, the vermilion has a tendency to sink and separate itself from the others; and if this is overlooked, a varying tint of unpleasing effect will be imparted to the object coloured.

130. *Steel or Wrought Iron.*—Fig. 3. The colour by which these metals are expressed is obtained from pure Prussian blue laid on light—being lighter and perhaps brighter for steel than for wrought- iron. The Prussian blue generally met with in cakes has a con- siderable inclination to a greenish hue, arising from the gum with which it is made up. This defect may be considerably amended by the addition of a little carmine or crimson lake—the proper proportion depending on the taste of the artist.

131. *Cast-Iron.*—Indigo is the colour employed for this metal; the addition of a little carmine improves it. The colours termed *Neutral Tint*, or *Payne's Gray*, are frequently used in place of the above, and need no further mixture. They are not, however, so easy to work with, and do not produce so equable a tint.

132. *Lead* and *Tin* are represented by similar means, the colour being rendered more dull and gray by the addition of China ink and carmine or lake.

133. *Copper.*—Fig. 5. For this metal, pure carmine or crimson lake is proper. A more exact imitation of the reality may be ob- tained by the mixture, with either of these colours, of a little China ink or burnt sienna—the carmine or lake, of course, considerably predominating.

134. *Brass or Bronze.*—Fig. 6. These are expressed by an orange colour, the former being the brighter of the two; burnt Roman ochre is the simplest pigment for producing this colour. Where, however, a very bright tint is desired, a mixture should be made of gamboge with a little vermilion—care being taken to keep it constantly agitated, as before recommended. Many draughtsmen use simple gamboge or other yellow.

135.—*Wood.*—Fig. 7. It will be observable, from preceding examples, that the tints have been chosen with reference to the actual colours of the materials which they are intended to express— carrying out the same principle, we should have a very wide range in the case of wood. The colour generally used, however, is

burnt umber or raw sienna; but the depth or strength with which
it is laid on, may be considerably varied. It is usual to apply
a light shade first, subsequently showing the graining with a
darker tint, or perhaps with burnt sienna. These points are susceptible of great variation, and very much must be left to the
judgment of the artist.

136. *Leather, Vulcanized India-Rubber, and Gutta Percha.*—
Fig. 8. These are all represented by very similar tints. Leather
by light, and gutta percha by dark sepia, whilst vulcanized india-
rubber requires the addition of a little indigo to that colour.

We may here remark, that if the student is unwilling to obtain
an extensive stock of colours, he may content himself with merely
a good blue, a yellow, and a red—say Prussian blue, gamboge or
yellow ochre, and crimson lake. With these three, after a little
experimental practice, he may produce all the various tints he
needs; but, of course, with less readiness and facility than if his
assortment were larger.

137. *The Manipulation of the Colours.*—We have seen by what
mixtures each tint may be obtained, and we shall proceed to give
a few hints relative to their application. It may be imagined that
it is an easy matter to colour a geometrical drawing—that is, simply
to lay on the colours; but a little attention to the following
observations will not be misplaced, as the student may thereby at
once acquire that method which conduces so much to regularity
and beauty of effect, and which it might otherwise require some
practice to teach.

The cake of colour should never be dipped in the water, as this
causes the edges to crack and crumble off, wasting considerable
quantities. Instead of this, a few drops of water should be first
put in the saucer, or on the plate, and then the required quantity
of colour rubbed down, the cake being wetted as little as is
absolutely necessary. The strength or depth of the colour is
obtained by proportioning the quantity of water, the whole being
well mixed, to make the tint and shade equable throughout.
When large surfaces have to be covered by one shade, which it
is desired to make a perfectly even flat tint, it is well to produce
the required strength by a repetition of very light washes. These
washes correct each other's defects, and altogether produce a soft
and pleasing effect. This method should generally be employed
by the beginner, as he will thereby more rapidly obtain the art of
producing equable flat tints. The washes should not be applied
before each preceding one is perfectly dry. When the drawing-
paper is old, partially glazed, or does not take the colour well,
its whole surface should receive a wash of water, in which a very
small quantity of gum-arabica or alum has been dissolved. In
proceeding to lay on the colour, care should be taken not to fill
the brush too full, whilst, at the same time, it must be replenished
before its contents are nearly expended, to avoid the difference in
tint which would otherwise result. It is also necessary first to
try the colour on a separate piece of paper, to be sure that it will
produce the desired effect. It is a very common habit with
water-colour artists to point the brush, and take off any superfluous colour, by passing it between their lips. This is a very
bad and disagreeable habit, and should be altogether shunned.
Not only may the colour which is thus taken into the mouth be
injurious to health, but it is impossible, if this is done, to produce

a fine even shade, for the least quantity of saliva which may be
taken up by the brush has the effect of clouding and altogether
spoiling the wash of colour on the paper. In place of this un-
cleanly method, the artist should have a piece of blotting-paper at
his side—the more absorbent the better. By passing the brush
over this, any superfluous colour may be taken off, and as fine a
point obtained as by any other means. The brush should not be
passed more than once, if possible, over the same part of the drawing before it is dry; and when the termination of a large shade is
nearly reached, the brush should be almost entirely freed from the
colour, otherwise the tint will be left darker at that part. Care
should be taken to keep exactly to the outline; and any space
contained within definite outlines should be wholly covered at one
operation, for if a portion is done, and then allowed to dry, or become
aged, it will be almost impossible to complete the shade, without
leaving a distinct mark at the junction of the two portions. Finally,
to produce a regular and even appearance, the brush should not be
overcharged, and the colour should be laid on as *thin* as possible;
for the time employed in more frequently replenishing the brush,
because of its becoming sooner exhausted, will be amply repaid by
the better result of the work under the artist's hands.

CONTINUATION OF THE STUDY OF PROJECTIONS.
THE USE OF SECTIONS—DETAILS OF MACHINERY.
PLATE XI.

138. We have already shown, when treating of the illustrations
in Plate VIII., that it is advisable to section, divide or cut
through, various objects, so as to render their internal organization clearly intelligible; and we may now proceed to demonstrate,
with the aid of sundry examples, brought together in Plate XI.,
that in particular cases sections are indispensable, and even more
necessary, than external elevations. It is with this object that,
in many of our geometrical drawings, we have given representations of objects, cut or sectioned through their axes or centres, so
as to accustom the student to this description of projections, the
importance and utility of which cannot be overrated.

139. *Footstep Bearing.*—Figs. 1 and 1ᵃ are the representations,
in plan and elevation, of a footstep, formed to receive the lower
end of a vertical spindle or shaft. This footstep consists of several pieces, one contained within the other; and it is evidently
impossible to say, from the external views, what their actual
entire shape may be, although a part of each is seen in the horizontal projection, fig. 1. If, however, we suppose the whole to
be divided by a vertical plane in the line, 1—2, fig. 1, we shall be
enabled to form another vertical projection, fig. 1ᵇ, showing the
internal structure, and which is termed a vertical section, or sectional elevation. This figure shows, first, the thickness of the
external cup-piece, or box, A, as also the dimensions of the opening, a, which is made in its base, for the introduction of a pin, to
raise the footstep proper, B, when necessary; secondly, the thickness and internal depth of the footstep, B, as also the internal
vertical grooves, b, which serve for the introduction of the key,
c; thirdly, the form and manner of adjustment of the centre-bit,
c, which sustains the foot of the vertical spindle or shaft. This

centre-bit, which, of course, should not turn with the spindle-foot, is prevented from doing so by means of the key, c, which fits into a cross groove in its under side, the key itself being held firmly by the grooves, b, into which its projecting ends are made to fit. Of these details, the cup-piece, A, is of cast-iron, the footstep, B, of gun-metal or brass, the centre-piece, C, of tempered steel, and the small key, c, of wrought-iron. Therefore, bearing in mind what has already been said, we may indicate these various materials in the sections, either by line-shading, of different strengths, as in the figure, or by means of colours, corresponding to those employed in Plate X.; and we may here remark, that where line-sectioning is used, brass, gun-metal, or bronze, is frequently expressed by a series of lines, which are alternately full and dotted. There are, besides, many ways of varying the effect produced by line-shading. For example, the spaces between the lines may be alternately of different widths, or the lines may be alternately of different strengths.

Strictly speaking, figs. 1 and 1 are all that are necessary for the representation of the object under discussion. The cup-piece, A, however, which is externally cylindrical, has, at four points, diametrically opposite to each other, certain projecting rectangular plane surfaces, d, which are provided to receive the thrust of the screws which adjust the footstep accurately in the centre. The width of these facets is shown in the plan, fig. 1, whilst their depth is obtainable from the elevation, fig. 1ᵃ. If, instead of these facets, d, being, as they are, tangential to the cylinder, A, they had projected, in the least, at their centres, their depth would necessarily have been given in the section, fig. 1ᵇ, and in such case the elevation, fig. 1ᵃ, might have been altogether dispensed with. Whilst referring to the representation of the projecting facets, in connection with the cylinder, A, we may remark, that when a cylinder is intersected by a plane, which is parallel to its axis, the line of intersection is always a straight line, as e f, figs. 1 and 1ᵃ.

140. *Stuffing-box cover, or gland.*—In pumps and steam-engine cylinders, the cover is furnished, at the opening through which the piston-rod passes, with a stuffing-box, to prevent leakage. The hemp, or other material used as packing, is contained in an enlargement of the piston-rod passage, and is tightly pressed down by a species of hollow bush with flanges, as represented in plan in fig. 2, and in elevation in fig. 2ᵃ. In this instance, the necessity of a sectional view is still more obvious than in the case of the footstep already treated of. In the vertical section, fig. 2ᵇ, it is shown, that the internal diameter is not uniform throughout, and that there is a ring or ferule, B', let in at the lower part of the interior. The cylindrical opening, a, of the gland, coincides exactly with the diameter of the piston-rod; the internal diameter of a portion, b, of the ring, B', is also the same. The part, c, however, comprised between these two, is greater in diameter, so as to lessen the extent of surface in frictional contact with the piston-rod, and it also serves for the lodgment of lubricating matter. It is further discernible in the section, that the flanges or lugs, d, which project on either side of the upper portion of the gland, have each a cylindrical opening, e, throughout their whole depth. These are the holes for the bolts, which force down the gland, and secure it to the corresponding flanges, or lugs, on the

stuffing-box. The annular hollowing out, f, at the upper and internal part of the gland, acts as a reservoir, into which the lubricating oil is first poured, and whence it gradually oozes into the interior. The ring, B', is forcibly fitted into the bottom of the gland, and terminates below in a wedge, in the same manner as the gland itself, the double wedge jamming the packing against the piston-rod and the sides of the stuffing-box, and thus forming a steam-tight joint. The ring, B', is generally made of brass, both with a view to lessen the friction, and to its being replaced with facility when worn, without the necessity of renewing the whole gland. The latter is generally made of cast-iron, though the whole is sometimes made of brass or gun-metal.

141. *Spherical Joint.*—In some cases, a locomotive receives water from its tender by means of pipes which are fitted with spherical joints, as a considerable play is necessary in consequence of the engine and tender not being rigidly connected together, and also to obviate any difficulty of attachment from the pipes in the locomotive not being exactly opposite to those in the tender. This species of joint, represented in plan and elevation in figs. 3 and 3ᵃ, gives a free passage to the water, in whatever position, within certain limits, one part may be with respect to the other. For its construction to be thoroughly understood, the vertical section fig. 3ᵇ is needed. This view, indeed, at once explains the various component parts, consisting —first, of a hollow sphere, A, of the same thickness as the pipe, B, of which it forms the prolongation ; and, second, of two hemispherical sockets, C, D, which embrace the ball, A, and which are firmly held together by bolts passing through lugs, a, a. When this species of joint is used of a small size, as at the junction of a gas chandelier with the ceiling, the two half-sockets are simply screwed together—this method, indeed, being adopted in many locomotives. It must be borne in mind, that our object in this work is simply to instruct the student to accurately represent mechanical and other objects, and for this purpose we employ both precept and example ; but such examples do not necessarily comprise the latest and most improved or efficient forms. The half-socket, C, forms part of the continuation, E, of the feed-pipe, whilst the half-socket, D, is a detached piece, necessarily moveable, to allow of the introduction of the spherical part, A. This half-socket, D, is partially cut away at the lower part, and does not fit closely to the neck of the ball. This allows the pipe, B, to move to a slight extent from side to side in any direction ; and the upper end of the ball, A, is cut away to a corresponding extent, to prevent any diminution of the opening into the pipe, E, when the two portions are thus inclined to each other. The pipe, E, with its half-socket, C, is an example of the combination of a cylinder with a sphere, and gives us occasion to observe, that the intersection formed by the meeting or junction of these solids is always a circle in one projection, and a straight line in the other. The subject of such intersections will be discussed more in detail in reference to Plate XIV.

The sockets, C and D, are formed with four external lugs, or eye-pieces, a, for connection by bolts, as before stated. The curved outlines of these lugs, which glide tangentially into that of the body of the socket, give rise to the solution of a problem which may be thus put : *To draw with a given radius an arc tangential to two given arcs.* The solution is thus obtained : with the centres, *o, o,* and radii equal to those of the respective arcs given, plus that of the required arc, describe arcs at about the position in which the centres of the required arcs should be ; the intersections of these arcs will give the exact centres, as F, &c., and the lines joining F, with the centres, *o, o,* give the points of junction of the arc, G H, with the other two. This spherical joint, which requires great accuracy of adjustment of the different parts, is generally cast in brass, being finished by turning and grinding.

142. *Safety-Valve.*—To insure, as far as is practically possible, the safe and economical working of steam boilers, they are usually fitted with pressure gauges, level indicators, alarm whistles, and safety-valves. The object of the safety-valve is to give an outlet to the steam as soon as it reaches a greater pressure than has been determined on, and for which the valve is loaded. Figs. 4, 4ª, and 4ᵇ, respectively, represent a horizontal section, elevation, and vertical section of a safety-valve in common use. This apparatus consists of two distinct parts : first, the cast-iron seat, A, permanently fixed to the boiler-top by three or four bolts, the joint being made perfectly steam-tight by means of layers of canvas and cement ; second, the valve itself, B, which is sometimes cast-iron, sometimes brass. The valve-piece, B, is cast with a central spindle, c, hollowed out laterally into the form of a triangle with concave sides, for the purpose of giving a passage to the steam, and, at the same time, of lessening the extent of frictional contact of the spindle with the sides of the passage—some contact, however, being necessary for the guidance of the valve. The method of drawing the horizontal section of this valve-spindle is similar to that given for fig. A, Plate III. (34), with this difference, that it is drawn in an equilateral triangle, instead of in a square. The base of the valve-piece, or the part by which it rests on the seat, A, consists of a very narrow annular surface ; the upper edge of the seat is bevilled off internally and externally, so that the surface on which the valve-piece rests exactly coincides with that of the latter. The upper external surface of the valve-piece is hollowed out centrally to receive the point of the rod through which the weighted lever acts upon the valve ; this lever is adjusted and weighted to correspond with the pressure to which it is deemed safe to submit the boiler, so that, when this pressure is exceeded, the valve rises, and the steam blows off as long as relief is necessary.

143. *Equilibrium or Double-beat Valve.*—Steam engines of large dimensions, such as those for pumping, met with in Cornwall, as well as marine engines, are often furnished with a species of double-beat or equilibrium valve in place of the ordinary D slide. An example of this description of valve is given in figs. 5, 5ª, and 5ᵇ. It possesses the property of giving a large extent of opening for the passage of the steam, with a very little traverse, and very little power is required to work the valve. The valve here represented consists of a fixed seat, A, of cast-iron or brass, and forming part of the valve chamber ; and a bell-shaped valve-piece, B, also in brass, fitted with a rod, c, by means of which it is moved. The contact of the valve with its seat is effected at two places, *a* and *b*, which are formed into accurate conical surfaces—one, *a*, being internal, and the other, *b*, external. When the valve is closed, these surfaces coincide with similar ones on the seat, and when it is lifted, as in fig. 5ᵇ, two annular openings are simultaneously formed, thus giving a double exit to the steam—which issues from the upper opening,

through the central part of the valve-piece, B. The rod or spindle of this piece is fixed to a centre-piece cast in one with the valve piece, and connected to it by four branches, c. The seat is similarly constructed. The external contour of this valve presents a series of undulations, involving the following problems in their delineation :—*To draw the curved junction of the body of the valve with the upper cylindrical part.* This is similar to the one treated of in reference to fig. 5, Plate III. (37), and may easily be drawn with the assistance of the enlarged detail, fig. 5ᶜ (Plate XI). Next, for the junction of the branch, c, with the more elevated boss, we require : *To draw an arc tangent to a given straight line, and passing through a given point.* The solution of this is extremely simple : we have merely to erect a perpendicular on the line, *e f,* fig. 5ᶜ, at the point of contact, *e,* of the tangential arc ; to join *e* and the given point, *g,* through which the arc is to pass ; on the centre of the line, *e g,* to erect a perpendicular, *h i,* and the point, *i,* of intersection of this line with the perpendicular, *i e,* will be the centre of the arc sought, *e h g,* and *i e,* the radius.

The central leaves or feathers of the seat, A, are drawn according to a problem already discussed (38).

The student will now see the imperative necessity of internal views or sections for the perfect intelligibility of the construction and action of various pieces of mechanism. With reference also to the examples collected together in this plate, a little consideration will show that the internal formation could not generally be sufficiently indicated by dotted lines ; for, besides the complication and confusion that would result from such a method, many such lines would confound themselves with full ones representing some external outline.

We have not thought it necessary to enter more into detail respecting the methods of constructing the various outlines, being persuaded that the dotted indications we have given will be quite sufficient for the student who has advanced thus far, the more so since the requisite operations bear great resemblance to those treated of in reference to Plate III.

SIMPLE APPLICATIONS.

SPINDLES, SHAFTS, COUPLINGS, WOODEN PATTERNS.

PLATE XII.

144. For the conveyance of mechanical action, under the form of rotatory, or partial rotatory motion, details, technically known as shafts or spindles, of wrought and cast-iron and wood, are used. Shafts of the latter description, namely, cast-iron and wood, are employed chiefly in hydraulic motors, water and wind mills, and in all machines where a great strain has to be transmitted, rendering considerable bulk necessary. Of these two kinds, wooden shafts, being more economical, have been preferred in some cases, particularly when the length is great, since they will better sustain severe shocks. Wrought-iron shafts are employed for the transmission of motion in factories and workshops, and for the main paddle-shafts of steam-vessels. Wrought-iron has the advantage of being less brittle than cast, and of possessing greater tenacity and elasticity.

145. *Wooden Shaft.*—Figs. 1, 4, 5, and 6, represent different

projections of a wooden shaft, such as is used for a water-wheel. Fig. 4 shows, on one side, a lateral elevation of the shaft, furnished with its iron ferules or collars, and its spindle; and at the same time, on the other side, a vertical section, passing through the centre of the shaft, giving the ferules in section, but supposing the central spindle, with its feathers, to be in external elevation. Generally, in longitudinal sections of objects enclosing one or more pieces, the innermost or central piece should not be sectioned, unless it has some internal peculiarity—the object of a section being to show and explain such peculiarity where it exists, and being quite unnecessary where the object is simply solid. In the same manner, it is not worth while sectioning the various minutiæ of machinery, such as bolts and nuts, simple cylindrical shafts and rods and screws, unless these are constructed with some intrinsic peculiarity.

Fig. 5 is a transverse section through the middle of the shaft, and merely shows that it is solid, and that it has the external contour of a regular octagon. Fig. 6 is an end view of the same shaft, showing the fitting of the spindle, with its feathers, into the socket and grooves, formed in the end of the shaft to receive them, and the binding of the whole together by the ferules or hoops. These views are what are required to determine all the various parts of the shaft. It manifestly consists, in fact, of a long prismatic beam of oak, A, of an octagonal section, and of which the extremities, b, are rounded, and slightly conical. The spindles, B, which are let into the ends, are each cast with four feathers, c, and a long tail-piece, d, uniting and strengthening them. Some engineers construct the spindles without the additional tail-piece, d. Though this simplifies the thing considerably, it is an arrangement which does not possess so much strength as when the spindle is longer. The beam-ends are turned out and grooved to receive these spindles, the grooves for the feathers being made rather wider than the feathers themselves. When the spindles are introduced into the sockets, b, thus formed for them, the whole are bound together by means of the iron hoops, f, which are forced on whilst hot. After this, hard wooden wedges are jammed in on each side of the feathers, thus tightening and solidifying the whole mass. In addition to this, iron spikes, g, are sometimes hammered in, to jam up the fibres of the wood still closer. Fig. 1, which is a shaded and finished elevation of one end of the shaft, gives an accurate idea of its appearance when complete and ready for adjustment.

146. *Cast-iron Shaft.*—There are several descriptions of cast-iron shafts. Some are cast hollow, others quite solid, and cylindrical or prismatical in cross section. Such as are intended to sustain very great strains, are generally strengthened by the addition of feathers, which project more towards the middle. These give great rigidity to the piece. A shaft of this description is represented in elevation in fig. 7, half being sectioned through the irregular line, 1—2—3—4, and half in external elevation. Fig. 8 is an end-view of it; and fig. 9 a transverse section through the line, 5—6, in fig. 7. In practice, it is not considered absolutely necessary that a section should follow a straight line. Frequently a much greater amount of explanation may be given in one view, by supposing the object sectioned by portions of planes at different parts, and solid and easily comprehended portions are generally

shown in elevation, as the feathers of the shaft, in the present instance, or the spokes of a spur-wheel or pulley. The shaft under consideration is such a one as is employed for hydraulic motors. The body, A, is cylindrical and hollow, and it is cast with four feathers, B, disposed at right angles to each other, and of an external parabolic outline, so as to present an equal resistance to torsion and flexure throughout. Near the extremities of these feathers, four projections are cast, for the attachment of the bosses of the water-wheel. These projections are formed with facets, so as to form the corners of a circumscribing square, as shown in fig. 8; and they are planed to receive the keys, i, by which they are fixed and adjusted to the bosses or naves, which are grooved at the proper places to receive them. The spindles, D, which terminate the shaft at each end, are cast with it, and are afterwards finished by turning. The shaft thus consists of only one piece, or casting.

147. Although we have already shown the method of drawing a parabola, in Plate ▼., the outline of the shaft feathers affords a practical exemplification, which it will be useful to illustrate. We here also give the method generally adopted—because of its simplicity—when the curve is a very slow or obtuse one, such as is given to the feathers of shafts, beams, side-levers, connecting-rods, and similar pieces. It is understood, in these cases, that two points in the curve are given; the one, a, fig. 7, being at the summit, and at the same time in the middle of the piece, and the other, b, situated at the extremity. In the present instance, we suppose the heights, a c and b d, from the axial line, m n, of the shaft to be given. This line, m n, may also be taken as the centre line of a beam, or connecting-rod. After having drawn through the point, b, a line, e b, parallel to the axis, divide the perpendicular, a e, into any number of equal parts, and transfer these divisions to the line, b i, the prolongation of the line, d b; then draw lines from the points, 1, 2, 3, to the summit, a. Further, divide also the length, c d, into the same number of equal parts as the perpendicular, and, through the divisions, 1', 2,' 3', draw other perpendiculars, the respective points, f, g, h, of intersection of these with the lines already drawn, will be points in the required curve. As the lower feather is an exact counterpart of the upper one, the perpendiculars may be prolonged downwards, and corresponding distances, as 1'—f', 2'—g', 3—h', set off on them. To draw, also, the half of each feather to the left, it is merely necessary to erect perpendiculars of corresponding lengths, at corresponding points in the axis. A different method of drawing this curve is sometimes adopted; namely, the one which we have already given in Plate IX., for the entasis of the Tuscan column. As, however, it does not possess the advantages of the true parabolic form, and as the curve becomes too sudden towards the extremities, we think the method given in Plate XII. is to be preferred.

Fig. 3 represents a portion of the shaft just discussed, shaded and finished, the lines running in different directions, the better to distinguish the flat from the round surfaces.

148. *Shaft Coupling.*—In extensive factories, and other works, where considerable lengths of shafting are necessary, they have to be constructed in several pieces, and coupled together. These couplings are generally of cast-iron, and formed of one or more pieces, according to their size. One form consists of a species of

cylindrical socket, accurately turned internally, which receives the ends of the two shafts to be connected, these being scarfed or halved into each other, so as to be bound well together, and revolve like one continuous piece. According to another form, two sockets are employed, of increased diameter at the part where they meet, and formed at this part into quadrant-shaped clutches, gearing with each other. The coupling represented in side elevation, in fig. 10, is of this kind; and in front elevation, as separated, in fig. 11.

This coupling was designed for a shaft, of which the diameter at the collars was 28 centimètres. The socket, A, of the coupling, is adjusted on the end of the first part of the shaft, c. The other socket, A', is similarly adjusted on the end of the other part, c', of the shaft. These two socket-pieces gear with each other, when brought together, by means of the projections or clutches, B and B', concentric portions, however, being adapted to fit the one into the other, to insure the coincidence of their centres. Fig. 11, which is a front view of the socket-piece, A, shows the exact shape and dimensions of these projecting clutches, each occupying a quadrant of the circle on the face of the socket-piece. Those of the second piece, A', are precisely the same, occupying, however, the intervals of those on A, so that the two may fit exactly into each other, as shown in fig. 10. The perfect and accurate union of these coupling-pieces with the two portions of shafting is obtained, in the first place, by means of two keys, a, diametrically opposite to each other, and let half into the shaft, and half into the socket-piece; and secondly, by screws, b, one of which is visible in fig. 10. The keys, a, are for the purpose of fixing the coupling-pieces to the two portions of shafting, making them solid therewith; and the screws, b, prevent the longitudinal separation of the two halves of the coupling.

THE METHOD OF CONSTRUCTING A WOODEN MODEL OR PATTERN
OF A COUPLING.

149. After the design for any piece of mechanism which it is proposed to cast has been decided on, it is generally necessary to construct a model or pattern in wood, by which to form the moulds for the casting. The proper formation of such a pattern is no easy matter, and requires considerable skill on the part of the pattern-maker, as also a knowledge of the kind of wood most appropriate, and of the various precautions needed to insure success when the mould comes to be prepared.

It is customary to construct the patterns of deal, because of its cheapness. Sometimes, however, plane-tree or sycamore or oak is used; and for small patterns, and such as require great precision, mahogany, box, or walnut. Whatever kind of wood is used, it should be perfectly dry, and well seasoned. The pattern is made solid, or hollow and built up, according to the dimensions of the object. For a drum, for instance, a column of any considerable width, a steam-engine cylinder, or for a coupling of large size, such as that represented in figs. 12, 13, and 14, the pattern is generally hollow, for economizing the wood, and reducing the weight of the piece. Also, if built up, there is less risk of warping or alteration of form, from changes of temperature. In fig. 13, the pattern of a coupling-piece is represented, partly in external side elevation, and partly in longitudinal section, being cut by

a vertical plane, passing through the axis. Fig. 12 is a front elevation, showing the projecting clutches. It is easy to see from these views, that the pattern is formed of two boards, D D', round the circumferences of which are fitted a series of staves, E, secured to the boards by screws. The wood for these staves is first cut up into pieces of the required thickness, and the sides are then bevilled off, to coincide with the radii, c d, c e, fig. 14. They are then fitted to the boards, D D', and at this stage present the appearance of the left-hand portion of fig. 14. The drum is afterwards put into the lathe, and the circumference is reduced to a cylindrical surface, like the right-hand portion of the same figure.

On one of the ends, D, of this drum, is fixed the projecting clutch-piece, B, which has been previously cut out of a board of greater thickness, so as to present the outline of fig. 12. On the opposite end, D', of the drum, are fixed several discs, or thicknesses, of wood, F, which are turned down to a diameter proportionate to the central socket which it is intended to form in the coupling-piece. After having been turned where necessary, the pattern is treated with sand-paper to make the surface as smooth as possible, and to prevent the adherence of the loam of which the mould is formed. Such patterns, particularly when of small size, are moreover coated with black-lead, well rubbed in, to give a polish and hardness to the surface. The diameter of the core-piece, F, is less than that of the shaft to which the coupling is to be fitted, so as to leave some margin in the casting for turning and grinding down the socket to the exact dimensions. The core itself, which gives form to the socket, is a cylinder of loam placed in the centre of the mould, fitted into the recess formed for that purpose by the piece, F. As in the present example, the mould would be constructed on end, and the core is very short, it would not require further support; but where a core is very long, or placed in a horizontal position, it requires to be supported at both ends, and, further, to be strengthened by wires or rods passing through its centre. For this reason, a core-piece, as F, is only attached to one end of the drum. It will be observed that this is slightly conical; the drum is so also, but to a less extent; the core itself, however, is quite cylindrical.

150. DRAW, or Taper, and SHRINK, or Allowance for Contraction.—In order that the pattern may be lifted from the mould without bringing away portions of the sides, it is necessary to form its sides with a slight taper, or draw, as it is technically called. For example, the diameter of the core-piece, F, as well as that of the drum itself, must be less at the lower extremity, or at the part first introduced into the mould, than at the opposite extremity. A very slight difference of diameter is sufficient for the purpose.

Cast-iron, as is the case with all the metals of the engineer, is of less bulk when cold than when in a state of fusion, and, because of this contraction, it is necessary to make the patterns of somewhat larger dimensions than the casting is to be when finished. It follows, then, that when the pieces to be cast have afterwards to be planed, turned, ground, or grooved, it is necessary to bear in mind, in constructing the wooden pattern, not only the after reduction due to the contraction, or, as it is termed, the shrink, of the metal, but also that which is occasioned by the reducing processes involved in finishing the article. In general, grey iron requires an allowance for shrink of from 1 to $1\frac{1}{10}$ per cent.; white iron, however, requires a much larger allowance. The allowance to be made for the reduction caused by the finishing processes, depends entirely on their nature.

When, with a view to avoid the expense of constructing a pattern, the mould is formed from the actual object which is to be reproduced or multiplied, the mould-makers obtain the necessary margin by shifting the model slightly during the formation of the mould. This, of course, can only be done with advantage when the piece is not of intricate shape.

ELEMENTARY APPLICATIONS

RAILS AND CHAIRS FOR RAILWAYS.

PLATE XIII.

151. In railways, the two iron rails on which the trains run are placed at the distance apart, or gauge, of $1\frac{1}{2}$ mètres, and are generally formed of lengths of $4\frac{3}{4}$ to 5 mètres. In England, the gauge is generally 4 feet $8\frac{1}{2}$ inches, and the rails are rolled in lengths of from 12 to 15 feet. These rails are supported by cast-iron chairs, placed at from 9 to 10 décimètres asunder, and adjusted and bolted on oak sleepers, lying across the rails, imbedded even with the surface. Those chairs which occur at the junctions of the lengths of rails are made wider at the base, and of greater length, so as to embrace the end of each length of rail, and render their rectilinear adjustment and union as perfect as possible.

In Plate XIII. we give details of a very common form of rail and chair. There are many different forms in use; but the method of drawing or designing each will be similar, and may be thoroughly understood from the exemplification here given. Figs. 1 and 2 represent the elevation and plan of a chair, with a portion of the rail which it supports. Fig. 3 is a vertical section through the line, 1—2. in the plan; but supposing the chair to be turned round, or to belong to the right-hand rail—showing, in connexion with fig. 1, the relative positions of the two lines of rails, with their respective chairs. Fig. 4 is a side view of the chair alone, and fig. 5 is an end view of a length of rail. This chair, which is designed with the view of combining solidity and strength with economy of material, consists of a wide base, A, by which it is seated on the sleeper, and of two lateral jaws, B, B′, strengthened by double feathers, C, C′. The base, B, is perforated at a—the holes being cylindrical, and slightly rounded at their upper edges. These holes are for the reception of the bolts which secure the chair to the sleeper. The space between the jaws of the chair is for the reception of the rail, D, and the wooden wedge, E, which holds it in position.

In this example, the vertical section of the rail, D, presents an outline which is symmetrical with reference both to the vertical centre line, $b\,c$, and also to the horizontal line, $d\,e$, fig. 5. This permits of the rail being turned when one of the running surfaces is worn. The section of the wedge, E, is also symmetrical with reference to its diagonals, so that it is immaterial which way it is introduced, whilst it also fits equally well to the rail when the latter is reversed.

The outline of the rail is composed of straight lines and arcs, which are geometrically and evenly joined, as shown in fig. 5. The necessary operations are fully indicated on the drawing itself. These operations are, for the most part, but the repetition and combination of the problems treated of in the first division of the subject. We have, moreover, given some of the problems detached, and on a larger scale, in figs. 6, 7, 8. Fig. 6 recalls the problem (35), which has for its object the drawing of an arc, $i\,j\,k$. tangent to the straight lines, $f\,g$ and $g\,h$, the radius, $o\,k$, being given, equal to $31\cdot5^{m}\,l_{m}$. (fig. 2, Plate III.) This problem meets with an application at $f\,g\,h$, fig. 5. In fig. 7 we have the problem (37), which requires that an arc, $l\,m\,n$, be drawn tangent to a straight line, $n\,p$, and to a given arc, $q\,r\,t$, the point of contact, n, being known (fig. 6, Plate III.) This meets with its application at $l\,m\,n$, fig. 5.

The problem illustrated by fig. 8 is, to draw a tangent, $g^{2}\,j^{1}$, to two given circles of radii, $s\,t$ and $o^{1}\,k^{2}$, respectively. In this problem (9), we require to find a common point, u, on the line, $o\,s$, which joins the centres of the two circles. To effect this, we draw through the centres, o and s, any two diameters, $v\,x$ and $v'\,x'$, parallel to each other. Join two opposite extremities of each, as v and x', by the straight line, $v\,x'$, which will cut the line, $o'\,s$, in the point, u. The problem then reduces itself to the drawing of a tangent to any single circumference (fig. 4, Plate I.), from a given point, u. The tangents obtained, in the present instance, will lie in one straight line, and be the line required—tangent to both circles. The application of this problem is at $x\,k^{2}\,t$ in fig. 4.

On fig. 9 we have also indicated the solution of a problem (41), which is—to draw an arc, $y\,z$, of a given radius, $a'\,b'$, tangent to two other arcs, having the radii, $c'\,d'$ and $e^{1}f^{2}$ (fig. 8, Plate III.) This problem is called for in drawing the outline of the jaw of the chair, where it runs into the base, A, near the edge of the bolt-hole, a, fig. 3.

To complete the outline of the chair, it remains for us to show how to determine the lines, $g'\,h'$, which represent the intersections of portions of cylindrical surfaces, as will be gathered from figs. 1 to 4. To avoid a confusion of lines, we have reproduced this portion in figs. 10, 11, and 12, which represent—the two former, vertical sections of each cylindrical portion, and the latter, the line of intersection in plan.

We must first determine on fig. 12, which corresponds to fig. 2, the horizontal projection, i', of any point, as i, taken on the arc, $g'\,h'$, in fig. 10; letting fall from this point, on the base line, L T, a perpendicular, $i\,i'$, and also drawing from it a horizontal line, $i\,i^{2}$. This latter line meets the cylindrical outline, $g'\,h'$, fig. 11, in i^{2}. Project i^{2} in i^{3} on the base line, transferring it to a line at right angles to the base line, by means of a quadrant of a circle, and draw through the point thus obtained a line parallel to the base line, and meeting the line $i\,i'$ in i', which will be a point in the curve required; other points, as j', n', are found in a similar manner.

It must be observed, that when the two cylindrical portions are of equal diameters, their intersection with each other, $g'\,h'$, as will be demonstrated hereafter, is projected horizontally as a straight line; the greater the difference between the two cylinders, the more curved will the line of their intersection be, as is apparent in figs. 10, 11, 12.

The outlines of the feathers, c and c′, glide into that of the base, A, with a curve which, in the plan, is projected in the arc, k′ l′. The operation necessary to determine these curves, is quite analogous to that treated of in reference to the preceding figures, and will be found sufficiently explained in figs. 13, 14, and 15. We should here remark, that we have given explanatory diagrams of all the sweeps or combinations of curves, both that the student may be well exercised in many of the problems already discussed, and also with a view of collecting, in one plate, several of the difficulties which more frequently meet the draughtsman in the course of his practice. In such objects as that chosen for exemplification, very little of the nicety here carried out is observed, and the curves are generally obtained by measurements with callipers from the object itself, or are formed of arcs determined by the eye.

The rails are not adjusted in their chairs perpendicularly, but are inclined slightly towards each other, in such a manner that their centre lines, c b, form a slight angle with the vertical, c b²: this inclination is given to counteract any tendency that the carriages may have to run off the rails, as is the case more particularly in curves, from the effort made by the wheels to run in a straight line. The expedient of laying the outer or convex rail at a level slightly higher than the other, is also resorted to in quick curves, for the like purpose of keeping the trains on the line.

RULES AND PRACTICAL DATA.

STRENGTH OF MATERIALS.

152. The various materials employed in mechanical and other constructions, differ considerably in their several natures, both with reference to the amount of force they will bear or resist uninjured, and the description of force or mode of applying it, to which they offer the greatest resistance.

Such forces are termed, according to the mode in which they are applied—tension, compression, flexure, and torsion.

A series of practical rules have been deduced from often repeated experiments, which serve as guides for readily calculating the dimensions of any piece of mechanism, with reference to the description and degree of force to which it will be subjected.

RESISTANCE TO COMPRESSION OR CRUSHING FORCE.

153. Compression is a force which strives to crush, or render more dense, the fibres or molecules of any substance which is submitted to its action.

According to Rondelet's experiments, a prism of oak, of such dimensions that its length or height is not greater than seven times the least dimension of its transverse section, will be crushed by a weight of from 385 to 462 kilogrammes, to the square centimètre of transverse section, or a weight of from 5,470 to 6,547 per square inch of transverse section.

In general, with oak or cast-iron, flexure begins to take place in a piece submitted to a crushing force, as soon as the length or height reaches ten times the least dimension of the transverse section. Up to this point, the resistance to compression is pretty regular.

Wrought-iron begins to be compressed under a weight of 4,900 kilog. per square centimètre, or of nearly 70,000 per square inch, and bends previously to crushing, as soon as the length or height of the piece exceeds three times the least dimension of the transverse section.

We show, in the following table, to what extent per square inch we may safely load bodies of various substances.

Table of the Weights which Solids—such as Columns, Pilasters, Supports—will sustain without being crushed.

WOODS AND METALS.

Description of Material.	Proportion of length to least dimension.				
	Up to 12.	Above 12.	Above 24.	Above 48.	Above 60.
	lb.	lb.	lb.	lb.	lb.
Sound oak, ...	426·750	355·625	213·375	71·125	35·562
Inferior oak,...	270·275	119·490	71·125	"	"
Pitch pine, ...	533·437	440·975	266·007	106·687	"
Common pine, .	137·982	116·645	69·702	"	"
Wrought-iron, .	14225·000	11877·875	7112·500	2375·575	1194·900
Cast-iron, ...	28450·000	23755·750	14225·000	4741·666	2375·575
Rolled copper, .	11707·175	"	"	"	"

STONES, BRICKS, AND MORTARS.

Description of Material	Length being less than 12 times least dimension.
	lb.
Basaltic Marble, Swedish and Auvergnese,..........	2845
Granite from Normandy, ...	996
" green, from Vosges,.....................	882
" grey, from Bretagne, ...	925
" " from Vosges, ...	597
" ordinary,.............................	569
Marble, hard, ...	1422
" white and veined, ...	427
Freestone, hard, ...	1280
" soft,..................................	6
Stone from Châtillon, near Paris, ...	242
Very hard freestone, or lias, from Bagneux, near Paris,.	726
A softer stone, from the same place,..............	185
Stone from Arcueil, near Paris,..................	355
" from Saillancourt, near Pontoise, best quality, ..	199
" from Conflans, much used at Paris, ...	128
Hard calcareous stone, ...	711
Ordinary calcareous stone,.......................	427
Calcareous stone from Givry, near Paris,..........	441
" " ordinary, from the same place, ...	171
An inferior stone, termed *Lambourde*,................	33
Bricks, very hard, ...	171
" inferior, ...	57
" hard and well-baked,...................	213
" red, ...	85
A soft stone, *Lambourde vergetée*,...................	85
Plaster, mixed with water,.......................	71
" mixed with lime-water, ...	104
Mortar, best, eighteen months old, ...	57
" ordinary, eighteen months old, ...	36
" " of lime and sand, ...	50
Cement, ...	68
" Roman, or Neapolitan,..................	53

Rule.—To find, by means of this table, the greatest compressing weight to which any piece may be submitted with safety:— *Multiply the transverse sectional area of the piece by the number in the table corresponding to the material, and to the proportionate length of the piece.* And inversely, from the weight which a piece is to support, its smallest transverse section may be determined. *By dividing this weight, expressed in pounds, by the number in the table corresponding to the material, and to the proportionate length.*

First Example.—What weight can be put with safety upon a pillar constructed of ordinary bricks, the pillar being of a rectangular section, of 50 inches by 60, and the height being below 12 times the length of this cross section?

We have $50 \times 60 = 3000$ square inches of transverse sectional area. Then, according to the table, we have—

$$3000 \times 57 = 171,000 \text{ lbs.}$$

Second Example.—What must be the transverse sectional area of a square post of sound oak, 19 feet 8 inches in height, and which will safely bear a load of 60,000 lbs.?

According to the table, if we suppose the length to be not more than 12 times the least cross section, the number or coefficient of compression, in pounds per square inch, is 426·75.

Then,
$$\frac{60,000}{426 \cdot 75} = 140 \text{ square inches;}$$

and

$\sqrt{140} = 11 \cdot 8$ inches, the length of the supposed side.

Comparing this 11·8 inches with the given height, we find that

$$\frac{19 \text{ ft. } 8 \text{ in.}}{11 \cdot 8 \text{ in.}} = \frac{236}{11 \cdot 8} = 20.$$

This shows—and we have constructed the example with this view—that in this instance the proportionate length has not been correctly estimated; and therefore, instead of taking the number 426·75, as in the first column, we must take that in the second column, for a proportionate length of between 12 and 24 times the cross section. The calculation will, consequently, have to be rectified thus—

$$\frac{60,000}{355 \cdot 625} = 168 \cdot 7 \text{ square inches,}$$

and $\sqrt{168 \cdot 7} = 13$ inches nearly, the proper dimension for the cross section of the post.

Third Example.—What is the greatest load that can be borne with safety by a solid cast-iron column, 3 inches in diameter, and 12 feet in height?

It is, in the first place, evident that the ratio of the diameter to the height is 12 feet, or 144 inches, $\div$ 3 inches $= 48$.

Consequently,
the section $\cdot 785 \times 3^2 \times 4741 \cdot 666 = 33,500$ lbs.

In shops and warehouses, builders employ solid cast-iron columns, instead of brick pillars, so as to take up less space. These columns are generally calculated to support loads of above 33,000 lbs. each. They are usually about 3 inches in diameter, and 12 feet high. In which case, supposing a cubic foot of cast-iron weighs 452 lbs., they will weigh (3 inches being equal to ·25 foot)—

$$\cdot 785 \times \cdot 25^2 \times 12 \times 452 = 266 \text{ lbs.}$$

If, instead of these columns being massive or solid, we employ, in place of two of them, a hollow one, to support the proportionate load of 66,000 lbs., and being 6 inches in diameter, this increase

in the diameter makes the ratio of the length to it 24, instead of 48; and the coefficient to be taken from the table will consequently be 14,225, instead of 4742.

Now, $66,000 \div 14,225 = 4 \cdot 64$ square inches, would be the cross section of a solid pillar, equivalent to that of which the thickness is sought. Since, however, the diameter of the latter is 6 inches, its section of solidity would be—

$$\cdot 785 \times 6^2 = 28 \cdot 26 \text{ square inches.}$$

Then, deducting from this area 4·64 square inches, as above determined, we have $28 \cdot 26 - 4 \cdot 64 = 23 \cdot 62$, for the cross sectional area of the central hollow. From this we deduce the internal diameter, thus—

$$\sqrt{\frac{23 \cdot 62}{\cdot 785}} = 5 \cdot 485 \text{ inches.}$$

And, finally, the thickness of the column will be—

$$\frac{6 - 5 \cdot 485}{2} = \cdot 2575 \text{ inches.}$$

The weight of such a column, if 12 feet in height, will be—

$$\frac{4 \cdot 64}{144} \times 12 \times 452 = 174 \cdot 77 \text{ lbs.}$$

This result shows very markedly how great an economy results from the employment of hollow in place of solid cast-iron columns. The thickness, determined as above, of ·2575 inch, is theoretically sufficient, but in practice we seldom find such castings under half an inch thick.

In the above examples, too, the mouldings usually added to the columns are not taken into the account. With these, the weight will be a tenth or so more, according to the description of moulding.

TENSIONAL RESISTANCE.

155. A tensile force is one which acts on a body in the direction of its length, tending to increase the length, and when carried to a sufficient extent, to cause rupture.

As with reference to compression, many experiments have been made to determine the sectional area to be given to bodies of various materials submitted to a tensile strain, so that they may safely resist a given force.

First Example.—Required the sectional area for four square tension rods of wrought-iron, to connect the top and bottom of a hydraulic press, in which the force which tends to separate these two ends, and consequently to rupture the rods, is equal to 500,000 lbs.

Each rod must be capable of resisting

$$\frac{500,000}{4} = 125,000 \text{ lbs.}$$

According to the table, the best wrought-iron may be safely subjected to a strain of 14,225 lbs. per square inch of cross section. We have, consequently,

$$\frac{125,000}{14,225} = 8 \cdot 79 \text{ square inches.}$$

for the area of the cross section; and

$$\sqrt{8 \cdot 79} = 2 \cdot 964, \text{ or nearly 3 inches,}$$

for a side of the square rod. If the rod were round, we should have—

$$D = \sqrt{\frac{8 \cdot 79}{\cdot 785}} = 3 \cdot 345 \text{ inches, for the diameter.}$$

In the same manner, the diameter proper for steam-engine piston-rods may be calculated, when the pressure on the piston is known.

Table of Weights which Prisms and Cylinders will sustain when submitted to a Tensile Strain.

Description of Material.	Per square inch of cross section.	Per square centimètre of cross section.
	lbs.	kilog.
WOODS.		
Oak, with the grain, sound, ...	1,138	80
Oak, with the grain, ordinary, ...	853	60
Oak, across the grain, ...	228	16
Deal, with the grain, ...	1,138 to 1,280	80 to 90
Deal, across the grain, ...	60	4·2
Ash, with the grain, ...	1,707	120
Elm, "	1,479	104
Beech, "	1,138	80
METALS.		
Wrought or bar iron, superior and select samples, ...	14,225	1,000
Wrought or bar iron, inferior, indiscriminately selected	5,917	416
Wrought or bar iron, medium, ...	9,474	666
Sheet iron, in the direction in which it was rolled,	9,957	700
Sheet iron, in the direction perpendicular to this,	8,535	600
Hoop iron, soft	1,069	750
Unannealed iron wire, *De Laigle,* ·009 inch, or ·23 $^m/_m$ in diameter, ...	21,337	1,500
Unannealed iron wire, inferior, and of considerable diameter, ...	11,850	833
Unannealed iron wire, best, from ·02 to ·04 inch, or ·5 to 1 $^m/_m$ in diameter,......	18,996	1,333
Unannealed iron wire, medium quality, ·04 to ·12 inch, or 1 to 3 $^m/_m$ in diameter, ...	14,225	1,000
Iron wire rope, ...	7,112	500
Iron cables, ordinary, oblong links,........	5,690	400
Iron cables, strengthened by stays,........	7,587	533
Grey cast iron, run vertically, strongest kind,	3,201	225
Grey cast iron, run horizontally, inferior, ..	3,087	217
Steel, cast or wrought, selected, ...	23,702	1,667
Steel, inferior, badly tempered, taken indiscriminately, ...	8,535	600
Steel, medium, ...	17,781	1,250
Gun metal, average, ...	5,448	383
Copper, rolled lengthwise, ...	4,979	350
Copper, of superior quality, ...	6,117	433
Copper, hammered, ...	5,932	417
Copper, cast, ...	3,314	233
Unannealed copper wire, superior, under ·04 inch, or 1 $^m/_m$ in diameter, ...	16,600	1,167
Unannealed copper wire, medium, from ·04 to ·08 inch, or 1 to 2 $^m/_m$ in diameter, ...	11,850	833
Unannealed copper wire, inferior, ...	9,488	667
Yellow copper, or fine brass.............	2,987	210
Unannealed brass wire, superior, under ·04 inch, or 1 $^m/_m$ in diameter, ...	20,143	1,416
Unannealed brass wire, medium,....................	11,850	833
Platinum wire, hardened, unannealed, ·0045 inch, or ·127 $^m/_m$ in diameter,......	27,511	1,933
Platinum wire, hardened, annealed,.............	8,066	567
Cast tin, ...	711	50
Cast zinc, ...	1,422	100
Sheet zinc, ...	1,185	83·3
Cast lead, ...	303	21·3
Sheet lead, ...	320	22·5
CORDAGE.		
Hawsers and cables of Strasburg hemp, ·5 to ·6 inch, or 13 to 14 $^m/_m$ in diameter, ...	6,259	440
Do. of Lorraine hemp.	4,623	325
Do. of Lorraine or Strasburg hemp, ·9 inch, or 23 $^m/_m$ in diameter, ...	4,267	300
Do. of Strasburg hemp, 1·5 to 2 inch, or 40 to 54 $^m/_m$ in diameter, ...	3,912	275
Old rope, ·9 inch, or 23 $^m/_m$ in diameter, ...	2,987	210
Black leather bands, ...	284	20

Second Example.—Required the amount of tensile or tractive force which can safely be resisted by a carriage draw-shaft, made of ash, and having a cross-sectional area of 15·5 square inches. According to the table, we have—

$$1707 \text{ lbs.} \times 15 \cdot 5 = 26 \cdot 460 \text{ lbs.}$$

155. *Pulley Bands.*—The following simple formula may generally be employed in practice, to determine the dimensions proper for pulley bands:—

$$L = \frac{20 \times H P}{v};$$

in which L is the width of the band in inches; H P, the force in horse power; and v, the velocity in feet per minute.

By *horse power* is meant a force equal to 33,000 lbs., raised 1 foot high in a minute. French engineers call it 75 kilogrammes, raised a mètre high per second, which is very nearly the same as the English measure. To suit the French system, the above formula would be—

$$L = \frac{1500 \times H P}{v},$$

v, in this case, signifying the velocity in centimètres per second, and L, the width in centimètres. The thickness of the leather is supposed to be that of strong ox-hide, say about ·2 inch, or 5 $^m/_m$.

The above formula gives rise to the following rule:—*Multiply the horse power by the constant multiplier, 20, and divide the product by the velocity in feet per minute, and the quotient will be the width of the band in inches.*

Example.—Let H P = 2 horse power, v = 10 feet per minute, then,

$$L = \frac{20 \times 2}{10} = 4 \text{ inches.}$$

This formula satisfies the following conditions—that the band do not slide round the pulley which it embraces; that it be not liable to increase perceptibly in length; and that it be capable of resisting the strain transmitted by it.

It is found advisable never to make the respective diameters of two pulleys, coupled together, in a greater ratio to each other than 1 : 3.

RESISTANCE TO FLEXURE.

156. The resistance of a piece of any material to flexure, is the effort which it opposes to all strain acting upon it in a direction perpendicular to its length, as in the case of levers, beams, or shafts.

Bodies may be submitted to the strain of flexure in several ways. Thus, the piece may be firmly fixed in a wall by one end, whilst the straining weight or force is applied at the other; or it may be securely fixed at both ends, and the weight applied in the centre; or it may be supported at the centre, and have the weight applied at both extremities.

We shall first consider the case of a piece fixed by one end, and subjected to a strain at the other.

Let W be the weight in pounds, placed at a distance, L, in inches from the wall, in which the piece under experiment is fixed; C, a coefficient varying with the material; a, the horizontal dimension in inches of cross section; b, the vertical dimension, similarly expressed;—then the greatest weight that the piece will bear, without undergoing alteration, will be determinable by the following formula, the piece being of rectangular section, and fixed at one end, and weighted at the other.

$$W = \frac{C \times a\,b^2}{6\,L}$$

Now,   C = 8,535, for wrought-iron;
10,668, for cast-iron;
854, for oak and deal.

Substituting these values of C, in the preceding formula, we shall have, for pieces of rectangular section, according to the material—

For Wrought-Iron.

$$P = \frac{8535 \times a\,b^2}{6\,L}, \text{ or more simply, } = \frac{1422\cdot5 \times a\,b^2}{L}.$$

For Cast-Iron.

$$P = \frac{10,668 \times a\,b^2}{6\,L}, \text{ or more simply, } = \frac{1778 \times a\,b^2}{L}.$$

For Wood.

$$P = \frac{854 \times a\,b^2}{6\,L}, \text{ or more simply, } = \frac{142 \times a\,b^2}{L}.$$

These formulæ lead us to the following rule for pieces of rectangular section:—*Multiply the horizontal dimension in inches of cross section, by the square of the vertical dimension in inches, and by a coefficient depending on the material: then divide the product by the length in inches, and the quotient will be the weight in pounds, which the piece will sustain without alteration.*

This rule is derived from the fact, that the transverse resistance of pieces submitted to a deflective strain is inversely as their length, directly as their width, and as the square of their vertical thickness.

According to this, pieces fixed at one end, and intended to bear a strain at the other, should be placed on edge; in other words, the greatest cross section should be parallel to the direction of the strain.

First Example.—What weight can be suspended, without causing deflection, to the free end of a wrought-iron bar, fixed horizontally into a wall at one end, and projecting 5 feet (= 60 inches) from it; the bar being of a rectangular cross section, having its horizontal dimension, a = 1·2 inches, and its vertical dimension, b = 1·6 inches?

We have

$$P = \frac{1422\cdot5 \times 1\cdot2 \times 1\cdot6^2}{60} = 72\cdot8 \text{ lbs.}$$

This result is obtained on the supposition that the bar is placed on edge; but what would be the weight, other things being equal, supposing the bar to be placed on its side—that is, when 1·6 inches is its horizontal dimension, a, and 1·2 its vertical dimension, b?

We have, in this case,

$$P = \frac{1422\cdot5 \times 1\cdot6 \times 1\cdot2^2}{60} = 54\cdot6 \text{ lbs.}$$

This inferior result shows the advantage of placing the bar on edge.

When the piece under experiment is of square instead of oblong section, a necessarily = b, and a b² becomes b³, and this is consequently to be substituted in the formula for the former.

If, however, the piece is cylindrical, the formula will be—D representing the diameter,

$$\text{For wrought-iron, } P = \frac{854 \times D^3}{L}.$$

$$\text{For cast-iron, } \quad P = \frac{1066 \times D^3}{L}.$$

$$\text{For wood, } \quad P = \frac{85 \times D^3}{L}.$$

In each of the cases just referred to, the transverse sectional dimensions of pieces fixed at one end, and submitted to a strain at the other, are determined by the following formulæ:—

MATERIAL.	FORM OF SECTION.					
	Rectangular.		Square.		Circular.	
Wrought-Iron, ..	$a\,b^2 =$	$\frac{P\,L}{1,422\cdot5}$	$b^3 =$	$\frac{P\,L}{1,422\cdot5}$	$D^3 =$	$\frac{P\,L}{854}$
Cast-Iron,.....	$a\,b^2 =$	$\frac{P\,L}{1,778}$	$b^3 =$	$\frac{P\,L}{1,778}$	$D^3 =$	$\frac{P\,L}{1066}$
Wood, ...	$a\,b^2 =$	$\frac{P\,L}{142}$	$b^3 =$	$\frac{P\,L}{142}$	$D^3 =$	$\frac{P\,L}{85}$

The rule derivable from these formulæ for the determination of the transverse section, whether *rectangular, square,* or *circular,* of a bar or beam fixed by one end and loaded at the other is thus stated:—*Multiply the weight in pounds by its distance in inches from the support; divide the product by a coefficient varying with the material and form of section; and extract the cube root, which will give in inches the vertical dimension, the side of the square, or the diameter of the circle, according as the bar or beam is rectangular, square, or circular in cross section.*

First application: What should be the transverse section of a rectangular wrought-iron bar, intended to carry at its free end, and at a distance of 5 feet from its support, a weight of 72·8 lbs., the bar being supposed to be placed on edge?

We have here,

$$a\,b^2 = \frac{72\cdot8 \text{ lbs.} \times 60 \text{ in.}}{1,422\cdot5} = 3\cdot071;$$

then, if a be taken = 1·2 inches,

$$b = \sqrt{\frac{3\cdot071}{1\cdot2}} = 1\cdot6 \text{ inches, the vertical dimension.}$$

Second application: What should be the side of the cross section measure, of a *square* bar, under similar circumstances otherwise?

$$b^3 = \frac{72\cdot8 \times 60}{1422\cdot5} = 3\cdot071, \text{ and}$$

$$b = \sqrt[3]{3\cdot071} = 1\cdot454 \text{ in., the thickness of the bar.}$$

157. OBSERVATIONS.—When the bar, or beam, under experiment possesses in itself any weight capable of influencing its resistance; or, besides the weight suspended or acting at one end, has a weight equally distributed throughout its length; the transverse-sectional dimensions are, in the first place, determined with-

out taking the additional weight into consideration. This is, then, calculated approximately, and the half of it added to the suspended load, a fresh calculation being made with this sum as a basis.

A bar, or beam, fixed by one end, and loaded at the other, has always a tendency to break off at the shoulder, or point of junction, with its support, because it is on that point that the weight or strain acts with the greatest leverage. When, therefore, the transverse section of the piece has been determined, in accordance with the formulæ given above, which are calculated for the dimensions of the piece at the shoulder; the section may be beneficially diminished towards the free extremity, thereby economising the material, and lessening its own overhanging weight. The curve proper to give the outline is the parabola, as described in reference to Plates V. and XII. It may also be obtained in the following manner, for the particular case under consideration :— Calculate the transverse section for different lesser lengths of the piece, the other data remaining as before, and the required curve will be one which passes through the outline of each section, when they are placed at distances from the load equal to the lengths for which they are calculated. This curve is also given to bars, beams, or shafts, fixed at both ends and loaded in their middle, or sustaining a uniform weight throughout their length. The cast-iron shaft represented in Plate XII. may be taken as an example of this. Steam-engine beams and side levers are also formed with feathers of this shape, as it gives them a uniform resistance throughout, so that they are not liable to break or give way in any one point rather than another.

A bar, or beam, supported in the centre, and loaded at either end, will support double the weight capable of being carried by one of similar dimensions, supported at one, and loaded at the other end; it is, indeed, evident that each weight will only act with half the leverage, being only half the distance from the point of support.

Similarly, a bar, or beam, freely supported at both extremities, and loaded in the centre, will support a weight double that sustained by a piece of the same dimensions fixed at one, and loaded at the other end. Therefore, in calculating the proportions for these two last-mentioned cases, it is necessary simply to double the coefficient, c, given for the first case.

A bar, or beam, firmly and solidly fixed by both ends, will support a load four times as great as one of the same dimensions fixed at one end, and loaded at the other extremity. It will, consequently, be necessary to quadruple the above coefficient in this case.

For calculating the diameters of the spindles, or journals, of cast-iron shafts for hydraulic motors, which are intended to sustain great weights, the following particular formula may be employed :—

$$D = \sqrt[3]{W} \times \cdot 1938,$$

where D expresses the diameter in inches, and W the weight to be sustained in pounds.

TABLE OF THE DIAMETERS OF THE JOURNALS OF WATER-WHEEL AND OTHER SHAFTS FOR HEAVY WORK.

Total load in Pounds.	Diameter of Journal in Inches.		Total load in Pounds.	Diameter of Journal in Inches.	
	Cast-Iron.	Wrought-Iron.		Cast-Iron.	Wrought-Iron.
17·2	$\frac{1}{2}$	·4315	70343	8	6·9040
137·4	1	·8630	84373	$8\frac{1}{2}$	7·3355
463·7	$1\frac{1}{2}$	1·2945	100156	9	7·7670
1099·0	2	1·7260	117793	$9\frac{1}{2}$	8·1985
2146·7	$2\frac{1}{2}$	2·1575	137388	10	8·6300
3709·5	3	2·5890	158604	$10\frac{1}{2}$	9·0615
5890·5	$3\frac{1}{2}$	3·0205	182864	11	9·4930
8805·6	4	3·4520	208950	$11\frac{1}{2}$	9·9245
12619·5	$4\frac{1}{2}$	3·8835	237296	12	10·3560
17175·5	5	4·3150	268012	$12\frac{1}{2}$	10·7875
22858·0	$5\frac{1}{2}$	4·7465	311666	13	11·2190
29676·0	6	5·1780	338026	$13\frac{1}{2}$	11·6505
37730·0	$6\frac{1}{2}$	5·6095	376993	14	12·0820
43873·0	7	6·0410	418845	$14\frac{1}{4}$	12·5135
58915·7	$7\frac{1}{2}$	6·4725	463685	15	12·9450

According to this formula, the diameter of the cast-iron spindle, or journal, is found by extracting the cube root of the weight, or strain, in pounds, and multiplying it by the constant, ·1938, the product being the diameter in inches.

The diameter for wrought-iron spindles, or journals, may be derived from that for cast-iron, by multiplying the latter by ·863; or, directly, by employing the multiplier, ·1673, in the above formula.

Example.—Of what diameter must the spindle of a water-wheel shaft be, the total strain being equivalent to 70,000 lbs.? Here,

$$D = \sqrt[3]{70,000} \times \cdot 1938 = 7 \cdot 987, \text{ or } 8 \text{ inches nearly.}$$

A wrought-iron spindle of $(7 \cdot 987 \times \cdot 863 =)$ 6·9 inches, will answer the same purpose.

RESISTANCE TO TORSION.

158. When two forces act in opposite directions, and tangentially to any solid, tending to turn its opposite ends in different

directions, or to twist it, it is said to be subjected to *torsion*, and offers more or less resistance to this action according to its form and composition. Taking, for example, the main shaft of a steam-engine, at one end of which the power acts through a crank, set at right angles to it, and at the other the load, by means of wheel gear—the *resistance* which this load presents, on the one hand, and on the other, the *power* applied to the crank, represent two forces which tend to twist the shaft, subjecting it to the action of torsion.

In machinery, all shafts and spindles which communicate power by a rotatory, or partially rotatory, movement on their axes, are subject to a torsional strain: Those which sustain the greatest torsional efforts are those shafts denominated first movers, the first recipients of the power. Such are the fly-wheel shafts of land engines, and the paddle-shafts of marine engines. In these the action is further complicated and heightened by the irregularity with which, in reciprocating engines, the power is communicated to them. Such shafts as carry very heavy toothed gearing, but receive and transmit the power in an equable manner, and without a fly-wheel, are termed second movers; and finally, such as carry only pulleys, or comparatively small toothed wheels, are comprised in the class of third movers. Such shafts, again, as meet with an intermittent resistance, as is the case with all cam movements, require increased strength to meet this irregularity of action.

In constructing formulæ for the determination of the diameters of shafts, regard must always be had to the class to which they belong, and also to the description of work they have to perform.

As the journals are the parts of a shaft on which the greatest strain is concentrated, it is obviously to the determination of their dimensions that our investigation should be directed. The practical formula, for ascertaining the diameter proper for the journal of a cast-iron first-mover shaft, is—

$$d = \sqrt[3]{\frac{H\,P}{R} \times 419}.$$

Here, d = diameter of journal in inches.

H P = the horse power transmitted by the shaft.

R = the number of revolutions of the shaft per minute.

This formula is expressed in the following rule.

159. To determine the diameter at the journals of a cast-iron first-mover shaft:—*Divide the horse power of the engine by the number of revolutions of the shaft per minute, multiply the quotient by the constant, 419, and extract the cubic root, which will be the diameter required in inches.*

For the journals of cast-iron shafts which are second movers, the formula is—

$$d = \sqrt[3]{\frac{H\,P}{R} \times 206};$$

and for third movers—

$$d = \sqrt[3]{\frac{H\,P}{R} \times 106}.$$

These are, in fact, similar to the formula given for first movers, with the exception, that for these the constant multiplier is 419, whilst for the latter it is 206 and 106, respectively.

160. For the journals of wrought-iron shafts the same formulæ are employed, the multipliers only being changed; these are 249 for first movers, 134 for second movers, and 67·6 for third movers.

If, with a view of suppressing the radical sign in the above formulæ, we raise both sides of the equation to their third or cubic power, and further express the multiplier by m, we have

$$d^3 = \frac{H\,P}{R} \times m;$$

from which formula it will be seen, that the cube of the diameter of the journal is proportional to the force transmitted. Similarly, the resistance of a journal is proportional to the cube of its diameter. In other words, one journal, of which the diameter is double that of another, is capable of sustaining a strain eight times greater, since the cube of 2 is 8.

161. As, in consequence of the necessity of extracting cubic roots, the calculation, according to these formulæ, becomes very tedious and complex, we have rendered it much simpler by means of the table on the next page.

We may, however, first observe, that the formula,

$$d^3 = \frac{H\,P}{R} \times m,$$

may be put in the form—

$$\frac{d^3}{m} = \frac{H\,P}{R};$$

or again, reversing the terms,

$$\frac{m}{d^3} = \frac{R}{H\,P}.$$

If now we divide the coefficient, m, by the cubes of the series, 1, 2, 3, 4, &c., representing the diameters of the journals in inches, we shall obtain a series of numbers corresponding to

$$\frac{R}{H\,P}.$$

Thus, if 419 be successively divided by the cubes, 1, 8, 27, 64, &c., the numbers in the second column of the table will be obtained; and by dealing with the other multipliers in like manner, the numbers in the 3d, 4th, 5th, 6th, and 7th columns, will be found.

Rule.—When the table is used, the rule for determining the diameter of the journal of a shaft is thus stated:—

Divide the number of revolutions per minute of the shaft by the horse power, and find the number in the table which is nearest to the quotient thus obtained, bearing in mind the class and material, and the corresponding number in the first column will be the diameter required.

First Example.—What should be the diameter at the journals of a cast-iron first-motion shaft, for an engine of 20 horse power, the shaft in question to make 31 revolutions per minute?

We have—

$$\frac{R}{H\,P} = \frac{31}{20} = 1·55.$$

It will be observed that this quotient is the nearest to the number 1·526 in the second column of the table, and that 1·526 is opposite to $6\frac{1}{2}$; the diameter, d, of the shaft journal should consequently be $6\frac{1}{2}$ inches in diameter.

If a shaft for the same purpose as the above be made of wrought-iron, we must look in the fifth column for the number to which 1·55 approaches nearest. It will be observed that it lies between the numbers 1·992 and 1·497, respectively opposite to 5 and $5\frac{1}{2}$ inches; the diameter of the journal should consequently be between these—say about $5\frac{3}{8}$ inches.

TABLE OF DIAMETERS FOR SHAFT JOURNALS, CALCULATED WITH REFERENCE TO TORSIONAL STRAIN.

Diameter in Inches.	Journals of Cast-Iron Shafts.			Journals of Wrought-Iron Shafts.		
	First Movers.	Second Movers.	Third Movers.	First Movers.	Second Movers.	Third Movers.
¼	3352·000	1568·000	848·000	1981·200	1072·000	540·800
1	419·000	206·000	106·000	249·000	134·000	67·600
1½	124·133	61·037	31·408	73·778	39·704	20·030
2	52·375	25·750	13·250	31·125	16·750	8·450
2½	26·816	13·190	6·790	15·872	8·576	4·327
3	15·519	7·630	3·922	9·222	4·963	2·504
3½	9·773	4·805	2·475	5·808	3·123	1·577
4	6·547	3·219	1·656	3·891	2·094	1·563
4½	4·598	2·266	1·163	2·732	1·475	·742
5	3·352	1·648	·848	1·992	1·072	·541
5½	2·519	1·239	·637	1·497	·806	·406
6	1·940	·954	·491	1·153	·620	·313
6½	1·526	·750	·386	·906	·488	·246
7	1·222	·601	·309	·726	·391	·197
7½	1·002	·493	·253	·595	·325	·162
8	·838	·402	·207	·487	·261	·130
8½	·682	·335	·173	·405	·218	·110
9	·575	·282	·145	·341	·184	·093
9½	·489	·240	·124	·290	·156	·079
10	·419	·206	·106	·249	·134	·068
10½	·362	·178	·092	·215	·116	·058
11	·314	·155	·079	·187	·101	·051
11½	·275	·135	·069	·163	·089	·044
12	·242	·119	·061	·144	·078	·039
12½	·214	·105	·054	·127	·068	·034
13	·191	·094	·049	·114	·061	·031
13½	·170	·084	·043	·101	·054	·027
14	·153	·075	·038	·091	·049	·024
14½	·137	·067	·035	·082	·044	·022
15	·124	·061	·031	·074	·039	·020
1	2	3	4	5	6	7

Second Example.—We require to ascertain the diameter proper for the journals of a shaft of the second class, intended to transmit a force, equal to 15 horse power, at the rate of 40 revolutions per minute.

Here,

$$\frac{R}{HP} = \frac{40}{15} = 2 \cdot 67.$$

This quotient lies between the numbers 3·219 and 2·266 in the third column, and between 3·123 and 2·094 in the sixth. It follows, then, that if the shaft is to be of cast-iron, its journals must be between 4 and 4½ inches in diameter; or, if it is to be of wrought-iron, between 3½ and 4 inches, there being about half an inch of difference between the two materials in this instance.

Third Example.—A shaft, intended for a third mover, is to transmit a force equal to 6 horse power, at a velocity of 50 revolutions per minute, what should be the diameter of its journals in cast or wrought-iron?

Here,

$$\frac{R}{HP} = \frac{50}{6} = 8 \cdot 333.$$

This number, in the third column, lies between 13·25 and 6·79; therefore the diameter for cast-iron should be between 2 and 2½, say, 2⅜ inches. For wrought-iron the diameter should be 2 inches, as the number, 8·45, opposite to this in the seventh column, almost coincides with the quotient above obtained.

The length of the journals and their bearings should always be greater than their diameter. For large sizes, it should be 1·2d to 1·4d, and for smaller sizes, 1·5d to 2d. Thus, the length of a wrought-iron journal, 1·5 inches in diameter, should be from (1·5 × 1·5 =) 2·25 to (1·6 × 2 =) 3 inches.

When shafts have to resist both a torsional and a lateral or transverse strain, the diameter of their journals should be determined with reference to that strain which is the greatest, or which of itself would require the greatest dimensions.

When shafts are not of any great length—3 to 6 feet, for example—their diameter need not be above a tenth greater than that of their journals. Solid cast-iron shafts of above six feet in length should have a diameter one-fifth, or even one-fourth greater than that of their journals.

FRICTION OF SURFACES IN CONTACT.

162. Friction is the resistance which one surface offers to another—moving or sliding on it. Friction may be distinguished as *sliding friction*, and the *friction of rotation.* The former is that which arises from the simple rubbing of one surface upon another; the latter, from the rotation of one surface upon another.

The friction caused by the rubbing of plane surfaces is independent of the extent of surface or velocity of movement; it depends essentially on the weight of the body, or, more accurately, the pressure binding the two surfaces together. It may therefore be said, that the friction is in proportion to the pressure.

Similarly, the friction of a journal in its bearings is independent of the length of these, but is proportional to the diameter and to the pressure.

We give tables for each of these classes of friction, indicating the ratio of the friction to the pressure, and consisting of a series of coefficients, whereby the pressure must be multiplied in order to ascertain the amount of resistance due to friction.

Table of the Ratios of Friction for Plane Surfaces.

Description of Materials	Disposition of the Fibres.	Condition of the Surfaces.	At Starting.	In Motion.
	Parallel.	Dry.	·62	·48
	Do.	Lubricated with dry soap.	·44	·16
Oak on oak,............	Across.	Dry.	·44	·34
	Do.	Wet with water.	·71	·25
	Endwise (on one piece).	Dry.	·43	·19
Oak on elm,...............	Parallel.	Do.	·38	"
Ash, beech, or deal on oak, ..	Do.	Do.	·53	·38
Hempen cord on oak,........	Do.	Do.	·80	·52
Wrought-iron on oak,........	Do.	Do.	·62	·49
Cast-iron on oak,...........	Do.	Wet with water,	·65	·22
Pump leather on cast-iron,...	Flat or on edge.	Do.	·62	"
Belt { on oaken drums, ... on cast-iron pulleys,...	} Flat.	Oiled or greased. Dry.	·12 ·47 ·28	" ·27 "
Cast-iron on cast-iron,.......	.. .. ..	Do.	·16	·15
Wrought iron on cast-iron, ..	.. .. ..	Do.	·19	·19

Example.—What power is necessary to raise an oaken floodgate weighing 30 lbs., and against which a pressure is exerted equal to 700 lbs.?

We have

(·71 × 700 =) 497 + 30 = 527 lbs. at starting,

and   (·25 × 700 =) 1.5 + 30 = 205 when in motion,

supposing the pressure continues the same.

Table of the Ratios of Friction for Journals in Bearings.

Description of Materials.	Condition of the Surfaces.	Ratio of Friction to Pressure, with regular Lubrication.
Cast or wrought-iron journals, in cast or wrought-iron, brass, or gun-metal bearings,.....	Lubricated with oil or lard, ...	·07 to ·08
Cast-iron in cast-iron	Similarly lubricated and wet with water	·08
	Lubricated with ordinary oil, and wet with water, ...	·14
Cast-iron in brass or gun-metal,	Greased, ...	·16
	Greased and wet, ...	·19
	Unlubricated, ...	·18
Cast-iron in lignumvitæ, ...	Lubricated with oil and lard, ...	·10
	Lubricated with a preparation of lard and plumbago, ...	·14
Wrought-iron in brass or gun-metal,.................	Greased, ...	·09
	Greased and wet, ...	·19
	Badly lubricated, ...	·25
Wrought-iron in lignumvitæ,.	Lubricated with oil and lard,.............	·11
	Lubricated with ordinary oil, ...	·19

Rule.—To determine the frictional pressure, F, acting on the bearings of a journal, always bearing in mind the weight of the shaft and the gear carried by it, the power transmitted, as also the resisting load: *Multiply the product of these, P, by the coefficient, c, to obtain the amount of friction; next multiply this by the constant ·08, and by the diameter d., in inches, (or by ·08d.,) to obtain the amount per revolution; and, finally, multiply this by the number of revolutions in a minute, which will give the amount of power consumed by friction during this unit of time.*

Example.—What amount of power, A, is absorbed by the friction of the journals of a cast-iron shaft revolving in bearings; also, of cast-iron, under the following conditions?

The diameter at the journals = 5 inches.

The pressure of the shaft and gear = 20,000 lbs.

The velocity = 5 revolutions per minute.

According to the table, the coefficient, c, is ·075.

Here we have—

$$F = ·08\, d \times c \times P,$$
$$= ·08 \times 5 \times ·075 \times 20,000 = 3,000 \text{ lbs.}$$

CHAPTER IV.

THE INTERSECTION AND DEVELOPMENT OF SURFACES, WITH APPLICATIONS.

163. Nowhere is descriptive geometry more useful, in its application to the industrial arts, than in the determination of the lines of intersection, or junction, of the various solids, whether the intersection be that of two similar solids with each other, as a cylinder with a cylinder; or of dissimilar ones, as a cylinder with a sphere or a cone. With the aid, however, of this branch of geometry, we can determine, in the most exact manner, the proportions of all the curves—of double as of single curvature—which may be produced by the intersections of surfaces of revolution, the constructive or generative data of which are known.

The applications of forms in which such curves occur are exceedingly numerous; they abound in the works of the brazier, the tinsmith, the joiner, the carpenter, the builder, and the architect, as well as in all descriptions of machinery. This treatise would, indeed, be incomplete, were we not to render the delineation of these curves quite familiar to the student. Intimately connected also with this branch of the subject, is the development of curved surfaces; that is, the determination of the dimensions of such surfaces when extended in a plane, so that the workman may be able to cut out such pieces with the certainty of their taking the form, and fitting the place assigned for them.

The study of projections, moreover, comprises the methods of delineation of such curves as helices, spirals, and serpentines, which frequently occur in mechanical and architectural construction.

THE INTERSECTIONS AND DEVELOPMENT OF CYLINDERS AND CONES.

PLATE XIV.

PIPES AND BOILERS.

164. The intersections of cylindrical or conical surfaces may be curves of either single or double curvature. A curve is said to possess a *double curvature*, when it is not situated wholly in one plane. The problem to be considered in representing the lines of intersection, reduces itself to the determination in succession of the projections of several points in the curve, and the completion, by tracing the projections of the entire curves through the points thus found. The principle generally to be followed in these cases is, to imagine the two cylinders, for instance, to be cut by one and the same plane—their intersection in that plane being a point in the line sought. Thus, to obtain a point in the line of intersection of two right cylinders, A and B, represented in figs. 1 and 2, draw any plane, c d, parallel to the axes of both cylinders. This plane cuts the vertical cylinder, A, as projected horizontally in the points, e' f, and as projected vertically through the lines, $e^1 e^2$, and $f^1 f^2$. The horizontal cylinder, B, is cut in c d in the horizontal projection, and in c' d' in the vertical projection, which latter is obtained as follows:—The semi-base, g i, of the cylinder, B, is drawn in plan as in fig. 1ᵃ; then prolonging c d until it cuts this plan in c^2, it will give the distance, $c^2 h$, of the cutting plane from the axis of the cylinder; this distance is then transferred to i c', fig. 2, and through c' the line, c' d', is drawn as required. The points, e^2, f^2, of intersection of this line, c' d', with the lines, $e^1 e^2$, $f^1 f^2$, are points in the intersecting line respectively on each side of the vertical cylinder, A.

By repeating this operation with another plane, as m n, parallel to the first, other two points will obviously be found, as l^2 and o^2. The extreme points, a', k', are naturally determined by the intersection of the outlines of the cylinders. As for the point, b', it is found by means of the imaginary plane, g p, tangential to the vertical cylinder, A, and also to the horizontal one, B, when, as in this case, the two are of equal diameter.

As many points having been found as constitute a sufficient guide, according to the scale or size of the drawing, and the proportion between the intersecting solids, their reunion into one continuous line completes the delineation of the curve of intersection. It will be observed that, in fig. 2, the vertical projection of this curve is a straight line, as a' b', or b' k', these two being at right angles to each other; this results from the fact, that the cylinders, A and B, chosen for this illustration are of equal diameter, and have their axes situate in the same plane, and at right angles to each other, in such a manner that the curves of intersection, which are elliptical, lie in a plane at right angles to the plane of the vertical projection. It follows, then, that this peculiarity being known, all that is necessary in similar cases—that is, when two equal right cylinders, having their axes in the same plane, cut each other—is simply to draw lines from the extreme points, a' and k', to the summit, b', the projection of the point of intersection of their axes—the operations above described being, in such cases, altogether dispensed with.

165. When the cylinders are of unequal diameters, the curve of intersection becomes one of double curvature, notwithstanding that the axes of the cylinders may lie in the same plane. Thus, figs. 7 and 8, which represent two intersecting cylinders, A and B, of very different magnitudes, show that the curve of intersection, a' b' k', drawn according to the method before given, is one of double curvature, becoming the more flattened at b', according as the diameters of the cylinders differ more. To render it quite plain that the operation is the same, we have indicated the various points obtained, by the same letters which mark the corresponding points in figs. 1 and 2. We must further remark, that in figs. 7 and 8 the curve is determined with the assistance of two elevations, taken at right angles to each other; whilst, in figs. 1 and 2, an elevation and a plan were employed, similarly, at right angles to each other.

We show the application or exemplification of this curve in figs. 4 and 5, which represent a steam-engine boiler, c, seen partly in elevation and partly in section. The tubular piece, D, which is a species of man-hole, is supposed to be cylindrical, and is attached to the body of the boiler by means of a flange, which gives rise to the external intersectional curves, a b, c d, and the internal one, e f.

THE INTERSECTION OF A CONE WITH A SPHERE.

166. Whenever a cone is cut by a plane parallel to its base, the section presents an outline similar to that of the base; then, when the cone under consideration is a right cone of a circular base, all such parallel sections are circles. Thus, in figs. 3 and 3ᵃ, representing a right cone, A' B' s', the plane, a' b', parallel to its base, A' B', cuts the cone so as to present a circle, of which the diameter is exactly contained within the extreme generatrices, A' s', B' s'. If, then, with the centre, s, and radius, a s = a' b' ÷ 2, we describe a circle, it will be the outline of that part of the cone intercepted by the cutting plane.

The section of a sphere, c, by any plane whatever, is also a circle. When this cutting plane, a' b', for instance, is perpendicular to the plane of projection, it is necessarily projected as a straight line, as in fig. 3ᵃ, and as a circle, as in fig. 3, in the plane of projection to which it is parallel. It follows, from the existence of these respective properties, that we have at hand a very simple method for determining the curve of intersection of a cone with a sphere, whatever may be the relative position of their axes. This method consists in supposing a series of parallel planes to cut both the cone and the sphere, so as to produce circular sections of both—the intersections of the outlines of which will consequently be points in the curve sought, as indicated in fig. 3.

The intersection, $a'\,b'$, is a circle, the diameter of which is limited by the extreme generatrices, $s'\,a'$, $s'\,b$, of the cone, where they encounter the great circle of the sphere, c. The same method holds good when the cone is cut by any plane, $a'\,g$, inclined to the base, the outline of the section being in this case an ellipse, which is projected in the plan, fig. 3, by the line, $a\,i''\,g'\,n'$, the resultant of the various intersections in the planes adopted in the construction and obtainment of the curve.

The same occurs with the intersection of a cone, $a'\,b'\,s'$, with a cylinder, $a'\,b'\,d\,f$; and when their axes lie in the same straight line, the intersection, $a'\,b'$, is also a circle, the diameter of which is equal to that of the cylinder.

167. If their axes are parallel, though not in the same straight line, the intersection of these two surfaces becomes a curve of double curvature, which may be determined either according to the method adopted in reference to figs. 1 and 3, or by supposing a series of planes to cut the cone parallel to its base, and consequently at right angles to the generatrix lines of the cylinder; by this means circular sections will be produced, those of the cylinder being always the same, but those of the cone varying according to the distance of the planes from its apex. The points of intersection of the various circles representing, respectively, sections of the cone and cylinder, will be points in the curve of intersection sought.

DEVELOPMENTS.

168. By this term is meant the unrolling, extending, or flattening out upon a plane, of any curved surface, in order to ascertain its exact superficial measurement.

The more generally used surfaces or forms which are capable of development in this manner, are—the cylinder, the cone, prisms, pyramids, and the *frusta*, or fragments of these solids.

Tin and copper-smiths and boiler-makers, who operate upon metals which come into their hands in the form of thin sheets, have continually to transform these sheets into objects which are analogous in form to these solids.

To do their work with skill and exactitude, and not by mere guess, and also to avoid the cutting of the material to waste, they should make plans of the whole or part of the object as finished, so that they may calculate the exact development of the surface, both as to form and size, and cut it at once from the sheet of metal with all possible precision.

THE DEVELOPMENT OF THE CYLINDER.

169. Here, taking fig. 2, which we have on a former occasion considered as a couple of solid cylinders, to represent, in the present case, two pipes or hollow cylinders formed of thin sheet metal, let us set about ascertaining what should be the shape and size of the pieces of metal as extended out flat, of which these

two cylinders are to be formed. It is to be observed, in the first place, that the rectification or development into a straight line of a circle, is equal to its diameter multiplied by 3·1416, &c.; whence the development of the base, P Q, of the right vertical cylinder, A. fig. 2, of which the diameter measures ·322 mètres, is obviously equal to ·322 × 3·1416 = 1·012 m.

This length, then, 1·012 m., is set off on the line, M M, fig. 10, and the circumference having been divided into a number of equal parts, as was done to obtain the curve of intersection of the two cylinders in fig. 1; the line, M M, is divided into the like number of equal divisions. Through each of these points of division, perpendiculars are erected upon the line, M M, representing so many generatrix lines corresponding to those of the cylinder, A, fig. 2; and for the sake of greater intelligibility, we have marked the corresponding lines by the same letters. Next, on each of these are set off distances, M b', $e'\,e^2$, $l'\,l^2$, P a', $f'\,f^2$, $o'\,o^2$, Q k', &c., equal to the respective distances in fig. 2. By this means are obtained the points, b', e', l', &c., in fig. 10, through which the curve passes which forms the contour of intersection corresponding to that portion of the semi-cylinder, $b'\,a\,b''$, fig. 1, which is intersected by the horizontal cylinder, B; and as the other half of the cylinder is precisely the same, the curve has simply to be repeated, as shown in fig. 10.

It is unnecessary to detail the method of finding this development of the horizontal cylinder, B, as it is identical in principle to that just discussed.

It may be gathered from the above exemplification, that the principle generally to be followed in obtaining the development of cylindrical surfaces, is, first, to unfold it in a direction at right angles to one of its generatrices, or in the direction the generatrix takes in the construction of the solid, and then to set off from the straight line thus produced, at equal distances apart, any number of distances previously obtained from the projections of the outline or line of intersection when the cylinder is joined to another, or of its section when cut by any plane. The curve of this outline is finally obtained by tracing a line through the extremities of the generatrices, drawn perpendicular to the base.

THE DEVELOPMENT OF THE CONE.

170. As in the case of the cylinder, so likewise, in order to find the development of the cone, do we unfold it, as it were, in the direction of motion of its generatrix. Now, as all the generatrices of a right cone are equal, and converge to one point, the apex, it follows that, when the conical surface is developed upon a plane, these generatrices will form radii of a portion of a circle; consequently, if with one of the generatrices, as a radius, we describe a circle, and cut off as much of the circumference as shall be equal to that of the base of the developed cone, we shall obtain a sector of a circle equal in area to the lateral surface of the cone, as developed upon a plane.

Fig. 9 represents the development of the frustum, or truncated cone, $a'\,b'$, $a'\,b'$, as projected in fig. 3°, and of which the apex would be s', were the cone entire. The operation is as follows:—

We shall suppose the cone to be developed in the direction taken by the generatrix, $s'\,a'$, fig. 3°; therefore, with a radius equal to s⁣ A′, and with the centre, s′, describe the fragment of a circle, A′ B′ A², fig. 9.

Having divided the circular base, A B, fig. 3, of the cone into some arbitrary number of equal parts, say 16, and having drawn the respective generatrices, 1 s, 2 s, 3 s, &c., set off on the arc, A B A², fig. 9, an equal number of arcs, each equal to the respective arcs obtained by the subdivision of the circle, A B, fig. 3. From the points thus obtained, 1′ 2′ 3′, &c., fig. 9, draw the radii, 1′ s′, 2′ s′, 3′ s, &c., representing generatrices corresponding to those projected in fig. 3.

By this operation we obtain the development of the entire cone, and find that it produces the figure s′ A′ B′ A″, fig. 9, the circular perimeter of which is equal to that of the base of the cone itself. The cone, however, under consideration, is divided by a plane, a′ b′, fig. 3, parallel to its base, which reduces it to a frustum of a cone; the development of the conical surface of which is equal to the space contained between the arc, A′ B′ A², corresponding to the base of the cone, as just determined, and the arc, a c b, of lesser radius, drawn with the same centre, s′, and with a radius equal to the generatrix, s′ a′, of the portion of the cone taken away.

The development, then, of the truncated cone, is the fragment of an annular space, distinguished in fig. 9 by a flat tinted shade.

171. In the case of a truncated cone, of which the dividing plane is inclined to the base, as a′ g, fig. 3ᵃ, instead of being parallel, or if the cone is joined to a cylindrical or spherical body, and the line of intersection is curved in any way, the development of this edge of the conical surface will no longer take the form of the arc, a c b, fig. 9. Its true representation will be obtainable by setting off, on the several radii, fig. 9, lengths corresponding to the respective generatrices as intercepted by the plane, or curve, of intersection. In order to obtain the lengths of the respective generatrices, which can be done from the vertical projection, fig. 3ᵃ, each intermediate one, as 4′ i, &c., must be squared across to an extreme one, as at A′ i′, and indicated by the horizontal lines; this will give the exact length of each—being otherwise, as projected, considerably foreshortened. Thus, the division of the cone by the inclined plane, a′ g, fig. 3ᵃ, produces an ellipse, the development of which, in fig. 9, takes the form of the curve, a i g b.

In the construction of the boiler, represented in figs. 4 and 5, which is formed of several pieces of sheet metal, we shall find extensive applications of the principles just discussed. It must be borne in mind that, in calculating the development, or the size and shape of the component pieces, an allowance must be made for the *lap* of the pieces over each other, for the purpose of joining them together, as indicated in the drawing.

172. In cylindrical steam boilers, the extremities are generally constructed in the shape of hemispheres—this form offering the greatest resistance to internal or external pressure.

As the sphere cannot be developed upon a plane, these hemispherical ends cannot be made in a single piece, unless cast or forged. In practice this difficulty is overcome, by forming this portion in from 5 to 8 gores, according to the size of the boiler, these being surmounted by a central cap-piece. After being cut out, these several pieces are hammered to give them the necessary sphericity.

In fig. 6, we give a practical method of approximately determining the development of one of such gores; this consists in drawing with the centre, o′, an arc, m n, corresponding to the radius of the hemisphere. On this arc, from m to n, set off the circular length of the gore; set off, also, the length, p q, corresponding to one of the six divisions, as seen in the end view, fig. 5. On the arc, m n, fig. 6, mark an arbitrary number of points, at equal distances asunder, as 1, 2, 3, 4, 5; draw through these horizontal lines, cutting the vertical, m o′, thereby giving the various radii, o′ 1″, o′ 2″, o′ 3″, &c., with which arcs are drawn as indicated; the rectification, or development, of these arcs, contained between the radii, p o′, g o′, are then obtained, and transferred to perpendiculars drawn through the points, 1′, 2′, 3′, &c., on the line, o′ n′, which is the rectification, or development, of the arc, m n, with its series of divisions. Thus, from the arc, p q, is obtained the line, p′ q′, and similarly the entire figure, p′ n′ q′, which is an approximation to the surface of the gore, as supposed to be flattened out. The necessary allowance for lap is superadded, as shown by the flat tinting in the drawing, fig. 6. The gore cut to this outline in sheet metal is then hammered to a proper form upon a mandril, or anvil, with a spherical surface.

THE DELINEATION AND DEVELOPMENT OF HELICES, SCREWS, AND SERPENTINES.

PLATE XV.

HELICES.

173. That curve is called a cylindrical helix, which may be said to be generated by a point caused to travel round a cylinder, having, at the same time, a motion in the direction of the length of the cylinder—this longitudinal motion bearing some regular prescribed proportion to the circular or angular motion. The distance between any two points which are nearest to each other, and in the same straight line parallel to the axis of the cylinder, is called the *pitch*—in other words, the longitudinal distance traversed by the generating point during one revolution.

This definition at once suggests a method of drawing the lateral projection of this curve, when the two projections of the cylinder and the pitch are known. This method consists in dividing the circumference of the base of the cylinder into any number of equal parts, and drawing parallels to the axis through the points of division projected on the vertical plane; at the same time a portion of the axis, equal to the pitch, must be divided into the like number of equal parts, and as many lines must be drawn perpendicular to the axis. The intersections of the corresponding lines of each set will be points in the curve.

Let A and A′, figs. 1 and 2, be the horizontal and vertical projections of a right cylinder, and a^1—a^2 the length of the pitch of the helix, generated by the traverse, as already defined, of the point projected in a and a′.

The circle described with the radius, a o, and representing the base of the cylinder, is divided into 12 equal parts, starting from the point, a. Through each of the points thus obtained, a vertical line is drawn. The pitch, a^1 a^2, is similarly divided into 12 equal parts, and a corresponding number of horizontal lines are drawn to cut the vertical ones in the points, 1′, 2′, 3′, &c.; these points are next connected by the continuous line, a', $1'$, $3'$, $6'$, $9'$, a^2, which forms the vertical or lateral projection of the helix.

Half of this curve is indicated by a sharp full line, as being on the front surface, a, 3, 6, of the cylinder, whilst the other half is in dotted lines, representing the portion of the curve which is on the other side, a, 9, 6.

The number of divisions of the circumference of the cylinder is a matter of indifference as regards the accurate delineation of the curve, and it is therefore natural to choose a number that calls for the simplest operations—an even number, for example, as 6, 8, or 12; and in the present instance, wherein the starting point, a, lies in the horizontal diameter, a 6, of the base, it will be observed that two points occur in the same vertical line, as 2—10, which gives the points, $2'$, $10'$, in the vertical projection.

The operations will be similar, if the given starting point be diametrically opposite to a, as b', the pitch, b^1 b^2, being equal to a^1 a^2.

174. The conical helix is different from the cylindrical one, simply in that it is described on the surface of a cone instead of on that of a cylinder, and the operation consequently differs very slightly from the one before described; the horizontal and vertical projections of the cone are given, and also the pitch. Fig. 3 is the vertical projection of a truncated cone, c, the bases of which, a' b', c' d', are represented in the plan, fig. 1, by the concentric circles described, with the respective radii, a o and c o. The outer circle having been divided as already shown, radii are drawn to the centre, o, from all the points of division, 1, 2, 3, &c., which cut the inner circle in the points, e, f, g, &c. . These points are then projected upon the upper base, c' d', in fig. 3, those on the outer circle being similarly projected on the lower base, a' b'; the respective points in each base are next joined, thus forming a series of generatrices of the cone, as 1^2—e^2, 2^2—f^2, o^1—o^2, &c., which would all converge in the apex, if the cone were complete. These lines are cut by horizontals drawn through a corresponding number of divisions in the length of the given pitch, a' c', and the points of intersection thus obtained lie in the curve which it is required to draw. The horizontal projection of the curve is then obtained by letting fall from the points of intersection last obtained, a series of verticals which cut the respective radii in the plan, fig. 1. This produces a species of spiral, or volute, e^3, f^3, g^3, h^3, 2^3, &c. By following out the same principles, helices may be represented as lying upon spheres, or any other surfaces of revolution.

THE DEVELOPMENT OF THE HELIX.

175. It will be recollected that a cylinder, and also a cone, are capable of being developed upon a plane surface, and that the base of either, when rectified, or converted into a straight line, is equal to the diameter multiplied by 3·1416. Let, then, a 6, fig. 4, be a portion of the development of the base of the cylinder, A, figs. 1 and 2; to obtain the development of the helix drawn upon this cylinder, we must first divide it off into lengths, corresponding and equal to the arcs obtained by the division of the circle, a o. On each of the divisions thus obtained, as 1, 2, 3, &c., we then erect perpendiculars, making them equal respectively to the distances from the starting point, a, of the several divisions

of the pitch. The extremities of these perpendiculars, as $1'$, $2'$, $3'$, &c., will be found to lie in the same straight line, a $6'$, which consequently represents the development of a portion of the helix. In general, the development of a helix is a straight line, forming the hypothenuse of a right-angled triangle, the base of which is equal to the circumference of the cylinder, and the height to the pitch of the helix.

Several helices drawn upon the same cylinder, and having the same pitch, or a helix which makes several convolutions about a cylinder, is represented by a series of parallel curves, the distance between which, measured on any line parallel to the axis, is always equal to the pitch.

The development of the conical helix may be obtained by means of an operation analogous to that employed for the development of the cone (Plate XIV.); and in this case the result will be a curve, instead of a straight line.

We meet with numerous applications of the helical curve in the arts, for all descriptions of screws; and staircases, and serpentines.

SCREWS.

176. Screws are employed in machinery, and in mechanical combinations, either for securing various pieces to each other, so as to produce contact pressure, or for communicating motion. Screws are formed with triangular, square, or rounded threads or fillets.

A screw is said to have a triangular thread, when it is generated by a triangle, isosceles or not, the three angles of which describe helices about the same given axis, situate in the same plane as the triangle. Figs. 5 and 5^a represent the projections of a triangular-threaded screw, such as would be generated by the helical movement of the triangle, a' b' c', of which the apex, a', is situate on a cylinder of a radius equal to a o, and of which the other angles. b', c', are both situate on the internal cylinder, having the radius, b o, which is called the core of the screw, and is concentric with the first. The difference, a b, between the radii, a o and b o, indicates the depth of the thread.

When, as in the case taken for illustration, the screw is single-threaded, the pitch is equal to the distance between the two points, b' and c'; that is, to the base of the triangle. The screw is one of 2, 3, 4, or 5 threads, according as the pitch is equal to 2, 3, 4, or 5 times the base of the generating triangle. From what has already been discussed, the method of delineating the triangular-threaded screw will be easily comprehended; for all that is necessary is to draw the helices, generated by the three angular points, in the manner shown in reference to figs. 1 and 2. We have, notwithstanding, given the entire operation for one semi-convolution of the thread, in figs. 5 and 5^a. When one of the curves, as a' $3'$ $6'$, is obtained, it is repeated as many times as there are convolutions of the thread on the length of the screw. To do this with facility, and without repeating the entire operation, it is customary to cut out a pattern of the curve in hard card-board, or, by preference, in veneer wood; then setting this pattern to the points of division, d' e' f', previously set off, the curves are easily drawn parallel to one another. The same may be done with the inner helical curves.

It must be observed, that, to complete the outline of the screw, these various curves require to be joined by the portions, b' d', d' i', which, though in fig. 5ᵃ they are drawn as simple straight lines, should, if it is wished to be precise, be shown by lines slightly curved and tangential to the curves passing through the points, a and b', as in fig. 5ᵇ. These curves are the result of a series of helices, traced by the component points of the lines forming the sides, a' b', a' c', of the generating triangle. In practice, this nicety is disregarded, and simple straight lines are employed.

177. A screw is termed square-threaded when it is generated by a square or by a rectangle, the parallel sides of which lie in right concentric cylinders, and the angles or corners of which describe helices about the axes of these cylinders. Figs. 6 and 6ᵃ, represent projections of a square-threaded screw—the thread being generated by the square, a' c' b' d'. The horizontal side, a' c', determines the depth. The height, a' d', marks the width of the thread, and d' c' is the width of the interval, which is generally equal to that of the thread.

When the screw is single-threaded, the pitch, a' e', is equal to the sum of the widths of the thread and of the interval. or, in the case before us, to twice the side of the square. Of course, when the pitch is equal to 2, 3, or 4 times a' e', the screw is 2, 3, or 4-threaded, in all cases having as many intervals as threads. The operations called for in delineating the screw of a single square thread, are fully indicated upon the figures. The delineation of a screw of several threads does not possess any additional points of difficulty.

INTERNAL SCREWS.

178. An internal screw, or nut, is a screw in *intaglio*, cored out of a solid body—instead of being in relief, and having the material cut away from it—in such a manner. that its more indented portions correspond to the more elevated portions of the common or external screw, whilst the more indented portions of the latter correspond to the more elevated portions of the former. In order to represent the helical fillets or threads of the internal screw, it is necessary to section it by a plane passing through its axis; it is in this manner that we have represented the nuts, m n p q, in figs. 5ᵃ and 6ᵃ, the first having a triangular thread fitting to and embracing the screw, D, which is represented as just introduced into it; the other has a square thread similarly adapted to the screw, E.

It follows, from these nuts being represented in section, that we only see the half of each corresponding to the posterior portion of their respective screws, D and E; and in consequence of this, the helical curves are inclined in the opposite direction to those representing the anterior portions of the screws.

Those screws are distinguished as right-handed screws, of which the thread in relief rises from the left to the right, as in the screws, D, E; and as left-handed when the thread takes the direction from right to left—that is, for example, in the direction taken by the curves representing the nuts, D, E.

SERPENTINES.

179. Serpentine is the name given in practice to a pipe or tube bent to the helicoidal form; but, in geometry, it is the term given to the solid generated by a sphere, the centre of which traces a helicoidal path.

This form is often employed, whether hollow, as for pipes, such as the worm of a distilling apparatus, or solid, as for metal springs

The first thing to be done in delineating this solid, is to determine the helix traced by the centre of the generating sphere, its pitch, and the radius of the cylinder on which it runs, being given. The helix having been drawn, a series of circles are described with the radius of the sphere, and with various points of the curves as centres; curves drawn tangential to these circles, will then form the outline of the object. Figs. 7 and 7ᵃ represent the plan and elevation of a serpentine formed in this manner. The circle drawn with the radius, a o, is the base of the cylinder, on which lies the helix generated by the traverse of the point projected vertically in a'. Next is given the radius, a' b', of the generating sphere, and the pitch, a^1 a^2, of the helix. This helix is then projected according to the operation indicated on the drawing, and already described, by the curve, a^1, $1'$, $2'$, $6'$, $9'$, and a^2; it may be continued indefinitely, according to the number of convolutions desired. With different points of this curve as centres, and with the radius, a' b', are then described a series of circles pretty near to each other, and two curves are drawn tangential to these, as shown on fig. 7ᵃ.

In going over this figure with ink, it is of importance to limit these curves to the portion of the outline, which is quite apparent or distinct; thus, for the anterior portion, a, 1, 2, 3, 6, fig. 7, of the serpentine, the lower curve, c e f g, ends at the point of contact, c, with the circle whose centre is a^2, whilst the upper one, h i d, ends in the point, d, on the circle described with the centre, 6'. The posterior portions of these curves are limited by the points, g and i, where the bend of the serpentine goes behind, and is hid by the anterior portion.

The horizontal projection of the serpentine is always comprised within two concentric circles, the distance asunder of which is equal to the diameter of the generating sphere, as in fig. 7.

Fig. 7² represents a tubular serpentine, which is supposed to be divided by a plane, 1—2, in fig. 7, passing through its axis. It is, consequently, the posterior portions that are visible, and they are inclined from right to left; the section at the same time shows the thickness of the tube, or pipe.

In the arts, we also see serpentines, both solid and hollow, generated by conic or other helices; of this description are the springs employed in the moderator lamps, and the forms of distillery worms are sometimes varied in this way.

180. *Observation.*—The curves representing the outline of screws and serpentines, the rigorously exact delineation of which we have just explained, are considerably modified when these objects come to be represented on a very small scale; thus the triangular-threaded screw may be represented, as shown in fig. 8, by a series of parallel straight, instead of curved, lines—these being inclined from side to side to the extent of half the pitch. These lines should be limited by two parallels to the axis on each side, marking the amount of relief of the thread. When the scale of the drawing is still smaller, and greater simplicity desirable, the draughtsman is content with a series of parallel lines, as in fig. 9, limited by a single line on each side parallel to the axis.

For the square-threaded screw, the helical curves may similarly be replaced by straight lines, as in fig. 10. The same also applies to the serpentine, as shown in fig. 11.

THE APPLICATION OF THE HELIX.

THE CONSTRUCTION OF A STAIRCASE.

PLATE XVI.

181. The staircases, which afford a means of communication between the various floors of houses, are constructed after various systems, the greater number of which comprise exemplifications of the helix. The cage, or space set apart for the staircase, varies in form with the locality. It may be rectangular, circular, or elliptic.

Figs. 1 and 2 represent a staircase, the cage of which is rectangular this space being provided for the construction of the main frame of the stair, with its steps and balustrade, and with a central space left sufficient for the admission of light from above. In the case of a cylindrical cage, the curve with which the steps rise is helical from bottom to top; but in a staircase within a rectangular cage, the steps rise for some distance in a straight line, and only take the helical twist at the part forming the junction between the rectilinear portions running up alternate sides of the rectangle. Stairs are sometimes made without this curved part, a simple platform, or "resting-place," connecting the two side portions.

For the division of the steps, we take the line, $e f g h i$, passing through the centre of their width, and taking exactly the direction it is intended to give the stairs. The first or lowest step, A, which lies on the ground, is generally of stone, and is larger and wider than the others.

For the stairs, as for the helix, the pitch or height, say 3·38 m., from the basement to the floor above, is divided into as many equal parts as it is wished to have steps. The centre line, $e f g h i$, is also divided into a like number of equal parts. In general, the number of steps should be such, that the height of each does not exceed 19 or 20 centimètres. The larger the staircase is, the more may this height be reduced—say, perhaps, as low as 15 or 16 centimètres. The width, 1—2, of the step should not be under 18 to 20 centimètres.

If, for example, in the given height of 3·38 m., we wish to make 21 steps, we must divide this height into 21 equal parts, and draw a series of horizontal lines through the points of division, which will represent the horizontal surfaces of the steps.

For those steps which lie parallel to each other, it is simply requisite to erect verticals upon the points of division on the centre line in the plan. The points of intersection of these with the horizontals above, as 1, 2, 3, 4, fig. 2, indicate the edges of these steps. For the turning steps, however, or winders, as those steps are called which are not parallel to each other, a particular operation is necessary, termed the balancing of the steps, the object of which is to make the steps as nearly equal in width as possible, without, at the same time, making them very narrow on the inner edges, or rendering the twist or curve too sharp or sudden. Where the stairs are narrow, as in the case we have illustrated, the balancing should commence a step or two before reaching the curved portions. This balancing may be obtained in the following manner:—A part of the rectilinear portion, $p l$, equal to three steps, is developed, and then a part of the curved portion, $l m n$,

equal to three more steps. On the vertical, $t q$, fig. 3, set off the heights of the first three steps; and through the point, q, draw the horizontal, q 4, representing the development of the widths of the steps in a straight line. Also, on the prolongation, $t q'$, of the vertical, $t q$, set off the heights of other three steps. Through the point, q', draw a horizontal, and make q' 10 equal to the arc, $l m n$, in the plan, fig. 1, as rectified. The straight line, t 10, will then be the development corresponding to the curve of the framepiece. At the latter point, n, erect a perpendicular on this line, and at the point, 5, a perpendicular to the straight line, t 4. The point of intersection, o, of these two perpendiculars, gives the centre of the arc, $p k n$, which is drawn tangentially to these lines. Then, through each point of division on the vertical, $q q'$, draw horizontals, meeting this curve in the points, j, k, l, m, through which draw parallels to $q q'$. Then transfer the respective distances, j 6, $k t$, l 8, m 9, comprised between the arc and the two straight lines, t 4 and $t u$, on the line of the framepiece, $p k n$, in the plan, fig. 1, as at $j k$, $k l$, $l m$, $m n$. Next, draw straight lines through the points, j, k, l, m, and through the respective points of division, 6, 7, 8, 9, on the centre line, which will give the proper inclination for the steps as balanced. The second half of the curved portion is obviously precisely the same as the first in plan, and may easily be copied from it.

Having thus determined the position of the steps in the horizontal projection, they must next be projected on the vertical plane, by means of a series of verticals, which cut the respective horizontals drawn through the points of division, 1, 2, 3, 4. As in fig. 2, the anterior wall of the cage is supposed to be cut away by the line, a 6′ 10′, in the plan, the outer edges of the steps are seen and are determined by erecting verticals on the corresponding points, 6′, 7′, 8′, 9′, &c.

The perpendicular portions, $v v'$, of the steps, which are overhung by the horizontal portions, and consequently invisible in the plan, fig. 1, are, nevertheless, indicated there in dotted lines, parallel to the edges of the steps. To render them quite distinct, however, and at the same time to show the manner in which they are fitted into the framepiece, we have represented them, in fig. 4, without the actual steps, supposing them to be cut in succession horizontally, through their middles.

The framepiece is the principal piece in the staircase. It is situated in the centre of the cage, and sustains each step, and, consequently, must be constructed very accurately, for upon it, in a great measure, depends the strength and solidity of the staircase. For a staircase of proportions, like those of the one represented in the plate, the framepiece is generally made of oak, in three pieces; the middle piece, c, corresponding to the curved portion, whilst the other two, B and D, joined to that one, form the rectilinear portions. A special set of diagrams is necessary, to determine the shape and proportions of the various parts of this framepiece. The method here to be followed is, in the first place, to draw the joints, by which the vertical portions of the steps are attached to the framepiece. These can easily be obtained by squaring them over from fig. 4 to fig. 5, in which last are the horizontal division lines, corresponding to fig. 2. It will be observed, that the joints referred to are bevilled off, so as not to be apparent externally, The faces on the framepiece are seen on fig. 5, at the parts, B. C.

and the method of obtaining them is sufficiently indicated by the dotted lines. The framepiece has a certain regular depth throughout, and is cut on the upper side, to suit the form of the steps, and below, to the curvilinear outline, a' b' c' d' e' f', which is nothing but the combination of a helix with a couple of straight lines. These straight lines, a' b' and e' f', are naturally parallel to the curve passing through the edges of the steps, 1, 3, 5, 13, 16, 19. The curved part, b^1 c^1, which corresponds to the anterior face, b^2 c^2, of the framepiece, is drawn in precisely the same manner as a common cylindrical helix. It is the same with the part, d^1 e^1, which corresponds to the interior portion, d^2 e^2. If, in order to better indicate the space occupied by the framepiece, it is wished to construct an end view of it, this may be done, as in fig. 6, from the data furnished by figs. 4 and 5.

In figs. 12, 13, and 14, we have given, on a larger scale, the different views of the curved part, c, of the framepiece, so as to show its construction more plainly, as well as the form of the joint connecting the three parts of the framepiece together. Each of these figures is inscribed in a rectangle, indicated by dotted lines, and representing the rectangular parallelopiped, in which the piece may be said to be contained. To strengthen the junction of this piece with the portions, B and D, they are connected by iron straps or binding-pieces let in, or by bolts passing through, the entire thickness of the wood.

Figs. 7 and 8 represent, in plan and elevation, the details of the landing-stage, which forms the top step of one flight of the stairs, and is on a level with the upper floor. It is with this piece that the upper portion, D, of the framepiece is connected, by a joint similar to that uniting the other portions. Fig. 9 is a section, through the centre of this step-piece, through the line, 1—2, in the plan; whilst fig. 10 is another section, through the line, 3—4; and fig. 11 a third, through the line, 5—6. The form, dimensions, and joint of this piece, are all fully indicated in this series of figures.

The shaft of the staircase, or the open space left in the centre of the cage, is partially occupied by a balustrade, formed by a number of rods of iron or wood, attached at their lower extremities to the framepiece, as shown in fig. 15, and united above by a flat bar of iron, surmounted by a hand-rail of polished furniture-wood, of the form given in Plate III., fig. ©. The position of the rods, as given in the plan, fig. 1, is sufficient for the determination of their vertical projection or elevation.

THE INTERSECTION OF SURFACES.

APPLICATION TO STOPCOCKS.

PLATE XVII.

182. We have already discussed several examples of intersections of surfaces, as in pipes and boilers, and we shall now proceed to give some others, which are pretty generally met with, particularly in the construction of stopcocks; and for that reason we take one of these contrivances as an illustration.

A stopcock is a mechanical arrangement, the function of which is to establish or interrupt at pleasure the communication through pipes, for the passage of gases or liquids. It consists of two distinct parts, one called the cock, and the other—adjustable and moveable in the first—termed the key or plug.

Stopcocks are generally made of brass, composition-metal, or cast-iron, and the cock is formed with or without flanges, for attachment to vessels or piping. The key is generally conical, so as to fit better in its seat. The degree of taper given to the key varies with different constructors. We have shown in dotted lines. in fig. 2^b, various degrees of taper to be adopted, according as greater tightness or greater facility of movement is wanted. The part of the cock which receives the key is, of course, turned out to a corresponding conical surface. This portion of the cock is connected to the tubular portions by shoulders, of a slightly elliptical contour. A stopcock answering to this description is represented, in plan and elevation, in figs. 1 and 1^a.

In these figures will be seen the conical part, A, which embraces the key, the cylindrical portions, B, united to the former by the shoulders, D, and terminated by the flanges, C.

The conical key, E, adjusted in the cock, is surmounted by a handle, F, by means of which it is turned. The key is retained in the cock by a nut, G, working on a screw, formed on the lower projecting end of the key. Fig. 1^b represents an end view of this cock, and fig. 2^b is a vertical projection of the key alone. Fig. 2^a is a view of the key, looking on the lower end. Fig. 2 is a horizontal section through the line, 1—2, in fig. 1^a; and fig. 2^a is a vertical section through the line, 3—4, fig. 1.

It will be easy to see, from these various views, that, in order to represent the stopcock with exactitude, it has been necessary to find, on the one hand, the projection of the intersection of the elliptic shoulder, D, with the external conical surface of the central part, A, of the cock; and on the other, that of the cylindrical surfaces of the handle, F, of the key, as well when this is placed in a position parallel to the vertical plane, as in fig. 2^a, or inclined to this plane, as in fig. 1^a. We have, moreover, to determine the intersection with the external surface of the key of the rectangular opening, H, provided for the passage of fluids; and also the intersection of a prism with a sphere, which occurs in the shape of the nut, G, which secures the key in its place. The various operations here called for are indicated on the figures, which we shall proceed to explain.

Figs. 3 and 3^a show the geometrical construction of the intersection of the horizontal cylinder, F', of the handle, with the vertical cylinder, E', of the key. The curve is obviously obtained according to the method already described in reference to figs. 1 and 2, Plate XIV. We have, however, repeated the operations, the exemplifications being a variation from that previously given.

183. When the horizontal cylinder, F', figs. 3^b and 3^c, becomes inclined to the vertical plane, its curve of intersection with the vertical cylinder, E', assumes a different appearance as projected in this plane. Its construction, however, is precisely the same, as follows:—To obtain any point in the curve, we proceed just as in the preceding example, drawing the vertical plane, d' e', parallel to the axes of the cylinders, this plane cutting the vertical cylinder through the lines, d f and e g. This same plane cuts the horizontal cylinder, as projected in plan, at d' e', whence the vertical projection is obtained, after drawing the semi-cylindrical end view, as in fig. 8. The distance, i i', being set off on h h', the horizontal

line, *d e*, drawn through the point, *h'*, represents the intersection of the plane with the horizontal cylinder, *h h'*, being, of course, measured from its axis. It will be seen that the line, *d e*, is cut by the vertical lines, *d f* and *e g*, in the points, *d*, *e*, which lie in the curve sought; and the same construction will apply to every other point in the curve, *d b e c*.

184. Figs. 4 and 5 represent the intersection of an elliptical cylinder with a right cone of circular base, corresponding to the external conical surface, A, of the cock, at its junction with the shoulders, D. Fig. 5 is a plan, looking on the cock from below, and which shows the horizontal projection of the intersectional curves.

The solution of the problem requiring the determination of these curves consists in applying a method already given—namely, in taking any horizontal plane which cuts the cone, so as to present a circular section on the one hand, and the cylinder in two straight lines on the other—the points of intersection of these straight lines with the circle representing the section of the cone. Thus, by drawing the plane, *c d*, fig. 4, we obtain a circle of the diameter, *c d*, which is projected horizontally, as with the centre, *o*, fig. 5; we have also two generatrices of the cylinder, both projected in the vertical plane in the line, *a b*, and in the horizontal plane in the lines, *a' b'* and *a² b²*. Having drawn the semibase of the cylinder, *d e*, as at *d' f e'*, and having taken the distance, *f g*, fig. 4ª, and set it off, in fig. 5, from the axis, as from *g'* to *a'*, and to *a²*, we thereby obtain the generatrices, *a' b'* and *a² b²*, which cut the circle of the diameter, *c' d'*, in the four points, *h' i'*, which are squared across to, and projected in, the vertical plane in the points, *h*, *i*. In the same manner we obtain any other points, as *m*, *n*; *k l* being the plane taken for this purpose. The extreme points of the curve are obtained in a very simple and obvious manner, as *f*, *g*, *r*, *s*, being the points of intersection of the extreme generatrices, or the outlines of the two solids. With regard to the points, *t*, *u*, which form the apices of the two curves, their position may be obtained from the diagram, fig. 4ª, by drawing from the point, *s*, which would be the apex of the entire cone, a tangent, *s t*, to the base, *d' f e'*, of the cylinder, and projecting the point of contact, *t*, in the line, *x y*, representing a plane cutting the cone, which must be projected in the horizontal plane. Then, making *g' x'*, fig. 5, equal to *t v*, fig. 4ª, and drawing horizontals through *x'*, their intersections, *t' u'*, with the circular section of the cone, will be the points sought, which are accordingly squared over to fig. 4. The operations just described are analogous, it will be observed, to those employed in obtaining the intersection of two cylinders.

If, in the case of the cone and cylinder, the latter had been one of circular instead of elliptical base, as is frequently the case, still the construction, as a little consideration will show, must be precisely the same, and the resulting curves would be analogous—that is, when the diameter of the cylinder is less than that of the cone at the part where it meets the lowest generatrix of the cylinder; the curves, however, assume a different appearance when the diameter of the cylinder exceeds this, as is shown in figs. 6 and 7. In this case the intersections are represented by the curves, *s t r* and *p u q*; the method of obtaining these is fully indicated on the diagrams.

185. The opening or slot, H, cut through the key of the stopcock, is generally rectangular, rather than circular, or similar to the tubular portions of the cock. The object of this shape is to make the key as small as possible, and yet retain the required extent of passage. This rectangular opening gives rise, in fig. 2ª, to the intersectional curves, *a b*, *c d*, which are portions of the *hyperbola*, resulting from the section made by a plane, cutting the cone parallel to its axis. The operations whereby they are determined are indicated in figs. 10, 11, and 12.

To render the character of the curve more apparent, we have, in these figures, supposed the generatrices of the cone to make a greater angle with the axis than in fig. 2ª. The line, *a b*, represents the vertical plane in which the curve of intersection lies. It is evident that, if we delineate a series of horizontal planes, as *c d*, *e f*, *g h*, *i k*, fig. 10, we shall obtain a corresponding series of circles in the horizontal projection, these circles cutting the plane, *a b*, in the points, *l'*, *m'*, *n'*, *p'*, &c. These points are squared over to the vertical projection, fig. 10, giving the points, *l*, *m*, *n*, *p*; and the apex, *o*, of the curve is obtained, by drawing in the plan, fig. 12, with the centre, *s*, a circle tangent to the plane, *a b*, and then projecting this on the vertical plane, fig. 10, as shown. From these diagrams, it is easy to see that the opening, H, will be partly visible when the key is seen from below, as in fig. 2ª.

186. Figs. 8 and 9 represent the vertical and horizontal projections of the nut, G, which secures and adjusts the key in its socket. This nut is hexagonal, being terminated by a portion of a sphere, the centre of which lies in the axis of the prism. Each of the facets of the prism cuts the surface of the sphere, so as to present at their intersection portions of equal circles, which should be determined in lateral projection. The diameter of the sphere is generally three or four times that of the circle circumscribing the nut, but, to render the curves more distinct, we have adopted a smaller proportion in the case under examination. The sphere, *y*, is represented by two circles of the radius, *o* A; and the nut by an hexagonal prism, the axis of which passes through the centre of the sphere. The anterior facet, *a' b'*, of this nut, cuts the sphere, so as to show a circle of the diameter, *c' d'*. This circle, projected vertically on fig. 8, cuts the straight lines, *a e* and *b f*, of the prism, in the points, *a* and *b*; and the portion of the circle comprised between these two points, consequently, represents the intersection of this facet with the sphere. The other two facets, *a g'* and *b' h'*, which are inclined to the vertical plane, also cut the sphere, so as to produce, at their intersection with the surface, arcs of equal radii with that of the facet, *a b*. From their inclination, these arcs become slightly elliptical, being comprised, on the one hand, between the points, *a* and *g*, and *b*, *h*, on the other. The summits of these ellipses are obtained by drawing horizontal lines tangential to the arc, *a b*, and cutting it in the points, *k*, *l*, by perpendiculars drawn through the middle of the lateral facets. In practice, it is quite sufficient to describe circular arcs, passing through the points, *g*, *k*, *a*, and *b*, *l*, *h*.

We have already seen, in reference to Plate XIV., that the intersection of a right cylinder with a sphere, through the centre of which its axis passes, gives a circle projected laterally as a straight line. Thus, the opening *o'*, which passes through the nut, being cylindrical, produces, by its intersection with the sphere, a

H

circle of the diameter, m' n', in the plan, projected vertically in the straight line, m n.

Fig. 8^a indicates the analogous operations required to determine the same intersections when the nut is seen with one of the angles in the centre, and only two facets visible, as represented in fig. 1^b.

The elliptic curve, b^2 l^2 h^2, corresponding to the one, b l h, must obviously be comprised between the same two horizontal lines passing through these points, and an arc is drawn through them as before.

We may here observe, that the proficient draughtsman will, doubtless, deem it unnecessary, except in extraordinary cases, to enter into such minute details of construction for the various intersectional curves as those we have discussed, being guided simply by his own judgment, and the appearance presented by different experimental proportions. All draughtsmen, however, will find that some practice in obtaining the exact representation of the various curves, according to the methods here given and rules laid down, will be of immense advantage to them—enabling them, from possessing a thorough theoretical knowledge of the relations of the various forms of solids to each other, to approach much nearer truth, when, at a more advanced stage, they relinquish the aid of such constructive guides.

RULES AND PRACTICAL DATA.

STEAM.

187. All liquids become changed to vapour when their temperature is sufficiently elevated. When water, contained in a close vessel, is elevated to a temperature of 212° Fahrenheit, it produces steam of a pressure or force equal to that of the atmosphere.

The pressure of the atmosphere is a force capable of sustaining, in a vacuum, a column of water 33 feet high, or a column of mercury 30 inches high. This force is equal to a weight of about 15 lbs. per square inch.

Thus, taking the square inch as the unit of superficial measurement, the pressure or tension of the steam at 212° Fahrenheit is also equal to 15 lbs.

When the containing vessel is hermetically closed, as in a boiler, if the temperature be increased, the steam becomes endued with more and more expansive force—this increase of force, however, not being directly proportionate to the increase of temperature.

The tension or expansive force of steam, as also of gases generally, is inversely as the volume; thus, at the pressure of one atmosphere, for example, the volume of the steam or gas being one cubic foot, the same quantity of steam would occupy only half the space at a pressure of two atmospheres, and reciprocally.

TABLE OF PRESSURES, TEMPERATURES, WEIGHTS, AND VOLUMES OF STEAM.

Pressure in Atmospheres.	Pressure in Inches of Mercury.	Pressure per Square Inch.	Temperature Fahrenheit.	Temperature Centigrade.	Weight of a Cubic Foot of Steam.	Volume of a Pound of Steam.
			Degrees.	Degrees.	Lb.	Cubic Feet.
1·00	30·0	15·00	212	100·0	·3671	2·7236
1·25	37·5	18·75	224	106·6	·4508	2·2183
1·50	45·0	22·50	234	112·4	·5332	1·8852
1·75	52·5	26·25	243	117·1	·6144	1·6281
2·00	60·0	30·00	250	121·5	·6936	1·4433
2·25	67·5	33·75	258	125·5	·7729	1·2938
2·50	75·0	37·50	264	128·8	·8491	1·1777
2·75	82·5	41·25	270	132·1	·9284	1·0771
3·00	90·0	45·00	275	135·0	1·0058	·9942
3·25	97·5	48·75	280	137·7	1·0826	·9237
3·50	105·0	52·50	285	140·6	1·1582	·8634
4·00	120·0	60·00	294	145·4	1·3086	·7642
4·50	135·0	67·50	301	149·1	1·4572	·6862
5·00	150·0	75·00	308	153·3	1·6033	·6236
5·50	165·0	82·50	314	156·7	1·7494	·5716
6·00	180·0	90·00	320	160·0	1·8946	·5273
6·50	195·0	97·50	326	163·3	2·0359	·4912
7·00	210·0	105·00	331	166·4	2·1777	·4583
8·00	240·0	120·00	342	172·1	2·4562	·4071

With the assistance of this table, we can solve the following problems:—

First Example.—What is the amount of steam pressure acting on a piston of 10 inches diameter, corresponding to a temperature of 275 degrees? It will be seen that the pressure corresponding to 275° is equal to three atmospheres, or to 45 lbs. per square inch.

The area of a piston of 10 inches in diameter is equal to

$$10^2 \times \cdot 7854 = 78\cdot54 \text{ sq. inches;}$$

consequently,

$$78\cdot54 \times 45 = 3534\cdot3 \text{ lbs.}$$

Thus, to solve the problem, we look in the table for the pressure corresponding to the given temperature, and multiply it by the area of the piston expressed in square inches.

Second Example.—What weight of steam is expended during each stroke of the piston, the length of stroke being 3 feet?

We first obtain the volume expended,

$$\frac{78\cdot54}{12} \times 3 = 19\cdot635 \text{ cubic feet.}$$

At a pressure of three atmospheres, a cubic foot of steam weighs 1·0058 lb.; consequently,

$$19·635 \times 1·0058 = 19·75 \text{ lbs.}$$

To solve this problem, then, we ascertain the volume expended in cubic feet, and multiply it by the weight corresponding to the given temperature, or pressure—the product is the weight in pounds.

UNITY OF HEAT.

188. With a view to facilitate various comparisons connected with the subject of steam, the French experimentalists have adopted the term *calorie*, or unity of heat. This is defined as the amount of heat necessary to raise the temperature of a kilogramme (= 2·205 lbs.) of water, one degree centigrade.

Thus, a kilogramme of water at 25° contains 25 unities of heat; and, in the same manner, 60 kilog. of water at 50° contains

$$50 \times 60 = 3000 \text{ unities.}$$

The number of unities of heat is obtained by multiplying its weight in kilogrammes by the temperature in degrees centigrade.

The amount of heat developed by different descriptions of fuel varies according to their quality, and according to the construction of the furnaces.

According to M. Péclet, the mean quantity of heat developed by a kilogramme of coal is equal to 7500 *calories*, or unities of heat.

According to M. Berthier, that developed by a kilogramme of wood charcoal varies from 5000 to 7000 unities.

In the following table will be found the results of experiments with different descriptions of fuel:—

Table of the Amount of Heat developed by one Kilogramme of Fuel.

Description of Fuel.	Number of unities of heat developed by 1 kilog.	Quantity of steam practically obtainable from 1 kilog.
		Kilog.
Wood Charcoal,	6000 to 7000	5·6 to 6
Coke,	6000	7· " 8
Medium Coal,	7500	5·75 " 7
Dry Turf,	4800	"
Common Turf, containing 20 per cent. of water,	3000	1·8 " 2
Inferior Turf,	1500	"
Dry Wood of all descriptions,	3600	3·7
Common wood, containing 20 per cent. of water,	2800	2·7
Turf Charcoal,	5800	2·8 to 3

In the last column of this table, we have given the quantities of steam produced by the combustion of one kilogramme of fuel, being such as are practically obtainable in apparatus most commonly met with.

Example.—What is the quantity of coal necessary for the supply of a furnace intended to produce 250 kilog. of steam? The average produce of 1 kilog. of coal being 6·5 kilog., we have

$$\frac{250}{6·5} = 84 \text{ kilog. of coal.}$$

189. The boilers in which the steam is to be produced, may be of the shape represented in figs. 4 and 5, Plate XIV.—that is, cylindrical, and terminated by hemispheres. They are frequently accompanied by two or three tubular pieces in connection with the main portion of the boiler by pipes. Boilers answering to this description are termed French boilers, being of French origin; they are found very effective, and are much used in the manufacturing districts of England. These boilers are made of plates of wrought-iron, the thickness of which varies, not only according to the size of the boilers, but also according to the pressure at which it is intended to produce steam.

The proper thickness for the plates of cylindrical boilers may be determined by the following formula, which is the one adopted by the French Government in their police regulations:—

$$T = \frac{18 \times d \times p}{10} + 3;$$

where

T = thickness in millimètres;
d = diameter of boiler in mètres;
p = pressure in atmospheres, less one.

The rule derivable from the formula is—

To multiply the *effective* pressure of the steam in atmospheres by the diameter of the boiler, and by the constant 18, dividing the product by 10, and augmenting the quotient by 3, which will give the thickness in millimètres.

To simplify these calculations, we give a table showing the thickness proper for boiler plates, calculated up to a diameter of 2 mètres, and to a pressure of 8 atmospheres above the atmosphere:—

Table of Thicknesses of Plates in Cylindrical Boilers.

Diameter of Boiler.	Pressure of Steam in Atmospheres.						
	2.	3.	4.	5.	6.	7.	8.
Mètres.	Millim.	Millim.	Millim.	Millim.	Millim.	Millim.	Millim.
·50	3·9	4·8	5·7	6·6	7·5	8·4	9·3
·55	4·0	5·0	6·0	7·0	7·9	8·9	9·9
·60	4·1	5·1	6·2	7·3	8·4	9·5	10·5
·65	4·2	5·3	6·5	7·7	8·8	10·0	11·2
·70	4·3	5·5	6·8	8·0	9·3	10·5	11·8
·75	4·3	5·7	7·0	8·4	9·7	11·1	12·4
·80	4·4	5·9	7·3	8·8	10·2	11·6	13·1
·85	4·5	6·1	7·6	9·1	10·6	12·2	13·7
·90	4·6	6·2	7·9	9·5	11·1	12·7	14·3
·95	4·7	6·4	8·1	9·8	11·5	13·3	15·0
1·00	4·8	6·6	8·4	10·2	12·0	13·8	15·6
1·10	5·0	7·0	8·9	10·9	12·9	14·9	"
1·20	5·2	7·3	9·5	11·6	13·8	16·0	"
1·30	5·3	7·7	10·0	12·4	14·7	"	"
1·40	5·5	8·0	10·6	13·1	15·6	"	"
1·50	5·7	8·4	11·1	13·8	"	"	"
1·60	5·9	8·8	11·6	14·5	"	"	"
1·70	6·1	9·1	12·2	15·2	"	"	"
1·80	6·2	9·5	12·7	16·0	"	"	"
1·90	6·4	9·8	13·3	"	"	"	"
2·00	6·6	10·2	13·8	"	"	"	"

To suit English measures, the formula is—

$$T = \frac{18 \times d \times p}{10,000} + ·1182.$$

And here,

T = thickness in inches;

d = diameter in inches;

p = pressure in atmospheres, less one.

HEATING SURFACE.

190. In practice it is generally calculated that a square mètre of heating surface will produce from 18 to 25 kilog. of steam per hour, whatever be the form of boiler, whether cylindrical, with or without additional tubes, or waggon-shaped.

The amount of heating surface, per horse power, generally adopted, is from 1 to 1·5 sq. m.

In this surface is not only included that which is directly exposed to the action of the fire, but also that which receives heat from the smoke and gases which traverse the flues; this last being, of course, much less effective in the production of steam.

According to circumstances, one-half or a third of this surface may be exposed to the direct action of the fire, which will give, for the whole heating surface, two-thirds of the entire surface of the boiler.

In the following table we give the principal dimensions, corresponding to given horses power of boilers of the French description—that is, cylindrical with two tubes or smaller cylinders below.

Table of Dimensions of Boilers and Thickness of Plates for a Pressure of five Atmospheres.

Horses Power.	Length of Boiler.	Length of the two Tubes.	Diameter of Boiler.	Diameter of the Tubes.	Thickness of Plates for the Boiler.	Thickness of Plates for the Tubes.
	M.	M.	M.	M.	$^M/_m$.	$^M/_m$.
2	1·65	1·75	·66	·28	8	8
4	2·10	2·20	·70	·30	8	8
6	2·70	2·85	·75	·35	9	10
8	3·40	3·60	·80	·35	9	10
10	4·10	4·30	·80	·38	10	10
12	4·80	5·00	·80	·38	10	10
15	5·60	5·80	·80	·45	10	10
20	6·60	6·80	·85	·50	10	10
25	8·00	8·20	·85	·50	10	10
30	8·30	8·50	1·00	·60	10·5	10
35	9·50	9·70	1·00	·60	11	10
40	10·00	10·30	1·00	·70	11	10

In cylindrical boilers, without additional tubes, the water should occupy two-thirds of the whole space, and in boilers, with the tubes, it should occupy about one-half the main cylindrical body of the boiler, in addition to the tubes.

In order that the steam may not carry along with it small quantities of water, which action is termed "*priming*," the boiler is surmounted by a cylindrical chamber, or dome, in which the steam collects, and from the highest part of which it makes its exit, quite out of reach of the water thrown up by the ebullition.

CALCULATION OF THE DIMENSIONS OF BOILERS.

First Example.—What is the proper length for a cylindrical boiler, without additional tubes, capable of supplying an engine of 6 horses power, supposing the diameter to be ·8 m., and the heating surface 1·3 sq. m., per horse power?

We have $1·3 \times 6 = 7·8$ sq. m., total heating surface.

Now, as the heating surface should be two-thirds of the entire surface of the boiler, it follows that

$$7·8 \text{ sq. m.} = L \times 2\,\pi\,R \times \frac{2}{3} = L \times \frac{4\,\pi\,R}{3},$$

where L represents the length sought, and R the semi-diameter, = ·4 m.; so that, substituting for π and R their respective numerical values, we have—

$$7·8 \text{ sq. m.} = L \times 3·14 \times ·4 \times \frac{4}{3} = L \times 1·675;$$

whence,

$$L = \frac{7·8}{1·675} \times 4·65 \text{ m.}$$

As it may be well to know the capacity of the boiler for water and steam, this may be ascertained according to the rules previously given for the contents of cylinders, spheres, &c. (121—124). The boiler being terminated by hemispheres, the length of the cylindrical portion will be equal to

$$4·65 - (·4 \times 2) = 3·85.$$

We shall have, then, for the volume corresponding to the cylindrical portion—

$$V = \frac{2}{3} \times 3·14 \times ·4^2 \times 3·85 = 1·29 \text{ cub. m.}$$

and for that of the hemispherical ends—

$$V = \frac{2}{3} \times \frac{4}{3} \times 3·14 \times ·4^3 = ·179 \text{ cub. m.}$$

The whole volume of water is, consequently,

$$1·29 + ·179 = 1·469 \text{ cubic mètres.}$$

The remainder of the volume, which is occupied by the steam is obviously

$$\frac{1·469}{2} = ·734 \text{ cubic mètres.}$$

and the contents of the entire boiler,

$$1·469 + ·734 = 2·203 \text{ cubic mètres.}$$

This result might have been obtained by the following general formula:—

$$V = L \times \pi R^2 + \frac{4}{3}\pi R^3 =$$

$$3·85 \times 3·14 \times ·4^2 + \frac{4}{3} \times 3·14 \times ·4^3 = 2·203 \text{ cubic mètres.}$$

191. We here quote the portion of the regulations enforced by the French Government, relating to the steam-boilers, as showing what conditions are deemed necessary in France for the insurance of public safety, and also as forming a good basis for calculations:—

" (33.) The boilers are divided into four classes.

" The capacity of the boiler, including that of the tubes, if there be any, must be expressed in cubic mètres, and the maximum steam pressure must be expressed in atmospheres; and these two quantities multiplied into each other.

" If the product exceeds fifteen, the boiler is of the first class. It is of the second class, if the product is more than seven, but does not exceed fifteen. Of the third, when more than three, and not exceeding seven. And of the fourth, when not exceeding three.

" If two or more boilers are arranged to work in concert, and have any communication with each other, direct or indirect, the term taken to represent the capacity must be the sum of the capacities of each.

" (34.) Steam-boilers of the first class must be stationed outside of all dwelling-houses or workshops.

" (35.) Nevertheless, in order that the heat, which would otherwise be dissipated by radiation, may be better economised, the officer may allow a boiler of the first class to be stationed inside a workshop, provided this does not form part of a dwelling-house.

" (36.) Whenever there is less than 10 mètres in distance between a boiler of the first class and a dwelling-house or public road, a wall of defence must be built, in good and solid masonry, and 1 mètre thick. The other dimensions are specified in article 41. This wall of defence must, in all cases, be distinct from the masonry of the furnaces, and separated from it by a space of at least 50 centimètres in width. It must, in a like manner, be separated from the intermediate walls of the neighbouring houses.

" If the boiler be sunk into the ground, in such a manner that no part of it is less than 1 mètre below the level of the ground, the wall of defence shall not be required, unless the boiler is within 5 mètres of a dwelling-house or of the public road.

" (38.) Steam-boilers of the second class may be stationed inside a workshop which does not form part of a dwelling-house, or of a factory or establishment consisting of several stories.

" (39.) If a boiler of the second class be within 5 mètres from a dwelling-house or the public road, an intermediate wall of defence shall be erected, as prescribed in article 36.

" (41.) The authority given by the inspecting-officer for boilers of the first and second class, shall indicate the situation of the boiler, its distance from dwelling-houses and the public roads, and shall determine, if there be space enough, the direction to be given to the axis of the boiler.

" This authority shall also specify the situation and dimensions, as to length and height, of the wall of defence, where this 'is required, in conformity with the above regulations.

" In determining these dimensions, regard must be had to the capacity of the boiler, to the pressure of the steam, as well as to all circumstances tending to make the boiler more or less dangerous or inconvenient.

" (42.) Steam-boilers of the third class may be stationed in workshops which do not form parts of dwelling-houses, and it is not necessary to erect a wall of defence.

" (43.) Steam-boilers of the fourth class may be stationed in any workshop, even if this forms part of a dwelling-house.

" In this case, the boilers must be furnished with an open manometer.

" (44.) The furnaces of steam-boilers of the third and fourth class shall be entirely separated, by a space of at least 50 centimètres, from any dwelling-house."

According to these regulations, a boiler of the dimensions taken for illustration, and supposing the maximum pressure to be 3 atmospheres, would be in the second class, for—2·203 × 3 = 6·609, which is below 7.

Second Example.—What should be the dimensions of a cylindrical boiler, with two additional tubes, intended to supply an engine of 16 horses power, the diameter of the main body being ·9 m., and that of the tubes ·45 m. ?

Assuming 1·2 sq. m., per horse power, for the heating surface, we shall have 1·2 × 16 = 19·2 sq. m., for the entire heating surface. Half of the surface of the main cylinder of the boiler, and three-fourths of that of the tubes, is the best disposition of this heating surface. These data give rise to the following formula :—

$$19\text{·}2 \text{ sq. m.} = \frac{2\pi \, R \times L}{2} + r \, 2\pi \times L \times 2 \times \frac{3}{4} =$$
$$\pi \, R \, L + 3\pi \, r \, L \text{—.}$$

L here represents the length of the boiler and tubes, which is the only unknown term.

Substituting for R and r their numerical values, ·45 and ·225, we have—

19·2 sq. m. = 3·14 × ·45 × L + 3 × 3·14 × ·225 × L; or
19·2 sq. m. = L (3·14 × ·45) + 3 × 3·14 × ·225 =
L (1·413 + 2·12) ;

whence,

$$L = \frac{19\text{·}2}{1\text{·}413 + 2\text{·}12} = \frac{19\text{·}2}{3\text{·}533} = 5\text{·}43 \text{ m.}$$

Thus, the total length of the boiler is 5·43 m., but the ends being hemispherical, the length of the cylindrical portion is equal to—

$$5\text{·}43 - \text{·}9 = 4\text{·}53 \text{ m.}$$

The tubes usually project in front of the main body, to a distance of about 50 centimètres; but, for convenience in constructing the return flues, they do not extend as far back, so that they are of about the same length as the main body.

192. In distillery boilers, a horse power is understood to mean the capability of evaporating 25 kilogrammes of water in an hour. Thus, a boiler of 10 horses power should be capable of evaporating 250 kilog. of water in that time. Now, assuming 1·12 sq. m. of heating surface, per horse power, for a steam-engine, we should only have an evaporation of from 18 to 20 kilog. per hour, per horse power, and per square mètre of heating surface.

DIMENSIONS OF FIRE-GRATE.

193. In practice, 1 square mètre of grate will burn from 40 to 45 kilog. of coal per hour. Thus, a boiler intended to produce 280 kilog. of steam per hour, will require, for this purpose—assuming that 1 kilog. of coal produces 6·65 of steam—

$$\frac{280}{6\text{·}65} = 43 \text{ kilogrammes of coal;}$$

and the furnace of this boiler should have a grate, measuring 1 square mètre.

The grate-bars are generally of cast-iron, of from 30 to 35 millimètres in width, but having between them a space of only 7 or 8 millimètres, so that the intervals only occupy a fourth or a fifth of the whole area.

It has been found that greater strength and durability is obtained by making the bars straight above, and strengthened by parabolic feathers below.

CHIMNEYS.

194. The height of chimneys is very variable, and cannot be subjected to any fixed rule. The cross section at the summit depends upon the size of the grate and is generally about a sixth of

this. In the following application will be found calculations respecting chimneys, and examples of the various rules we have just given.

APPLICATION.

We propose calculating the dimensions of the furnace of a boiler, with its chimney, for an engine of 8 horses power, for example, to be worked on the high-pressure system, consuming, as a maximum, 5 kilogrammes of coal, per horse power, per hour, the amount of heating surface being taken at 1·52 sq. m., per horse power.

For 8 horses power, the heating surface will be—

$$1·52 \times 8 = 12·16 \text{ sq. m.}$$

Each square mètre of heating surface producing, at an average, 18 kilogrammes of steam, we have—

$$12·6 \times 18 = 218·88 \text{ kilog. of steam.}$$

As 5 kilog. of steam are produced by 1 kilog. of coal, then—

$$\frac{218·88}{5} = 43·8 \text{ kilog.,}$$

representing the quantity of coal consumed per hour.

The grate area, corresponding to this consumption, assuming that one square décimètre is sufficient for 1·2 kilog. per hour, will be—

$$\frac{43·8}{1·2} = 36 \text{ square décimètres,}$$

supposing a fourth of this area to be free to the passage of air.

It now only remains to calculate the cross sectional area of the chimney. With reference to this we must remark, that 18 cubic mètres of air are required for the consumption of 1 kilog. of coal; therefore, 43·8 kilog. will require

$$43·8 \times 18 = 788·4 \text{ cubic mètres.}$$

This air, in traversing the fire, relinquishes a portion of its oxygen, which is partially replaced by carbonic acid gas and steam. If the gases escape from the chimney at a mean temperature of 300° centigrade, the volume being, according to M. Péclet, at the rate of 38·54 cubic m. per kilog. of coal, will be $43·8 \times 38·54 = 1688$ cubic mètres per hour. If we divide this by 3600, we shall obtain the quantity which escapes per second; namely,

$$\frac{1688}{3600} = ·4689 \text{ cubic m.}$$

If we assume, as is usually the case with boilers of the proportions here discussed, that the chimney is 22 mètres high, the external atmosphere being at a temperature of 15° centigrade, the rate of exit of the gases may be obtained by the following formula:—

$$V = \sqrt{2g \ H \ a \ (t'—t)}.$$

In the case under consideration, H = 22 m., a is the constant multiplier, ·00365, t' = 300°, t = 15°, and $2g$ = 19·62. Substituting, then, for the letters their numerical values, we have

$$V = \sqrt{19·62 \times 22 \times ·00365 \times (300 — 15)} = 21.$$

This signifies that the gas will escape from the chimney-top at the rate of 21 mètres per second, if it meets with no resistance from the lateral surfaces of the flues and chimney; the actual rate, however, is only 70 per cent. of this—or,

$$21 \times ·7 = 14·7 \text{ m.}$$

If we divide the volume of gas which escapes per second by the rate at which it escapes in that time, as just determined, we shall obtain the cross sectional area proper for the upper part of the chimney; as thus—

$$\frac{·4689}{14·7} = 3·2 \text{ square décimètres.}$$

Thus the chimney, which is supposed to be square, will only require to measure, internally, something less than two décimètres each way at the point of exit; this, however, is a minimum dimension, and it will be advisable to give it greater dimensions than these. Thus it might be made 25 centimètres square, or even 30 or 35 centimètres, if there is any likelihood of the power of the boiler being increased afterwards, such increase being frequently called for in manufactories. A damper, however, should always be provided at the base of the chimney, by means of which the draught may be suited to the requirements.

SAFETY VALVES.

Table of Diameters of Safety Valves.

Extent of Heating Surface.	Pressure in Atmospheres.									
	1½	2	2½	3	3½	4	5	6	7	8
Sq. M.	M/m.	M/m.	M/m.	M/m.	M/m.	M/m.	M/m.	M/m.	M/m.	M/m.
1	25	21	18	16	15	14	12	11	10	9
2	35	29	25	23	20	19	17	15	15	13
3	43	36	31	29	26	24	21	19	17	15
4	50	41	36	32	29	27	24	22	20	19
5	56	46	40	36	33	30	27	24	22	21
6	61	50	44	39	36	34	30	27	25	23
7	66	54	48	43	39	36	32	29	27	25
8	70	58	51	46	42	39	34	31	29	27
9	75	62	54	48	44	41	36	33	30	28
10	79	65	57	51	47	43	38	35	32	30
11	83	68	60	54	49	45	40	36	33	31
12	87	71	62	56	51	47	42	38	35	33
13	90	74	65	58	53	49	44	40	36	34
14	93	77	67	60	55	51	45	41	37	35
15	96	80	70	62	57	53	47	42	38	36
16	100	82	72	65	59	55	48	44	40	38
17	103	85	74	67	61	56	50	45	42	39
18	106	87	76	68	63	58	51	47	43	40
19	109	90	78	70	64	60	53	48	44	41
20	111	92	80	72	66	61	54	49	45	42
21	114	94	82	74	68	63	56	50	46	43
22	117	97	84	76	69	64	57	51	47	44
23	119	99	86	77	70	66	58	53	48	45
24	122	101	88	79	72	67	59	54	49	46
25	125	103	90	81	74	69	60	55	50	47
26	127	105	91	82	75	70	62	56	51	48
27	129	107	93	84	77	71	63	57	52	49
28	132	109	95	85	78	73	64	58	53	50
29	134	111	97	87	80	74	65	59	54	51
30	136	113	98	88	81	75	66	60	55	52
32	140	116	100	90	82	76	67	62	57	53
34	145	119	104	94	86	79	69	64	59	55
36	149	122	107	96	87	82	71	65	61	57
38	151	125	110	97	90	83	74	66	62	58
40	156	130	113	101	92	86	75	69	64	59
45	167	137	119	107	97	91	80	73	68	63
50	174	145	125	113	104	96	84	76	70	67
55	184	151	132	119	107	101	88	80	75	70
60	193	158	137	121	113	106	94	84	78	73

195. Steam-engine boilers are always provided with various accessories, as *safety valves, manometers, floats, alarm whistles.*

The manometer is an instrument which serves to indicate the pressure of the steam inside the boiler in atmospheres, and fractions of atmospheres. These instruments are constructed after various systems.

The float serves to indicate the level of the water, and the whistle to give the alarm when the water is much below the proper level.

The safety valve provides an exit for the steam when the pressure is too high.

We have given a drawing of one at fig. 4, Plate XI. Their diameters vary with the dimensions of the boilers and the pressure of the steam.

The regulations of the French Government contain the following rules and the above table for their determination. To find the proper diameter for the safety valve, the heating surface of the boiler, expressed in square mètres, must be divided by the maximum pressure of steam intended to be maintained, expressed in atmospheres, previously diminished by the constant ·412: the square root of the quotient being extracted, is to be multiplied by 2·6, and the product will be the diameter sought, expressed in centimètres. This rule may be put as a formula, thus:—

$$d = 2\cdot6 \sqrt{\frac{s}{n - \cdot412}};$$

where d is the diameter of the valve in centimètres, s the heating surface of the boiler, including both fire and flue surface, expressed in square mètres, and n the number expressing the pressure in atmospheres.

CHAPTER V.

THE STUDY AND CONSTRUCTION OF TOOTHED GEAR.

196. Toothed gear is a mechanical expedient, universally employed for the transmission of motion. It is met with of all proportions, from the minute movements of the watch, to the gigantic fittings of manufacturing workshops. Toothed gear is generally constructed with a view to the following principle of action—that the lateral acting-surfaces develop the same arc during the same duration of contact, whilst their angular velocities vary inversely as their diameters. By the angular velocity of any body, turning about a centre, is meant the angle passed through by the body in a unit of time; whilst the real or linear velocity of any point is the space passed through by this point, whether the direction of motion be rectilinear or circular. Thus, various points on a crank, taken at different distances from the centre of the shaft, have all the same angular velocity, whilst their actual velocity differs considerably, because of their respective distances from the centre. It is the same with a pendulum, which vibrates through an angle, or has an angular motion about its centre of suspension. The angular velocity of a body is greater, as the angle passed through in the same time is greater. Two points may have the same angular velocity, although the space passed through by each may be very different. Thus, all the points in the pendulum are affected with an equal angular motion, whilst their actual velocities, or the course traversed by each, vary as the distance from the centre of motion.

This description of gear consists of a series of projections, or teeth, regularly arranged on straight, cylindrical, or conical surfaces, termed *webs*, and disposed so as to act on each other during a limited time.

In order, however, that the gearing action may take place in a regular, even manner, it is indispensably necessary that the surfaces of the teeth should bear upon each other tangentially, throughout the entire duration of their contact; and for this purpose, far from being arbitrarily designed, their form should be determined with the utmost geometrical exactitude, for on their form entirely depends their accurate and easy working. It is,

therefore, obviously incumbent on the student to give particular attention to the delineation of these teeth.

The curves generally adopted in practice for the outline of teeth, are the involute, the cycloid, and the epicycloid.

It is useful to investigate the nature and construction of these curves, both on account of their application to the teeth of wheels, and also because of their employment in several other mechanical contrivances.

INVOLUTE, CYCLOID, AND EPICYCLOID.

PLATES XVIII. AND XIX.

INVOLUTE.

FIGURE 1.—PLATE XVIII.

197. When a thread is unwound from the circumference of a circle, and is kept uniformly extended, its extremity will describe the curve known as the involute.

This definition serves as a basis for obtaining the geometrical delineation of the involute. Let A B C be the given circle of the radius, A O, and A the extremity of a thread wound upon it. Starting from the point, A, mark off, at equal distances apart, several points, as a, b, c, so near to each other, that the intervening arcs may be taken for straight lines without sensible error. Through each of these points draw tangents to the circle, or perpendiculars to the corresponding radii; and on these tangents set off distances, equal to the rectifications of the respective arcs, A a, A b, A c, &c.; by which means are obtained the points, a', b', c', &c., and the curve passing through these points is a portion of the involute. By continuing the development or unwinding of the thread, the curve may be extended to a series of convolutions, increasing more and more in radius, and becoming a species of spiral. After one complete evolution of the circumference, the shortest distance between two consecutive convolutions is always the same, and equal to the development or rectification of the circumference of the generating circle, which forms the nucleus of the curve.

The points, a, b, c, being taken at equal distances apart on the circumference, the tangents are respectively double, triple, &c., that of the first, A a; and if, as we directed, these points are sufficiently near to each other, the curve may be drawn, with closely approximate accuracy, by describing a succession of arcs, having these tangents for radii. Thus, with the point, a, as centre, and radius, a a', the first arc, A a', is drawn; and with the centre, b, and radius, b b', the second arc, a' b', in like manner; and similarly with the rest.

We shall show the application of the involute to touched gear, worm wheels, and also for *cams* and *eccentrics*.

CYCLOID.

FIGURE 2.—PLATE XVIII.

198. When a circular disc is rolled upon a plane surface in a rectilinear direction, any point in the circumference of this disc generates the curve called the *cycloid*. Thus, any point taken on the outside of a locomotive wheel in motion, describes as many repetitions of the curve as the wheel makes revolutions.

In order that the curve may be perfect and true throughout, it is necessary that the motion should take place without any sliding upon the plane; in other words, the length of the straight line forming the path of the disc should be equal to the portion of the circumference which, during the motion, has been applied to, or in contact with, the plane throughout that length.

We propose to delineate the cycloid generated by the point, A, of a circle of the given radius, A O, and rolling upon a given straight line, B C.

There are several methods of solving this problem.

1st Solution.—Set off on the circumference, starting from the point, A, a number of distances equal to A a, so small that the arcs so divided may be taken as straight lines. Set off the same distance a like number of times along the straight line, A C, and at the points, a b c, erect perpendiculars, cutting the line, o o', generated by the centre of the rolling circle, and parallel to the given straight line, B C. In this way are obtained the points of intersection, o, o^1, o^2, which are the centres of the circle when in the positions corresponding to the points of contact, a, b, c, d. With each of these points as centres, then describe portions of circles, on each of which successively set off the lengths of the arcs, A a', A b', A c', &c., from a to a'', b to a^2, and from c to b^2, and so on throughout. The curve, A a'' a^2 b^2 c^2, passing through the points thus obtained, is the cycloid required.

2d Solution.—The points in this curve may also be obtained by drawing horizontal lines through the points of division, a' b' c', of the original circle, and then intersecting these by the arcs drawn with the respective centres, o, o^1, o^2.

3d Solution.—In place of drawing arcs of circles with the various centres, as indicated on the right-hand side of fig. 2, the curve may be obtained by setting off successively from the vertical, A O, on the horizontals, as before drawn, distances equal to those respectively contained between the original circle and the perpendiculars through the several corresponding positions of the centre;

thus, the distances, e e', f f', g g', h h', &c., are set off from 1 to a^2 2 to b^2, 3 to c^2, &c.

To avoid confusion, we have constructed the diagram appertaining to this last solution to the left-hand side of fig. 2, which shows a portion of a second cycloid similar to the first.

When the generating circle has made half a revolution, the summit of the curve is obtained, as at D', the point corresponding to the diameter, A D. The length, A C, of the given straight line, is obviously equal to the rectification of the semi-circumference of the generating circle, whose radius is A O.

By continuing the construction, a complete curve may be obtained, having equal and symmetrical portions on either side of the vertical, C D, and having for its base a line double the length of A C, and consequently equal to the rectification of the entire circumference of the generating circle.

The cycloid is the curve more generally given to the teeth of wheel gear and endless screws.

EXTERNAL EPICYCLOID.

FIGURE 1.—PLATE XIX.

199. The epicycloid only differs from the cycloid, in that the generating circle, instead of rolling along in a straight line, does so around a second circle, which is fixed. When the two circles are in the same plane, the point taken generates a *right* or *cylindrical* epicycloid; when the two circles are situate in different planes, but maintaining a uniform angle to each other, the generated curve becomes a *spheric* epicycloid; in this case the generating circle is supposed to revolve about a fixed centre, at the same time rolling along the circumference of the stationary circle.

1st Solution.—For the delineation of the right epicycloid, the methods of construction to be adopted are analogous to that given for the cycloid. Thus, let A O be the radius of the generating circle, and A c the radius of the fixed circle; divide the former into a number of equal parts in the points, a', b', c', d', &c., and on the latter divide off as many arcs equal to the arcs of the former, starting from A, as at a, b, c, d, &c. Through these latter points of division draw radii, c a, c b, c c, and prolong them so as to cut a circle, the radius of which is c o; this circle being generated by the centre of the moving one during its rotation about the stationary one; in this way are obtained the points, o, o^1, o^2, o^3, which are the successive positions of the centre of the generating circle, as during its rotation it is successively in contact at the points, a, b, c, d, of the fixed circle. Then, with these points as centres, describe the several arcs of equal radii with the generating circle, making them severally equal to the corresponding arcs, A a', A b', A c', as from a to a^2, b to b^2, c to c^2, &c. The curve passing through the points, a^2, b^2, c^2, is the epicycloid required.

2d Solution.—The points of this curve may also be determined by drawing, with the centre, c, arcs passing through the points of division, a', b', c', d', and cutting the arcs described with the various centres, o, o^1, o^2, o^3, in a^2, b^2, c^2, d^2, which are so many points in the epicycloid.

3d Solution.—The curve may also be delineated by transferring the distance between the points, e, f, g, &c., of the generating circle in its original position, and the radii, c h, c i, c k, passing through the different points of contact on the stationary circle, measured upon the arcs described with the centre, c, to the same arcs, but so that the extremities of the whole may lie in the prolongation of the radius, c B. Thus the distances, ee', ff', gg', &c., are set off, from 1 to a^2, 2 to b^2, 3 to c^2, &c. The diagram referring to this construction forms the right-hand portion of fig. 1.

When the generating circle has made an entire revolution, the curve obtained is an entire epicycloid, A D B, comprising two equal and symmetrical portions on either side of the line, D E, which is equal to the diameter of the moving circle.

EXTERNAL EPICYCLOID DESCRIBED BY A CIRCLE ROLLING ABOUT A FIXED CIRCLE INSIDE IT.
FIGURE 3.—PLATE XIX.

200. For this diagram, which is analogous to the preceding one, the radii of the circles are given, c A being that of the fixed circle, and B A that of the moving one. Divide the first circle into any number of equal parts, in the points, a, b, c, d, &c., and divide off, on the larger circle of the radius, B A, a like number of arcs, equal to those on the other circle, as from A to a', a' to b, &c. Then with the point c as centre, and with the radius B C, describe a circle, cutting the radii, c A, c a, c b, c c, in the points, B, B^1, B^2, B^3, and with each of the last as centres, and with the radius, A B, describe arcs, which will be tangents to the fixed circle, at the different points of contact, a, b, c, in succession. Then, with the centre, c, describe arcs, passing successively through the points, a', b', c', d', on the moving circles, as in its first position. These last will cut the arcs tangential to the given circle, in the points, a^2, b^2, c^2, d^2, and the curve passing through these points is the epicycloid sought.

The other two methods given, of drawing the common epicycloid, are also applicable to this last case.

INTERNAL EPICYCLOID.
FIGURE 2.—PLATE XIX.

201. The epicycloid is termed internal, when the generating circle rolls along the concave side of the circumference of a fixed circle.

Let c A be the radius of the fixed circle, and B A that of the generating circle. As in preceding cases, so also here, we commence by dividing the moving circle into a certain number of equal parts, and then dividing the fixed circle correspondingly, so that the arcs thus obtained in each may be equal. We then proceed as in the case of the external epicycloid, according to whichever of the three solutions we propose adopting, all being alike applicable. The operations are fully indicated on fig. 2, and the same distinguishing letters are employed as in fig. 1.

When the generating circle is equal to half of the fixed circle, the epicycloid generated by a point in the circumference is a straight line, equal to the diameter of the fixed circle. Thus, in fig. 3, Plate XVIII., the epicycloid generated by the point, A, of the moving circle of the radius, A c, after a semi-revolution, coincides exactly with the diameter, A B.

If, with circles of the same proportions as those in fig. 3, Plate XVIII., we take a point, D, outside the generating circle, but preserving a constant distance from it, the epicycloid generated

by it will be the ellipse, D F E G, having for its transverse axis the line, D E, equal to the diameter, A B, of the fixed circle, augmented by twice the distance, D A, of the point, D, from its extremity; and for conjugate axis, the line, G F, equal to twice the same distance, D A, alone. If it is wished to determine this curve according to its properties as an epicycloid, and without having recourse to the methods given in reference to Plate V., and proper to the ellipse, it may be done by adding the distance, A D, to that of the radius, c A, in each successive position occupied by the generating circle during its rotation. If the generating point be taken inside the moving circle, the curve produced will also be an ellipse.

The epicycloid is the curve most employed for the form of the teeth, whether of external or internal spur or bevil wheels.

Toothed gearing may be divided generally into two categories; namely, right, cylindrical, or "spur" wheels, and conical, angular, or "bevil" wheels. In the first are comprehended the action of a rack and pinion, that of a worm or tangent-screw with a worm-wheel, and finally, that of two wheels. We may remark, that in all these modes the teeth are so formed and arranged, as to act equally well whichever of each couple be the driver, and in whichever direction the motion takes place.

THE DELINEATION OF A RACK AND PINION IN GEAR.
FIGURE 4.—PLATE XVIII.

202. A rack is a species of straight and rigid rod or bar, formed with teeth on one side, so as to take into or gear with the teeth of a right wheel, generally of small diameter, and in such case termed a pinion. Such a rack is represented at A B in the figure.

In proceeding to construct this design, as well as for all kinds of toothed gear, it is necessary to have determined beforehand the thickness, $a b$, of the teeth, as this dimension varies according to the power or strain to be transmitted; and rules and tables, for this purpose, will be found at the end of the chapter.

When the rack and pinion are made of the same metal, the thickness of the teeth should be the same in both. The spaces or intervals between the teeth ought also to be equal in such case. Theoretically speaking, the intervals should be equal to the thickness of the teeth; but in practice, they are made a little wider, to admit of freer action.

203. The *pitch* of the teeth comprises the width of the tooth and that of the interval. In a wheel this pitch is measured upon a circle of a given radius, termed the *primitive* or *pitch circle*, and in the rack on a straight line tangent to the pitch circle of the pinion, and also called the *primitive* or *pitch line*.

204. Let o c be the radius of the pitch circle of a pinion gearing with a rack, of which the pitch line is A B. We propose, in the first place, to determine the curve of the teeth of the pinion, so as to gear with and drive the rack, and we shall subsequently determine the curve of the teeth of the rack, enabling it to gear with and drive the pinion.

The operations consist in rolling the straight line, A c, tangentially to the pitch circle, o c; during this movement, the point, c. will generate an involute, c D, which may be drawn in the manner indicated in fig. 1—a construction which is further repeated at a' d', on one of the teeth of the pinion. fig. 4.

This curve possesses this property, that if the teeth are formed

I

to it, and the pinion be turned on its axis, the point of contact, c, will always be in the straight line, A, B, traversing this line at precisely the same velocity as the pinion at that distance from the centre, that is, at the pitch circle; consequently, we divide this pitch circle into as many equal parts as there are to be teeth and intervals in the pinion, and at each of the points of division repeat the involute curve, c d, which will, of course, fulfil the same conditions at the various positions; then, each of these divisions rectified is set off on the pitch line, A B, of the rack, as many times as is necessary. For each tooth the curves are placed symmetrically with reference to the radius which passes through their centres, as indicated at o d', so that the pinion may act equally well when turning in one direction as in the other.

205. Since the teeth cannot have an indefinite length, they may be limited as far as is compatible with the following considerations:—The tooth of the wheel, which is the driver, should not relinquish contact with the one upon which it acts, until the tooth immediately succeeding it has taken up its original position, which, in the working of two wheels, corresponds to the line joining the centres, and in that of a pinion and rack, to the radius, o c, perpendicular to the pitch line, A B.

Thus, supposing the pinion to move in the direction indicated by the arrow, the tooth, E, which is acting on the tooth, H, of the rack, should continue to impel it until the following tooth, G, shall have taken its place, when it will itself have taken the place of the tooth, F, having made the tooth, H, of the rack traverse to I. It will be observed that the curved part of the tooth is in contact at the point, c, on the pitch line, A B; the tooth might be cut away at this point; but in practice, in order that the pinion teeth may act through a somewhat greater interval, and to avoid the play resulting from wear, they are truncated at a little beyond this point, c, a circle being described with the centre, o, cutting the curves of all the teeth at equal distances from the centre.

To allow of the passage of the curved portion of the teeth of the pinion, the rack must be grooved out, so as to present bearing surfaces, which are determined simply by the perpendiculars, b f, c d, g b, to the pitch line, A B, and passing through the points of division already set out on this line.

These perpendiculars, at the same time, form the sides or flanks of the rack teeth.

Rigorously speaking, the depth of the intervals on the rack should be limited by the straight line, m n, tangential to the external circle of the pinion; but, to prevent the friction of the teeth against the bottom, it is preferable to augment the depth of the hollows by a small quantity, joining the sides of the teeth with the bottom by small quadrants, which, avoiding sharp angles, gives greater strength to the teeth.

206. As in practice, toothed gear is constructed so as to drive, or be driven, indifferently, we require yet—to complete the design under consideration—to give to the teeth of the rack such curvature as is necessary to enable them to drive the pinion with which they are in gear in their turn, always fulfilling the conditions of a regular and uniform motion, both of the rack at its pitch line, and of the pinion at its pitch circle.

With a view to the determination of this curve, we may remark, that if with the radius, o c, as a diameter, we describe the circle,

o L c, and cause it to roll along the straight line, A B, the point of contact, c, will generate a cycloid, c K, which may be constructed according to the methods indicated in fig. 2.

If the same circle is made to roll along the interior of the pitch circle, G c J, of the pinion, the same point, c, will generate a right epicycloid, coinciding with the radius, o c, as has been seen in reference to fig. 3.

Then, if we give to the teeth of the rack the curve, c K, and to the flanks of the pinion teeth the straight line, c o, the arrangement will exactly fulfil the condition sought; that is to say, that, in impelling the pinion teeth from right to left, the curve, c K, of the rack teeth will constantly apply itself to the straight line, o c, being always tangential to it.

For example, suppose the curve, c K, to be traversed to the position, c' L, the radius, o c, will then be in the position, o L; then, if from the point, L, the straight line, L c, be drawn, the angle, o L c, will be a right angle; that is to say, the line, o L, will be perpendicular to L c, and, consequently, tangential to the curve, L c', in the point, L. If, therefore, the motion of the rack is regular and uniform, that of the pinion will be equally so. The same curve, c K, is drawn at each of the points of division of the pitch line of the rack, as was already done for the teeth of the pinion.

To find the proper length to give to the teeth, all that is necessary is to place, in the generating circle, o L c, a chord, L c, equal to twice c b², and through the point, L, thereby obtained, to draw a straight line, M N, parallel to A B. If, through all the points of division in the pitch circle of the pinion, are drawn radii converging in the centre, o, they will give the flanks of the teeth, as i j, k l, &c., which are limited by a circle described with the centre, o, and tangential to the straight line, M N; for the same reason as that assigned in the case of the rack, however, the spaces between the teeth are made a little deeper, and the sides of the teeth are joined to the bottoms by quarter circles, the circle in which the bottoms lie being described with a radius somewhat less than that of the circle last drawn.

As it would be a tedious process to repeat the operations for determining the curves in the case of each individual tooth, it is a convenient plan to cut a piece of card or thin wood to the curve, so as to form a pattern or template, by the application of which to each of the points of division, the sides of the teeth may be drawn, care being taken to make the two sides of each perfectly symmetrical with reference to the centre line of the tooth.

Even the labour of making a template or pattern is often dispensed with, and, in place of the curve, a simple circular arc is employed for the side of the tooth, the arc being of such a radius as to approximate as near the true curve as possible. With this view the arc should be tangential to the side of the tooth, and passing through the external corner. Thus, supposing it is wished to substitute an arc for the true curve of the rack teeth, such as o r of the tooth, F, since this arc has to pass through the point, r, corresponding to L, and obtained by making r' r equal to L q, and to be a tangent at o, to the vertical, o p, draw the chord, o r, and bisect it by the perpendicular, s t, and its point of intersection, s, with the pitch line, A B, will be the centre of the required arc, and the sides of all the teeth may afterwards be drawn with the same radius, care being taken to keep the centres in the line, A B.

An analogous operation will give the proportions of the arc, substituting the curve of the pinion teeth.

THE GEARING OF A WORM WITH A WORM-WHEEL.

FIGURES 5 AND 6.—PLATE XVIII.

207. This system of gear is constructed on the same principles as that of a rack and pinion, which method requires that, in the first place, the worm and worm-wheel be supposed to be sectioned by a plane passing through the axis of the former, and at right angles to that of the latter. The representation of this section becomes analogous to the diagram, fig. 4; that is to say, the pitch circle, G C J, of the worm-wheel being given, and also the straight pitch line, A B, of the worm tangential to this circle, and parallel to the axis of the worm, the involute curve, C D, is sought for the teeth of the wheel, and the cycloid, C K, for those of the worm. The lengths of these curves are limited, as in the preceding example, and when the whole is complete, an outline will be produced similar to the tinted portions of fig. 6. It is in this manner that the gearing of the worm and worm-wheel is made to depend upon the same principles as that of a rack and pinion, and the same method may be employed in construction in determining the outline of the teeth, as we have shown.

To represent the worm and worm-wheel geometrically in external elevation, instead of a section of the teeth alone, it is necessary to know the diameter and pitch of the worm on the one hand, and the thickness of the worm-wheel, fig. 5, on the other.

Let M′ A′ be the distance of the pitch line, A B, from the axis, M′ N, of the worm, and $a b$ the width of the wheel. When the worm is single-threaded (177), the pitch of the helix is the same as that of the teeth, and, therefore, the thickness of a tooth, added to the width of an interval. In this case, each revolution of the worm turns the wheel to the extent of one tooth, and this is the arrangement represented in the figures. If the worm, however, is double or triple-threaded, its helical pitch will be correspondingly two or three times the pitch of the teeth; and in such case, each revolution will turn the wheel to the extent of two or three teeth.

The worm-wheel being of a certain thickness, and requiring to gear with the convolutions of the worm, must necessarily have its teeth inclined to correspond with the obliquity of the worm-thread. It is further to be observed, that the sides of the wheel-teeth being simply tangential to the worm-thread, contact cannot, rigorously speaking, take place in more than one point of each tooth and convolution. This point constantly changes with the motion, but always lies in the plane, O′ M′, of the section.

In delineating the convolutions of the worm-thread, helices have to be drawn passing through the external corners, d, e, and internal corners, f, g. We have repeated these points to the left-hand side of fig. 6, where the required operations are fully indicated, in connection with the projection, fig. 5, and in accordance with the principles already explained (173). The corresponding points in the two figs. (5 and 6) are distinguished by the same letters and numbers.

208. For the representation, in external elevation, of the teeth of the worm-wheel, it is required to develop a portion of the cylindrical surface generated by the revolution of the pitch-line, A B, about the axis of the worm, and containing the portion, A $i k l m$, for example, of the helix, described by the central point of contact, A. To obtain this, make the line, E′ A′, fig. 7, equal to the semi-circumference, A′ m E², rectified. At the point, E′, erect the perpendicular, C′ E′, and make it equal to C E, fig. 6, or half the pitch, and join E′ A′, whereby will be obtained the actual inclination of the worm-thread. On each side of the point, m, on E′ A′, mark distances, $m a′$ and $m b′$, equal to $m′ a$ and $m′ b$, fig. 5, and through these points draw parallels to C′ E′, and the portion, $p q$, of the enclosed line comprised within them, will serve to determine the width and inclination of the teeth of the worm-wheel. Through the points, p, r, draw $p t$ and $r s$ parallel to E′ A′, and mark off the distances, $t s$ and $s q$, which are equal, on the pitch circle of the wheel, fig. 6, from s to t and q, after having drawn through the points, s, but only in faint pencil or dotted lines, the contours of the teeth as sectioned at F and G′. It is then sufficient to repeat these outlines through the points, t and q, limiting their length by the same internal and external circles.

Finally, the edge view of the worm-wheel, fig. 5, being the lateral projection of the teeth, is determined by squaring across the points, u, v, x, to u^1, v^1, x^1, which give the interiors of the teeth; and the points, u^2, v^2, x^2, being squared over to u^3, v^3, x^3, give their exterior edges.

Worm-wheels are sometimes constructed with the form of the teeth concave, and concentric with the axis of the worm, with the view of their being in contact with the convolutions of the worm-thread throughout a certain extent, in place of only touching at single points.

This arrangement, which requires a particular operation for its construction, is generally adopted when great precision is required, and when it is wished to avoid, as much as possible, any play between the teeth and the worm-thread during the transmission of motion.

CYLINDRICAL OR SPUR GEARING.

PLATE XIX.

THE EXTERNAL DELINEATION OF TWO SPUR-WHEELS IN GEAR.

FIGURE 4.

209. Spur-toothed wheels are such as have their teeth parallel, and lying upon a cylindrical surface or web. When a couple of such wheels are of unequal size, the smaller one is generally called a pinion, and the larger one a spur-wheel. Two wheels, which are intended to gear together, cannot work satisfactorily in concert, unless their radii or pitch circles are exactly proportional to the number of teeth contained by each. Consequently, in order to construct designs for couples of toothed wheels, it is necessary to know—the number of teeth of each, and the radius of one or other of them; or the radii or diameters of both, and the number of teeth of one; or the distance between their centres, and the radius or number of teeth of one; or finally, the number of revolutions of each in the same time, and the distance between

their centres, or the radius and number of teeth of one of them. In the rules and data at the end of this chapter, will be found the solution of the several problems involved in these various cases.

If we assume the following data, A B = 240, and B C = 400, these being the respective radii of the pitch circles of two right wheels, and $n = 24$, the number of teeth of the pinion—we at once ascertain the number of teeth, N, of the spur-wheel, by the following proportional formula:—

A B : B C :: n : N, or 240 : 400 :: 24 : N = 40.

Then describe the pitch circles of the radii, A B and B C, and divide them respectively into 24 and 40 equal parts, thereby obtaining the pitch, or the central point of each tooth, which is exactly the same on both pitch circles. Next subdivide the pitch into four equal parts, to obtain the centres of the intervals, and, at the same time, the points through which the flanks of the teeth pass. If, with the line, A B, on the line of the centres, A C, as a diameter, we describe a circle, the centre of which is at o, and suppose this circle to roll round the pitch circle, D B E, of the spur-wheel, the point, B, at present in contact, will generate an epicycloid, B F, as shown previously in reference to fig. 1; and this curve is the one proper to give to the side of the teeth of the spur-wheel, and it is accordingly repeated symmetrically on each side of the several teeth, as shown in the diagram. If, further, we suppose the same circle of the radius, o B, to roll round the interior of the pitch circle, G B H, of the pinion, we shall obtain the internal epicycloid (sometimes called hypocycloid), B o, as already explained in reference to fig. 3, Plate XVIII., and a portion, B a, of this, forms the flank of the pinion tooth.

Supposing the curve, B C, to form a part of the wheel, turning about the centre, c, in the direction of the arrow, I, it will fulfil the condition of impelling the flank, B a, which forms part of the pinion, so as to turn about the centre, A, in the like uniformity. In other words, the space passed through by the point, B, on the pitch circle, G B H, shall be exactly the same as that passed through by the same point, B, considered as belonging to the spur-wheel, on the pitch circle, E B D.

210. In proceeding to the determination of the length to give to the tooth, it is first to be observed that the epicycloidal curve should be sufficiently long to bear upon the side of the tooth, through an extent of circumferential movement equal to the length of the pitch from the line of centres; that is to say, until the flank, at present in the position, B a, shall have arrived to the position, c d. At this moment, it will be observed that the curve, B F, has reached the position, $b f$, and is in contact with the flank of the pinion tooth in the point, f, on the circumference of the generating circle of the radius, A o. It will thus be obvious that the point, f, may be obtained by simply cutting off, on the generating circle, an arc, B f, equal to the length of the pitch. Through this point, f, describe a circle having c for its centre, and it will cut all the teeth at the proper length.

The depth of the intervals is theoretically determined by describing, with the centre, A, a circle tangential to the first; but in practice, as it is necessary to leave a slight space between the ends of the teeth and the bottoms of the intervals into which these work, the circle in question is described with a somewhat smaller radius, as A a.

211. Hence it is manifest, on the supposition that the spur-wheel is intended always to be the driver, without being driven at any time by the pinion, the teeth of the spur-wheel would only require to be of the form indicated at J, and those of the pinion, like the portion of a tooth, K, slightly tinted for the sake of distinction; but generally, and for obvious reasons, all spur gear is so constructed as to act reciprocally, and equally well, whichever be the driver, and we must, therefore, shape the teeth of the pinion, so that it may, in turn, perform that function.

With this view, describe a circle with the centre, o', of the radius. B C, taken as a diameter; and suppose this circle to roll round the pitch circle, H B G, of the pinion, the point, B, at present in contact, will generate the epicycloid, B L, which is the proper curve to be given to the teeth of the pinion. The same point, B, considered as on the spur-wheel, will, as we have seen, generate a straight line, B' o', when rolling in the same manner round the interior of the circle, E B D, and this line forms the flank of the tooth of the spur-wheel. The operation proceeds in the same manner as for the pinion, the length of the teeth of which is determined by making the arc, B f', equal to the length of the pitch, and describing, with the centre, A, a circle passing through the point, f'.

The depth of the intervals of the spur-wheel is, in like manner, limited by a circle described with the centre, c, and radius, c g, which is somewhat short of being a tangent to the external circle of the pinion, so as to allow a little play to the teeth in their passage, as already explained. In this manner are obtained the complete forms of the teeth, which are regular, symmetrical, and similar to each other, and satisfy the conditions of reciprocal gearing.

In the graphic operations here discussed, we have supposed the intervals between the teeth to be exactly equal in width to the teeth themselves; but as, in practice, it is necessary to allow of some play between the teeth, in order that they may work into each other with facility, this object is attained by reducing the thickness of the teeth a little; and in the drawing, when the scale is not very large, it will be sufficient to delineate the ink lines just within the thickness of the pencil lines. Where it is wished to be more precise, this allowance may be calculated at about $\frac{1}{15}$th or $\frac{1}{20}$th of the pitch. To give strength to the teeth, the interior angles of the intervals are rounded, as shown at each tooth in fig. 4.

When the pinion is but of small diameter, the web, M, which carries the teeth, is cast solid with the boss, the interval being filled up with a disc; but when the wheel is larger, as in the case of the spur-wheel, the web, M', is attached to the boss, P', by arms, Q, which are strengthened by feathers, rounded in at the angles, as represented in fig. 4.

DELINEATION OF A COUPLE OF WHEELS GEARING INTERNALLY.

FIGURE 5.—PLATE XIX.

212. The principles observed in determining the relative numbers of the teeth, with reference to the example just discussed, apply in like manner to the case before us; that is, such numbers must be in the exact ratios of the diameters of the pitch circles. The curvature of the teeth is also determinable by means of the

same operations, modified to suit the different positions of the parts with respect to each other. Thus the curve, B L, of the pinion tooth, is generated by the rolling round the pitch circle, G B H, of the circle described with the centre, o, and radius, o B, equal to the half of B C, the radius of the pitch circle, D B E, of the larger wheel. This is an application of the operations explained in reference to fig. 3. The flanks, B a, or the sides of the teeth, are obtained by simply drawing radii, or lines converging in the point, c.

In the same manner, the curve, B F, of the teeth of the large wheel, is generated by rolling along the interior of its pitch circle, B D E, a circle described from the centre, o′, and radius, B o′, equal to half the radius, B A, of the pitch circle, G B H, of the pinion. These curves being obtained, the outlines of the teeth are completed in the manner explained in reference to fig. 4. It may, however, be observed that, in the diagram, fig. 5, though the teeth might be cut off by a circle passing through the point, f, and described with the centre, A, they are prolonged beyond that, so that the teeth remain longer in contact, and a greater number of teeth are, consequently, engaged at one time, allowing the strain to be distributed over a greater number of points. It is the fact of the curvatures of the two lines of teeth being in the same direction, which admits of a greater number of teeth being engaged at once, without that increase of friction, and other disadvantages, which would result from such an arrangement with wheels like fig. 4.

THE PRACTICAL DELINEATION OF A COUPLE OF SPUR-WHEELS.

PLATE XX.

213. In the cases treated of in the preceding sections, which comprehend the general principles involved in rack and wheel gearing, we have assumed that the rack and pinion, or pinion and spur-wheel. are constructed of the same material, and in this case the thickness of the teeth is the same in any two working together. It very often happens, however, in actual construction, that one of the two has wooden, and the other cast-iron teeth, or of other dissimilar material. When this is the case, the thickness of the one description must necessarily be greater than that of the other, to compensate for the difference in the strength of the materials. The pitch, however, will still be the same for both wheels; for, since the intervals on one wheel correspond to the teeth on the other, a tooth and an interval on one must obviously be equal to an interval and a tooth on the other. A couple of wheels of this description are represented in plan and elevation, in figs. 1 and 2.

We here assume the wheels to be in the ratio to one another of 3 : 4; whence, giving the pinion 36 teeth, the spur-wheel must have 48. After dividing the pitch circle of the spur-wheel, drawn with the radius, C B, into 96 equal parts, the points of division representing the centres of the teeth and of the intervals, and the pitch circle of the pinion drawn with the radius, A B, likewise, into 72 equal parts—with the centres, o and o′, describe the circles which generate the epicycloidal curves, B F and B L. Take $\frac{11}{21}$ of the pitch, b c, for the thickness of the wooden tooth, d e, and $\frac{9}{21}$ for that of the cast-iron tooth, allowing the remaining $\frac{1}{21}$ for the play in working. Next draw a series of radii, to indicate the

flanks of the teeth, both of the pinion and spur-wheel, and at the point of their junction with the pitch circle, draw the curved portion of each, with the aid of a small pattern or template, cut to the curves, B L and B F; and, finally, limit the lengths of the teeth and the depths of the hollows in the manner already pointed out, in reference to Plate XIX.

As draughtsmen are generally satisfied with representing the epicycloidal curves by arcs of circles which almost coincide with them, and nearly fulfil the same conditions, such arcs must be tangential to the radial sides of the teeth at their points of intersection with the pitch circle. They are determined in the following manner:—Let fig. 10 represent one of the pinion teeth, drawn to a larger scale. Through the point of contact, B, draw a tangent, B o, to the pitch circle; then bisect the chord, B n, which passes through the extremities of the curve, by a perpendicular, which will cut the tangent, B o, in the point, o. This is the centre of the arc, B m n, which very nearly coincides with the epicycloidal curve. The same arc is repeated for each side of all the teeth of the pinion, the radius, B o, being preserved throughout. An analogous operation determines the radius of the arc to be substituted for the curve in the teeth of the spur-wheel.

It is generally advisable to make wooden teeth about three-fourths as long as the pitch, and cast-iron teeth about two-thirds as long. In no case, however, should the lengths of the teeth in the two wheels geared together be less than those obtained by calculation, and determined by the points, f, f′, situated on the circles described with the centres, o, o′, by which the epicycloids are generated. The ratio of the curved external portion, n m, of the tooth to the flank, n p, is 4 : 5. In other words, the whole height or length of the tooth being divided into 9 equal parts, 4 of these are to be taken for the length of the curved portion, and 5 for the rectilinear flanks. When the teeth are of cast-iron, the thickness, p q, of the web should be equal to the thickness, r s, of the tooth. Sometimes it is made only $\frac{3}{4}$ths of this; but in that case it is strengthened by a feather on the interior.

For wooden-toothed wheels, since it is necessary that the tenon, t, of the tooth be firmly secured, the web is made of a thickness, p q, often double that of the tooth. The tenons of the teeth must be adjusted very carefully and accurately in the web. They are made with a slight taper, and are secured on the interior of the web either by iron pegs, as at u, passing through them, or by a series of wooden keys or wedges, v, driven in between them, and forming strong dove-tail joints. These two methods of fixing the teeth are shown at different parts on fig. 1, and more in detail in fig. 7. There is a third modification, which also possesses some advantages. We have represented it at T, fig. 3, whence it will be seen that it consists in forming the teeth with a couple of shoulders, z, which allow of the tenons, t, being made much stronger, and also take away thereby some of the weight of metal, two objects of great importance.

The width, x y, of the teeth is equal to two or three times their pitch. In wheels entirely of cast-iron, the web is of the same width as the teeth; but it is much broader when the teeth are of wood, for it requires to be mortised, to receive the tenons of the teeth, and should have a width equal to that of the teeth, plus an amount equal to once and a half or twice their thickness. We have already mentioned, that in wheels of moderate size, the web, M', is attached to the boss, P', by arms, Q. The number of these arms varies, 4, 6, or 8 being used according to the diameter. In the present case the wheels have six arms; this number, amongst other reasons, being more particularly convenient, because the number of teeth are divisible by 6. Whence it follows, that the feathers which strengthen the arms on either side of the wheel, can be made to lie between two of the teeth, at each of the six points of attachment to the web.

The feathers are joined to the body of each arm by cavetto **or** concave quarter-round mouldings, with or without fillets, as indicated in figs. 5 and 6, which represent sections of the arms taken through 1—2, 1—2, in fig. 1

At other times the feathers are united to the body of the arm by plain chamfer portions, as shown in fig. 8; or, even more simply still, and without filling up the angle formed, as in fig. 9, the feathers being united, as it were, to the body of the arm without any additional moulding.

In all cases, however, these feathers are made with a taper, being thicker at their point of union with the body, and gradually decreasing in thickness outwardly.

Figs. 3 and 4 represent cross sections of the wheels, taken through the irregular line, 3—4—5, on fig. 1. We may observe, in reference to these sections, that at the upper part of each the plane of section is supposed to be parallel to the arm, or the arm is, as it were, turned so as to be parallel to the plane, c c', or A A', fig. 1, in order that it may be projected in the sectional view without foreshortening. At the lower parts of these views, however, the arms are projected, as in the oblique position represented in fig. 1.

In this description of drawings, these oblique projections are generally dispensed with, and are, indeed, avoided, as they do not readily give the exact measurements of the parts represented.

The operations indicated on the figures complete the general design of Plate XX., whether of the plan, elevation, or sections.

THE DELINEATION AND CONSTRUCTION OF WOODEN PATTERNS FOR TOOTHED WHEELS.

PLATE XXI.

SPUR-WHEEL PATTERNS.

214. If, as we have already endeavoured to impress upon the student, great care is required in the construction of wooden patterns in general, above all is this care and extreme accuracy called for in the execution of the patterns of toothed wheels, because of the great exactitude absolutely needed in the proportions of the various parts—as that, for example, between their diameters and numbers of teeth. .

The pattern-maker must make allowance, not only for the shrinking of the cast-iron, but also for the quantity of metal to be taken away by turning and finishing afterwards. Moreover, the pattern, which is necessarily in many pieces, must be joined together so strongly and solidly, that it may not run the risk of changing its shape during the construction of the mould.

For wooden-toothed wheels, the web must be pierced with a

number of openings or mortices to receive the tenons of the teeth. But in place of producing these mortices on the wooden patterns— which system, besides weakening it, would render the formation of the mould much more difficult—small projections corresponding to the teeth are fixed externally to the web. These projections form sockets in the mould, in which the actual loam cores are fixed, which form the mortices when the piece is cast.

Bearing in mind these various considerations, we may proceed to the construction of the patterns for two spur-wheels, such as are represented in Plate XX.

PATTERN OF THE PINION.

215. Figs. 1 and 2 show a half plan and a vertical section of the wooden pattern of the pinion. It is composed of many principal pieces—namely, the web, or crown, and its teeth; the boss, with its core-pieces; and the arms, or spokes, with their feathers. We shall proceed to examine these various parts in succession.

WEB OR CROWN.

The pattern-maker takes planks, of from 25 to 30 millimètres in thickness, and cuts out of it a series of arcs, A, of a uniform radius, corresponding to that to be given to the pinion, with the addition of the allowance for shrinkage and loss from finishing. These arcs are built up like brickwork, the joints of one layer, or series, being opposite to solid portions of the contiguous layers, as shown in fig. 3. This arrangement prevents the liability to warp or change the form, from variation in the humidity of the atmosphere, as would be the case were the crown made of a single piece.

This piece being finished and glued together, and the joints quite dry, is put into a lathe, and there turned quite true, both externally and internally. The two surfaces are here made perfectly parallel, and the whole is reduced to the exact dimensions determined on, and shown upon a large working drawing of the actual size, previously prepared, generally by the pattern-maker himself.

At this stage, the external surface of the crown is divided off by lines, showing the positions of the teeth, which are then sometimes simply screwed or nailed on. It is, however, much preferable, and conduces very much to the solidity of the wheel, to cut out grooves of a trifling depth on the periphery, into which the teeth are fixed, being formed with a dovetail for that purpose, as shown at B, in fig. 1.

BOSS.

The boss is made in two pieces, each one solid block of wood, D, except when the wheel is of a large size, in which case the boss requires to be built up of several pieces.

These blocks are each turned separately to the exact dimensions given in the plans, and they secure between them the thickness of the body part of the arm.

ARMS OR SPOKES.

The body of each arm, c, fig. 4, is also cut out of planks of a uniform thickness, being formed not only to the external contour of that part of the arm which is afterwards the only part visible in the casting, but also comprising, above and beyond this, the projections by which, in the pattern, it is attached to the boss on the one hand, and to the crown on the other. The extremity, a, of the boss end of the arm is in the form of a sector, corresponding to a sixth part of the circle of the boss, the pinion having six arms; the lateral facets, b, of this part are grooved out, to receive small tongue-pieces, or keys, c, fig. 1, so as to form a strong joint when glued together. The other extremity, d, of the arm is cut circularly, to the form of the crown, or web, into which it is fitted, penetrating to a slight extent, the crown being previously formed with a socket to receive it.

Next, the feathers have to be attached to the body, c, of the arm. These feathers, B, are each cut out in separate pieces, to the shape indicated in fig. 5: they have supplementary projections, e and f, at their opposite extremities, whereby they are fixed into the crown and boss. When all these feathers are in their place, and the arms glued into the crown, the two portions, D, D, of the boss are fixed to them, the grooves for the reception of the ends of the feathers being glued, as well as the other parts, to give greater solidity. Finally, the boss is surmounted by the conical projecting pieces, F, F, which serve to produce in the mould the cavities, or sockets, which retain the loam core in position, the core being provided to produce the eye of the wheel, into which the shaft is fitted.

To give compactness and strength to the whole, a bolt, G, is passed through the centre; and this method of securing permits of the core projections, F, F, being changed for larger or smaller ones, if desired, without having to pull the entire wheel to pieces. If, to add to the elegance of the shape of the wheel, it is wished to ornament the arms with mouldings, as at i, these are applied at the angles of junction of the feathers with the body of the arm. These are simply glued or nailed on. The sectional view, fig. 6, shows the form and position of these mouldings.

It is to be observed that, in wheels of a moderate size, when cast-iron teeth are to work on cast-iron, they are at once cast to the exact shape, and the pattern is constructed accordingly; but it is almost always indispensable, where cast-iron and wooden teeth have to work together, to finish and reduce the former after being cast; and the projections, B, on the pattern answering to them, must consequently be made of larger proportions every way, to provide for the quantity of metal taken away in the finishing process.

PATTERN OF THE WOODEN-TOOTHED SPUR-WHEEL.

216. Figs. 7, 8, and 9 represent, in elevation, plan, and vertical section, the wooden pattern of the spur-wheel, which gears with the pinion just described. It consists, like that wheel, of the crown or web, the boss, and the arms; and these various parts, which are designated by letters corresponding to those employed in the preceding example, are constructed exactly in the same manner.

There is, however, an essential difference in the exterior of the crown: in place of this carrying the projections, B, cut to the shape of the teeth, and such as will actually be produced on the casting, it has other projections, B', of a simpler form, intended to produce in the mould the sockets for receiving the core-pieces

which form the mortises in the casting, to receive the tenons of the wooden teeth. These projections are let into the crown, or simply applied thereto, and fixed by nails, as at l, or by screws, as at m, the latter method being preferable, as it has the advantage of permitting the number of teeth to be changed without injury to themselves or to the crown. In the wooden pattern, the length of the projections, B', is carried to the edge of the face of the crown, on that side which descends into the lower half of the mould-frame, to allow of the more accurate adjustment of the core-pieces, and also to facilitate the recovery of the pattern from the mould. These core-pieces, however, are so formed as to make the mortises no wider than is necessary, and to leave a sufficient thickness of metal for the strength of the crown, as already pointed out in reference to Plate XX.

CORE-MOULDS.

217. The core-pieces for the mortises should not only be placed at equal distances apart throughout the circumference of the crown, but they must all also be of precisely the same form and dimensions throughout, so that the mortises may be perfectly equal. With this view, a wooden core-box or mould is made; and there are several methods of doing this. Thus, fig. 10 represents a face view, and fig. 11 a horizontal section, through the line 3—4 in fig. 10, of one form of core-mould, consisting of a single piece. The portion, n, of the cavity corresponds to the projecting core-piece, B', outside the crown, and the portion marked o, to the mortise, or hollow socket, in the crown: this last has the same section as the crown in the width of the cut-out part. The moulder fills the cavity of the core-mould with loam, previously prepared, and after pressing it well in, levels it off with a straight-edged doctor or scraper; he finally inverts the mould, thus releasing the core complete. The operation is repeated as many times as there are teeth; and when the cores are all dry, they are placed with great care in the mould, their supplementary projections, B', being let into the sockets formed to receive them—thereby insuring the accuracy of their adjustment.

Figs. 12, 13, and 14, show another construction of wooden core-mould, formed in two separate pieces, H and I. These have between them the cavity, n o, corresponding to that in the one just described. In this last case, the surface of the core which requires to be levelled off with a scraper, is only at one of the extremities instead of on the lateral faces, as in the other, and the cores are released by separating the two pieces, H, I, which are rendered capable of accurate adjustment to each other by means of marking-pins, k.

To return to the wheel itself: when it is of very large dimensions, the blocks, D, of the boss are secured together by two or more bolts, G, in place of one.

The mould for the wheel is in two pieces, the lower frame, or "drag," being let into the ground in the moulding shop; the upper frame or top part, is moveable, and it will be obvious that very great care is required to lift this off the pattern, so as not to injure the regularity and sharpness of the impression; and for this purpose, sufficient "draw" or taper must be given to the various parts, as the crown, the boss, and the feathers on the arms, as already pointed out.

When the patterns are heavy, two screw-staples, or "draw-plates," L, fig. 1, 8, and 15, of iron or brass, are countersunk into the crown, and into these draw-handles are screwed, by which the pattern is lifted out of the mould.

In figs. 1, 2, 8, and 9, are combined, in single views, several different projections, to avoid repetitions of the diagrams, and to simplify the whole drawing, and bring it into a small space. This system is very much used in drawings, or plans, made for actual construction.

RULES AND PRACTICAL DATA.

TOOTHED GEARING.

218. It has been already laid down, as a fundamental rule, that in order to work well, all toothed wheels coupled together must have the same ratio between the numbers of their teeth as between their diameters.

It follows from this principle, that when we know the radii of the pitch circles of two wheels, and the number of teeth of one of them, we can determine that of the other, and reciprocally.

Thus, putting N to represent the number of teeth of a wheel of the radius, R; and n to represent the number of teeth of a wheel of the radius, r, we have the direct proportionals, $N : n :: R : r$; whence we can, at any time, ascertain any one of the terms when the other three are known.

First Example.—Let the radius of the pitch circle of a spur-wheel be 12 inches, and the number of teeth on it 75, what should be the number of teeth on a pinion gearing with it, the radius of the pitch circle of which is 8 inches?

We have

$$75 : n :: 12 : 8; \text{ whence}$$

$$n = \frac{75 \times 8}{12} = 50 \text{ teeth.}$$

Second Example.—Let 75 and 50, respectively, be the number of the teeth of a spur-wheel and pinion, and 12 inches the radius of the pitch circle of the former, the radius of the pitch circle of the latter may be found by means of the proportion—

$$75 : 50 :: 12 : r; \text{ whence,}$$

$$r = \frac{50 \times 12}{75} = 8 \text{ inches.}$$

219. The velocities of rotation, or the numbers of revolutions of the shafts of a spur-wheel and pinion in gear with each other, are in the inverse ratio of the respective diameters, radii, or numbers of teeth of the two.

Consequently, putting V to represent the velocity of rotation of the pinion shaft, the radius of the pitch circle of which equals r, and the number of the teeth n, and putting v to represent the velocity of the spur wheel shaft, of which the pitch circle radius equals R, and number of teeth N, we have the inverted proportions—

$$V : v :: r : R,$$

and

$$V : v :: n : N.$$

In either of these proportions, we can determine, as in the former example, any one term when the three others are known.

First Example.—A spur-wheel, the pitch circle radius of which is 10 inches, has a velocity of 25 revolutions per minute; what is the pitch circle radius of a pinion to gear with it, and make 60 revolutions in the same time? By the inverse proportion,

$$25 : 60 :: r : 10;$$

whence,

$$r = \frac{25 \times 10}{60} = 4\frac{1}{6} \text{ inches,}$$

the pitch circle radius of the pinion.

A spur-wheel has 60 teeth, and is required to run at 25 revolutions per minute, and at the same time to drive a pinion at the rate of 75 revolutions per minute, what should be the number of teeth of the latter?

Here,

$$75 : 25 :: 60 : n;$$

whence,

$$n = \frac{25 \times 60}{75} = 20,$$

the number of teeth the pinion must have.

These principles apply equally to pulleys or drums put in communication with one another by cords or belts, and known as belt-gearing.

Sometimes, in systems of geared spur-wheels, all that is known is the distance apart of their centres, the number of teeth which they are to carry, or the number of their revolutions in the same time. In this case we have, on the one hand, an inverse proportion between the distance of their centres, the sum of their revolutions, and between their respective radii and revolutions; and, on the other hand, a direct proportion between the distance of the centres, the sum of the teeth on both wheels, and their respective radii, or the number of teeth of each.

Let D be the distance apart of the centres of a spur-wheel and pinion of the respective radii, R, r, and number of teeth, N, n, or the reciprocal velocities, v and V; we have first the following inverse proportion,

$$D : V + v :: R : V;$$

and, secondly, the direct proportion,

$$D : N + n :: N : R.$$

First Example.—Let 45 inches be the distance between the centres of a spur-wheel and pinion, the former of which is to make 22 revolutions per minute to the other's 15½, what should be their respective radii?

We have, first,

$$45 : 22 + 15\cdot5 :: R : 22;$$

whence,

$$R = \frac{45 \times 22}{22 + 15\cdot5} = 26\cdot4 \text{ inches,}$$

and

$$45 : 22 + 15\cdot5 :: r : 15\cdot5;$$

whence,

$$r = \frac{45 \times 15\cdot5}{22 + 15\cdot5} = 18\cdot6 \text{ inches.}$$

When the pitch circle radius of one of the wheels is ascertained, it is evidently unnecessary to search for the other radius by means or the second proportion, for it is sufficient to subtract the one found from the sum of both; thus,

$$45 - 26{\cdot}4 = 18{\cdot}6; \text{ or,}$$
$$45 - 18{\cdot}6 = 26{\cdot}4.$$

Second Example.—The distance, D, between the two centres being known = 45 inches, and one wheel carrying 31 teeth and the other 44, what are their respective radii?

We have here, in the first place,

$$45 : 31 + 44 :: R : 44;$$

whence,

$$R = \frac{45 \times 44}{31 + 44} = 26{\cdot}4,$$

and

$$45 : 31 + 44 :: r : 31;$$

whence,

$$r = \frac{45 \times 31}{31 + 44} = 18{\cdot}6,$$

or, more simply,

$$r = 45 - 26{\cdot}4 = 18{\cdot}6 \text{ inches.}$$

In like manner, the respective radii of a spur-wheel and pinion, to gear together, may be determined geometrically, when the distance between their centres is known, as well as the numbers of revolutions of each, by the following rule:—

Divide the distance into as many equal parts as there are of any measure contained exactly in the sum of the velocities, such measure being also contained exactly any number of times in each of the velocities alone. Then, for the pinion radius, take as many of these measures as are contained in the lesser velocity, and for the radius of the spur-wheel, the remainder of them.

Example.—Let 16 inches be the distance between the centres of a spur-wheel and pinion which make 6 and 4 revolutions respectively, or any equi-multiples or equi-submultiples of these, as 12 and 8, or 3 and 2. Divide the distance into 10 equal parts, and take 4 of these for the pinion radius, and 6 for the spur-wheel radius.

This rule is of very simple application when the ratios of the numbers of revolutions are whole numbers, such as 1 : 4, or 2 : 5; for all that is necessary is to add the two together, to divide the distance between the centres to correspond, and to take the respective numbers of measures for each wheel.

The following table will be of great assistance in the solution of various problems connected with systems of gearing, when the number of teeth, the pitch, or the radius are known.

TABLE FOR CALCULATING THE NUMBERS OF TEETH AND DIAMETERS OF SPUR GEAR, FROM THE PITCH, OR *VICE VERSA.*

Number.	Coefficient.	Number.	Coefficient.	Number.	Coefficient.	Number.	Coefficient.	Number.	Coefficient
10	3·183	39	12·414	68	21·644	97	30·875	126	40·106
11	3·501	40	12·732	69	21·963	98	31·193	127	40·424
12	3·820	41	13·050	70	22·281	99	31·512	128	40·742
13	4·138	42	13·369	71	22·599	100	31·830	129	41·061
14	4·456	43	13·687	72	22·917	101	32·148	130	41·379
15	4·774	44	14·005	73	23·236	102	32·467	131	41·697
16	5·093	45	14·323	74	23·554	103	32·785	132	42·016
17	5·411	46	14·642	75	23·872	104	33·103	133	42·334
18	5·729	47	14·960	76	24·191	105	33·421	134	42·652
19	6·048	48	15·278	77	24·509	106	33·740	135	42·970
20	6·366	49	15·597	78	24·827	107	34·058	136	43·289
21	6·684	50	15·915	79	25·146	108	34·376	137	43·607
22	7·002	51	16·233	80	25·464	109	34·695	138	43·925
23	7·321	52	16·552	81	25·782	110	35·013	139	44·244
24	7·639	53	16·870	82	26·100	111	35·331	140	44·562
25	7·957	54	17·188	83	26·419	112	35·650	141	44·880
26	8·276	55	17·506	84	26·737	113	35·968	142	45·199
27	8·594	56	17·825	85	27·055	114	36·286	143	45·517
28	8·912	57	18·143	86	27·374	115	36·604	144	45·835
29	9·231	58	18·461	87	27·692	116	36·923	145	46·153
30	9·549	59	18·780	88	28·010	117	37·241	146	46·472
31	9·867	60	19·098	89	28·329	118	37·559	147	46·790
32	10·186	61	19·416	90	28·647	119	37·878	148	47·108
33	10·504	62	19·734	91	28·965	120	38·196	149	47·427
34	10·822	63	20·053	92	29·284	121	38·514	150	47·745
35	11·140	64	20·371	93	29·602	122	38·833	151	48·063
36	11·459	65	20·689	94	29·920	123	39·151	152	48·382
37	11·777	66	21·008	95	30·238	124	39·469	153	48·700
38	12·095	67	21·326	96	30·557	125	39·788	154	49·020

RULES CONNECTED WITH THE PRECEDING TABLE.

f. To find the diameter of a spur-wheel, when the number and pitch of the teeth are known.

Multiply the coefficient in the table, corresponding to the number of teeth, by the given pitch in feet, inches, mètres, or other measures, and the product will be the diameter in feet, inches, or mètres, to correspond.

K

First Example.—What is the diameter of a spur-wheel, of 63 teeth, having a pitch of 1½ inches?

Opposite the number 63, in the table, we find the coefficient, 20·053. Then—

$$20·053 \times 1·5 = 30·08 \text{ inches,}$$

the diameter of the spur-wheel.

Second Example.—What are the diameters of two wheels, of 41 and 150 teeth respectively, their pitch being ¾ inch?

On the one hand, we have

$$13·05 \times ·75 = 9·7875 \text{ inches,}$$

the diameter of the pinion of 41 teeth; and on the other,

$$47·745 \times ·75 = 35·8 \text{ inches,}$$

the diameter of the spur-wheel of 150 teeth.

II. To find the pitch of a spur-wheel, when the diameter and number of teeth are known.

Divide the given diameter by the coefficient in the table corresponding to the number of the teeth, and the quotient will be the pitch sought.

First Example.—What is the pitch of a wheel of 30·08 inches diameter, and of 63 teeth?

Here—

$$30·08 : 20·053 = 1·5 \text{ inch,}$$

the pitch required.

Second Example.—It is required to construct a spur-wheel, of 126 teeth, to work with the preceding, what must be its diameter?

Here—

$$1·5 \times 40·106 = 60·159 \text{ inches,}$$

the diameter of a wheel of 126 teeth, and of the same pitch.

III. To find the number of teeth of a wheel, when the pitch and diameter are known.

Divide the given diameter by the given pitch, the number in the table corresponding to the quotient will be the number of teeth sought.

If the quotient is not in the table, take the number corresponding to that nearest to it.

First Example.—The diameter of a spur-wheel is 30·08 inches, and the pitch of the teeth is 1·5 inch, what number of teeth should the wheel have?

$$30·8 : 1·5 = 20·53;$$

which quotient corresponds to 63 teeth.

Second Example.—What should be the number of teeth of a pinion, the diameter of which is 875 millimètres, and which is intended to gear with a rack, of which the pitch is 25 millimètres?

$$875 : 25 = 35.$$

The number most nearly corresponding to this is 110, the number of teeth to be given to the pinion.

ANGULAR AND CIRCUMFERENTIAL VELOCITY OF WHEELS.

519. When it is known what is the angular velocity of the shaft of a fly-wheel, spur-wheel, or pulley, the circumferential velocity may be found by the following rule :—

Multiply the circumference by the number of revolutions per minute, and the product will give the space passed through in the same time; and this product being divided by 60, will give the velocity of the circumference per second.

Example.—Let the diameter of a wheel be 4 feet, and the number of its revolutions per minute 20, what is the velocity at the circumference?

The circumference of the wheel $= 4 \times 3·1416 = 12·5664$; then

$$12·5664 \times 20 = 251·328 \text{ feet,}$$

the space passed through per minute by any point in the circumference; and

$$\frac{251·328}{60} = 4·2,$$

the velocity in feet per second.

When the velocity at the circumference is known, the angular velocity, or the number of turns in a given time, may be ascertained by the following rule :—

Divide the circumferential velocity by the circumference, and the quotient will be the angular velocity, or number of revolutions in the given time.

In the preceding case, 4·2 feet being the circumferential velocity per second, and 4 feet the diameter, we have

$$\frac{4·2}{4 \times 3·1416} = ·334,$$

the angular velocity per second; and

$$·334 \times 60 = 20,$$

the number of revolutions per minute.

In practice, it is easy to ascertain the velocity of a wheel, the motion of which is uniform. With this view, a point is marked with chalk on the rim of the wheel, and note is taken of how often this point passes a fixed point of observation in a given time; then this number of revolutions is multiplied by the circumference described by the marked point, and the product divided by the duration of the observation expressed in seconds. The result will be the velocity of the circumference of the wheel. Every other point on the wheel will have a different velocity, proportioned to its distance from the centre of motion.

Example.—A wheel, 2 feet in diameter, having, according to observation, made 75 revolutions per minute, what is its circumferential velocity (per second)?

$$\frac{75 \times 3·14 \times 2}{60} = 7·83 \text{ feet,}$$

circumferential velocity of the wheel.

Reciprocally, when the circumferential velocity (per second) is known, the number of revolutions per minute is found by means of the formula—

$$N = \frac{V \times 60}{3·14 \times D};$$

or, with the data of the preceding case,

$$N = \frac{7·83 \times 60}{3·14 \times 2} = 75 \text{ revolutions per minute.}$$

When several spur-wheels or pulleys are placed on the same shaft, the circumferential velocity of every one of them is found in the same manner, by multiplying the number of revolutions by the respective circumferences, and dividing the products by 60.

Example.—Three wheels or pulleys, a, b, c, are fixed on one shaft; the radius of the pulley, a, is equal to 1·1 feet; that of the pulley, b, 1·6 feet; and that of the pulley, c, 2·15 feet; and the shaft makes 12 turns per minute,—what is the circumferential velocity of these three pulleys?

For the pulley, *a*, we have—

$$V = \frac{6\cdot28 \times 1\cdot1 \times 12}{60} = 1\cdot38 \text{ feet per minute;}$$

for the pulley, *b*—

$$V' = \frac{6\cdot28 \times 1\cdot6 \times 12}{60} = 2 \text{ feet;}$$

and for the pulley, *c*—

$$V'' = \frac{6\cdot28 \times 2\cdot15 \times 12}{60} = 2\cdot7 \text{ feet.}$$

DIMENSIONS OF GEARING.

220. In designing tooth-gearing of all descriptions, it is necessary to determine—first, the strength and dimensions of the teeth; second, the dimensions of the web which carries the teeth; and, third, the dimensions of the arms.

THICKNESS OF THE TEETH.

221. The resistance opposed to the motion of the wheel or the load, may be considered as a force applied to the crown, to prevent its turning, and the power, during its greater strain, as applied to the extremities of the teeth. The teeth then should be considered as solids fixed at one end, and loaded at the other; and the equation of equilibrium for them is—

$$P \times h = k \times t^2 \times w;$$

in which formula, P signifies the pressure in kilogrammes at the extremity of the tooth; *h*, the amount of projection of the teeth from the web in centimètres; *k*, a numerical coefficient; *t*, the thickness of the teeth in centimètres; *w*, their width in centimètres.

In this formula, the numerical coefficient, *k*, which is calculated with reference to the motion of toothed gearing, varies with the material of which the teeth are constructed.

From Tredgold's experiments with well-constructed cast-iron wheels, this coefficient has been calculated to be 25 for that metal; and adopting it, the preceding formula will then become

$$P \times h = 25 \times t^2 \times w;$$

whence,

$$P = \frac{25 \times t^2 w}{h},$$

a formula in which three dimensions are variable.

The following ratios usually exist between these quantities:—

w varies between 3 *t* and 8 *t*.

h = 1·2 *t* to 1·5 *t*.

Let, then, *w* = 5 *t*, and *h* = 1·2 *t*, so that, substituting these values in the equation, it becomes—

$$P = \frac{25 \times 5 \times t \times t^2}{1\cdot2 \times t} = 104 \times t^2;$$

whence,

$$t^2 = \frac{P}{104} \text{ and } t = \cdot098 \sqrt{P}.$$

If the above ratio between the thickness, *t*, and width, *w*, be adopted for all proportions; for low pressures or small loads, we shall have teeth much too thin and small; and for high pressures, on the other hand, the defects of too great thickness and

pitch. To retain, then, the thicknesses within convenient limits, it is well to vary the ratio of *t* to *w*, according to the pressures; and in order that the pitch may not be too great, the width of the teeth is determined at the outset, according to the pressure or load which they have to sustain, in the following manner:—

I.	For	100 to	200 lb.,	make	$w =$	3 *t*;	when	$t =$	$\cdot126 \sqrt{P}$
II.	"	200	300	"	$w =$	3·5 *t*	"	$t =$	$\cdot117 \sqrt{P}$
III.	"	300	400	"	$w =$	4 *t*	"	$t =$	$\cdot110 \sqrt{P}$
IV.	"	400	500	"	$w =$	4·5 *t*	"	$t =$	$\cdot104 \sqrt{P}$
V.	"	500	1,000	"	$w =$	5 *t*	"	$t =$	$\cdot098 \sqrt{P}$
VI.	"	1,000	1,500	"	$w =$	5·5 *t*	"	$t =$	$\cdot093 \sqrt{P}$
VII.	"	1,500	2,000	"	$w =$	6 *t*	"	$t =$	$\cdot089 \sqrt{P}$
VIII.	"	2,000	3,000	"	$w =$	6·5 *t*	"	$t =$	$\cdot084 \sqrt{P}$
IX.	"	3,000	5,000	"	$w =$	7 *t*	"	$t =$	$\cdot082 \sqrt{P}$
X.	"	5,000 and upwards,		"	$w =$	8 *t*	"	$t =$	$\cdot077 \sqrt{P}$

The height, or projection, *h*, should be comprised between 1·2 *t* and 1·5 *t*, the latter applicable to low powers or loads, and the former to high ones.

For teeth of wood, which are ordinarily made of beech or elm, the coefficient should be augmented by a third in each of the last given formulæ, which become—

I.	$t = \cdot168 \sqrt{P}$	making	$w = 3\cdot0$ *t*.
II.	$t = \cdot156 \sqrt{P}$	"	$w = 3\cdot5$ *t*.
III.	$t = \cdot147 \sqrt{P}$	"	$w = 4\cdot0$ *t*.
IV.	$t = \cdot139 \sqrt{P}$	"	$w = 4\cdot5$ *t*.
V.	$t = \cdot131 \sqrt{P}$	"	$w = 5\cdot0$ *t*.
VI.	$t = \cdot124 \sqrt{P}$	"	$w = 5\cdot5$ *t*.
VII.	$t = \cdot119 \sqrt{P}$	"	$w = 6\cdot0$ *t*.
VIII.	$t = \cdot112 \sqrt{P}$	"	$w = 6\cdot5$ *t*.
IX.	$t = \cdot109 \sqrt{P}$	"	$w = 7\cdot0$ *t*.
X.	$t = \cdot103 \sqrt{P}$	"	$w = 8\cdot0$ *t*.

All these formulæ are constructed on the supposition that, although there are generally several teeth in contact at the same time, yet each should be capable of sustaining the whole strain as if there were only one in contact, and they should be strong enough to compensate for wear, and sustain shocks and irregularities in the strain for a considerable length of time.

The pressure, P, on the teeth may be determined according to the amount of power transmitted by the wheels per second at the pitch circumference.

This pressure is obtained by dividing the strain to be transmitted, expressed in kilogrammètre, by the velocity per second of the pitch circumference. A kilogrammètre is a term corresponding to the English expression, "one pound raised one foot high per minute." A kilogrammètre is equal to one kilogramme raised one mètre high per second: it is written shortly thus—k. m.

First Example.—A spur-wheel is intended to transmit a force equal to a power acting at the pitch circumference of 500 kilogrammètres, at the rate of 2·09 m. per second, what pressure have the teeth to sustain?

Here,

$$\frac{500 \text{ k. m.}}{2\cdot09} = 239 \text{ kilog.,}$$

the strain that each tooth must be capable of resisting without risk of breakage, even after considerable use and wear.

Second Example.—A spur-wheel, 2 mètres in diameter, transmits a force equal to 20 horses power, and makes 25 revolutions per minute, what is the pressure on the teeth?

We have, in the first place,

$$20 \text{ H.P.} = 75 \times 20 = 1500 \text{ kilogrammètres,}$$

and

$$V = \frac{3\cdot14 \times 2 \times 25}{60} = 2\cdot62 \text{ m. per second;}$$

whence,

$$\frac{1500}{2\cdot62} = 573 \text{ kilog.,}$$

the pressure on the tooth.

When the power that a wheel has to sustain at its circumference is known, the thickness proper for the tooth may be calculated by one of the preceding formulæ, according to the material of which it is constructed.

Thus, in the former of the last two examples, in which P = 239 kilog., the thickness of the tooth, if of cast-iron, should be making $w = 3\cdot5\,t$:

$$t = \cdot117 \sqrt{239} = 1\cdot8 \text{ cent.} = 18 \text{ millimètres.}$$

And, in the second example, where P = 573 kil., the thickness will be, supposing the teeth to be of beech, and $w = 5\,t$,

$$t = \cdot131 \sqrt{573} = 3\cdot23\,c, \text{ or } 32\cdot3 \text{ millimètres,}$$

$$w = 5 \times 32\cdot3 = 161\cdot5 \text{ millimètres.}$$

Third Example.—A water-wheel of 4·2 mètres diameter makes 4½ revolutions per minute, and transmits a force equal to 25 horses power by means of a spur-wheel, the radius of which is 1·65 m., it is required to determine—first, the pressure on the teeth of this spur wheel; and, secondly, the thickness of their teeth.

In the first place,

$$25 \times 75 = 1875 \text{ kilogrammètres,}$$

and

$$V = \frac{1\cdot65 \times 2 \times 3\cdot14 \times 4\cdot5}{60} = \cdot777 \text{ m.;}$$

whence,

$$P = \frac{1875}{\cdot777} = 2413 \text{ kilogrammètres;}$$

consequently, making $w = 6\cdot5\,t$, the thickness of the tooth will be

$$t = \cdot084 \sqrt{2413} = 3\cdot7\,c = 37 \text{ millim.,}$$

and

$$w = 37 \times 6\cdot5 = 240\cdot5 \text{ millim.}$$

Fourth Example.—The cast-iron pinion of a powerful machine is 1·06 m. in diameter, it is fixed on a shaft which should transmit an effective force of 200 horses power, at the rate of 45 revolutions per minute, what is the pressure on the teeth and their dimensions?

The power transmitted is

$$200 \times 75 = 15,000 \text{ kilogrammètres,}$$

and

$$V = \frac{1\cdot06 \times 3\cdot14 \times 45}{60} = 2\cdot37 \text{ mètres per second.}$$

The pressure on the teeth is—

$$P = \frac{1500}{2\cdot37} = 6333 \text{ k.m.;}$$

consequently, making $w = 8\,t$; we have, for the thickness of the teeth, in cast-iron,

$$t = \cdot077 \sqrt{6333} = 61\cdot2 \text{ }^m/_m.$$

and

$$w = 8 \times 61\cdot2 = 489\cdot6 \text{ }^m/_m.$$

For a pinion of the above proportions, actually constructed, the thickness was made 75 millim., and the width 525 millim.

PITCH OF THE TEETH.

222. It will be recollected (203) that the pitch of cast-iron spur-wheel teeth, measured on the pitch circumference, comprises the thickness, t, of the tooth, and the width of the interval, which last is, in ordinary cases, made equal to t, augmented by one-tenth; this gives, $p = 2\cdot1\,t$.

Thus, with the data of the preceding examples—

$$\text{In the 1st,}\dots\dots p = 2\cdot1 \times 18 \ = \ 27\cdot8 \text{ }^m/_m.$$
$$\text{3d,}\dots\dots p = 2\cdot1 \times 37 \ = \ 77\cdot7 \text{ }^m/_m.$$
$$\text{4th,}\dots\dots p = 2\cdot1 \times 61\cdot2 = 128\cdot5 \text{ }^m/_m.$$

When the spur-wheel is intended to carry wooden teeth, as in the second of the preceding examples, it will generally be coupled with a pinion, having cast-iron teeth, which should be of about three-fourths the thickness of the wooden ones; in this case the pitch will be equal to

$$t + \cdot75\,t + \cdot1\,t = 1 + \cdot85\,t = 1\cdot85\,t.$$

Thus, in this example, we should have—

$$p = 32\cdot3 \times 1\cdot85 = 59\cdot8 \text{ }^m/_m.$$

After this is done, that is, when the pitch is ascertained, which, as has already been observed, should be precisely the same on the pitch circles of any two wheels working together, the number of teeth of one of the wheels may be obtained by the following formula—

$$N = \frac{2\pi R}{p},$$

where N signifies the number of teeth of the spur-wheel; R, the radius of the pitch circle; and p, the pitch, measured on this circle.

First Example.—What is the number of teeth on a spur-wheel of two mètres diameter, and the pitch of which is ·0278 mètres?

Here—

$$N = \frac{2 \times 3\cdot14 \times 1}{\cdot0278} = 225 \text{ teeth.}$$

It will be easily understood, that the fraction arising from the operation must be neglected, since we cannot have a part of a tooth. In cases, therefore, where there is a fraction, the pitch must be slightly increased. Thus, in the example under consideration, the pitch becomes

$$p = \frac{2\pi R}{N} = \frac{6\cdot28}{225} = \cdot0279 \text{ m.,}$$

instead of 0·278 m.

Second Example.—It is required to determine the number of wooden teeth to be carried by a spur-wheel of two mètres diameter, the pitch being ·0598 m.

Here,

$$N = \frac{3\cdot14 \times 2}{\cdot0598} = 105.$$

When a spur-wheel is to have wooden teeth, it is necessary that the number of these be some multiple of the number of arms of the wheel, in order that they may be conveniently attached to the web; thus, in the present example, if the wheel is to have 6 arms, the number of teeth must be 102 or 108, to be divisible by that number; and if the former be adopted instead of 105, the pitch will be slightly augmented in consequence.

To obviate the necessity of making long and tedious calculations, a table is subjoined, showing the thickness and pitch of teeth of spur-wheels, in which is adopted the coefficient ·105 of M. Morin, which makes the formula,

$$t = ·105 \sqrt{P}$$

for cast-iron teeth, and

$$t = ·145 \sqrt{P}$$

for wooden teeth: the width being constantly equal to nearly 4·5 the thickness.

Table of the Pitch and Thickness of Spur Teeth for different Pressures.

Pressure in Kilogrammes.	Of Cast-Iron.		Of Wood.	
	Thickness of Teeth in Millimètres.	Pitch in Millimètres.	Thickness of Teeth in Millimètres.	Pitch in Millimètres.
5	2·3	4·9	3·2	5·9
10	3·3	6·9	4·7	8·7
15	4·0	8·5	5·6	10·4
20	4·6	9·7	6·4	11·8
30	5·7	12·0	7·9	14·4
40	6·6	13·9	9·1	16·9
50	7·4	15·6	10·2	18·9
60	8·1	17·0	11·2	20·8
70	8·7	18·4	12·1	22·4
80	9·4	19·7	12·9	23·9
90	9·9	20·8	13·7	25·3
100	10·5	22·0	14·5	26·8
125	11·6	24·4	16·1	29·8
150	12·8	26·9	17·7	32·7
175	13·8	29·1	19·1	34·8
200	14·8	31·1	20·2	37·4
225	15·7	33·0	21·7	40·1
250	16·6	34·8	22·9	42·4
275	17·3	36·3	23·9	44·2
300	18·2	38·1	25·1	46·4
350	19·6	41·2	27·1	50·1
400	21·0	43·2	29·0	53·6
500	23·4	49·1	32·4	59·9
600	25·7	54·0	35·5	65·7
700	27·7	58·2	37·2	69·1
800	29·7	62·4	41·0	75·8
900	31·5	66·1	43·8	83·0
1000	33·2	69·6	45·8	84·7

With the assistance of this table, and the preceding rules, we can always determine, not only the thickness and pitch of the teeth, but also their height and width, since these are in proportion to their thickness.

DIMENSIONS OF THE WEB.

223. The width of the web is ordinarily equal to that of the teeth when the whole is of cast-iron. Nevertheless, in some cases—such as, for example, where very great irregularities in the pressure and speed, and reiterated shocks have to be borne in the heavy machinery in engine shops—the web is made wider than the teeth,

projecting also on either side of the teeth, so that these are wholly or partially imbedded, which increases their power of resistance very considerably. These lateral webs are generally, each made of about half the thickness of the tooth.

The thickness of the web, or crown, is never made less than three-fourths that of the tooth, and very frequently it is further strengthened by an internal feather, as already mentioned.

213. When the teeth are of wood, the web is much thicker, to give sufficient hold to the tenons of the teeth; it is generally made about 1·5 to 2· times the thickness of the tooth.

NUMBER AND DIMENSIONS OF THE ARMS.

224. The number of arms, or spokes, which a spur-wheel ought to have, has not, up to the present time, been precisely and scientifically determined. According to general experience, up to a diameter of 1 mètre, or about 3 feet, four arms are sufficient; from 1 mètre to 2 mètres, or 3 feet to 6 or 7 feet, six are necessary and sufficient; beyond 2·5 m., or 8 feet, eight arms are used: and for 5 m., or 16 feet, ten are given; it is seldom this last number is exceeded, except for wheels of extraordinary dimensions.

The section of the arms of the wheel is always in the form of a cross, the stronger portion of which lies in the plane of the circumferential strain, whether these arms are cast in one piece with the boss and the crown, as is the case with wheels of small diameter—that is, of such as have not a greater radius than 2 m. or 6½ feet; or whether they are cast in separate pieces, and afterwards fitted together. The thicker part, then, of the arm must be strong enough to bear the circumferential strain. Experience has shown, that when a spur-wheel is in motion, and acted upon by a considerable force, this strain has a tendency to make the arms assume a twisted shape, and produce on them a lateral inflexion. It is to obviate and prevent this, that the arms are strengthened by feathers.

The power acts with greatest effect near the boss of the wheel, so that it is necessary to make them wider at this part than near the crown, so as to approximate to the form which presents an equal resistance throughout. This will be observed in the figures in Plate XX. The boss must have such a thickness as will allow of the wheels being solidly fixed on the shaft. A thickness of 5 inches may be considered a maximum for the bosses of moderately-sized wheels. The dimensions of the arms should be in proportion to the width of the web or crown, their thickness being ordinarily about ⅓ that of the crown. This proportion is a good one for wheels under 6½ feet in diameter. For larger sizes, ¼ the width of the web is considered sufficient.

The lateral feathers should have, at the very most, only the thickness of the arm. Generally, the width of the arm near the web is made about ⅔ of its width near the boss. The following table, calculated from Tredgold's experiments, shows the proportions to be given to the arms or spokes of spur-wheels, according to the strain acting at their circumferences; supposing the diameter of the wheels to be 1 m., and the number of arms 6, their thickness being taken equal to ⅓ the width of the crown. The dimensions given are the averages, or those to be applied to the arm, half-way between the boss and the crown.

Table of the Dimensions of Spur-wheel Arms.

Tangential Strain on the Wheel in kilog.	Width of the Arm in centimètres.	Width over all, of the Feathers in centimètres.
10	4·20	1·21
10	6·00	2·00
80	8·00	3·00
158	8·50	3·90
244	9·70	4·85
336	10·67	6·30
430	11·64	6·80
680	12·12	8·25
730	13·10	8·73
870	13·80	9·70
1100	14·50	10·67
1210	15·50	11·64
1500	16·00	12·60
1750	16·50	13·68
2200	17·00	14·06
2300	17·50	16·50
2660	18·00	17·00
2840	18·50	17·95
3220	19·00	19·50
3500	19·50	19·40

To apply the numbers in this table to wheels of other diameters, they must be multiplied by $\sqrt{R}$, R being the radius of the wheel for which the dimensions are to be calculated.

WOODEN PATTERNS.

225. When a casting has not to be turned, or otherwise reduced, about 1 per cent. must be allowed in the dimensions of the pattern, and if the piece has to be turned, a little more than this. It is, however, impossible to give any rule in this last case, as the allowance to be made depends entirely upon the nature and destination of the piece. The larger the piece, the greater should be the per centage given.

No piece can be cast with mathematical precision—whether it is, that, on the one hand, the pattern loses its true shape, and lines, which have been made perfectly straight or circular, become twisted, notwithstanding that every precaution has been taken in perfecting it; or, on the other hand, that, in lifting it from the loam, the moulder is forced to move it laterally, to some slight extent, so that the casting becomes larger at one part, or twisted at another; or, again, that the metal does not shrink equally at all parts. With regard to the last-mentioned source of error, it has often been found that the diameter of a wheel, measured through the line of the arms, is sensibly less than as measured across the centres of the spaces between the arms. This difference is indeed so great, that in wheels of 10 to 15 feet diameter, it reaches an eighth or a sixth of an inch.

It is manifest, that all these considerations must be borne in mind when constructing wooden patterns for castings; otherwise, errors of considerable magnitude will arise.

CHAPTER VI.

CONTINUATION OF THE STUDY OF TOOTHED GEAR.

CONICAL OR BEVIL GEARING.

226. Cylindrical or spur-wheels are only capable of transmitting motion between shafts which are parallel to each other; and when the shafts are inclined, or form any angle with each other, the wheels require to be made conical, and are then called bevil-wheels.

In order that this description of gear may be capable of working well and regularly, and of transmitting considerable power when needed, as with spur gear, it is essential that the shafts or axes of any pair working together be situated in the same plane; in this case, the axes will meet in a point which is the apex common to the two wheels.

Formerly, when it was required to transmit power through shafts intersecting each other at right angles, a species of lantern-wheel was employed for one of the wheels, consisting of a couple of discs with cylindrical bars for teeth, passing from one to the other parallel to the axis; and the wheel to gear with this one was formed with similar teeth, also parallel with the axis, but projecting up from a single disc or ring. This form of gearing is still to be found in old mills; but it is very defective, and very inconvenient when any speed is required.

Sometimes, as for some descriptions of spinning machinery—the cotton-spinner's fly or roving-frame, for example—bevil-wheels are used, in which the axes are not situate in the same plane; these are termed "skew bevils," from the teeth having a hyperboloidal twist in order that they may act properly on each other. This kind of wheel does not work well, and is seldom employed, except where the size is very small, or where a small power only has to be transmitted; the peculiar form of their teeth also renders them very difficult to construct. Their use is so limited, that further details respecting them are uncalled for. Indeed, they ought rather to be avoided, since there are very few cases in which common bevil-wheels cannot be substituted for them with advantage.

The teeth of bevil-wheels are made of wood or metal, similarly to spur-wheel teeth, and their geometrical forms are determined on the same principles.

DESIGN FOR A PAIR OF BEVIL-WHEELS IN GEAR.

PLATE XXII.

227. We propose, in the present example, to give the larger wheel wooden teeth, and the smaller ones cast-iron ones, as was done with the pair of spur-wheels last described.

Let A B and A C, figs. 1 and 2, be the axes of the two wheels assumed here to be at right angles to each other; though we must observe, that what follows will apply equally well to the construction of a couple of wheels, the axes of which make any angle with each other, acute or obtuse.

Let B D = ·220 m., and E F = ·440 m., the radii of the pitch circles of the two wheels. It is, in the first place, necessary to determine the position these circles should occupy on their respective axes. With this view, on any point, B, taken on the axis, A B, erect a perpendicular, B D, and make it equal to the radius of the smaller wheel, and through the extremity, D, draw a line, D L, parallel to this axis; in the same way, at any point, E, taken on the axis, A C, erect the perpendicular, E F, equal to the radius of the larger wheel, and through the extremity, F, draw F H parallel to A C. The point of intersection, G, of these two lines, F H and D L, is the point of contact of the two pitch circles, the radii of which are G I and G K. Make I H and K L, respectively, equal to the radii, and join the points, H G L, to the common apex, A, thereby determining what are termed the "pitch" cones, A H G and A G L, of the two wheels, the straight line or generatrix, A G, being the line of contact of the two cones. These pitch cones possess the same properties as the pitch circles, or, more correctly, pitch cylinders, of spur-wheels; that is to say, their rotative velocity is in the inverse ratio of their diameters, and their diameters are proportional to the respective numbers of their teeth.

The proportions of the pitch cones being thus obtained, with the centres, o and o', figs. 2 and 3, taken on the prolongation of the given axes, describe the pitch circles, A H' I' and G' K' L'. Divide these circles into as many equal parts as there should be teeth; that is to say, in the present case, 24 and 48, respectively, which operation will give the pitch; each part is then bisected to obtain the centres of the teeth and of the intervals, and on each side of the centre lines are set off the demi-widths of the teeth, regard being had to the difference to be made between the wooden and cast-iron teeth, as already explained (213).

The external contours of the teeth will be situated in cones, the generatrices of which are perpendicular to those of the pitch cones; they are obtained by drawing through the point of contact, G, on the line, A G, a perpendicular, B C, meeting the axis of the smaller wheel in B, and that of the larger one in C; the points, B and C, are the apices of the two cones, B H G and C G L.

If these last-mentioned cones be developed upon a plane, it will be easy to draw upon it the exact forms of the teeth. Now, we have seen (170) that the development of a cone on a plane surface takes the form of a sector of a circle, which has for radius the generatrix of the cone, and for arc the development of the base of the cone. As it is unnecessary to develop the entire cone in the present case, it is sufficient to describe with any point, B', fig. 4, with a radius equal to B G, an arc, a e b, on which, starting from the point, c, are divided off distances—one, c d, equal to the thickness of the tooth of the smaller wheel, fig. 3, and the other, c e, to that of the tooth of the larger wheel, fig. 2. The same operation is performed for the larger wheel; that is, with the point, c', situated on the prolongation of B' c, and with a radius equal to c G, describe the arc, f c g, on which are measured the distances, respectively, equal to the former ones, e d and c e.

This done, the outlines of the teeth are obtained by means of precisely the same operations as those explained in reference to the spur-wheels. Thus, on the radius, B' c, considered as a diameter, describe a circle, i c j, which, in rolling round the circle, f c g, considered as the pitch circle of the larger wheel, determines the epicycloid, e h, which gives the curvature of the teeth of the larger wheel; in the same manner, the circle, k e l, described on the radius, e c', as a diameter, and rolling round the circle, a c b, gives the epicycloid, c m, which is taken for the curve of the teeth of the smaller wheel. After having repeated these curves symmetrically on each side of the teeth, these are limited by drawing chords in the generating circles from the point, e, each equal to the pitch of the teeth, as c n, c k, and then with c' and B' as centres. describe circles passing, one just outside the point, n, and the other just outside the point, k; and to indicate the line of the web, describe a second couple of circles, nearly tangents to the preceding. Then project the points, o and p, which indicate the depth and extremities of the teeth, over to the line, B c, in o' and p'; through these last draw straight lines to the apex, A, which will represent the extreme generatrices of the teeth, as in vertical section.

As all the teeth converge in one point, it is obvious that the contour of the inner ends of the teeth cannot be the same as that of the outer ends; the difference is the greater, according as the width, G r, on the generatrix line of contact is itself greater, in proportion to the entire cone, and to the greater or less angle formed by the extreme generatrices.

In other respects, this contour is determined in the same manner as the first. Thus, through the point, r, is drawn the straight line, s t, perpendicular to A G, which cuts the two axes, and gives the proportions of the two cones, on the surface of which lie the contours of the inner ends of the teeth. Continuing the operation as above, portions of the cones are developed, arcs being described with the points, s' and t', as centres, and radii equal to r s and r t. The diagram, fig. 5, which is analogous to fig. 4, fully explains what further is to be done.

What has been said so far, has referred only to one tooth of each wheel. In proceeding with the execution of the design, after cutting out templates to the form of the teeth as obtained by means of them, the outline is repeated, as often as is necessary, on the external cones, the generatrices of which are B G and G C, for the outer ends of the teeth, and on the internal cones, the generatrices of which are r s and r t, for the outlines of the inner ends of the teeth. At the same time, and in order that the operation may be performed with regularity, a series of lines should be drawn through the points, o, p, of the two wheels, lying on the surface of the external cones, A H G, A G L, and uniting at the apex, A, by means of a "false square," of a form analogous to that represented at x, in fig. 3, Plate XXIII., for the smaller wheel, and like that represented at T, fig. 4, of the same Plate, for the larger wheel.

The forms of the teeth being thus obtained, the partial section, fig. 1, of the two wheels is drawn, the radii of the shafts being given, as well as the thickness of the bosses and webs, the proportions employed in the present example being indicated on the drawings. It will be observed that those teeth which are of wood are adjusted in the web of the larger wheel, in the same manner as in the spur or cylindrical wheels, the forms of the tenons being modified, so that their sides all incline to the common apex, A

The sections, together with the developments, figs. 4 and 5, are sufficient for the purposes of construction, as all the required measurements can be obtained from them; but when it is desired to produce a complete external elevation of the two wheels, it will be necessary to find the projections of the teeth and other parts. With this view, the teeth are first actually drawn upon the planes of projection parallel to the bases of the wheels, as shown in figs. 2 and 3. It will be recollected, that divisions have already been made on the pitch circles, A H' I', and L' K' G', indicating the centre lines, as well of the teeth as of the intervals, and marking the positions of the flanks; and, consequently, all that remains is to draw the external outlines and the curved portions. For the smaller wheel, the operation consists in projecting to p', in fig. 3, the point, p, fig. 1, which limits the lower and outer edge of the tooth, and in describing with the centre, o, and radius, o p', a circle limiting the whole of the teeth externally, and corresponding to the section of the cone in which the points, p p', fig. 1, lie. In this circle, also, terminate the curves of the outer portions of the teeth, and their exact points of intersection are obtained by measuring on each side of the centre lines, v o, distances, v u, v p, equal to the corresponding distances, v' u', v' p', in fig. 4. Then, through the points. u, p, draw a series of lines, converging to the centre, o; and through the points, e, e, found in a similar manner, draw similarly converging lines, indicating the inner angles of the intervals. Further, find the circular arc to represent the epicycloidal curve, passing through the points, u, p, and tangential at the same time to the lines, o e, at the points, e, e.

The method of doing this is shown in fig. 3: it consists in drawing through the point, e, a line, e z, at right angles to the radius, o e, and in bisecting the chord, e u, by a perpendicular cutting, e z in z, which will be the centre of the required arc. Arcs of the same radius, e z, are employed for the curves of all the teeth on the smaller wheel, and the outline of these is completed by determining, in a similar manner, the arcs for the corresponding curved portions of the inner ends of the teeth, after having projected and drawn circles through the points corresponding to r and p², of fig. 1. Finally, the lines of the web between the teeth—that is, the bottom lines of the intervals—are drawn, the projections of the points, y and y', being found, and circles described with the centre, o, passing through them. It will be observed that, on a portion of fig. 3, is represented a view of a quarter of the lower and inner side of the wheel, whilst the other portion of the figure is an external view, showing the teeth as in plan; in the former case, the outline resembles that of a spur-wheel, for, as it is the larger ends of the teeth and web on which we are looking, the narrower and inclined portions are hid behind.

The lateral projection of the teeth of the small wheel, fig. 1, is obtained, first, by successively projecting or squaring over, from the plan, fig. 3, the points, e, e, to the pitch line, G H; and secondly, by similarly squaring over the points, p p, to the external line, p p'. Through the points, e, e, draw a series of lines converging at the apex, B, and representing the flanks of the teeth, and limited by the line, y y; then draw curves tangential to these flanks at the points, u, p, making them pass through the extreme points, e, e. Where the scale of the drawing is very large, and it is wished to be particularly precise in delineating these curves,

points intermediate between u, p, and e, e, may be obtained by describing intermediate circles in fig. 3, representing sections of the cone, projected in straight lines in fig. 1, over to which are projected the points of intersection of the curves, with the circles in fig. 3. Through the points, u p, draw straight lines, converging in the apex, A, and find the lateral projection of the inner ends of the teeth, supposing planes to pass through the points, r, y' and p²; these points in the circular projection of the planes, fig. 3, being squared over to the corresponding rectilinear projections in fig. 1. The inner ends of the teeth are then completed by drawing the flanks, e', y', all converging in the apex, s, and joined by arcs passing through the points, e', p'.

The upper left-hand quadrant, M, of fig. 2, is a face view of the teeth of the larger bevil-wheel, with wooden teeth, the whole being drawn in the same manner as in fig. 3. The method of finding the centre, z, of the arc, which is substituted for the curved portion of each tooth, is shown in fig. 2ª. From this view (fig. 2) are obtained the various points required to produce the lateral projection of the teeth in fig. 1. The operations are precisely the same as those just described in reference to fig. 3, and the smaller wheel; the same distinguishing letters are also used to point out the similarity.

The same figure (2) also comprehends at N a second quadrant of the wheel, drawn as seen from the under side, so as to show a face view of the tenons of the wooden teeth, the sides of which all converge in the point, o'. A third quadrant, P, gives a view of the outer side of the web or crown, the teeth being supposed to be removed, so that the mortises are seen. The last quadrant, R, gives a back view of the web, also without the teeth.

Fig. 6 is a section of one of the arms of the larger bevil-wheel, made through the line, 1—2, in fig. 2. Fig. 7 is a section of the web made through the line, 3—4, fig. 2, passing through the centre of the mortise; and fig. 8 comprehends a lateral projection and two end views of one of the wooden teeth.

Bevil, as well as spur-wheels, are fixed on their shafts by means of keys, and pressure screws, v, are often added to insure their perfect adjustment centrally.

The measurements given in the diagrams will enable the student to form an accurate idea of the actual proportions of the various parts.

THE CONSTRUCTION OF WOODEN PATTERNS FOR A PAIR OF BEVIL-WHEELS.

PLATE XXIII.

228. The observations we have already made with reference to the patterns of spur-wheels, are evidently equally applicable to the construction of patterns for bevil-wheels; still, at the same time, the difference in the form of the latter calls for further details, more especially appertaining to them.

PATTERN OF THE SMALLER BEVIL-WHEEL.

229. Figs. 1 and 2 represent the two projections of the pattern of the smaller of the two wheels in the preceding Plate. Fig. 3 is a vertical section through the line, 1—2, of fig. 2, showing on one side the layers of wood put roughly together, and intended to

form the crown; and on the other, a view of the same as finished, with the arm and its feathers.

It will be seen from these figures that the crown is built up in the same manner as that of the pinion in Plate XXI.; the layers of wood are, however, in steps, increasing in diameter downwards, so as to give the required conical form when turned. When these pieces are glued together, the whole is turned externally and internally in such a manner as to conform exactly to the full-sized drawing, previously made on a board planed smooth for the purpose. "Squares," also, should be made from the drawings, to serve as guides in producing the correct conical inclination.

After turning the top face, b' b', perpendicular to the axis of the cone, the pattern-maker proceeds to turn the external conical surface, a' b', of the web or crown. As a guide in doing this, he takes a "false square," T, fig. 4, of which one side, b b, corresponds to the plane face, b' b', and the other, a b, to the inclination of the conical generatrix, a' b': it is very easy with this to take off just as much of the wood as is necessary, without the liability of going too far. It is also necessary to determine the inclination of the generatrix, B a', of the outer cone, perpendicular, it will be recollected, to the contact generatrix, G r, by means of the square, x, fig. 3, the side, a b, of which is applied exactly to the conical surface, a' b', and the side, a c, then gives the inclination of the conical surface, a' c'; and the same square being turned round will give the inclination of the internal conical surface, b' d', the generatrix of this, the smaller cone, being s r, parallel to B G, that of the larger one.

Finally, the thickness at a' c' and b' d', is measured on the wooden web, so as to obtain the proportions of the internal conical surface, c' d', to be turned out in a similar manner.

Mortises have now to be cut in the crown to receive the ends of the arms, c, and their feathers, E. As the wheel under consideration is of very small diameter, the number of arms is limited to four; these arms are so placed inside the crown that the feathers are all on one side, and towards the wider end of the cone. Their attachment to the web is by means of a circular groove or mortise, seen at e' f', fig. 2, and at g' d', fig. 3, and they are united at the centre to each other and to the boss, in the same manner as the arms of the pinion, described in reference to Plate XXI. The arms are not placed in the middle of the boss, as in the spur-wheel and pinion, but are simply applied to the base of the boss, which may, consequently, be of a single piece; and the feathers are let into a groove extending their whole length, and are fixed into the boss and crown at either extremity. The boss is slightly coned, so as to give the "draw" necessary in the construction of the mould. Its outer edges are indicated by the lines, m n, m n, whilst the other lines, o p, which are, on the contrary, parallel to the axis, show the depth of the grooves cut to receive the feathers of the arm. These last, as shown in the section, fig. 10, are thicker near the arms.

The core pieces, E, are added on either end of the boss, and the whole is held firmly together by means of a central bolt.

The pattern being so far advanced, the external conical surface is divided into as many equal parts as there are to be teeth and intervals, and, with the assistance of the "false square," T, lines which represent generatrices of the cone, are drawn through the

points of division, to indicate the positions of the teeth or of the grooves to receive them.

Each tooth is cut out separately according to the full-size drawing made, as already mentioned, which, besides containing the vertical section, fig. 3, should also show the exact form of each end of the tooth, B', and of the dovetail joint attaching them to the web. Fig. 5 shows a portion of this drawing for the larger ends of the teeth.

PATTERN OF THE LARGER BEVIL WHEEL.

230. Figs. 6 and 7 represent the elevation and plan of the pattern of the larger bevil wheel, with wooden teeth, represented in Plate XXII. Fig. 8 is a vertical section through the axis of the wheel, showing on one side the arrangement of the pieces of wood built up upon one another, and forming the crown, A, and on the other side, the same piece, turned and finished, attached by the arm, c, to the boss, D.

Fig. 9 represents the false square, T, employed as a guide for giving the proper inclination to the external conical surface, a' b', of the crown.

Fig. 11 is a transverse section of one of the arms, or spokes, taken through the line 7—8 in fig. 7.

Whatever explanations are called for regarding the construction of the crown, A, the arms, c, and the boss, D, as well as the uniting of these parts with each other, have already been given in reference to preceding examples. We have distinguished all corresponding parts and working lines by the same letters.

The only difference between this last and the preceding example consists in the disposition of the tooth pieces, B', placed on the outside of the crown, to form the sockets in the mould for receiving the core pieces for the mortises, into which the wooden teeth are to be fixed after the piece is cast.

It must be observed, in the first place, that these projections must be shaped so that the end, k l, is inclined to the surface, b' a', instead of being perpendicular to it. This inclination must be sufficient to allow of the easy disengagement of the piece from the mould. This disposition is necessary, because the lower half of the mould takes the impression of the outside of the crown, with the tooth pieces and the upper portions of the arms, whilst the top part of the mould takes the inside of the crown, the feathers of the arms, and the boss, the position of the whole being the reverse of that in which they are represented in the drawing.

The core pieces for the teeth are formed by the moulder in core boxes, similar to those described in reference to figs. 10 and 11, Plate XXI., which we have reproduced in Plate XXIII., figs. 12, 13, and 14, as modified to suit the different form of tooth. Fig. 12 is a face view, and figs. 13 and 14 are sections made through the lines 9—10 and 11—12 of fig. 12. It will be observed that, at the larger end of the tooth, the part to project is formed with an inclination corresponding to k l, in fig. 7, already referred to as required in this case.

The operations called for in delineating these patterns are all fully indicated, and are analogous to those in the preceding plates. The observations, also (149 and 214), already made, with reference to calculating the allowance to be made for shrinking, and for the turning and finishing processes, are equally applicable to the case before us.

INVOLUTE AND HELICAL TEETH.

PLATE XXIV.

DELINEATION OF A COUPLE OF SPUR-WHEELS WITH INVOLUTE TEETH.

FIGURES 1 AND 2.

231. In the various systems of gearing just discussed, wherein epicycloidal teeth have been employed, it will have been observed—

1st. That the outline of the teeth of one wheel depends on the diameter of the other wheel with which it is in gear.

2d. That the distance between the centres of any couple of wheels cannot be altered in the slightest degree without deteriorating the movement.

3d. That the distance from the respective centres of the point of contact varies throughout the duration of the contact; from which must obviously result irregularity in the action and inequality in the amount of friction.

The practical defects arising from these causes have induced a search after other forms, and amongst these a modification of the involute has been tried. The form in question possesses the following advantages :—

1st. The form of the teeth of such a wheel is quite independent of the diameter of the wheel with which it is to gear.

2d. The distance between the centres of the wheels may be varied without disadvantage.

Some authors also attribute to this form the property of transmitting the pressure uniformly throughout the duration of the contact. This, however, cannot be the case altogether, for the distance of the point of contact from the centres of the wheels is constantly varying—the variation not being accurately proportional in the two wheels. This system of gearing is constructed on the following principles :—

Let the centres, o and o', fig. 1, of the two wheels be given, and the radii, o A and A o', of the respective pitch circles; also, let o B be the radius of any circle described with the centre, o ; to the circumference of this last draw a tangent, A B, passing through the point, A, and prolong it indefinitely in either direction. From the centre, o', let fall on this line a perpendicular, o' c, on which will accordingly be the radius of a second circle tangent to the same line. These circles of the radii, o B and o' c, are those from which are derived the involute curves, a b and c d, forming the outline of the teeth. For the rest, the wheels are drawn just as in Plate XVIII. (197.)

It must be observed that the curve, a b, which is the involute of the circle of the radius, o B, is that for the tooth of the spur-wheel, the centre of which is the same, and the radius, o A ; and, in like manner, the curve, c d, the involute of the smaller circle, is that for the teeth of the pinion of the radius, o' A. It thus follows that the form of the teeth of the spur-wheel is quite independent of the diameter of the pinion, whilst that of the pinion teeth is independent of the diameter of the spur-wheel. From which it follows, that wheels constructed in this manner may be set to gear with any wheels whose teeth are formed on the same principle, and whose pitch is the same, whatever may be their respective diameters. The epicycloidal system does not admit of this,

although, when the wheels are large, and there is not much difference between their diameters, a slight deviation from strict mathematical proportions is not found practically inconvenient.

The involute curves, a b and c d, are repeated symmetrically on either side of the division lines representing the centre lines of the teeth. If we now suppose the two involutes, A b' and A c', to be in contact at the point, A, on the line of centres, o o', and we measure off on the common tangent, A B, a distance, A e, equal to the pitch, f g, as measured at the pitch circle, and then, with the centre, o', describe a circle passing through the point, e, this circle will be the external limit of the pinion teeth.

In like manner, if, on the other portion, A c, of the tangent, we measure a distance, A e', also equal to the pitch, f g, and with the centre, o, describe a circle passing through the point, e', it will be the limit of the spur-wheel teeth. It is further obvious, that circles passing a little within the point, e', on the one hand, and e, on the other, will determine the depth of the intervals, or the line of the web of the pinion and spur-wheel respectively.

Fig. 3 is a diagram to show—first, how that the point of contact of the two involute curves is always in the line of the common tangent, B c. Thus, referring again to fig. 1, and supposing the pinion to turn in the direction of the arrows, the point of contact, as A of the involute, A b, is gradually removed away from the centre, o', of the pinion, whilst it approaches nearer and nearer to the centre, o, of the spur-wheel. Returning to fig. 3, it is shown, in the second place, that the distance between the two centres, o, o', may be varied without its being necessary to alter the curves ; but, in such case, the inclination of the tangent will be different, becoming, for example, as B c', when the two centres are brought nearer together.

In practice, instead of determining the radius, o B, arbitrarily, and then deriving the other radius, o c, from it, or vice versâ, the circles which serve for generating the involutes may be found, as well as the inclination of the tangent, by the following method :—On one of the pitch circles, that of the pinion, for example, take an arc, A i, equal to the pitch of the teeth; draw the radius, o' i, and on it let fall a perpendicular, A m, from the point, A ; o m then be the radius of the generating circle for the involute curve of the teeth of the pinion, and by prolonging m A to n, which is, in fact, the common tangent, and drawing the radius, o n, perpendicular to it, or, what is the same thing, parallel to o' m, o n will be the radius of the generating circle for the involute of the teeth of the spur-wheel.

If this rule is applied to wheels of large diameters, it will give curves differing very slightly from epicycloids.

By taking for the generating circles, as in the first case, radii, o B and o' c, sensibly less than the radii of the pitch circles, the inclination of the common tangent to the line joining the centres is greater, and the resulting form of tooth possesses greater proportionate width and strength at the roots, which is desirable for gearing intended to transmit great or irregular strains.

It will be observed further, that, according to this system, the rectilinear portion of the flank of the tooth is almost reduced to nothing, indeed the curve may be continued down to the line of the web with advantage, as the tooth will, in consequence, be much stronger near the web, which is not the case with the epicycloidal teeth, for in these the flanks all converge towards the centre of the wheel, and the tooth is, in consequence, narrower at the neck, close to the web, than at the pitch circle.

Fig. 2 is a fully shaded elevation, or vertical projection of the spur-wheel separated from the pinion. The portions of these wheels not particularly referred to, are constructed on the same general principles as those previously discussed.

HELICAL GEARING.

FIGURES 4 AND 5.

232. If to a worm-wheel we apply, instead of a worm, a pinion with teeth helically inclined to correspond to the similarly inclined teeth of the worm-wheel, we shall have a spur-wheel and pinion constructed on the helical principle.

This system, invented in the seventeenth century by Hooke, but reproduced since by White and others, claims to possess two properties which have been often thought to be incompatible with each other—namely, uniformity of angular velocity, and freedom from other than rolling friction between the teeth. In other words, the arcs described by driver and follower will be equal in equal times, and the contact between the teeth will resemble that of circles rolling on planes.

Added to these properties, and consequent to them, are the advantages of a constant contact, and of an insusceptibility to the play between the teeth, which invariably exists more or less palpably in gearing constructed according to the systems before described.

The form of the helical teeth, as taken in a sectional plane at right angles to the axis of the wheel, may be derived either from a couple of epicycloids, or a couple of involutes; it is only the sides which, in common spur-gearing, are parallel to the axis that here follow the inclination of a succession of helices coming in contact one after the other. The arrangement is such that the contact of each tooth commences at one side of the wheel and crosses over to the other, and does not cease until the following tooth shall have commenced a fresh contact.

The helicoidal system may be applied either to wheels having their axes parallel, as spur-wheels, or intersecting, as bevil-wheels, or again inclined, but not intersecting, as skew bevils.

In figs. 4 and 5 are represented, in face and edge view, a spur-wheel and pinion, constructed according to this system of Hooke's, this being its simplest and most common application:—Let A o and A' o be the radii of the respective pitch circles of the two wheels, these radii being, of course, in the same ratio as the numbers of the teeth, as in common gearing. The radii are supposed to lie in a vertical plane, B' C', and it is on this plane, as turned at right angles, that the operations represented in fig. 4 are supposed to be performed.

These operations have for their object the obtainment of the outline of the teeth, and are precisely the same as for any other epicycloidal system of gearing. Thus, the curves, A b and A c, are derived from the generating circles, O D A and A D' O', as also the flanks, A d and A e; but it is unnecessary to repeat a detailed explanation of the proceeding.

Supposing, then, the outline of the teeth to be drawn as on the

plane, B' C', representing say the anterior face or base of the wheels, next draw the line, E F, (fig. 5,) representing the opposite face, and parallel to the first, limiting also the breadth of the wheels.

To proceed methodically, the teeth should also be drawn as seen on this plane, E F being behind the outlines of the anterior ends of the teeth, a distance equal to A A', or rather more than the pitch. These last outlines need only be represented in faint dotted or pencil lines in fig. 4, as the parts they represent are not actually seen in that view when complete. Thus, starting from the point, A', on the pitch circle of the spur-wheel, and from the point, G', on the pitch circle of the pinion, we repeat the contours of the teeth, as obtained at e A i and d A n, respectively.

As the result of this disposition, it will be observed, that if the curve, A i, of the tooth, A, of the spur-wheel is in contact, at the pitch circle, with the flank, G d, of the tooth, G, of the pinion at the anterior face, B' C', and if the wheels be made to turn to a certain extent in the direction of the arrows, the curve, A' i', on the opposite face, E F, will in time be found to be in contact with the corresponding flank, G' d', of the pinion. In other words, if the space between the curves, A i and A' i', be filled up by a helicoidal surface, as also the space between the flanks, G d and G' d', all the points of one such surface will be in contact successively with the corresponding points on the other; so that when, for example, the curve A i', shall have reached the position, A² i''; that is, when it shall have passed through a distance equal to A A', the posterior curve, A' i, will have assumed the position held originally by A i; or rather, a position directly behind this in the plane passing through the axis, and the point of contact between A' i' and G' d' will then obviously be in the line of centres, O O'. It thus follows, that any two teeth which act on each other will be constantly in contact on the line of centres throughout a space equal to A A'. This space, A A', is, as before stated, somewhat greater than the pitch of the teeth, so as to allow a following couple of teeth to act on each other, and be in contact on the line of centres before the couple in advance shall be quite free, and thus a constant contact on the line of centres is preserved throughout the entire revolution.

In order to delineate the lateral projection, fig. 5, it will be necessary to find the curves which form the outline of the helicoidal surfaces of the teeth. The principle, according to which this is to be done, is precisely what has already been explained (208). In the present case, however, as we have but fragments of helices to draw, in place of finding the pitch of the helix, and then dividing it and the circumference proportionately, it will be sufficient to divide the width, B' E, of the wheels, into a certain number of equal parts; and through the points of division, to draw lines parallel to B' C'. Further, the arcs, A A', e e', i i', must be divided into a like number of equal parts.

To render the diagram clearer, these divisions are transferred to 1, 2, 3, 4, &c., and 1', 2', 3', 4', &c. (fig. 4.) Each point, 1, 2, 3, 4, being squared over, in succession, to the corresponding lines in fig. 5—namely, the lines of division first obtained, and lying parallel to the faces of the wheels, the operation will give the curve, 1, 3, 5, 6, (fig. 5,) corresponding to the outline of the external edge, extending from i to i'. The curve, 1', 3', 5', 6', similarly gives the other edge. It is also obvious that the line of junction of the tooth with the web will be represented by the helical curve, $a\,a'$, (fig. 5), having the same pitch as the last, but lying on a cylinder of a somewhat smaller diameter.

The lateral projections of all the teeth are determined in the same manner, but they will, of course, assume various aspects, from the different positions in which they lie with respect to the vertical plane.

233. In construction, in order to determine the exact inclination of the teeth, the following proportional formula is employed. The four terms of the formula being, the radius of the wheel, its width, the given circumferential distance, corresponding to A A', and the pitch of the helix; that is, A A' : A O :: B' E : x, x being the helical pitch for the spur-wheel, or the quantity sought. It may be obtained geometrically, simply thus :—Make the straight line, M N, (fig. 6,) equal to the arc, A A', as developed; at the extremity, N, of this line, erect a perpendicular, N L, equal to the width, B' E, of the wheels; join L M, which will give the mean inclination of the tooth, corresponding to the pitch circle. Then make N I equal to the arc $i\,i'$, rectified, and N J equal to the arc, $e\,e'$, rectified, which will give the inclinations, L I and L J, of the helices, passing through the extremity, i, of the tooth, and the line, e, of junction of the tooth to the web.

It will be understood that the helices of the pinion-teeth will have the same inclination as those of the spur-wheel teeth, with which it is in gear, and the helical pitch is, in consequence, different; for, the radius is smaller, and the corresponding proportional formula becomes A A' or A G' : A O' :: B' E : x.

The motion of wheel-work, constructed according to the helical system, is remarkably smooth, and free from vibratory action, but it has the defect of producing a longitudinal pressure upon the axes, from the obliquity of the surfaces of contact to the plane of rotation. This, however, may be obviated, and the longitudinal action balanced, by making the wheels duplex; that is, as if two wheels, on each axis, were joined together—the inclination of the helices being in contrary directions, or right and left handed. Such wheels, though duplex, need not be wider or thicker, in proportion, than simple ones; for the arrangement would permit of a much greater obliquity of the teeth, the only limit, indeed, to the degree being the tendency to jam, which would arise were the inclination very great.

When the wheels are placed on axes which are inclined to each other, as in common bevil-wheels, the helices become such as are described upon conical surfaces, and require to be drawn in the manner already shown (174), the form of the tooth being previously determined, for each end, by means of the developed planes of the opposite faces of the wheels.

Besides the epicycloid and involute and their various combinations, other and more complex curves have at different times been proposed for the forms of wheel teeth. The most worthy of notice amongst these is that derived from the "hour-glass" curve, the properties of which have lately been investigated in a very scientific manner by Professor Sang of the Imperial School at Constantinople.

If a couple of discs, with their pitch circles touching, be made to revolve at a rate proportionate to the required number of teeth in each, a point may be imagined as travelling along a curve, returning upon itself in such a manner that it will describe the forms of the respective teeth on each disc. In the system of teeth alluded to, this point is made to travel along the "hour-glass" curve, a curve similar to that described by the piston-rod attachment in Watt's parallel motion, and also exhibited by the vibration of a straight wire, whose breadth is double its thickness. The form of tooth obtained in this manner is demonstrated by its inventor to be theoretically superior to all others yet known. The chief advantage appears to be, that whilst according to the epicycloidal and involute systems, the form of the entire tooth is made up of two curves of different natures, whose junction cannot, in consequence, be perfectly smooth or fluent, the point of inflexion or passage from one curve to the other, occurring, moreover, precisely where the best action would otherwise be. The "hour-glass" curve produces one continuous analytic curve for the entire outline of the wheel, thereby avoiding all sudden transitions, such outline, at the same time, allowing of the interchange, in any way, of wheels of the same pitch.

The great exactness and nicety obtainable by and called for in the construction of teeth on this system, is, however, far beyond the requirements of ordinary machinery. Indeed the practical engineer and machinist will not be at the trouble of employing even epicycloidal or involute curves, but contents himself with arcs of circles approximating pretty nearly to these curves. The method generally pursued in determining the best proportions for the radii of these substitutive arcs is as follows: A pair of templets or thin boards are cut to the curvature of the pitch circle and generating circle, respectively, of the wheel, the shape of whose teeth is sought. The generating templet carries a point which is made to describe the outline of the tooth on an additional board, by rolling its edge on that of the pitch templet. The operator then finds by trial with a pair of compasses, a centre and radius which will give an arc agreeing as nearly as possible with the curve traced by the templet. Through the centre thus found he describes a circle concentric with the pitch circle, and in which the centres for the arcs of all the teeth will obviously lie, and retaining the radius, he steps from tooth to tooth in both directions, until all the teeth are marked out.

A very ingenious and useful scale was invented some years ago by Professor Willis, which renders unnecessary this preliminary operation for obtaining the radii and centres. This scale, termed the "Odontograph," is now largely employed, and is found to give very excellent forms of teeth. Its application is very convenient. A graduated side of the instrument has a certain inclination to another, which is first made to coincide with a radius of the wheel, whilst its point of intersection with the first is placed in the pitch circle. The graduated side gives the direction in which the centres lie, whilst the lengths of the radii are obtained from tables calculated for the purpose, indicating the respective distances on the graduated scale, and corresponding to the given pitch and number of teeth.

Wheels with teeth formed according to this scale are capable of being interchanged, which is not the case with those in which the arcs are determined according to other rules.

After going through the explanations given, and rules laid down in the last few sections, the student should be quite competent to design practical arrangements and combinations of toothed gear according to whichever of the systems may be preferred.

CONTRIVANCES FOR OBTAINING DIFFERENTIAL MOVEMENTS.

THE DELINEATION OF ECCENTRICS AND CAMS.

PLATE XXV.

234. Eccentrics and cams are employed to convert motion, whilst toothed-wheel work is for the simple transmission of it.

Endued themselves with a continuous circular movement, they are so constructed as to give to what they act upon, an alternate rectilinear movement, or an alternate circular movement, as the case may be, the motion so produced being obtainable in any desired direction.

CIRCULAR ECCENTRIC.

235. There are several descriptions of eccentrics. The simplest and most generally employed, consists of a circular disc, completely filled up, or open and with arms, according to its size, and made to turn in a uniform manner, being fixed on a shaft which does not pass through its centre. Such eccentrics are represented in Plate XXXIX.

The stroke of such a piece of mechanism is always equal to twice the distance of its centre from that of the shaft on which it turns; that is to say, to the diameter of the circle described by its centre during a revolution of the shaft. The motion of the piece acted upon is uninterrupted during either back or forward stroke, but is not uniform throughout the stroke, although that of the actuating shaft is so; the velocity, in fact, increasing during the first half of the stroke, and decreasing during the second half.

HEART-SHAPED CAM.

FIGURE 1.

236. When it is required to produce an alternate rectilinear motion which shall be uniform throughout the stroke, the shape of the eccentric or cam is no longer circular; it is differentially curved, and its outline may always be determined geometrically when the length of the stroke is known, together with the radius of the cam, or the distance of its centre from the nearest point of contact.

An example of this form of cam is represented in the figure.

Let $a\ a'$ be the rectilinear distance to be traversed, and o, the centre of the shaft on which the cam is fixed, it is required to make the point, a, advance to the point, a', in a uniform manner during a semi-revolution of the shaft, and to return it to its original position in the same manner during a second semi-revolution.

With the centre, o, and radii, $o\ a$, and $o\ a'$, describe a couple of circles, and divide them into a certain number of equal parts by radii passing through the points, 1, 2, 3, 4, &c. Also divide the length, $a\ a'$, into half as many equal parts as the circles, as in the points, 1', 2', 3', &c. Describe circles passing through these points, and concentric with the first. These circles will successively intersect the radii, o 1, o 2, o 3, &c., in the points, b, c, d, e, &c., and the continuous curve passing through these points will

be the theoretical outline of the cam, which will cause the point, a, to traverse to a', in a uniform manner, for the equal distances, a' 1', 1' 2', 2' 3', &c., passed through by the point, a, correspond in succession to the equal angular spaces, a' 1, 1—2, 2—3, &c., passed through by the cam during its rotation.

As it is not possible to employ a mathematical point in practice, it is usually replaced by a friction roller of the radius, $a\ i$, which has its centre constantly where the point should be; and it will be seen, that in order that this centre may be made to travel along the path already determined, it will be necessary to modify the cam, and this is done in the following manner :—With each of the points, b, c, d, &c., on the primitive curve as a centre, describe a series of arcs of the radius, $a\ i$, of the roller, and draw a curve tangent to these, and such curve will be the actual outline to be given to the cam, B.

It will be seen from the drawing, that the curve is symmetrical, with reference to the line, $a\ e$, which passes through its centre; in other words, the first half which pushes the roller, and consequently the rod, A, to the end of which the roller is fitted, from a to a', is precisely the same as the second half, with which the roller keeps in contact during the descent of the rod from a' to a. Thus the regular and continuous rotation of the cam, B, produces a uniform alternate movement of the roller, and its rod, A, which is maintained in a vertical position by suitable guides.

In actual construction, such a cam is made open, and with one or more arms, like a common wheel, or filled up, and consisting of a simple disc, according to its dimensions; and it has a boss, by means of which it is fixed on the shaft. When it is made open, it is cast with a crown, of equal thickness all round, and strengthened by an internal feather, curved into the boss at one side, and into the arm or arms at the other.

Examples of the heart-shaped cam are found in an endless variety of machines, and particularly in spinning machinery.

CAM FOR PRODUCING A UNIFORM AND INTERMITTENT MOVEMENT.

FIGURES 2 AND 3.

In certain machines, as, for example, in looms for the "picking motion," cases occur where it is necessary to produce a uniform rectilinear and alternate motion, but with a pause at each extremity of the stroke. The duration of the pause may be equal to, or greater, or less, than that of the action. Fig. 2 represents the plan of a cam designed to produce a movement of this description; and in this case the angular space passed through by the cam, in making the point, a, traverse to the position, a', is supposed to be equal to half the angular space described by it, whilst the point, a, is stationary, whether in its position nearest to the centre, or its furthest, a', from it. For this reason, the circles of the radii, $o\ a$, and $o\ a'$ are each divided into six equal parts in the points, a', 1, f, g, h, and j. Of these portions, the two opposite, 1 f and $j\ h$, correspond to the eccentric curves, $b\ f$ and $l\ h$, which produce the movement, whilst the other portions correspond to the pauses.

After having drawn the diameters, 1 h, and $f\ j$, the eccentric curves, $b\ f$, and $l\ h$, are determined in precisely the same manner as the continuous curve already discussed, and represented in fig. 1. That is to say, the arcs 1 f, and $j\ h$, are to be divided into a certain number of equal parts by radial lines; and the line, $a\,a'$, being divided into a like number of equal parts in the points, 2′, 3′, 4′, &c., concentric circles are to be drawn through these points, which will be intersected in the points, c, d, e, by the radial division lines. Lines passing through these points of intersection will be the curves sought, $b\,f$, and $l\,h$.

The arcs, $b\,a\,l$, and $f\,g\,h$, which unite the extremities of the curves, are concentric with the shaft, and consequently, as long as the point remains in contact with these arcs, it will continue without motion, although the cam itself continue its rotation.

The observation made with reference to the preceding example of a cam, applies equally to the one, c, under consideration—that is, with regard to the actual shape to be given to it, which is derived from the substitution of a friction roller of the radius, $a\,i$, for the mathematical point, a. The operation is fully indicated on the diagram.

This eccentric not being intended to overcome any great resistance, is made very light, a considerable portion of the metal being cut away, and merely a couple of arms left for stiffness. The crown, arms, and a great part of the boss, are, in fact, all of a thickness, as will be more plainly seen in fig. 3, which is simply a section made through the line, 1—2, in fig. 2. Fig. 3 also shows the proportions of the roller, and its spindle.

When the moving point, or the roller, is constrained to move through an arc, instead of a straight line, being, for example, at the end of a vibratory lever, the curves of the cam are no longer symmetrical, but the operations by which they are determined are still the same, the difference arising from the divisions of the arc, which takes the place of the straight line, $a\,a'$.

TRIANGULAR CAM.
FIGURES 4 AND 5.

238. A species of cam, in the form of a curvilinear equilateral triangle, is sometimes employed in the steam-engine, to give motion to the slide valve. This valve is generally of cast-iron, of a rectangular form, as at T, figs. A and B. It is hollowed out in its inner side, to form a passage, and it applies itself, with its inner planed edges, to a surface, $a\,b$, on the cylinder, D, also planed true, and called the valve face. Its function is to allow the steam to pass alternately to the upper part of the cylinder, by the port, c, or to the lower part, by the port, d, whilst the hollow part of the valve forms a communication alternately between either of these ports, c, d, with the escape pipe, E. To obtain the desired effect, it is necessary that the slide valve be actuated with an alternate rectilinear reciprocatory movement; for this purpose it is attached to a vertical rod, t, passing through a stuffing-box in the valve casing, and connected to the rod, u, represented in fig. C, and forming one piece, with the rectangular frame, F, inside, which works the triangular cam, G.

It is the last piece which has to effect the raising and lowering of the valve a certain distance and intermittently, in such a manner that the port, c, for example, may be open to the entering steam for a certain time, whilst the other, d, is in communication with the escape pipe, and reciprocally.

Let $o\,e$, fig. 4, be the whole stroke of the valve, or the distance through which it traverses; with the centre, o, and with this

distance, $o\,e$, for a radius, describe a circle, and divide it into six equal parts, in the points e, 1, 2, 3, 4, and 5. With any two adjacent points, as 1 and 2, and with the same radius, $o\,e$, describe two arcs, $o\,2$, and $o\,1$, so as to form the curvilinear triangle, o—1—2, which is exactly the outline of the eccentric, G, each side of which is equal to a sixth of the circumference.

Draw the parallels, 5—1 and 4—2, tangential to the two sides of the triangle, G, and we shall thus obtain the upper and lower internal surface of the frame, F.

The cam is made of steel, as well as the two sides of the frame, F, which bear upon it. It is adjusted and secured by the screwbolt, h, to the disc, H, keyed on the shaft, J, as shown in the horizontal section, fig. 5, taken through the line, 3—4, in fig. 4.

It will be easily conceived, that if the shaft turns in the direction of the arrow, the curved side, $o\,1$, of the cam, acting against the upper side of the frame, will cause it to rise, carrying with it the rod, u, in such a manner, that when the point, 1, shall have reached the position, e; that is, when the cam shall have made a sixth of a revolution, this side of the frame will occupy the position, $m\,n$, thereby indicating that the slide-valve has been elevated to a distance equal to half $o\,e$, and that, in consequence, the port, d, is uncovered, so as to allow the steam to enter the lower part of the cylinder (fig. B); whilst, on the other hand, a communication is established between the upper port, c, and the escape orifice, E, so that the steam can pass out from the upper end of the cylinder. If the movement of the cam be continued during a second sixth of a revolution, the slide-valve will remain in the same position, because the arc, 1—2, which is concentric with the axis, does not change the position of the frame, as long as it is in contact with its side, $m\,n$. As soon, however, as the point, 2, of the cam reaches the position, e, the side, $o\,1$, will be in the position, $o\,5$, and it will, in consequence, be in contact with the lower side of the frame, which is in the position of the horizontal centre-line, 3—4. The further revolution of the cam, therefore, makes the frame descend from its pressure on the lower side, until the side, $o\,1$, of the cam, occupies the position, $o\,3$, when the lower side of the frame will occupy the position, $m'\,n'$, corresponding to the position of the valve, represented in fig. B.

It follows from this arrangement, that the valve will remain stationary when it arrives at each extremity of its stroke, and the pause each time will be of a duration corresponding to one-sixth of a revolution of the cam shaft. The upward and downward movements each take place during a third of a revolution, and the velocity of the valve will not be uniform, although the rotation of the cam-shaft is so. In actual construction, the angles of the cam are slightly rounded off, to avoid a too sudden change of motion, and to prevent the too rapid wear of the sides of the frame.

INVOLUTE CAM.
FIGURES 6 AND 7.

239. In certain industrial arts, an instrument is employed for pounding, crushing, and reducing substances, such as plaster or tanbark, for example, in which the direct-acting force is the weight of the instrument itself brought into play by its descent through a determined height. The mechanical forge-hammer is a well known working application of this expedient.

In these cases, the stamp, or hammer, has to be raised or tilted up preparatory to each succeeding stroke, and it is obvious that this may be most economically done in a gradual manner. It is generally effected by a cam, the outline of which is the involute curve already described; this form being preferable on account of the uniformity of its action.

The office, then, which the cam under consideration has to fulfil, is the raising of the stamp, or load, to a certain height, and then the letting it fall, without impediment, upon the object submitted to its action.

The diameter of the cam-shaft being predetermined, as well as that of the generating circle, which last is usually the same as that of the boss of the cam, the design is proceeded with as follows:—

Letting A be the cam-shaft, and taking A o as the radius of the generating circle, whilst a a' is the height to which the projection, B, fig. D, formed on the stamp, c, is to be raised, develop the circumference (197) of the circle of the radius, A o, by means of a series of tangents which give the points, c, d, e, &c., the curve passing through which forms the involute, b f i. The inner portion, b o, is not a continuation of the involute, but simply joins the boss with a circular turn, because the stamp projection, B, does not approach the cam-shaft, A, nearer than the point, a, to which b corresponds. Through the point, a, draw the vertical, a a', and make it equal to the height to which the stamp has to be raised; then with the centre, A, and a radius equal to A a', describe the arc, a' m i, which will cut the involute in the point, i, and this point is consequently the outer limit of the cam. A little consideration will show that if the cam-shaft, A, be turned in the direction of the arrow, supposing that it is originally placed, so that the point b, coincides with a, it must necessarily raise the lifting-piece, B, the lower side of which is indicated by the line, m a, and will carry it by equal increments up to the position, m' a'. The point, i', will then have attained the position, a', and the rotation continuing, the next moment it will pass it, when the cam will be entirely clear of the lifting-piece, B, and this last being unsupported, must fall by its own weight.

The involute might have been derived from a generating circle of the radius, A a, and had this radius been adopted, the resulting curve would have been shorter, notwithstanding that it would give the same extent of lift. The angular space passed over would also be less, and this would admit of a higher velocity of the camshaft, and the strokes might be given in more rapid succession, whilst on the other hand, a greater power would be required to raise the same weight.

The cam we have represented in fig. D, is such as is employed to actuate the chopping stamp of mills for reducing oak, or other bark, for the preparation of tan. The bark is placed in a kind of wooden trough, E, solidly fixed into the floor. The stamps are armed with a series of cutters, n, in the form of crosses. The side of the trough next to the stamp is vertical, whilst the opposite side is elliptical in shape, and the matter under operation has, consequently, always a tendency to fall under the stamp. The stamps are kept vertical by slides in which they work. They are generally from 450 to 700 pounds weight, and fall through a height of from 16 to 20 inches.

Fig 7 is a plan of the cam as seen from below, and fully indicates the width of the rim, and of the boss, and the thickness of the feather or disc uniting the two.

A series of such cams are frequently employed in different planes on the same shaft, actuating a corresponding series of stamps, and in such case they are arranged in steps so as to come into action one after the other. Two or more are also sometimes employed in the same plane, and working a single stamp. In this latter case, the generating circle requires to be of much larger diameter in proportion, but the principle of construction is however the same.

CAM TO PRODUCE INTERMITTENT AND DISSIMILAR MOVEMENTS.

FIGURES 8 AND 9.

240. In certain examples of steam engines, the valve movement is obtained from a species of duplex cam, which being formed of two distinct thicknesses, affords a means of adjustment whereby the valve may be made to move intermittently and at different rates, the proportions of which are variable at pleasure. The object of this is to form and shut off the communication between the cylinder with the steam-pipe, at any required point of the stroke. In other words, the arrangement permits of the working of the machine on the *expansive* principle, and of varying the "cut-off" point at pleasure within certain limits. We shall see, at a more advanced period, what is to be understood by the foregoing expressions. In designing cams of this class, we primarily determine the radius o a, of the cam boss, and the entire length, b c, of the stroke to be given to the valve-rod. This distance, which in the present instance we shall take as equal to three times the height of the port, must not be traversed at one movement. On the contrary, a third only of this is at first passed through, with some rapidity, and the remaining two-thirds are traversed at a later period, in a continuous manner: in other words, after a third of the stroke has been traversed, a slight pause takes place before the remainder is traversed, and a second pause also occurs before the commencement of the return stroke.

After describing a couple of concentric circles with the respective radii, o a, and o c, and having determined the angular spaces, a d, and f g, corresponding to the times during which the valve is to remain stationary, and the spaces, g h, and c f, corresponding to the duration of the movements; divide the whole stroke, b c, into three equal parts in the points, i, j, through which describe circles concentric with the preceding. Through the points, f, g, h, draw radii, and produce them to f', g', and h'.

As the cam will act on two friction rollers, G, diametrically opposite to each other, their radius is determined, as a e; one is drawn with its centre, e, on the radius, o a produced, and tangential to the circle described with that radius; the other, with its centre, e, on the radius, o c produced, is, in like manner, tangential to the circle described with this radius.

Between the two points, d and k, and comprised within the given angle, g o h, a curve, k l d, is drawn and united by tangential arcs at either extremity with the circles of the radii, a o and o c, respectively, in such a manner as to avoid any sudden change of direction. Next divide the arc, g h, into a certain number of equal parts in the points, 1, 2, &c., and carry the radii across to 1', 2, &c.; then, on each of these radii, as a centre line, describe an arc corresponding to the radius of the roller, G, and tangential to the curve, k l d. By this means will be obtained the points, r s t, indicating the successive positions of the centre of the roller on the line, e e', when impelled by the curve, k l d. If, then, starting from these several points, we measure on the corresponding cross 'lines, 1—1', 2—2', &c., distances equal to e e', which is obviously constant, we shall obtain the positions, r', s', t', of the centre of the opposite roller, G', corresponding to those of the first. Then, with these points, r, s, t, as centres, describe arcs of the radius of the roller, and draw the curve, d' l' f', tangential to them, and unite them to the circles of the radii, c o and j o, in a similar manner to the opposite curve. The curve, d' l' f', will obviously, from its construction, be in contact with the roller, G', whilst the first, d l k, is in contact with the other roller, G.

In order that the rollers, G, G', may maintain their relative position, and move in the same rectilinear direction, they are carried in bearings, H, forming, with four tierods, I, a frame which embraces the cam and cam shaft, the middle of the rods being planed to rest and slide upon the latter.

To one end of the frame is bolted the cast-iron connecting rod, J, fig. ⑨, jointed to the bell-crank lever, K. This last vibrates on the centre, u, and by its second arm actuates the link, v, connected to the rod, x, of the valve T, fig. Ⓔ, above. In the position given to the cam and roller frame, in fig. 8, the valve is not covering the upper part, c', and this remains open whilst the cam rotates through the angle, a o d, because the arc, a d, and its opposite, c d, are both concentric with the axis of the cam shaft, o.

When, however, the point, d, shall have arrived at the position, a, supposing the cam shaft to continue to turn in the direction of the arrow, the cam will shortly pass through the angle, d o g, and the projecting curve, d l k, will push the roller, G, to the right, and the opposite roller, G', being drawn in the same direction, will roll along the corresponding curve, d' l' g'. This movement will cause the valve to be raised to the extent of a third of its stroke, corresponding exactly to the width of the port, c'. This port will, in fact, be completely closed when the radius, o k, of the cam shall have reached the position, o e. At this point, the valve is required to remain stationary for a short time, during which the cam, in continuing to revolve, describes the angle, g o f. As soon, however, as the radius, o f, reaches the position, o e, the valve, and its actuating gear, will again move, and continue to do so, until the lower port, c², be completely open. This movement will take place whilst the cam describes the angle, f o e, and is caused by the curve, a' b' c', which pushes the roller, G, and the frame still further to the right. The curve, a' b' c', is united by a gradual turn to the circles of the radii, o k and o c, in the same manner as the curves previously drawn. The opposite and corresponding curve, a m n, is obtained in the same manner as d' l' g', opposite to, and derived from, the first curve, d l k. The operations in both cases are fully indicated on the diagram, and it has merely to be borne in mind that the object is to keep the two rollers, G and G', in contact with the cam in every position of the latter.

After the cam has passed through the angle, f o c, the valve, with its gear, remains stationary during another interval, in which the angle, c o d", is traversed, and then the first curve will commence to act upon the roller, G', and cause it, with the frame, to return from right to left, and the movements and intervals will take place in the same order as to time as in the up stroke of the valve already described in detail; but the direction will be reversed—that is, the valve will perform its return stroke—until it reaches its original position, as represented in fig. Ⓔ.

To proceed: it is easy to conceive the cam, as constructed in two pieces, precisely alike in all respects, and laid upon one another, as M and M', fig. 9, one M being fast to the shaft, whilst the other, M', is capable of being adjusted to the first in any relative position. Since the rollers, G, G', are long enough to be in contact with both, it will follow they will, in any given position, be acted upon by that half of the cam which projects most at that particular point; so that, if the curved portion, d l k, of one is turned slightly in advance, it will come into action sooner, and, by consequence, will cause the valve to shut off the communication between the steam pipe and the cylinder at an earlier period of the stroke. In this manner is obtained a means of varying the rate of expansion at which the engine is worked.

Fig. 9 is a horizontal section, showing the two halves, M M', of the eccentric, and the arrangement of the details of the friction rollers, G G', and frame, H I.

Fig. Ⓕ is a front view of the valve face of a steam-engine cylinder, showing the disposition of the ports.

An innumerable variety of movements may be produced by the agency of cams; but the principles of their construction are mostly the same as those just discussed, and the examples given will be a sufficient guide in designing others.

RULES AND PRACTICAL DATA.

MECHANICAL WORK, OR EFFECT.

241. To work, considered in the abstract, is to overcome, during any certain period of time, a continuously replaced resistance, or series of resistances. Thus, to file, to saw, to plane, to draw burdens, is to work, or produce mechanical effect.

Mechanical work is the effect of the simple action of a force upon a resistance which is directly opposed to it, and which it continuously destroys, giving motion in that direction to the point of application of the resistance. It follows from this definition, that the mechanical work or effect of any motor is the product of two indispensable quantities, or terms :—

First, The effort, or pressure exerted.

Second, The space passed through in a given time, or the velocity.

The amount of mechanical work increases directly as the increase of either of these terms, and in the proportion compounded of the two when both increase. If, for example, the pressure exerted be equal to 4 lbs., and the velocity 1 foot per second, the amount of work will be expressed by 4 × 1 = 4. If the velocity be double, the work becomes 4 × 2 = 8, or double also; and if, with the velocity double, or 2 feet per second, the pressure be doubled as well—that is, raised to 8 lbs.—the work will be, 8 × 2 = 16, or the quadruplicate of its original amount.

In the term "velocity," "time" is understood; so that, in fact, just as space or solidity is represented in terms of three dimensions, length, breadth, and depth, so also is mechanical effect defined by the three terms representing pressure, distance, and time. This analogy gives rise to the possibility of treating many questions and problems, relating to mechanical effects, by means of geometrical diagrams and theorems.

The unit of mechanical effect (corresponding to the geometrical cubical unit) adopted in England, is the horse power, which is equal to 33,000 lbs. weight, or pressure, raised or moved through a space of 1 foot in a minute of time. The corresponding unit employed in France is the kilogrammètre, which is equal to a kilogramme, raised one mètre high in a second. Thus, supposing the pressure exerted be 20 kilog., and the distance traversed by the point of application be 2 mètres in a second, the mechanical effect is represented by 40 k. m.; that is, 40 kilog., raised 1 mètre high. This unit is much more convenient than the English one, from its lesser magnitude. Indeed, when small amounts of mechanical effect are spoken of in English terms, it is generally said that they are equal to so many pounds raised so many feet high. That is to say, this takes place in some given time, as a minute, for example. The *time* must always be expressed or understood. It is impossible to express or state intelligibly an amount of mechanical effect, without indicating all the three terms—pressure, distance, and time. It is to the losing sight of this indispensable definition, that we may attribute the vagueness and unintelligibility of many treatises on this subject. The French engineers make the horse power equal to 75 kilogrammètres; that is, to 75 kilog., raised one mètre high per second.

The motors generally employed in manufactures and industrial arts are of two kinds—living, as men and animals; and inanimate, as air, water, gas, and steam.

The latter class, being subject only to mechanical laws, can continue their action without limit. This is not the case with the first, which are susceptible of fatigue, after acting for a certain length of time, or duration of exertion, and require refreshment and repose.

What may be termed the amount of a day's work, producible by men and animals, is the product of the force exerted, multiplied into the distance or space passed over, and the time during which the action is sustained. There will, however, in all cases, be a certain proportion of effort, in relation to the velocity and duration which will yield the largest possible product, or day's work, for any one individual, and this product may be termed the maximum effect. In other words, a man will produce a greater mechanical effect by exerting a certain effort, at a certain velocity, than he will by exerting a greater effort at a less velocity, or a less effort at a greater velocity, and the proportion of effort and velocity which will yield the maximum effect is different in different individuals.

TABLE OF THE AVERAGE AMOUNT OF MECHANICAL EFFECT PRODUCIBLE BY MEN AND ANIMALS.

NATURE OF THE WORK.	Mean weight elevated or effort exerted.	Velocity or distance per second.	Mechanical effect per second.	Duration per diem.	Mechanical effect per diem.
	Lbs.	Feet.	Lbs. raised 1 foot high.	Hours.	Lbs. raised 1 foot high
A man ascending a slight incline, or a stair, without a burden, his work consisting simply in the elevation of his own weight,..............	143	·50	71·5	8	2,059,200
A labourer elevating a weight by means of a cord and pulley, the cord being pulled downwards,....................................	40	·65	26·0	6	561,600
A labourer elevating a weight directly, with a cord, or by the hand,....	44	·56	24·6	6	531,360
A labourer lifting or carrying a weight on his back, up a slight incline, or stair, and returning unladen,.......................	143	·13	18·6	6	401,760
A labourer carrying materials in a wheel-barrow, up an incline of 1 in 12, and returning unladen,...	132	·06	8·5	10	306,000
A labourer raising earth with a spade to a mean height of five feet,....	60	·13	7·8	10	280,000
ACTION ON MACHINES.					
A labourer acting on a spoke-wheel, or inside a large drum.					
At the level of the axis,..................................	132	·50	66·0	8	1,900,800
Near the bottom of the wheel,.................................	26	2·30	59·8	8	1,722,240
A labourer pushing or pulling horizontally,.........................	26	1·97	51·2	8	1,474,560
A labourer working at a winch handle,..............	17½	2·46	43·0	8	1,238,400
A labourer pushing and pulling alternately in a vertical direction,.....	11	3·61	39·7	8	1,143,360
A horse drawing a carriage at an ordinary pace,.....................	154	2·95	454·3	10	16,354,800
A horse turning a mill at an ordinary pace,......................	99	2·95	292·0	8	8,409,600
A horse turning a mill at a trot,............................	66	6·56	433·0	4½	7,014,600
An ox doing the same at an ordinary pace,.........................	143	1·97	281·7	8	8,112,960
A mule do. do.	66	2·95	194·7	8	5,607,360
An ass do. do.	31	2·62	81·2	8	2,338,560

It may be gathered from this table that a labourer turning a winch handle can make its extremity pass through a distance of 2·46 feet per second, or 60 × 2·46 = 147·6 feet per minute. Then, supposing the handle has 13¾ inches, = 1·147 feet radius, which corresponds to a circumference of 6·28 × 1·147 = 7·2 feet

at the point of application, the labourer is capable of an average velocity of

$$\frac{147 \cdot 6}{7 \cdot 2} = 20 \text{ turns (nearly) per minute.}$$

Also, the same labourer exerting a force equal to 17½ lbs. with

M

the velocity of 2·46 feet per second, will produce a mechanical effect equal to

$17\frac{1}{2} \times 2\cdot46 = 43$ lbs. raised 1 foot high per second, or of

$43 \times 60 = \quad 2580$ per minute, and

$2580 \times 60 = 154{,}800$ lbs. raised 1 foot high per hour.

And as he can work at this 8 hours per diem, the total mechanical effect during this time will be, as indicated in the table, equal to 1,238,400 lbs. raised 1 foot high.

We may then calculate that, as a day's work, a labourer turning a winch-handle can elevate in a continuous manner $17\frac{1}{4}$ lbs. 2·46 feet high per second; when, however, the labourer has only to apply his strength at intervals to a crane, a windlass, or a capstan, he can develop a much greater force for a few minutes. According to experiments tried in England with a discharging crane, a man can in 90″ raise a load of 1048·6 lbs. to a height of $16\frac{1}{4}$ feet. Now, to compare this with the tabulated quantities, we must multiply the weight raised, 1048·6 lbs., by the height, $16\frac{1}{2}$ feet, and divide the product by the duration of the action, or 90″; the quotient, 192, indicates the number of pounds raised 1 foot high in a second, to which the mechanical effect is equal.

It has been proved by experiments, that under the most favourable circumstances, an Irish labourer of extra strength can, by great exertion, raise to the same height, $16\frac{1}{4}$ feet, a load of 1·474 lbs. in 132″, which is equal to a mechanical effect of

$$\frac{1474 \times 16\cdot5}{132} = 184\cdot25 \text{ lbs. raised 1 foot high per second.}$$

A man can evidently only exert such a force during a very limited period; we cannot, therefore, compare this kind of labour with that which continues through several consecutive hours. Although the load and velocity as given in the table are those most conveniently proportioned to each other, still, when the case requires it, they might be altered to some extent; thus, if it is necessary to apply a force of 25 lbs. to the extremity of the winch-handle instead of $17\frac{1}{4}$, then the velocity would be reduced, and would become

$$\frac{43}{25} = 1\cdot72 \text{ feet per second, instead of } 2\cdot46.$$

It has been ascertained from actual observations, that a horse, going at the respective rates of 1, 3, 5, and 10 miles per hour, cannot exert a greater tractive force than the corresponding weights, 194, 143, 100, and 24 lbs., and cannot draw anything appreciable when going at the rate of 15 miles per hour.

Thus, when it is wished to increase the force exerted, a decrease takes place in the velocity; and reciprocally, when it is wished to gain time and speed, it can only be done at the expense of the load. Thus, in the case of the winch-handle, the two factors must always produce an effect equal to 43 lbs. raised 1 foot high per second, whatever ratio they may have to each other.

In all cases of the direct action of forces, a certain *velocity* is **impressed**, for without *movement* there could not be the action of **a force.**

There are two kinds of motion—uniform and varied motion.

243. UNIFORM MOTION.—A body is said to have a uniform motion when it passes through equal distances in equal times. Thus, for example, if a body traverses 5 feet in the first second, 5 feet in the second, and so on throughout, its motion is uniform.

Putting D to represent the distance, V the velocity, and T the time, the formula, $D = V \times T$, indicates that the distance is equal to the velocity multiplied by the time.

First Example.—The velocity of a body subject to a uniform motion is 3 feet per second, through what distance will it have passed in 15 seconds?

$$D = 3 \times 15 = 45 \text{ feet.}$$

From the preceding formula, $D = V \times T$, is obtained $V = \dfrac{D}{T}$; that is to say, the velocity per second is equal to the distance divided by the time.

Second Example.—The distance passed through in 15 seconds is 45 feet, what is the velocity?

$$V = \frac{45}{15} = 3 \text{ feet.}$$

The wheel-gear of machinery, as well as many other instruments of transmission, is, for the most part, actuated in a uniform manner.

244. VARIED MOTION.—When a body passes in equal times through distances which augment or decrease by equal quantities, the motion is called uniformly varied.

The distance in motion uniformly varied is equal to half the sum of the extreme velocities multiplied by the time in second.

First Example.—What is the distance passed through in 4 seconds by a body in motion, the velocity of which is 2 feet per second at starting, and 6 feet per second at the termination?

$$D = \frac{2 + 6}{2} \times 4 = 16 \text{ feet.}$$

Second Example.—What is the distance passed through in 4 seconds by a body in motion, which at starting has a velocity of 6 feet per second, but which is gradually reduced to 2 feet?

$$D = \frac{6 + 2}{2} \times 4 = 16 \text{ feet.}$$

It will be seen from these two examples, that, with like conditions, the total distance is the same for motions uniformly accelerated or retarded.

The velocity at the end of a given time, in uniformly accelerated motion, is equal to the velocity at starting, plus the product of the increase per second into the time in seconds.

First Example.—What velocity will a body have at the end of 8 seconds, supposing the initial velocity = 1, and that it increases at the rate of 3 feet per second?

$$V = 1 + (8 \times 3) = 25 \text{ feet.}$$

The velocity which, at the end of a given time, a body uniformly retarded should have, is equal to the initial velocity minus the product of the diminution per second, multiplied into the time in seconds.

Second Example.—A body in motion starts with a velocity of 22 feet per second, and its velocity decreases at the rate of 2 feet per second, what will be the velocity at the end of 10 seconds?

$$V = 22 - (2 \times 10) = 2 \text{ feet.}$$

245. The motions of which the various parts of machines are capable are of two principal kinds—continuous, and alternate or back and forward motion.

These two kinds of motion may take place either in straight or curved lines, the latter generally being circular.

In the actual construction of machinery, we find that, from these principal descriptions of motions, the following combinations are derived:—

Continuous rectilinear motion is converted into	Continuous rectilinear. Continuous circular. Alternate circular.
Alternate rectilinear motion is converted into	Continuous rectilinear. Continuous circular. Alternate circular.
Continuous circular motion is converted into	Continuous rectilinear. Alternate rectilinear. Continuous circular. Alternate circular.
Alternate circular motion is converted into	Alternate rectilinear. Continuous circular. Alternate circular.

THE SIMPLE MACHINES.

246. This term is applied to those mechanical agents which enter as elements into the composition of all machinery, whether their function be to elevate loads, or to overcome resistances.

The simple machines are generally considered to be six—the lever, the wheel and axle, the pulley, the inclined plane, the screw, and the wedge.

A much more scientific and comprehensive arrangement of the elementary machines is that lately suggested by Mr. G. P. Renshaw, C.E., of Nottingham. According to his system, the elementary machines, or mechanical powers, are five—namely, the lever, the incline, the toggle or knee-joint, the pulley, and the ram.

The wheel and axle, of the first system, is evidently but a modification of the lever, and the screw and wedge are modifications of the inclined plane; whilst no mention is made of the toggle-joint and ram—the last so well represented by the hydrostatic press.

All these machines act on the fundamental principle, known as that of *virtual velocities*. According to this principle, the pressure or resistance is inversely as the velocity or space passed through, or that would be passed through, if the piece were put in motion.

The *momentum* of the power and resistance is equal when the machine is in *equilibrio*. By *momentum* is understood the product of the power by the space passed through by the point of application.

Time is occupied in the transmission of all mechanical force. In any mechanical action we do not see the effect and the cause at the same instant. Thus, in continuous motion, in which the time expended is not apparent at first sight, each succeeding portion of the motion is due to a portion of the impelling action exerted a certain time previously. This will be more obvious on observing the commencement and termination of any motion. The motion does not commence at the instant that the power is applied, nor does it cease at the exact moment of the power's cessation. The fiction of the *vis inertiæ* has been invented to account for these latter observed facts, but it explains them very awkwardly. Thus, bodies are said to possess a certain force which is opposed to a *change* of state, whether from rest to motion or motion to rest. If such a resistive *force* existed, it would require an effort to overcome it, in addition to what is actually

accounted for by the motion. If it is said that this is again given back at the termination of the motion, another fiction is required to account for it in the meantime, that is, during the continuation of the motion. Moreover, there is nothing analogous to it throughout the entire range of physical science.

The facts are described in a much more simple and philosophical manner, when they are said to arise from the *time* taken in the transmission of motive force. Why there should be this expenditure of time is a more abstruse question. It probably arises from the elasticity of the component particles of bodies and resisting media, and is regulated by the laws which govern the relation to time of the vibrations of the pendulum.

In all machines, a portion of the actuating power is lost or misapplied in overcoming the friction of the parts.

247. THE LEVER.—The lever, in its simplest form, is an inflexible bar, capable of oscillation about a fixed centre, termed the *fulcrum*. A lever transmits the action of a power and a resistance, or load; the distance of the power, or load, from the centre of oscillation, is called an arm of the lever.

There are two kinds of *power* levers, distinguished by the position of the fulcrum as regards the power and the resistance. These become *speed* levers, by transposing the power and resistance. By a *power* machine, is meant one which gives an increase of power at the expense of speed, and by a *speed* machine, one that gives an increase of speed at the expense of power, and all the simple machines are one or the other, according to the relative position of the power and resistance.

In all cases of the lever, *the power and the resistance are in the inverse ratio to each other of their distances from the centre of oscillation.* That is to say, that when, in *equilibrio*, the momentum of the power, $P \times A$, or the product of this power into the space described by the lever arm, A, is equal to the product, $R \times B$, of the resistance, into the space described by the lever arm, B: whence the following inverse proportion:—

$$P : R :: B : A;$$

Any three of which terms being known, the fourth can be found at once.

248. The wheel and axle is a perpetual lever. As a power, the advantage gained is in the proportion of the radius of the circumference of the wheel to that of the axle. That is to say, the power, P, is to the resistance, R, as the radius, b, of the axle, is to the radius, a, of the wheel, or the length of the winch handle—in the simpler form of this machine, consisting of an axle and a winch handle. The same rules and formulæ obviously apply to this, as to the first described form of lever.

Thus, multiply the resistance by the radius of the axle, and divide by that of the handle, and the quotient will be the power.

In windlasses and cranes, consisting of a system of wheel-work, the power is applied to a handle fixed on the spindle of a pinion, which transmits the power to a spur-wheel, fixed in the spindle of the barrel, about which the cord, or rope, carrying the load to be raised, is wound.

Where there are several pairs of such wheels, it is necessary to include in the calculations the ratios of the pinions to the spur wheels.

The proportional formula will, in this case, be the same as for a system of levers :—

$$P : R :: b \times b' \times b'' : a \times a' \times a'' ;$$

Or, the power is to the resistance, as the produst of the radii of the pinions and barrel is to the product of the radii of the spur-wheels and handle.

From this we derive the following rules :—

I. *Multiply the load to be raised by the product of the radius of the barrel into the radii of the pinions, and divide the sum obtained by the product of the radius of the handle into the radii of the spur-wheels, and the quotient will be the power, which, when applied to the handle, will balance the load.*

II. *Multiply the power applied by the radius of the handle, and by the radii of the spur-wheels, and divide the product by the radius of the barrel, and by the radii of the pinions, and the quotient will be the resistance which will balance the power.*

III. *Multiply the radii of the pinions and barrel, and divide the product by the radii of the handle and spur-wheels, and the quotient will be the ratio of the power to the resistance.*

249. THE INCLINE.—When a body is raised up a vertical plane, its whole weight is supported by the elevating power, and this power is consequently equal to the weight elevated.

When a body is drawn along a horizontal plane, the tractive power has none of the weight of the body to sustain, but merely to overcome the friction of the surface.

If, however, a body is drawn up an inclined plane, the power required to elevate it is proportionate to the inclination of the plane, in such a manner, that

If the power acts parallel to the plane, the length of the plane will be to the load as the height is to the power.

The advantage gained by the use of the inclined plane, as a power, is the greater the more its length outmeasures its height; it is then the ratio of the length to the height which determines that of the power to the resistance, whence we obtain the following rules :—

I. *The resistance, multiplied by the height and divided by the length of the plane, is equal to the power required to balance a body on the inclined plane.*

II. *The power, multiplied by the length of the plane and divided by the height, is equal to the resistance.*

III. *The resistance, multiplied by the height of the plane and divided by its length, is equal to the load on the plane.*

The wedge and the screw are noticeable modifications of the incline. An incline wrapped round a cylinder generates a screw. When used as a power-machine, it is generally combined with a lever, as in presses. The advantage gained depends upon the length of the lever and the pitch of the screw. Multiply the actuating force by the circumference described by the end of the arm or lever, and divide the product by the length of the pitch of the screw; the quotient, minus the friction, which is very considerable in these machines, will be the pressure exerted by the screw, and the velocity will, of course, be in the inverse ratio of the theoretical pressure to the actuating force.

250. THE TOGGLE.—This is met with chiefly in punching presses. Deflected springs and rods are also examples of it, and also the twisted cords used by carpenters to stretch their saws in

frames. As in the other machines, the resistance is to the power, as the space passed through by the latter is to the space passed through by the former.

251. THE PULLEY.—There are two kinds of pulleys, the one turning on fixed centres, the other on traversing centres.

The pulley, which turns on a fixed centre, serves simply to change the direction of the motive force, without altering the relations of power and velocity. It is, in fact, only the moveable pulleys which can be classed amongst the elementary machines.

A single moveable pulley, acting as a power, doubles it at the expense of the speed ; thus, if a weight of 10 lbs. be suspended to one extremity of the cord, it will balance 20 lbs. hung to the axis of the pulley. This arises from the fact that, from the arrangement of the cord, the pulley only rises through half the height passed through by the motive force ; thus, if the latter pass through 6 feet, the pulley will only rise 3 feet, and the resulting momentum of the power, 10×6, will be equal to that of the resistance, or 20×3, so that the two will be in equilibrium.

Though the stationary pulley cannot be considered as a mechanical power, yet, in changing the direction of the motion, it affords great facilities in the application of force ; thus, it is easier to pull downwards than upwards, as the labourer brings his weight to bear in the former case.

When several pulleys or sheaves are placed on one axis in a suitable frame, it is called a block. Where two or more blocks are employed, it is only the moveable ones which increase the power, and this increase is equal to double the number of sheaves, or pulleys, in the block or blocks.

The mechanical advantage of the block, as a power, arises from the fact, that the space traversed by the motive power is equal to the sum of the doublings of the cord round the pulleys, whilst the load is only elevated to a distance corresponding to this space divided by the number of these doublings.

A clock line and weight, in which the line goes round a pulley fixed in the weight, is an example of a speed-pulley, that is, one in which the power, or resistance, is transposed, for the weight, or motive power, causes the moveable end of the cord to pass through twice the space it passes through itself.

252. THE RAM.—This is the most economical augmentor of power that we have. It is freer from friction and other disadvantages than the other simple machines, and it is, in its action, very closely allied to the pulley. Each derives its advantage from the division of the points of support, for the proportionate area of the piston in the Bramah press represents the number of points over which the pressure, or resistance, is diffused.

253. REMARKS.—It is essential that, to avoid illusive mistakes, the student should perfectly understand, that when, in employing mechanical forces, the effect of the power applied is augmented, the distance passed through by the resistance, or load, is diminished, with reference to that passed through by the power, *in exactly the same ratio that this is increased.* This is true in all cases, and may be stated thus : What we gain in force, by means of machinery, we lose in speed, and reciprocally.

It follows from this, that the true object of machinery cannot be to augment the work performed by the motive agent, but to convert any primary action in a manner appropriate to the circumstances in which the power is to be used. Thus we can make a very small force, as that of a man, elevate an enormous weight, but with a speed proportionately slow.

Finally, *The mechanical effect developed in a given time by a given force, through the instrumentality of machinery, must always equal the useful effect obtained, plus the amount lost in overcoming frictional and other resistances; and the useful effect of machinery will be the greater, according as the causes of these resistances are diminished.*

CENTRE OF GRAVITY.

254. All bodies are equally subjected to the action of weight. Gravity, or weight, is the action of that universal attraction which draws all bodies towards each other, and by which, in the case of bodies on the surface of the earth, these are drawn towards its centre. The power, of whatever nature it may be, which balances this action, is equal to the weight of the body.

The curvature of the surface of the earth being quite inappreciable for small distances, gravity is considered as acting in parallel lines, and its direction is given by the plumbline.

The centre of gravity is that point in any body in which the action of its entire weight may be said to be concentrated. If the body be suspended by this point it will be in *equilibrio*, in whatever position it is put.

The position of the centre of gravity depends upon the nature and form of any body; it may generally be found in the following manner:—

Suspend the body by a thread attached to any point whatever in it; when the body is motionless, the line of the suspension thread will pass directly through the centre of gravity. Suspend the body by any other point, and the centre of gravity will also be in the continuation of the line of the thread, so that the actual centre must be at the point of intersection of the two lines thus obtained. This simple expedient reminds us of the application of the square to the finding of the centres of circles—the unknown centre on the endface of a shaft, for example—where the intersection of any two lines, drawn along the blade of the square, when the head is laid against the periphery of the shaft in two different positions, gives the required point of centre.

The centre of gravity of regular bodies, as spheres, cylinders, prisms, is in the centre of their configuration.

The centre of gravity of an isosceles triangle is one third up the centre line which bisects the base.

The centre of gravity of a pyramid, with a triangular or polygonal base, is one fourth up the line which joins the summit with the centre of gravity of the base. It is the same with a cone.

The centre of gravity of a hemisphere is situated three-eighths up the radius at right angles to the base.

The centre of gravity of an ellipse is in the point of intersection of the axes.

When a body is placed in a vertical or inclined position on a plane, it is necessary, in order that it may rest upon it in that position without falling, that the vertical line passing through the centre of gravity shall fall within the external outline of the side in contact with the plane. This limit, however, allows of considerable deviation from the vertical in the general contour of bodies, as is instanced in the case of leaning or inclined edifices. The stability of bodies increases as the extent of their bases is greater in comparison with their height, and also, as the vertical line, passing through the centre of gravity, meets the plane on which the body rests nearer to the centre of the base. A body is said to be more stable when it requires a greater force to overturn it. A cone is more stable than a cylinder of the same height and base. The stability of walls depends greatly on the kind of foundations given to them, and on the proportionate extension of their bases.

ON ESTIMATING THE POWER OF PRIME MOVERS.

255. As we shall see further on, the power of prime movers may be calculated from the dimensions of the various parts of the engine. Still, the many different modes of construction tend to modify considerably the actual useful effect, and engineers have endeavoured to construct an apparatus, by means of which the actual power, or useful effect of engines, may be measured with exactitude.

Prony's brake, which is the instrument most generally used for this purpose, acts on the principle of the lever, and consists of a cast-iron pulley in two halves, united by screws. This is fixed on the main shaft of the prime mover, the force of which it is wished to measure. It is embraced by two jaws, which may be tightened down upon the pulley by screws. To the lower jaw is attached a long lever, from the end of which is suspended a scale for weights. If it is known what power the engine was designed to possess, it is simply necessary to put into the scale the weight corresponding to this power, that is, the weight which, by the action of the lever, will give a pressure equal to the supposed power of the machine.

Having fixed the apparatus on the engine, and provided means of efficiently lubricating the frictional surface of the pulley with soap and water, and having balanced the apparatus in such a manner that it will not be necessary to take into the calculation anything but the weight placed in the scale, the steam may be gradually let on. The engine will perhaps shortly acquire a greater velocity than that for which it was designed; if this is the case, the jaws are gradually screwed closer and closer upon the pulley. As the friction thereby increases, the velocity will diminish, and full steam may be let on. After a short time, and when the friction is so great that the lever is raised slightly above the horizontal line, and the engine is going at its proper velocity, and the pressure of the steam at its correct point, so that the power of the engine balances the load on the lever, it may be concluded that the engine develops the power for which it was intended. If the lever rises considerably, it will be necessary to increase the weight in the scale, so as to obtain the actual maximum power of the engine; and, on the contrary, if the engine does not appear to have the desired power, the weight must be reduced, by which means its actual power will be ascertainable.

CALCULATION FOR THE BRAKE.

256. The weight which will balance the force of a machine may be calculated when the length of the lever arm is known, or, more correctly, the radius from the centre of the shaft to the point of suspension of the weight, and the nominal horse-power, by the following rule:—

Multiply the nominal horse-power by 33,000, and divide the product by the circumference described by the end of the lever, and by the number of revolutions per minute, and the quotient will be the weight sought.

Let us take, for example, the main shaft of a steam-engine of 16 horse-power, which runs at the rate of 30 revolutions per minute, the radius of the brake being nine feet—

$$\text{Here we have } w = \frac{16 \times 33,000}{6\cdot28 \times 9 \times 30} = 311\cdot4 \text{ lbs.}$$

Such is the net weight to be suspended from the end of the lever, the brake being previously balanced by being suspended on its centre of gravity.

The actual power, or maximum effect of an engine, may likewise be calculated by means of the following rule :—

Multiply the circumference described by the lever, by the number of revolutions of the shaft per minute and by the weight in the scale, and divide the product by 33,000 and the quotient will be the actual force of the engine in horses power.

For example, let us suppose that the main shaft of a steam-engine makes 30 revolutions per minute, that the radius of the lever is 9 feet, and that the net weight in the scale is 311·4 lbs., what is the maximum force of the engine ?

$$F = \frac{6\cdot28 \times 9 \times 30 \times 311\cdot4}{33,000} = 16 \text{ H. P.}$$

TABLE OF HEIGHTS CORRESPONDING TO VARIOUS VELOCITIES OF FALLING BODIES.

Velocity.	Height.	Velocity.	Height.	Velocity.	Height.	Velocity.	Height.	Velocity.	Height.
Inches.	Inches.	Inches.	Inches.	Inches.	Inches.	Inches.	Inches.	Inches.	Inches.
·1	·0001	5·7	·165	16·5	1·388	44·5	10·094	72·5	26·794
·2	·0002	5·8	·171	17·0	1·473	45·0	10·322	73·0	27·164
·3	·0005	5·9	·177	17·5	1·561	45·5	10·553	73·5	27·538
·4	·0009	6·0	·184	18·0	1·651	46·0	10·786	74·0	27·914
·5	·0013	6·1	·190	18·5	1·745	46·5	11·022	74·5	28·292
·6	·0019	6·2	·196	19·0	1·840	47·0	11·260	75·0	28·673
·7	·0026	6·3	·202	19·5	1·938	47·5	11·501	75·5	29·057
·8	·0034	6·4	·209	20·0	2·039	48·0	11·744	76·0	29·443
·9	·0043	6·5	·215	20·5	2·142	48·5	11·990	76·5	29·832
1·0	·0051	6·6	·222	21·0	2·248	49·0	12·239	77·0	30·223
1·1	·0062	6·7	·229	21·5	2·356	49·5	12·490	77·5	30·617
1·2	·0074	6·8	·236	22·0	2·467	50·0	12·744	78·0	31·013
1·3	·0087	6·9	·243	22·5	2·580	50·5	13·000	78·5	31·412
1·4	·0101	7·0	·250	23·0	2·696	51·0	13·258	79·0	31·813
1·5	·0115	7·1	·257	23·5	2·815	51·5	13·520	79·5	32·217
1·6	·0131	7·2	·264	24·0	2·936	52·0	13·784	80·0	32·624
1·7	·0148	7·3	·272	24·5	3·060	52·5	14·050	80·5	33·033
1·8	·0166	7·4	·279	25·0	3·186	53·0	14·319	81·0	33·445
1·9	·0185	7·5	·287	25·5	3·315	53·5	14·590	81·5	33·859
2·0	·0204	7·6	·295	26·0	3·446	54·0	14·864	82·0	34·275
2·1	·0225	7·7	·302	26·5	3·580	54·5	15·141	82·5	34·695
2·2	·0247	7·8	·310	27·0	3·716	55·0	15·420	83·0	35·116
2·3	·0270	7·9	·318	27·5	3·855	55·5	15·701	83·5	35·541
2·4	·0294	8·0	·326	28·0	3·996	56·0	15·986	84·0	35·968
2·5	·0319	8·1	·334	28·5	4·140	56·5	16·272	84·5	36·397
2·6	·0345	8·2	·343	29·0	4·287	57·0	16·562	85·0	36·829
2·7	·0372	8·3	·351	29·5	4·436	57·5	16·854	85·5	37·264
2·8	·0400	8·4	·360	30·0	4·588	58·0	17·148	86·0	37·701
2·9	·0429	8·5	·368	30·5	4·742	58·5	17·445	86·5	38·141
3·0	·0459	8·6	·377	31·0	4·899	59·0	17·744	87·0	38·583
3·1	·0490	8·7	·386	31·5	5·058	59·5	18·046	87·5	39·028
3·2	·0522	8·8	·395	32·0	5·220	60·0	18·351	88·0	39·475
3·3	·0555	8·9	·404	32·5	5·384	60·5	18·658	88·5	39·925
3·4	·0589	9·0	·413	33·0	5·551	61·0	18·968	89·0	40·877
3·5	·0624	9·1	·422	33·5	5·721	61·5	19·280	89·5	40·832
3·6	·0660	9·2	·431	34·0	5·893	62·0	19·595	90·0	41·290
3·7	·0697	9·3	·441	34·5	6·067	62·5	19·912	90·5	41·750
3·8	·0735	9·4	·450	35·0	6·244	63·0	20·232	91·0	42·212
3·9	·0775	9·5	·460	35·5	6·424	63·5	20·554	91·5	42·677
4·0	·0816	9·6	·470	36·0	6·606	64·0	20·879	92·0	43·145
4·1	·0856	9·7	·480	36·5	6·791	64·5	21·207	92·5	43·615
4·2	·0899	9·8	·490	37·0	6·978	65·0	21·537	93·0	44·088
4·3	·0942	9·9	·500	37·5	7·168	65·5	21·869	93·5	44·563
4·4	·0986	10·0	·510	38·0	7·361	66·0	22·205	94·0	45·041
4·5	·1032	10·5	·562	38·5	7·556	66·5	22·542	94·5	45·522
4·6	·1078	11·0	·617	39·0	7·753	67·0	22·883	95·0	46·005
4·7	·1125	11·5	·674	39·5	7·953	67·5	23·225	95·5	46·490
4·8	·1174	12·0	·734	40·0	8·156	68·0	23·571	96·0	46·978
4·9	·1228	12·5	·797	40·5	8·361	68·5	23·919	96·5	47·469
5·0	·1274	13·0	·861	41·0	8·569	69·0	24·969	97·0	47·962
5·1	·1325	13·5	·929	41·5	8·779	69·5	24·622	97·5	48·458
5·2	·1378	14·0	·999	42·0	8·992	70·0	24·978	98·0	48·956
5·3	·1431	14·5	1·072	42·5	9·207	70·5	25·336	98·5	49·457
5·4	·1486	15·0	1·147	43·0	9·425	71·0	25·696	99·0	49·960
5·5	·1541	15·5	1·225	43·5	9·646	71·5	26·060	99·5	50·466
5·6	·1598	16·0	1·305	44·0	9·869	72·0	26·425	100·0	50·975

THE FALL OF BODIES.

258. When bodies fall freely of their own weight, the velocities which they acquire are proportionate to the time during which they have fallen, whilst the spaces passed through are as the squares of the times.

It has been ascertained by experiment that a body falling freely from a state of rest, passes through a distance of 16 feet and a small fraction, in the first second of time. At the end of this time it has a velocity equal to twice this distance per second.

From this it follows that if the times of observation are—

	1″	2′	3″	4″
The corresponding velocities will be	32 ft....	64 ft....	96 ft....	128 ft.
The spaces passed through from the commencement,	16 "...	64 "...	144 "...	256 "
The spaces passed through during each second,	16 "...	48 "...	80 "...	112 "

That is to say, that the times are as the numbers, 1, 2, 3, 4
The velocities also as, 1, 2, 3, 4
The spaces passed through as the squares, 1, 4, 9, 16
And the space for each interval as the odd numbers, 1, 3, 5, 7

These principles apply equally to all bodies, whatever may be their specific gravity, for gravity acts equally on all bodies; the effect, however, being modified by the resistance of the media through which the bodies pass, which is greater in proportion, as the specific gravity is less.

259. The velocity which a body will acquire in a given time when falling freely, will be found by multiplying the time expressed in seconds by 32 feet.

Example.—Let it be required to ascertain the velocity acquired by a body falling during 12 seconds.

$$V = 12 \times 32 = 384 \text{ feet per second.}$$

When a body falls from a given height, H, the ultimate velocity, or that acquired by the time the base is reached, will be given by the formula (g being the velocity gravity causes a body to acquire in the first second)

$$V = \sqrt{2\,g\,H}, \text{ or } V = \sqrt{64 \times H},$$

which leads to the following rule :—Multiply the given height in feet by 64, and extract the square root, which will be the velocity in feet per second by the time the body shall have fallen through the height, H, not taking resistance into consideration.

Example.—What will be the ultimate velocity of a body falling a distance of 215 feet ?

$$V = \sqrt{64 \times 215} = 117 \cdot 3 \text{ feet per second.}$$

From the above formula,

$$V = \sqrt{2\,g\,H},$$

we obtain $V^2 = 2\,g\,H$, then

$$H = \frac{V^2}{2\,g} = \frac{V^2}{64};$$

whence we have this rule :—Divide the square of the velocity in feet per second by 64, and the quotient will express the height through which a body must fall unimpeded, from a state of rest, in order to obtain that velocity.

Example.—A body has acquired a velocity of 117·3 feet per second, through what height must it have fallen ?

$$H = \frac{117 \cdot 3^2}{64} = 215 \text{ feet, the height of the fall.}$$

To obviate the necessity of calculating the corresponding heights and velocities, we give a very extensive table, calculated for tenths of inches. The numbers, however, being equally correct as representing feet or yards, those of both columns being of the same denomination.

MOMENTUM.

260. The force with which a body in motion strikes upon one in a state of rest, is equal to the product of the mass of the moving body multiplied into the velocity; this product is termed its momentum. If a body with a mass, m, is animated with a velocity, v, its momentum is equal to m v. The term, m, however, may be taken as signifying the mechanical effect of a weight falling during a second of time, or through 32 feet, therefore, $m = \dfrac{w}{g}$, that is, the weight in pounds divided by 32 feet, whence, $m\,v = \dfrac{w \times v}{g}$.

What distinguishes the simple momentum or force of impact of a body from the mechanical effect of a prime mover is, that whilst the former is due to a single impulse, we have in the latter to consider the continuous action of the impelling force.

261. When a motive force imparts continuously a certain velocity to a body, the result of its action is what may be termed *vis viva*, or continuous momentum; it is numerically the product of the (moving) mass multiplied into the square of the velocity imparted to it.

Putting M to represent the mass of a body, and V the velocity impressed upon it,

$$M V^2 \text{ or } \frac{W V^2}{g}$$

is the expression of the *vis viva* of the body. This force is double that developed by gravity. For, in fact, when a body of the weight, W, falls from a height, H, it acquires from its fall an ultimate velocity, V, which we have already shown to be equal to

$$\sqrt{2\,g\,H} = \frac{V^2}{2\,g},$$

and the mechanical effect, W H, is consequently expressed by

$$\frac{W V^2}{2\,g};$$

now, putting for P, its value, M g, the formula becomes $\dfrac{M V^2}{2}$.

Thus, the mechanical effect developed by gravity is equal to half the *vis viva* imparted to a body.

CENTRAL FORCES.

262. When a body revolves freely about an axis, it is said to be subjected to two central forces; the one, termed "centripetal," tends to draw the body to the axis; the other, termed "centrifugal," or tangential, and due to the tendency of bodies in motion to proceed in straight lines, strives to carry the body away from the centre. These forces are equal, and act transversely to each other.

The centrifugal effort exerted by a body in rotative motion, and which tends to separate the component particles, is expressed by the following formula :—

$$F = \frac{W V^2}{g \times R},$$

in which W represents the weight of the body; V, the velocity in feet per second; and R, the radius, or distance of the centre of motion from the centre of the revolving body.

Example.—Let a ball of the weight W = 23 lbs., attached to a radius, R, measuring 5 feet, rotate with a velocity, V = 40 feet

per second, what is the centrifugal effort, or the pull of the ball on the radius?

$$F = \frac{23 \times 40 \times 40}{32 \times 5} = 230 \text{ lbs. raised 1 foot high per second.}$$

CHAPTER VII.

ELEMENTARY PRINCIPLES OF SHADOWS.

263. We have already, when treating of shadow lines, laid it down as a rule to be observed generally, in mechanical or geometrical drawing, that the objects represented shall be supposed to receive the light in parallel rays, in the direction of the cubic diagonal, running from the upper left hand corner of the anterior face of the cube, down to the lower right hand corner of the posterior face.

We have also shown that the horizontal and vertical projections of this cubic diagonal make angles of 45° with the horizontal or base line.

The advantages of this assumption of the direction of the rays of light will, no doubt, have been appreciated. Amongst these, it has the merit of at first sight plainly pointing out the relative degrees of prominence of the various parts of an object, even with the aid of a single projection or view.

264. This point, then, being determined, on considering an object of any form whatever, as receiving in this way the parallel rays of light, it may be conceived that these rays will form a cylindrical or prismatical column, the base of which will be the illumined outline of the object. The part met by these rays of light will be fully illumined, whilst the portions opposite to this will be as entirely void of light. The absence of light on this latter part may be termed the *shadow proper* of the object—that is, its own shadow upon itself.

265. If, further, we suppose the luminous rays surrounding the object to be prolonged until intercepted by the surface upon, or adjacent to which it lies, a portion of such surface will be unillumined, because of the interception of some of the rays by the object; the outline of this unillumined portion will be limited by, and depend upon the contour of the object, and it is termed the shadow *cast*, or *thrown*, by an object on any surface.

The line which separates the illumined from the unillumined portion is termed the line of separation of light and shade, or the outline of the shadow. This is modified by the form of the recipient surface, as well as by that of the object which gives rise to it. It is always bounded by straight lines when the generating surfaces are planes; and by curves when either or both are cylindrical, conical, spherical, or otherwise curved.

266. As a general rule, the determination of the outlines of shadows proper, and cast, reduces itself to the problem of finding the point of contact of a straight line representing a luminous ray, with a plane or other surface. The application, however, of this general principle, though apparently so simple, gives rise to many difficulties in practice, from the variety of cases presented by the different forms of objects and it is necessary to give several special

examples, to explain the most simple and expeditious expedients which may be employed in such cases, always with a due regard to geometrical accuracy.

We shall primarily choose for these applications objects of simple form, and bounded by plane surfaces; next, such as are wholly or partially cylindrical; and we shall proceed, in succession, to objects of more complex forms. The objects which we have taken in preference, as examples, are such as are most frequently met with in machinery and architecture; they will, notwithstanding, afford quite sufficient illustration in connection with what has to be said respecting the study of shadows.

SHADOWS OF PRISMS, PYRAMIDS, AND CYLINDERS.
PLATE XXVI.
PRISMS.

267. Let the figures 1 and 1 *a* be given, the horizontal and vertical projections of a cube, it is required to determine the form of the shadow cast by this cube on the horizontal plane.

In the position given to this cube it is easy to see that the sides which are in the light are those represented by A D and A C, in the horizontal projection, and projected vertically in A' E' and A' C'. The opposite faces, B C and B D, fig. 1, and B' C', B' E', fig. 1 *a*, are consequently in the shade; as, however, these latter faces are reduced to mere lines in the representations, the shadow proper can only be shown by a thick shadow line, produced by China ink in line drawings, and by a narrow stroke of the brush in watercolour drawings.

These lines, which distinguish the illumined sides of the cube from those which are not so, are termed, as we have said, the lines of separation of light and shade. It now only remains to find the shadow cast by the cube on the plane, L T.

268. When the object rests on the horizontal plane, as supposed in this case, and is at a greater distance from the vertical plane than is equal to its height, the entire shadow cast by it will be in the horizontal plane; and to determine its outline here, it is merely requisite to draw straight lines from each corner of the cube, representing the rays of light, as c c, B b, D d, parallel to R, and to find the points, c, b, d, in which these lines meet the plane.

To effect this, through the points, c', and A', fig. 1 *a*, the projections of the two first, B D, draw the rays, c' c', and A' B', parallel to R', and meeting the base line, L T, in c' and B'. If now, through these points, we draw perpendiculars to the base line, as c' c B' B, these will cut the first rays in c, b, and d. The contour of the shadow cast is, in consequence, limited by the lines c c, c b, b d, and d D.

The face, E′ B′, being that on which the cube rests, has no prominence, and cannot therefore cast any shadow. It follows, then, that the shadow, as above determined, is all that is apparent. It is generally represented by a flat, uniform shade, laid on with the brush, and produced by a greyish wash of China ink.

269. It will be observed that the lines, $d\,b$ and $b\,c$, are parallel to the straight lines, D B and B C. This is because these are themselves parallel to the horizontal plane; for when a line is parallel to a plane (82), its projection on this plane is a line parallel to itself; and hence we have this first consequence, that—

When a straight line is parallel to the plane of projection, it casts a shadow on the plane, in the form of an equal and parallel straight line.

270. It will also be observed, that the straight lines, D d, B b, C c, which are the shadows cast by the verticals, projected in D, B, and C, are inclined at an angle of 45° to the base line; whence we derive the second consequence, that—

When a straight line is perpendicular to the plane of projection, it casts a shadow on the plane in the form of a straight line, parallel to the rays of light, and consequently inclined at an angle of 45° to the base line.

271. These observations suggest a means of considerably simplifying the operations. Thus, in place of searching separately for each of the points, c, b, d, where the rays of light pierce the horizontal plane, it is sufficient to determine one of these points, such as b, for example, and through it to draw the straight lines, $b\,d$, $b\,c$, parallel and equal to the sides, D B and B C, of the cube and intersecting lines, inclined at an angle of 45° drawn from the points, D C.

In the actual case before us, we may even entirely dispense with the vertical projection, fig. 1ᵃ, since it would have been sufficient to prolong the diagonal, A B, to b, making b B equal to B A, or to make the inclined lines, D d, or B b, equal to the diagonal, A B; because the vertical projection, c′ c′, and horizontal projection, c c, of the same ray of light, are always of the same length, which follows from our having taken the diagonal of the cube for the direction of this ray, the two projections, A B and A′ B′, of this diagonal being obviously equal. Whence follows the third consequence, that—

If, through any point of which the two projections are given, we draw a straight line, representing the ray of light, and if we ascertain the point in which this ray meets either plane, the length of the ray in the other plane of projection will be the same.

272. Finally, it is to be observed that the distance, B d, taken on the prolongation of the vertical line, C B, is equal to the entire height, c′ B′, namely, that of the cube; and consequently, in place of employing the diagonal to obtain the various points, d, b, c, we may make the distance, B d, equal to the height of the cube, and draw, through d, a straight line, $d\,b$, parallel and equal to D B, and through b a second, $b\,c$, parallel and equal to B C, and then join d D, c C.

Thus the shadow cast on a plane by a point, is at a distance from the projection of the point, equal to the distance of the point itself from the plane.

273. Figs. 2 and 2ᵃ represent a prism of hexagonal base, supposed to be elevated above the base line, but at the same time at such a distance from the vertical plane, that all the shadow cast will be in the horizontal plane.

It will be seen that the vertical faces, A B, B C, and A F, are illumined, whilst the opposite ones, E D, D C, and E F, are in the shade.

Of these latter faces, C D is the only one visible in the vertical projection, fig. 2ᵃ, and represented by the rectangle, c′ D′ H G, which should be shaded to a deeper tint than the cast shadows, to distinguish it.

274. The operation by which we determine the shadow cast upon the horizontal plane, is evidently the same as in the preceding case; still, since the lower base, J H, does not rest upon the horizontal plane, it will not be sufficient merely to draw the rays of light through the points, C, D, E, F, of the upper side; it is, in addition, necessary to draw corresponding rays through the points, J, I, G, H, of the base.

It is to be observed, as in the preceding case, that as these two faces are parallel to the horizontal plane, the shadow cast by each upon this plane will be a figure equal and parallel to itself; so that, in place of seeking all the points of the shadow, it would have been quite sufficient to obtain one of these points, as d, for example, of the upper side, and k, of the lower side, and then, starting from them, to draw a couple of hexagons, parallel and equal to A B C D E F.

It will also be understood, that as it is only the outside lines, those of the separation of the light and shade, which make up the contour of the shadow, it is not necessary to determine the points which fall within this contour, and correspond to those points in the object itself which do not lie in the lines of separation of the illuminated and shaded parts.

275. Thus it is unnecessary to find the points, a, b, e, h; and generally, in making drawings, we do not seek the shadows cast by points fully illuminated, or within the borders of the shaded portion; and the contour of the shadow is derived simply from points lying in the line of separation of the light and shade on the object.

276. From what we have already explained, it will be gathered, that the projection in one plane of the shadow, cast by a point, can be obtained by drawing the diagonal of the square, a side of which is equal to the distance of the point from the plane, as shown in the other projection.

For example, the shadow, k, on the horizontal plane of the point, the two projections of which are F and I, figs. 2 and 2ᵃ, may be got by forming the square, F $l\,k$, a side of which, F l, is equal to the distance, I $l′$, of the point from the horizontal plane.

In the same way, we have the points, g, i, f, corresponding to G, I, F, which are the same height as the first above the plane.

For the points, c, d, e, f, which correspond to the upper side, A′ D′, of the prism, we draw the diagonal, D′ $d′$, of the square having for a side the height, D′ m, of the point, D′, above the horizontal plane, and set out this diagonal from C to c, D to d, E to e, &c.

PYRAMID.

277. When several straight lines converge to a point, the shadows they cast on either plane of projection must necessarily

N

also, converge to a point. Thus, in the pyramid, figs. 3 and 3ᵃ, the apex of which is projected in the points, s and s', the edges of all the sides being directed to this point, cast shadows on the horizontal plane, bounded by lines converging to the point, s, the shadow cast by the apex on the same plane. In order, then, to find the shadow cast by a pyramid, on either of the planes of projection, it is sufficient to draw the ray of light through the apex, and ascertain the point at which this ray meets the plane; then to draw lines to this point from all the angles of the base of the pyramid, if this rests upon the plane. If, however, the pyramid is raised above the plane, it will be necessary to find the shadows cast by the various angles of the base, and then draw straight lines from these to the shadow of the apex.

TRUNCATED PYRAMID.

278. When we have only the frustum of a pyramid to deal with, and the apex is not given, it is necessary to find the shadows cast both by the angles of the base, and by those of the surface of truncation. Thus, the points, E, F, G, H, of the upper side, cast their shadows on the horizontal plane, in the points, e, f, g, h, which are obtained by drawing through each point, in the vertical projection, E', F', G', H', the rays, inclined at an angle of 45°, meeting the base line in the points e', f', g', h', which are squared over to the horizontal projection, so as to meet the corresponding rays, drawn through the points, E, F, G, H. Then, if we draw lines from the points, e, f, g, h, to the angles, A, B, C, D, situated in the horizontal plane, we shall obtain the shadows cast by each of the lateral edges of the pyramid.

For the same reason that these edges are diversely inclined to the horizontal plane, the shadows cast by them on this plane have also different inclinations to the base line; but the edges of the upper side or surface of truncation being parallel to this plane, cast a shadow, which in figure is equal and parallel to this side; this would not have been the case had it been inclined to the plane. It is evident that, in the position in which the pyramid is represented with regard to the rays of light, the two faces, A E H D and A E F B, are in the light, whilst their opposites, D H G C and C G F B, are in the shade. This last, which is the only one visible in fig. 3ᵃ, is there distinguished by a moderate shade of colour.

CYLINDER.

279. A cylinder with a circular base being a regular solid, all that is wanted, in determining the lines of separation of light and shade, is, when the cylinder is vertical, to draw a couple of planes tangential to it, and parallel to the rays of light, as in figs. 4 and 4ᵃ. These tangential planes are projected in the horizontal plane, in the lines, A a, B b, tangents to the circle, and inclined at the angle of 45°. By their points of contact with the circle, these tangents give the lines of separation of light and shade, which are projected vertically in A' c and B' D. One of these lines is apparent on this view, but the other is not. We have thus the portion, A E B, of the cylinder, in the light, and its opposite, A F B, in the shade. A very small portion of this last is seen in fig. 4ᵃ, and is there slightly shaded.

280. With reference to the cast shadow, it is to be remarked, that for the very reason that the lines of separation of light and

shade are vertical, the shadows they will cast on the horizontal plane will be in two lines, c a and d b, with an inclination of 45°, as already explained, these lines being identical with the prolongation of the tangential rays. The two bases of the cylinder being parallel to the horizontal plane, their shadows will be circles equal to themselves; and all that is required is to find the shadows, n, o, cast by their respective centres, N and o', and with the points, n, o, as centres, to describe circles, with a radius equal to o A. The entire shadow cast by the cylinder is comprised between the two semicircles and the two tangents, c a, d b.

SHADOW CAST BY ONE CYLINDER UPON ANOTHER.

281. Hitherto we have only considered the shadow cast by an object upon one of the planes of projection. It frequently happens, however, that one body casts a shadow on another, or that the configuration of the body itself is such, that one part of it casts a shadow on another.

Let fig. 6 be the vertical projection of a short cylinder, A, with a concentric cylindrical head, B. We have, in the first place, to find the line of separation of light and shade upon these two cylinders; and for this purpose we require to draw a second vertical projection, fig. 6ᵃ, at right angles to the first, and in the line of its axis. In this figure, the projection of the ray of light also makes an angle of 45° with the base line. We must, consequently, draw the two straight lines, c' c' and D' d', tangential to the circles, A' and B, and project, or square over, the points of contact, c' and d', to fig. 6, drawing the lines, a b and D d, which separate the light from the shaded part of the objects. Instead of drawing these tangents, we can directly obtain both points of contact, by drawing the radius, o c' d', at right angles to the ray of light.

282. The shadow cast by the projecting head, B, upon the cylinder, A, is limited to that due to the portion, d' c' H', of the circumference. Different points in the outline of this shadow are determined, by first taking any points, c', E', F', G', upon the arc, d' c' H', and drawing through each of them lines, representing the parallel rays of light, and meeting the circumference of the cylinder, A', in the points, c', e', f', g'. Having projected the first-mentioned points on the base, d H (fig. 6), draw through the points, c, E, F, G, a series of lines parallel to the first, and likewise representing the rays of light, and square over the points of contact, c', e', f', g', which will give the points, c, e, f, g, of the curve, which is the outline of the shadow upon the cylinder, A.

As seen in a former example, instead of squaring over the points, c', e', f', g', we can obtain the same result by making the corresponding rays, c c, E e, F f, G g, equal to the lines, c' c', E' e', F' f', G' g'.

SHADOW CAST BY A CYLINDER UPON A PRISM.

283. Figs. 7 and 7ᵃ represent two vertical projections of a prism, A, of an octagonal base, having a cylindrical projecting head, B.

As in the preceding case, draw the radius, o d', perpendicular to the ray of light, thereby obtaining the point of contact, d', and, in consequence, the line of separation, D d, of light and shade on the cylindrical head, B.

The inclined facet, c' i', of the prism, being in the direction of the ray of light, and, consequently, inclined at an angle of 45° with the vertical plane, is considered to be completely in the shade. The edge line, *a b*, fig. 7, is therefore the line of separation of light and shade on the prism-shaped portion of the object, and the surface, *a b i d*, is consequently tinted. The shadow cast upon the prism by the overhanging head, B, reduces itself to that due to the portion, c' F' H', merely, of the circumference of the latter, and it falls upon the two faces, c' *f* and *f'* h', of the latter.

The lines indicated on the diagram, with their corresponding letters, when compared with those of the preceding example, will show that the operations are precisely the same in both cases, and, in the latter, the curves, *c e f* and *f g h*, are the resulting outlines of the shadow. In general, it is unnecessary to obtain more than the extreme points of the curve, and another near the middle. Through the three points thus obtained, arcs of circles can then be drawn. The curves are, however, in reality elliptical.

SHADOW CAST BY ONE PRISM UPON ANOTHER.

284. Figs. 8 and 8ᵃ represent a couple of vertical projections, at right angles to each other, of a prism of an octagonal base, surmounted by a similar and concentric, but larger prism. Although the operations called for in this case are precisely the same as in the two preceding, still it is an exemplification which cannot be omitted; and its chief use is to show, that

The shadow cast by a straight line upon a plane surface is invariably a straight line; and, consequently, it is sufficient to determine its extreme points, in order to obtain the entire shadow in any one plane.

Thus, the straight line, E' c', casts a shadow upon the plane facet, *f c*, which is represented by the straight line, *e c*.

It is further obvious, that

The shadow cast upon a plane surface, by any line parallel to it, must be parallel to that line.

Thus, the straight line, E' G', of the larger prism, B, being parallel to the plane facet, *f g'*, of the prism, A, casts a shadow upon the latter, which is represented by the straight line, *f g*, parallel to the line, F G, the vertical projection of the edge, F' G'. It is not, however, the same with the portion, *e f*, because the corresponding portion, E' F', of the edge of the larger prism, is not parallel to the facet, *f e'*.

SHADOW CAST BY A PRISM UPON A CYLINDER.

285. Figs. 9 and 9ᵃ represent vertical projections, at right angles to each other, of a portion of an iron rod, A, surmounted by a concentric head, B, of a hexagonal base. The main object of this diagram is to show, that

When a right cylinder is parallel, or perpendicular, to a plane of projection, any straight line, which is perpendicular to the axis of the cylinder, and parallel to the plane of projection, casts a shadow upon the cylindrical surface, which is represented by a curve, similar to the cross section of such surface.

If, therefore, the cylinder is of circular base or cross section, as we have supposed in the present case, the shadow cast upon it will be a portion of a circle, of the same radius as the cylinder. Thus, the straight line, D' F', situated in a plane, at right angles to the axis of the cylinder, A, and being, at the same time, parallel to the vertical plane, casts a shadow upon the cylinder, which is re-

presented by the portion, *c e f*, of a circle, the centre, o', of which is obtained by drawing through the point, O, a line, O I, representing the ray of light, and extending to the prolongation of the edge, D' F'. The line, O I, cuts the circumference of the cylinder in the point, i', which is squared over to *i*, upon the other projection, H *i*, fig. 9, of the ray, O I. The lower point, *c*, is obtained from the upper one, *i*, being symmetrical with reference to the axis of the cylinder. The ray, H *i*, being continued to the axis, cuts it in the point, o', which is, consequently, the centre of the arc, *c e i*, the radius, *i o'* or *c o'*, of which is equal to that, O i', of the cylinder.

286. The edge, F' H', although situated in a plane perpendicular to the axis of the cylinder, is not parallel to the vertical plane, and does not, therefore, cast a shadow of a circular outline upon the cylinder, but one of an elliptical outline, as *f g h*, which is obtained by means of points, the operations being fully indicated on the diagrams. If the head, B, which casts a shadow upon the cylinder, were square, instead of hexagonal, as is often the case, one of the sides of the square, as I H', fig. 9ᵃ, being perpendicular to the vertical plane, would cast a shadow on the cylinder, having for outline the straight line, H *i*, making the angle of 45° with the axis.

Thus, whenever a straight line is perpendicular to the plane of projection, not only is its shadow, as cast upon this plane, a straight line, inclined at the angle of 45°, but it is also the same on an object projected in this plane, no matter of what form.

OBSERVATION.—In the four examples last discussed, we have only represented half views of the objects in the auxiliary vertical projections, figs. 6ᵃ, 7,ᵃ 8ᵃ, and 9ᵃ, this being quite sufficient for determining the shadow, as it is only that produced by this half which is seen. It is obvious, that the same operations will answer the purpose, whether the axis of the object be horizontal or vertical.

SHADOW CAST BY A CYLINDER IN AN OBLIQUE POSITION.

287. In figs. 5 and 5ᵃ, we have given the horizontal and vertical projections of a right cylinder, having its axis horizontal, but inclined to the vertical plane. As in this oblique projection we cannot obtain the points of contact of the luminous rays with the base in a direct manner, it becomes necessary to make an especial diagram, in order to determine the lines of separation of light and shade, which are always straight lines, parallel to the axis of the cylinder.

To this effect, we shall make use of a general construction, susceptible of application to a variety of such cases. This construction consists in determining the projection of the luminous ray, in any given plane, perpendicular to either of the geometrical planes, whence may be derived its form and aspect in either of the latter planes. It follows, that if we have any curve in the given plane, we can easily find the point of separation of the light and shade situated upon this curve, by drawing a couple of tangents to it, parallel to the ray of light projected in this plane, and transferred to the other plane of projection.

Thus, let R O and R' o' be the projections of the luminous ray. it is proposed to find the projection of this ray upon the plane, *a b*, of the base of the cylinder. To obtain this, project the point, E to *r*, by means of a perpendicular to *a b*, and *r c* represents the horizontal projection of the ray of light upon the plane, *a b*, and the vertical projection, $r'\,o'$, is obtained by squaring over the point, o to o', on the base line, and the point, r to r', on the horizontal, R' e', and then joining $o'\,r'$. Next, draw tangents to the ellipses, which represent the vertical projections of the ends of the cylinder, fig. 5^a, making these tangents parallel to the ray of light, $r'\,o'$. Their points of contact give, on the one hand, the first line, $c'\,d'$, of separation of light and shade, which is visible in the vertical projection, and, on the other hand, the second line, $e'\,f'$, which is not visible in that projection.

By squaring over these points of contact, respectively, to the two ends, $a\,b$ and $g\,h$, of the cylinder, in the horizontal projection, we obtain the same lines of separation of light and shade, $c\,d$ and $f\,e$, as in this projection; the former of which lines is invisible, whilst the latter is visible.

The same lines, $c\,d$ and $f\,e$, fig. 5, can be obtained independently of the vertical projection, fig. 5^a, in the following manner:—Draw an end view of the cylinder, as at $a^2\,b^2$, having its centre in the continuation of the cylinder's axis. Upon this end view, also, draw the ray of light, as projected upon the base, after describing the circle, $a^2\,m\,b$, with the radius, $o\,a$; make $r\,r^2$ equal to the height of the point, R', above the bottom of the cylinder, thereby obtaining the line, $o\,r^2$, representing the ray of light upon the end view of the cylinder. Next, draw a couple of tangents to the circle, $a^2\,m\,b^2$, parallel to $o\,r^2$, and their points of contact, c^2, f^2, will represent the end view of the lines of separation of light and shade, which are transferred to the horizontal projection, fig. 5, by perpendiculars drawn from them to the straight line, $a\,b$.

288. When the shadow proper, of the cylinder, has been thus determined, it will not be difficult to find the outline of its shadow cast upon the horizontal plane. In the first place, the shadows of the two bases are found, being in the form of ellipses; and next, those, $c''\,d''$ and $f''\,e''$, cast by the lines, $c\,d$ and $f\,e$; namely, those of the separation of light and shade upon the object itself. These lines will necessarily be tangents to the ellipses, representing the shadows of the bases. It may be observed, that the transverse axes of the ellipses are parallel to the line, $r^2\,o$.

If the cylinder were inclined at an angle of 45° to the vertical plane, still remaining parallel, however, to the horizontal plane, the lines of separation of light and shade would, in the horizontal projection, be confounded with the extreme generatrices, or outlines, of the cylinder, the visible semicylinder being wholly in the light, and the opposite semicylinder wholly in the shade. In the vertical projection, the line of separation would be in the line of the axis, and would divide the figure horizontally into two equal parts.

PRINCIPLES OF SHADING.

PLATE XXVII.

289. Before proceeding to the further study of shadows, we must observe that shadows, proper and cast—which are simply represented by flat-tints, so as not to render the diagrams confused—should be modified in intensity according to the form of the objects, and the position of their surfaces with reference to the light.

The study of shading carries us somewhat into the province of the non-mechanical painter, who is guided by his taste rather than

by mathematical rules; still, whilst we acknowledge the difficulty of laying down an exact theory on this subject, we would recommend the following systematic methods, which will render the first difficulties of the study more easily surmountable.

In painting, and in every description of drawing, the effects of light and shade depend upon the following principles:—

ILLUMINED SURFACES.

290. *When an illumined surface has all its points at an equal distance from the eye, it must receive a clear shade of uniform intensity throughout.*

In geometrical drawing, where all the visual rays are supposed to be parallel and perpendicular to the plane of projection, all surfaces parallel to this plane have all their points equally distant from the eye: such is the plane and vertical surface, $a\,b\,c\,d$, of the prism, fig. Ⓐ.

291. *Of two such surfaces, disposed parallel to each other, and illumined in the same manner, that which is nearer to the eye should receive a shade of less intensity.*

292. *Any illumined surface, inclined to the plane of the picture, having its points at varying distances from the eye, should receive a shade of varying intensity.*

Now, according to the foregoing principle, it is the most advanced portion of an object which ought to be the lightest in colour; this effect is produced on the face, $a\,d\,f\,e$, which, as shown in the plan, fig. 1, is inclined to the vertical plane of projection.

293. *Of two illumined surfaces, that which is more directly presented to the rays of light should receive a shade of less intensity.*

Thus, the face, $e'\,a'$, fig. 1, being presented more directly to the light than the face, $a'\,b'$, is covered with a shade which, being graduated because of the inclination to the plane of the picture, is still, at the more advanced portion, of less intensity than that of the latter face. It is near the edge, $a\,d$, that the difference is more sensible.

SURFACES IN THE SHADE.

294. *When a surface in the shade is parallel to the plane of projection, or of the picture, it must receive a deep tint of uniform intensity throughout.*

An exemplification of this will be seen on the fillet, B, fig. Ⓒ, Plate XXVIII., which is parallel to the vertical plane: the difference of shade upon this fillet, in comparison with that upon the more projecting portion, A, which is parallel to it, but in the light, distinctly points out the difference between an illumined surface and one in the shade, in conformity with the two principles, 290 and 294.

295. *Of two parallel surfaces in the shade, that nearer the eye should receive the deeper tint.*

Thus, the shadow cast upon the fillet, B, fig. Ⓒ, Plate XXVIII., is sensibly deeper than that cast by it upon the vertical plane, which is more distant.

296. *When a surface in the shade is inclined to the plane of the picture, the part nearest to the eye should receive the deepest tint.*

The face, $b\,g\,h\,c$, fig. Ⓐ, Plate XXVII., projected horizontally in $b'\,g'$, fig. 1, is thus situated. The shade is made considerably deeper near the edge, $b\,c$, than near the more distant one, $g\,h$.

297. *When two surfaces in the shade are unequally inclined, with reference to the direction of the rays of light, the shadow cast by any object should be deeper upon that which receives it more directly.*

Thus, the shadow, *a d f e*, cast upon the face, F, of the prism, fig. 3, Plate XXVI., should be slightly stronger than that cast upon the face, G, because the first is more directly presented to the light than the second, as shown by the lines, *f' h'* and *f' c'*, fig. 7ª.

These first principles are exemplified in the finished figures on Plate XXVI., XXVII., and subsequent ones.

As, in order to produce the gradations of shades, it is important to have some knowledge of actual colouring or shading by means of the brush, we shall proceed to give a few short explanations of this matter.

Two methods of producing the graduated shades are in use—one consisting in laying on a succession of flat tints; the other, in softening off the shade by the manipulation of the brush.

We have already said two or three words about the laying on of flat tints, when treating of representing sections by distinguishing colours. (137.) These first precepts may serve as a basis for the first method of shading, which is the less difficult of the two for beginners. In fact, according to it, the graduated shade is produced by the simple superposition of a number of flat tints.

FLAT-TINTED SHADING,

298. Let it be required to shade a prism, A, Plate XVII., with flat tints :—

According to the position of this prism, with reference to the plane of projection, as seen in fig. 1, it appears that the face, *a' b'*, is parallel to the vertical plane, and is fully illumined; it should, consequently, receive a clear uniform tint, spread over it by the brush, and made either from China ink or sepia, as has been done upon the rectangle, *a, b, c, d*, fig. A. When the surface to be washed is of considerable extent, the paper should first be prepared by a very light wash, the full intensity required being arrived at by a second or third. (137.)

The face, *b' g'*, being inclined to the vertical plane, and completely in the shade, should receive a tint (294) deepest at the edge, *b c*, and gradually less intense towards *g h*; this is obtained by laying on several flat shades, each of different extent. For this purpose, and to proceed in a regular manner, we recommend the student to divide the face, *b' g'*, fig. 1, into several equal parts, as in the points, 1', 2', and through these points to draw lines parallel to the sides, *b c, g h*, fig. A. These lines should be drawn very lightly indeed, in pencil, as they are merely for guides. A first greyish tint is then spread over the surface comprised between the first line, 1—1, and the side, *b c*, as in fig. 2; when this is quite dry, a second like it is laid on, covering the first, and extending from the side, *b c*, to the line, 2—2, as in fig. 3. Finally, these are covered with a third wash, as in fig. A, extending to the outer edge, *g h*, and completing the graduated shade of the rectangle, *b c g h*.

The number of washes by which the gradation is expressed, evidently depends upon the width of the surface to be shaded; and it will be seen that the greater the number of washes used,

the lighter they should be, and the lines produced by the edges of each will be less hard, and a more beautiful effect will result.

The student must remember to efface the pencilled guide-lines, as soon as the washes are sufficiently dry.

299. This method of overlaying the washes, and covering a greater extent of surface at each succeeding time, is preferable to the one sometimes adopted, according to which the whole surface, *b g h c*, is first covered by a uniform wash; a second being then laid over *b 2—2 c*; and finally, a third over the narrow strip, *b 1—1 c*. When the shade is produced in this manner, the edges of the washes are always harder than when the washes are laid on as we recommend—the narrowest first—for the subsequent washes, coming over the edge of each preceding one, soften it to a considerable extent.

The face, *e' a'*, fig. 1, being likewise inclined to the vertical plane, but being wholly illumined, should receive a very light shade (292), being, however, a little bolder towards the outer edge, *e f*, fig. A. The shade is produced in the same way as that of the face, *b' g'*, but with much fainter washes.

300. Let it be proposed to shade a cylinder, fig. B, with a series of flat tints :—

In a cylinder, it is necessary to give the gradations of shade, both of the illumined and of the non-illumined portion. In reference to this, it will be recollected that the line of separation, *a b*, of light and shade, is determined by the radius inclined at an angle of 45°, as *o a*, fig. 4, perpendicular to the ray of light; consequently, all the shadow proper, which is apparent in the vertical projection, fig. B, is comprised between the line, *a b*, and the extreme generatrix, *c d*. Consequently, according to the principle already laid down (296), the shade of this portion of the surface should be graduated from *a b* to *c d*, as was the case with the inclined plane surface, *b' g'*, fig. 1, the greater intensity being towards *a b*.

On the other hand, all that part of the cylinder comprised between the line, *a b*, and the extreme generatrix, *f g*, is in the light: at the same time, from its rounded form, each generatrix is at a different distance from the vertical plane of projection, and makes different angles with the ray of light. Consequently, this portion of the surface should receive graduated shades. (292.) To express the effect in a proper manner, it is necessary to know what part of the surface is the clearest and most brilliant; and this is evidently the part about the generatrix, *e i*, fig. B, situated in the vertical plane of the ray of light, R O, fig. 4. In consequence, however, of the visual rays being perpendicular to the vertical plane and parallel to the line, V O, the portion which appears to the eye to be the clearest will be nearer to this line, V O, and may be limited, on the one hand, by the line, T O, bisecting the angle made by the lines, R O and V O, and on the other, by the line, R O; squaring over, then, the points, *e'* and *m'*, fig. 4, and drawing the lines, *e i* and *m n*, fig. B, we obtain the surface, *e i m n*, which is the most illumined.

301. This surface is bright, and remains white, when the cylinder is polished, as a turned iron shaft, for example, or a marble column · it is covered with a light shade, being always clearer, however, than the rest of the surface, when the cylinder is unpolished, as a cast-iron pipe.

302. After these preliminary observations, we may proceed to

shade the cylinder, f' m' a' e', fig. 4, dividing it into a certain number of equal parts, the more numerous according as the cylinder is greater. These divisions are squared over to the vertical projection, and straight lines drawn lightly with the pencil, as limiting guides for the colour. We then lay a light gray shade on the surface, a c d b, fig. 5, to distinguish at once the part in the shade ; when this is dry, we lay on a second covering, the line, a b, of separation of light and shade, and extending over a division on either side of it, as shown in fig. 6 ; we afterwards lay on a third shade, covering two divisions to the right and to the left, as in fig. 7 ; and proceed in the same manner, covering more and more each time, always keeping to the pencil lines. The different stages are represented in figs. 8, 9, and 10.

303. We next shade the part, f e i g, laying on successive shades, but lighter than the preceding, as indicated in figs. 8, 9, and 10.

The operation is finally terminated by laying a light wash over the whole, leaving untouched only a very small portion of the bright surface, e m n i, fig. ⒝. This last wash has a beautiful and softening effect.

SHADING BY SOFTENED WASHES.

304. This system of shading differs from the former in producing the effects of light and shade by imperceptible gradations, obtained by manipulation with the brush in the laying on of the colour : this system possesses the advantage over the first, of not leaving any lines, dividing the different degrees of shade, which sometimes appear harsh to the eye, and seem to represent facets or flutings, which do not exist.

For machinery, however, the former system is very effective, bringing out the objects so shaded in a remarkable manner. Indeed, we recommend all machinery to be shaded in this manner, whilst architectural subjects will look better treated according to the second system.

In this, the laying on of the shade is much more difficult, requiring considerable practice, which will be aided by proceeding in the following systematic course.

305. Let it be proposed to shade a truncated hexagonal pyramid, fig. ⒟, Plate XXVII.

The position of this solid, with reference to the vertical plane of projection, is the same as that of the prism, fig. ⒜. Thus the face, a b c d, should receive a uniform flat shade of little intensity ; rigorously keeping to rules, this should be slightly graduated from top to bottom, as the face is not quite parallel to the vertical plane.

The face, b g h c, being inclined, and also in the shade, should receive a deep shade, graduated from b c to g h ; to this effect apply a first light shade to the side, b c, fig. 15, softening it off to the right, taking the line, 1—1, as a limiting guide in that direction : this softening is produced by clearing the brush, so that the colour may be all expended before the lighter side is reached ; and when the shade is wide, a little water should be taken up in the brush once or twice, to attenuate the colour remaining in it. By these means an effect will be produced like that indicated in fig. 15., care being taken not to extend the wash beyond the outline of the object.

When this first wash is well dry, a second is laid over it, produced exactly in the same manner, and extending further to the right, covering the space, b c 2—2, as shown in fig. 16. Proceeding in the same manner, according to the number of divisions of the face, we at length cover the whole, producing the graduated shade, b g h c, fig. ⒟.

The operations are the same for the face, e a d f, which is nearly perpendicular to the rays of light, but is considerably inclined to the plane of projection.

In rigorously following out the established principles, the shade on this face should be graduated, not only from e f to a d, but also from e a to f d. Also, on the face, b g h c, in the shade, the tint should be a trifle darker at the base, c h, being graduated off towards b g. But for objects so simple in form as the one under consideration, this nicety may be neglected—at any rate, by the beginner—as only increasing his difficulties ; the proficient, on the other hand, is well aware how attention to these refinements assists in producing effective and truthful representations.

306. Let it be proposed to shade a cylinder with softened washes, fig. ⒞, Plate XXVII.

By following the indications given in fig. 4, for the regular imposition of the shades, as explained with reference to the flat-wash shading, the desired effect may be similarly produced by substituting the softened washes. It is scarcely necessary to divide the circumference into so many parts as for the former method ; a first shade must be laid on at the line, a b, of separation of light and shade, and this must be softened off in both directions, as in fig. 11 ; a second and a third wash must then be applied and similarly softened off, and in this manner we attain the effects rendered in figs. 12, 13, and ⒞.

We have not deemed it necessary to give diagrams of all the stages, as the method of procedure will be easily understood from preceding examples. The student should practise these methods upon different objects of simple form, and he will thereby rapidly acquire the necessary facility.

307. When spots or inequalities arise in laying on a wash, from defects in the paper or other accidents, they should be corrected with great care. If they err on the dark side, they should, if possible, be washed out ; the best means of doing this, in very bad cases, is to let the drawing become perfectly dry, and then slightly moisten the spots, and gently rub off the colour with a clean rag. Lights may be taken out in this way, where, from their minuteness or intricate shape, it would be difficult to leave them whilst laying on a flat shade, in the midst of which they may happen to be. A defect on the light side is more easily corrected, by applying more colour to the spots in question—being careful to soften off the edges, and to equalize the whole wash.

Figs. ⒜, ⒝, ⒞, ⒟, ⒠, Plate XXVI., represent several shaded objects, the shadows of which have already been discussed, as indicated in figs. 1 to 9. These may serve as guides, also, in shading with washes of colour, although the shades in that plate are produced by lines, whilst the figures in Plate XXVII. represent the actual appearance of the wash-shading method.

Finally, we have to recommend the adoption of a much larger scale for practice, as it is desirable to be able to produce large washes with regularity and smoothness of effect.

CONTINUATION OF THE STUDY OF SHADOWS.

PLATE XXVIII.

SHADOW CAST UPON THE INTERIOR OF A CYLINDER.

308. When a hollow cylinder, as a steam-engine cylinder, a cast-iron column, or a pipe, is cut by a plane passing through its axis, we have, on the one hand, a straight projecting edge, and, on the other, a portion of one of the ends, which cast shadows upon the internal surface of the cylinder.

We propose, then, to determine the form, as projected, of the shadow cast upon its interior by a steam-engine cylinder, A, sectioned by a plane passing through its axis, figs. 1 and 1ᵃ. In the first place, we seek the position of the shadow cast by the rectilinear projecting edge, B C, which is, in fact, produced by the intersecting plane, B′ A′. This straight line, B C, being vertical, is projected horizontally in the point, B′, and casts a shadow upon the cylinder, as represented by the straight line, b f, which is also vertical, and is determined by the point, b, of intersection of the ray of light, B′ b′, with the surface of the cylinder, B′ b′ o′. Thus, when a straight line is parallel to a generatrix of the cylinder, the shadow cast by it will be a straight line parallel to the axis. It is, therefore, evidently quite sufficient to find a single point, whence the entire shadow may be derived.

309. We next proceed to determine the shadow cast upon the interior of the cylinder by the circular portion, B′ E′ F′, of the upper end. If we take any point, E′, on this circle, and square it over to E in the vertical projection, and draw through this point a ray of light, E′ e′, E e, it will be found to meet the cylindrical surface in the point, e′, which is squared over to e, the length of the ray being equal in both projections, according to the well known rule. This applies to any point in the arc, E′ F′. The extreme point on one side is obtained by a tangent to the circle in the point, F′, giving the point, F, in the vertical projection; the opposite extreme point, b, being already given as the top point of the straight edge, B C; we have, therefore, the curve, F e b, for the upper outline of the shadow due to the circular portion, B′ E′ F′.

310. If, as in figs. 1 and 1ᵃ, we suppose the piston, P, with its rod, T, to be retained unsectioned in the cylinder, we shall have to determine the form of the shadow cast by the projecting part of the piston upon the interior of the cylinder, and represented by the curve, d h o. For this purpose we take any points, B′, H′, O′, on the circumference of the piston, and draw through them, in both projections, the rays of light which meet the surface of the cylinder, B′ b′ o′, in the points, b′ h′ o′, which are projected vertically in d h o: the curve passing through these points is the outline of the shadow sought. The curved portions of these shadows are elliptical.

The piston-rod, T, being cylindrical and vertical, casts a shadow, of a rectangular form, upon the interior of the cylinder, the vertical sides, i j, k l, being determined by the luminar tangents, I′ i′, K′ k′, parallel to the axis.

SHADOW CAST BY ONE CYLINDER UPON ANOTHER.

311. Let figs. 2 and 2ᵃ be the projections of a convex semi-cylinder, A, tangential to a concave semicylinder, B, forming a pattern often met with in mouldings.

This problem, which consists in determining the shadow proper of a convex cylinder, together with that cast by it upon the surface of a concave cylinder, in addition to that cast by the latter upon itself, is a combination of the cases discussed in reference to figs. 4 and 4ᵃ, Plate XXVI., and to figs. 1 and 1ᵃ in the present plate. The operations called for here are fully indicated on the diagram; and we have merely to remark, that it is always well to start by determining the extreme points, as C′, D,′ which limit the shadow proper C G, and cast shadow, D c g: these points may be obtained more exactly, as already pointed out, by drawing the radii, O c′ and D′ E, perpendicular to the luminous rays.

SHADOWS OF CONES.

312. In this branch of the study, we propose to determine, first, the shadow proper, or the line of separation of light and shade upon the surface of the cone; second, the shadow cast by the cone upon the vertical plane of projection; and, third, the shadow cast upon the cone, and upon the vertical plane of projection, by a prism of a square base, placed horizontally over the cone.

313. First: We have laid it down as a general principle, that, in order to determine the shadow proper of any surface, it is necessary to draw a series of parallel luminous rays tangential to this surface. When, however, the body is a solid of revolution generated by a straight line, as a cylinder or a cone, it is sufficient to draw tangential planes parallel to the luminous rays, to obtain the lines of separation of light and shade.

In the case of the cone represented in figs. 3 and 3ᵃ, and of which the axis, S T, is vertical, the operation consists in drawing from the apex, s and s′, two lines, making angles of 45°, as s s and s′ s′, giving, in the point, s′, the shadow cast by this apex upon the horizontal plane. From this point we draw a straight line, a′ s′, tangential to the base, A′ c′ B′, of the cone. This straight line represents the plane, tangential to the cone, as intersecting the horizontal plane of the base; and the contact generatrix is then obtained by letting fall from the centre, s′, a radius, s′ a′, perpendicular to the line, a′ s′; and this line, s′ a′, is the horizontal projection of one of the lines of separation of light and shade. The vertical projection of this straight line is obtained by squaring over the point of contact, a′, to a, and then drawing the straight line, s a. The other line, s b, of the separation of light and shade, is similarly obtained by means of the tangent, s′ b′. Its vertical projection is, however, not apparent in fig. 3ᵃ.

314. Second: The shadow cast by the cone upon the vertical plane is limited, on the one hand, by the line of separation of light and shade, and, on the other, by the portion of the illumined base comprised between the two separation lines. Now, the straight line, s a, casts a shadow, represented by the straight line, s² a², as indicated in the diagram; and the base, A′ E′ c′ B′, casts a shadow, represented by the elliptic curve, f e d a², which is determined by points, as in the case considered in reference to fig. 5, Plate XXVI.

315. Third: The shadow cast by the lower side, G H, of the rectangular prism, P, upon the convex surface of the cone, is found in accordance with the principle already enunciated—that when a straight line is parallel to a plane of projection, it casts a shadow

upon this plane, which is represented by a straight line, equal and parallel to itself. It follows, then, that if we cut the cone by a plane, M N, parallel to its base, the shadow cast by the straight line, G H, upon this plane, will be found by drawing from the point, I, of the base, situated upon the axis of the cone, and projected horizontally in the point, s', a luminous ray, which meets this plane, M N, in the point, i, projected horizontally in the point, i', upon the projection of the same ray. If, next, we make $i^1\ i^2$ equal to s' J', and through i^2 draw the straight line, $G^2\ H^2$, this last will be the shadow cast by the edge, G H, of the prism, upon the plane, M N. This plane, however, cuts the cone in a circle, the diameter, M N, of which is comprised between the extreme generatrices, whilst the circle is projected horizontally in M' L' N'. The intersection of the straight line, $G^2\ H^2$, with the circle, gives the two points, i^2 and i^2, which being projected vertically in i, i'', upon the straight line, M N, constitute two points in the outline of the shadow cast upon the cone.

Continuing the operations in this manner, and taking any other intersecting plane parallel to M N, any number of points may be obtained. It will be observed that these planes are taken at a convenient height, when the projections of the straight line, G H, cut the corresponding circles; and with regard to this, much useless labour may be avoided, by at first determining the limiting points of the curve. Thus, in the example before us, we get the summit, g, of the curve, by making I J, fig. 3^a, equal to J' s', fig. 3. Through the point, J, we then draw a luminous ray, and the point, g'', at which it meets the extreme generatrix, A s, of the cone, is squared over to the generatrix, s T, by means of the horizontal, g'' g, whence g is the summit of the curve. We next obtain the extreme points, h, h', of the same shadow, by making s' G'', fig. 3, equal to s' G', and squaring over G'' to G^2, in fig. 3^a. Through G^2 draw the straight line, $G^2\ h'$, parallel to the luminous ray, as situate in a vertical plane, passing through it; the ray, as we have already seen, making, in this plane, an angle of 35° 16' with the base line. The point, h', at which this ray meets the extreme generatrix, s A, determines the plane, h' h, which is intersected by the luminous rays, making angles of 45°, and drawn through the points, I and G, in the points, h, h', the limits of the curve sought.

The shadow cast by the prism, P, upon the vertical planes, presents no peculiarity apart from the principles already fully explained.

SHADOW OF AN INVERTED CONE.

316. When the cone, instead of resting upon its base, has its apex downwards, as is the case with the one represented in figs. 4 and 4^a, the rays of light illumine a less portion of its surface; and the lines of separation of light and shade are determined by drawing from the apex, s s', lines at an angle of 45°, which are prolonged towards the light, until they intersect the prolongation of the plane of the base, A B.

It will be observed, that the points of intersection, s, s', lie to the left, instead of to the right of the cone. Through the point, s', the horizontal projection of the point, s, draw a couple of lines, s' a', s' b', tangential to the circumference, A' B' D', of the base. The radii, s' a' and s' b', drawn to the points of contact, represent the horizontal projection of the two lines of separation of light and shade, and show that the illuminated portion of the cone, consisting

of the surface, b' G^2 a' s', is smaller than the portion, b' D' a' s', in the shade. In the case of the cone with its apex uppermost, the contrary would be observed, the portion in the shade being there less than that in the light; and the method given of determining the proportion of shadow of the inverted cone is suggested by the consideration, that this proportion must be exactly the reverse of that for the cone with its apex uppermost.

The first-mentioned line, s' a', is the only one apparent in the vertical projection, fig. 4^a. It is found by squaring over the point, a', to a, and joining this last to the apex, s. As the cone is truncated by the plane, D E, the line of separation obviously terminates at the point, c, of its intersection with this plane.

317. The cone, thus inverted, is surmounted, moreover, by a square plinth, the sides of which, F G' and C' H', cast shadows upon its convex surface. The side, F G', as projected vertically in G', fig. 4^a, is perpendicular to the vertical plane, and consequently its cast shadow is a straight line, making an angle of 45°, as G f. The extreme limit, f, is determined by proceeding as in previous examples; that is to say, by making I G^2, in fig. 4^a, equal to s' G', in fig. 4, and then drawing through the point, G^2, the straight line, $G^2\ h''$, parallel to the ray of light, as in the diagonal plane, that is, at an angle of 35° 16' to the horizon; next draw the horizontal line, h'' h, and it will be intersected by the straight line, G f, in the point, f, which is consequently the shadow cast by the corner, G.

The following method, although more complicated, is of more universal application:—Draw the vertical projection of the outline of the body which receives the shadow, as sectioned by the vertical plane, in which the ray of light lies, which passes through the point whose shadow is sought; draw the same ray of light as projected in the vertical plane, and its intersection with the projection of the sectional outline will be the projection of the shadow of the point.

Thus, in the present instance, as the plane of the ray, G' f, passes through the apex of the cone, the latter will present a triangular section, the vertical projection of which may be obtained by squaring over the point, G^2, fig. 4, to the base line, A B, fig. 4^a; then, if a straight line is drawn from the vertical projection of this point to the apex, s, it will represent the projection of the section of the cone, and it will be intersected by the luminous ray, G f, in the point, f, which is the point sought.

If the plane passing through the point does not likewise pass through the axis of the cone, the section will be a parabola, which may be drawn according to methods already discussed. If the object is a sphere instead of a cone, the section will be a circle, whether the plane passes through the centre or not, and the vertical projection will, in all cases, be an ellipse. As a good idea of the whereabouts of the point sought may always be formed on inspection, it will generally be sufficient to find one or two points in the parabola or ellipse, near the supposed position, when a sufficient length of the curve may be drawn to give the intersection of the luminous ray, as G f.

As the plinth is square, the summit, g, of the curved outline, corresponding to the shadow of the front edge, G H, is obtained directly by the intersection in g'' of the line, G f, with the extreme generatrix, A s, the horizontal line, g'' g, being drawn through this point. Any other point in the curve, as i'', is afterwards found by means of the sectional plane, M N ; G² H, fig. 4, is the shadow of the edge, G H, in that plane, and it cuts the circle representing the section of the cone in the same plane in the point, i'', which is obviously a point in the outline of the shadow.

SHADOW CAST UPON THE INTERIOR OF A HOLLOW CONE.

318. Fig. 5 represents a plan of a hollow truncated cone, and fig. 5ᵃ is a vertical section through the axis of the object. It is required to determine the horizontal projection of the shadow cast upon the internal surface of the cone by the portion of the edge, A′ B C, and the vertical projection of the shadow cast by the sectional edge, D s, and by the small circular portion, A′ D′, projected vertically in A D.

It is to be observed, in the first place, that the straight line, D s, which is a generatrix of the cone, casts a shadow upon the latter, in the form of a straight line, for the plane parallel to the ray of light, and passing through this line, D s, must cut the cone in a generatrix ; we therefore draw through the point, D′, the ray of light, D′ d′, making an angle of 45° with the base line, and from the centre, s′, let fall the perpendicular, s′ E′, this straight line representing the horizontal projection of the intersection of the cone by the plane passing through the line, D′ s′, and at the same time parallel to the ray of light. By squaring over the point, E′, to E, fig. 5ᵃ, and joining E s, we have the vertical projection of this line of intersection, and consequently the shadow cast by the line, D s. The diagonal ray of light, D d, drawn through the point, D, determines the limit, d, of the shadow. The horizontal projection of the extreme points, A′ and c, of the curved outline of the shadow, is also obtained by means of the tangents, s′ A′ and s′ c, drawn from the point, s, in which the ray of light passing through the apex intersects the plane of the base of the cone. The determination of the central or symmetrical point, b′, of the same curve, is derived from the straight line, D b, drawn from the point, D, parallel to the ray of light, s R², as in the diagonal plane, that is, as at s R² ; the point, b, in which this straight line meets the generatrix directly opposite to that passing through the point, D, is projected horizontally in the point, b′, upon the prolongation of the diagonal ray of light, s′ s′.

319. The operation for finding any intermediate point in the curve, is based on principles already explained ; namely, that when a line or a surface is parallel to a plane, the shadow cast is also a line or a surface equal and parallel to the first. If, then, we draw a plane, M N, parallel to the base, D F, of the cone, the shadow cast by this base upon the plane, M N, will be a circle ; it will consequently be sufficient to draw through the centre, o, fig. 5ᵃ, a ray, o a, which will meet the plane, M N, in a, which must be squared over to a′, on the horizontal projection of the same ray. Next, with the point, a′, for a centre, and with a radius equal to D o, describe a circle, H′ I J ; this will represent the entire shadow that would be cast by the base, D F, of the cone upon the plane, M N ; this plane, however, cuts the cone in the circle, of which M N is the diameter and vertical projection, whilst H′ M′ J N′ is the horizontal projection ; this circle is cut by the former in the points, H′ and J, which are consequently two points in the outline of the shadow in fig. 5, and the one of these which is seen in the vertical projection is squared over to H, upon the line, M N.

320. In this plate, as well as in Plate XXVI., we have given shaded and finished representations of several objects, which serve as applications of the several principles we have just pointed out, whether referring to shadows proper, or cast, or to graduated shading. Thus, fig. Ⓐ represents the interior of a steam-engine cylinder with piston and rod. In this example, regard has been had to the general principle, that shadows are the stronger the brighter the surfaces on which they fall would be, if illumined—that is, when such surfaces are perpendicular to the rays of light, any shadow cast upon them will be most intense ; the shade is consequently made deepest about the generatrix, corresponding to G h, in fig. 1ᵃ, and situate in the vertical plane of the rays of light passing through the axis of the cylinder : to the right and left of this line, the shade is softened off.

321. In the graduation of the shade, regard has also been had to the effects of the reflected light, which prevents a surface in the shade from being quite black. In a hollow cylinder, for the portion in the shade, it is the generatrix, F F², fig. 1ᵃ, which should receive the shade of least intensity, as it receives the reflected rays of light more directly. It will be recollected that the point, F′, is obtained by means of the radius, T F′, perpendicular to the ray of light.

Fig. Ⓑ represents a portion of a common moulding, and shows how the distinction made between the shadow proper, and the cast shadow, tends to bring out and show the form of the object.

Fig. Ⓒ is an architectural fragment from the Doric order, given as an application of shadows cast upon cones, as well as those cast by cones upon a vertical plane.

This example also shows how necessary it is, in producing an effective representation, to make a difference in the intensity of shadows cast upon planes parallel to the plane of projection, and at different distances from the eye ; and also to give gradations to such shadows when cast upon rounded surfaces.

Fig. Ⓓ is a combination of a cylinder with a couple of cones, with their apices in opposite directions, showing how differently the effects of light and shade have to be rendered upon each.

There is less shadow upon the upper cone than upon the cylinder, whilst there is more upon the lower cone ; the reasons of these differences have already been explained in reference to figs. 3ᵃ and 4ᵃ.

Fig. Ⓔ represents an inverted and truncated cone, showing the manner of shading the same, and the form of the shadow cast by the square tablet above ; and fig. Ⓕ is a view of a hollow cone, sectioned across the axis, presenting a further variety of combinations

---

TUSCAN ORDER.

PLATE XXIX.

SHADOW OF THE TORUS.

322. In geometry, the torus is a solid, generated by a circle, revolving about an axis, continuing constantly in the plane of this axis, in such a manner, that all sections made by planes passing through the axis are equal circles, and all sections by planes perpendicular to the axis will also be circles, but of variable diameters.

We have seen, that in architecture, the torus is one of the essential parts of the base, and of the capital of the column, of each order. It will, therefore, be useful to give the methods of determining the shadows upon it, or cast by it, in the quickest and most accurate manner.

Figs. 1 and 1ᵃ represent the two projections of a torus, A, supposed to be generated by the semicircle, $a\,f\,c$, revolving about the vertical axis, o P; namely, that of the column.

323. We propose to determine the shadow proper of this torus, or the line of separation of light and shade upon its external surface. It will be convenient, in the first place, to seek the principal points, which, for the most part, present little difficulty. Thus, by drawing, parallel to the ray of light, R o′, a couple of tangents to the semicircles, $a\,f\,c$, which limit the contour of the torus in the vertical projection, we at once obtain the two extreme points, b, d, of the curved line of separation. These points are more exactly defined by letting fall perpendiculars from the centres, o, o', of the semicircles, upon the tangents. Then, by drawing through the point, b, the horizontal, $b\,e$, the middle point, e, of the curve will be obtained upon the vertical line, o P.

To obtain the curve in the horizontal projection, square over the points, b, e, d, of fig. 1ᵃ, to b', e', d', fig. 1, which will lie in a circle, having $b\,e$ or $o\,d$ for radius. An additional point, g', is obtained by drawing the diagonal, o′ g′, perpendicular to the ray, R′ o′; this radius cuts the outer circumference, $f'\,h\,f'$, of the torus, in the point, g'. This circumference, $f'\,h\,f'$, is projected vertically in the horizontal line, $f\,f$, passing through the centres, o, o, of the semicircles, and the point, g', is squared over to g, in fig. 1ᵃ.

To find the point, i, which seems to be the lowest in the curve, and which is situated in the vertical plane passing through the luminous ray, $i\,o$, of the horizontal projection, fig. 1—2, we proceed as follows:—Suppose the vertical plane, $i'\,o'$, to be turned about the axis, o P, so as to coincide with the plane of projection, when the section of the torus by the plane, $i'\,o'$, being obviously a semicircle, will coincide with the semicircle, $a\,f\,c$, draw a tangent, $k\,i^2$, to the last, parallel to the ray of light, as in the vertical plane, $i'\,o'$—that is, at an angle of 35° 16′, as has been already explained —the point of contact, i^2, is the one sought. But it has to be transferred to the original position of the vertical plane; and for this purpose it is squared over to i^3, in the horizontal projection. Then o′ i' is made equal to o′ i^3, and the point, i', again squared over to i, in the horizontal, $i^3\,i$, drawn through i^3.

It is generally sufficient to find five principal points, as b, i, e, g, and d, in the curved line of separation of light and shade; but if, because of the large scale of the drawing, it is wished to obtain intermediate points, this may be done by drawing planes passing through the axis; such, for instance, as o′ B′, which cuts the torus in a circle of the same radius as the generating circle. We then proceed to find the point of contact of the ray of light, according to the method indicated in figs. 5 and 5ᵃ, Plate XXVI.; that is to say, we seek the projection of the luminous ray upon this plane, o′ B′. For this purpose, we let fall upon this plane a perpendicular, R′ i', from any point taken upon the luminous ray, R′ o′, and we obtain a face view of this ray, as projected upon the plane, o′ B′, by supposing the latter to be turned about the axis, o′, until it coincides with f' o′, r' then coinciding with r''. Then, as the

height, $r''\,r$, of the point, r', above the horizontal plane, is equal to that of the point, R, the line joining $r\,o$ will be the face view of the projection of the ray in the plane, o B′. In turning round the plane, o′ B′, the section of the torus will become coincident with the semicircle, $a\,f\,c$, as in a previous operation. If, therefore, we draw a straight line, $m\,n$, tangential to this semicircle, and parallel to the ray, $r\,o'$, the point of contact, n, will be the point of separation of light and shade, as in the plane, o′ B′. Finally, we square n over to n', fig. 1; make o′ n^2 equal to o′ n', by describing an arc with the centre, o′, and radius, o′ n', and cutting the line, o′ B′, in n^2. This point, n^2, we again square over to n^2, upon the horizontal, $n\,n^2$, in fig. 1ᵃ, and n^2 is the point sought. Or we might have drawn the vertical projection of the section of the torus by the plane o′ B′, which would have been an ellipse, similar to that in fig. 5ᵃ, Plate XXVI.; and we might have proceeded, as shown in reference to that figure, the result being the same in both cases.

If the circular arc be prolonged to beyond the radius, o′ g′, and upon it, $g\,l$ be made equal to $g'\,n^2$, another point, l', will be obtained, symmetrical with n^2, with reference to the radius, o′ g, which is at an angle of 45° to the base line, and perpendicular to the luminous ray. This point, l', is to be squared over to l, in the vertical projection, and upon the horizontal, $p\,l$, drawn at a distance, $q\,p$, above the centre line, $f\,f$, equal to the distance, $q\,s$, of the horizontal passing through the point, n^2, below it.

324. When the shadow proper of a torus is known, it is very easy to determine the shadow which it will cast upon the horizontal plane—the plinth or pedestal below it, for instance—by drawing, through any points in the line of separation of light and shade, a number of lines parallel to the luminous ray, and then finding the points at which these lines intersect the horizontal plane. Thus, in figs. 2 and 2ᵃ, a portion of the torus, A, casts a shadow upon the horizontal plane, B C, the outline of which is a curve; but the portion, $a'\,b'\,c'$, of this curve is all that is visible.

Any point, b, b', in this curve is determined by the meeting of the ray of light drawn from the point, $l\,l'$, with the plane, B C.

The half of the line of separation of light and shade upon the posterior portion of the torus, fig. 1ᵃ, which is not seen in the front elevation, is similar to the anterior half; it is indicated in dotted lines, the portion, o b, being similar to the front portion, $e\,d$, whilst o d is similar to $e\,b$.

325. When the torus is surmounted by a cylindrical fillet, the line of separation of light and shade upon the latter will cast a shadow upon the surface of the torus. Thus, in figs. 2 and 2ᵃ, this will be the case with the fillet, D, the line of separation of light and shade of which is $f\,h$. This line, being vertical, casts a shadow, which is a straight line, $f'\,i'$, parallel to the luminous ray, and determined by drawing through the point, f, a luminous ray, $f\,i$, meeting the horizontal plane, $a\,a$, in i, which point, i, is squared over to the horizontal projection. It remains to determine the shadow cast by the circular portion, $f'\,j'$, which is in the shade: this may be done according to the general method explained in reference to figs. 3, 4, and 5, of Plate XXVI., and which we shall have occasion to repeat on figs. 3 and 3ᵃ of the present plate. This method is also applicable for the determination of the shadow, $n\,j$, $n'\,j'$, cast by the cylinder or shaft, E, upon the annular gorge, which unites this cylinder with the fillet, D.

SHADOW CAST BY A STRAIGHT LINE UPON A TORUS OR QUARTER-ROUND.

326. Fig. 3 represents the horizontal projection, as seen from below, of a fragment of a Tuscan capital, of which fig. 3ᵃ is the vertical projection, the object of these figures being to show the form of the shadow cast by the larmier, F, which is a square prism, upon the quarter-round, A, which is annular.

We yet again recall the general principle, that when a straight line is parallel to a plane, its shadow upon this plane is a straight line parallel to itself. For the rest, it will be sufficient to compare the operations indicated with those of figs. 3 and 3ᵃ, Plate XXVIII., to see that they are precisely the same : thus, on the one hand, we have the diagonal, G f, for the shadow cast upon the quarter-round, where it is limited by the curve, b e l, the line of separation of light and shade upon this ; and, on the other hand, we have the curve, i″ g i′, likewise limited by the same curve, for the shadow cast by the edge, G H, of the larmier upon the quarter-round.

Figs. 3 and 3ᵃ complete what refers to the shadow of the capital of a column ; they show the operations necessary to determine the shadow cast by the line of separation of light and shade of the quarter-round upon a cylinder, as well as that cast on the same cylinder by a portion of the larmier. The operation, in fact, simply consists in drawing the luminous rays through various points, i″ e, in a portion of the line of separation of light and shade upon the quarter-round, finding their intersection with the cylindrical surface of the shaft, E, by means of the horizontal projection. There is no peculiarity or difficulty in this procedure, and the whole being fully indicated upon the diagrams, we need not pause to detail it further.

To render the diagrams just discussed more generally applicable and intelligible, we have not given to the different parts the precise proportions prescribed by this or that architectural order ; such proportions, however, will be found in fig. A, which represents the model fully shaded and finished, being the entablature and column of the Tuscan order. A double object is intended to be gained by this beautiful example of drawing ; namely, to show the application of the principles laid down regarding shadows, and the distinctness and niceties to be observed in the various intensities of the washes, and in the general shading.

SHADOWS OF SURFACES OF REVOLUTION.

327. It will be recollected, that a solid or surface of revolution is that which may be said to be generated by a straight or curved line, caused to turn about a given fixed axis, and maintaining a uniform distance therefrom ; thus, the cylinder, the cone, the sphere, the torus, are all surfaces of revolution ; so, also, is the surface generated by the curve, a b c, revolving about the axis, A B, figs. 4 and 4ᵃ. It follows, from the above definition, that every section made perpendicularly to the axis will be a circle, and all such sections will be parallel. Every section made by a plane passing through the axis will give an outline equal to the generating curve, and which may be termed a *meridian*.

328. The shadow of a surface of revolution may be determined in two different ways : by drawing sectional planes perpendicular to the axis, and then considering the sections made by these planes as bases of so many right cones ; or by imagining a series of planes passing through the axis, and then projecting the ray of light upon these planes, so as to draw lines tangential to the different parts of the outline, and parallel to the projections of the ray of light, the points of contact of which will be points in the line of separation of light and shade sought. This latter method having been applied in the preceding figs. 1 and 1ᵃ, Plate XXIX., and figs. 3 and 4, Plate XXVIII., we deem it more useful, in the present instance, to explain the operations called for in the first method.

Take, then, any horizontal plane, b d, figs. 4 and 4ᵃ, cutting the surface of revolution in a circle, the radius of which is b e, and the horizontal projection, b′ e′ d′, through the points, b and d, draw a couple of tangents to the generating curve which forms the outline of the surface of revolution. These tangents will cut each other in the point, s, upon the axis, this point being the apex of an imaginary cone, s b d ; through this apex draw a luminous ray, s f and A′ b′, meeting the horizontal plane of the section, b d f, in f, f′ ; from this latter point, the horizontal projection, draw two straight lines, f′ g′ and f′ i′, tangents to the circle, b′ c′ d′ ; then the points of contact, g′ and i′, will be the two points of the line of separation of light and shade intersected by the plane, b d, and they are therefore squared over to the vertical projection, fig. 4ᵃ, i, only being there visible.

It is in a similar manner that the points, h and j′, are determined, these points being situated in planes, C D and E F, parallel to the first. It is to be observed, however, that, in these two last cases, the imaginary cones will be inverted, and the luminous ray must consequently be drawn to the left instead of to the right, as has already been explained in reference to figs. 3ᵃ and 4ᵃ, Plate XXVIII.

329. When the tangents to the generating curve are vertical, as is the case with the sectional planes, M N and a l, the points, m and n, of the line of separation of light and shade, are determined by lines, inclined at an angle of 45°, and tangential to the circular sections in the horizontal projection, because these circular sections are the bases of imaginary cylinders and not cones.

When a sufficient number of points have been obtained in this manner, as in fig. 4ᵃ, a curved line is drawn through them all, which will give the visible portion, m i n h j E, of the line of separation of light and shade upon the surface of revolution. This method is general, and may be applied to surfaces of revolution of any outline whatever.

As it is well to determine directly the lowest point, k, of this and similar curves, it may be done in the same manner as for the torus, figs. 1 and 1ᵃ, namely, by drawing the ray of light, R B, at the same inclination to the base line, as it is in the diagonal and vertical plane, and then drawing parallel to it a tangent to the outline of the surface of revolution, the projection for the moment being supposed to be in a plane parallel to the ray of light, R′ A′ ; the distance of the point of contact, k, from the axis, being then measured upon the horizontal projection, R′ A′, of the luminous ray gives the point, k′, which is finally squared over to k, in the horizontal line in the vertical projection passing through the same point of contact.

A portion of this curve, namely, the lower part, E k j, casts a shadow upon the cylindrical fillet, c o ; to determine this shadow it will, in the first place, be necessary to delineate the horizontal projection of the curve, E $k\,j$, and then to draw luminous rays through one or two points in the latter, to meet the circle, $c'\,o'$, the horizontal projection of the fillet. The points in which the luminous rays intersect the circle, are then to be squared over to the vertical projection of the same rays, whence is derived the curve, $c\,p\,q$. The various operation lines are not indicated on the figures, to avoid confusion, but the proceeding will be easily comprehended.

330. Fig. 4ᵃ represents the vertical projection of a baluster, such as is often seen in balconies of stone or marble, and sometimes also in machinery, serving as an isolated standard, or as a portion of the framing. Below the fillet, $c\,o$, is an annular gorge, upon the surface of which the base of the fillet casts a shadow. It is easy to see that this shadow is obtained in precisely the same manner as those occurring in figs. 3 and 3ᵃ, Plate XXVIII., as well as in subsequent diagrams.

Figs. Ⓑ and Ⓒ represent the shaded models of two descriptions of baluster, consisting of surfaces of revolution. We recommend the student to draw them upon a large scale, and to determine the outline of the shadows in rigorous accordance with the principles which we have laid down. Such balusters are generally made of stone, and are susceptible of various sizes and proportions. We have, however, supposed them to be drawn to a scale of one-tenth their actual size.

Many forms and combinations, of which we have said nothing, will be met with in actual practice; but our labours would be interminable were we to give them all. Our exemplifications involve all the principles that are needed, and each case will suggest the modification of operations applicable to it.

RULES AND PRACTICAL DATA.

PUMPS.

331. There are three kinds of pumps.

I. *Lifting pumps*, in which the piston or bucket lifts the water, first drawing it up by suction. We engrave one of this kind in Plate XXXVII.

II. *Forcing pumps*, in which the piston presses or forces the water to any distance. The feed pumps of steam-engines are of this class, and one is represented in Plate XXXIX.

III. *Lifting and forcing pumps*, in which both the above actions are combined.

HYDROSTATIC PRINCIPLES.

332. Whatever be the height at which a pump delivers its water —whatever be the calibre or inclination of the suction or delivery pipe—the piston has always to support a weight equal to a column of water, the base of which is equal to the area of the piston, and the height is equal to the difference of level of the water below, from which the pump draws its supply, and the point of delivery above.

Thus, putting H to represent the difference in the level, D for the diameter of the piston, and P for the weight or pressure on the piston—

$$P = \frac{\pi\,D^2\,H}{4}.$$

To express this pressure in pounds, it must be multiplied by 62·5, that being the weight in pounds of a cubic foot of water; the formula then becomes—

$$P = 62\cdot5\,\frac{\pi\,D^2\,H}{4}\,\text{lbs.,}$$

the measurement being expressed in feet.

333. Independently of this load, which corresponds to the useful effect of the machine, the power employed in elevating the piston has other passive resistances to overcome, namely—

1st. The friction of the piston against the sides of the pump.

2d. The friction of the water itself in the pipes.

3d. The retardation of the water in its passage to the pump by the suction valve.

4th. The weight of this valve.

These resistances can only be determined approximately. Still it follows, from the experiments of M. d'Aubisson, that the load to be overcome in raising the piston is equal to

$$62\cdot5\,\frac{\pi\,D^2}{4} \times H \times 1\cdot08;$$

or, more simply,

$$52\cdot5\,D^2\,H.$$

It is sufficient to add to this the weight of the piston and rod.

The power exerted in depressing the piston, being assisted by the weight of itself and the rod, is always less than that required to raise it.

334. In ordinary pumps, the volume of water delivered for each stroke of the piston, instead of being given by the formula,

$$\frac{\pi\,D^2}{4} \times l, \text{ or } \cdot785\,D^2\,l,$$

where l is the length of stroke, is determined by an expression which varies between

$$\cdot6\,D^2\,l \text{ and } \cdot7\,D^2\,l.$$

The velocity of the piston generally ranges between a minimum of 50 feet and a maximum of 80 feet per minute. The diameter of the suction and discharge pipes is generally equal to ⅜ or ¼ of that of the body of the pump.

It may be remarked, that the height to which liquids rise in vacuo, by the pressure of the atmosphere, is in the inverse ratio of their specific gravities. Thus this pressure, which is equal to 15 lbs. to the square inch, makes water rise to 33 feet, whilst mercury only rises to 30 inches, its specific gravity being 13·59 times that of water. If the atmosphere presses on a liquid lighter than water, it will cause it to rise higher in vacuo than 33 feet, in proportion to the difference of the specific gravity. In practice, more than 29 or 30 feet cannot be calculated on for the lift of the pump, because of the difficulty of obtaining a perfect vacuum.

FORCING PUMPS.

335. What has been here said of lifting pumps, applies as well to forcing pumps. The resistance, however, to be overcome, is somewhat greater in the latter case—for instance, at the moment of opening the discharge valve; and in general this occurs with

all valves having a great body of water above them, and with their upper surface greater than the area of the orifice above.

LIFTING AND FORCING PUMPS.

336. A pump of this description ordinarily consists of a cylinder with a short suction pipe, a discharge pipe, a solid piston, termed a plunger, and suction and discharge valves.

Two such pumps are frequently coupled together, in which case a single suction and discharge pipe serves for both.

337. The power necessary to work one or more pumps is expressed by $52.5 \, D^2 \, H \, v$; or, taking into account the force necessary to work the piston by itself, $55.7 \, D^2 \, H \, v$; v signifying the velocity in feet per minute.

This velocity is obviously obtained by multiplying the number of strokes per minute by the length of stroke; thus—
$$v = 2n \, l,$$
n being the number of back-and-forward movements per minute; consequently, the power required is equal to
$$55.7 \, D^2 \, H \times 2n \, l = 111.4 \, D^2 \, H \, n \, l;$$
this product representing pounds raised one foot high per minute, the measurements being in feet.

With these premises, we can solve such problems as the following:—

First: What force, F, is required to work a pump, having a piston 6 inches in diameter, a stroke of 18 inches, and a velocity of 15 double-strokes per minute; the whole height between the well and the point of delivery being 70 feet?

The velocity $v = 2n \, l = 30 \times 1\frac{1}{2} = 45$ feet. Then $F = 55.7$ $D^2 \times H \times v = 55.7 \times .25 \times 74 \times 45 = 46,997$ lbs. raised one foot high per minute.

To express this in horses power, we must simply divide it by 33,000; therefore,
$$F = \frac{46,997}{33,000} = 1\frac{1}{2} \text{ horses power, nearly.}$$

Second: What quantity will the same pump raise in ten hours?

Assuming, according to the formula (333), the effective volume, $V = .6 \, D^2 \, l$, or $V = .6 \times .25 \times 1.5 = .225$ cubic feet per stroke;

and the volume per minute,
$$.225 \times 15 = 3.375 \text{ cubic feet};$$
and per hour,
$$3.375 \times 60 = 202.5 \text{ cubic feet.}$$
The quantity of water raised in ten hours will consequently be
$$202.5 \times 10 = 2,025 \text{ cubic feet.}$$

Third: What diameter should be given to the piston of a pump which raises 202.5 cubic feet of water per hour, the velocity being 45 feet per minute, the length of stroke 18 inches, and the height to which the water is raised 75 feet?

The formula above, relative to the effective discharge per stroke,
$$V = .6 \, D^2 \times l,$$
by transposition, becomes
$$D^2 = \frac{V}{.6 \times l}.$$

Now, the volume, 202.5 cubic feet, discharged per hour, is, per minute,
$$\frac{202.5}{6.} = 3.375 \text{ cubic feet.}$$

This last again reduces itself to
$$\frac{2 \times 1.5 \times 3.375}{45} = .225 \text{ cubic feet per stroke};$$
consequently,
$$D^2 = \frac{.225}{.6 \times l}.$$
Whence,
$$D = \sqrt{\frac{.225}{.6 \times 1.5}} = 6 \text{ inches.}$$

THE HYDROSTATIC PRESS.

338. This powerful machine is an application of the lifting and forcing pump. It consists of a bulky piston, or plunger, termed a ram, working in a cylinder to correspond, and communicating, by a pipe of small bore, with a small but very strong forcing pump. To the top of the large piston is fixed a table or platform, which compresses or crushes what is submitted to the action of the machine.

The pressure exerted upon the water by the smaller piston, is, by means of the fluid contained in the pipe, transmitted to the base of the ram; and as, according to the well-known hydrostatic law, the pressure is equal on all points, the total force acting on each piston will be in proportion to their area; so that if, for example, the diameters of the pistons are to each other as 1 to 5, the pressure on the larger one, the ram, will be 25 times as great as that exerted by the pump-piston. Suppose a man can apply a force equal to 60 lbs. to the end of a lever 3 feet long, and that the point of connection with the piston-rod is only $1\frac{1}{2}$ inch from the fulcrum, the leverage of the power will be 24 times as great as that of the resistance, and the pressure upon the ram will consequently be $24 \times 25 \times 60 = 36,000$ lbs., an effort equal to that of 600 men acting at once.

In the hydrostatic press, we have, consequently, to consider two mechanical advantages—that of the simple machine, the lever, and that of the ram: these advantages are, however, necessarily compensated for by the diminution in the velocity of the ram.

On these principles, enormously powerful presses and lifting-machines have been constructed. The one capable of lifting 18,000 tons, at the Menai Tubular Bridge, is an unparalleled example.

HYDROSTATICAL CALCULATIONS AND DATA—DISCHARGE OF WATER THROUGH DIFFERENT ORIFICES.

339. The discharge of a volume of water, in a given time, varies according to the velocity of the water, and depends upon the area and form of the discharge orifice.

Surface Velocity.—The velocity of water at the surface of a water-course or river, of which it is wished to ascertain the discharge, is obtained by means of a float, which is thrown into the part where the current is strongest. As the wind, if there is any, affects the result very considerably, the float must project above the surface as little as possible. A distance of as great a length as convenient is measured on the part of the stream where the current is most regular, and the time occupied by the float in passing that distance is noted by a seconds watch. The space passed through is then divided by the time expressed in seconds, and the quotient will be the surface velocity per second.

It is usual to try several floats in different parts of the current.

Example.—Suppose the space passed through by each float is 150 feet in 35 seconds, what is the surface velocity?

$$V = \frac{150}{35} = 4\cdot 28 \text{ feet per second.}$$

If the velocity is not uniform throughout the length of the canal, the velocity at any point may be obtained by means of a small paddle-wheel, the floats of which just dip into the water. The number of revolutions per minute of this instrument being multiplied by its mean circumference—that is, the circumference corresponding to the centre of the immerged part of the float—the product expresses the velocity per minute; and, by dividing by 60, the surface velocity per second is obtained.

Example.—Suppose that the wheel makes 120 revolutions per minute, and that the mean circumference is equal to 1½ foot, what is the surface velocity of the current?

$$\frac{120 \times 1\cdot 5}{60} = 3 \text{ feet per second.}$$

340. *Mean Velocity.*—The velocity above obtained is only that at the surface; now, the mean velocity, V', of the whole body of water, which is what is necessary to know for the gauging of the river or canal, is deduced from the first, by multiplying it by a coefficient, which varies in the following proportions :—

For a surface velocity equal to The ratio of V to V' is	·5 ft.	1·5 ft.	3 ft.	5 ft.	6·5 ft.	8 ft.	10 ft.	11·5 ft	13 ft.
	·77	·78	·81	·83	·85	·86	·87	·88	·89

Example.—What is the mean velocity of a current of which the surface velocity is 5 feet per second?

It is equal to ·83 × 5 = 4·15 feet.

The mean velocity of water in an open water-course or river of uniform cross-section is determined by the following formula :—

$$V' = 56\cdot 86 \times \sqrt{\frac{A}{P} \times \frac{H}{L}} - \cdot 236.$$

This formula requires the obtainment of the exact level of the surface of the water throughout a certain length, L, the greater the better; the cross-sectional area, A; the form of the immerged perimeter or profile of the bed; and the height of the fall, H, corresponding to the length, L.

Example.—What is the mean velocity of the water in a water-course of uniform rectangular cross-section, having a width of 35 feet, a depth of 12 feet, and with a fall of ·8 feet in a distance of 1400 feet?

The cross-sectional area, A,

$$= 35 \times 12 = 420 \text{ square feet.}$$

The immerged profile, P,

$$= 35 + (2 \times 12) = 59 \text{ feet.}$$

Then,

$$V = 56\cdot 86 \times \sqrt{\frac{420 \text{ sq. ft.}}{59} \times \frac{\cdot 8}{1400}} - \cdot 236 = 3\cdot 39$$

feet per second.

Thus, according to this formula, it is necessary to extract the square root of the product of the quantities placed under the radical sign $\sqrt{}$; next to multiply this root by the co-efficient 56·86;

and, finally, to subtract from the product ·236 feet. When the measurements are in mètres this last item is ·072.

COMPARISON OF FRENCH AND ENGLISH MEASURES OF CAPACITY.

The French litre is equal to a cubic mètre, and therefore to 10·76 cubic feet, or ·220 gallon. The gallon is equal to 4·543 litres or cubic mètres, and the cubic foot to ·9929 litres or cubic mètres.

THE GAUGING OF A WATER-COURSE OF UNIFORM SECTION AND FALL.

341. When we know the mean velocity of a water-course of regular section and uniform fall, the discharge per second can be obtained by the following formula :—$D = A \times V$, in which D signifies the discharge per second; A, the cross-sectional area and V', the mean velocity.

Example.—What is the discharge of a water-course, the cross-section of which is 4·2 square mètres, and the mean velocity 1·065 mètres?

$D = 4\cdot 2 \times 1\cdot 065 = 4\cdot 473$ cubic mètres, or 4·473 litres per second

VELOCITY AT THE BOTTOM OF WATER-COURSES.

342. The velocity of water at the bottom of water-courses is still less than the mean velocity.

Putting V to represent the surface velocity, V the mean velocity, and V'' the ground velocity, the relation of the three will be expressed by $V'' = 2 V' - V$. That is to say, the velocity at the bottom of a canal is equal to twice the mean velocity minus the surface velocity.

Example.—The surface velocity of a water-way is found to be 2 mètres, and the mean velocity calculated to be 1·55 mètres, what is the ground velocity?

$$V'' = 2 \times 1\cdot 55 - 2 = 1\cdot 10 \text{ mètres.}$$

Too great a velocity at the bottom of a water-course tends to loosen and carry away the bed, undermining the sides and causing a great deal of damage; too small a velocity, on the other hand, by allowing the matter suspended in the water to settle, is a cause of obstruction.

The following table shows the limit of velocity according to the nature of the bed, which cannot be exceeded without danger :—

Nature of the Bed.	Limit of the Velocity per second.	
	Mètres.	Feet.
Soft brown earth,	·076	·25
Soft clay,	·152	·49
Sand,	·305	1·00
Gravel,	·609	2·00
Flint stones,	·614	2·02
Shingle,	1·220	4·00
Agglomerated stones, soft schist,	1·524	5·00
Rock fragments,	1·830	6·00
Solid rock,	3·050	10·00

343. *Prony's measure.*—The produce of any source may also be measured by damming up the entire width of the stream with thin planks pierced with holes of 20 millimètres in diameter, disposed in a horizontal line. These holes are at first covered, and are opened in succession, until the level of the water within them

is maintained above their centres; so that when this is effected, the discharge is calculated from the number of orifices which require to be open.

The quantity of water discharged by each orifice of ·02 m. in diameter, in a board ·017 m. thick, and under a column ·03 m. above the centre, is 20 cubic mètres in 24 hours.

Another method of gauging a stream of water, consists in setting up an under or overshot sluice-gate at a similar dam, the discharge being calculated according to the following rules in reference to this subject :—

CALCULATION OF THE DISCHARGE OF WATER THROUGH RECTANGULAR ORIFICES OF NARROW EDGES.

344. As it is of importance, in a majority of circumstances, to be able to calculate the discharge of water by sluice-gates, or by the vertical discharge-gates of hydraulic motors, so as to know the volume, and, consequently, the value of a stream of water, we shall commence by giving a table, which enables us to determine this discharge in a very simple manner, and places these operations within the capacity even of labourers and working mechanics.

TABLE OF THE DISCHARGES OF WATER THROUGH AN ORIFICE ONE METRE IN WIDTH.

Height of the orifices in centi-metres.	Volume discharged in litres per second, corresponding to the heights:—																	
	·2 m.	·3 m.	·4 m.	·5 m.	·6 m	·7 m.	·8 m.	1·0 m.	1·2 m.	1·4 m.	1·6 m.	1·8 m.	2·0 m.	2·5 m.	3·0 m.	3·5 m.	4·0 m.
4	50	61	71	79	86	93	99	110	121	130	138	146	154	172	188	201	215
5	62	76	88	98	107	116	124	138	151	162	173	182	191	214	255	251	268
6	75	91	107	117	128	139	148	165	181	194	207	218	229	257	281	301	321
7	86	106	122	136	148	161	172	192	210	226	241	255	267	299	327	350	374
8	98	120	139	155	170	184	196	219	240	258	275	290	305	341	374	400	427
9	109	135	156	174	191	208	220	246	267	289	309	326	343	382	420	450	481
10	122	149	173	193	212	228	246	272	298	321	342	362	380	424	466	500	533
11	133	164	189	212	230	249	267	299	327	353	376	398	418	466	511	550	587
12	145	178	206	230	251	272	291	326	356	384	409	434	455	507	557	599	640
13	157	192	222	249	272	294	314	352	385	416	443	469	492	549	602	647	693
14	168	206	238	267	292	316	338	379	414	446	476	504	530	590	648	697	745
15	179	220	255	285	312	338	361	405	443	477	509	539	566	631	693	747	799
16	190	234	271	304	330	360	385	432	472	509	542	574	603	673	739	797	852
17	201	248	287	322	350	382	414	456	501	540	575	610	638	715	784	847	905
18	213	262	304	340	370	403	432	484	529	571	608	644	677	757	830	896	958
19	223	276	324	358	392	425	454	510	558	601	641	680	715	799	876	946	1011
20	235	291	337	377	414	447	485	536	586	627	675	715	753	841	922	996	1065
21	247	305	354	396	431	470	512	563	615	664	708	751	790	884	968	1046	1118
22	259	320	370	417	451	492	538	590	645	695	742	787	828	926	1014	1096	1171
23	271	334	388	434	472	515	550	616	674	726	776	823	865	968	1060	1146	1224
24	282	348	404	452	492	537	574	643	703	758	809	859	903	1010	1106	1195	1278
25	294	363	420	471	516	559	598	670	733	790	843	895	941	1052	1152	1245	1331
26	306	377	437	490	538	581	626	697	762	822	877	930	978	1094	1198	1295	1384
27	318	392	454	509	559	604	645	724	791	853	911	966	1016	1136	1245	1345	1437
28	329	406	471	527	573	626	679	740	820	885	944	1001	1054	1172	1291	1395	1491
29	340	421	487	546	602	649	693	777	850	916	978	1037	1092	1220	1337	1444	1544
30	353	434	504	564	624	670	718	804	880	948	1010	1073	1129	1262	1385	1494	1597
31	364	449	521	583	635	694	741	831	909	980	1046	1109	1167	1305	1429	1544	1650
32	376	463	538	602	655	715	765	857	939	1011	1079	1144	1205	1366	1475	1594	1703
33	388	477	555	622	676	737	789	884	969	1043	1113	1180	1242	1389	1521	1644	1756
34	400	491	572	640	696	759	813	911	998	1074	1147	1216	1279	1431	1568	1693	1810
35	415	507	588	659	717	782	837	938	1027	1103	1180	1252	1317	1473	1614	1743	1863
36	424	520	605	677	737	804	861	965	1057	1138	1214	1288	1355	1515	1660	1793	1916
37	436	534	622	696	758	826	885	981	1086	1169	1248	1324	1392	1557	1706	1843	1969
38	450	549	638	715	778	849	909	1018	1115	1201	1283	1359	1430	1599	1752	1893	2023
39	462	564	653	734	798	872	933	1045	1145	1232	1315	1395	1468	1641	1798	1943	2076
40	484	577	671	753	819	894	957	1070	1174	1266	1351	1431	1506	1683	1844	1992	2129
41	,,	591	688	772	840	915	981	1097	1203	1298	1384	1467	1543	1725	1890	2042	2182
42	,,	606	705	790	860	936	1005	1124	1233	1329	1419	1503	1581	1768	1936	2092	2236
43	,,	620	722	809	881	961	1028	1151	1262	1361	1453	1538	1618	1809	1982	2142	2289
44	,,	635	737	828	901	983	1053	1171	1291	1393	1486	1574	1656	1851	2029	2192	2343
45	,,	649	754	847	920	1005	1076	1204	1321	1424	1520	1609	1694	1894	2075	2241	2394
46	,,	663	771	866	941	1028	1100	1231	1350	1456	1554	1636	1731	1936	2121	2291	2449
47	,,	677	787	885	961	1050	1124	1257	1380	1488	1588	1681	1769	1978	2167	2341	2504
48	,,	691	804	903	982	1072	1148	1284	1409	1519	1622	1716	1807	2020	2213	2391	2559
49	,,	706	820	922	1002	1095	1172	1311	1438	1551	1656	1753	1845	2062	2339	2440	2614
50	,,	719	836	940	1023	1115	1194	1337	1468	1583	1690	1789	1882	2104	2395	2490	2669

This table has been calculated by means of the following formula :—

$$D = w.h \times \sqrt{2\,g\,H} \times 1000;$$

in which

D represents the volume of water discharged in litres per second;

w, the width of the orifice in mètres;

h, the height of the orifice;

H, the column, or the height of the pressure, in mètres, measured from the centre of the orifice to the upper level of the reservoir;

g, signifies the action of gravity, being equal to 9·81 mètres;

$v, = \sqrt{2\,g\,H}$, the velocity due to the height H (see 258); and, finally,

m is a coefficient, which varies in practice according to the heights, h and H, from ·59 to ·66, supposing the contraction of the orifice to be complete; that is to say, it occurs on all four sides of the orifice.

In the first column of the table we give the heights of the orifices in centimètres, and in the following columns the results of the discharge effected, in litres per second, for various heights of the column of pressure, from ·20 to 4 mètres.

By means of this table we can now determine, by a very simple operation, the volume of water discharged through a vertical floodgate, or through a rectangular orifice, of which the edges are narrow; the level of the reservoir being above the top of the orifice, and the contraction complete. We have, in fact, simply to *find the number in the table corresponding to the given height of the orifice, and to the column of water acting at its centre, and then multiply this number by the given width.*

Example.—What is the volume of water discharged by the orifice of a vertical water-gate, 1·5 mètres wide, the height of the orifice being ·25 m., and the height of the column, from the centre of the orifice to the upper level in the reservoir, 2·5 m., and the contraction being complete?

In the table, on a line with the height, 25 centimètres, and in the column corresponding to 2·5 m., will be found the number 1052.

We have, therefore,

1·5 × 1052 = 1578 litres for the actual discharge per second.

It will be equally easy to estimate very approximately the discharge of water, corresponding to data which do not happen to be in the table.

First Example.—What is the volume of water discharged by a vertical sluice-gate, ·8 m. in width, the height of the orifice being 16 centim., and the column upon the centre 2·75 m.?

This height of column, 2.75 m., is not in the table, but it lies between that corresponding to 2·5 m. and 3 m.; consequently, the discharge for the height of orifice, 16 c., will be comprised between the numbers 673 and 739, and it will be about 706; therefore the discharge will be 706 × ·8 = 664·8 litres per second.

Second Example.—Suppose the height of the orifice to be 6·5 c., instead of 16, the other data remaining the same. As this height is comprised between 16 and 17 centimètres, the discharge effected will evidently be between the numbers 673 and 715, corresponding to a column of 2·5 m., and between the num-

bers 839 and 784, for a column of 3 mètres. It will therefore be very nearly a mean between these four numbers;

$$\text{or } \frac{673 + 715 + 739 + 784}{4} = 727·75 \text{ litres.}$$

Whence we obtain 727·75 × ·8 = 582·2 litres for the effective discharge.

345. INCOMPLETE CONTRACTION.—When one or more sides of the orifice are simply the prolongation of the sides of the reservoir or stream, the contraction is sensibly diminished, and the corresponding coefficient is consequently greater.

In this case, in order to calculate the effective discharge, the numbers must be multiplied by

1·125, if the contraction is only on one side.

1·072,   "   "   "   two sides.

1·035,   "   "   "   three sides.

Example.—Required the volume of water discharged by an orifice of ·25 m. in height, 1·3 m. in width, and with a column of ·8 m. measured from the centre of the orifice, the bottom of the opening being in a line with the bottom of the reservoir; that is to say, the contraction taking place only on the three sides?

It will be found, according to the table, that the effective discharge is 598 litres for a width of one mètre, and consequently 598 × 1·3 = 777 litres, is the discharge for 1.3 m., when the contraction is complete. We have, therefore, 777 × 1·035 = 804 litres, the actual discharge sought.

346. INCLINED SLUICEGATE.—It very often happens that the sluicegate is inclined. In this case, if there is no contraction on the sides or bottom of the orifice, the coefficient needs to be considerably augmented. Thus, to calculate the effective discharge, it is necessary to multiply the numbers in the preceding table by 1·33 if the sluice is inclined at an angle of 45°, or with 1 mètre of base to 1 in height, and by 1·23, if the inclination is 60°, or 1 mètre of base to 2 in height.

Example.—It is desired to know the volume of water discharged through an orifice inclined at an angle of 45°, having 17 m. in height vertically, 1·25 m. in width, and at a distance of 1·2 m. below the surface of the reservoir; the two vertical sides and the bottom being in a line with the sides of the reservoir.

From the table we shall find 398 × 1·25 = 622·5 litres for the discharge with a vertical orifice and complete contraction; consequently, 622·5 × 1·33 = 828 litres will be the effective discharge sought.

347. When vertical floodgates have their lower edges very near the bottom of the reservoir, as is generally the case, to determine the discharge,

Multiply the numbers given in the table by 1·04.

Example.—What is the volume of water discharged per second by a sluice, the orifice of which is opened to a height of ·38 m. having ·8 m. in width, and 2·5 m. being the distance from the centre to the upper level?

The table gives 1,599 litres for the discharge effected through an orifice of a mètre in width. Whence 1,599 × ·8 × 1·04 = 1,330·0 litres, the effective discharge sought.

When two sluices are at not more than three mètres distance from each other, and are open at the same time, the discharge will be obtained by

Multiplying the numbers given in the table by ·915.

Example.—If the orifices of two sluices, situated at a couple of mètres distance from each other, have together a width equal to 1·5 m., and are both opened to a height of ·45 m., the column of water upon their centres being 1·8 m., what will be the effective discharge of the two together per second?

In the table, we find that 1609 litres corresponds to a column of 1·8 m., and a width of 1 m. Therefore, 1609 × 1·5 × ·915 = 2208·35 litres is the required discharge.

TABLE OF THE DISCHARGE OF WATER BY OVERSHOT OUTLETS OF ONE METRE IN WIDTH.

Heights of the reservoir level above the bottom of the outlet.	Discharge in litres per second.		Heights of the reservoir level above the bottom of the outlet.	Discharge in litres per second.		Heights of the reservoir level above the bottom of the outlet.	Discharge in litres per second.	
	1st Case.	2d Case.		1st Case.	2d Case.		1st Case.	2d Case.
5·0	20	21	28·5	259	283	52·0	639	698
5·5	23	24	29·0	266	290	52·5	648	708
6·0	26	27	29·5	273	298	53·0	658	718
6·5	29	31	30·0	280	306	53·5	667	728
7·0	32	34	30·5	287	313	54·0	676	738
7·5	36	38	31·0	293	321	54·5	685	748
8·0	40	42	31·5	301	329	55·0	694	758
8·5	43	46	32·0	309	337	55·5	704	769
9·0	47	50	32·5	315	344	56·0	713	779
9·5	51	54	33·0	323	353	56·5	724	790
10·0	56	59	33·5	330	361	57·0	733	800
10·5	60	63	34·0	338	369	57·5	743	811
11·0	64	68	34·5	345	377	58·0	753	822
11·5	68.	73	35·0	353	385	58·5	762	832
12·0	72	77	35·5	360	393	59·0	771	842
12·5	77	82	36·0	368	402	59·5	781	853
13·0	82	87	36·5	375	410	60·0	791	864
13·5	86	92	37·0	382	419	60·5	801	875
14·0	92	98	37·5	392	428	61·0	811	886
14·5	97	103	38·0	399	436	61·5	821	896
15·0	101	108	38·5	408	445	62·0	831	907
15·5	107	114	39·0	415	453	62·5	841	918
16·0	111	119	39·5	423	462	63·0	851	929
16·5	117	125	40·0	431	471	63·5	861	940
17·0	121	130	40·5	439	479	64·0	871	951
17·5	127	136	41·0	447	488	64·5	882	963
18·0	132	142	41·5	455	497	65·0	892	974
18·5	138	148	42·0	463	506	65·5	902	985
19·0	143	154	42·5	472	515	66·0	912	996
19·5	149	160	43·0	481	525	66·5	922	1007
20·0	154	166	43·5	488	533	67·0	932	1018
20·5	160	173	44·0	497	543	67·5	943	1030
21·0	166	179	44·5	506	552	68·0	954	1042
21·5	171	185	45·0	514	561	68·5	965	1054
22·0	176	192	45·5	523	571	69·0	976	1066
22·5	182	199	46·0	531	581	69·5	987	1078
23·0	188	205	46·5	540	590	70·0	998	1090
23·5	194	212	47·0	549	599	70·5	1008	1101
24·0	202	219	47·5	558	609	71·0	1019	1113
24·5	207	226	48·0	567	619	71·5	1030	1125
25·0	212	233	48·5	576	629	72·0	1041	1137
25·5	220	240	49·0	584	638	72·5	1052	1149
26·0	226	247	49·5	593	648	73·0	1063	1161
26·5	233	254	50·0	603	658	73·5	1073	1172
27·0	239	261	50·5	612	668	74·0	1084	1184
27·5	245	268	51·0	621	678	74·5	1095	1196
28·0	253	276	51·5	630	688	75·0	1106	1208

CALCULATION OF THE DISCHARGE OF WATER THROUGH OVER-
SHOT OUTLETS.

348. The practical formula employed by engineers to determine the quantity of water which escapes in a second of time, through an overshot or open-topped outlet, is the following :—

$$D = W \times H \times \sqrt{29\,H} \times m \times 1000 ;$$

in which formula,

D represents, as before, the discharge in litres per second;

W, the width of the outlet in mètres;

H, the depth of the outlet, as measured vertically from its bottom edge, to the level of the water in the reservoir.

The following table is calculated by means of this formula, it being supposed,

First, That the width of the outlet is 1 mètre.

Second, That the heights of the outlet increase at the rate of ·005 m., from ·05 m. up to ·75 m. These heights are expressed in centimètres in the first column of the table, the corresponding velocities being given in the table at page 94.

Third, That the outlet is supposed to be narrower than the reservoir, or water-course, in which case, MM. Poncelet and Lesbros give the following numerical values for the term m. :—

	m.	m.	m.	m.	m.	m.	m.	m.
For the height, H, of	·03	·04	·06	·08	·10	·15	·20	·22
The term, m, is........	·412	·407	·401	·397	·395	·393	·390	·385

The corresponding discharges in this case are given in the second column of the table. They are expressed in litres per second.

Or, fourth, that the outlet is virtually of the same width as the reservoir, or water-course, having its lower edge only a little, if anything, above the bottom. In this case, according to M. d'Aubuisson (M. Costal's experiments), the coefficient, m, is equal to ·42 on the average. The corresponding discharges will be found in the third column of the table.

RULE.—With the aid of this table, the calculation for determining the effective discharge of water by an overshot outlet, reduces itself to the following:—

Multiply the width of the outlet, expressed in mètres, by the number given in the second column, and corresponding to the height of the outlet in the first column, when the outlet is narrower than the watercourse, and when the water is discharged freely into the air ;

And by the number in the third column corresponding to the same height, when the water-course is of the same width as the outlet, its depth, likewise, not being sensibly greater than that of the lower edge of the outlet.

First Example.—It is necessary to determine the volume of water discharged per second by an overshot outlet, the width of which is 2·5 m., and the height of the overflow ·22 m., the case being supposed of the first description.

It will be seen from the second column of the table, that the discharge effected through an outlet of a mètre in width, and of ·22 m. in depth, is 176 litres per second; whence we have

$$176 \times 2{\cdot}5 = 440 \text{ litres, the volume sought.}$$

Second Example.—Required to determine the discharge with the same data ; the case being supposed of the second description.

In the third column, the number corresponding to the depth of ·22 m. will be found to be 192 litres ; whence,

$$192 \times 2{\cdot}5 = 480 \text{ litres, the volume sought.}$$

REMARK.—If the given height happen to fall between some of the numbers given in the table, it will be necessary to take a mean proportional between the two corresponding results, in order to obtain the actual discharge.

Example.—What is the quantity of water discharged by an overshot outlet of 3 mètres in width, and of a depth equal to ·183 m. ?

In the first case, the discharge effected, for 1 mètre in width, will be between 132 and 138 litres, the mean between which is very nearly 136.

Consequently, $136 \times 3 = 408$ litres, the effective discharge per second.

And in the second case, the discharge effected for 1 mètre in width, being comprised between the numbers 142 and 148, will be about 146.

Whence, $146 \times 3 = 438$ litres effective discharge.

TO DETERMINE THE WIDTH OF AN OVERSHOT OUTLET.

349. When the volume of water to be discharged per second is known, and it is wished to calculate the width to be given to an overshot outlet, or sluice-gate, so as to effect the desired discharge with a given height of water, this may be done in the following manner :—

Take from the table the number corresponding to the given height (this number expressing the discharge for a width of 1 mètre), *and divide the given volume, expressed in litres, it will give the required width in mètres.*

First Example.—What width must be given to an outlet, required to discharge 600 litres per second, with a depth above the bottom edge of ·12 m. ?

In the second column of the table, and opposite ·12 m., will be found the number 72.

We have, then—

$$600 \div 72 = 8{\cdot}33 \text{ m., the width sought.}$$

Second Example.—What width must be given to an open sluice, required to discharge 448 litres of water per second, with a depth of ·205 m. ?

From the table, we find that 160 litres is the effectual discharge, corresponding to a width of 1 mètre.

Whence—

$$448 \div 160 = 2{\cdot}8 \text{ m., the width sought.}$$

TO DETERMINE THE DEPTH OF THE OUTLET.

350. Cases may occur where we are limited as to width. It is then necessary to ascertain the least depth necessary to effect the required discharge, which may be done by means of the following rule :—

Divide the discharge expressed in litres per second, by the width in mètres, and take the number in the second column which is nearest to the quotient obtained, the number in the first column corresponding will give the depth sought, or very nearly so.

Example.—With what depth of outlet will a discharge of 350 litres per second be effected, the width being limited to 2 mètres?

We have

$$350 \div 2 = 175 \text{ litres.}$$

In the second column of the table will be found the number 176, corresponding to a height of ·22 m. in the first column, which will therefore be the required height, within a millimètre.

351. OBSERVATION.—When it is not possible to measure the depth, H, with exactness, the lesser depth, *h*, must be taken immediately over the lower edge of the outlet, and multiplied by 1·178, so as to obtain the actual value of H, corresponding to the numbers given in the table, according as the outlet is narrower than the reservoir, or water-course, or equal to it in width.

First Example.—Determine the discharge effected through an outlet, 4 mètres wide, the depth, *h*, immediately above the lower edge being equal to ·11 m., the width being about four-fifths of that of the reservoir.

We have ·11 m. × 1·178 = ·13 m., for the assumed height, H, of the reservoir level.

Corresponding to this height, we have, in the second column, the quantity, 82 litres.

Then 82 × 4 = 328 litres, the effective discharge sought.

TABLE OF THE DISCHARGE OF WATER THROUGH PIPES.

Mean velocity in mètres per second.	Diameters of the Pipes.									
	·10 m.		·15 m.		·20 m.		·25 m.		·30 m.	
	Discharge in litres per second.	Fall per mètre in length in centimètres.	Discharge in litres per second.	Fall per mètre in length in centimètres.	Discharge in litres per second.	Fall per mètre in length in centimètres.	Discharge in litres per second.	Fall per mètre in length in centimètres.	Discharge in litres per second.	Fall per mètre in length in centimètres.
0·10	0·8	0·02	1·8	0·01	3·1	0·01	4·9	0·01	7·07	0·01
0·15	1·2	0·04	2·6	0·03	4·7	0·02	7·4	0·02	10·60	0·01
0·20	1·6	0·07	3·5	0·05	6·3	0·03	9·8	0·03	14·14	0·02
0·25	2·0	0·10	4·4	0·07	7·8	0·05	12·3	0·04	17·67	0.03
0·30	2·3	0·15	5·3	0·10	9·4	0·07	14·7	0·06	21·20	0·05
0·35	2·7	0·19	6·1	0·13	11·0	0·10	17·2	0·08	24·74	0·07
0·40	3·1	0·25	7·1	0·17	12·6	0·12	19·6	0·10	28·27	0·08
0·45	3·5	0·31	8·0	0·21	14·1	0·16	22·0	0·12	31·81	0·10
0·50	3·9	0·38	8·8	0·25	15·7	0·19	24·5	0·15	35·34	0·13
0·55	4·3	0·46	9·7	0·30	17·3	0·23	27·0	0·18	38·88	0·15
0·60	4·7	0·54	10·6	0·36	18·8	0·27	29·4	0·22	42·41	0·18
0·65	5·1	0·63	11·5	0·42	20·4	0·32	31·9	0·25	45·95	0·21
0·70	5·5	0·73	12·4	0·49	22·0	0·36	34·4	0·29	49·48	0·24
0·75	5·9	0·83	13·2	0·56	23·6	0·42	36·8	0·33	53·01	0·28
0·80	6·3	0·95	14·1	0·63	25·1	0·47	39·3	0·38	56·55	0·31
0·85	6·7	1·06	15·0	0·71	26·7	0·53	41·7	0·43	60·08	0·35
0·90	7·0	1·19	15·9	0·79	28·3	0·59	44·2	0·48	63·62	0·40
0·95	7·5	1·32	16·8	0·88	29·8	0·66	46·6	0·53	67·15	0·44
1·00	7·8	1·46	17·7	0·97	31·4	0·73	49·1	0·58	70·7	0·49
1·10	8·6	1·76	19·4	1·17	34·5	0·88	54·0	0·70	77·7	0·59
1·20	9·4	2·09	21·2	1·39	37·7	1·04	58·9	0·83	84·8	0·69
1·30	10·2	2·44	23·0	1·63	40·8	1·22	63·8	0·98	91·9	0·81
1·40	11·0	2·82	24·7	1·88	44·0	1·41	68·7	1·13	98·9	0·94
1·50	11·8	3·24	26·5	2·16	47·1	1·62	73·6	1·29	106·0	1·08
1·60	12·6	3·68	28·3	2·45	50·3	1·84	78·5	1·47	113·1	1·22
1·70	13·3	4·14	30·6	2·76	53·4	2·07	83·4	1·66	120·2	1·38
1·80	14·1	4·64	31·8	3·09	56·5	2·32	88·3	1·85	127·2	1·55
1·90	14·9	5·16	33·6	3·44	59·7	2·58	93·3	2·06	134·3	1·72
2·00	15·7	5·71	35·3	3·80	62·8	2·85	98·2	2·28	141·4	1·90
2·10	16·4	6·29	37·1	4·19	66·0	3·14	103·1	2·51	148·4	2·10
2·20	17·2	6·89	38·9	4·60	69·1	3·45	108·0	2·76	155·5	2·30
2·30	18·0	7·53	40·6	5·02	72·2	3·76	112·9	3·01	162·6	2·50
2·40	18·8	8·19	42·4	5·46	75·4	4·09	117·8	3·28	169·6	2·73
2·50	19·6	8·88	44·2	5·91	78·5	4·44	122·7	3·55	176·7	2·90
2·60	20·4	9·60	45·9	6·40	81·7	4·80	127·6	3·83	183·8	3·20
2·70	21·2	10·34	47·7	6·89	84·8	5·17	132·5	4·14	190·8	3·44
2·80	22·0	11·11	49·4	7·41	88·0	5·56	137·4	4·45	197·9	3·70
2·90	22·8	11·92	51·2	7·94	91·1	5·95	142·3	4·77	205·0	3·97
3·00	23·6	12·74	53·0	8·50	94·2	6·37	147·3	5·10	212·1	4·25

Second Example.—With the like data, what would be the effective discharge, supposing the outlet to be of the same width and depth as the reservoir?

We have, as before, ·11 × 1·178 = ·13 m. for the depth, H, to which 87 litres is the corresponding discharge, as in the third column.

Whence—

$$87 × 4 = 348 \text{ litres, the actual discharge.}$$

OUTLET WITH A SPOUT, OR DUCT.

352. It may happen that a spout or duct, slightly inclined, or even horizontal, is fitted to the outlet, and that it is more contracted, both at the bottom and at the sides, than the reservoir. In such case, the discharge is sensibly different; and to determine it, it is necessary to multiply the numbers in the second column of the table by ·83, when the height is ·2 m., or upwards; by ·8, when the height is ·15 m.; and by ·76, when the height is only ·1 m.

PIPES FOR THE CONDUCTION OF WATER.

353. The formulas employed in calculating the proportions of a conduit for water of uniform section, consisting of cylindrical tubes, are the following :—

$$V = 53·58 \sqrt{\frac{d\,F}{4}} - 0·025;$$

and

$$D = S V = \frac{\pi d^2}{4} × V.$$

In which,

V is the mean velocity ;

D, the volume in litres;

d, the internal diameter of the conduit :

F, the fall per mètre, or the length, L, of the conduit, divided by the difference between the levels at either extremity ; and

S, the section of the conduit.

In order to abridge the calculations, we give a table, with the aid of which, various questions relative to the laying down of water-ducts, formed by cylindrical tubes, may be solved very speedily.

First Example.—What fall must be given to a conduit, ·1 m. in diameter, in order that it may discharge 11 litres of water per second ?

From the table it will be seen, that the fall, in this case, should be ·1 c., or 1 millimètre, per mètre.

Second Example.—What diameter must be given to a conduit, 500 mètres in length, in order that it may discharge 168 cubic mètres of water per hour, the whole fall being ·265 m.?

We have 168 cubic mètres, or 168,000 litres, ÷ (60 × 60) = 46·65 litres, discharged per second ;

and   ·265 ÷ 500 = ·53 c., the fall per mètre.

It will be seen from the table, that the diameter necessary for this discharge, and with this fall, is ·25 m., or 25 centimètres.

CHAPTER VIII.

APPLICATION OF SHADOWS TO TOOTHED GEAR.

PLATE XXX.

SPUR WHEELS.

FIGURES 1 AND 2.

354. We have already pointed out, that before shading an object in a finished manner, it is generally necessary to lay down the outlines of all the shadows, proper and cast, which may happen to be occasioned by the form of each part.

Thus, before proceeding to apply the finishing shades to the spur-wheel and pinion, fig. A, we must first determine, separately, on each wheel, both the shadow proper of the external surface of the web, and the shadows of the teeth upon it, and also upon themselves. The operations called for with one of the wheels are indicated in the figures.

The external surface, A c, of the web, A, of the spur wheel, being cylindrical, the line of separation of light and shade will be obviously determined by a tangent parallel to the luminous ray, or better, by the radius, o D, at right angles to this. By squaring over the point of contact, D, in the horizontal projection, we obtain the line, D′ E, in the vertical projection. Similarly, by squaring over the point, E, we get the straight line, F′ G, for the line of separation of light and shade on the outer ends of the teeth,

which are likewise cylindrical. A portion of the lateral surface of the teeth is also in the shade, as will easily be determined, by drawing lines through the extreme angles, as a, b, c, &c., parallel to the luminous rays. Thus the surfaces, a d, b e, and c f, do not receive any light, and are, therefore, shaded in the elevation, as within the outlines, a′ d′ g h, b′ e′ i j, and c′ f′ k l.

Each of these teeth, also, casts a shadow upon the cylindrical surface of the web; and as their edges, a′ h, b′ j, c′ l, are vertical, their shadows on the web are also vertical. These last are determined by drawing the luminar lines through the points, a, b, c, and a′, b′, c′, and then squaring over the points of contact, m, n, o, to m′, n′, o′.

To complete the shadows of the teeth upon the web, it is further necessary to obtain the outline corresponding to the edges, a d, b e, c f, &c. We already have the extreme points, d′, e′, f′, and m′, n′, o′, and in most cases these are sufficient. Where, however, greater exactness is required, it is well to find a few intermediate points. The lower edge of the tooth, also, casts a shadow upon the web, which is obtained in the same manner, by drawing luminar lines through the points, p, q, r, meeting the surface of the web in points projected vertically in r′, v′.

Some of the teeth, also, cast shadows upon each other; but as their surfaces are vertical, these shadows are simply determined by the contact of the luminar lines with them. Thus, the edges projected in s, t, y, &c., have for shadows the straight lines projected vertically in u' u^2, x' x^2, z' z^2.

Finally, when we have drawn the horizontal projection of the wheel, as in the present example, we have to determine the shadow cast by the web upon the tenons of the teeth, and upon the arms, or spokes. All these surfaces being horizontal and parallel, the shadow cast upon each will be a circle equal to the one, H I L, which is the projection of the inner edge of the web. All that is necessary, then, is to draw through the centre, o, o', a line parallel to the luminous ray; and to find the points of intersection, o² and o³, with the planes, M o″ and N o‴, in which lie the upper surfaces of the tenons and of the arms, and to describe arcs with the points, o² and o³, as centres, and with the common radius, o H (280). In the same manner we obtain the shadows cast by the boss of the wheel, and by the feathers upon the arms.

When we have thus gone through the requisite operations for each wheel, we proceed with the shading, according to the principles laid down (289, *et seq.*), covering first the portions which require a more pronounced shade, and leaving the lighter parts to the last.

The specimen, fig. A, which we recommend to be copied on a larger scale, indicates the various gradations of shade required to produce the proper effect, according to the different positions of the planes, and to the contour of the surfaces. These wheels are also supposed to be mounted upon their shafts, which are shaded as polished cylinders.

BEVIL WHEELS.

FIGURES 3 AND 4.

355. The procedure here called for will be the same as in the preceding case—that is to say, we must first draw the outlines of the shadows, proper and cast, for each wheel. The figures represent a horizontal and vertical projection of a bevil wheel with cast-iron teeth, the shadows being indicated on the different surfaces.

The external surfaces of the teeth and of the web being conical, the shadows proper are determined in the same manner as for the cone, by drawing through the apex a plane parallel to the luminous ray, and finding the generatrix at which this plane touches the conical surface (313).

It is in this manner that, for the outer ends of the teeth, we obtain the generatrix projected in o A, fig. 3, and for the outer surface of the web, that projected in o B. These generatrices, which are the lines of separation of light and shade, are projected vertically in the straight lines, c' A' and D' B', converging to the apex of the cone; since, however, these lines occur between two teeth in the present example, they are not apparent in fig. 4.

Some of the teeth have their lateral faces in the shade, whilst all the lower conical surface corresponding to the wider ends of the teeth is in deep shade, as indicated in fig. 4 by a darker tint.

We have, besides, merely to determine the shadows cast by the outer edges, $a\,d$, $b\,e$, $c\,f$, and by the curved portions, $d\,g$, $e\,h$, and $f\,i$. Now, the outer edges, $a\,d$, $b\,e$, $c\,f$, cast shadows upon the conical surface of the web, which are represented by straight lines coinciding with generatrices on this surface; and therefore, to determine them, we must draw through the corresponding edges a series of planes parallel to the luminous ray; the whole of these necessarily passing through the common apex, o, it is simply requisite, therefore, to find the shadow cast by any one point in these edges. Let us take, for example, the points, d, e, f, all situate in the same circle, E d F; the operation, then, is to find the shadow of this circle upon the conical surface, and is the same as that which we have already indicated and explained several times; it consists, in fact, in drawing any planes, G H and I J, perpendicular to the cone's axis, and, consequently, parallel to the plane of the circle, E d F.

356. We have seen that the shadow cast by the circle, E d F, upon each of the planes, will be a circle equal to itself; and it is, therefore, simply necessary to find the shadow cast by the centre, o, o'. This shadow falls in o, o', on the plane, G H, and in o², o³, on the plane, I I; if, then, with the points, o and o², as centres, and with the radii, o K' and o² J', equal to the radius, o E, we draw a couple of arcs, these arcs will cut the circles, G' K' H' and I' L' J', the projections of the sectional planes, in the points, K' and J', which, being squared over to the vertical projection in the points, K and J, will give two points in the curve, J K M N, representing the shadow cast by the circle, E d F, upon the conical surface of the web. Consequently, if we draw the luminar lines through the points, d', e', f', &c., the respective points of their intersection with the curve, as M, P, Q, will represent their shadows cast upon the web surface. These points are squared over to M', P', Q', in the horizontal projection.

The points, g, h, i, situated upon the upper base of the cone, obviously cast no shadows, the shadows of the teeth, however, springing from them; if it is wished to determine any points between these and those already found, it will be necessary to describe an imaginary circle, such as G', K', H', passing between the points, d and g, the outer and inner angles of the teeth. The curve, R S T, as projected in the elevation, will be found to represent the shadow cast by this circle upon the conical surface of the web.

As the edges, $a\,d$, $b\,e$, $c\,f$, cast shadows which coincide with generatrices of the cone, they may be obtained simply by drawing straight lines through the several points, M', Q', and P', converging in the apex of the cone in both planes of projection.

Finally, the shadows cast by some of the outer edges of the teeth, such as $f\,c$, upon the teeth immediately behind, are defined by drawing the luminar line, $f\,l$, through the point, f, meeting the flank, $l\,m$, of the other tooth, which lies in a vertical plane. This point of contact is projected vertically in l', on the vertical projection, $f'\,l'$, of the luminar line. It now remains to draw a line, $l'\,n$, through this point, l', and through the apex of the cone, and this line will represent the shadow cast by the edge, $f\,c$.

357. In the case where the luminar line passing through the extremity of the tooth—as that, for example, drawn through the point, p—falls upon a curved portion of the tooth behind, it is necessary, if great accuracy is required, to imagine a vertical plane passing through this point and through the luminar line, and then to find the intersection of this plane with the curved surface of the tooth. This would require a separate diagram; but

the operation is very simple, and has been explained in reference to previous examples (287).

358. The example, fig. ⓑ, represents the application of finished shading to a bevil wheel with wooden teeth, in gear with a pinion on each side, each with cast-iron teeth. It is to be remarked, that although the shadows are not the same upon each of these wheels, because of their different positions with regard to the light, these are, nevertheless, determined by means of the same operations as those which we have just explained.

In shading this example, the principles and observations already discussed must be borne in mind, and note taken of the various lights and shades. It is also to be observed, that, from the positions of the two pinions, the inner end of the shaft of one is completely in the shade, whilst the inner end of the other is illuminated.

APPLICATION OF SHADOWS TO SCREWS.

PLATE XXXI.

359. It has already been shown, that a screw may be generated by a triangle, a rectangle, or by a circle, the plane of which passes through the axis of the screw, the generating movement being along a helical path. The screw is, consequently, called triangular, square, or round-threaded. In each of these cases, the outer edges cast shadows upon the core of the screw, or upon the twisted surface of the consecutive convolutions of the thread itself. If the screw is surmounted by a head, there will be, in addition, the shadow cast by this upon the outer surface of the thread, as well as upon the other parts. We shall proceed to explain the methods of determining the various shadows upon these different kinds of screws.

CYLINDRICAL SQUARE-THREADED SCREW.

FIGURES 1, 2, 2ᵃ, AND 3.

360. The limit of the shadow proper upon the screw, is obtained in the same manner as that upon a right cylinder, by drawing the radius, o A, at right angles to the ray of light, R O, and then squaring over the point, A, to A' and A², and drawing a line through these parallel to the axis of the cylinder. In the same manner we obtain, by projecting the point, B, the line of separation of light and shade, B' B², upon the surface of the core.

The shadows cast by the outer edge of the threads upon the cylindrical surface of the core, are simply determined by means of the straight lines c c, D d, drawn parallel to the luminous ray, R O, and meeting the circle, E d B, the projection of the core, in c and d; then, by squaring over the points, c D, to c' D', and drawing through the latter the straight lines, c c', D d', parallel to the ray of light, R', we obtain the points, c', d', for the shadows sought. We can, in the same manner, obtain as many points as are necessary to complete the curved outline of the shadow.

When the threads of the screw are inclined to the left, as in figs. 2ᵃ and 3, instead of being inclined to the right, as in figs. 1 and 2, the operations necessary for determining the curve of the shadows are still the same. This is rendered sufficiently plain by the employment of the same letters to represent similar and symmetrical

points; it only requires to be observed, that the end view, fig. 3, is that of the right half of the screw, whilst that in fig. 1 is one of the left half, or, one may be supposed to be the turning over of the end of the screw to the right, whilst the other is to the left; the ray of light is similarly respectively represented to the right and left; this, however, does not make any difference, as it is the length of the line merely, as D d, which is required. The luminous ray, in both cases, makes an angle of 45° with the axis of the screw, which is horizontal.

The polygonal head, F G H I, which separates the right-handed from the left-handed portion of the screw, casts a shadow upon a part of the latter, represented by curves, which will be easily determined, in accordance with previous examples (285 and 286), and the principal points in which are f, g, in figs. 2ᵃ and 3.

SCREW WITH SEVERAL RECTANGULAR THREADS.

FIGURES 4 AND 5.

361. The construction of the shadows of a rectangular-threaded screw is the same, whether it be in a horizontal or vertical position, or whether it be right-handed or left-handed. Thus, the screw with several rectangular threads, represented in figs. 4 and 5, has in the first place a shadow proper, limited by the vertical line, A' A², as squared over from the point, A, and next, the shadow, c' d' f', cast upon the core by the outer edge of the thread, c' D' E'; there is, moreover, a portion of the shadow cast by the circular shoulder, G H I, upon the threads, and also upon the core. The outlines of these shadows are found in precisely the same manner as those in figs. 1, 2, and 3 (361).

TRIANGULAR-THREADED SCREW.

FIGURES 6, 6ᵃ, 7, AND 8.

362. When the screw is generated by an isosceles triangle, such as c a d, fig. 6, of which the height, a b, is greater than the half of the base, c d, there will be a shadow cast by the outer edge of the thread upon the twisted surface of the succeeding convolution. In proceeding to determine the outline of this shadow, in accordance with the general method, which consists in finding the points of contact of the luminous rays with the surface, we are led to seek, in the first place, the curve of intersection of this surface, with a plane passing through the luminous ray, and parallel to the axis of the screw.

For this purpose, let E o, fig. 7, be the sectional plane; its intersection with the outer edge, c G' p, of the screw-thread will be in the point, E, E', figs. 6 and 7, and similarly its intersection with the inside, a l g, will be in the point, r, r'. To obtain intermediate points of the sectional curve, we must describe various circles with the centre, o, and radii, o m, o n, representing the projections of so many cylinders, on which lie the helices comprised between the inner one, a l g, and outermost, d E² s, being of the same pitch as these latter. We thereby obtain the points of intersection, h, i, fig. 7, which are to be squared over to h', i', in fig. 6, and then, by joining the several points, E², h', i', r, we get the curve of intersection of the plane with the helical surface of the thread; so that, if we draw a luminar line, E' e', through the point, E', in the same plane, its intersection with the curve, E² h' i' r, will give a point, e', in the outline of the shadow sought.

In like manner, by drawing other planes, as F H and G I, parallel to the first, E O, we shall obtain the intersectional curves, F² f' H' and G² j' g l, and further upon these the points, f' and g', of the outline of the shadow. By proceeding thus, we can obtain as many points as may be deemed necessary for the construction of the shadow cast by the outer edge, c G' p, of the thread, and the curve obtained is, of course, repeated on the several convolutions of the thread. We would remark, that there is no shadow cast when the depth of the thread is such, only that a b, fig. 6, is less than the half of the base, c d, of the generating triangle.

The diagrams, figs. 6° and 8, which represent a portion of a left-handed screw, will show that the operations required in this modification, to determine the outlines of the shadows, are precisely the same as those last explained.

The core, N, which separates the two portions of the double screw, as well as the end, N', receives a shadow cast by the outer edge of the adjacent convolution of the thread.

SHADOWS UPON A ROUND-THREADED SCREW.

FIGURES 9 AND 10.

363. These figures represent a species of screw generated by a circle, a b c d, the plane of which passes through the screw's axis, and of which each point describes a helix about the same axis. The intervals or hollows between the convolutions of the thread are also formed with a helical surface generated by a semicircle, d e f, tangential to the first. We have, then, to determine the limiting line of the shadow proper upon the screw, and the shadow cast by this line upon the hollows.

The projecting thread being a species of spiral torus or serpentine, the determination of its shadow will be similar to that of the shadow of the ring (323).

Thus, if the screw be sectioned by a vertical plane, G O, passing through its axis, its intersection with the thread will evidently be a circle, as projected in j' l', fig. 9. This circle, being inclined to the vertical plane of projection, fig. 10, is projected therein in the form of an ellipse, the principal points, j, k, l, of which are obtained by squaring over the points, j', k', l', respectively, upon the helices corresponding to the points, a, b, c. If, then, upon the plane, G O, which we suppose to be reproduced at o g, fig. 10°, we project the luminous ray, R o, it will be sufficient to determine the point of contact of this ray with the curve, j k l; for this purpose, find the projection of the ray upon the vertical plane in g' o', fig. 10°; then draw a line, g² o³, tangential to the ellipse, j k l, and parallel to the straight line, g' o', its point of contact, m, with the ellipse will be a point in the line of separation of light and shade upon the outer surface of the screw-thread. By proceeding in this manner, any number of points in this line may be obtained.

By continuing the sectional plane, G O, across the hollow of the screw, we shall likewise obtain the elliptic curve, n o², the principal points in which are equally situated upon the helices which pass through the points, d, e, f; it is sufficient to prolong the luminar line, g² o³, until it cuts the ellipse, n o² p, so as to obtain the point, o², which is the shadow cast by the corresponding point, m, of the

line of separation of light and shade upon the hollows or intervals between the convolutions of the thread.

It is to be remarked, that the prolongation of the line of separation of light and shade, s t, casts a shadow upon the outer surface of the convolution immediately below; and, in the same manner, the shoulder above casts a shadow over the projection and hollow of the adjacent thread.

APPLICATION OF SHADOWS TO A BOILER AND ITS FURNACE.

PLATE XXXII.

SHADOW OF THE SPHERE.

FIGURE 1.

364. It will be recollected, that a sphere is a regular solid, generated by the revolution of a semicircle about its diameter. From this definition it follows, that its convex or concave surface, according as it is considered solid or hollow, is a surface of revolution, of which every point is equally distant from the centre of the generating circle. To determine, then, the shadow proper, upon the surface of a sphere, we can proceed according to the general principle (328); but, in this particular case, the following will be the simpler method.

Let us suppose the sphere to be enveloped in a right cylinder, having its axis parallel to the luminous ray; this cylinder will touch the sphere at a great circle, which is, in fact, the line of separation of light and shade, and the plane of which is perpendicular to the luminous ray, and, consequently, inclined to the planes of projection; it follows, therefore, that the projection of this line upon these planes will be an ellipse.

Thus, let fig. 1 represent the horizontal projection of a sphere, whose radius is O A, the projections of the extreme generatrices, B C and D E, of the cylinder, parallel to the luminous ray, touch the external contour of the sphere in the points, C, E, which are diametrically opposite to each other, and are the extremities of the transverse axis of the ellipse.

As, in general, this curve can be drawn when its two axes are determined, it merely remains to find the length of its conjugate axis. To this effect let us imagine a vertical plane to pass through the luminous ray, R O, and let us take two lines tangent to the section of the sphere in this plane, and parallel to the luminous ray; if now we turn this plane about the line, R O, considered as an axis, so as to fold it over upon, and make it coincide with, the horizontal plane, the great circle, which is its section with the sphere, will obviously coincide with the circle drawn with the radius, A O. The luminous ray will, as already seen (287), be turned over to R' O, making an angle of 35° 16' with the line, R O. It may also be obtained by making the line, R' R, perpendicular to R O, and equal to a side of the square, as G R, and then joining R' O. The two luminous rays tangential to the sphere will then coincide with the straight lines, H L and M N, parallel to R' O, their points of contact with the great circle will be the extremities of the diameter, L N, perpendicular to R' O. If now we imagine the plane to be returned to its original position, the points, L and

N. will be projected in L′ and N′, thereby giving the length, L N, of the conjugate axis of the ellipse sought.

365. If, in place of constructing this ellipse by the ordinary methods, it is preferred to determine the various points by means of a series of analogous sections, with their subsequent operations, it will be sufficient, for example, to draw the plane, a b, parallel to R O, and then to turn over, as it were, the section of the sphere formed by this plane, so that it shall coincide with the horizontal plane, making its centre, at the same time, to coincide with the centre, O, of the sphere, the section in question being a circle, described with the radius, c o, equal to a c. Next draw the tangent, e d, parallel to R′ O, and then project the point, d, on the diameter, L N, to d′, upon the original line of section, and a point in the elliptic curve. In this manner, as many points may be obtained as are wished. The distance, c d², being made equal to c d′, d² will be the symmetrical point in the opposite, and now apparent part of the ellipse.

If the projection of the sphere were supposed to be upon the vertical plane, the operations would be identical, only the transverse axis of the ellipse, instead of being in the direction, c E, would, on the contrary, be in the direction, A I, perpendicular to it, as seen on fig. ⑧, representing the hemispherical end of a boiler, shaded and finished.

SHADOW CAST UPON A HOLLOW SPHERE.

FIGURE 2.

366. When a hollow sphere is cut by a plane passing through its centre, and parallel to the plane of projection, the inner edge of the section will cast a shadow upon the concave surface, the outline of which will be an elliptic curve, which may be determined in accordance with the general principle of parallel sections, already explained (287), or by means of the simpler system of sections and auxiliary views adopted in the preceding example, and of which we shall proceed to give another instance, in fig. 2.

This figure represents the projection of a hollow sphere upon the vertical plane, being, in fact, the section through the line, 1—2, of the boiler, represented in figs. 4 and 5. If this hemisphere be sectioned by a diametrical plane, A B, parallel to the luminous ray, the section represented in the auxiliary view, fig. 3, will be a semicircle, A′ c′ B′. The luminous ray, lying in this plane, and passing through the point, A, A′, will, in fig. 3, be represented by the line, A′ c′, parallel to the line, R′ A, obtained, as indicated in fig. 2, by the method already explained. This straight line, A′ c′, cuts the circle, A′ c′ B′, in the point, c′, which must be squared over to c, on the line, A B, fig. 2, when c will be the shadow cast by the point, A.

In the same manner we obtain the points, b, d, by means of the sectional planes, a b, c d, parallel to A B, and cutting the sphere in semicircles, represented by a′ b′ e, in fig. 3. This semicircle is cut in the point, b′, by the line, a′ b′, parallel to A′ c′. The extreme points, D, E, are obviously situated at the extremities of the diameter, D E, perpendicular to the luminous ray, R O, and representing the transverse axis of the ellipse. These shadows are frequently met with in architectural and mechanical subjects; as, for example, in niches, domes, and boilers.

APPLICATIONS.

367. Fig. 4 represents a longitudinal section, at the line, 3—4, in fig. 5, of a cylindrical wrought-iron boiler, with hemispherical ends, and surmounted by a couple of cylindrical chambers, one of which serves for a man-hole, and has a cover fitted to it.

Fig. 5 is a plan of the same boiler, looking down upon it, and showing the cylindrical chambers.

Fig. 6 is a transverse section, made at the line, 5—6, in figs. 4 and 5.

For this boiler, we have to determine—

First, In fig. 4, the shadows, D d c and E b c, cast upon the spherical surfaces at either end of the boiler, as well as those, c g i and j k l, upon the cylindrical surface, together with the shadows cast on the interior of the cylindrical chambers.

Second, In fig. 5, the shadows proper of the external cylindrical and spherical portions of the boiler, and the shadows cast upon these by the cylindrical chambers.

In fig. 7, we apply the same letters as to the analogous diagram, fig. 3, this view being drawn for the purpose of obtaining the elliptic curve, D d c, of the shadow cast by the circular portion, A c D, upon the internal spherical surface of the end of the boiler.

In the same manner is obtained the portion, E b c l, by means of the diagram, fig. 8, observing that the sections made parallel to the ray of light, above the line, a b, give semicircles, whilst those made below, such as F c, give the circular portion to the right of the line, a o, but an elliptical portion to the left of this line, in consequence of this portion of the plane cutting the cylindrical part of the boiler obliquely. It must be remarked, that the cylindrical chambers, situated on the top of the boiler, give rise to the intersections, I J K F, which cast shadows upon the interior of the boiler, instead of the rectilinear portion, I F, of the extreme generatrix of the cylinder, which would have cast a shadow, had the cylindrical chambers not been there.

The shadow cast by the edge of these intersecting surfaces is limited to the curves, J K F, which may be easily delineated with the aid of the section, fig. 6, by squaring over the points, J, K, L, F, to the arc, J′ K′ L′ F′, and then drawing a series of luminar lines through these points; that is, lines parallel to the ray of light. These will meet the internal surface of the cylinder in the points, j′, k′, l′, which are squared over again to the longitudinal section, fig. 4, by means of horizontals, intersecting the luminar lines, drawn through the corresponding points in the edges of each chamber, in the points, j, k, l. The rectilinear portion, F I, of the uppermost generatrix of the cylinder, has for its shadow, on the internal surface thereof, the similar and equal straight line, l i, which coincides, in the projection, with the axis, o o (308).

A part of the extreme left-hand generatrix, I N, of each cylindrical chamber, likewise casts a shadow upon the internal surface of the boiler, the outline of which is a curve, i m j, which is simply an arc of a circle, described with the centre, o, and with the radius, o i, equal to that, c o, of the boiler. This shadow is circular, because the straight line, I N, which casts it, is perpendicular to the axis of the cylinder; whilst the axis and itself lie in a plane, parallel to the plane of projection.

We can, however, determine the points, i, m, j, of the curve, independenuy, with the assistance of the auxiliary projection, fig. 6, at right angles to fig. 4.

It is the same with the curve, n p q, which is likewise an arc of a circle, because the straight line, N P, the edge of the cover which closes the top of the chamber, is at right angles to the axis of the latter, and at the same time parallel to the vertical plane of projection. The edges, N R and R M, being vertical, have for shadows upon the internal surface of the chamber, a couple of vertical straight lines, parallel to themselves (309). The chamber to the right having a circular opening in the cover, has a shadow upon its internal surface, necessarily different from that in the other chamber. It is, however, easily obtained, and in the same manner as in figs. 1 and 1ᵃ, Plate XXVIII. It must be observed, however, that a portion, s t u, of this shadow is due to the under edge, s T U, of the cover-piece; whilst the other part, s v, takes its contour from the upper edge, v x, of the same piece. A comparison of figs. 4 and 5 will render these points easy of comprehension.

There remains, finally, the curve, c e g h, and the rectilinear portion, h i, together extending from the first, D d c, to the straight line, i i, and which represents the shadow cast by the arc, A F, G H, of the hemispherical end of the boiler, and the straight part, H I, of the upper edge of the cylindrical portion.

The whole curve, D d, c g i, representing the shadow cast by the edge of the section of the boiler upon the internal surface of the latter, is precisely the same as that distinguished in architecture by the name of the *niche shadow*. It is to be observed, however, that the position in this case is different, as the axis of the niche is vertical.

We have now to draw the shadows, proper and cast, upon the outer surface of the boiler, as seen in horizontal projection, fig. 5. As for the shadow proper, it consists partly in that limited by the line of separation of light and shade, d d, obtained by the tangential line, making an angle of 45° with the horizon, and touching the circle in the point, c, and partly in that bounded by the elliptic curves, c d and d c′ E, upon the spherical ends of the boiler, the manner of determining which has already been thoroughly discussed in reference to fig. 1.

368. As to the shadows cast by the cylindrical chambers, either on their neck pieces, or upon the outside of the boiler itself, they are simply represented by lines inclined at an angle of 45°, as A′ D′, B′ E′, drawn tangential to the outsides of the cylinders, and which are prolonged in straight lines, as far as the line of separation of light and shade, upon the cylindrical portion of the boiler; that is, in case they stand out far enough from the boiler surface. If, on the contrary, they do not rise very high, as exemplified in the end view, fig. 9, it will be necessary to determine the outline of the shadow cast by a portion of the upper edge, B′ c′, as lying either upon the cylindrical part of the boiler, or upon one of the spherical ends. To find the shadow in this last case, we have supposed an imaginary vertical plane to pass through the luminous ray, R′ o′, fig. 5, producing an elliptical section of the cylinder, and a circular one of the spherical part. This plan being reproduced at R² o², fig. 9, and turned about, to coincide with the horizontal plane, we have the curve, F² G² H², representing the section in question. The point of contact, B′, being transferred to B², is also turned down, as it were, upon the horizontal plane, to the

point, B²; so that if we draw a line, B² I², through this point, B², parallel to the luminous ray, R² o², similarly brought into the horizontal plane, this line, B² I², will cut the intersectional curve in the point, I²; the horizontal projection, I², of this point, upon the line, R² H², being obtained by letting fall the perpendicular, I² I², upon the latter. The corresponding point, I′, in fig. 5, is taken at a distance from B′, equal to B² I², in fig. 9. Proceed in the same manner with another sectional plane, parallel to the first, and passing through the point, c′, in order to obtain a second point, c′, of the shadow. The operations necessary for determining the intersectional curves are sufficiently indicated in figs. 5 and 9.

369. The cylindrical steam-boiler, represented in longitudinal section in fig. Ⓐ, in end elevation in fig. Ⓑ, and in transverse section in fig. Ⓒ, conjoins the various applications of shadows, of which we have been treating, in reference to spheres and cylinders; whilst, at the same time, they serve as examples of shading, by lines or by washes, indicating the effects to be aimed at, and to be attained by the following out of the various principles already laid down.

370. We must remind the student, that, in order to produce tnese effects, he must not always confine himself to the representation of the shadows proper and cast merely. He must, further, show the gradations of the light or shadow upon each part, as has already been explained with reference to solid and hollow cylinders. As upon a cylinder or a cone, there is always a line of pre-eminent brilliancy, so likewise, upon the surface of a sphere, will there be a point of greater brilliancy than the rest.

This point is actually situated upon the luminous ray, passing through the centre of the sphere, fig. 1. Since, however, the visual rays are not coincident with the luminous rays, the apparent position of this point is somewhat changed. Thus, if we bring the vertical plane, R o, fig. 1, into the horizontal plane, the luminous ray will coincide, as has been seen, with the line, R′ o′, and, consequently, its point of intersection with the sphere will coincide with the point, i. On the other hand, the visual rays which are perpendicular to the horizontal plane will coincide with parallels to o o, when brought into the horizontal plane. This latter line intersects the sphere in the point, c; and as the light is reflected from any surface in the direction of the visual rays, so as to make the angle of incidence equal to the angle of reflection, if we divide the angle, i o c, into two equal angles, by the line, n o, the point, n, will be that which will appear to the eye most brilliantly illuminated. The positions, n′ and i′, in the vertical plane of the points, n and i, are obtained by letting fall perpendiculars upon the line, o A, representing this plane.

In shading up a drawing it is preferable to place the bright or lightest part between the two points, n′ and i′, a more pleasing effect being obtained thereby. When the sphere is polished, as a steel, brass, or ivory ball, a circular spot, of pure white, must be left about the point in question. When, however, the body is rough, as is supposed in fig. Ⓑ, this part is always lighter than the rest; but, at the same time, it is covered by a faint wash.

In the case of a hollow sphere, figs. 2 and 3, we have to bear in mind, not only to indicate the position of the bright spot, which is projected, in the same manner, upon the luminous ray, A B, and lies between the points, n′, i′, but also the point in the cast shadow, which should be the least prominent. This latter will be found to be at m', fig. 2, as determined by the radius, o' m, fig. 3, drawn perpendicularly to the ray of light, A' c', as brought into the same plane as fig. 3.

371. The boiler is represented as placed in its furnace, which is built entirely of bricks, with a diaphragm passing down the middle of its length, to oblige the flames and gases issuing from the grate to pass along the flue to the left, then to return by that to the right, and passing through a third flue, before it reaches the chimney. In this third flue is placed an auxiliary boiler, full of water, and in communication with the main boiler by a pipe passing to the bottom of each. In this auxiliary boiler, the feed-water becomes heated before entering the main boiler, so as not to reduce the temperature of the latter to a serious extent, upon its introduction into it.

The main boiler is represented as half full of water. It should generally be two-thirds full, but is delineated as but half full; so that a greater portion of the shadow cast upon its interior may be visible. The remainder of the space, as well as the cylindrical chambers, is supposed to be filled with steam. The base of the chimney is of stone, whilst the stalk is of brick. The foundations of the furnace are likewise of stone.

Besides this present example of a boiler, we give a further exercise for finished shading in Plate XXXIII., the objects in which we recommend the student to copy, on a scale two or three times as large, so as to acquire the proper skill and facility of treatment.

SHADING IN BLACK.—SHADING IN COLOURS.

PLATE XXXIII.

372. In a great number of drawings, and particularly in those termed working drawings, and intended for use in actual construction, the draughtsman contents himself by shading the objects with China ink—sometimes, perhaps, covering this with a faint wash of colour, appropriate to the nature of the material. The shading, on the one hand, brings out the parts in relief, and renders the forms of the object intelligible to the eye; whilst, on the other hand, the colours indicate of what material they are made. This duplex artistic representation makes the drawing much more life-like, and more easily comprehended. A drawing may be coloured in several ways. The simplest plan is first to shade up the various surfaces with China ink, having due regard to the respective forces and gradations of tone, according to the lights and shades, as has been done in the preceding plates. The entire surface of each object is then covered with an especial wash of colour, the line of which is quite conventional. It must be laid on in flat washes, according to the instructions given in reference to Plate X. This first method of operating may suffice in many cases, but it leaves out much to be desired in the effective appearance of the drawing, its aspect being generally without vigour, cold and monotonous. A better result is obtainable by not carrying the China ink shading to so great a depth, and by covering the surfaces by two or three washes of colour, laid on in gradations, as was done with the China ink itself, so as to produce a sufficient strength of colour at the darker parts, whilst the light

parts are left very faint; and where the objects are polished, a pure white line or spot is left, which will add considerably to the brilliancy of the whole. A softer and more harmonious effect can be produced by the use of a warm neutral tint, instead of the China ink, for the preliminary shading. This colour, however, is very difficult to mix, and to keep uniform.

When a little practice has given some skill and facility in the preparation and combination of the colours, the draughtsman may proceed, at the outset, in a more direct and vigorous manner, leaving out altogether the preliminary shading with China ink, and laying on at once the successive coloured washes, rendering, at the same time, the effects of light and shade, and indicating the nature of the material. This last method has the merit of giving to each part of the drawing a richer translucence, more warmth, and a more satisfactory fulfilment of all desirable conditions.

In general, all drawings intended to be shaded should be delineated with faint gray instead of black outlines, as for a simple outline drawing; the faintness of such lines avoids the necessity of making them very fine, and their greater breadth affords a much better guide to the shading-brush. A black outline, however fine it may be, always produces a too sharp and hard appearance, whilst there is much greater risk of overstepping it in laying on the washes.

373. In Plate XXXIII. we give a few good examples of objects shaded in colours, comprising the materials most in use in construction.

Fig. 1 represents the capital of a Doric column in wood. Although the woods are naturally very different in colour, still, in mechanical drawings, a single tint is used indiscriminately: it is, as we have said, entirely conventional.

In fixing upon these colours, the object in view has been to avoid confusion, and to employ a distinct and intelligible colour for the representation of each substance, without seeking to copy the natural colour in all its varieties.

In colouring this wooden capital, after the preliminary operations which we have mentioned, for determining the outlines of the shadows, proper and cast, it is first shaded throughout with China ink, and when this shading has reached a convenient depth, and is thoroughly dry, the whole surface is to be covered with a light wash, which may be a mixture of gamboge, lake, and China ink, or burnt umber alone. The colour, in fact, should be analogous to that of fig. 4, Plate X.; it should, however, always be fainter than in that example, which represents the material in section, and is, therefore, stronger.

This proceeding may be easily modified, and made to resemble the effect of the second method, by leaving certain parts of the object uncoloured, and by softening off the shade in those places where the light is strongest, with a nearly dry brush. If, however, the draughtsman has become somewhat familiarized with the use of the brush and the mixture of the colours, he may, as we have said, omit the preliminary shading in black, by modifying each shade as laid on, mixing the China ink directly with the colours, and then gradually bringing up the shades, either according to the system of flat washes, or the more difficult one of softened shades. Care must be taken in laying on these shades to commence at the deeper parts, and then to cover these over again by the subse quent washes, which gradually approach the bright part of the object; for in this way a more brilliant and translucent effect will bo obtained.

When the objects are of wood, it is customary to represent the graining in faint irregular streaks, care being taken to make these as varied as possible. A general idea of the effect to be produced will be obtained from fig. 1.

Following out these principles, the draughtsman may proceed to colour various other objects composed of different materials, merely varying the mixtures of colour according to the instructions given in reference to Plate X.

Fig. 2 represents the top of a chimney of brickwork, the form being circular. In this external view, the outline of each brick is indicated; and to render them more distinct from each other, a line of reflected light has been shown on the edges towards the light, near the brighter part of the chimney. Indeed, it is generally advisable to leave a narrow, pure white light at the edges of an object which are fully illuminated, as it gives an effective sharp appearance.

Fig. 3 represents the base of a Doric column in stone, showing the flutings. This being an external view, the tint to represent the stone is not made nearly so strong as for the sectional stone-work, represented in Plate X. A yellowish grey may be used for it, made by mixing gamboge, the predominant colour, with a little China ink, adding a little lake to give warmth.

These three examples of wood, brick, and stone, represent bodies with rough surfaces, and which, therefore, can never receive such brilliant lights as objects in polished metal; no part, indeed, should be entirely free from some faint colour.

Fig. 4 represents a nut or bolt-head of wrought-iron; and, as we have supposed it to be turned and planed, and polished upon its entire surface, it has been necessary to leave pure white lights at the brighter parts, to distinguish the surfaces from those which are rough and dull. It is the same in the example, fig. 5, representing the base of a polished cast-iron column, and in the lateral projection, fig. 6, of polished brass upper and lower shaft-bearings or brasses.

We would hope that the principles of shadows and shading, explained and exemplified in the last two chapters, may serve as sufficient guides for the various applications which may present themselves to the draughtsman—whether his skill be called forth to render the simple effects of light and shadow, or to produce the gradations of shade and colour due to roundness or obliquity of surface—to the various positions of the objects in their polished or unpolished state, and to the various materials of which they may be composed.

Thus, it will be understood, that although two objects are precisely alike in material and form, if they are situated at unequal distances from the spectator, the nearer one of the two must be coloured more strongly and brilliantly than the more distant, more force and depth being given to the darker shades.

CHAPTER IX.

THE CUTTING AND SHAPING OF MASONRY.

PLATE XXXIV.

374. The operation of stone-cutting has for its object, the preparing and shaping stones in such manner that they may be built up into any desired form in a compact and solid manner; great care and skill, as well as mathematical knowledge, is more particularly required in the preparation of stones for arches, vaults, arcades, and such like structures.

The study of the shaping of stones is based entirely upon descriptive geometry, being indeed but a particular application or branch of it, and in it have to be considered the generation of surfaces, as well as their intersections and developments.

In proceeding to adapt the stones to the position they are to occupy, the mason should prepare a preliminary drawing of the actual size of each stone, as well as a general view of the entire erection, indicating the joints of each stone; these, according to the various positions to be occupied by them, are called *key stones, arch stones,* &c.

It is not our intention to give a complete treatise on the shaping of masonry; but, as this study seems to belong, in part, to geometrical drawing, we have thought it quite within the design of the present work to give a few applications, sufficient to show the line of procedure to be followed out in operations of this nature.

THE MARSEILLES ARCH, OR ARRIERE-VOUSSURE.

FIGURES 1 AND 2.

375. We propose to prepare the designs for the bay and arch of a door or window, to be built of stonework, the upper part being cut away, so as to present a twisted surface, analogous to that known as the *arrière-voussure* of Marseilles.

This surface is such as would be generated by a straight line, c A, kept constantly upon the horizontal, c′ K′, projected vertically in the point, c, and moved, on the one hand, upon the semi-base, B E D, of a right cylinder, having c′ K′ for its axis; and, on the other, upon the circular arc, F K A, situated in a plane parallel to that of the base, B E D.

The lateral faces, F B L N and A R Q D, of the bay, are vertical, and are projected horizontally in F′ B′ and A′ D′, fig. 2. These faces intersect the twisted surface at the curves, F B and A D, which we shall proceed to determine.

For this purpose, the first thing to be done is to seek the projections of the straight generator line, c A, as occupying different positions, so as to obtain their points of intersection with one of the oblique planes.

We may remark, that if the arc, F K A, be prolonged to the right, for example, of fig. 1, and a number of lines be drawn through the point, c, as c J, c a, c b, and c G, they will represent so many vertical projections of the generatrix, c A, in different positions. These straight lines meet the semicircle, B E D, in the points, I, c, d, e, which are projected horizontally in the points, I′, c′, d′, e′. These same lines also cut the circular arc, F A G, in the points, J, a, b, G, which are projected upon the line, F′ G′, the horizontal projection of this line, in the points, J′, a′, b′, G′. By drawing lines through these last, and through those first obtained, I′, c′, d′, e′, we obtain the straight lines, c² J′, c³ a′, c⁴ b′, c⁵ G′, which are the horizontal projections of the generatrix, c A, and correspond to the vertical projections in fig. 1.

These straight lines cut the plane, A′ D′, in the points, M′ f′ i′, which are then projected vertically to M, f, i, upon the straight lines, c J, c a, c b; the curve, A M f i D, passing through each of these points, is the line of intersection sought, and it is reproduced symmetrically at F B, to the left hand of fig. 1, so as to avoid the necessity of repeating the diagram.

To obtain this line of intersection full size, it is necessary to bring the plane, D′ A′, into the plane of the picture, by supposing it to turn about the vertical, D Q, projected horizontally in D′, as an axis; during this movement, each of the points, A′, M′, f′, will describe an arc of a circle about the centre, D′, finally coinciding with the points, M², A², f², and i². Through the corresponding points, A, M, f, i, in the vertical projection, we must draw a series of horizontal lines, A A″, M M″, f f″, upon which, square over the preceding points, M², A², f², i², by which means will be obtained the curve, A″ M″ f″ D, representing the exact form or parallel projection of the line of intersection.

376. The preliminary design thus sketched out, gives nothing but the outline of the surface of the erection, and it now remains to divide it into a certain number of parts, to represent the individual stones of which it is to be built up.

The number of divisions necessarily depends upon the nature of the material and sizes of stone at the mason's disposal; the number snould, however, in all cases, be an odd one, so that a central space may be reserved for the principal piece, known as the key-stone.

The divisions are struck upon the semicircle, B E D, by a series of radii converging in the centre, c; it is these lines which represent the divisions of the stones. Below the arched part, the regular pieces, as X, consist of a series of stones of equal dimensions, the joints of which are horizontal.

The horizontal projections of each of the stones forming the arch are straight lines, because the joints lie in planes perpendicular to the vertical plane, whose intersection with the twisted surface is always a straight line corresponding to a generatrix; thus, the planes, o c and P c, of the joints on either side of the key-stone, K, are perpendicular to the vertical plane, and pass through the axis, c K′; and the portions of them, n h and o l, comprised between the directing circles, B E D and F K A, are represented in the horizontal projection by the straight lines, n′ h′ and o′ l′, which are the joints of the stones as seen from below—that is, the lines of their intersection with the twisted surface.

It is the same with the planes, m c and J c, in which lie the

joints of the corner stones, Y Z; the portions, k g and I R, of the joints falling upon the twisted surface, are likewise projected horizontally at the straight lines, k′ g′ and M′ I′.

377. The design of the erection being thus completed, the shaper should delineate each individual stone as detached from the arch, in such a manner as to represent all the faces of the joints, and he then takes for each, a stone of the most convenient dimensions from amongst those at his disposal, which are generally hewn out roughly in the shape of rectangular parallelopipeds; on each of these pieces he marks off the parts to be cut away, to reduce the stone to the required form and dimensions.

Thus, supposing he commences with the key-stone, K, for example, detailed in front view and vertical section through the middle, in figs. 3 and 4; he takes a parallelopiped, of which the base, p q r s, is capable of circumscribing the two parallel faces of the upper part of the key-stone, and of which the height is at least equal to the length, t u′. After having cut and finished the two vertical faces, t′ o′ and u′ v, of the prism, as well as the horizontal face, t′ u′, he measures off upon the anterior face, fig. 3, the parallel and vertical sides, t o and u P, and then the oblique lines, o h and P l, which, it will be remembered, converge to the same point, c, the axis of the voussure. He next sets off upon a template the arcs, n o and h l, fig. 1, and reproduces them thence upon the parallelopiped, fig. 3, at n o and h l. After this preliminary marking out, the stonecutter reduces and takes away all the material upon the sides of the parallelopiped which lies outside the lines, o h and P l; these faces being finished, the shape-designer lays out upon them the lines projected at n h and o l. In order that the form of this joint may be more easily comprehended, we have brought the face, P l, into the plane of the picture, representing it in fig. 4ᵇⁱˢ, as parallel to the plane of projection.

This view, it will be seen, is easily obtained; for, on the one hand, we have the line, P′ y, equal to K K², representing the thickness of the wall or of the arch; and, on the other hand, all the other dimensions, as projected horizontally in fig. 2, so that the inclination of the line, o′ l′, can be determined with the most rigorous exactness.

This straight line, as well as the corresponding one on the opposite face, o h, serves as a guide to the stonecutter in reducing the twisted portion of the surface of the key-stone, comprised between them; and as affording a means of verification, it may be remarked, that this surface should be cut in such a manner, that a rule or straight edge may be applied to all parts of it, being guided by the arcs, n o and h l; the former of which springs from the point, o′, and the latter from the point, l′, on the face, P′ x, fig. 4ᵇⁱˢ.

To determine the faces of the joints of either of the two corner pieces, Z, represented in detail, and detached in figs. 5 and 6, but on which the faces are not represented in their full dimensions, it is necessary to proceed in the same manner as before, bringing each face into the plane of projection—that is, delineating auxiliary views of them, as if parallel to this plane.

Thus, to obtain the actual dimensions of the face of the joint projected at o h, with the point, w, as a centre, describe a series of arcs, with the respective radii, o w, n w, h w, so as to reproduce the points, o, n, h, at o², n², h², upon the vertical, o² w; then, by setting off, $h^2 h'$, equal to $n' h'$, fig. 2, and joining the points, $h' n^2$, fig. 7, we get the inclination of the generatrix line, $n^2 h'$, which is projected vertically at $n h$, fig. 1. The form of the joint face is completed by drawing the horizontal lines, $o^2 w$, $h' z'$, $y' v'$, and the verticals, $u' v'$ and $z' y'$, which last are already given full size in fig. 6. It will be observed that fig. 7 is on the plate removed a little to the right of the vertical, $o^2 w$; but this is a matter of no importance, and is merely done for convenience sake.

The same system of auxiliary projections is applicable to the determination of the dimensions of the other face of this piece—namely, that projected at $m g$, which is brought round to the horizontal, $m^2 g^2$, and drawn with full dimensions in fig. 8; only, for this last face, it is necessary to bear in mind the portion of the line of intersection of the sides with the arched part which it contains, and which is obtained in its actual proportions, as at $a^2 m^2$, by means of a template formed to the curve, $A'' M''$, in fig. 1. The stone, Y, beneath, of course, contains the remainder of the intersectional curve.

The methods just explained, in regard to the shaping of the keystone and one of the corner-stones, may be extended, without difficulty, to the remaining portions of this Marseilles arch.

In this application it has been necessary to determine the proportions of the twisted bay of the arch, as well as the faces of the joints; but in the more general case of straight bays, such as that represented in fig. 1bis, the operations are considerably simplified, and the designer has merely to attend to the form of the joint faces, making use, for this purpose, of the auxiliary projections, as above described. The delineation of the various parts of this figure presenting no new peculiarity, it need not further detain us.

378. Let it be proposed to delineate a circular vault with a full centering, bounded by two plane surfaces oblique to its axis, figs. 9 and 10. This example is taken from the entrance to the tunnel on the Strasbourg Railway, near the Paris terminus, and it is a form frequently met with in the construction of railways.

In the representation of this vault, we have supposed one of the oblique planes to be parallel to the vertical plane of projection, and it consequently follows that the axis of the arch is inclined to this plane.

Let A B be this axis, and C D the horizontal projection of a plane at right angles to it; with the point, B, as a centre, describe the semicircle, C A D, representing the arch in its true proportions, as brought into the plane of the picture. Let us suppose this semicircle to be divided into some uneven number of equal parts, as in the points, a, b, c, d, e, f; through each of these points draw straight lines, passing also through the centre, B, and representing the joints, $a g$, $b h$, $c i$, of the arch stones, being, of course, normal to the circular curvature of the arch, and being limited in depth, as we shall suppose, by the second outer semicircle, $g i l$, concentric with the first. Each of these joint faces intersects the centering of the arch in a straight line parallel with its axis, and the horizontal projections of these intersections, as seen from below, are obtained simply by drawing through the points, a, b, c, d, lines parallel to the axis, B A; these last extend as far as the vertical plane, A E, which bounds a portion of the vault. The external faces of the key and arch stones are limited by straight vertical lines, such as $m h$, $i n$, $o j$, and horizontals, as $m i$ and $n o$.

We have now to obtain the projections on the vertical plane, fig. 10, of the intersection of each of the arch stones by the plane, A E.

We may remark, in the first place, that since this plane is oblique to the axis of the cylindrical arch, it produces an elliptical section, having for its semi-transverse axis the length, $c' A$, and for its semi-conjugate axis, the length, A B, equal to the radius, $A' B$. As much of this ellipse as is required is drawn according to one or other of the many methods given (53, et seq.)—say as at $c' b^2 B'$ fig. 9, which curve is reproduced at $c'' b'' a''$, in the elevation, fig. 10.

If we, in like manner, obtain the projection of the semicircle, F $i l$, which limits the radial joints, we shall also obtain the portion of an ellipse, $F'' g''$. i'', and we have further merely to project the points, a', b', c', upon the first ellipse, in $a'' b'' c''$; as also on the second one, the points, g'', h'', i'', corresponding to $g h$ and i. The straight lines, $F'' c''$, $g'' a''$, $h'' b''$, $i'' c''$, represent the intersections of the faces of the arch stone joints, with the plane, A E.

The vault being supposed to extend no further back than the plane, C D, it will be necessary to represent the intersection of this last with the arch stones which extend thus far upon this plane, C D. We have, therefore, to project the elliptic curves, $c''' b''' c'''$ and $F''' g''' i'''$, corresponding to the quarter circles of the radii, F B and C B. As the arch stones cannot extend the entire length of the vault, they are limited by planes, M N, perpendicular to the axis, and, consequently, parallel to C D. so that the projections of these joints will be but repetitions of portions of the same elliptic curve; care is taken so to dispose the blocks of stone, that no two joints form a continuous line, the joints in one course being brought between those in the adjacent ones, as is customary in all brick and stone work.

379. We have now to determine the intersection of the oblique plane, A G, with the remaining half of the same circular vault, and then to obtain the projection of this intersection upon the vertical plane.

The plane, A G, also produces an elliptical section of the vault; this is represented at $G' gt$, as brought into the picture in the auxiliary diagram, fig. 11, which gives its actual proportions; the semi-transverse axis, G' O, of this ellipse is equal to G A, and its semi-conjugate axis is equal to the radius, $A' B$, of the vault.

After having divided this curve into a certain uneven number of equal parts, draw normals,[*] $p u$, $q v$, $r x$, $s y$, and $t z$, through the points of division representing the joints of the arch stones, the remaining sides of the external faces of which are limited by horizontals and verticals, as before.

If the vault is supposed not to extend beyond the plane, A G, the arch stones will have to be shaped as facing stones, and their joints will require to be set off upon the first ellipse, G' $q t$, and to be limited by the second, $H' q^2 t^2$, obtained from the intersectional plane, H I, drawn parallel to A G; by drawing straight lines from the points of division obtained upon the ellipse, G' $q t$, to the centre, O, we obtain the points, p^2, q^2, r^2, s^2, of intersection of these lines upon the second ellipse, and the straight lines, $p p^2$, $q q^2$, $r r^2$, $s s^2$, representing the intersections of the arch stones with the inside of the

* A line is said to be normal to a curve, when it is perpendicular to a tangent to the curve passing through its point of intersection with the curve (73).

vault; these straight lines are projected horizontally in p' p'', q' q'', r' r'', &c., fig. 9, where they are visible, because the diagram is supposed to be a projection of the vault, as seen from below; the two diagrams, figs. 9 and 11, will render the determination of the vertical projection, fig. 10, very easy, the same lines there being designated by the same letters.

To limit the arch facing stones, and unite them conveniently with the regular courses of the vault, they must be cut by planes, such as J K and L P, fig. 9, perpendicular to the axis, A B. The intersections of these planes with the vault produce portions of circles, which are projected as ellipses in fig. 11, such as L' q^2 V and U' r^2 X', for the inside of the vault, and J' Q R' and L' S' P', for their outer extremities, these various ellipses corresponding to the radii, C B and F B. The joints of these stones are finally completed by planes, such as K' P'' S Q, fig. 11, passing through the axis, A B, and through horizontal lines, Y' Z' and O S, in the vault, the latter and inner one of which only is visible in the elevation, fig. 10.

380. In constructing this vault, it is necessary to make detailed drawings of each particular stone, showing the dimensions of all the faces. In figs. 12 to 15, we have represented one of these arch stones, Ⓖ, in plan and elevation, as detached from the erection, fig. 10, and showing more particularly such lines as are not apparent in fig. 11. Thus, in these views may be distinguished:—

1st. The anterior face, v q r x, which is projected horizontally upon the line of the plane, A G; this face, it will be remembered, intersects the vault at the elliptic curve projected at q r.

2d. The face of the joint, x r r^2 w, of which the one edge, x r, is projected upon the same plane, G A, at x' r', whilst the opposite edge, w r^2, is projected upon the line, v'' r'', parallel to G A; and the lower edge, r r^2, the line of intersection of this face with the interior of the vault, is projected in the line, r' r'', whilst, finally, the upper and fourth edge, x w, is projected at x' w'.

3d. The second joint face, v q q^2 w, is opposite to the first, and projected at v' q' q^4 w.

4th. The face, Q S Z Y, the horizontal projection of which is q' s' z' y'; this face is situated in a plane passing through the axis of the vault, and is additionally represented in the diagram, fig. 14, on the radius, P Q''.

5th. The species of dovetail joint, q q^2 Y Z r^2 r, of which the edges, q q^2 and r r^2, are projected, as has been seen, at q q^4 and r' r''; whilst the sides, q r and z r^2, are similarly projected at q' r and z' r'', and finally the side, q^2 Y at q^4 Y'.

6th. Lastly, the posterior face, Q, of which it will be easy to render an account by means of the distinctive letters, which are invariably the same for the same points, although additional special marks are superadded to obviate confusion amongst the various figures. To render this vertical projection more intelligible, we have added the subsidiary view, fig. 14, representing the projection of the block in the plane, L P, as brought into the plane of the picture; we have thus the actual proportions of the faces projected in the planes, s' r'' and P' Q''. To obtain the various points seen in this view, it is sufficient to set off the vertical distances from the line, G O, of the elevation, figs. 11 and 13, obtaining in this manner, for instance, the points, r^3, q^3, v^3, x^3, &c., corresponding to r^2, q^2, v, and x.

The examples chosen for this plate (XXXIV.) combine the more difficult problems and applications met with in the shaping and arrangement of stonework, and will make the student acquainted with the operations upon which designs for these purposes are based, as well as with the general methods to be adopted in obtaining oblique projections by the employment of auxiliary projections, taken, as it were, in planes parallel to the different surfaces, and then brought into the plane of the picture; this system, at the same time, being of much use in ascertaining the exact proportions of various surfaces, such as the joints of masonry.

RULES AND PRACTICAL DATA.

HYDRAULIC MOTORS.

381. The fall of a stream of water varies with the locality, and gives rise to the employment of different kinds of hydraulic motors, which are denominated as follows, according to their several peculiarities.

First, Undershot water-wheels, which receive the water below their centres, and the buckets or floats of which pass through an enclosed circular channel, at the part where the water acts upon them.

Second, Overshot water-wheels, which receive the water from above.

Third, Wheels with vertical axes, known as turbines, and which are capable of working at various depths.

Fourth, Water-wheels, with plane floats or buckets, receiving the water below their centres, and working in enclosed channels, through a portion of their circumference.

Fifth, Similar wheels, with curved buckets.

Sixth, Hanging wheels, mounted on barges, and suspended in the current.

UNDERSHOT WATER-WHEELS, WITH PLANE FLOATS AND A CIRCULAR CHANNEL.

382. The most advantageous arrangement that can be adopted in the construction of an undershot water-wheel, with plane floats, and working in an enclosed circular channel, is that in which the outlet is formed by an overshot sluice-gate, and when the bottom of this outlet is ·2 to ·25 m., or about 8 inches, below the general level of the reservoir.

Let it be required to determine the width of an undershot water-wheel, with the following data:—

First, The discharge of water is 1,200 litres per second.

Second, The height of the fall is 2·475 mètres.

Third, The depth of the water at the sluice-gate is to be ·23 m.

WIDTH OF THE WHEEL.

It will be seen, in the table at page 113, that, with an outlet of ·23 in depth, a discharge can be effected of 188 litres of water per second, for a width of 1 mètre; consequently, the width to be given to the sluice, to enable it to discharge 1,200 litres per second, should be—

$$1200 \div 188 = 6·38 \text{ mètres.}$$

DIAMETER OF THE WHEEL.

383. The diameter to be given to a wheel of this description has not been accurately determined, because it has not a direct influence upon the useful effect that may be obtained from it. Nevertheless, it is manifest that it should not be too small; for in that case the water would be admitted too nearly in the horizontal line passing through the centre, or even above it, which would cause great loss of power. Neither should it be too great, for in that case the exaggerated dimensions would but involve an increased bulk and weight, and, consequently, a greater load and more friction, without any compensating advantage.

In general, for a fall of from 2 to 3 mètres, it is advisable to make the extreme radius of the wheel at least equal to the mean height of the fall, augmented by twice the depth of the water upon the edge of the outlet.

Thus, in the case before us, the height of the fall being limited to 2·475 m., the outer radius of the wheel should not be less than 2·475 m. plus twice the depth of the overflowing body of water when at its fullest—say ·6 m.; that is to say, in all, 3·075 m., which corresponds to a diameter of 6·15 mètres.

Water-wheels, on the same system, with a fall of water of from 2·6 to 2·7 mètres, have often an extreme diameter no greater than this.

VELOCITY OF THE WHEEL.

384. Theoretically speaking, the velocity which it is convenient to give to an undershot water-wheel should be equal to half that due to the height of the overflow of the water; that is to say, equal to from 1· to 1·1 m. in the present case. Nevertheless, practice shows that this rule may be departed from without inconvenience, and the wheel may be made to attain a velocity of from 1·5 to 1·6 m. per second at pleasure, which is a very great advantage in many circumstances.

If the wheel makes three turns per minute, the mean velocity at the outer circumference, and at the edges of the floats, will be—

$$\frac{6·15 \times 3·1416 \times 3}{60} = 1·021 \text{ m. per second.}$$

Thus, when the height of the overflow is ·24 m., the corresponding velocity of the water being 2·17 m. nearly, as shown in the table at page 94, which gives the heights, 23·56 and 24·67 cent., therefore, the ratio of the velocity of the wheel to that of the water is ·47 : 1.

If the height of the overflow were reduced to ·15 m., which supposes that the discharge would only be

101 litres × 6·32 m. = 638 litres per second,

the corresponding velocity of the water would not be more than 1·72; and in this case, the ratio of the velocity of the wheel, supposing it to be still the same, to that of the water, would be—·595 : 1.

NUMBER AND CAPACITY OF THE BUCKETS.

385. Although the number of buckets cannot be determined in accordance with any exact rule, it is, nevertheless, of importance that their pitch should not be much greater than the depth, or thickness, of the overflowing body of water acting upon them. It

is also necessary that the number of the buckets should be divisible by that of the arms of the wheel, so that the whole may be put together conveniently.

Now, since the outer circumference of the wheel is

6·15 × 3·1416 = 19·32 mètres,

we can very conveniently give it 8 arms and 64 buckets; and the pitch of these last will be ·32 m. With this distance between the buckets, there should not generally be a greater depth of overflow than ·25 or ·26 m.; because, at ·27 m. the water will begin to choke, as it will not be admitted easily into the buckets, and will rebound against the interior of the channel, giving rise to a continual shaking action.

Thus, then, in determining the number of buckets for an undershot water-wheel, receiving the water from an overshot outlet, it is necessary to calculate the spaces between them, so as to be about a third, or at least a fourth, greater than the depth of the water at the outlet, whilst their number must be divisible by the number of arms of the wheel.

For water-wheels of from 3·5 to 4·75 mètres in diameter, six arms for each rim or shrouding; for wheels of 5 to 7 mètres in diameter, there should always be eight arms for each shrouding; and the number of arms should obviously increase for wheels of greater diameters than 7 mètres, of which, however, there are but few examples.

With regard to the capacity of the buckets, and the channel, taken together, it should be equal to at least double the volume of water discharged. Therefore, on this basis, we can always easily determine the depth to be given to the buckets, when the maximum discharge is known.

Thus allowing, in the present instance, the maximum discharge to be 1,340 litres per second, instead of 1,200, since the velocity at the outer circumference is 1·021 m. per second, the number of buckets contained in this space is equal to

1·021 ÷ ·32 = 3·19.

Then—

1·340 ÷ 3·19 = ·43 cubic mètres nearly,

the quantity which should be in each bucket during the revolution of the wheel. If, then, the capacity is to be double this, it will be equal to ·86 cubic mètres. The product, however, of the width, 6·38 m., of the wheel, multiplied by the space between two consecutive buckets, ·32 m., is equal to 2·022 m.

We have, then, ·86 ÷ 2·022 = ·42 m., for the depth of the buckets. The distance between the buckets, however, is not the same at the inside as at the extremities, and the capacity is also further diminished by the thickness of the sides of the buckets, and by the inner portions, which make an angle of 45° with the outer portions. For these reasons, the depth should be somewhat increased. When the discharge of water is considerable, and we are limited as to the width of the wheel, it is preferable to do away with the inner inclined portion of the buckets, as indicated in the drawing, Plate XXXVI., prolonging them considerably towards the centre of the wheel.

USEFUL EFFECT OF THE WATER-WHEEL.

386. The absolute force of a stream of water is the product of the water discharged per second, expressed in kilogrammes, by

the height of the fall expressed in mètres, or the weight in pounds by the height in feet.

Thus, when the discharge is 1300 litres or kilog. per second, and the total height of the fall 2·475 m., the product of 1300 kilog. by 2·475 m. expresses in kilogrammètres the absolute force; this may be converted into horses-power by dividing the result by 75: we have, therefore—

1300 × 2·475 = 3217 km., and 3217 ÷ 75 = 43 horses-power.

Undershot water-wheels, with plane-bottomed buckets and circular channels, when well constructed, are capable of utilizing from 70 to 75 per cent. of the absolute force of a stream of water.

OVERSHOT WATER-WHEELS.

387. Let it be proposed to construct a water-wheel to receive the water from above, under the following circumstance :—

1st. The effective vertical height of the fall, or the distance between the upper and lower level, is 4·56 m., without sensible variation.

2d. The quantity of water discharged per second is supposed to be almost uniform, and is measured by a vertical sluice-gate, with complete contraction at the outlet.

3d. The width of the sluice-gate is ·5 m., the height of the opening ·14 m., and the charge or height of the reservoir level above the centre of the outlet, ·55 m.

Solution.—From the table at page 111, of the discharges of water, we find that 280 litres per second is the quantity which escapes at an orifice ·14 m. in height, by 1 mètre wide; and with a pressure upon the centre due to a height of ·55 m., we have, consequently,

$$280 \times \cdot 5 = 140 \text{ litres.}$$

This discharge being known, if we are not limited to any particular width of wheel, it may be constructed thus, for it gives as great a useful effect as can be expected in ordinary circumstances.

In such case, the velocity, v, should be regulated to about one mètre per second at the circumference, because the advantage that might result from a less velocity would be counterbalanced by the consequent increase in the width of the wheel.

If we adopt the velocity, v, of 1 mètre, we find that V, of the water, at its point of escape from the outlet, should be 2 mètres per second, to act with proper effect upon the buckets; now it will be seen in the table, at page 94, that this velocity corresponds to a height of ·205 m. above the centre of the orifice.

This height has to be deducted from the total fall.

For small discharges of water, it is advisable to make the height of the orifice as small as possible, so that the depth of the water may be trifling, which will permit of its entering the buckets much more freely: it may be taken at ·06 m., or H = ·06 m.

The half of this height, or ·03 m., must be added to the first ·205 m., to give the whole height of the water in the duct behind the outlet; that is, from the upper level to the lower edge of the orifice.

Taking also ·01 for the extent of the trifling fall of the small spout reaching from the front of the outlet to the top of the wheel, and ·01 m. for the play-space which may be supposed to exist between the end of the spout and the latter; after deduct-

ing all these quantities from the total fall, namely, 4·56, we shall have remaining—

$$4 \cdot 56 - (\cdot 205 + \cdot 03 + \cdot 01 + \cdot 01) = 4 \cdot 305 \text{ m.}$$

for the extreme diameter, d, of the wheel.

The channel which conducts the water to the wheel, and the width of the outlet orifice, should be disposed as much as possible, so that it may not meet with contraction from the lateral or bottom edges of the sluice-gate. Referring again to the table on page 111, the discharge, 140 litres, must be divided by the number 75, corresponding to the height ·06 m., and to the charge ·2 m.; it must also be divided by the coefficient, 1·125, when we shall have—

$$\frac{140}{75} \div 1 \cdot 125 = 1 \cdot 66 \text{ m.}$$

for the width of the outlet orifice.

By adding ·1 m. to this, we have 1·76 m. for the width of the wheel.

The depth of the buckets is determined thus :—

$$d = \frac{8 \times \cdot 140 \text{ m.}}{3 \times 1 \cdot 78 \text{ m.} \times 1 \text{ m.}} = 214 \text{ m.};$$

consequently, the internal diameter, d, of the wheel becomes—

$$d' = 4 \cdot 305 - (\cdot 214 \times 2) = 3 \cdot 877 \text{ m.}$$

By augmenting this depth about a fifth, which will make it ·257 m., we get the distance to be allowed between the buckets; so that, as the internal circumference is equal to—

$$3 \cdot 14 \times 3 \cdot 877 = 12 \cdot 174 \text{ m.,}$$

dividing this by ·257, it becomes

$$\frac{12 \cdot 174}{\cdot 257} = 47 \cdot 3 \text{ ; say 47 buckets.}$$

For a water-wheel, however, of 4·305 mètres in extreme diameter, there should be eight arms; and if it is intended to make the shroudings of cast-iron, and in segments, it is advisable that the number of buckets be divisible by 8; it will, therefore, be convenient to have 48 instead of 47, and in this case the space allowed between each will be reduced to—

$$12 \cdot 174 \div 48 = \cdot 254 \text{ m.}$$

It now merely remains to draw the wheel; for this purpose, the concentric internal and external circles are described with the determined radii: the first is then to be divided into 48 equal parts, and radii are drawn through each point of division, as indicated in Plate XXXVI.; on each of these, outward from the internal circle, is marked off a distance equal to a little more than half the depth of the buckets, say ·12 m., to indicate the bottoms of the buckets.

The water-wheel, when constructed in this manner, may give off 79 or 80 per cent. of the absolute force of the fall of water. Now this force, expressed in horses-power, is equal to—

$$\frac{140 \times 4 \cdot 56}{75} = 8 \cdot 51 \text{ horses-power.}$$

Deducting 5 or 6 per cent. at the most, for the friction of water-wheel shaft in its bearings, we may still calculate, with certainty, that the power utilized and transmitted by this wheel will be equal to 74 or 75 per cent., or

$$8 \cdot 51 \times \cdot 75 = 6 \cdot 38 \text{ horses-power.}$$

The number of revolutions which this wheel should make per minute is—

$$60 \div 4\cdot305 \times 3\cdot14 = 4\cdot44,$$

since its velocity, v, is 1 mètre per second, or 60 mètres per minute.

In tracing out the preceding solution, it will have been seen that the width to be given to the wheel is 1·76 m.; a much less width might have been obtained, by making the wheel revolve faster, and by augmenting the velocity of the water also. Let us suppose, for example, that the question has to be solved on the hypothesis, that the velocity of the water-wheel is to be 1·5, instead of 1 mètre, per second; it will then be necessary, in order that the water may escape from the orifice at double this velocity, that it be equal to 3 mètres per second.

For this velocity, the height of the upper level, above the centre of the orifice, should be ·46 m.

Allowing ·06 m. for the height of the open part of the sluice-gate, the whole height above the wheel will be

$$\cdot46 + \cdot03 + \cdot02 = \cdot51 \text{ mètres};$$

consequently, the outer diameter of the latter should be

$$d = 4\cdot56 - \cdot51 = 4\cdot05 \text{ mètres},$$

the width of the sluice-gate, or

$$w = \frac{\cdot140}{\cdot06 \times 3 \times \cdot7} = 1\cdot11 \text{ mètres},$$

and consequently the width of the wheel

$$= 1\cdot11 + \cdot10 = 1\cdot21 \text{ mètres}.$$

This width, it will be seen, is considerably less than that first calculated. This wheel, however, which is narrower, and revolves at the rate of 1·5 mètres per second, will not be capable of transmitting so great a useful effect, by four or five per cent. Nevertheless, it may be preferable in many circumstances to adopt this lesser width, either to render the wheel lighter and less costly in construction, or to avoid the necessity of much intermediate gear between the wheel and the machinery to be actuated. Thus, it is evident that this wheel should make

$$(60 \times 1\cdot5) \div (4\cdot305 \times 3\cdot14) = 6\cdot66 \text{ revolutions per minute,}$$

whilst the first wheel only made 4·44.

The other parts of the wheel are proportioned according to the above rules; they will, however, differ but slightly from those of the first wheel.

The proportions of the water-wheel might still be otherwise modified; thus, the depth of water at the outlet might be allowed to be greater than that taken for a basis in the preceding calculations. Thus, the outlet might be opened to the height of ·1 m. instead of only ·06 m.: in this case, the width of the outlet and of the wheel would be much less. But this arrangement would have many disadvantages, for it would be necessary to make the buckets more open; that is to say, the angle made by the outer portion of the bottom of the bucket with the tangent to the circumference passing through its extremity, instead of being 15° or 16°, as is usual, would have to be 30° or 32°; the buckets would have to be deeper and more capacious; they would empty themselves sooner: from all which causes would follow a decrease in the useful effect given out, which might reach even to 15 per cent.

It is true, on the other hand, that the width of the outlet would be reduced to 1 mètre, supposing the wheel to revolve at the

rate of 1 mètre per second, and that it would not be more than ·67 m. when the wheel revolves at the rate of 1·5 m. per second; in which case, the depth of the buckets would be about ·34, and the spaces between them ·4 m. each.

It will be easily conceived that such an arrangement cannot be advantageously adopted, except where there is plenty of water to spare, and when the constructor is limited as to the width of the wheel.

WATER-WHEELS WITH RADIAL FLOATS.

388. In old mills we sometimes meet with water-wheels which have plane floats placed radially, working in straight inclined channels, with a vertical outlet more or less distant from the centre of the wheel.

These wheels generally give out 25 to 35 per cent. of useful effect of the absolute force of the stream. In them the floats are three or four centimètres clear of the sides of the channel; when a greater space than this is allowed, the useful effect is sensibly diminished. Generally, the width of such wheels is equal to that of the outlet.

At the present day, water-wheels are never constructed with plane floats arranged in this way. When a wheel is required to have a great velocity, it is preferable to construct it to work in an enclosed circular channel, and to receive the water from above, or from an orifice with a sufficient column above it, to give the proportionate velocity to the water.

Such wheels are constructed in the same manner and with the same care as undershot water-wheels; in fact, they do not differ from the latter, except in that these receive the water from an open topped or overshot duct. The useful effect given out by them varies from 40 to 50 per cent., according as the sluice-gate is more or less near to the upper level of the water. Thus, the nearer the channel approaches to the upper level, the more like the wheel becomes to a common undershot one, and, in consequence, the useful effect is greater.

In the construction of a water-wheel of this kind, the same rules are followed as are already laid down for common undershot wheels with open outlets.

Thus, let it be proposed to construct a wheel for a fall of 1·75 mètres, and with a discharge of 440 litres of water per second; let the centre of the outlet orifice be at ·4 m. below the upper level, and the height of the orifice itself, ·15 m.

By referring to the table on page 111, it will be seen that the discharge of water through an orifice, under these circumstances, is 255 litres per second for a width of one mètre, and it will therefore be evident that the wheel should have

$$\frac{440}{255} = 1\cdot72 \text{ mètres in width.}$$

The velocity of the water at the sluice-gate, corresponding to the column of ·4 m., is 2·802 per second; consequently, if we make the velocity of the wheel equal to ·55 times that of the water, it will be

$$2\cdot802 \times \cdot55 = 1\cdot54 \text{ mètres per second.}$$

The diameter of the wheel is of itself a matter of indifference: it should be reduced as much as possible, so as to lessen the cost of construction; notwithstanding, it should never be less than twice

R

the whole height of the fall; thus, in the present example, it should not be less than 4 mètres.

It has often been asserted that the power is increased by increasing the diameter; it seems incontrovertible, however, that the power transmitted must be in proportion to the height of the fall, and to the quantity of water discharged. If the diameter of the wheel is increased, the angular or rotative velocity is diminished, and, consequently, the momentum and actual force communicated remain the same.

Taking the diameter at 4 mètres, we have

$$\frac{1\cdot54 \times 60}{4 \times 3\cdot1416} = 7\cdot2,$$ the number of revolutions per minute.

If a wheel of this diameter were adapted to an open-topped or overshot duct, with a depth of water at the sluice-gate equal to ·2 m., the velocity of the water being then reduced to 1·981 mètres, the velocity at the circumference of the wheel would not be more than

$$1\cdot981 \times \cdot55 = 1\cdot09 \text{ m.,}$$

and, consequently, the number of turns only

$$\frac{1\cdot09 \times 60}{4 \times 3\cdot1416} = 5\cdot2 \text{ per minute.}$$

But then, as the discharge in such case, at an overshot outlet of ·2 m. in depth and 1 mètre in width, is 166 litres per second (see table, page 113), the width of the wheel must be made equal to

$$\frac{440}{166} = 2\cdot7 \text{ mètres.}$$

Thus, it will be seen that the water-wheel which revolves more rapidly is narrower than the one with the same discharge of water by an open outlet, and it is, consequently, less costly in construction; but then, it only gives out, as useful effect, about 50 per cent. of the absolute force of the stream, whilst that given out by the other description may reach, as we have seen, as much as 70 per cent.

With regard to the other dimensions of the wheel, we have merely to refer to what has been said about the common undershot water-wheel.

WATER-WHEELS WITH CURVED BUCKETS.

389. These wheels are fitted with inclined ducts for the water, the inclination being equal to a base of 1 mètre for every 1 or 2 mètres in height—that is to say, to 45 to 600; they are enclosed for a short distance in a circular channel, and between two side walls.

They are seldom constructed except for low falls of from ·5 to 1·3 mètres, and when a great velocity is required; the useful effect they give out varies from 45 to 55 per cent.

It is of importance that the water duct be brought as close up to the circumference of the wheel as possible, and that, at its lower part, it should have an enlargement of 10 or 15 centimètres, to facilitate the disengagement of the water, and render its action freer; this enlargement should commence at a distance from the vertical line passing through the centre of the wheel, equal to the space between two consecutive buckets. The velocity of the wheel should be from ·5 to ·55 times that of the water at its exit from the duct.

The width of these wheels is to be calculated in the same manner

as that for the preceding ones; as to the diameter, it may be reduced in proportion to the fall, but it should never be less than three times the height of the latter.

The depth of the curved buckets, or the width of the shrouding in the direction of the radii of the wheel, should be equal to *one-fourth of the fall augmented by the height of orifice open.*

For falls of less than 1·2 m., the height of the orifice, or the depth of the outflowing water, should be from ·2 to ·22 m.; it may be reduced to ·18 or ·16 m. for falls of from 1·2 to 1·5 m.

The buckets or floats are in the form of a cylindrical curve, being a single circular arc, tangential to the radius at the inner part, and making an angle of about 24° or 25° with the stream of water flowing towards the inside of the crown of the wheel. The space between two consecutive buckets is measured at the outer circumference by an angle of 25°, and their thickness is 24 to 28 hundredths when made of wrought-iron plates, and 32 to 35 when of wood. The bottom of the channel should have a fall or inclination of about $\frac{1}{12}$th or $\frac{1}{15}$th—that is to say, equal to that of the hypothenuse of a triangle, the base of which is 12 or 15, and the height 1 mètre.

TURBINES.

390. Among the varieties of turbines which receive the action of the water throughout their whole circumference, may be distinguished those which discharge the water at their outer circumferences, and those which allow it to escape behind. The useful effect given out by these wheels varies from 55 to 65 per cent. of the absolute force of the stream of water.

For these descriptions of wheel, the discharge of water is calculated in accordance with the rules and tables already cited. For the first kind, termed centrifugal turbines, the internal diameter is determined by multiplying the fourth or fifth of the velocity due to the total fall by 785·4; then dividing the quantity of water to be discharged by the result obtained, and finally extracting the square root of the quotient.

Example.—Let us suppose that the fall is 2·2 m., and the discharge of water 800 litres per second. It will be gathered from the table on page 111, that the velocity due to the height,

$$2\cdot2 \text{ m.} = 6\cdot57 \text{ m.}$$

We have then,

$$\frac{6\cdot57}{4} = 1\cdot642, \text{ and } \frac{6\cdot57}{5} = 1\cdot314;$$

and further,

$$D = \sqrt{\frac{800}{785\cdot4 \times 1\cdot642}} = \cdot787;$$

or,

$$D = \sqrt{\frac{800}{785\cdot4 \times 1\cdot314}} = \cdot874 \text{ mètres,}$$

for the internal diameter of the cylindrical tank above the turbine.

Add 4 or 5 centimètres for the internal diameter of the latter, which gives

$$\cdot82 \text{ to } \cdot91 \text{ m.}$$

The external diameter should be equal to the internal diameter multiplied by 1·25 or 1·45, and is, therefore,

$$1\cdot025 \text{ to } 1\cdot189 \text{ m.;}$$

or,

1·137 to 1·319 m.

When the height of the fall and the discharge of water are variable, the diameters should be calculated for the extreme cases, so that the most advantageous proportion may be adopted—that is, the one which will give the best result throughout the greater part of the year.

If the variation is very considerable, there should be two or more turbines employed, some calculated for the lowest discharges, others for the mean, and others again for the maximum discharges.

The height of the buckets—that is to say, the vertical distance between the two discs which form their top and bottom—is generally about a fifth, or a fourth at most, of the radius of the interior of the wheel.

Thus, in the case before us, the diameter being ·787 or ·874, the radius is ·3985 or ·437, and, consequently, the height of the buckets should be ·1 to ·11 m.

The buckets being cylindrical in form, their entrance is normal to the conducting channels which direct the water against them, and for these low discharges of water should make angles of 68° to 70° with the internal circumference of the wheel—that is to say, the conducting channels should make angles of 20° to 22° with the circumference. When the discharges are large, this angle may be increased to 30° or 45°; thus, for a discharge of 600 to 700 litres per second, it is considered that the angle should be about 30°.

In order to obtain the maximum useful effect, the velocity of the wheel should be equal to about ·7 times that of the water; in practice, one-tenth may be added to this ratio, or one-fifth to one-sixth, without materially diminishing the useful effect.

The space between each bucket, taken at the internal circumference, should be nearly equal to the distance between the top and bottom discs of the turbine; it should, however, never exceed 18 to 20 centimètres. The internal and external distances between the buckets are necessarily in the ratio of the internal and external diameters of the wheel.

In the following table we give the principal dimensions, data, and results of several descriptions of turbines, constructed, within the last few years, by MM. Fourneyron, Fontaine, and André Kœchlin.

These results have been selected under circumstances where the best useful effects were given out :—

TABLE OF DIMENSIONS AND PRACTICAL RESULTS OF VARIOUS KINDS OF TURBINES.

Data and Results.	Names of the Turbines and of their Constructors.			
	Moussay Turbine. Fourneyron.	Mulbach Turbine. Fourneyron.	Bouchet Turbine. Fontaine.	Vadenay Turbine. Fontaine.
Total fall,	7·56 m.	3·45 m.	1·00 m.	1·40 m.
Discharge per second,	527 lit.	2500 lit.	218 lit.	1400 lit.
External diameter,	·850 m.	1·9 m.	1·33 m.	1·940 m.
Depth of shrouding,	·110 m.	·335 m.	...	·23 m.
Height of outlet,	·071 m.	·270 m.	·04 m.	...
Number of buckets,	....	32	58	64
Number of director curves,	....	24	24	32
Number of revolutions per minute,..	185	55	36	...
Useful effect	35 H. P.	90 H. P.	2 H. P.	18 H. P
Ratio of useful effect to absolute force,	70°/₀	70°/₀	71°/₀	71°/₀

Data and Results.	Jonval Turbines, constructed by M André Kœchlin, Mulhouse		
Total fall,	2·720 m.	2·77 m.	1·70 m
Discharge per second,	684 lit.	470 lit.	355 lit.
External diameter,	·800 m.	·800 m.	·810 m.
Width of buckets,	·410 m.	·100 m.	·120 m.
Number of buckets,	16	18	18
Area of outlets,	·290 sq. m.	·220 sq. m.	·0706 sq. m.
Area of escape outlet below the wheel,	·450 sq. m.	·45 sq. m.	·2977 sq. m.
Number of revolutions per minute,	90 to 158	90 to 168	90
Useful effect,	13 H. P.	15 H. P.	6 H. P.
Ratio of useful effect to absolute force,	...	72°/₀	72°/₀

REMARKS ON MACHINE TOOLS.

VELOCITY OF THE TOOL, OR OPERATING PIECE, IN MACHINES INTENDED TO WORK IN WOOD AND METAL.

391. The principal machine tools, employed in machine shops, are—

1. The simple lathe, the self-acting lathe, and the wheel-cutting lathe, with adjustable table.

2. Boring machines of various dimensions, and radial drilling machines.

3. Horizontal and vertical shaping machines.

4. Planing machines with a fixed tool, or with a moveable one, so as to work both ways.

5. Mortising or slotting machines, having a vertical tool with a revolving table below.

6. Machines for finishing nuts and screws.

7. Machines for cutting screws and bolts.

8. Dividing engines, for dividing and cutting toothed-wheels of all dimensions.

9. Straight and curved shears, for shearing plates.

10. Punching and riveting machines.

11. Steam and other hammers.

12. Straight and circular saws.

The velocity of the cutting tools, in these machines, varies according to the nature of the material, and the quality of work desired.

In general, for soft cast-iron, it is convenient to give a velocity of seven to eight centimètres per second to the tool, in such machines as lathes, and planing and slotting machines. This velocity should be reduced, at least, to four or five centimètres in shaping, drilling, and screwing machines. When the cast-iron is hard, the velocity is considerably diminished.

For wrought-iron, the velocity may be advantageously increased one half, because the tool is kept well lubricated with oil, or with soap and water; thus, in turning or planing, the velocity may be raised to eleven or twelve centimètres; and in shaping and screwing, to about six centimètres per second.

For copper, brass, and other analogous metals, with which the tool does not become heated whilst working, the velocity may be very much greater; and for wood, its only limits are those determined by the size of the tool, and by the powers of the machine.

With regard to the pressure and rate of advance of the tool per revolution, or per stroke, it necessarily varies according to the dimensions of the machine itself, and also according to the degree of finish which is to be given to the surface; we evidently cannot give as much pressure to the tool upon a small lathe as to that upon a large one — to a small drill, as to a powerful shaping machine. This variation extends, for the different metals, from a tenth of a millimètre, in some cases, to as much as two millimètres in others. Amongst other things, the following table shows the rotative velocity to be given to the tool—when it revolves, and the work is fixed; or to the latter when it revolves, and the cutting tool does not;—in lathes, and shaping and drilling machines.

TABLE OF VELOCITY AND PRESSURE OF MACHINE TOOLS OR CUTTERS.

Diameter in centimètres.	Turning.				Drilling and Shaping.			
	Number of revolutions per minute.		Work performed per hour with ½ ᵐ/ₘ of pressure.		Number of revolutions per minute.		Work performed per hour with ½ ᵐ/ₘ of pressure.	
	Cast Iron.	Wrought Iron.	Cast Iron.	Wrought Iron.	Cast Iron.	Wrought Iron.	Cast Iron.	Wrought Iron.
			cent.	cent.			cent.	cent.
1	152·9	229·4	458·5	687·8	76·4	114·6	229·2	343·9
2	76·4	114·6	229·2	343·9	38·2	57·3	114·6	171·9
3	50·9	76·4	152·8	229·2	25·5	38·2	76·4	114·6
4	38·2	57·3	114·6	171·9	19·1	28·7	57·3	85·9
5	30·6	45·8	91·7	137·5	15·3	22·9	45·8	68·7
6	25·5	38·2	76·4	114·6	12·7	19·1	38·2	57·3
8	19·1	28·7	57·3	85·9	9·5	14·3	28·6	42·9
10	15·3	22·9	45·8	68·7	7·6	11·5	22·9	34·3
12	12·7	19·1	38·2	57·3	6·4	9·5	19·1	28·6
15	10·2	15·3	30·5	45·8	5·1	7·6	15·2	22·9
			With 1 ᵐ/ₘ of pressure.				With 1 ᵐ/ₘ of pressure.	
20	7·6	11·5	45·8	68·7	3·8	5·7	22·9	34·3
25	6·1	9·2	36·6	55·0	3·0	4·6	18·3	27·4
30	5·1	7·6	30·5	45·8	2·5	3·8	15·2	22·9
35	4·4	6·5	26·1	39·0	2·2	3·3	13·0	19·6
40	3·8	5·7	22·9	34·3	1·9	2·9	11·4	17·1
45	3·4	5·1	20·3	30·5	1·7	2·5	10·1	15·2
50	3·1	4·6	18·3	27·4	1·5	2·3	9·1	13·7
55	2·7	4·2	16·2	24·9	1·4	2·1	8·2	12·6
60	2·5	3·8	15·2	22·9	1·3	1·9	7·6	11·4
65	2·3	3·5	14·1	21·1	1·2	1·8	7·0	10·5
70	2·2	3·3	13·0	19·6	1·1	1·6	6·5	9·7
75	2·0	3·0	12·1	18·3	1·0	1·5	6·0	9·0
80	1·9	2·9	11·4	17·1	·9	1·4	5·7	8·5
90	1·7	2·5	10·1	15·2	·8	1·3	5·0	7·6
100	1·5	2·3	9·1	13·7	·8	1·1	4·5	6·8
110	1·4	2·1	8·2	12·6	·7	1·0	4·1	6·2
120	1·3	1·9	7·6	11·4	·6	·9	3·7	5·7
130	1·2	1·8	7·0	10·5	·6	·9	3·4	5·2
140	1·1	1·6	6·5	9·7	·5	·8	3·2	4·8
150	1·0	1·5	6·0	9·0	·5	·8	3·0	4·5
175	·9	1·3	5·1	7·8	·4	·6	2·6	3·9
200	·8	1·1	4·5	6·8	·4	·6	2·2	3·4
225	·7	1·0	4·0	6·0	·3	·5	1·9	3·0
250	·6	·9	3·6	5·4	·3	·4	1·8	2·7
275	·5	·8	3·3	4·9	·3	·4	1·6	2·4
300	·5	·7	3·0	4·5	·2	·4	1·5	2·2
350	·4	·6	2·5	3·9	·2	·3	1·2	1·9
400	·3	·5	2·2	3·4	·2	·3	1·1	1·6

This table will serve as a guide in designing machine tools for the various combinations of movements, the application of which may be called for according to the nature and dimensions of the work to be submitted to their action. Thus, a lathe which is only intended to turn articles of from four to twenty or thirty centimètres in diameter, should have a considerable rotative velocity, whilst one that is to be chiefly applied to turning and shaping bulky pieces, or such as measure from one to two mètres in diameter, should, on the contrary, be actuated by a combination of very slow, but, at the same time, very powerful movements.

CHAPTER X.

THE STUDY OF MACHINERY AND SKETCHING.

VARIOUS APPLICATIONS AND COMBINATIONS.

392. Hitherto we have had to occupy ourselves with industrial drawing, as regards only the geometrical delineation of the principal elements of machinery and architecture. This preliminary study being of great importance, we have thought it well to dwell more particularly upon it, since also it is the very basis of all designing, with a view to actual construction, comprehending not only the mere outline of objects, but also the proportions between the various parts, as dependent upon the functions which each is required to perform.

Machines are, indeed, but well calculated and thoughtfully arranged combinations of these elements, and afford innumerable applications of the rules and instructions laid down in reference to them. The study, therefore, of machines in their complete state, naturally suggests itself as the next step to be taken.

393. Machines may, in general, be classified under three categories—machine tools, productive or manufacturing machinery, and prime movers.

By machine tools are meant those by the instrumentality of which we work upon raw materials, as wood, metal, stone ; lathes, wheel-cutting machines ; drilling, boring, and shaping machines ; mortising, slotting, planing, and grooving machines ; riveting machines ; shears, saws, hammers—are of this class. The movements of these machines should be so combined, that the tool or cutting instrument—that is, that part which attacks the material—should move with a velocity properly proportioned to the nature of the work.

In the few notes accompanying our text will be found some experimental deductions, which may serve as guides for adjusting the movements in designing and constructing machinery of this description.

Amongst productive or manufacturing machinery, are comprised spinning, weaving, and printing machines ; pumps, presses, corn, and oil mills ; and, finally, prime movers consist of those worked by animals ; windmills, water-wheels, turbines, and steam-engines.

For the study of complete machines, we have selected from each of these categories those possessing most interest and generality—as a drilling machine, an instrument so very useful and so much employed in machine-shops and railway works ; a pump for raising water, serving for domestic purposes as well as for important manufacturing establishments ; two examples of water-wheels, showing various arrangements and forms of floats or buckets ; a high pressure expansive steam-engine, with geometrical diagrams, determining the relative positions of the principal pieces in various circumstances ; and, finally, a set of belt-driven flour mills, constructed on a system recently adopted.

Before proceeding to the description of these machines, it will be necessary to habituate the student to draw from the reality, for up to the present time he will have done nothing but copy the various graphic examples to this or that scale. The operation in question consists in drawing with the hand, the elevation, plan, sections, and details of a machine, preserving, as much as possible, the forms and proportions of each part ; and then taking the actual measurement of each part, and laying it down in figures in its particular position upon the drawing : this duplex operation of sketching and measuring constitutes the study of the rough draughting of machinery.

THE SKETCHING OF MACHINERY.

PLATES XXXV. AND XXXVI.

394. Before commencing the sketch or rough draught of a machine, it is absolutely necessary to look carefully into its organization, the action of the various working parts, the motion of the intermediate mechanical connections, and finally, its object and results. The object of this preliminary examination is to give the draughtsman a good general idea of the more important parts—those which he will have to render most prominent and detailed when he comes to make a complete drawing of the whole ; such drawing comprising a series of combined views, together with separate diagrams of such details as may not be apparent in the former, or require to be drawn to a different scale to render them intelligible. In fact, this must be done in such a manner, that, with the aid of the sketch, a perfect representation of the machine may be got up, which, if necessary, may serve in the construction of other similar machines.

DRILLING MACHINE.

PLATE XXXV.

395. In order to give an exact idea of the manner of sketching machinery, we take a simple machine as an example ; this we suppose to be represented in perspective* in fig. A, this view being instead of the machine itself.

This machine is for drilling metals : it consists of a vertical cast-iron column, A, which forms part of the building or workshop. This column is hollow, and rests by an enlarged base upon a stone plinth, B, imbedded in the ground, and at its upper end it supports the beam, C.

Upon one side of this column is cast the vertical face, D, which is planed to receive three cast-iron brackets, E, F, G, attached to it by bolts. To the opposite side, D', of the same column, is in like manner attached the bracket, H, which, with the middle one, F, on the other side, serves to carry the horizontal spindle, I. This spindle carries on one side the cone-pulley, J, over which passes the driving-belt, K, and on the other extremity it has keyed upon it the bevil-pinion, L, which gears with a larger bevil-wheel, M. This last is attached to the vertical shaft, N,

* In a subsequent chapter, we shall explain the general principles of parallel and exact perspective.

which is, in fact, the drill-holder, and is moveable in the bracket-bearings, F and G. This shaft receives a duplex movement, that of continuous rotation, which is more or less rapid, according as the belt, K, is on the less or greater diameter of the cone-pulley; and the other vertical and rectilinear, due to the action of the screw, O, which works in an internal screw in the end of the bracket, E. This screw carries at its upper end a spur-wheel, P, gearing with a small pinion, Q, the shaft, R, of which is prolonged downwards, and terminates in a small hand-wheel, S.

The object to be drilled is held between a pair of jaws, a, a', set in grooves upon the table, T, and capable of adjustment back and forward by means of the screw, b, the head of which has a sliding handle. The table, T, is made in two pieces, so as to form a collar about the column, A, and it is fixed at any convenient height upon this column by means of the pressure screw, c; the exact distance of the table from the drill, d, according to the thickness of the piece of metal to be drilled, is settled by means of the vertical rack, U, which is fitted to the front of the column, and into which gears a pinion on the shaft, e, carrying the handle, f, at its extremity. The rotation of this handle and the pinion necessarily causes the ascent or descent of the table, T.

The drilling machine, then, fulfils the following conditions: on the one hand, the drill, d, is worked at a greater or less speed of rotation, whilst it descends vertically with a very slow motion, which latter varies, of course, with the nature of the material acted upon; and, on the other hand, the table which carries the object to be drilled is capable of being set at the most convenient height, according to the forms and dimensions of the objects, whilst it may also be set eccentrically, when necessary, by turning it to the required extent round the column.

396. After having thus taken note of the construction and action of each individual piece and element of the machine, the draughtsman may proceed to make his sketch. He should commence by drawing a rough general view, indicating, in mere outline, the relative positions of the various pieces.

For example, in fig. 1 will be seen the geometrical elevation of the column, A, with the positions of the brackets and the table, which are merely in outline. It is advisable, even in this rough draught, as well as in the finished drawing, with or without the assistance of a rule, to draw the centre lines for guides; thus, after drawing the first centre line, g h, of the column, A, draw upon each side of it the portions forming its contour; then draw parallel to it the centre line, i j, of the drill-stock, N; then the horizontal, k l, which represents the centre line of the bevil-wheel, L, and the driving-pulleys, J, and likewise the straight lines, m n, o p, q r, which are the centre lines of the brackets, E, F, and G; finally, draw the lines, s t and u v, of the table, T, and of the bracket, H; and likewise the extreme lines, x y, w z, of the bottom and top of the column. At this stage it is necessary to lay down the measurements upon the sketch. The column being fitted with the principal parts of the drilling apparatus, so that no clear space can be found upon it for the height to be measured close to it, a plumb-line is suspended from the point, z, on the beam, c, which rests upon the column, and this line is measured either by a foot-rule, or by a measuring-tape, and the measurement in feet, or mètres, and frac-

tions thereof, may be written upon the centre line, g h, of the column.

The draughtsman must next measure the diameters at the base and summit of the column, as well as those of the various mouldings. These diameters may be measured with callipers, which open to such an extent that they can be applied to the place in question, the amount of opening being then measured upon the rule, and written down upon the corresponding place in the sketch; or the diameters may be obtained by applying a cord, or a very flexible rule, to the circumference. This latter method is always employed for cylinders of large diameter, when it is not possible to obtain the measurement from either base. In this case, to obtain the actual diameter, it is necessary, as has been seen (72), to divide the circumference found, by 3·1416.

To obtain the distance of the line, i j, from g h, the centre line of the column, place the extremity of the rule at i', against the surface of the column, and let it lie across the centre, i, of the spur-wheel, P, or screw, O; the measurement read off the rule will be that of i' i, to which must be added the radius, i' i², of the column.

If the centre, i, were not approachable with the rule, we should have to take the internal distance between the surface of the column and that of the screw, and then add the respective radii of the screw and column. When these distances are greater than the length of the measuring-rule, a rod or tape must be employed. When, indeed, the draughtsman has attained a reasonable amount of skill, he may take the measurement, i i², directly, by applying the rule upon the surface of the column opposite to its centre, and also opposite to the axis of the screw, in such a manner that the rule shall be tangential to the column, when the space between the two points will be the measurement sought.

It is further necessary to quote upon the sketch, the vertical distances between the different horizontal lines, m n, o p, q r, s t. The measurements indicated upon fig. 1 will show how all these are obtained.

The preceding operations will allow of the finished drawing being commenced, by laying off the relative position of the main parts which go to compose the machine to be sketched. We have next to sketch and measure all the minor details of each separate piece of the machine. To this effect, and to avoid confusion, it is necessary to treat each of these pieces as detached, and to draw different views of them, upon which the dimensions of every part may be properly indicated.

Figs. 2 and 3 represent, in elevation and plan, the detail of the principal bracket, F, which supports the shafts, I and N, with the bevil-wheels, L and M. Even these views are not sufficient to represent thoroughly all the dimensions of this bracket; thus it is necessary to draw a section such as that made at the line, 1—2, and projected in fig. 4, so as to show the exact form of the feathers of the bracket; it is likewise necessary to make a side view (fig. 5) of the bearing, b', which holds up the shaft, N, to the bracket, and also a vertical section (fig. 6) made at the line, 3—4, to show the brasses which embrace the journal of the shaft, I. These details should always, if possible, be drawn to a larger scale, so as to indicate the adjustments clearly, and to give room for the measurements; and it may be observed, that, for a draughtsman who has not much practical knowledge of machinery details, it will be necessary to take down or separate various parts, such as the cap and the upper brass. With regard to wheel-work, it will be sufficient to give the section of the web and boss, as indicated in figs. 2 and 7, and a section, as fig. 8, of one of the arms when the wheel has any, and then the numbers of teeth and arms must be counted and set down.

When all the parts of any detail are thus sketched out in elevation, plan, or section, the draughtsman must take the measurements of each, and set them down in their appropriate positions upon the sketches, as indicated in the figures; being mindful to see that the principal measurements coincide with those laid off in the complete general view already commenced. The measurements of the diameter of the pitch-circle, and of the width of the teeth, will be sufficient, in addition to what has already been directed to be done in reference to wheel-work, the proper ratios being maintained between those in gear with each other. As many parts of machinery require to be in proportion to each other, a knowledge of such relations will enable the draughtsman to dispense with a great deal of tedious measuring and sketching, as in the case just alluded to, of wheels working together.

The remaining parts of the machine are to be detailed in the same manner. Thus, figs. 9, 10, and 11, represent a vertical section, a plan, and a side view of a portion of the table, T, with its holding-jaws, and its elevating pinion and shaft. Fig. 12 is a vertical section of the lower extremity of the drill-stock, or spindle, N, with the drill, d, in elevation. Fig. 13 is a section of the cone-pulley, J. Figs. 14 and 15 show, in vertical and horizontal section, the manner of jointing the screw, O, into the upper end of the spindle, N. Finally, figs. 16 and 17 give a complete detail of the mechanism for elevating the table, T, as well as that for fixing or adjusting it at any required height.

397. On all the preceding details, we have quoted the measurements of the different parts exactly as they should be upon an actual machine. These measurements are expressed in millimètres, as in former examples, this measuring unit being adopted because its minute scale renders fractions unnecessary. We have also slightly shaded various parts, as is generally done where the complication and variety of forms would otherwise lead to confusion and error. Besides, in this manner, a few touches of the pencil show at once whether this or that portion is round or square, and, in many instances, the labour of drawing additional views will thereby be dispensed with.

In order to facilitate the proceedings of beginners in sketching, we would recommend them to delineate the main centre lines with the aid of a rule, and the circles with compasses, though the dimensions of the latter need not be exact. This will give the sketch a much neater appearance, and render the various objects or details more regular. It is with this view that sketchers frequently employ cross-ruled paper, with horizontal and vertical lines equally spaced. That portion of Plate XXXV., upon which are sketched figs. 9, 10, and 11, is of this description.

It will be understood, that, if the lines ruled upon the paper are at equal distances apart, corresponding to one or more units of the scale to which the sketches are being made, these may be drawn in correct proportions at once, in which case it will be unnecessary to write on the various measurements.

The example which we have given as an introduction to the study of sketching machines, will have somewhat familiarized the student with his operations even now. The applications contained in the subsequent examples will suffice to complete this study, which is one of great importance to the draughtsman and constructive engineer.

MOTIVE MACHINES.

WATER-WHEELS.

PLATE XXXVI.

398. The water-wheel, represented in fig. 1, has plane floats, and works, through a portion of its circumference, in a concentric circular channel. It receives the water from over a sluice-gate, a little below its centre, and is of the undershot description.

The wheel is composed of several parallel shroudings, A, in which are fitted the radial wooden bearers, B, carrying the floats, C. When the shroudings are of cast-iron, as is supposed in the present example, they are cast in one piece with the arms, D, and central boss, E, and are firmly secured by keys, a, upon the shaft, F, also of cast-iron.

The head of the channel, G, which embraces the lower part of the wheel, is constructed with a piece, H, in cast-iron, called the neck-piece, which is fitted upon the cross timber, I, and let into the two lateral walls. Against this neck-piece works the wooden sluice, J, above which overflows a certain depth of water, falling, in succession, upon each float of the wheel as it comes round, causing it to turn in the direction of the arrow. The rotatory movement of this water-wheel is taken off by the cast-iron spur-wheel, K, mounted upon the end of the shaft, F, and gearing with the cast-iron pinion, L, the shaft of which communicates with the machinery to be set in motion.

In giving this example, our object has been to examine this motor, not only with reference to its accurate delineation, but also with a view to sketching similar wheels, as well as to constructing and setting them up, with their channel and sluice gear.

THE CONSTRUCTION AND SETTING UP OF THE WATER-WHEEL.

399. The channel, G, is built up of hewn stones, the lateral joints of which converge towards the centre, o, of the wheel, and they are imbedded upon a foundation of ordinary stone-work. All this masonry is put together with mortar, made with hydraulic lime, the joints being finished with Roman cement. In some localities the channel is of bricks or freestone, and sometimes even of wood. The apparent concave surface of the channel should be perfectly cylindrical, and concentric with the external circumference of the wheel. Also, before placing the latter in its proper position, this surface should be finished, and rendered quite smooth and true, which may be done with the assistance of a temporary shaft, o, with the actual shaft of the wheel, in the following manner:—

The shaft, F (146), is adjusted to the exact height at which it is to be afterwards, and it is made capable of rotation in appro priate bearings, adjusted upon iron plates, let into and firmly bolted to the lateral walls.

Upon this shaft are fitted the shroudings, A, each connected to its boss by eight arms. To the outside of these arms are then temporarily attached two radial pieces of wood, having a cross piece attached to them, the outer edge of which is made true and parallel to the shaft, and coincident with the external edges of the complete wheel. It will be evident that, if the shaft is now made to revolve, this frame upon it will describe a cylindrical surface, which is precisely that which the channel should possess; it will serve, therefore, as an accurate guide in giving the channel its appropriate contour.

The lower part of the channel is continued on in a straight line, commencing at the vertical, $o\, b$, and in a direction, $b\, c$, slightly inclined to a short distance away from the wheel, to facilitate the escape of the water.

The cross timber, I, which surmounts the masonry of the channel, and which receives the neck-piece, H, is also rendered concave internally, like the channel, so as to allow the sluice-gate to be brought closer up to the wheel. The neck-piece, H, which forms the crest of the channel, is more frequently constructed of cast-iron than of either wood or stone, as that material does not require to be so thick, for resisting the pressure of the water. The top of the neck-piece is at a distance below the upper water-level, corresponding to the greatest depth of water which it is proposed to admit to the wheel at any time. This depth of water varies very considerably, according to the quantity of water to be discharged, and the width which it is wished to give the wheel. Behind the neck-piece, a cavity, M, is formed in the masonry, which is intended to receive the sluice, J, when lowered, and is of a sufficient size to allow of its being cleaned out, so that it may not become choked up with sediment. The small raised portion of masonry behind this, again, serves to arrest floating bodies, as trees, &c., independently of a grating placed further behind, and preventing their reacting, and injuring the wheel.

The sluice consists of two strong oaken planks, having grooved and tongued joints, and being made thicker at the middle than at the extremities, where the wheel is of a greater width than $1\frac{1}{2}$ mètre. The amount of inclination of this sluice, J, is determined by drawing a perpendicular to the extremity of the radius, $o\, f$, drawn near the middle, or, perhaps, two-thirds of the depth of the overflowing body of water. The sluice is moveable in grooves, in two wooden side-posts, N, entirely imbedded in the lateral walls. At the upper parts of these are iron bearing-pieces, to receive two straight cast-iron racks, o, which rise above the cross timber, P, attached to the two side-posts, N. These racks rest, on one side, upon the friction-pulleys, h, which also guide them, and, on the other side, they gear with the pinions, g, keyed upon one horizontal axis. This latter is at one end prolonged, to receive the worm-wheel, Q, actuated by the worm, R, which may be worked at pleasure from above—a winch-handle, or hand-wheel, being fixed upon the upper extremity of its vertical spindle for this purpose. This arrangement permits of the regulation of the position of the sluice, and, consequently, of the depth of the overflowing water, with the greatest nicety, as well as of the total shutting off of the water from the wheel.

The shrouding, A, of the wheel, being of cast-iron, the weight has been reduced, by making panels in it, as at h, i, shown in the elevation, fig. 1, and section, fig. 2, made at the circular line, 1—2. It is also cast with mortises, to receive the tenons, or ends, of the carrier-pieces, B, to which the floats are bolted.

When the wheel has counter-floats, as represented at the lower part of figure 1, which is only the case when the discharge, and consequently the depth, of water at the sluice-gate is very small, the carrier-pieces are very short, and do not project far upon the inner side of the shrouding. But when the wheel is without counter-floats, which is the case when the discharge, and consequently the depth, of water at the sluice is considerable, the floats, c, and their carrier-pieces, B, are prolonged to a considerable distance inside the shroudings, as has been supposed to be the case in the upper part of fig. 1. In both cases, the tenons, or ends, of the carrier-pieces, always lie in the direction of radii from the centre of the wheel, and they are retained by iron-keys, j, upon the inside of the shroudings. Sometimes, in order to facilitate the adjustment of the carrier-pieces upon the shroudings, in place of fitting them into closed mortises, they are received into slightly dovetailed recesses, formed upon the side, as shown in figs. 3 and 4, being retained in position by wedges, j. When this last arrangement is adopted, it is unnecessary to cut holes in the carrier-pieces for the reception of the keys.

When the shroudings are of wood, they must necessarily be composed of several pieces, which are fitted together with mortise and tenon joints, as shown in figs. 5 and 6; and to consolidate the joint, iron straps, k, are added, secured at one side by bolts, and at the other by keys, or tightening screws, by means of which the perfect union of the component pieces can at all times be obtained, should they begin to get loose. In this system, the carrier-pieces are adjusted with tenons, keyed on the inside of the shrouding, as indicated in figs. 7 and 8, and the oaken arms are joined to the shrouding with tenons, being further secured by iron straps, as shown in figs. 9 and 10.

The floats, c, of the wheel, are formed of oaken boards, and are attached to the carrier-pieces, B, by means of the bolts, l.

The counter-floats, s, extend from the inner ends of the floats, c, to the bottom pieces, s′, and are nailed down upon the small triangular pieces, m. The open spaces left between the ends of the floats and the bottom pieces serve for the escape of the air. When the floats are lengthened, they are, of course, formed of several boards, joined edge to edge.

DELINEATION OF THE WATER-WHEEL.

400. The explanations just given will have enabled the student to comprehend the details and peculiarities of construction of the wheel, channel, and sluice apparatus. He should now proceed to delineate these various objects in the following manner:—Place the centre, o, of the wheel, at the intersection of two lines which form a right angle; and with this centre, describe a first circle, with a radius equal to that of the wheel and channel. Divide this circle into as many equal parts as there are to be floats. The number of the floats should always be divisible by that of the arms of the shrouding, so as not to be restricted as to space in fitting in the carrier-pieces. Through each point of division draw

lines passing through the centre, and representing the sides of the carrier-pieces upon which each float is placed. Two circles must next be described, expressing the depth of the shrouding. Then the complete outline of one of the carrier-pieces must be drawn, with the dimensions quoted on the figure; and the key and bolts may also be indicated upon it. Afterwards, to complete the drawing, it will be sufficient to describe a series of circles, passing through the bolts, the ends of the floats and carrier-pieces of the key, and of the counter-float. With regard to the floats, and to the arms of the shrouding, as well as to the spur-gear for transmitting the motion, the student may refer back to the diagrams and explanations already given concerning similar objects. The same remark applies to the lifting apparatus of the sluice-gate, which is also composed of gearing already treated of in the course of the studies.

DESIGN FOR A WATER-WHEEL.

401. If it is in contemplation to make a design for the construction of a water-wheel, analogous, we shall suppose, to the one above described, it is simply necessary to ascertain the height of fall, and the amount of discharge per second, of the water at our disposal, and to refer to the calculations and practical rules which accompany our text, to be able to determine, on the one hand, the diameter and width of the wheel, and, on the other, the depth and interstices of the floats, and their number. By referring back, also, to the tables and notes relating to the resistance of materials (Chapter III.), we shall be able to complete the remaining dimensions for the shaft and its journals, the shrouding and its arms.

The study of water-wheels of this description will be much simplified, if we consider that certain dimensions, such as the thickness of the floats, the section of the carrier-pieces and shrouding, and the diameter of the bolts, as well as the details of the sluice apparatus, do not sensibly vary; and for them the draughtsman may refer entirely to those indicated upon the drawing, which are themselves examples of actual construction.

SKETCH OF A WATER-WHEEL.

402. The sketch of a water-wheel, already constructed and set up, is a very simple matter; for the apparatus consists of a repetition of various pieces, and it is sufficient to obtain the measurements of one only of each kind. Thus, after having measured the diameter and extreme width of the wheel with the aid of a long rule or tape, and counted the number of buckets or floats, of the shroudings, and of the arms, we have merely to take the sketch of a single float, with its carrier-piece and accompaniments, then to make a section of one of the shroudings, another of one of the arms, and, finally, a third of the boss and shaft.

The details given in figs. 2 to 10 show the various parts of which the sketches have to be made, as detached, together with the corresponding measurements. Fig. 20 is a transverse section of one of the arms, D, of cast-iron, taken near the boss.

The sketching of the sluice apparatus consists in making a section of the side-posts, with their cap-piece, and of the sluice itself; then a detailed view of one of the racks, with its pinion and friction-pulley, and of the worm-wheel and worm. As to the amount of inclination of the sluice and side-posts, it has already

been seen that it is determined by a perpendicular to the radius, entering near the middle of the depth of water at the outlet, at the circumference of the wheel. It may, however, be found by means of a plumb-line, let fall from one of the edges of the cap-piece down to the level of the water, by measuring the horizontal distance, $r\ s$, of the plumb-line, from one of the sides of the side-post, and then the vertical height, $r\ t$. By applying a rule against the side-post, and down to the neck-piece, H, we can always obtain the actual distance of the top of the latter, either from the prolongation of the horizontal, $r\ s$, or from the cap-piece, P, of the sluice. To obtain the horizontal distance, $r\ s$, with exactitude, it should generally be taken at a given distance above the level of the water, and chalked upon one of the side-walls of the channel; it is also advisable to make use of a spirit-level. (Plate I.)

In order to take an accurate sketch of the neck-piece and the channel, it is almost always necessary to stop the water behind by means of a dam, so that the parts requiring to be examined may be dry and open. The sluice must also be taken away, as well as a few of the floats of the wheel. We may remark, that this labour may be avoided, when it is known that the height and thickness of the neck-piece are nearly always equal to those indicated in fig. 11; and as to the arrangement of the masonry or brickwork, of which the channel may be constructed, it will be recollected that all the lateral joints are pointed towards the centre of the wheel.

OVERSHOT WATER-WHEEL.

FIGURE 12.

CONSTRUCTION OF THE WHEEL, AND ITS SLUICE APPARATUS.

403. Overshot water-wheels, with buckets, receive the water from a duct placed immediately above them, and allow it to escape from as low a part only as possible. They are constructed of wood, or of cast-iron. In the first case, which is the simpler and more economical, the shaft, the arms, and the shroudings are of oak. The lower part of the wheel, represented in the drawing, fig. 12, is of this description. The buckets and the inner-rim are likewise of oak, or of iron plates. As this wheel is of small diameter, its shaft, F, has only six sides; and consequently, each shrouding, A, of the wheel has only six arms, D, which are recessed into, and bolted upon, a central cast-iron frame, E, which is itself keyed upon the shaft. The transverse section, fig. 13, shows the manner in which the arms are attached to this frame. The wooden shroudings, A, are generally composed of two rings, placed one on the other in such a manner that the joints of each are opposite to solid portions of the other, to "break bond," and obviate the tendency to warp. A portion of the shrouding is represented as detached in figs. 14 and 15. These rings are held together by screws, v, or by nails or pegs; and at their junction with the arms, a couple of bolts are passed through all, as indicated in the transverse section, fig. 16. The buckets, c, are either let into grooves of small depth, upon the inner face of the shrouding, as seen at c', in figs. 14 and 15, or they are retained by bracket-pieces, c; and, added to this, strong tension-rods, B, hold the whole together, being secured to

the shroudings, A, on either side of the buckets. These tension-rods are fixed, when the inner rim, s, or bottom of the buckets, has been nailed or screwed to the inner edges of the shroudings. The shroudings are further strengthened externally by a circular iron strap, G, similar to the felloe of an ordinary wheel, and covering up the joints of the duplex shrouding.

Sometimes the buckets are partly of wood, and partly of iron plate, to give them greater strength. The edges, indeed, should always be defended with metal, as they are most apt to wear soon. The lower portion of the drawing, fig. 12, shows three different ways of constructing these buckets.

When the wheel is of cast-iron, if it is not of a very great dia-meter, but of the size represented in the upper part of fig. 12, the arms and the boss, E′, may be cast in one piece with the shroud-ings, A′. Where the diameter is considerable, these consist of several pieces bolted together. The bottom piece, or inside rim, s′, and the buckets, c′, are of iron plates, of about ⅛th inch in thick-ness. To secure the latter, a series of feathers, figs. 12, 17, and 19, are cast upon the inner faces of the shroudings, to which they are fixed by screw-bolts, l. In the width of the wheel, the buckets and the bottom rim are riveted together, as at i, or are fixed together by small screw-bolts, i′, figs. 17 and 18.

The advantage of making the buckets of iron plates, consists in the being able to give them a curved form, which enlarges their capacity, and allows of a more favourable introduction of the water; whilst the wooden buckets necessarily consist of two rectilinear portions, one of which is directed towards the centre of the wheel, whilst the other is inclined.

The water is conducted by the wooden channel, M, to the top of the wheel, and its outflow is regulated by a sluice, J, moving in side grooves, and worked by means of a couple of vertical racks, o, and pinions, d, the shaft of which last carries the winch-handle, Q. The two vertical sides, N, of the channel, are prolonged beyond the actual summit of the wheel, and their distance asunder should be a little less than that of the two shroudings of the wheel, with the twofold object of better directing the water into the buckets, and of avoiding the splashing and loss of water by allowing the air to escape laterally. The depth of the outflow of water depends on the distance of the lower edge of the sluice above the bottom of the channel, and should always be less than the smallest distance existing between two consecutive buckets. The pressure of the water upon the buckets, produces the rotation of the wheel in the direction of the arrow, and this motion is given off by an internally-toothed wheel, attached to the outside of one of the shroudings. This wheel, which in the drawing is simply indicated by its pitch circle, K, gears with the pinion, L, mounted on the extremity of the shaft, which communicates with the machinery in the interior of the factory or workshop.

DELINEATING, SKETCHING, AND DESIGNING OVERSHOT WATER-WHEELS.

404. The delineation of the principal parts of an overshot bucket water-wheel, is effected in the same way as that of the undershot wheel with floats, the only difference being, in fact in the receptacles for the water. It has been seen, that when these buckets are of wood, they are composed of two boards, one of

which lies in the direction of a radius of the wheel, the other being inclined according to the direction of the water, and make an angle of 15 or 30 degrees, as the case may be, with the tangent, to the outer circumference of the wheel, drawn through its extremity, as will be seen by the angle, a b c, in fig. 17. When the bucket is made of iron plates, the same angle is adopted near the outer edge, although the whole contour is a continuous curve, which may be made up of two or three arcs of circles, as shown in figs. 12, 17, and 18.

In sketching this wheel, the directions given in the preceding case may be likewise followed here, by counting the number of buckets, and taking an accurate sketch of one of them, together with the accompanying measurements. We must also measure the internal and external diameters of the shroudings; then the least space existing between two consecutive buckets; also the depth from b to d, fig. 17. Finally, if it is required to obtain the exact form or curvature of the bucket, it will be necessary to take one down, and to make a pattern of it, by applying a sheet of paper against one edge, and pencilling out the shape, as is done for the forms of wheel-teeth, or other curves, which are difficult to measure. As to the sketch of the other parts of the wheel, such as the boss, the arms, and also the sluice apparatus, no peculiarity or difficulty can present itself which need detain us here. The drawing, moreover, indicates all the figures and measurements which are necessary.

In designing an overshot water-wheel, it is necessary to know the height of fall, and the daily discharge of the water. With regard to these particulars, we must simply refer to our accompa-nying Rules and Practical Data.

WATER-PUMPS.

PLATE XXXVII.

GEOMETRICAL DELINEATION.

405. We have already indicated, in preceding notes and calcula-tions, the various classes of pumps, with their proper dimensions. in proportion to the quantities of water to be furnished by them. We now propose to enter upon more detailed and complete expla-nations, with regard to their construction, action, and performance. For this purpose we have selected, by preference, a combined lifting and forcing pump, the discharge of which is almost continu-ous, although its construction is analogous to what is termed a single-acting pump.

Figure 1, on Plate XXXVII., represents a vertical section, taken through the axis of this pump. It consists of a cast-iron cylinder, A, turned out for the greater portion of its length, and resting upon a feathered base, B, cast in one piece with the suction or lift-pipe, c, below. This base is bolted down either to stout timbers, D, or to a stonework foundation. It encloses the valve-seat, E, which consists of a rectangular frame, divided by a central partition, a, and having the sides formed so as to present two in-clined edges, upon which the brass clack, F, rests when shut. The pipe, c, terminates below in a flange, by means of which the suction-pipe is attached, extending down to the water to be ele-vated. Towards the upper part of the pump cylinder, A, is cast a curved outlet, G, likewise terminating in flanges, to which the discharge-pipe is secured. The piston, or bucket, of this pump is composed of a brass ring, or short cylinder, H, upon the outer circumference of which is formed a groove, b, (fig. 2,) to receive a packing-ring, c, which fits, air-tight, to the inside of the pump cylinder. The bucket, H, has also a central partition, d, to the top of which are jointed the two clacks, I, which rest upon inclined seats, formed by the elevated sides, e, of the bucket. This is further cast with a bridle, f, perforated in the middle, to receive the screw-bolt, g, which secures it to the stout hollow piston-rod, J. This rod, which, in the generality of pumps, is made of but small diameter, like the upper part, K, of the one represented in the plate, is, in the present instance, of a sectional area, equal to half that of the pump cylinder. It follows from this, as will be more particularly explained further on, that the water is discharged during both the up and down stroke of the piston.

The clacks, F, have projections, h, cast upon them, which prevent their opening too far, and falling over against the sides of the casing, B, so as not to shut again when required to do so. The clacks, I, in the bucket, have similar projections, i, for a like purpose, these projections striking against the top of the bridle, f, when the clacks open. It will have been observed, that the seats of these valves are inclined at an angle of 45°, with the view of facilitating their opening movement, and diminishing the concussive action of their own weight. The edges of the valve-seats are generally defended with a strip of leather, to facilitate their tight closing.

Figure 2 represents, detached and in elevation, the bucket, H, with its clacks, I. Fig. 3 is a horizontal section of the bucket, taken at the line, 1—2. Figs. 4 and 5 give the details of the valve-seat, E, in elevation and plan, the clacks being removed.

To prevent the entrance of air to the pump cylinder, it is closed at the top by a cast-iron cover, L, which is fitted with a stuffing-box for the passage of the piston-rod; the packing is compressed by the gland, M, similar in general form to that represented in Plate XI. (81.)

ACTION OF THE PUMP.

406. The upper extremity of the piston-rod, K, carries a cross-head, l, (fig. 6,) and is there jointed to the lower extremity of a connecting-rod, N, which is itself jointed to the pin of a crank, o; this latter is mounted on the end of a horizontal shaft, P, actuated by a continuous rotatory movement. This movement is transformed by means of the crank and connecting-rod into an alternate rectilinear motion—that is, into the up-and-down strokes of the pump bucket—this last being forced to move in a straight line, the cross-head, l, sliding in vertical guide-grooves, to maintain the piston-rod, K, in the same line with it.

It follows, from this disposition of parts, that when the crank, o, is in the position, P—o, fig. 6, the piston will be at the bottom of its stroke, that is, at H'; consequently, during the time the crank turns, the piston must rise, tending to leave a vacuum below it, because the space between the clacks, F, and its under side increases, as well as the volume of air that may be therein enclosed. Consequently, the pressure of this air upon the clacks is diminished, whilst that upon the surface of the water remains

the same, and causes the water to rise up the suction-pipe, and, raising the clacks, F, to enter the pump cylinder, filling it up nearly to the under side of the piston; or if the apparatus is in a perfectly air-tight condition, it will rise quite up to the piston.

When the crank has reached the position, P—12,—that is, when it shall have described a semi-revolution,—the piston itself will likewise be at the highest point of its stroke, and, in this position, all the space left behind it in the body of the pump will be filled with water; if now the crank, continuing its rotation, makes a second semi-revolution, the piston will descend, and, pressing upon the water below it, will cause the clacks, F, to shut. Now, as the water is incompressible, it must find an exit, or else prevent the descent of the piston; and it therefore raises the bucket-clacks, I, thus opening up for itself a passage through the piston, H, above which it then lodges. But as the piston-rod, J, is of a large diameter, and therefore occupies a considerable space in the pump cylinder, a part of the water must necessarily escape through the outlet, G, in such a manner that, when the piston shall have reached the bottom of its stroke, there will not remain in the pump cylinder more than half the quantity of water which was contained in it when the piston was at the top of its stroke.

Such is the effect produced by the first turn of the crank, which corresponds to a double stroke of the piston—that is, an ascent and a descent.

At the second turn, when the piston again rises, it sucks up, as it were, anew, a volume of water about equal to the length of cylinder through which it passes, because the suction-clacks, F, which were shut, now open again, and the bucket-clacks, I, which were open during the descent, are now shut by the upward movement of the piston.

During this stroke, all the water which previously remained above the piston, finds itself forced to pass off through the pipe, G, so that, with this arrangement of piston and rod, or plunger, of large diameter, it follows that, at each up-stroke of the piston, the quantity of water which rises into the pump is equal to the length of cylinder through which the piston passes, the half of which quantity rises in the discharge-pipe during the descent, and the other half during the subsequent ascent of the piston, and the jet is consequently rendered almost continuous and uniform.

When, on the contrary, the piston-rod is made very small in diameter, as in ordinary pumps (fig. 6), the discharge of the water only takes place during the ascent of the piston, and it is consequently intermittent.

In a pump, as in all other machines in which an alternate rectilinear is derived from a continuous rotatory motion, by means of a crank and connecting-rod, the spaces passed through in a straight line by the piston do not correspond to the angular spaces described by the crank-pin; in fact, it will be seen from the diagram, fig. 6, that if the crank-pin is supposed to describe a series of equal arcs, beginning from the point, 0, the corresponding distances, 0' 1', 1' 2', 2' 3', passed through by the piston will not be uniform; very small at the commencement of the stroke, they will gradually increase towards the middle, after passing which they will similarly decrease whilst the piston approaches the other end of its stroke. The successive positions of the piston may be obtained by describing with each of the points, 1, 2, 3, 4, upon the circumference traced by the crank-pin as centres, and with a radius equal to the length of the connecting-rod, a series of arcs or circles cutting the vertical, passing through the centre, P, in the points, 0^2, 1^2, 2^2, which indicate upon this line the various positions of the point of attachment, l, of the connecting-rod to the piston-rod: these points are then repeated at $0'$, $1'$, $2'$, on the same line, at distances from the points, 0^2, 1^2, 2^2, equal to the length of the piston-rod, measured from the point, l, to the bottom of the piston.

It will be easily understood, that, in consequence of this irregularity in the motion of the piston, the force and volume of the jet of water will vary throughout the whole stroke. We have endeavoured to show the nature of this variation in the diagram, fig. 7, which represents the comparative volumes of the jet of water at successive periods for a single-acting pump, such as the one in fig. 6.

This diagram is constructed by laying off upon any line, $x\,y$, as many equal parts as we have taken in divisions on the circle described by the crank-pin; then through each of these points, as 1, 2, 3, 4, drawing perpendiculars to $x\,y$. As during the ascent of the piston from 0 to 12 (figs. 6 and 7) there is no discharge, as the piston only sucks up the water, there is nothing to indicate upon these first divisions; as soon, however, as the crank-pin passes the highest point, and the piston begins to descend, it will produce the jet of water; it is considered then, that when it has passed through the first rectilinear space, $12'$ to $11'$, the quantity of water forced out by it may be represented by its base multiplied by the height, $11'$—$12'$. It is this distance which is set off from 13 to a, upon the perpendicular drawn through the point, 13; in the same manner, when the piston descends from $11'$ to $10'$, it is also taken as represented by its base multiplied by the height, $11'$—$10'$, which last is therefore set off from the point, 14 to b. It will be seen from this, that, in proceeding with the diagram, it is simply necessary to set off upon each of the perpendiculars drawn through the points of division, 15, 16, 17, the successive distances passed through by the piston during its descent, so as to represent intelligibly the actual volumes of water discharged for each portion of the stroke, since these volumes are proportional to the distances passed through by the piston, the section of the cylinder remaining constant.

If, through the various points, a, b, c, d, fig. 7, obtained in this manner, we trace a curve, we shall obtain the outline of a surface which we have distinguished by a flat shade, and which will give a good idea of the amounts of water discharged in correspondence with any position of the crank. On continuing the rotation of the crank, the piston next ascends and sucks up the water, consequently the jet of water is interrupted during this upstroke, but recommences on the down-stroke due to the subsequent part of the revolution; the quantity of water then discharged is indicated in fig. 7, by a curve equal to the first, and on which the same points are distinguished by the same letters.

To avoid this irregularity in the discharge, pumping apparatus is sometimes constructed with two, or with three, distinct cylinders, in which the disposition of the pistons is such, that the points of

attachment to the several crank-pins divide the circle described by them into two or three equal parts.

Figure 8 represents a geometrical diagram of the performance of a two-cylinder pump; it is evident that the product of each of the pistons is alternately the same, since one descends whilst the other rises; it is thus that one of the pistons, having produced a jet corresponding to, and expressed by, the curve, $a'\,b'\,c'$, the other one immediately afterwards produces a jet, expressed by the curve, $a\,b\,c\,d$; so that this diagram only differs from fig. 7, in that the unoccupied intervals, from 0 to 12, and 24 to 12, in the latter, are in the former filled up by an equal figure, covered by an equal flat shade.

This diagram of the performance of a two-cylinder pump may also be considered as representing that of the pump, fig. 1, which, because of its trunk piston-rod, acts as a double-acting pump, as already explained.

Fig. 9 represents the diagram of the performance of a three-cylinder pump, of which the pistons, H, H′, H², represented, for convenience' sake, as in the same cylinder, occupy the positions corresponding to those of the three crank-pins, 0, $0'$, $0''$, as placed at the angles of an equilateral triangle, inscribed in the circle described by them with the centre, P. In consequence of this disposition, there are at one time two pistons ascending and one descending, and at another time, on the contrary, only one ascending and two descending. It is easy to represent the combined performance of these pumps in a diagram, by using different colours, or different depths of shade, for the performance of each, as dependent upon the successive positions, 1, 2, 3, 4, taken up by their successive crank-pins. By this means all confusion will be avoided, and it will be necessary to find the positions, N, N′, N″, of the attachment of the connecting-rod to the piston-rod upon the vertical line passing through the centre, P, only as for one cylinder, as the distances will be the same for all, being merely placed at different parts of the diagram.

In the diagram, fig. 10, we have laid down the performance of each of the three pumps, supposing them all to be of the same diameter, and taking care, when two pumps are discharging together, to add together their performance; thus, for example, when one of the pistons elevates a quantity of water, corresponding to the perpendicular, $13\,a$, that which is also discharging at the same time furnishes a quantity expressed by the distance, $a\,a'$; consequently, the total volume of the discharge at this instant is represented by the total height, $13a'$; when, on the other hand, only one of the three pumps discharges, whilst the pistons of the other two are ascending, as in fig. 9, the volume discharged is represented by a single length of perpendicular, such as $18\,f$. Now, it will be observed, that it is precisely at the moment when only one pump is discharging that it gives out its maximum performance; from which it follows, that the jet of water is continuous, and almost uniform throughout its duration, as will be very evident from a consideration of the diagram, fig. 10, the outline of which is determined by perpendiculars, or ordinates, reaching nearly to the straight line, $m\,n$, throughout.

To compare the combined effect of a three-cylinder pump with that of two or of three double-acting pumps, we have, in figs. 8 and 11, repeated the corresponding diagrams for the two last arrange ments; and it will be remarked, that although, with cylinders of an equal sectional area, we necessarily obtain a much larger discharge, yet the regularity of volume is not so great as in the previous example.

STEAM MOTORS.

HIGH-PRESSURE EXPANSIVE STEAM-ENGINE.

PLATES XXXVIII., XXXIX., AND XL.

407. When the steam generated in a boiler is led into a vase or cylinder which is hermetically closed, it acts with its entire expansive force upon the sides and ends of the cylinder, so that, if this encloses a diaphragm, or piston, capable of moving through the cylinder in an air-tight manner, the force of the steam, in seeking to enlarge its volume, will make the piston move. It is in this way that a mechanical effect is derived from the expansive action of the steam, and it is on the same principle that the generality of steam-engines are constructed.

Thus, in most apparatus to which this name is given, the action of the steam is caused to exert itself alternately on the upper and under surface of the piston, enclosed in the cylinder, thereby causing it to make a rectilinear back and forward movement or stroke. (187.)

Steam-engines are said to be low or high pressure engines, according as the tension of the steam is only of about 1 atmosphere on the one hand, or of 2, 3, and upwards, on the other. Low-pressure engines are generally condensing engines, and high-pressure ones non-condensing; so that the terms, low pressure or condensing, high pressure or non-condensing, are used indiscriminately, although, in modern engineering practice, what are called high-pressure condensing engines are extensively employed.

When the steam is made to act alternately above and below the piston, the engine is said to be double-acting; and of this description are most of those employed at the present day; but if the steam acts only on one side of the piston, as is the case in many mine-pumping engines, the engine is called a single-acting one.

Low-pressure engines are generally also condensing engines; that is to say, that after the steam has exerted its expansive action upon the piston, and is on its way out of the cylinder, it passes into a chamber immersed in cold water, and termed a condenser, where it is condensed or reduced to the state of water. This condensation produces a partial vacuum in the cylinder, and consequently considerably diminishes the resistance to the movement of the piston.

In high-pressure engines, the steam which has produced its effect upon the piston escapes directly to the atmosphere, so that the piston has always to overcome a resistance equal to one atmosphere, or about 15 lbs. per square inch, acting in a direction opposite to its motion.

Steam-engines are further distinguished as expansive and non-expansive; of the latter description are those wherein the steam enters the cylinder throughout the entire stroke of the piston; so that the pressure is uniform, since the volume of steam of a given pressure which enters is always equal to the space passed through by the piston.

In expansive engines, on the contrary, the steam is only allowed to enter the cylinder during a portion of the stroke; so that the expansive power of the steam is called into action during the remainder of the movement.

The machine detailed in Plates XXXVIII., XXXIX., and XL., is a high-pressure engine, with a variable expansion valve.

Fig. 1, Plate XXXVIII., represents an external elevation or front view of the machine, the frame of which consists of a hollow column, with lateral openings.

Fig. 2 is a horizontal section, taken at the height of the line, 1—2.

Fig. 3 is an elevation of a fragment of the lower part of the column.

Fig. 4 is another horizontal section, taken at the line, 3—4; and fig. 5 is an elevation of the capital of the column.

Figs. 6 and 7 are diagrams, relating to the movement of the governor, with its balls.

Fig. 8, Plate XXXIX., represents a vertical section, taken through the axes of the column and the steam cylinder, at the plane, 5—6, parallel to that of the fly-wheel.

Fig. 9 is another vertical section, at right angles to the preceding figure.

And, finally, fig. 10 is a horizontal section, taken at the broken line, 7—8—9—10.

This machine consists of a cast-iron cylinder, A, truly bored out, and enclosing the piston, B. On one side of the cylinder are cast the passages, a, b, by which the steam enters alternately above and below the piston. These passages are successively covered over by a cup or valve, D, the details of which are given in figs. 28 to 31, Plate XL.; and the valve is itself contained in the cast-iron chamber, E, called the *valve casing*, and communicating with a second chamber, F, called the *expansion-valve casing*; it is into this latter chamber that the steam is first conducted by the pipe, G, from the boiler. The communication between the two valve casings is intercepted for short periods during the action of the machine, by the expansion valve, H, detailed in figs. 38 to 41, Plate XL.

The vertical rod, I, of the piston, B, is attached at its upper extremity to a short cross pin, e^2, which connects it to the wrought-iron connecting-rod, J, hung on the pin, f, of the crank, K; this is adjusted and keyed upon the extremity of the horizontal shaft, L, which carries on one side the fly-wheel, M, and on the other the eccentrics, N, O, P. The first of these eccentrics is intended to actuate the distributing valve, D, the rod, g, of which is connected to it by the intermediate adjustable rod, N'. The second works the expansion valve, H, by means of the rods, o' and h; and, finally, the third eccentric, P, gives an alternate movement to the piston or plunger, Q, of the feed-pump, R.

The steam cylinder is bolted in a firm and solid manner, by its upper flanges, to the top of the hollow cast-iron plinth or pedestal, S, on which also rests, and is bolted, the column, T. The pedestal is square; and, at the corners of its base, lugs are cast, by means of which it is firmly bolted down to a solid stone foundation.

The column, T, is cast hollow, and with four large lateral openings diametrically opposite to each other, their object being to diminish the weight of the column, and to afford the necessary passages for the introduction of the various pieces when being put together, or when taken down. This column also serves as a frame for the entire machine, and above the capital is placed a cast-iron pillow-block, U, furnished with bearing brasses to receive the principal journal of the first motion shaft, as well as the supporting brackets, k, k', of the spindle, l, of the ball governor. To its inner side are also bolted the two supports, i, of the parallel motion, and guide, j, of the valve-rod, g.

ACTION OF THE MACHINE.

408. Before proceeding further, we shall give some idea of the general action of the machine. As already mentioned, the steam is generated in a boiler, such, for example, as that represented in Plate XIV. (189), and is conducted by the steam-pipe, G, into the first chamber, F; when the valve, H, in this chamber uncovers the orifice, or port, d, the steam finds its way into the valve-casing, E, whence it passes either to the upper or to the lower end of the cylinder, accordingly as the valve, D, uncovers one or other of the two ports or passages, a, b. Now, when the piston is, for example, at the top of its stroke, the passage, a, is almost fully open, whilst the channel, b, is in communication with the exit orifice, c, from which the two pipes, e^4, conduct it to the atmosphere. If, on the introduction of the steam to the cylinder, it has a pressure of, say four atmospheres, it follows that it will act upon the piston with all this force to cause it to descend; since, however, the lower part of the cylinder is at this time in communication with the external atmosphere, there is a resistance equal to one atmosphere opposed to its movement, therefore the actual effective pressure acting on the top of the piston will be equal to three atmospheres.

It is the same when the piston reascends; the valve uncovers the port of the passage, b, to allow the steam to enter the lower end of the cylinder, whilst the port, a, is put in communication with the exit orifice, c, by the cup of the valve, to give an outlet for the steam which has just acted on the upper side of the piston during the down-stroke.

It is to be remarked, that if the introduction of the steam takes place during the entire up-and-down stroke of the piston, which might be the case if the steam-pipe, G, communicated directly with the valve-casing, E, and if the valve, D, kept one of the ports uncovered throughout the entire stroke, the pressure of the steam would remain constant; in such case, it would be said that the machine was a high-pressure non-expansive engine—that is to say, that it worked with a full allowance of steam.

In the machine, however, which at present occupies our attention, the steam first introduces itself into the casing, F, the valve, H, of which, at each stroke, closes the passage, d, communicating with the second casing, E, before the piston reaches either end of its stroke. It follows, that the steam contained in the cylinder at the time of closing the passage, d, must augment in volume or expand, whilst its pressure will consequently decrease during the remaining advance of the piston: the engine is then said to be working *expansively*; and in this case a quantity of steam is expended for each stroke, equal only to a third, half, or two-

thirds of the capacity of the cylinder, according as the introduction of the steam is intercepted at one-third, one-half, or two-thirds of the stroke; it is the ratio between the quantity of full steam-pressure introduced, and the entire capacity of the cylinder, which expresses the degree of expansion at which the engine works.

PARALLEL MOTION.

409. The rectilinear alternate movement of the piston is transformed into a continuous circular motion on the first motion shaft, L, by the intervention of the connecting-rod, J, and crank, K; but with this arrangement there is naturally a lateral strain upon the top of the piston-rod, I, and in order that its movement may be perfectly rectilinear and vertical, it is jointed to a system of articulated levers, forming what is termed a parallel motion.

This mechanism is composed of two wrought iron rods, V (figs. 1, 4, and 8), which oscillate on the fixed centres, i, and are articulated at their opposite extremities to the levers, X, near their middle, by means of the pin, n. The levers, X, are also of wrought-iron. and are jointed at one end to the cross pin, e^2, fig. 9, of the piston-rod end; and at the other to the rod, Y, attached to a cross spindle, o o, and oscillating in bearings, in a couple of cast-iron brackets, Z, bolted to the lower part of the frame.

The head of this last-mentioned oscillating rod is detailed separately, in figs. 21 and 22, Plate XL. It has brasses, to embrace the journal of the spindle, p^4, by which it is connected to the ends of the levers, X.

The combination of this mechanism is such, that the point of attachment, e, constantly moves in a straight line throughout the entire stroke. It may be designed on geometrical principles, as indicated in the diagrams, figs. 8 and 11. To this effect we have supposed, that after having drawn the horizontal line, e^2 p, and the vertical, e e^3, distances, e e^2 and e e^3, are set off on the latter, equal to the half stroke of the piston, or to the radius of the crank; then, with the points, e e^3, describe an arc, with a radius, e p, equal to the length of the lever, X, which is taken at pleasure, but should never be less than the stroke of the piston. If we next lay off this distance from e^2 to p^2, the space, p p^2, will express the amount of oscillation of the rod, Y, the centre of oscillation, o, of which we place below, on the vertical line, drawn at an equal distance from and between the two points, p, p^2. We next fix the point, n, of attachment of the rods, V, to the lever, X. This point, n, during the movement of the parallel motion, necessarily describes a circular arc, of which it is requisite to find the centre. In investigating this problem, it is to be observed that, whatever may be the position of the lever, the point, n, is always at an equal distance from the extremity, p, or the other one, e. If, then, we in succession draw the lines, p e, p^1 e^1, p^2 e^2, p^3 e^3, indicating the different positions of the lever, corresponding to those, e, e^1, e^2, e^3, of the piston-rod end, we shall, on each of these lines, obtain the several positions, n, n^1, n^2, n^3, by laying off on them either of the distances, p n or e n. We can then very easily find the centre of the arc passing through these points. (10.)

Fig. 10 represents the diagram of an analogous parallel motion, but one in which the rods, V, are so disposed, that their point of attachment is exactly in the middle of the levers, X; and in this case, their axis of oscillation lies in a plane passing through the vertical axis, $e\ e^2$.

DETAILS OF CONSTRUCTION.

STEAM CYLINDER.

410. The cylinder is cast in one piece with its bottom cover and lateral steam passages. As it should be bored with great care, so as to be perfectly cylindrical in the interior, a central opening is made in the bottom for the passage of the spindle of the boring tool; this opening, however, is afterwards closed by the small cover, a^2, cemented at its junction surfaces, and bolted down to the bottom of the cylinder. The upper end of the cylinder is closed by a cast-iron cover, A', which is formed into a stuffing-box in the centre, to embrace the piston-rod, which works steam-tight through it. The packing is compressed or forced down for this purpose by a gland (140), bolted to the stuffing-box, and hollowed out at the top to receive the lubricating oil. The valve-face, on the outside of the cylinder, and on which the valve works, is planed very carefully, so as to be a true plane throughout. The same is done with the valve-casing at the flanges, where it is fitted to the valve-face.

PISTON.

The piston (figs. 8, 9, 19, and 20) is composed of two cast-iron plates, which have an annular space between them for the reception of two concentric cast or wrought-iron or brass packing-rings, c'. These rings are cut through at one side, and are placed one within the other in such a manner, that the breaks in each are diametrically opposite to each other; their thickness gradually diminishes on each side towards the break, and they are hammered on the inside in a cold state, which renders them elastic, giving them a constant tendency to open. Since the diameter of the outer ring is equal to that of the cylinder when the two edges are brought together, the elasticity of the inner ring, combining with that of the outer one, tending constantly to enlarge them, it follows that there must be a perfect coincidence between the outside of the ring and the inside of the cylinder throughout the whole extent of the latter. Thus the contact of the piston with the sides of the cylinder only takes place through the packing-ring, and not by the plates, which are of a slightly less diameter. To prevent the passage of the steam through the break in the outer packing-ring, a rectangular opening is made in the two edges of the ring, and in this is placed a small tongue-piece, a^2, screwed to the inner ring, this piece serving to close or break the joint without preventing the play of the rings. The principal plate of the piston is fixed to the piston-rod by means of a key (fig. 9). The piston-rod is consequently of increased diameter at its lower end. The upper end of the piston-rod is likewise fixed in a socket, l', (figs. 9 and 13,) which terminates in two vertical branches to receive the middle of the spindle, e^2, which is held down by means of a key.

CONNECTING-ROD AND CRANK.

411. The connecting-rod, J, (figs. 8, 9, 14, and 15,) terminates at its lower end in a fork, by means of which it is jointed to the spindle, e^2, brasses being fitted in either side, and secured by bridle-pieces passing under them and keyed above. The fork is jointed to the spindle, e^2, on each side of the piston-rod head, sufficient space, however, being left between them for the levers, X. The head of the connecting-rod (figs. 15 and 16) is likewise fitted with brasses to embrace the pin, f, of the crank; these brasses are tightened up by means of the pressure screw, f'.

The crank, K, like the connecting-rod, J, is of wrought-iron, being adjusted on the end of the first motion shaft, and secured to it by a key. This crank is very often made of cast-iron in stationary engines, but in marine and locomotive engines it is generally forged, so as to be better suited for resisting severe strains and shocks.

The first motion shaft, L, is likewise either of cast or wrought-iron. In the notes, we have already given tables and rules for determining the respective dimensions of this detail. It is not only supported by the brasses of the pillow-block, U, but also by those of a similar one, fixed, we shall suppose, upon the wall which divides the engine-house from the workshop or factory. It should always be larger in diameter where it receives the fly-wheel, M.

FLY-WHEEL.

412. The fly-wheel is of cast-iron—of a single piece in the present example, because its diameter is only 3·5 mètres. When of larger dimensions, the rim and the arms are cast in separate pieces, and then bolted together. For wheels of from 5 to 8 mètres in diameter, the rim is made in several pieces, and the arms are also cast separate from the boss, and all the parts are then bolted together. The arms are sometimes made of wrought-iron of small dimensions, with the view of reducing the weight near the centre, without reducing the effect of the wheel.

FEED-PUMP.

413. This pump serves to force into the boiler a certain quantity of water, to replace that which is converted into steam and expended in actuating the engine. It is a simple force-pump, consisting of a cylinder, R, in which works the solid piston or plunger, Q. The piston is not in contact with the sides of the pump cylinder, and the latter consequently only requires to be turned out at its upper part, where it is formed into a stuffing-box and guide for the plunger, being necessarily air-tight.

On one side of the pump is cast a short pipe, to which is attached the valve-box, R, generally made of brass. To the lower part of this is secured the suction-pipe, T', communicating with a cistern of water, and having a stopcock, s', upon it, like the one represented in detail in Plate XVII. To one side of the valve-box is likewise fitted the discharge-pipe, carrying a similar stopcock, s^2; this last pipe is generally passed through the pipe which carries off the waste steam, so that the water may take up some of the heat of this steam before entering the boiler.

It will be seen, from figs. 9 and 23, that this valve-box contains two valves, s', s^2; the lower one of which, s', is the suction valve, and the upper one, s^2, is the discharge-valve. The latter is much larger in diameter than the former, so that its seat may be wide enough for the lower valve to be passed through it. The upper end of the valve-box is closed by a cover, which is firmly held down by the screw, r', and iron bridle, q'.

Both valves are made conical at the seat, as in fig. 24, so as to fit more easily. The under part of the valve is cylindrical, so as to guide it; but it is cut away at the sides, to allow of the passage of the water when it rises. It is from the appearance this gives that these valves are called *lantern valves*.

The pump cylinder is further furnished with a safety-valve, s^3, of which fig. 25 is a detailed view. The object of this is to permit the air to escape, when it accumulates within to such an extent as to destroy the action of the pump. This valve is horizontal, and is kept in its place by the bell-crank lever, u, upon the horizontal arm of which is suspended a weight, sufficient to counterbalance the internal pressure. (195.)

The top of the plunger is surmounted by a small rod, t, adjustable in the socket which terminates the long wrought-iron rod, P', figs. 9 and 18, the upper extremity of which is formed into a collar, embracing the circular eccentric, P. (142.)

The action of this pump is analogous to that of the pumps of which we have already given a description. Thus, when the machine is working, and the stopcocks, s' and s^2, are open, the water rises from the cistern by the pipe, R', the valve, s', opening, to give it passage into the body of the pump, into which it flows as long as the piston ascends. When, however, the piston descends, the water is driven back, and, closing the lower valve, s', necessarily opens the upper one, s^2, and proceeds along the discharge-pipe to the boiler. The quantity of feed-water is regulated by means of the stopcocks, and may be entirely shut off by closing them; but then, in such case, as the eccentric, P, with its rod, P', will continue to move, it will be necessary to loosen the plunger, Q, which is done by unscrewing the thumb-screw, v, by which the piston-rod is attached to the eccentric rod, in such a manner that the socket, b^3, fig. 18, at the end of the eccentric rod, P', will simply slide up and down the rod, without moving it.

BALL OR ROTATING PENDULUM GOVERNOR.

414. The object of this piece of mechanism is the regulation of the velocity of the machine, in proportion to the resistances to be overcome; and, accordingly, to this effect it opens or shuts a valve, c^3, placed in the steam-pipe, G, and called a throttle-valve. Just as a freer or narrower passage is left for the steam by the opening or closing of this throttle-valve, which is contained in an especial box, to facilitate adjustment, and is actuated by a rod, passing through a stuffing-box at the side—so is the quantity of steam which finds its way to the cylinder more or less; and, similarly, the consequent acceleration or retardation of the motion of the piston, as well as of the first motion shaft in connection with it.

It is composed, as seen in fig. 1, of a vertical spindle, l, stepped, at its lower extremity, in the end of a small bracket support, k', and is held higher up by a second bracket, k. To its upper end are jointed two symmetrical side rods, m', each terminating in cast-iron or brass spheres, o'. These side rods are also connected by means of the intermediate links, l', to the wrought-iron or copper socket or ring, i', moveable upon the main spindle.

A rotatory motion being given to the vertical spindle, and the balls being carried round with it, will have a constant tendency

to fly off from the vertical line, by reason of the centrifugal force due to the rotation (262); as long as the rotative velocity remains the same, the balls will tend to occupy the mean position indicated upon the drawing, and corresponding to the *normal* velocity; that is to say, the velocity to which the apparatus is regulated. When this velocity is exceeded—in consequence, as we may suppose, for example, of some parts of the machinery being put out of gear—the balls will fly asunder, and occupy the extreme position, o^2, indicated upon fig. 6. In this position of the balls, the socket, i', will be lifted up. Now this socket is embraced, at its circular groove, by the prongs of the forked lever, j, fig. 9, which is connected to the vertical rod, h, and this, by a suite of levers and bell-cranks, g^1, g^2, g^3, g^4, and g^5, communicates with the throttle-valve, c^3, drawn with its box, A^2, in figs. 26 and 27. It follows, from the combination of these connections, that, as the socket rises, the valve will be shut. If, on the contrary, the velocity should be reduced below the proper point, owing to an increased resistance, the balls will approach each other, and assume the position given in fig. 7. The socket, i', will descend, and, consequently, the throttle-valve will become more open, so as to allow a greater quantity of steam to enter the valve-casing, and thence pass into the cylinder. The extreme positions of the governor arms, beyond which they cannot go, are determined by the guides, m^2, fixed upon the spindle, l.

The motion of this spindle is derived from the first motion shaft, L, by means of the grooved pulley, p^3, fixed upon the intermediate spindle, r^2, placed close to the capital of the column, T, and by the bevil-wheels, r^3, receiving their motion from the pulley, r^4, so that a constant ratio is maintained between the rate of the machine and that of the governor.

The geometrical diagram, figs. 6 and 7, will sufficiently explain the respective positions of each of the pieces of the pendulum, and will show how the rising of the socket upon the spindle is caused by, and is in proportion to, the flying asunder of the balls, according to the number of revolutions of the spindle, and the length of the suspending arms.

MOVEMENTS OF THE DISTRIBUTION AND EXPANSION VALVES.

DISTRIBUTION VALVE.

415. We have seen that the valve, D, represented in different positions in figs. 28 and 31, and in horizontal section, fig. 32, is attached, by its rod, g, to the vertical rod, N', which is joined to the rod, N^2, of the circular eccentric, N, figs. 33 and 34. When, as was customary until lately, the centre of the eccentric lies in a radius perpendicular to the direction of the crank, the movements of the steam piston and valve are different to each other—that is to say, when the crank passes from the left horizontal to the right horizontal position, the piston makes a corresponding rectilinear movement; the eccentric, however, passes from the lower extremity of the vertical line, drawn through the centre of the first motion shaft, to the upper extremity, or *vice versâ*, and consequently gives the valve a rectilinear movement quite different to that of the piston, in such a manner that, when the latter is at the middle of its stroke, the valve, on the other hand, is at the end, and the steam-

ports are consequently fully open, to give the steam the freest passage into the cylinder.

Whilst the piston is accomplishing its stroke in one direction, the valve moves up or down, and returns again to its central position, the part which it covered being opened and again shut; when, however, the crank makes two fourths of a revolution in different directions, the piston rises and falls half a stroke each way, whilst the valve makes a single rectilinear movement in one direction.

Finally, for each of these movements, whilst the velocities of the piston are increasing from the commencement towards the middle of its stroke, those of the valve are decreasing, and reciprocally. It therefore follows, that the maximum space passed through by the piston, for a given portion of a revolution of the crank, corresponds to the minimum passed through by the valve.

LEAD AND LAP OF THE VALVE.

416. Of late years, engineers have recognised the advantage of inclining the radius of the eccentric, with regard to the radius of the crank, instead of placing them perpendicular to one another, in such a manner that, at the *dead points*—that is, the extreme high and low positions of the piston—the valve shall already have passed the middle of its stroke to a slight extent; it is this advance of the valve which is termed the *lead*.

The effect of giving this lead to the valve, is to facilitate the introduction of the steam into the cylinder at the commencement of the piston's stroke, and at the same time to allow a freer exit to the waste steam on the other side of the piston; a greater uniformity of motion is in consequence obtained, whilst less force is lost.

In order to avoid as much as possible the back pressure due to the slow exit of the waste steam, it is likewise customary, in addition to the lead, to give the valve more or less *lap*; that is to say, to make the width of that part of the valve which covers the ports, a, b, fig. 28, sensibly greater than that of the ports themselves.

In explanation of the effects due to the lead and lap of the valve, we have, in fig. 35, given a geometrical diagram, indicating the relative positions of the crank, the piston, the eccentric, and of the valve.

Let o o represent the radius of the crank; with this distance as a radius, and with the centre, o, describe a semicircle, which divide into a certain number of equal parts. From each of the points of division, let fall perpendiculars upon the diameter, o c. The points of contact, 1, 2, 3, 4, &c., represent upon this diameter, considered as the stroke of the piston, the respective positions of the piston, corresponding to those, 2^2, 3^2, 4^2, &c., of the crank pin. It is unnecessary to take into account the length of the connecting-rod, which connects the latter to the piston, because, in the present case, the connecting-rod is supposed to be of an indefinite length, and to remain constantly parallel to itself, so that it cannot modify the results.

With the centre, o, likewise describe a circle with a radius, o a', equal to that of the eccentric, N. We have assumed the point, a', to be the position the centre of the eccentric should have at the moment when the piston is at the end of its stroke—

that is to say, at o; the distance of this point, a', from the vertical m n, expresses the lead of the valve, and consequently the angle m o a', is called the angle of lead. The position of the point, a' may likewise be obtained, after the following data are decided on—namely, the height of the ports, a, b, fig. 28, the width, r s, of the flange of the valve, which is equal to the height of opening, t r which properly expresses the amount of lead given to the port augmented by twice the lap, together with the amount of the introduction of the steam to the cylinder, and the amount of opening, s' t', expressing the lead given to the escaping steam, and which is always greater than the former, so that the exit passages may be in communication as long as possible.

The diameter of the eccentric, N, is equal to the height of the port, augmented by the width, r s, of the flange of the valve, and the difference which exists between the two amounts of lead, s' t' and r t; it is, then, with the half of this as radius that the circle, a' b' c' d', must be described; and we then obtain the point, a', by setting off from the centre, o, to the right of the vertical, m n, a distance equal to the lead of introduction, r t, augmented by the lap. Starting from this point, a', we then divide this circle into as many equal parts as we previously divided the one into, described by the crank pin, and then through each of the points of division we draw perpendiculars to the vertical, m n.

We further draw the straight line, a' g', parallel to m n, when the distance of the several points of division from this line will indicate the successive positions of the valve in relation to those of the piston. Thus, after having drawn the horizontals, r u, through the extreme point, r, of the valve, at the moment when the piston is at the extremity of its stroke, make 1^2—1' equal to b^1 b^2, and the point, 1', indicates how far the valve has descended during the time the piston has traversed the space, o 1, whilst the crank has described the first arc, o 1'. In like manner, set off the distances, c^1 c^2, d^1 d^2, &c., which correspond to the third and fifth divisions, reckoning from the horizontal line, r u, from i^2 to 3', and from h^2 to 5', on the verticals corresponding to the third and fifth positions of the piston, and consequently the positions, 3^2 and 5^2, of the crank. It will then be seen that the valve continues to descend until the moment the centre of the eccentric reaches the point, f', upon the horizontal line, o f', corresponding to the sixth position, and the valve then wholly uncovers the port, a, as shown in fig. 29. During the continued revolution of the eccentric, on passing this point the distances of the points of division from the line, a' g', diminish, and the valve reascends, in such a manner as that, when the centre attains the point, p—that is to say, when the crank shall have performed a semi-revolution, and the piston have arrived at 18, at the other end of its stroke—the valve will occupy the position indicated in fig. 30. This figure shows that it uncovers the lower port, b, for the introduction of the fresh steam, and the upper one, a, for the escape of the used steam. If the respective positions, 6', 7', 8', 9', &c., of the valve, be determined throughout the entire stroke, by setting off upon the verticals, 6, 7, 8, 9, &c., the distances of the points of division of the eccentric from the straight line, a' g', as already explained, a curve will be formed, as at u 3' 6' 9' 18', which is a species of ellipse. This diagram has the advantage of bringing into a single view the relative positions of the crank, piston, eccen-

T

tric, and valve, and facilitates the determination of the position of the valve, corresponding to any position of the piston.

Thus, to obtain the position of the valve to correspond to that, y, of the steam-piston, it is sufficient to draw the vertical, $y\ x'$, which will cut the curve in the point, v'. The distance, $v'\ x'$, of this point, from the horizontal, $t\ u'$, passing through the upper edge of the introduction port, a, shows how much of this is uncovered by the valve. It will be seen, also, that the curve is cut by the horizontal, $t\ u'$, in the point, y', which indicates the moment at which the valve closes the port. In this position the piston will only as yet have reached the point, y^2, of its stroke; and it has, consequently, to traverse the distance, $y^2\ 18$, before it can receive any more steam from the boiler, which shows that, with a valve which has lead and lap, we actually work the steam expansively to a slight extent. In the case before us, the steam is cut off at four-fifths of the stroke.

It will be understood that, if the machine continues its action, the piston will retrace its stroke, the centre of the eccentric which had reached p will continue to ascend, and the valve will shortly attain the position indicated in fig. 31, this taking place as soon as the centre of the eccentric reaches the point, z. In this position, the ports, a, b, are completely open—the first to the exit aperture, the other to the introduction of the steam, whilst the valve is at the highest point of its stroke, as will also be found by continuing the curve, $u\ 9'\ 18'$, of which the prolongation, $18'\ 24'\ 30'$, is exactly symmetrical with regard to the inclined line, $u\ 18'$. On the same diagram, fig. 35, we have delineated a second elliptic curve, $0''\ 9''\ 18''$, equal and parallel to the first, and which indicates the respective positions of the point, s', of the lower flange of the valve, in relation to the port, b, so as to have, at first sight, the respective positions of this second flange. This outline is evidently obtained by setting off the constant distance, $r\ s'$, of the valve, fig. 28, upon the verticals, drawn through 1, 2, 3, 4, &c.

It may be remarked, that the distance between the ports, a and b, is arbitrary. It is, however, advisable to reduce it as much as possible, in order to diminish the surface of the valve, and, consequently, the pressure of the steam acting on the back of it. In all cases, it is necessary that the height of the exit port, c, should be greater than that of the introduction ports, by a quantity at least equal to the difference which exists between the lap and the lead, $t'\ s'$ and $t\ r$.

EXPANSION VALVE.

417. The action of the expansion eccentric, o, is analogous to that of the ordinary valve eccentric, except that the position of its centre is not regulated in the same manner.

We may observe, in the first place, that this eccentric is not immovably fixed upon the main shaft, L, as is the case with the preceding one. It is only attached to the adjustable collar-piece. P^2, figs. 36 and 37, by screws, u^2. This arrangement allows of its throw being increased or diminished; that is, of its centre being placed further from or nearer to that of the shaft, according to the length of stroke which it is wished to give it. To this end, its central opening is oblong in shape, and the holes for the securing screws are oblong likewise.

If the centre of this eccentric happens to be in the same direc-

tion as the crank, the expansion valve, H—the rod, h, of which is guided by the socket-bracket, h^2, attached to the pedestal, s, and drawn more detailed in fig. 43—is wholly open when the piston is at the end of its stroke; but we have supposed, as indicated in fig. 35, that the centre of this eccentric is in the point, a^4, upon the circle described with the centre, o, and radius, $L\ a^4$, of the eccentric, and that the valve does not therefore wholly uncover the entrance port, d, at this moment, so that the time of closing it may be later than would otherwise be the case.

As in the preceding case, we divide this circle into equal parts, starting from the point, a^4; through the point, a^4, draw a vertical line, and then set off on the various verticals, 1, 2, 3, 4, &c., the distances of the points of division from this line, measuring these from the horizontal passing through the upper edge, r'', of the valve, H; we thus obtain a second elliptic curve, $u\ m'\ n'\ p'$, the inside of which is flat—tinted with a slightly stronger shade than the ellipse corresponding to the distribution valve, so as to render the diagram more distinct. This curve cuts the horizontal line drawn through the upper edge of the port, d, in the point, n, which indicates at what time the valve, H, closes the entrance port, fig. 39. It will be seen that this point corresponds to the position, b', of the steam-piston, thereby signifying that the cut-off takes place when the piston has performed no more than a fourth of its stroke. Continuing the movement, it will be observed that the valve, H, rises higher and higher, so that it begins to uncover the entrance port a little before the piston reaches the end of its stroke; but it is evident that the steam cannot find its way into the cylinder at this point, for the distribution valve is in its turn closed, as soon as the position, $y\ y'$, is passed; no inconvenience, therefore, will be caused by the fact of the valve, H, being open before reaching the end of its stroke, as indicated in figs. 38 and 40, and as shown also in the diagram, fig. 35.

By varying the radius of the eccentric, o, and the position of its centre relatively with the radius of the crank, it will be easily understood, that within certain limits we can alter the time when the valve, H, opens and closes the entrance port, and are consequently enabled to vary the degree of expansion.

Figures 41 and 42 show that the rod of the valve is attached to it by a T joint, which leaves the valve sufficiently free for the steam to press it constantly against the planed valve face; and a similar adjustment is adopted with the distribution valve.

The general explanations which we have given in the preceding pages, with reference to the construction and action of this engine, evidently apply to other systems, which merely differ in some of the arrangements and forms of the component pieces. Moreover, in our notes, the student will find the rules and tables concerned in the calculations and designs of these engines.

RULES AND PRACTICAL DATA.

STEAM-ENGINES.

LOW-PRESSURE CONDENSING ENGINE, WITHOUT EXPANSION VALVE.

418. In those engines which are called low-pressure engines, the steam is produced at a temperature very little over that of boiling water, or 100° centigrade (212° Fahrenheit)—it is, in fact,

generally 105° cent.—in which case the tension of the steam will sustain a column of mercury of 90 centimètres in height: that is to say, 14 centimètres above that due to atmospheric pressure. It is, consequently, equal to a pressure of 1·17 atmospheres, or 1·2 kilog. per square centimètre. It is for this pressure that what are generally known as Watt's engines, without cut-off valves, are calculated; and the one we have been examining is regulated upon this datum.

There is, however, a great difference between the pressure of the steam in the boiler, and that to which the effective power of the machine is due. It is evident that a part of the pressure will be absorbed by the back pressure due to an imperfect vacuum, as well as by the friction of the piston, and other moving parts, and the leakage and condensation in the steam passages. So that, taking into consideration these various causes of loss, the effective force may be estimated at ·5 kilog. only, per square centimètre, in the majority of engines, whilst it may reach, perhaps, ·65 kilog. in the most efficient.

The rule for calculating the power of low-pressure steam-engines consists in—

Multiplying the mean effective pressure of the steam upon the piston by the area of the latter, expressed in square centimètres, and the product by the velocity in mètres per second.

The result of this calculation will be the useful effect of the engine in kilogrammètres.

To obtain the horses power, this result must be divided by 75.

Thus, the diameter of the cylinder of a low-pressure non-expansive steam-engine being ·856, and its section 5755 square centimètres, if the effective pressure upon the piston is ·63 kilog. per square centimètre, and the velocity 1·1076—

We have

$$·63 \times 5755 \times 1·1076 = 4015·67 \text{ k. m.}$$

Whence—

$$4015·67 \div 75 = 53·54 \text{ H. P.}$$

But the effective pressure upon the piston is not always ·63 kilog. per square centimètre; it is more frequently below than above this amount. It varies not only according to the power of the machine, but also according to the state of repair. Thus, sometimes the effective pressure will not be more than ·45 kilog. in small engines, whilst in large, powerful ones, it may at times reach ·65 kilog.

Single-acting engines, such as are employed in mines, are of the same dimensions as double-acting ones, but of only half the power. Thus, the cylinder of a low-pressure steam-engine, of 50 horses power, and only single-acting—that is to say, receiving the action of the steam during the descent only of the piston—is exactly the same as in a machine of 100 horses power, in which the steam acts alternately on both sides of the piston.

In the following table, which applies to this kind of steam-engine, we have given the diameters and velocities of the steam-piston from 1 to 200 horses power.

TABLE OF DIAMETERS, AREAS, AND VELOCITIES OF PISTONS, IN LOW-PRESSURE DOUBLE-ACTING STEAM-ENGINES, WITH THE QUANTITIES OF STEAM EXPENDED PER HORSE POWER.

Horses power.	Diameter of piston.	Area of Piston.		Length of stroke.	Number of revolutions.	Velocity of piston per second.	Velocity of piston per minute.	Effective pressure on the piston per square centimetre.	Weight of steam expended per horse power per hour
		Total.	Per horse power.						
	cent.	sq. m.	sq. cent.	m.	per 1′.	m.	m.	kilog.	kilog.
1	·15	·018	·181	·52	50	·85	51	·49	38·81
2	·21	·036	·178	·61	42	·86	52	·49	38·77
4	·30	·068	·171	·76	34	·90	54	·49	38·77
6	·35	·098	·163	·91	31	·94	57	·49	38·72
8	·40	·128	·160	1·07	27	·96	58	·49	38·72
10	·45	·159	·159	1·22	24	·98	59	·49	38·64
12	·49	·189	·157	1·22	24	·98	59	·49	38·64
16	·55	·240	·150	1·37	22	1·01	60	·50	37·80
20	·61	·292	·146	1·52	20	1·02	61	·51	37·38
24	·66	·346	·144	1·69	18	1·02	61	·52	36·88
30	·73	·414	·137	1·83	17	1·04	62	·53	36·04
40	·83	·535	·134	1·99	16	1·06	64	·53	35·70
50	·91	·658	·132	2·13	15	1·07	64	·54	35·32
60	1·00	·779	·130	2·28	14	1·07	64	·54	34·94
70	1·07	·903	·129	2·44	13	1·06	63	·55	34·36
80	1·14	1·032	·129	2·44	13	1·06	63	·56	34·31
90	1·21	1·138	·126	2·59	12	1·04	62	·57	33·01
100	1·27	1·264	·126	2·59	12	1·04	62	·58	32·97
120	1·39	1·512	·126	2·74	11	1·00	60	·59	31·92
160	1·60	2·005	·125	3·00	10	1·00	60	·60	31·67
200	1·78	2·480	·124	3·00	10	1·00	60	·61	31·47

DIAMETER OF THE PISTON.

By means of the above table, we can, in a very simple manner, determine the diameter and velocity of the piston of a low-pressure double-acting steam-engine, supposing the steam to be of the pressure of 1·17 atmospheres in the boiler, corresponding to a column of mercury of 90 centimètres in height.

Rule.—It is sufficient to obtain from the table the area of piston per horse power, and to multiply it by the number of horses power of the engine to be constructed, which will then determine the corresponding area of piston.

Example.—What should be the diameter of the piston of a low-pressure double-acting steam-engine of 25 horses power?

In the fourth column of our table, it will be seen that the area to be given to the piston should be 144 square centimètres per horse power for 24 to 26 horses, with a velocity of 1·02 m. per second.

We have, therefore, 144 × 25 = 3600 sq. cent. for the total area of the piston.

Whence—

$$\sqrt{3600} \times \cdot 7854 = 67\cdot7 \text{ cent.}$$

Thus, the diameter of the piston must be ·677 m.

VELOCITIES.

The velocities per second, and per minute, given in the seventh and eighth columns of the table, are what are generally adopted as the regular working rates in establishments and manufactories where steam-engines are employed, whatever may be the number of revolutions of the crank, or strokes of the piston, per minute, for this number varies according to the length of stroke which it is wished to give to the piston. Thus in stationary engines, the stroke of the piston is generally longer; and, therefore, fewer strokes are made per minute than in marine engines, since in these latter the engineer seeks, as much as possible, to reduce the height of the machinery; and the stroke is, consequently, much shorter for the same amount of power.

The length of stroke of the piston is regulated at pleasure by the constructor, according to what he may find most advantageous in the transmission of the power to the machinery; and he calculates so that the crank may make a few revolutions per minute more or less, without occasioning any very sensible difference in the velocity of the piston, with regard to the velocities laid down in the table.

If, notwithstanding, it is wished to construct an engine to work with a velocity somewhat less, or somewhat greater, than that given in the table, it will evidently be necessary to take this difference into consideration, and to augment or diminish the area of the piston in proportion, so as always to obtain the required power. The proper amount of alteration may be determined by a very simple operation.

Example.—Let it be proposed to construct our example engine of the effective power of 25 horses, with a velocity of piston of 1 mètre per second, in place of 1·02 m.

It will be sufficient to calculate the following inverse proportion:—

$$1 : 1\cdot02 :: 144 \text{ sq. c.} : x.$$

Whence—

$$x = 144 \times 1\cdot02 = 146\cdot8 \text{ sq. c.,}$$

the area, per horse power, to be given to the piston.

Consequently,

146·8 × 25 = 3675 sq. centimètres for the total area;

and

$$\sqrt{3675} \div \cdot 7854 = 68\cdot4 \text{ cent., for the diameter of the piston.}$$

As complemental to this table, we have given the expenditure of steam corresponding to the different powers, as well as the deductions from this of the expenditure per horse power per hour. It will be observed from the last column, which gives the expenditure of steam, that it is considerably more for engines of small force than for more powerful ones—the reason of which is self-evident. Thus, for an engine of 12 horses power, the expenditure of steam is 38·64 kilog. per horse power per hour; whilst for an engine of 100 horses power, the expenditure only reaches 32·97 for a like power in the same time.

The expenditures or weights of the steam have been calculated from the following formula:—

$$W = A \times S \times w \times 2 N \times 60.$$

A representing the area per horse power;

S, the stroke of the piston;

w, the weight of a cubic mètre of steam at the pressure employed;

N, the number of revolutions.

We need not here take into consideration the loss of steam resulting from leakage and condensation in the steam pipes and passages, which is generally estimated at one-tenth of the whole expenditure, as this item should evidently enter into the calculations respecting the boiler.

STEAM-PIPES AND PASSAGES.

The section of the pipe which conveys the steam to the cylinder, as well as that of the introduction ports and passages, should be equal to a twentieth of the area of the piston.

Whence it follows, that the diameter of the steam-pipe should be one-fifth of that of the cylinder.

We must, however, remark, that the greater the velocity of the engine, the greater should be the sectional area of the steam-pipes and passages. It is because of this that, in locomotive engines, this section is sometimes made a tenth or a ninth of that of the cylinder, and at the same time the pressure of the steam is much greater, being generally equal to 5 or 6 atmospheres, and sometimes more, in such engines.

AIR-PUMP AND CONDENSER.

The stroke of the air-pump piston is equal to half that of the steam-piston; and as it gives the same number of strokes, but does not discharge in ascending, it can only raise a quantity of air and water equal to its own cubic contents, at each double stroke.

Now, the sectional area of the pump is ·2827 sq. m.; and the length of stroke, ·923 m. Its capacity is, therefore, ·261 cubic mètres; and as twice the cubic contents of the steam-cylinder is 2·125 cubic m., it follows that the pump discharges only a little more than an eighth of the volume sent out by the steam cylinder. This capacity is quite sufficient for the effective action of the engine.

The sectional area of the condenser is the same as that of the pump, and its length is about 1 mètre; so that its capacity is, at least, as great.

As the quantity of water to be injected into the condenser varies according to the temperature of the injection water, it will be well to know how to regulate it.

To this end, the following rule will answer:—

RULE.—*Take the excess of the temperature of the steam over that of the injected water, and, after adding 550 to it, multiply it by the weight of steam to be condensed, and divide the product by the difference of temperature between the discharged and the injected water. The quotient will be the weight of cold water to be injected.*

Thus, let w represent the weight of the steam to be condensed; t, its temperature; W, the weight of the cold water to be injected into the condenser; t', its temperature; and T, that of the water discharged:—

We have

$$W = \frac{w\,(550 + t - T)}{T - t'}.$$

If we make $w = 26\cdot16$, $t' = 12°$ cent., $T = 38°$, and $t = 105°$, we shall have

$$W = \frac{26\cdot16\,(550 + 105° - 38°)}{38° - 12°}.$$

Whence, W = 621 kilog. or litres, for the expenditure per minute of cold water in the condenser.

That is to say, the quantity of water to be injected into the condenser should, in this case, be about 24 times the weight of the steam expended.

If the discharged water were of the temperature of 55°, the cold water remaining at 12°—

We should then have

$$W = \frac{26\cdot16\,(550 + 105° - 55°)}{55° - 12°}.$$

Whence—

W = 365 kilog. or litres.

That is to say, that in the last case the water injected would not be more than 14 times the steam expended.

But it is to be remarked, that in this case the force of the steam in the condenser, at a temperature of 55°, is equal to a column of mercury of 12·75 centimètres in height; whilst, in the first case, it would only be equal to a column of 5·5 cent. There is, therefore, an advantage in employing sufficient injection-water to produce the lower of the two temperatures.

From the preceding results, we may deduce what follows:—

First, That the stroke of the air-pump piston, in low-pressure double-acting steam-engines, is ordinarily equal to half the stroke of the steam-piston.

Second, That the diameter of the air-pump piston is equal to about two thirds of the diameter of the steam piston; and, consequently, its area is about half that of the latter.

Third, That the effective displacement of the air-pump piston—that is, the cubic contents of the cylinder generated by the disc of the piston—is equal to an eighth, or at least a ninth, of the contents of the cylinder generated by a double stroke of the steam-piston.

Fourth, That the capacity of the condenser is at least equal to that of the air-pump.

Fifth, That the sectional area of the passage communicating between the condenser and air-pump is equal to one-fourth the area of its piston.

Sixth, That the quantity of cold water to be injected into the condenser varies according to its temperature, and to the temperature of the water discharged.

Seventh, That this quantity is equal to 24 times the weight of steam expended by the cylinder, where the mean temperature of the cold water is 12°, and that of the water of condensation 38", which are generally what exist in low-pressure double-acting engines.

COLD-WATER AND FEED PUMPS.

The capacity of the cold-water pump should be the 24th or 18th of that of the steam cylinder. The capacity of the feed or hot-water pump should be the 230th or 240th, at least, of that of the steam cylinder.

HIGH-PRESSURE EXPANSIVE ENGINES.

Let the following dimensions be given for an engine analogous to that which we have just described:—

Diameter of the cylinder,.................. = ·275 m.
Stroke of the piston,..................... = ·680 m.
Area of the piston,........................ = ·0594 square m.
Number of double strokes per minute,...... = ·40

Let us suppose, in the first place, that when the steam reaches the cylinder, its pressure is equal to 5 atmospheres, and that it is cut off during three-fourths of the stroke; that is to say, that the cylinder only receives the steam during the first quarter of the stroke.

This pressure of 5 atmospheres is equal to $5 \times 1\cdot033 = 5\cdot165$ kilog. per square centimètre. Consequently, the total pressure exerted upon the surface of the piston is—

$$5\cdot165 \times 594 \text{ sq. cent.} = 3068 \text{ kilog.}$$

And as with this pressure the piston passes through a space equal to one-fourth of its stroke, or

$$·680 \div 4 = ·170 \text{ m.,}$$

it is capable, theoretically speaking, of transmitting an amount of force expressed by

$$3068 \times ·17 = 521\cdot56 \text{ kilogrammètres.}$$

Next, dividing the length, ·51 m., or the remaining three-fourths of the stroke, into an even number of equal parts—as four, for example—each of these parts will be equal to

$$\frac{51}{4} = ·1275 \text{ m.}$$

Now we know that, according to Mariotte's law, the successive volumes of a given quantity of any gas are in the inverse ratio of their tension or pressure, provided the gas is in the same condition throughout. This principle may be regarded as quite true in steam-engines, because the expansion is never carried very far, and as the steam passes through the cylinder with great rapidity, and is continually being renewed, after a certain time and when the cylinder has become warm, its temperature is very little below that of the steam itself, and the latter suffers no appreciable change in passing through it. Putting P for the pressure, 3068 kilog., as found for the first quarter of the stroke, we may state the relations of the volumes and pressures in the following manner; that is, at the points, 1, 2, 3, 4, 5, of the stroke, or for the successive spaces, ·170 m., ·295 m., ·425 m., ·5525 m., ·680 m.

The corresponding pressures will be—

$$\frac{P}{3068\,k}, \quad \frac{\cdot1700}{\cdot2975}P, \quad \frac{\cdot170}{\cdot425}P, \quad \frac{\cdot1700}{\cdot5525}P, \quad \frac{\cdot170}{\cdot680}P\;;$$

or finally,

$$3068\,k, \quad 1764\,k, \quad 1227\,k, \quad 944\,k, \quad 767\,k.$$

Next, according to Simpson's method, we have

The sum of the extreme pressures,.................... =   3068 + 767 = 3835
Twice the pressures at the odd intervals,.............. =   2 × 1227 = 2454
Four times the pressures of the even intervals,......... = 4 (1764 + 944)= 10832
                                                                          ——
                                         Total,....................... 17121

Taking the third of this quantity, and multiplying it by ·1275, we shall have the work given out during the cut-off. Thus—

$$\frac{17121 \times \cdot1275}{3} = 727\cdot64 \text{ k. m.}$$

Adding to this 521·56 k. m., the work given out before the cut-off, we shall have the total of the work given out by the steam during the entire stroke of the piston—

$$= 1249\cdot2 \text{ k. m.}$$

Deducting now from this the effect of the atmospheric pressure, which resists the motion of the piston throughout the stroke, and which is equal to

$$1\cdot033 \text{ k.} \times 594 \text{ sq. c.} \times \cdot68 \text{ m.} = 417\cdot25 \text{ k. m.,}$$

there remains for the effective force of the piston—

$$1249\cdot2 — 417\cdot25 = 832 \text{ k. m.,}$$

nearly, for each stroke; and as the piston gives 40 double or 80 single strokes per minute, the effective force per minute becomes $832 \times 80 = 56560$ k. m.; that is, 56560 kilogrammes, raised one mètre high.

The effective power of this, as well as of most other expansive steam-engines, will be obtained in a much more simple and less tedious manner, by taking advantage of the following table :—

TABLE OF THE FORCE, IN KILOGRAMMETRES, GIVEN OUT WITH VARIOUS DEGREES OF EXPANSION BY A CUBIC METRE OF STEAM AT VARIOUS PRESSURES.

Volume when expanded.	Force given out, corresponding with the pressure of							
	1 atmosph.	1½ atmosph.	2 atmosph.	2½ atmosph.	3 atmosph.	4 atmosph.	5 atmosph.	6 atmosph.
cubic mètres.	k. m.	k. m.	k. m.	k. m.	k. m.	k. m.	k. m.	k. m.
1·00	10333	15500	20666	25833	31000	41333	51666	62000
1·25	12639	18958	25278	31597	37917	50556	63195	75834
1·50	14523	21784	29046	36257	43568	58092	72615	87138
1·75	16116	24174	32232	40290	48348	64464	80580	86696
2·00	17496	26244	34992	43740	52488	69984	87480	104976
2·25	18713	28069	37426	46782	56139	74852	93565	112278
2·50	19802	29703	39604	49505	59406	79208	99010	118812
2·75	20787	31180	41574	51967	62361	83148	103935	124722
3·00	21686	32529	43372	54215	65058	86744	108430	130116
3·25	22513	33769	45026	56282	67539	90052	112565	135078
3·50	23279	34918	46558	58197	69837	93116	116395	139674
3·75	23992	35988	47984	59980	71976	95968	119960	143952
4·00	24658	36987	49316	61645	73974	98632	123290	147948
4·25	25285	37927	50570	63212	75855	101140	126425	151710
4·50	25875	38812	51750	64687	77625	103500	129375	155250
4·75	26434	39651	52868	66085	79302	105736	132170	158604
5·00	26964	40446	53928	67410	80892	107856	134820	161784
5·25	27467	41200	54934	68667	82401	109868	137335	164802
5·50	27949	41923	55898	69872	83847	111796	139745	167694
5·75	28408	42612	56816	71020	85224	113632	142040	170448
6·00	28848	43272	57696	72120	86544	115392	144240	173088
6·25	29270	43905	58540	73175	87810	117080	146350	175620
6·50	29675	44512	59350	74187	89025	118700	148375	178050
6·75	30065	45097	60130	75162	90195	120260	150325	180390
7·00	30441	45661	60882	76102	91323	121764	152205	182646
7·25	30804	46206	61608	77010	92412	123216	154020	183224
7·50	31154	46731	62308	77885	93462	124616	155770	186924
7·75	31494	47239	62986	78732	94479	125972	157465	188958
8·00	31820	47730	63640	79550	95460	127280	159100	190920
8·25	32139	48208	64278	80347	96417	128556	160695	192835
8·50	32447	48670	64894	81117	97341	129788	162235	194682
8·75	32747	49120	65494	81867	98241	130988	163735	196482
9·00	33038	49557	66076	82595	99114	132152	165190	198228
9·25	33321	49981	66642	83302	99963	133284	166605	199926
9·50	33597	50395	67194	83992	100791	134388	167985	201582
9·75	33865	50797	67730	84662	101595	135460	169325	203190
10·00	34127	51190	68254	85317	102381	136508	170635	204762

According to this table, if we have to calculate the force acting upon the piston in this engine, in the same circumstances, we must, in the first place, ascertain the original volume of the steam introduced into the cylinder during the first quarter of the stroke of the piston. This volume is equal to

$$·0594 × ·17 = ·010098 \text{ cubic mètres.}$$

Now it will be seen from the table, that the force given out when a cubic mètre of steam, of a pressure of 5 atmospheres, expands to four times its original volume, is equal to

$$123290 \text{ k. m.}$$

Consequently, that corresponding to a volume of ·010098 cubic mètres will be—

$$123290 × ·010098 = 1245 \text{ k. m.,}$$

And deducting from this the atmospheric pressure, which resists the motion of the piston, we have

$$1245 — 417 = 828 \text{ k. m.,}$$

a quantity which differs very little from that obtained by the more tedious calculation. Thus, the calculation for determining the effective power of a steam-engine, of which we know the diameter and stroke of the piston, the pressure of the steam, and the amount of cut-off, reduces itself to the following rule:—

RULE.—*Multiply the area of the piston by the portion of the length of the stroke, during which the steam acts with full pressure, and you will determine the volume of steam expended. Multiply this volume by the amount of kilogrammètres in the table, corresponding to the pressure of the steam and to the final volume, and then deduct from the product the amount, in kilogrammètres, of the atmospheric pressure opposed to the piston during the entire stroke,* and the result will be the theoretic amount of force, in kilogrammètres, given out by the steam during a single stroke of the piston.

A MEDIUM-PRESSURE CONDENSING AND EXPANSIVE STEAM-ENGINE.

Let the following data be assumed:—

The diameter of the steam-cylinder = ·330 m.
The stroke of the piston .... = ·650 m.
The diameter of the air-pump...... = ·180 m.
The stroke of its piston .... = ·325 m.
The diameter of the feed-pump.... = ·035 m.
The stroke of its plunger .... = ·235 m.

It follows, from these dimensions, that we shall have—

The area of the steam-piston ...... = 855·30 sq. cent.
The area of the air-pump piston ... = 254·47 "
The area of the feed-pump .... = 9.62 "

And for the displacement, or volumes of the cylinders generated by the pistons—

That of the steam cylinder .... = 55·594 cubic décim.
That of the air-pump .... = 8·270 "
That of the feed-pump .... = ·226 "

We shall suppose that, when the engine is in regular working condition, the pressure of the steam is $3\frac{1}{2}$ atmospheres; and we must ascertain what is the actual force given out, supposing the steam to be cut off during three-fourths of the stroke of the piston.

That is to say, that the steam is admitted into the cylinder only during a quarter of the stroke, which corresponds to ·1625 m.

Since the sectional area of the cylinder is ·0885 m., the volume of steam expended during a fourth of the stroke will be equal to

$$·0885 × ·1625 = ·0139 \text{ cubic mètres; or,}$$
$$13·9 \text{ cubic decimètres.}$$

Now, according to the table of the amounts of force given out by the steam at various pressures, it will be found that the force due to a cubic mètre of steam, of an initial pressure of $3\frac{1}{2}$ atmospheres, when allowed to expand to four times its volume, is equal to 86303 kilogrammètres. As the table does not give the actual amount for $3\frac{1}{2}$ atmospheres, it may be taken by adding together that for $2\frac{1}{2}$ and 1 atmospheres. Thus—

$$61645 + 24658 = 86303 \text{ k. m.}$$

We have, therefore, in the present case—

$$·0139 × 86303 = 1199·6 \text{ k. m.,}$$

as the force due to a single stroke of the piston.

From this quantity, however, we must deduct the back pressure due to the imperfect vacuum in the condenser. This back pressure is, in the generality of cases, equal to about ·27 kilog. per square centimètre, when the temperature of the water of condensation is about 65° cent.

Allowing this to be the case in the present example, we shall have to deduct from the preceding result the action of this back pressure upon the whole surface of the piston, and during the entire stroke. This is

$$·27 × ·0885 × ·65 × 150·1 \text{ k. m.,}$$

We have, consequently,

$$1199·6 — 150·1 = 1049·5 \text{ k. m.,}$$

for the actual force given out by the piston during a single stroke; and if this engine works at the rate of 42 revolutions per minute, which supposes the velocity of the piston to be ·9 m. per second, we shall find that the mechanical effect per minute will be equal to

$$1049·5 × 84 = 981588 \text{ k. m; or,}$$
$$881598 ÷ 4500 = 19·59 \text{ horses power.}$$

It is well known, however, that this amount is far from being all transmitted by the first-motion shaft, for a portion is absorbed in overcoming the friction of the various moving parts of the engine, and there are also other causes of loss.

If we reckon that the force which is really utilised is not more than four-tenths of that theoretically due to the steam, in which case we must suppose that six-tenths are completely lost, we shall have for the effective force transmitted to the first-motion shaft—

$$19·59 × ·4 = 7·84 \text{ horses power;}$$

or almost 8 horses power, of 75 kilogrammètres each.

If it is desired to know the quantity of fuel consumed per hour in producing this mechanical effect, we may remark, that a cubic mètre of steam, at a pressure equal to $3\frac{1}{2}$ atmospheres, weighs 1·8518 kilog.; and at a pressure of 4 atmospheres, it weighs 2·0291 kilog.

Now, although we have supposed the pressure in the cylinder to be $3\frac{1}{2}$ atmospheres, we, nevertheless, allow that it will be considerably more in the boiler, to compensate for the leakage in the valve-casing, passages, and valves.

Taking 4 atmospheres as the pressure in the boiler, it will be found that the weight of steam expended for each single stroke of the piston is—

·0139 × 2·091 = ·0291 kilog.;

and per hour—

·0291 × 84 × 60 = 146·204 kilog.

From which it follows, upon the hypothesis that one kilog. of coal generates 6 kilog. of steam, that the quantity of fuel consumed will be

146·64 ÷ 6 = 24·44 kilog. per hour.

And since the power obtained is 7·84 horses power—
We have

24·44 ÷ 7·84 = 3·1 kilog.

for the quantity of coal consumed, per horse power, per hour.

To complete the rules here given, we add the two following tables, relating to the principal dimensions given to steam-engines of different kinds :—

TABLE OF PROPORTIONS OF DOUBLE-ACTING STEAM-ENGINES, CONDENSING AND NONCONDENSING, AND WITH OR WITHOUT CUT OFF, THE STEAM BEING TAKEN AT A PRESSURE OF 4 ATMOSPHERES IN THE CONDENSING, AND AT 5 ATMOSPHERES IN THE OTHER ENGINES.

Horses power.	Stroke of piston.	Velocity of piston per second.	Number of revolutions per minute.	Condensing engines, cutting off at one-fourth of the stroke.			Noncondensing expansive engines, cutting off at one-fourth.		Noncondensing nonexpansive engines.	
				Diameter of the piston.	Area of piston per horse power.	Weight of steam per horse power per hour.	Diameter of the piston.	Area of piston per horse power.	Diameter of piston.	Weight of steam per horse power per hour.
	cent.	cent.		cent.	sq. cent.	kil·g.	cent.	sq. cent.	cent.	kilog.
1	40	70	52·5	16	189	24·90	14	148	10	50·76
2	50	75	45·9	20	160	22·62	19	135	14	49·56
4	60	80	40·0	27	148	22·38	25	124	18	46·98
6	70	85	36·4	32	138	22·08	31	123	21	45·30
8	80	90	33·7	36	127	21·54	33	106	23	42·00
10	90	95	31·7	39	119	21·36	36	100	25	41·34
12	100	100	30·0	42	112	21·18	38	92	26	40·86
16	110	105	28·6	46	104	20·58	42	87	29	39·96
20	120	110	27·5	49	94	20·28	45	81	31	38·82
25	130	115	26·5	54	92	19·80	49	76	34	38·52
30	140	120	25·7	57	86	19·32	52	72	36	37·56
35	150	125	25·0	59	77	18·54	55	68	38	37·38
40	160	130	24·3	62	75	18·06	57	64	39	36·60
50	170	135	23·8	67	70	17·28	62	60	43	36·18
60	180	140	23·3	72	68	17·22	66	58	46	35·76
75	190	145	22·9	78	67	17·16	72	54	50	35·04
100	200	150	22·5	85	57	16·62	84	56	56	34·08

TABLE OF PROPORTIONS OF MEDIUM PRESSURE CONDENSING AND EXPANSIVE STEAM-ENGINES, WITH TWO CYLINDERS ON WOOLF'S SYSTEM; PRESSURE, 4 ATMOSPHERES.

Horse power.	Diameter of cylinders in centimètres.		Area of pistons in square centimètres.				Stroke of pistons in metres.		Revolutions per minute.
	d.	D	Total.		Per horse power.		s.	S.	
			a.	A.	a.	A.			
4	16	27	201	572	50	143	·67	·90	30·0
6	19	35	283	962	47	160	·67	·90	30·0
8	21	38	346	1134	43	141	·75	1·00	30·0
10	23	42	415	1385	41	138	·75	1·00	30·0
12	25	46	491	1662	40	138	·82	1·10	27·3
16	28	52	616	2124	38	133	·90	1·20	27·5
20	30	54	707	2290	35	114	·97	1·30	25·4
24	32	59	804	2734	33	113	·97	1·30	25·4
30	34	63	908	3117	30	103	1·20	1·60	21·6
36	37	67	1075	3526	29	98	1·20	1·60	21·6
40	37	67	1075	3526	26	88	1·27	1·70	22·1
45	39	71	1194	3959	26	87	1·27	1·70	22·1
50	41	75	1320	4418	26	88	1·35	1·80	20·8
60	45	82	1590	5281	26	88	1·35	1·80	20·8
70	48	87	1809	5945	25	84	1·50	2·00	19·5
80	51	93	2043	6793	25	84	1·50	2·00	19·5
90	54	99	2290	7698	25	85	1·57	2·10	18·6
100	57	104	2552	8495	25	85	1·57	2·10	18·6
110	60	109	2827	9331	25	84	1·57	2·10	18·6
120	62	114	3019	10207	25	85	1·57	2·10	18·6
130	65	118	3318	10936	25	84	1·57	2·10	18·6

CONICAL PENDULUM, OR CENTRIFUGAL GOVERNOR.

The centrifugal ball-governor is compared, in physics, to a simple pendulum, the length of which is equal to the distance of the point of suspension from the horizontal plane passing through the centres of the balls; and the duration of an entire revolution of the ball-governor is equal to that of a complete oscillation of the pendulum.

The formula for determining the vertical height or the distance of the point of suspension above the plane of the balls is, consequently, the same as that employed to find the width of a pendulum, of which we know the number of oscillations. It may be reduced to the following rule:—

RULE.—*Divide the constant number, 89,478, by the square of the number of revolutions per minute.* The quotient will give the height in centimètres.

Example.—What is the vertical height or distance of the point of attachment, from the horizontal plane passing through the centres of the balls of a governor, revolving at the rate of 40 turns per minute?

We have $40^2 = 1600$,

and $89478 \div 1600 = 56$ centimètres,

for the height sought.

With this rule, it will be easy for us to calculate the heights of conical pendulums, from the velocity of 25 revolutions per minute, to that of 67; and within these will be found the rates of combinations more generally met with in practice. We have given them in the following table, adding a column, which gives the difference in height for each revolution. And as the angle which the arms of the governor make with the spindle is generally one of 30°, when the balls are in a state of repose, or are going at their minimum velocity, we have given, in the fifth column of the table, the lengths of these arms, from their point of suspension to the centres of the balls, assuming the angle of 30°, and making them to correspond with the number of revolutions given in the first column.

In calculating the lengths of the arms, we have employed the following practical rule:—

RULE.—*Divide the constant number, 103,320, by the square of the number of revolutions per minute, and the quotient will be the length in centimètres.*

Example.—Assuming the angle to be 30°, what should be the length of the arms of a conical pendulum, making 37 revolutions per minute?

We have $37^2 = 1369$.

Then— $\dfrac{10\cdot3320}{1369} = 75\cdot46$ centimètres,

for the length of the arms of the pendulum, or the diameter of the circle described by the balls.

It is evident, that if, on the other hand, the length of the arms, with this angle of 30°, is known, the number of revolutions which the balls make in a minute, will be found *by dividing the number,* 103,320, *by the length of the arms expressed in centimètres, and then extracting the square root of the quotient.*

The weight of the balls, according to the resistance they have to encounter, is as important to determine as the length of the suspending-arms, in order that the governing action of the pendulum may be sufficiently powerful and quick. It often happens, in badly designed engines, that the governor produces no effect, because the length of the suspending-arms is not proportionate to the velocity, or because the weight of the balls is not proportionate to the resistance to be overcome.

We have considered that it would be a great convenience to engineers and artisans to possess a table, showing at sight the velocities and corresponding lengths, for the conical pendulums, or ball-governors, generally employed in steam-engines, so as to enable them to determine with certainty the exact proportions to be given them, in relation to their spindles and driving-gear. When these points are determined, the weights of the balls may be easily adjusted.

TABLE RELATIVE TO THE DIMENSIONS OF THE ARMS AND TO THE VELOCITIES OF THE BALLS OF THE CONICAL PENDULUM OR CENTRIFUGAL GOVERNOR.

Number of Revolutions per Minute.	Square of the Velocities.	Length of Pendulum in Centimetres.	Difference of Length for one Revolution.	Length of Arms with an Angle of 30°.
		Cent.	Mill.	Cent.
25	625	143·1	108	16
26	676	132·4	96	153
27	729	122·7	86	142
28	784	114·1	77	132
29	841	106·4	70	123
30	900	99·4	63	115
31	961	93·1	57	107
32	1024	87·3	52	101
33	1089·	82·1	48	95
34	1156	77·4	44	89
35	1225	73·0	40	84
36	1296	69·0	37	80
37	1369	65·3	34	75
38	1444	61·9	31	71
39	1521	58·8	29	68
40	1600	55·9	27	64
41	1681	53·2	25	61
42	1764	50·7	23	58
43	1849	48·4	22	56
44	1936	46·2	20	53
45	2025	44·2	19	51
46	2116	42·3	18	49
47	2209	40·5	17	47
48	2304	38·8	16	45
49	2401	37·3	15	43
50	2500	35·8	14	41
51	2601	34·4	13	40
52	2704	33·1	12	38
53	2809	31·8	12	37
54	2916	30·7	11	33
55	3025	29·6	10	34
56	3136	28·5	10	35
57	3249	27·5	9	32
58	3364	26·6	9	31
59	3481	25·7	8	30
60	3600	24·8	8	29
61	3721	24·8	8	28
62	3844	23·3	7	27
63	3969	22·5	7	26
64	4096	21·9	7	25
65	4225	21·2	6	24
66	4356	20·5	6	24
67	4489	19·9	6	23
68	4624	19·3		23

NOTE.—With an angle of 30°, the centrifugal force is the same for all lengths of pendulum.

This table may also be consulted in the case of single-armed pendulums, which are occasionally employed, instead of centrifugal governors.

CHAPTER XI.

OBLIQUE PROJECTIONS.

APPLICATION OF RULES TO THE DELINEATION OF AN OSCILLATING STEAM CYLINDER.

PLATE XLI.

419. In geometrical drawing, the planes of projection on which the objects are represented, are chosen, when possible, so as to be parallel to the faces of such objects; from which it follows, that these are expressed in their exact shapes and dimensions. It is often, however, that the position of certain parts of the machine or apparatus to be drawn, are inclined in regard to the other parts, so that all the surfaces cannot be parallel to the geometrical planes. The projections of the inclined parts are oblique, and, consequently, are seen as foreshortened.

The general method employed in projections is evidently applicable to the delineation of oblique projections. It is, however, necessary first to represent the objects as if parallel to the plane of the drawing, so as to obtain the exact proportions and dimensions, such views being auxiliary to the production of the oblique representations.

420. Thus it is proposed to represent a hexagonally-based prism or a six-sided nut, the edges of which are inclined to both the horizontal and vertical plane.

We first of all represent this nut, in fig. 1, as placed with its base parallel to an auxiliary horizontal plane, represented by the line, L T, fig. 3. This gives the regular hexagon, $a\ b\ c\ d\ e\ f$.

If we were to make the vertical projection of this prism on a vertical plane, parallel to one of the faces, or to $a\ d$, we should, in this second auxiliary plane, have the projection of the edges, $a\ b\ c\ d$.

The straight line, L' T', fig. 3, indicates the line of intersection of these two auxiliary planes, when placed in their actual position with regard to the nut; and it is, therefore, the base line of the two projections. This line forms, we shall suppose, the angle, L o L', with the base line of the actual drawing in hand, which angle, likewise, expresses the amount of inclination of the top and bottom of the prism, with the actual horizontal plane; whilst the angle, $y'\ o\ o'$, formed by the perpendiculars, drawn to each of the lines through the point, o, expresses the amount of inclination of the edges and axis of the prism with regard to the vertical plane. After this, it is merely necessary, in order to obtain the points, a', b', c', d', to set off to the right and left of the point, o, on the line, L' T', the distances, $a\ o$ or $d\ o$, and $b\ g$ or $c\ g$, derived from fig. 1. Drawing perpendiculars to the line, L' T', through each of the points, a', b', c', d', and limiting them by the lines, $a^2\ d^2$ and $a^3\ d^3$, fig. 2, parallel to the former, we obtain the entire vertical projection of the prism, as upon the auxiliary plane, parallel to one of the faces, as $c\ b$. When one of the bases of the nut is rounded, or terminated by a spherical portion, which is generally the case, as already seen (186), its contour is limited by circular arcs, expressing the intersection of each face with the sphere.

We can then, by means of the two projections, figs. 1 and 2, obtain the oblique projection, fig. 4, upon the vertical plane, L T; fig. 1 giving the widths, the distances of each of the points from the axial line, $a\ d$, which passes through the centre, o, and fig. 2, defining the vertical heights or distances of the various points above the horizontal plane.

To this end, through any of the points, as c, for example, expressing the horizontal projection of the edge, $c^2\ c^3$, erect a vertical line, and through the corresponding points, $c^2\ c^3$, fig. 2, draw a couple of horizontal lines, cutting the vertical in c'' and c'''. The same operation is performed with regard to the points, b, a, d, &c., which are projected in b''', a''', d'', d''', fig. 4. The whole matter consists, therefore, in drawing vertical lines through each of the points in fig. 1, and horizontal lines through the corresponding points in fig. 2. The intersections of these lines give the projections of the extremities of each of the edges in the oblique view, fig. 4.

If it is wished to obtain the projections of the circular outlines with minute exactness, it will be necessary to determine, at least, three points in each arc; and as we have the extremities already, we only require now to find the middle of each. It is the same for the circle representing the central opening of the nut. Its oblique projection is necessarily an ellipse, the proportions of which are obtained by the projection of the two diameters perpendicular to one another, one of which, $m\ n$, is parallel to the vertical plane, and does not alter in magnitude; consequently, giving the transverse axis of the ellipse, whilst the other is inclined and foreshortened, and gives the conjugate axis.

421. In general, the oblique projection of any circle is always an ellipse, the transverse axis of which is equal to the actual diameter of the circle, whilst the conjugate axis is variable, according to the inclination or angle which the plane of the circle makes with one of the planes of projection. The application of this principle will be seen in figs. 5, 6, and 7. The two first of these figures represent the horizontal and vertical projections made upon the auxiliary planes of a portion of the cylindrical rod, A, of the piston, B, working in the oscillating steam-cylinder, C; and the last, fig. 7, is the oblique projection of this part of the piston-rod upon the vertical plane, corresponding to that of the drawing.

It will be remarked, that the upper part of the fragment of the rod being limited by a plane, $k\ l$, perpendicular to its axis, is projected as an ellipse, the transverse axis, $p\ q$, of which is equal to $k\ l$, whilst its conjugate axis, $l'\ k'$, is equal to the projection of this line, $k\ l$, on fig. 7. The cylindrical fillets, $r\ s,\ t\ u$, &c., of this rod, are projected obliquely, as similar ellipses, of which portions only are apparent. For the torus, or ring, which is comprised between these two fillets, the oblique projection is a curve, which results from the intersection of an elliptical cylinder, the generatrices of which are horizontal, and tangent to the external surface of the torus. If, therefore, we wish to determine this curve with great precision, we must use the very same method adopted in determining the shadow proper of the external surface of the torus (323). In practice, however, when the drawing is on but a small scale, we may content ourselves with determining the principal points in the curve, by projecting first the point, v, situated upon the middle of tne diameter, $y\,y'$, of the torus, and drawing through it the line, $v^1\,v^2$, equal to the diameter; and, secondly, drawing the horizontal lines touching the external contour of the torus in the points, z, z', fig. 6, over to z^2, z^3, upon the axial line, $l'\,o'$, fig. 7; then draw an ellipse with these two lines, $v^1\,v^2$ and $z^2\,z^3$, for the transverse and conjugate axes respectively. The key, D, which passes through the rod, A, being rectangular in section, is projected in fig. 7, by a couple of rectangles, as indicated by the dotted projection lines.

422. Proceeding upon these principles, we can make oblique projections, in a very simple manner, of various objects, more or less complicated in form, when we have already the projections of these objects upon auxiliary planes, making any known angle with the actual plane of the drawing. Thus, figs. 10 and 13 are the oblique projections of an oscillating steam-cylinder, the first representing the cylinder in external elevation, whilst the second is a section made through the axis of the cylinder.

It is easy to see that these projections have been obtained in the same manner as those already given in figs. 4 and 7; that is to say, the external projection, fig. 10, is derived from the two right projections, figs. 8 and 9—one made upon an auxiliary vertical plane, parallel to the axis of the piston-rod, and perpendicular to the axial lines of the trunnions, and the other upon a horizontal plane, parallel to the cylinder ends, and, consequently, perpendicular to its axis. All the different parts of this cylinder are, in fig. 10, projected by straight lines and ellipses, accordingly as they are rectilinear or circular in contour. It is the same with the section, fig. 13, and the horizontal projection, fig. 14, which are derived from the two right projections, figs. 11 and 12, made upon auxiliary planes; one vertical, and passing through the axis of the cylinder, and through the valve-casing, whilst the other is perpendicular to this axis, and passes through the line, 1—2, fig. 11. The dotted working lines, indicated upon the various figures, show sufficiently clearly the various constructions necessary to obtain these oblique projections. We have, moreover, applied numbers to the different parts projected, and more particularly to the axes or centre lines, which show at sight what parts correspond with each other upon the different projections.

423. These drawings represent the cylinder of a steam-engine,

different from that which we have already described. The present one is called an oscillating steam-engine, because, instead of the cylinder being vertical and immovable, it oscillates during the motion of its piston, B, upon the two trunnions, E, carried in suitable bearings in the engine-framing. This arrangement of oscillating cylinder has the advantage of dispensing with the parallel motion, and of attaching the rod, A, of the piston, directly to the crank-pin, to which its motion is transmitted, without the intervention of any connecting-rod. In the head, H, of the rod, there is, consequently, formed a bearing, which embraces the crank-pin.

The bottom of the cylinder is cast in the same piece with it, but it has a small central opening, for the passage of the spindle of the boring tool, by means of which the interior of the cylinder is turned smooth and true. This opening is closed by a cast-iron cap, F, bolted to the bottom of the cylinder. Against a planed face, upon one side of the cylinder, is fitted the valve-casing, G, which receives the steam direct from the boiler, and has within it the valve, H, which has an alternate rectilinear movement, at the same time oscillating along with the cylinder. During this movement, the valve alternately uncovers the ports, a, b, fig. 11, which conduct the steam to the top and bottom of the cylinder. A blade spring, I, attached to the inside of the valve-casing, at the back of the valve, constantly keeps the latter well up against the planed valve face.

The steam coming from the boiler introduces itself into the casing through the passage, c, fig. 12, which communicates with one of the trunnions, E, and the escape of the steam, when it has acted upon the piston, is effected through the exit channel, d, which communicates with the other trunnion.

The piston, B, is composed of a cast-iron body, on the outer surface of which is cut out a groove, to receive the hempen packing, i, partly covered by an elastic metal ring, h, coinciding exactly with the inside of the cylinder.

Oscillating cylinder-engines have always been admired for their simplicity and beautiful action; but it is only of late years, and now that such superior workmanship is attainable, that such engines have been constructed of considerable size. The aptness of this arrangement for engines of the largest size has lately been demonstrated by Penn, in the case of the *Great Britain*, and other large vessels.

CHAPTER XII.

PARALLEL PERSPECTIVE.

PRINCIPLES AND APPLICATIONS.

PLATE XLII.

424. We give the name of parallel perspective to the representation of objects by oblique projections, which differ from the preceding, in so far that the visual rays, which we have hitherto supposed to be always perpendicular to the geometrical planes, form, on the contrary, a certain angle with these planes, remaining, however, constantly parallel to each other; from which it follows, that all the straight lines, which are parallel in the object, maintain their parallelism in the picture, according to this system of perspective. Although, in general, it is immaterial what the angle of inclination is, it is nevertheless preferable, in regular

drawing, to adopt some particular angle as a matter of convention, which will have the advantage of giving the entire dimensions of the object in a single projection or view.

Let A B and A′ B′, figs. 1 and 2, be the two projections of a straight line, to which we wish to make the visual rays all parallel; the vertical projection, A B, of this straight line, forms an angle, C A T, with the ground line, L T, which angle is, we shall suppose, equal to 30°, and its horizontal projection, A′ B′, is such, that the distance of the point, A′, from the point, A, where it touches the horizontal plane, is equal to twice the length, A B, of its vertical projection, the point, B, being that at which it touches the vertical plane.

We shall proceed to show, by means of the various figures in Plate XLII., that, in taking the above straight lines as directrices for the visual rays, a single projection will be quite sufficient to express all the dimensions of any object. Instead of making the directrices of the different objects, represented in this plate, to coincide with the actual projection of the straight lines which we have just indicated, we have, by preference, chosen the mere setting of these same lines round at an angle of 30°. Thus, the lines, e′ d″, k′ i″, fig. 3, are the straight lines perpendicular to the planes of projection, set round to the angle in question; whilst, on the contrary, the straight line, y z, represents the projection of these lines properly parallel to the horizontal projection, A′ B′, in fig. 2.

425. The finished view, fig. A, is the representation in *parallel*, or, as it is sometimes called, *false* perspective, of a prism, E, with a square base, resting upon a plinth, F, also prism-shaped and square. In the first place, we suppose this prism to be represented in the horizontal projection, fig. 3, by two concentric squares, a′ d′ e f and h′ i′ k l; and in the vertical projection, fig. 4, by the rectangles, a b c d and g h i j. These projections are made upon the supposition, hitherto acted upon, that the visual rays are perpendicular to the geometrical planes.

If now, on the contrary, the visual rays make with the planes of projection an angle equal to that of the given straight line, figs. 1 and 2, each of the faces parallel to the vertical plane continues to be parallel to this plane, and is represented by a figure equal to itself, whilst all the faces perpendicular to the two planes are in projecting rendered oblique, in such a manner, that the lines horizontally projected become parallel to A′ B′, fig. 2; and those vertically projected, to A B, fig. 1. Consequently, if through the points of the projecting angles, a, h, i, j, fig. 4, are drawn straight lines, parallel to A B, they will express the directions of all the edges perpendicular to the vertical plane. Since then, as we have already stated, the length of the projection, A B, fig. 1, is equal to one-half the perpendicular, A A′, fig. 2, if from the points, a, h, i, j, and on each side of them, we measure off, upon the oblique lines just drawn, the distances, a a² and a f², h h² and h l², i i², and i k², &c., respectively equal to half the lengths, a′ m and h′ n, &c., we shall, in fig. 4, have the perspective representation of the various straight lines perpendicular to the vertical plane; and as all the other edges are parallel to this same plane, such lines as are actually vertical are represented as vertical, whilst all lines parallel to the base line remain horizontal. Thus, the edges, a b, h g, d c, i j, being vertical, are in the parallel perspective represented by the verticals, a² b², h² g², i² j², d² c²; and likewise the

edges, a d, b c, h i, &c., which are parallel to both planes of projection, are rendered by the straight lines, a² d², b² c², h² i², &c., parallel to the base line.

It will be easily seen, that by adopting the angle we have indicated for the direction of the visual, or more correctly termed, representative ray, that the one single view in parallel perspective is sufficient to make known all the dimensions of the object; for, on the one hand, we have the exact widths and heights of those faces which are parallel to the plane of the projection, as if the perspective view did not differ from an ordinary geometrical projection, in which the representative rays are supposed to be perpendicular to the plane; and, on the other hand, the oblique lines representing all the edges actually perpendicular to the vertical plane, and which are exactly equal to half the actual lengths of the latter.

We may here observe, that the base of the prism being square, the sides, k′ l and i′ k, are equal to the sides, h′ i′ or l k. Consequently, in order to construct the perspective or oblique projection, fig. 4, the plan, fig. 3, is not needed, since it would have answered the purpose equally well to have made the lines, d² e² or i² k², equal to the half of a d or h i.

426. The shaded view, fig. B, represents a frustum of a regular pyramid, G, resting upon an octagonal base, H, the horizontal projection of which is indicated in full, sharp lines, in fig. 5, and the vertical projection in dotted lines, in fig. 6.

According to the principle thus laid down, the perspective view is obtained, in the first place, by drawing all the lines which are perpendicular and parallel to the base line, fig. 5, and passing through the opposite angles of each of the octagons, representing the upper and lower bases of the pyramidal frustum, and of the plinth. Of these lines, all, a′ d′, f′ e′, h′ i′, &c., which are parallel to the base line, as well as the sides, p′ q′, t′ u′, v′ x′, which are likewise parallel to the former, remain horizontal in the perspective view, fig. 6, whilst, on the other hand, all the straight lines, such as p′ r′, t′ y′, v′ z′, as well as the sides, a′ f′, h′ l′, i′ k′, which are perpendicular to the base line, become inclined at an angle of 30° from this line, as in fig. 6, or, in other words, parallel to the straight line, A B, fig. 1.

If now, through the points, a, g, p, q, &c., and the points, h, o, i, of the two bases of the pyramidal frustum, we draw parallels to the straight line in question, and then mark off from each of those points, and on each side of them, the distances, a a², g g², p p², h h² &c., respectively, equal to the semi-lengths of the corresponding straight lines, m f′, g′ n, &c., of fig. 5, we shall have the parallel-perspective representation of all these lines; and consequently, by joining the extreme points of each of them, we shall also have all the lines representing the contours of the two bases; and further, by joining the angles of these bases, we define the lateral faces, and complete the view, fig. 6.

427. The parallel-perspective representation of a cylindrical object, of which the axis is perpendicular to the vertical plane, as in the finished example, fig. C, may be determined without the assistance of the horizontal projection; that is, when the length of the cylinder is known, as well as that of any other part which may be perpendicular to the vertical plane.

Let a b c d g f e, fig. 7, be the vertical projection of this object, the perspective of its base, *a b c d*, will be parallel to A B. The circles which have their centres at *o*, being parallel to the vertical plane, are represented in perspective by two circles equal to themselves; and their position is obtained by drawing through the point, *o*, the straight line, $o^1 o^2$, parallel to A B, fig. 1, and marking off a distance, lying equally on both sides of the point, *o*, equal to half the length of the cylinder, measured in the direction of the axis, perpendicular to the vertical plane. Then with the points, o^1, o^2, as centres, describe the circles with the equal radii, $o' f'$ and $o' i'$, straight lines, $f^1 f^2$ and $i^1 i^2$, drawn tangential to the circles, and parallel to the axis, $o^1 o^2$, express in perspective the generatrices of the two cylinders forming the contour of the object. The cylindrical pieces which join the cylinder to the base are determined in the same manner by means of the line, $n n^2$, drawn through the centre, *n*, of the circle, *d g*, parallel to $o^1 o^2$, and by the distances, $n n^1$, $n n^2$, together equal to half the actual length of these cylindrical surfaces. The base is drawn as in the preceding example.

428. The example, fig. Ⓓ, represents a cone resting upon a cylindrical base, both cone and base having the same axis perpendicular to the horizontal plane. This cone and cylinder are projected on the plan, fig. 8, in sharp lines, and in the elevation, fig. 9, in dotted lines.

The circles, fig. 8, representing the bases of the cone and cylinder, are to be divided into a certain number of equal parts; and through the points of division, 1, 2, 3, &c., perpendiculars are drawn to the ground line, and are prolonged as far as the horizontal line, *a' o'*, which is the vertical projection of the two bases. Through the points, *a'*, *b'*, *c'*, *o'*, are drawn straight lines parallel to A B, fig. 1; and on each of these are set off the distances, *a' 2'*, *b' 3'*, *c' 4'*, *o' 5'*, &c., respectively equal to half the lengths of the perpendiculars, *2 a*, *3 b*, *4 c*, *5 o*, &c., which operation gives the points, *2'*, *3'*, *4'*, *5'*, &c., through which an ellipse must be traced, to represent the perspective of the base of the cylinder. In the same manner we obtain the points through which passes the ellipse, representing the perspective of the base of the cone.

The heights of the cone and its base remain precisely what they really are, in consequence of their common axis being parallel to the vertical plane; but this is not the case with their bases, which, being horizontal, are projected obliquely, in the form of the ellipses we have just drawn. The apex of the cone, at the upper extremity of the vertical axis, does not change, and for the generatrices, or sides of the cone, it is simply necessary to draw through the apex the straight lines, $o^2 m$ and $o^2 n$, tangents to the ellipse representing the base of the cone, whilst the generatrices of the cylinder are tangents to the two ellipses representing its upper and lower bases.

429. The example, fig. Ⓔ, is the parallel-perspective representation of a metal sphere or knob, attached to a polygonal base by a circular gorge, forming altogether an ornamental head for a screw. Figs. 10 and 11 are the horizontal and vertical projections of this piece.

We must, in the first place, remark that the sphere, the radius of which is *o a*, may be determined in its perspective representation in several ways. First, by imagining the horizontal sections, *a b*, *c d*, *e f*, which give in plan the circles, with the radii, *a' o'*,

c' o', and *e' o'*, and the perspectives of each of these circles may be obtained by operations similar to the preceding, which will give a series of ellipses, to be circumscribed by another ellipse, tangential to them all. Second, by drawing the planes, *g h*, *i j*, parallel to the vertical plane, and which are projected in perspective as circles, with the radii, *l'' g*, *i m*, the centres being upon the oblique line, *n n'*, parallel to the line, A B, fig. 1, and passing through the centre, *o*, of the sphere. The external curve, drawn tangential to all these circles, will be elliptical, as in the preceding method, and represent the perspective of the sphere. Thirdly, by at first drawing through the centre, *o*, an oblique line, *n n'*; then a perpendicular, *e e''*, passing through the same point. Then set out from the centre, *o*, and on each side, the distances, *o e*, *o e''*, equal to the radius, *o a*, of the sphere, which gives the conjugate axis of the ellipse. To obtain the transverse axis, it will be necessary to draw tangents to the great circle of the sphere, parallel to the oblique ray of projection, A B, fig. 1, as brought into the vertical plane. This line is brought into the vertical plane, as at A'' B. in the following manner:—At the point, A, a perpendicular to A B is erected, and the distance, A'' A, is made equal to A A', when A'' B is joined.

These tangents touch the sphere in the points, *f*, *f'*, which may be obtained directly by drawing through the centre, *o*, the line, *f f'*, perpendicular to A'' B. These tangents, further, meet the line, *n n'*, in the points, *n*, *n'*; and the distance between these points is, consequently, the transverse axis of the ellipse, which represents the perspective of the sphere, and which may be drawn according to any of the known methods.

This last method is evidently the shortest and simplest of the three for obtaining the perspective of the sphere, but it is confined in its application; for any other surface of revolution, as, for example, the gorge, which unites the sphere to the hexagonal base, cannot be defined in this way. In cases where the axis of the surface of revolution is vertical, as in this example, it will be necessary to adopt the first general method, which consists in taking horizontal sections. When, on the other hand, the axis of the surface of revolution is horizontal, we must employ the second process, which consists in taking sections parallel to the vertical plane, or perpendicular to the axis. The perspective of the thread of the screw, of which the sphere is the ornamental head, is determinable in a manner analogous to that of a circle. It is sufficient, in fact, first to draw the two geometrical projections, figs. 8 and 12, of one or two convolutions of the thread, and to find the perspectives of the very points which have served for the construction of the helices. Thus, for example, we put the circle, *l p q*, fig. 8, into perspective, as at $l^4 p^4 q^4$, fig. 13, retaining for this purpose the same points, *l*, *p*, *q*, &c., which were employed in delineating the screw, fig. 12. Through these points, l^4, p^4, q^4, &c., draw vertical lines; and upon them set off the distances, $l^1 l^2$, $l^1 l^3$, $p^1 p^2$, &c. Then through the points, l^2, l^3, &c., draw the curve, which will be the perspective of the outer helix of the screw-thread. By going through the same operation for the inner circle, *r s t*, fig. 10, we shall obtain the similarly perspective outline of the inner helix.

An examination of fig. 13 will further show that the heights on the vertical lines are precisely the same for both helices, for they are taken upon radii common to the two circles, $l'' p''$ and $r s t$, considered as bases.

We have deemed it unnecessary to enter further into the development of this species of perspective, of which we have already given a general application in the boring-machine, represented at fig. 1, Plate XXXV., an example in which are collected almost all the various forms which present themselves for delineation amongst mechanical elements and machinery.

In that example, as well as in the figures in Plate XLII., which we have just been studying, we have supposed the representative or visual rays to be in all cases parallel to each other, and to be inclined at an angle of 30° with the ground line in the vertical projection, in such a manner that a single view serves to express all that two, or even three, geometrical projections can do, showing not only the external contours of the objects, but also whatever may be upon their surface.

It will be easy to comprehend the utility of this system of giving, at a single view, a general and precise idea of the actual *relieve* appearance of any object. It is a manner of representation often more intelligible to the generality of people than a series of geometrical projections, and in many cases it will greatly simplify the process of sketching buildings or machinery.

CHAPTER XIII.

TRUE PERSPECTIVE.

PRINCIPLES AND APPLICATIONS.—ELEMENTARY PRINCIPLES.

PLATE XLIII.

430. Perspective, properly so called—but here defined as true or exact perspective—differs from parallel or false perspective, in its being founded upon the actual manner in which vision takes place; that is, that instead of being parallel to each other, the visual rays converge to a point. An object is said to be drawn in perspective when, on viewing the drawing from a particular point, it presents the same appearance to the organs of vision as the object represented itself does when similarly viewed.

The visual rays, or impressions, travel from the object in straight lines, converging to a point at the eye, and forming a cone of rays. Let us suppose this cone to be intercepted by a transparent plane, or diaphragm, of any form—then, noting the points where the rays from the various parts of the object pierce this diaphragm, let us paint upon it the outline, and complete the picture with colours, which to the eye shall have the exact appearance of those of the object itself, modified, as they may be, by distance, position, form, and by their being in the light or shade. After doing this, we may remove the object, but the picture upon the diaphragm will make the same impression upon the eye that the object would itself. It is to the representation of objects in this exact and natural manner, that the art of drawing in perspective is devoted.

The fixed point, to which the rays converge, is called the point of sight; and in diagrams explanatory of perspective, it is shown, together with the converging rays, as projected into the plane of the picture. To determine the perspective delineation of an object mathematically, we must have given us the horizontal and vertical projections of the object; also those of the point of sight, and the position of the plane of the picture; and the general problem of perspective then reduces itself to conceiving the visual rays as passing from the various points of the object to the point of sight, and to find the intersection of these rays with the plane of the picture.

FIRST PROBLEM.

THE PERSPECTIVE OF A HOLLOW PRISM.

431. Let A and A′, figs. 1 and 2, be the horizontal and vertical projections of the prism which we wish to delineate in perspective, the point of sight being projected in v and v′, and the plane of the picture, in T and T′, being supposed to be perpendicular to the planes of projection, and vertical, as is generally the case.

Through the point, v, in the horizontal projection, draw visual rays from each of the points, a, b, c, d, appertaining to the external contour of the prism. The intersection of these points with the plane of the picture determines the points, b^2, a^2, c^2, d^2, which give, upon the horizontal projection, T o, of the latter, the perspective of the points, a, b, c, d.

In like manner, through the point, v′, in the vertical projection, draw the visual rays, a' v′, b' v′, f v′, e v′, intersecting the plane of the picture in the points, a'', b'', f'', and e''; these last being, consequently, the vertical projections of the perspective of the points, a', b', e, f.

As, because of the position given to the plane of the picture, the perspective of the object is not visible, since all the points are situated in the vertical line, T T′, the plane being represented on edge, we must imagine this plane as turned over upon the vertical plane of the drawing; whilst we must suppose the line, T o, the horizontal projection of the picture-plane, as turned about the point, o, as a centre, through a right angle, bringing it to coincide with the ground line, L M. When this is done, the points, a^2, b^2, c^2, d^2, will describe arcs of circles, and, finally, coincide with the points, a^3, b^3, c^3, d^3, on the ground line. Next, upon these last erect perpendiculars, to meet the horizontals, drawn through the points, a'', b'', f'', e''; the points of intersection of these cross lines will be the perspectives, a^4, b^4, c^4, d^4, of the corners, a, b, c, d, of the top of the prism. We have, likewise, the points, e^2, f^2, g, h, for the perspectives of the corners of the bottom of the prism, which is parallel to the top; consequently, by joining all these points together in couples, as indicated in fig. A, we obtain the entire perspective of the external outline of the prism. As the prism is hollow, we shall see in the perspective view the outline, $i' m' n' o'$, corresponding to the edges of the part hollowed out.

The point of sight, of which v and v′ are the geometrical projections, is projected upon the picture-plane in the points, v, v^2; and when the picture-plane is turned over, the point will be found at v'', which is the position of the point of sight upon the perspective drawing.

It must be observed, that in this example the lines, $a^4 b^4, a^4 d^4$, and $b^4 c^4$, which express the perspective of the corresponding lines, $a b, a d$, and $b c$, are the intersections with the plane of the picture, of planes passing through these lines, and through the point of sight. Now, since the intersection of two planes is always a straight line, the following conclusions may be drawn; that,

432. First, *The perspective of a straight line upon a plane is a straight line.*

It may also be remarked, that the verticals, such as $b^4 e^2, c^4 h, d^4 g$, are the perspectives of the vertical edges, projected in the points, b, c, d; whence we deduce that,

433. Secondly, *The perspectives of vertical lines are verticals, when the plane of the picture is itself vertical.*

It will further be seen, that the horizontals, $b^4 c^4, d^4 a^4, e^2 h, f^2 g$, of the perspective view, correspond to the straight lines projected horizontally in $b c$ and $d c$, which are parallel to the picture; whence it may be gathered, that,

434. Thirdly, *The perspective of any straight horizontal line, parallel to the picture, is itself horizontal.*

Further, it follows from the two preceding principles, that all lines parallel to the plane of the picture are represented, in perspective, by lines parallel to themselves.

Finally, the straight lines, $a^4 b^4, d^4 c^4, e^2 f^2$, and $h g$, which all converge to the same point, v'', the projection of the point of sight upon the plane of the picture, correspond to the edges, $a b, d c, e f$, which are horizontal, but perpendicular to the plane of the picture; whence it follows, that,

435. Fourthly, *The perspectives of lines which are horizontal, but perpendicular to the plane of the picture, are straight lines, which converge to the point of sight, and are consequently foreshortened.*

It will be seen, from figs. 1 and 2, that the whole width of the perspective representation, fig. A, is comprised between the points, b^2 and d^2, which lie on the outermost visual rays, drawn in the horizontal projection; and that its height is limited by the two points, a'' and e'', which correspond to the extreme visual rays in the vertical projection. The angle formed by the extreme visual rays is termed the *optical angle*. In the present example, this angle, $b^2 v d^2$, in the horizontal projection, differs from the angle, $a'' v' e''$, in the vertical projection.

The positions of the object and point of sight being given, the dimensions of the perspective representation vary according to the position of the plane of the picture. It will thus be seen, on referring to fig. 1, that if this plane be removed from T T′ to $t t'$, nearer to the object, the limits to the perspective representation

by the extreme visual rays will be enlarged; whilst, on the contrary, if we remove the plane of the picture to the position, $t'' t^4$, nearer to the point of sight, the limits will be sensibly narrowed.

Again, if, in place of moving the plane of the picture, the point of sight is removed further off, or brought nearer to, the size of the perspective outline will thereby be augmented or diminished. It may therefore be concluded, that,

436. Fifthly, *The dimensions in the perspective representation do not wholly depend, either on the actual size of the object, or on the distance from which it is observed, but also on the relative distances of the point of sight and of the object from the plane of the picture.*

Thus the sides, $d a$ and $c b$, fig. 1, are actually equal, but the former is further from the plane of the picture than the latter; so that whilst this is represented by the space, $c^4 b^4$, fig. A, that is limited to the much smaller space, $d^4 a^4$, in the perspective view.

SECOND PROBLEM.

THE PERSPECTIVE OF A CYLINDER.

FIGURES 3 AND 4.

437. To obtain the perspective outline of a vertical cylinder, such as the one projected horizontally in B, fig. 4, and vertically in B′, fig. 3, we proceed, as in the preceding example, to draw through the point of sight, v v, a series of visual rays, extending to the various points, a, b, c, d, e, taken on the upper end of the cylinder, by preference at equal distances apart. These lines intersect the plane, T T′, of the picture, in the points, d^2, c^2, a^2, g^2, &c., in the horizontal projection, and in the points, a'', c'', d'', &c., in the vertical projection.

By bringing the plane, T T′, of the picture, into that of the diagram before us, or what is equivalent to it, by finding the points, g^3, a^3, &c., by means of arcs, drawn with the centre, o, on which the plane is supposed to turn, and drawing the horizontal lines through the corresponding points in the vertical projection of the picture-plane, we obtain the points, c^4, d^4, a^4, g^4, &c., which are points in an elliptic curve representing the top of the cylinder in perspective, which is visible, in consequence of the point of sight being above it.

The same points, a, b, c, d, of the horizontal projection, give, in combination with their vertical projections, g', f'', c'', &c., the perspectives, d^5, e^5, f^5, g^5, of the bottom of the cylinder, of which, obviously, only a part is visible.

The two vertical generatrices, $d^4 d^5, g^4 g^5$, being drawn tangential to the upper and lower ellipses, complete the perspective outline of the cylinder, fig. B.

As this cylinder is hollow, an operation similar to the preceding will be called for in delineating the upper visible edge of the hollowed-out portion.

It must be observed that, in taking an even number of divisions, at equal distances apart, upon the horizontal projection of the cylinder, and setting them off from the diameter, $c g$, parallel to the plane of the picture, we have always a couple of points situated upon the same perpendicular to the plane, and of which the perspectives are, consequently, situated on the same straight line, drawn through the projection, v'', of the point of sight. This occurs with the points, b, d, the perspectives, b^4, d^4, of which, are situated upon the line, v' d^4, so that we have a means of verifying the preceding construction.

THIRD PROBLEM.

THE PERSPECTIVE OF A REGULAR SOLID, WHEN THE POINT OF SIGHT IS SITUATED IN A PLANE PASSING THROUGH ITS AXIS, AND PERPENDICULAR TO THE PLANE OF THE PICTURE.

FIGURES 5 AND 6.

438. Let v and v′ be the projections of the point of sight, situated in the vertical plane, v o, passing through the axis, o o', of the solid, c c′, and perpendicular to the plane, T T′, of the picture. It will be seen at once, that in the perspective view, fig. Ⓖ, this point must be projected on the vertical line, v'' v^2, representing the axis of the object, and in relation to which all the lateral edges of the object are symmetrical. Such are the sides, a b and c d, which are perpendicular to the plane of the picture, and which are represented in perspective by the lines, a^4 b^4 and d^4 c^4, both directed to the point of sight, v''. It is the same with the edges, f g, h i, of which the perspectives, f^4 g^4, h^4 i^4, likewise converge to the point of sight, v''.

As for the vertical edges, they retain their vertical position in the perspective, and the horizontal lines, a d, l m, n k, c b, parallel to the plane of the picture, are rendered in the perspective view by parallels, such as a^4 d^4, l^4 m^4, n^4 k^4, c^4 b^4.

It may be gathered from the solution of this problem, that whenever the point of sight is in a plane, passing through the axis of a regular solid, and perpendicular to the plane of the picture, the perspective representation will be symmetrical with reference to the centre line, and that it is, therefore, quite sufficient to go through the constructive operations for one side only of the figure.

FOURTH PROBLEM.

THE PERSPECTIVE OF A BEARING-BRASS, PLACED WITH ITS AXIS VERTICAL.

FIGURES 7 AND 8.

439. The point of sight being situated, as in the preceding example, in a vertical plane, passing through the axis of the object, and perpendicular to the picture-plane, the perspective will likewise be symmetrical in reference to the centre line, v'' v^2; and it is unnecessary to notice this peculiarity further. The inside of the brass being cylindrical, and being terminated by horizontal semi-circular bases, the perspective of these bases will be rendered by a couple of regular semi-ellipses, of which it will be sufficient to determine the axes. The transverse axis, a^4 c^4, is equal to the perspective of the straight line, a c, which is horizontal and parallel to the picture-plane; and the semi-conjugate axis, b^4 d', is equal to tne perspective of the line, b d or b' a', which is also horizontal, but is perpendicular to the plane of the picture, and is consequently foreshortened, whilst it coincides with a line passing through the point of sight, v''. It will be remarked, that the

transverse axis of the ellipse, corresponding to the upper end of the semi-cylinder, is equal to a^4 c^4, but that the conjugate axis is foreshortened to a greater extent than that, b^4 d^4, of the lower one, in consequence of being at a less distance below the point of sight. The effect of the perspective, in this case, is well rendered in fig. Ⓓ.

FIFTH PROBLEM.

THE PERSPECTIVE OF A STOPCOCK, WITH A SPHERICAL BOSS.

FIGURES 9 AND 10.

440. In carrying out the general principle, it will be conceived that, in obtaining the perspective representation of a sphere, we should draw through the point of sight a series of rays, tangential to the outer surface; but in order to ascertain the points of contact of these tangents, it will be necessary to imagine a series of planes as passing through the sphere, producing circular sections, and then to find the perspective of each of these circles. These being found, a curve, drawn to circumscribe them, will be the perspective of the sphere.

In the example, figs. 9 and 10, the point of sight being still chosen as before—that is, as situated in a plane passing through the centre of the sphere, and perpendicular to the picture-plane— the perspective of the sphere will, on this account, simply be an ellipse, having for conjugate axis the base, a^2 b^2, of the optical angle, a^2 v b, in the horizontal projection; and for transverse axis, the base, c^2 d^2, of the angle, c^2 v' d^2, in the vertical projection; because the right cone, formed by the series of visual rays tangential to, and enveloping the sphere, is obliquely intersected by the plane of the picture. If, however, the point of sight were situated upon a horizontal line, passing through the centre, o, of the sphere, the perspective of the latter would evidently be a circle.

The spherical part of the stopcock is traversed by a horizontal opening, for the reception of the key, and the edge, e f, of this opening, being situated in a plane parallel to the picture-plane, will, in the perspective, fig. Ⓔ, be rendered by a circle, of which the diameter is e^2 f^2.

As to the cylindrical flanges on either side of the stopcock, for forming its junction with a line of piping, the semicircle, a g b, is represented by a portion of an ellipse, having the horizontal line, a^4 b^4, corresponding to a b; and the vertical, g^4 o^2, being the perspective of g'' o''. The circle, a h b g, the horizontal projection of the surface of the uppermost flange, is represented in the perspective view by a perfect ellipse, as is also the upper visible edge of the inner tubular portion. But this is the same as the case in fig. 3, and the ellipses may be formed in a similar manner.

The perspective representation of a circle, however situated, otherwise than parallel with regard to the plane of the picture, is always a perfect ellipse; but the transverse axis of the ellipse does not coincide with, or is not the representation of, any diameter of the circle; for it is evident, that the more distant half of the circle must be more foreshortened in the perspective, and must occupy a less space than the anterior half, whilst the ellipse is equally divided by its transverse axis.

When the point of sight is in a line perpendicular to the circle, the rays from the latter will form a right cone ; and if the plane of the picture is not parallel to the circle, the section determined by it will be an ellipse, as is well known. Again, if the circle is not perpendicular to the central visual ray, the cone of rays will be elliptical, and the sections of such cone will be ellipses, of various proportions, that parallel to the circle, however, being a circle.

The transverse axis of the perspective ellipse is the perspective of that chord in the original circle, which is subtended by the arc, between the points of contact of the extreme visual rays, as projected in the plane of the circle.

SIXTH PROBLEM.

THE PERSPECTIVE OF AN OBJECT PLACED IN ANY POSITION WITH REGARD TO THE PLANE OF THE PICTURE.

FIGURES 11 AND 12.

441. In each of the preceding problems, we have supposed one or other of the surfaces of the objects to be parallel or perpendicular to the plane of the picture ; but it may happen that all the sides of the object may form some angle with this plane. It is this case which we propose examining in figs. 11 and 12.

Let $a\,b\,c\,d$ be the horizontal projection of a square, of which the sides are inclined to the plane, $\text{T T}'$, of the picture, and of which it is proposed to determine the perspective. The point of sight being projected in v and v', if we employ the method adopted in figs. 1 and 2, we shall find the points, a^2, b^2, c^2, d^2, to be the horizontal projections, and a'', b'', c'', d'', the vertical projections of the corners of the square ; and when we have brought the plane of the picture, $\text{T T}'$, into the plane of the present diagram, as before, we shall find the actual positions of these points to be at a^4, b^4, c^4, d^4. If we join these points, we shall have a quadrilateral figure, of which the two opposite sides, $a^4\,b^4$, $c^4\,d^4$, converge to the same point, f, whilst the other two sides converge to the point, f'. These two points are termed *vanishing points*. They are determined geometrically, by drawing through v, the horizontal projection of the point of sight, the straight lines, v T and v T', parallel to the sides, $a\,b$ and $b\,c$, of the given square, and prolonging these lines until they cut the line, $\text{T T}'$, representing the plane of the picture. Having drawn through v' the horizontal, v' v', termed the horizontal line or *vanishing plane*, set off the distance, v T, from v'' to f, and the distance, v T', from v'' to f', and f and f' will be the required vanishing points.

It follows from the preceding, that

When the straight lines which are inclined to the plane of the picture are parallel to each other, their perspectives will converge in one point, situated on the horizontal line, and termed the vanishing point.

When several faces or sides, situated in different planes, are parallel to each other, their perspectives all converge to the same vanishing point, which allows of a great simplification of the operations.

Thus, the edges of the horizontal faces, $h'\,i'$ and $h''\,i''$, of the quadrangular prism, being respectively parallel to the sides of the

square, $a\,b\,c\,d$, are represented in perspective by the straight lines, $i^3\,e^3$, $i^4\,e^4$, converging to the first vanishing point, f, and the straight lines, $i^3\,g^3$, $i^4\,g^4$, converging to the second point, f'.

The cone, F F', which is traversed laterally by the prism, has its apex projected horizontally in the point, s, fig. 12, and vertically in the point, s', which, with its axis, appertains to fig. 11. The perspective of the point, s s', on the plane of the picture, is found, in the usual way, to be at s in the horizontal projection, and at s' in the vertical projection ; and when the plane of the picture is brought into the plane of the diagram, these points are represented by the points, s^2 and s^2, upon the same vertical, $s^2\,o^2$, which is, consequently, the perspective of the axis, $o\,s'$, of the cone, and the point, s^2, is the perspective of the apex of the cone.

If we draw the perspectives of the two bases, $k\,l$ and $m\,n$, of the frustum of a cone, according to the methods already given, it will only remain to draw through the point, s^2, the two lines, $s^2\,m'$ and $s^2\,n$, tangential to the ellipses, representing the bases, which will complete the perspective of the entire object, as in fig. F.

APPLICATIONS.

FLOUR-MILL DRIVEN BY BELTS.

PLATES XLIV. AND XLV.

442. The elementary principles of perspective which we have laid down, will admit of application to the most complicated subjects, and, among other things, to complete views of mechanical and architectural constructions. In Plate XLV. we have given an example, which will enable the student to form a general idea of this branch of drawing. This Plate is the perspective representation of the machinery of a flour-mill driven by belts, and as fitted up by M. Darblay, at Corbeil. Before proceeding, however, to discuss this as a study of perspective, we propose to describe the various details of the mechanism composing the mill, and which we have represented, in geometrical projection, in Plate XLIV.

The construction of flour-mills has latterly undergone very important improvements, as well in reference to the principal driving machinery, as to the minor movements, and the cleaning and dressing apparatus. As such machinery belongs to a most important class, we have selected a mill, as an illustrative example of the subject before us, giving all the recently improved modifications now at work, both in this country and on the Continent.

443. Before the introduction of what is known as the American system, very large uncovered millstones, of upwards of six feet, or two mètres, in diameter, were employed ; and these gave what were then considered very good and economical results. These mills were worked by water-wheels or wind-wheels ; but as improvements gradually crept in, not only was the entire internal mechanism changed, but also the motor, and the description of stones. The American flour-mills, commonly known on the Continent as English mills, differed from the older mills in the employment of smaller stones, with furrowed surfaces, and in their being driven at a much greater speed, requiring, in consequence, more wheel-gear to bring up the speed. A mill on the old system, with large

x

stones of six feet in diameter, ordinarily goes at the rate of 55 to 60 revolutions per minute, being moved, we shall suppose, by a water-wheel, making 10 or 12 turns in the same time. Such a mill will only require a large toothed-wheel and a lantern-wheel; or better, a large bevil-wheel and a bevil pinion, in the ratio of 5 or 6 to 1.

But a modern mill, in which the stones are generally 4 feet or 1·3 m. in diameter, should make 115 or 120 revolutions per minute; whilst it may be impelled by an overshot water-wheel, making only 3 or 4 revolutions per minute; so that it is necessary to employ multiplying gearing between the power and the work. When this multiplication is obtained by gearing, two or three pairs of wheels are generally employed. The essential features of this gearing, consisting of a large horizontal spur-wheel, driving a spur-pinion on the mill-stone spindle, have recently been superseded, in many instances, by belt and pulley gearing. This arrangement has the advantage of rendering the motions more easy, and of allowing of the stoppage of a single pair of stones, without stopping the prime mover and the whole mill, which is a very essential point, more particularly in a large and important mill, where many pairs of stones are at work.

The drawing, Plate XLIV., represents a mill of this description, driven by belts, and erected by M. Darblay, at Corbeil. It comprises 10 pairs of stones, placed in two parallel rows. The establishment contains several sets of stones, exactly like these. Each set of mills is driven by a hydraulic turbine, on Fourneyron's system.

Fig. 1 represents the plan of a portion of the principal gearing, and one of the rows of stones. Fig. 2 is an elevation, prolonged as far as the vertical shaft of the turbine. Fig. 3 is a transverse vertical section, taken at right angles to the horizontal driving-shaft.

At A, in fig. 2, is represented the upper end of the vertical wrought-iron shaft, upon which the turbine is fixed lower down. This shaft is supported by a step-bearing at its lower extremity, and in a brass collar bearing, a, at its upper end; this bearing being in two pieces, adjusted in the top of the hollow casting, B, resting upon the foundation-plate, c, and also bolted by a bracket to the cast-iron pedestal, D, of the bearing, which receives the end journal, b, of the main driving-shaft, E.

This shaft, E, has fixed upon it, in the first place, the bevil-pinion, F, with strong thick cast-iron teeth, driven by the horizontal bevil-wheel, G, fitted with wooden teeth, and keyed upon the end of the turbine-shaft, A. This shaft is connected by a coupling-box, c, to a wrought-iron shaft, A', which passes up to the higher floors of the building, where it serves to drive the various accessory apparatus of the mill, such as the sack-hoists, pressing, washing, and dressing machines, and endless-chain elevators. At each floor, the shaft is supported by a collar-bearing, like that shown in section at d, in fig. 2.

The horizontal shaft, E, which drives the two rows of stones, is in several pieces, joined together by cast-iron couplings, as at e, and it is supported at different points of its length by the pedestal-bearings, f, each with its oil-receiver at the top, and bolted down to the base of the arched cast-iron standards, H. These standards are formed into receptacles at their tops, to receive the brass

footstep-bearings and steel pivot-piece, to support the lower case hardened extremities, g, of the vertical shafts, I. An adjusting-screw, i, is introduced from below, to raise the bearing when necessary; and the upper journal of the shaft revolves in the inverted cup-bearing, J, which is bolted to the cross beams of the ceiling.

Each of the vertical shafts, I, has keyed upon it a bevil-pinion, K, the teeth of which are cast upon it, as well as two horizontal pulleys, L, of the same diameter. The pinions gear with the wooden-toothed bevil-wheels, K', keyed upon the horizontal driving-shaft, E; and the pulleys are put in communication by means of the leather belts, h, with other similar pulleys, L', of the same diameter. These last are each keyed upon the cast-iron shaft of a pair of stones, M. A tension pulley, N, upon a short vertical spindle, supported by the two arms of a second vertical spindle, o, serves to stretch the belt of each pair of stones to the requisite degree of tightness. For this purpose, a lever, k, is fitted to the vertical spindle, o, and to its free extremity is attached a cord, passing over a couple of guide-pulleys, l, and sustaining a small weight, m. Thus, in the position given to each of the levers, k, in the drawing, the weights are supposed to be acting; and the belts are, consequently, in a stretched state, and the motion of the pulleys, L, is communicated to the pulleys, L'. But if the weight be lifted up, so as not to act, the levers, k, will be set free, and also the tension-pulleys, N; and the belts will be slack, so that the motion will no longer be communicated, and the pulleys, L', and consequently the pairs of stones, will be stopped. The vertical spindles, o, are supported in bearings, carried by cast-iron brackets, P, bolted to the under side of the cross beams. The tension-pulleys can thus assume various positions, whilst their supporting-arms vibrate upon the vertical spindles, o. In order that the belts may not fall when they are slack, iron fingers, n, are placed at intervals, attached to vertical rods, o, depending from the ceiling.

As the millstone shaft is generally made of cast-iron, its lower end is fitted with a case-hardened step, which revolves upon a steel pivot-piece, q, adjusted in the bottom of a brass footstep-bearing, fig. 4, which is itself contained in a cylindrical cast-iron cup, r, carried by the box, n', formed in the casting, p', which surmounts the solid masonry, o', upon which the entire framing of the mill is supported. Screws are introduced through the sides of the footstep-bearing receptacle, by means of which the centre of the shaft is adjusted; whilst the shaft is adjusted vertically, and, consequently, the distance between the stones, by means of the screwed spindle, s, which has a small spur-wheel, t, keyed upon it, with which a small pinion, u, is in gear, this last being actuated by the handle, v upon its vertical spindle. By turning this handle to the right or the left, the small wheels are set in motion; and as the spindle, s, cannot otherwise turn, it is forced to rise or fall, and with it the bearing and footstep of the millstone shaft. It is in this manner that the pitch, or distance, between the two stones is adjusted with all desirable precision, according to the kind of work required from the stones.

The upper end of the millstone shaft is also case-hardened, and is entered a certain distance into the boss of the centre-piece, w, fig. 3, which is fixed across the eye of the upper stone, or runner, Q, and firmly imbedded into the stone at either side. On the top of the boss of the centre-piece, w, is a species of metal saucer, .nto which dips the lower end of the pipe which conducts the grain down from the funnels, R, generally made of copper. These funnels, which receive the grain, communicate by the pipes, y, with a single hopper above, and rest upon the wooden cross-pieces, s, fig. 2, held down on one side by a hinge, z, and on the other by a vertical iron rod, z', by means of which they are raised or lowered at pleasure, so as to set the bottom of their pipes at a greater or less distance above the bottom of the saucer below. The object of this arrangement is to allow more or less grain to enter between the stones. The supports of the cross-pieces, s, are fixed upon a wooden casing, T, which covers each pair of stones, a space being left inside all round the stones, into which the produce of the grinding falls, as it issues from between the stones. It is thence conducted, by suitable channels, either to receiving-chests, or to the elevators, by which it is carried to the upper part of the building, to undergo the subsequent processes.

The lower immoveable stones, q', of the same diameter as the runners above, are fitted with metal eyes, b', furnished with brasses, which embrace the shafts of the runners, and assist in preserving their perfectly vertical position. These stones are grooved, as indicated in the plan of one of them, fig. 1; that is to say, shallow channels are cut out of their working surfaces, so as to present on one side a sharp edge, and act with the runner like scissors, cutting each grain as it comes upon them. The fine close-lined dressing, which is given to the surface between these channels, completes the fracture and crushing of the grain. These lower stones rest upon the cast-iron plates, U, but with the intervention of the three adjusting screws, a', which allow of the obtainment of an exact level; whilst four lateral screws, a^2, fig. 1, entered through the lateral cast-iron frame, serve to adjust with accuracy the centre of the stone.

The base plate and side frames are not only bolted to the cross beams of the building, but they are also supported at intervals by cast-iron columns, v, placed between each pair of stones, and resting upon the plates, o', and the solid masonry below them. The ceiling is additionally supported by the solid wooden columns, x, placed at the ends and between the two rows of stones. An iron railing, Y, is placed on each side of the driving-gear, to prevent accidents which might arise from persons passing too near the heavy wheels. Cavities are constructed in the masonry, for the reception of the mechanism for adjusting the footstep-bearings of the runner-shafts, already described. These openings are usually covered by suitable doors.

THE REPRESENTATION OF THE MILL IN PER-SPECTIVE.

PLATE XLV.

445. It was stated, in the preliminary instructions relating to perspective drawing, that the perspective dimensions depend on the position, both of the point of sight and of the object, from the plane of the picture, which is necessarily limited in size.

In the perspective delineation of one or more objects, we should consider, not only from what distance the object should be viewed,

but also at what height the eye, or the horizontal line, should be placed. In the example selected, we have supposed the point of sight to be placed at the height of a man's eye; but it is evident that this height of horizon is not invariable. It depends, more or less, on what part of the object we wish to develop more particularly in the perspective representation. Thus, for a machine of but little height, the point of sight should be lower; whilst it should, in all cases, be at a sufficient height to enable the spectator to take in the entire object, without changing his position.

In architectural subjects, the horizontal line should never be taken at a less height than that of a man's eye; whilst, in general, a good effect may be anticipated, when the distance of the spectator from the picture is equal to about one and a half times, or twice the width of the paper, provided there is, at least, as great a distance between the plane of the picture, and those parts of the object which are nearest to it.* Taste and practice in drawing in perspective will be the best guides in the choice of the dispositions leading to the happiest effects.

We have at t t', figs. 1 and 2, Plate XLIV., indicated the position assumed for the plane of the picture, which is supposed to be brought into the plane of the diagram in fig. 5, Plate XLV.

The point of sight, agreeably to the recommendation we have given, is supposed to be placed, with reference to the picture, at a distance equal to about twice the width occupied by the machinery of the mill in the vertical projection. It does not lie within the limits of the paper in the geometrical projections, Plate XLIV.; but it is projected into the plane of the perspective picture in the point, v', fig. 5.

In laying out the main design of this perspective picture, we must commence by finding the positions of the axial lines of all the columns, iron shafts, horizontal and vertical, and, in general, of all symmetrical objects. Thus, through the points, 1, 2, 3, 4, &c., fig. 1, we must draw a series of visual rays, converging to the point of sight, and cutting the projection, t t', of the plane of the picture, in the points, 1", 2", 3", 4", &c., which, in the picture itself, fig. 5, Plate XLV., are represented by the points, 1', 2', 3', 4', &c.

The vertical lines, drawn through each of these points, will be the axial lines sought. We next obtain the perspective of the objects situated nearest to the picture plane, as the column, x, for example. This column being very near the plane of the picture, and the visual rays tangential to each side of the cylindrical surface, being both very much inclined to the same side, its diameter in its perspective plane seems proportionately greater than it is in reality; but this is corrected by the obliquity with which this part of the perspective picture should be viewed. For it must be borne in mind, that all perspective pictures must be viewed from the single and precise point of sight in relation to which they are drawn; otherwise, the pictures will have an untrue and distorted appearance.

We next determine the perspective of the columns, v, the axes of all which are situated in a plane perpendicular to the plane of

---

* We do not see the force of this remark, for why should not a perspective representation be drawn full size, or even to a larger scale? In one case, the object must be supposed as close to the plane of the picture, and, in the other, as between it and the point of sight.—TRANSLATOR AND EDITOR.

the picture; so that they will diminish gradually in height, being limited by a couple of lines, converging in the point of sight, v'. It follows hence, that when the perspective of the first column has been obtained, it will be sufficient to draw through the principal points of the mouldings, and other parts, a series of lines, converging in the point of sight, v', which will give the perspective positions of the corresponding points on the other columns, together with their heights.

It is the same with the perspective of each of the runner shafts, the pulleys, and other details, the centres of all which lie in the vertical plane, passing through the axes of the columns, v.

As to the bevil-wheels, κ, the axes of which are vertical, and are projected horizontally in the points, 2, 10, 11, fig. 1, Plate XLIV., and consequently represented in perspective by the vertical lines, 2', 10', 11', &c., fig. 5, Plate XLV.—it is well to find the perspective of the apex, s', of the cone, of which the web carrying the teeth is a frustum; because the perspectives of all the edges of the teeth converge to this point.

The edges of the teeth of the bevil-wheel, κ', the axis of which is horizontal, are also represented in perspective by straight lines converging in this same point, s'; and as to the lines defining the sides or flanks of the teeth, as they also lie in cones, the surfaces of which, however, are perpendicular to the first, their perspectives likewise converge to a single point—the perspective of the apex of the cone, on the surface of which they lie.

The centre lines of the arms of the bevil-wheel, κ', converging to the centre of this wheel, are represented in perspective by lines which are directed towards the point, o², the perspective of that centre.

Since the perspectives of the objects which are repeated, and of which the axes lie in the same plane perpendicular to the picture plane, are always alike, and differ only in being of diminished dimensions according to their distance from the plane of the picture, it will be easily understood that when the perspective of one of them has been determined, the operations for determining the perspectives of the rest may be much simplified, especially by prolonging the various lines to the point of sight. This observation applies to the wheel gearing, the bearings and frames which support the various shafts, the pulleys, and other often-repeated details. It is thus that, in fig. 5, are drawn the principal converging lines, indicating the various heights, and giving the visual rays, which could not all be given in the horizontal projection, fig. 1, but which should, nevertheless, be drawn, in order to determine, by their intersection with the plane of the picture, t t', the whole of the horizontal widths.

Fig. 6 is a complete shaded representation of this perspective study, drawn to a larger scale, in order to render the various details more easily comprehended. This view only differs from fig. 5 in being more complete, and in being turned the reverse way. It is given with a twofold object—as an example of the delineation in perspective of mechanical and architectural objects, and to give an idea of shading such subjects, the shades being graduated in tone according to the distances and positions of the several surfaces, in strict accordance with the principles laid down in the sections treating of shading and colouring.

NOTES OF RECENT IMPROVEMENTS IN FLOUR-MILLS.

By far the best millstones used, in this or any other country, are made of French materials. The stones from the valley of the Marne have the credit of performing more work, and turning out better and whiter flour, than any others. They are purely siliceous in composition, and slightly tinged with ferruginous matter; they are now exported to every part of the world where the British system of grinding is followed. Formerly, great pains were taken to extract enormous stones from the quarry beds, to be used either as monolith grinders, or two or three only, combined into one, in a very rude manner, open faces being selected to grind upon, instead of the modern artificial furrows. The grand improvement of cutting furrows in the grinding faces, in such way as to improve the grinding action without interfering with the centrifugal effect, is an English invention, introduced only forty years ago. Hence the uncertainty attending the use of porous or partially cellular stones was removed; and the French makers gradually improved upon the idea, by building up together small fragments of stone of equal hardness, so as to insure a good grinding surface throughout—this being unattainable in large masses, where softer and more porous parts frequently occur alongside the harder areas. The makers thus contrived to get composite stones, each increment of the surface of which was of the same grain, hardness, porosity, and colour; and as the manufacture grew up to be an important branch of industry, the niceties of suiting the materials to the peculiarities of the country where the stones were to be used, the special system adopted by the millers, and even the character of the grain to be reduced, were all carefully attended to. Thus it is, that the millstone manufacture has become a precise art. In building such stones, the workman selects a solid centre-piece, or eye-stone; and round this he sets his choice-selected masses, previously bound together, and fixes the whole with plaster of Paris, such accuracy being observed in the fittings, that the entire structure hardly exhibits a joint. The smith then encircles the stone with a retaining hoop of wrought-iron, put on hot, so as to fit tightly on cooling. The dresser then reduces the yet uneven surface to a plane; and the furrow-cutter follows the dresser, first setting off, and then cutting out, the grooves which are to produce the sharp cutting edges. The eye is then completed, and the running stone balanced, to be of equal weight all round, cavities being left for the insertion of lead, when the stone is started in work, so that it may run with perfect steadiness. A second hoop of cold iron is then added to give further strength, and the stone is left to dry. M. Roger, a French maker of repute, produces annually some 500 millstones, and an immense number of the inferior or burr stones—all excavated from the valley of the Marne.

The ingenious and important contrivance of the "antifriction curve," by Mr. Schiele, has found an important application in the grinding surfaces of millstones, in which it has introduced a striking departure from old-established principles. The inventor was led to the consideration of this system of working surfaces by the irregularities of wear in the common conical plugged stopcock. Considering the truncated cone of the stopcock plug to be divided into a series of infinitely short lengths, he proposed to take a more obtuse cone for each larger portion, and in such progression, that it would require equal pressure for every portion of the surface to cause a uniform sinking of the plug in the course of wear. The contour thus obtained is of a peculiar curve, as shown in fig. 1. The main feature of the generating curve for such a surface, is the equality of all tangents drawn from the curve surface to the axis;

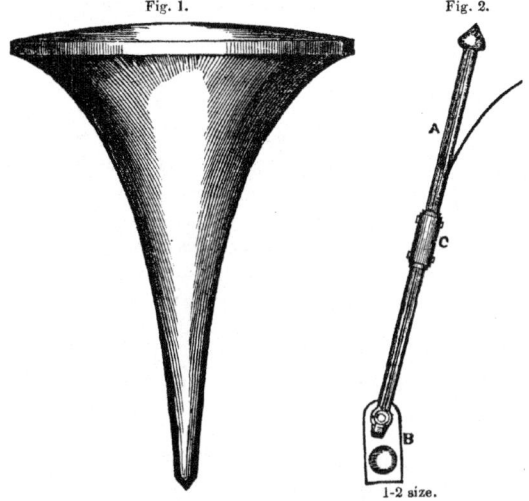

Fig. 1.   Fig. 2.

1-2 size.

hence the use of the simple instrument illustrated by fig. 2. This contrivance consists merely of a straight brass wire, A, jointed at one end by a pin to the upper surface of a small wooden slider, B, which is hollowed in the centre to receive the tip of the finger in drawing a curve. A small drawing-pen, c, ingeniously formed out of a slip of steel bent over the wire, A, and screwed to a brass bush, so as to form two broad nibs, is arranged to slide from end to end of the wire, being adjustable at any point by stiff friction, caused by a spring, which, fitting a groove in the wire, retains the vertical position of the pen. In drawing a curve, the rod or wire carrying the pen is set at right angles with the slider, B, which is drawn in a right line along the edge of a ruler, whilst the wire carrying the pen is left to find its way from its initial angular position, to that of a line in the same plane as the slider; and, in doing this, the pen describes the curve we have represented.

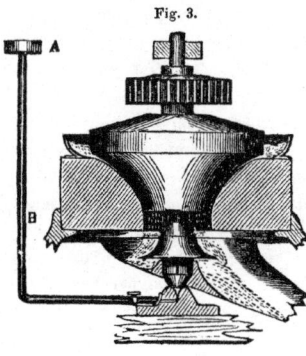

Fig. 3.

Fig. 3 is a vertical section of a millstone arrangement on this system, showing how the gradual variation of the curvature, in relation to the increasing distance of the parts from the centre of motion, equalizes the rubbing pressure in the most perfect manner. The same sketch

also shows the adaptation of the principle to footsteps, together with a new system of lubrication of these surfaces so liable to extreme abrasion. The oil supply is kept in an elevated vessel, A, whence a pipe, B, proceeds downwards to the footsteps, upon which a pressure is thus constantly kept by the oil column, a stop-cock being introduced to regulate the supply.

Mr. Schiele now makes independent or self-contained flour-mills of this kind, of such simplicity and compactness, that four complete mills, or sets of stones, placed together, may be worked in a room 10 feet square; a single shaft driving the set, from the centre, by means of a horizontal band-pulley, from which endless bands pass to corresponding pulleys on the spindle above the upper stone. In mills of this kind, when by wear the runner has sunk three inches, the adjusting screws of the steps arrive at the end of the 3-inch traverse allotted to them. The runner is then lifted from its seat, and the thin end is shortened to this amount. This plan of renovation may be repeated twice, thus allowing for 12 inches wear in a 26-inch runner; and the stones, so reduced, are still valuable for smaller mills.

The peculiar portability of these mills is a valuable feature of improvement. No fixtures are required, as the weight of the parts insures steadiness in working. Perfect uniformity of wear in the grinding surfaces is attained by the use of the curved face; and the expensive dressing necessary in flat stones is here entirely obviated, as the occasional grinding of hard substances roughens the faces to an extent sufficient for grinding all the softer materials, which gradually smooth down the faces.

Any of the materials ground in common mills, and many which the latter cannot properly act upon, are capable of reduction in these mills. For flour and other finely-ground substances, a few air-channels are formed down the face of the runner. Their best speed is only half that of common stones; and the inventor states that his experimental results go to show that a two-feet runner produces as much flour as a four-feet flat millstone, the power required being a minimum. If the stones run empty, no contact can take place, therefore there is no firing, nor does a variation in the feed or speed cause any difference in the relative position of the stones, on account of the firm and steady revolution on the curved pivots. The antifrictional qualities of these pivots are pretty well elucidated by the fact of the very minute consumption of oil upon them.

The "Ring Millstone," invented by Mr. Mullin of Gilford, Ireland, is proposed as the means of securing four special advantages—economy in manufacture, simplicity and effective ventilation, increased production of meal, and a saving of labour in repairs. Fig. 4 is a vertical section of the stone, and fig. 5 is a corresponding plan. The "eye," A, is made excessively large in proportion to the stone's diameter, exceeding, indeed, half the latter dimension. This increased area admits a

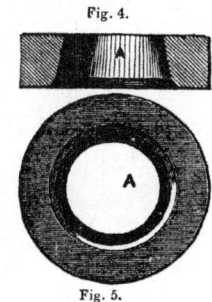

Fig. 4.

Fig. 5.

greater volume of air than is usual, and this air, coming in contact with the more rapidly revolving portion of the stone, is passed between the working surfaces by the action of the centrifugal force. Besides, the increased circumferential length of the eye admits of the formation of three or four times the ordinary number of leading furrows, for the distribution of the air over the grinding surfaces, and thus more grain is ground, without any risk of over-heating by friction. Finally, by getting rid of the great area of superabundant stone at the centre, the operation of dressing is obviously simplified very considerably.

Mr. Barnett of Hull has ingeniously enough contrived a permeable millstone, capable of dressing a great portion of the flour during the actual grinding process. Fig. 6 is a sketch of this stone. As soon as the grinding has commenced, the fine flour which is liberated passes over a set of radial wire-gauze openings in the lower stone, and the

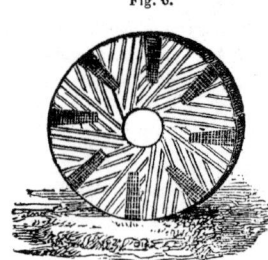

Fig. 6.

coarser particles are thus separated from the finer ones. In the upper stone, a series of openings are so arranged, and furnished with air-boxes, facing the direction of the stone's revolution, that the external air is forced down upon the grinding surfaces, to cool the meal, and facilitate the passing of the superfine flour through the wire-work in a cool state. The inventor alleges that he can thus separate a superfine flour from ordinary wheat, from one to two-thirds being delivered, ready dressed, into the bag, the rest being ready for immediate dressing.

Fig. 7 illustrates an arrangement by Mr. Hastie of Greenock, for the application of a separate steam-engine to each pair of stones, just as Mr. Nasmyth now works calico-printing machines, each with its own individual small engine. Here, a is the steam

Fig. 7.

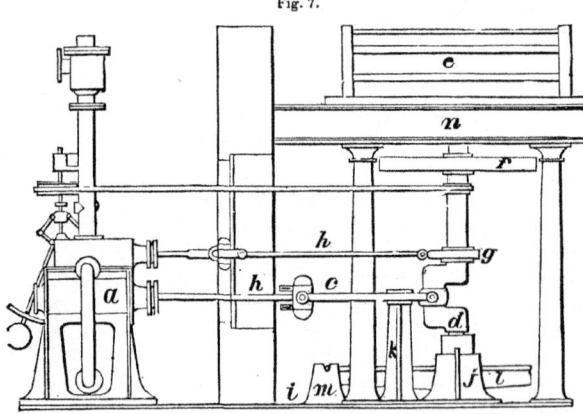

cylinder, and b the piston-rod, connected by a pair of connecting-rods, c, with the crank-shaft, d, which forms the axis of the upper millstone, e. The joints that unite the ends of the rods, c, with the piston-rod and crank-shaft are universal. The shaft, d, is provided with a fly-wheel, f, which serves to receive an endless belt for driving flour-dressing machines; and there is also an

eccentric, g, on the shaft, d, for communicating motion by the rod h, to the slide-valve belonging to the steam cylinder, a. The cylinder, a, is supported upon legs, bolted to the bed-plate, i; and from this plate rises a small standard, j, which carries the bearing for the lower end of the shaft, d, and likewise a standard, k, which sustains a guide for the end of the piston-rod. The lower end of the shaft, d, is not supported longitudinally by the bearing in the standard, j, but only laterally; and there is a hardened steel pivot in that lower end, which rests upon a similar plate lodged at the bottom of the cell formed in a bearing lever, l. This lever is sustained at one end by a centre pin or fulcrum in a low standard, m, and the other end of the lever is suspended from the frame, n, by a long screw-bolt, which, being turned, or a nut fitted upon the screw thereof being turned, when required, will raise or lower that end of the lever, and thus the upper millstone can be accurately set to the intended distance from the lower one. It is on account of the vertical movement which is occasionally required to be given to the shaft, d, that the connecting-rods, c, are united to that shaft and to the piston-rod by universal joints.

When two pairs of millstones are required to be worked by the same engine, this may be effected by causing the piston-rod to pass through both ends of the cylinder, a, and connecting it at each end with the shaft, d, of the upper millstone, belonging to the pair of millstones which are on that side of the steam-engine; and in case it should be desired at any time to work only one of the upper stones, the other may be disconnected by detaching the connecting-rods belonging thereto.

The efficient mingling of cold air with the grain as it passes between the grinding surfaces of millstones, is one of the most important of the modern improvements in grinding. The operating surfaces are thus kept cool, and the production is materially increased, whilst the quality of flour is very superior to that produced in the old way. It is this feature which holds a prominent place in a recent invention by Mr. J. Currie of Glasgow.

Fig. 8 of our engravings is a vertical section of one of his millstone arrangements, showing how the cooling air is mingled with the grain before it passes to the grinding surfaces. For this purpose he uses two grain feed-pipes, A, diverging downwards, like a forked branch of a tree, from the narrow bottom discharge opening of the hopper, B, the revolving feed-spindle, c, being passed up from the main spindle, D, through a joint-hole in the fork, into the main feed-pipe, receiving the grain from the hopper. After diverging downwards, until they reach the upper surface of the fixed stone, E, the two feed-pipes pass vertically through a pair of holes made directly through the upper stone, and set diametrically, one on each side the eye of the stone. An annular portion of the under surface of this stone, extending far enough to reach the feed apertures opening through it, is bevilled slightly upwards from the outer side of these holes towards the eye, so as to leave a narrow space between the two stones at this part, for the free entry of the grain and air, and precluding the chance of the commencement of the grinding action, before the air has fully reached the acting surfaces. The eye of the upper fixed stone, between the two feed-pipes, is covered over with a metal disc, G, passed over the feed-spindle, and capable of adjustment at any required height above the eye as a valve. The grinding surface of the lower running stone, H, is perfectly flat throughout, and its eye at the grinding level is covered over by a metal plate, F, with a central aperture round

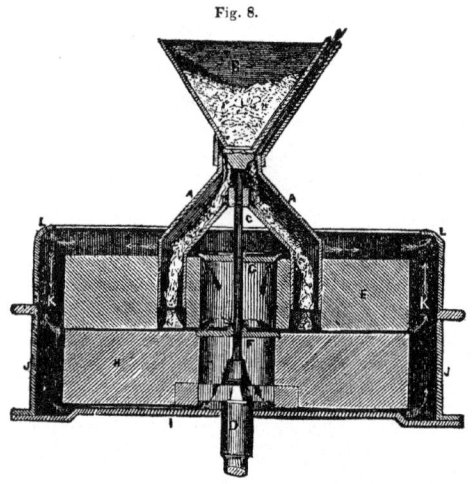

Fig. 8.

the feed-spindle, G, for the passage through of a portion of the air In this way, part of the air may be discharged at the eye of the upper stone, and part down through the eye of the runner beneath, whilst the main body of the air goes along with the grain, and is discharged with the grained material at the periphery of the stones. By this contrivance, the entire surface of both stones is kept encircled by a constantly changing air-bath or current, for the air, escaping at the eye of the upper stone, is directed by the valve disc over its entire surface, whilst that from the bottom of the lower eye passes over the whole bottom surface of the runner, between it and the bottom base plate, I. This has a ventilating effect; for on the upper edge of the iron casing, J, which surrounds the lower running stone, and supports the upper fixed stone, is placed an annular disc of wire-cloth, K, covering over the annular space left between the periphery of the stones and the interior of the casing. This wire-cloth stands a short distance above the level of the grinding surfaces, and from its periphery a light wooden casing, L, springs upwards, surrounding the upper stone, and bevilled inwards at some distance above the stone's surface. Thus there is a current of cold air passing from the running eye up outside the stone and inside the casing. There it meets the heated current from the grinding surfaces at right angles; and breaking this heated current, whatever grained material is held in suspension, falls back within the bottom casing, whilst the heated air passes off through the wire-cloth, again meeting at right angles with a cool current from the upper side of the top stone, which, in conjunction with the bevilled top of the upper case, still further separates the suspended flour, and aids the ventilation. Another modification of stones relates to the combination of three or more separate stones, instead of two, as hitherto used. In this plan, which is represented in fig. 9, the central stone, A, is the runner, the upper and lower ones, B, C, being fixed, so that the grinding is performed both between the under surface of the upper stone at D, and the upper surface of

the central runner, and between the under surface of the latter and the upper surface of the bottom fixed stone at E. The grain

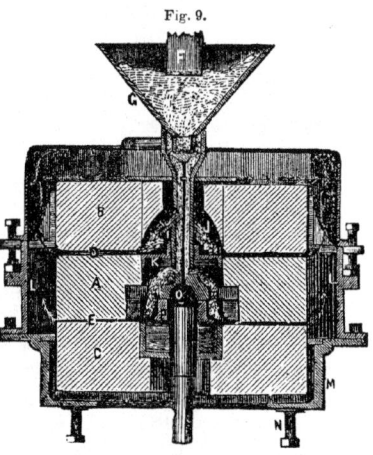

Fig. 9.

is fed through the pipe, F, into the hopper, G, through the adjustable feed-passage into the pipe, H. Hence the supply for the upper grinding surfaces passes out by the inclined lateral opening, I, into the hollow space, J, in the upper stone, forming the lower part of the eye thereof. Here it falls on to the disc, K, and is directed to the grinding surfaces. The supply of grain for the lower or secondary grinding action passes out at the bottom of the pipe, H, into the eye of the runner, A, and thence proceeds to the grinding surface. The upper stone is supported by side brackets, these brackets being carried on the lower annular casing, L, bolted down to the floor. The bottom stone is sunk in a casing, M, recessed into the floor or platform, being steadied laterally by an annular piece of metal level with the floor, whilst it rests on adjusting bolts, N, beneath. The spindle, driven by gearing from below, rests in an adjustable balanced footstep. It is fitted to the runner by a *Ryne*, made on the "balance" principle. The top of the spindle is spherically shaped, as at O, being passed through the collar disc, P, and fitted into a spherical recess in the under side of the Ryne, Q, connected to the stone, A. In this way, as the connection between the spindle and the stone

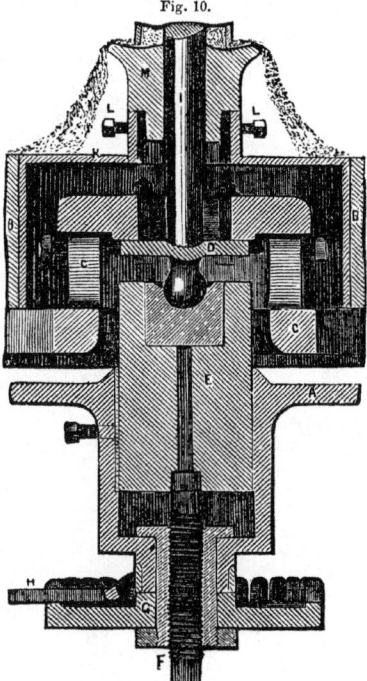

Fig. 10.

is entirely formed by this ball and socket, no derangement can arise from the spindle and runner getting out of truth.

Fig. 10 is a vertical section of the "balance Ryne," on a large

scale. A is the base plate, and B the lower running stone, driven
from above by the main spindle, I, which passes down through the
centre of the adjustable tubes of the feed-hopper, and terminates
in a convex foot. This foot rests in a concavity in the top of
the disc piece, D, which has formed upon the centre of its lower
surface a spherical journal or step piece, resting in a brass carried
in the top of the adjustable block, E. The bottom of the spindle
has a transverse piece, J, forged upon it, and arranged to gear
into slots in a projection standing up from the upper face of the
disc piece, D, so that the spindle cannot revolve without carrying
this disc with it. This disc is secured vertically to the upper disc
of the Ryne by bolts passed up from below, and it is adjustable
laterally by set screws passed through the vertical arms of the
Ryne, C, and bearing against the disc's periphery. These vertical
arms terminate in an annular piece, from which projections pass
into corresponding internal slots in the lower end of the eye of
the stone. A large box piece, K, is firmly wedged into the eye
of the runner from above, covering up the whole of the Ryne apparatus, and this box piece has an upper collar upon it, through
which side bolts, L, are passed. These bolts pass as well through
the feed-cup piece, M, and finally bear upon the spindle which
passes through the cup piece and into the box. By this arrangement the full benefit of the universal joint connection is obtained,
as the bolts admit of exact lateral adjustment, and the stones will
work accurately, even if they should get out of truth with the
spindle. The bottom block, E, rests on the top of the screw bolt,
F, which works in a brass nut, the latter carrying a notched end,
G, for turning by the adjusting lever, H. The forked end of
this lever embraces, and is jointed to, a loose ring by a pin on
each side, so that the lever may be engaged and disengaged from
the notches in the disc at pleasure. In this way, as the disc is fast
to the brass, the attendant, by urging round the lever when
engaged in one of the notches, can screw up the spindle, and thus
raise the block, O, as may be required. This movement resembles that of a ratchet-drill, wherein a few short strokes and a
succession of engagements with the disc notches, give a considerable power of traverse. The block, E, is capable of being fixed by
a set screw, passed through the projecting bottom collar of the
base plate.

Many of these improvements are now at work, at the patentee's
extensive and well-arranged "City of Glasgow Grain Mills."

In this country, Mr. Fairbairn of Manchester, perhaps, takes the
foremost position as a flour-mill engineer. Mr. Joyce, of the
Greenock Iron Works, has also produced some excellent work of
this kind. The Union Corn Mills, Birmingham, and the Bone Mills
of Mr. Lawes, at Deptford, may be mentioned as working examples
of the respective performances of these makers.

RULES AND PRACTICAL DATA.

WORK PERFORMED BY VARIOUS MACHINES.

FLOUR MILLS.

446. As we have stated in the preceding general description of
the machinery of flour mills, the diameter commonly adopted for

millstones on the English system is 1·3 m., whilst they are driven
at a velocity of 115 to 120 revolutions per minute. Such stones,
in some of the well-managed establishments in and around Paris,
grind on an average 15 or 16 hectolitres of wheat in 24 hours; but,
at the same time, 60, 62, and even 63 per cent. of that first quality
of flour is obtained, which is so much sought after by the Parisian
bakers.

When worked in this manner, we have ascertained that it requires an effective force of one horse power, equal to 75 kilogrammètres, to grind on an average from 20 to 22 kilogrammes of wheat
per hour, or about four horses power for from 80 to 88 kilogrammes. In this estimate we include the power necessary to
work, not only the millstones, but also all the accessory apparatus
of the mill.

It would appear, then, according to this, that in order to grind
from 15 to 16 hectolitres in the 24 hours—which corresponds to 50
or 51 kilogrammes per hour—it requires an effective force of $2\frac{1}{2}$
horses power, that required for the cleaning and bolting or dressing processes being included.

Supposing, then, that we have at our disposal an effective force
of 15 horses power, we should set it to work six pairs of stones,
together with the accompanying apparatus and machinery. We
must observe, however, that in this number we include the pair of
stones that may happen to be being redressed. As this operation
is made almost regularly every five or six days, or every week at
furthest, there is necessarily almost always a pair of stones not
working, but uncovered and undergoing the redressing operation;
an active manager, besides, always arranges that this work may be
well and quickly done, and as much as possible during the day-
time.

In mills where the stones are not screwed down so hard, and
consequently work further apart—as is the case in the greater part
of Burgundy and Lyons, and also in other countries—the mills are
made to grind from 24 to 25 hectolitres of wheat per pair of stones
per 24 hours, and often even more. The work done is, in these
cases, much more considerable; but then it is evidently at the expense of the quality of the flour, and almost always more seconds
than firsts are produced by these mills.

The power required by each pair of stones is necessarily greater,
although it does not increase in proportion to the quantity of flour
produced. In fact, it has been demonstrated by experiment, that
under the last-mentioned system, from 25 to 26 kilogrammes of
wheat can be ground by a force equal to one horse power of 75
kilogrammètres, whilst under the first system only 20 to 22 kilogrammes are ground. There is, therefore, an actual gain, as far as
regards this point; and it may be said, indeed, that with a power
of four horses, from 100 to 104 kilogrammes of wheat per hour can
be ground according to the system adopted at Lyons, Dijon, and
elsewhere, whilst, in the mills in and around Paris, the same power
serves to grind only from 80 to 88 kilogrammes.

In the mills intended for war purposes, in which, as we have
said, a much coarser flour is produced, and the stones consequently
work further apart, the expenditure of power is even still less,
proportionately, and the more so that the cleansing and dressing
apparatus is extremely limited in its action: thus, the work accomplished may be estimated at from 28 to 30 kilogrammes of wheat

ground per horse power per hour. In fact, experimental investigations have shown, that, with a steam-engine of from 24 to 25 horses power, working seven pairs of stones of 1·3 m. in diameter, 17,374 kilog. of wheat could be ground in the 24 hours. This corresponds to a power of 3½ horses, and 103·4 kilog. of wheat ground per pair of stones, or to 29·5 kilog. per horse power per hour.

We may, therefore, deduce from the preceding results:—

First—That with an effective power of one horse (or 75 kilogrammes raised one mètre high per second), a mill should grind a minimum of 20 kilog. of wheat, and a maximum of 30 kilog. per hour.

Second—That the minimum quantity applies to mills which are worked for commercial purposes, and particularly for the Parisian consumption, producing the greatest possible quantities of the higher qualities of flour.

Third—That the medium quantity (of from 25 to 26 kilog. per hour) is that produced by mills likewise worked for commercial purposes, but making a greater quantity of second quality flour, such as those at Lyons and other places.

Fourth—Finally, that the maximum quantity corresponds to the produce of those mills which only grind the coarser qualities, and in which the cleansing and dressing mediums are very simple.

TABLE OF THE POWER REQUIRED, THE QUANTITY OF WHEAT GROUND, AND THE NUMBER OF PAIRS OF STONES, WITH THEIR ACCESSORY APPARATUS.

Effective Force in		Quantity of Wheat ground in kilogrammes per hour.			Number of Pairs of Stones.		
Horses power.	k. m.	Minimum.	Medium.	Maximum.	Minimum.	Medium.	Maximum.
1	75	20	25	30	1	1	1
2	150	40	50	60	1	1	1
3	225	60	75	90	1	1	1
4	300	80	100	120	1 to 2	1	1
5	375	100	125	150	2	1 to 2	1 to 2
6	450	120	150	180	2 to 3	2	1 to 2
7	525	140	175	210	2 to 3	2	2
8	600	160	200	240	3	2 to 3	2
9	675	180	225	270	3 to 4	3	2 to 3
10	750	200	250	300	4	3	2 to 3
12	900	240	300	360	4 to 5	4	3
14	1050	280	350	420	5	4 to 5	4
16	1200	320	400	480	6	5	4 to 5
18	1350	360	450	540	6 to 7	6	5
20	1500	400	500	600	7	6 to 7	5 to 6
22	1650	440	550	660	8	7	6
24	1800	480	600	720	9	8	6 to 7
26	1950	520	650	780	10	8 to 9	7
28	2100	560	700	840	11	9	8
30	2250	600	750	900	12	10	8 to 9
32	2400	640	800	960	12 to 13	10 to 11	9
34	2550	680	850	1020	13	11	9 to 10
36	2700	720	900	1080	14	12	10
38	2850	760	950	1140	15	12 to 13	10 to 11
40	3000	800	1000	1200	16	13	11
45	3375	900	1125	1350	18	15	12 to 13
50	3750	1000	1250	1500	20	16 to 17	14
55	4125	1100	1375	1650	22	18	15 to 16
60	4500	1200	1500	1800	24	20	17
65	4875	1300	1625	1950	26	21 to 22	18 to 19
70	5250	1400	1750	2100	28	23	20
75	5625	1500	1875	2250	30	25	21 to 22
80	6000	1600	2000	2400	32	26 to 27	
85	6375	1700	2125	2550	34	28	24
90	6750	1800	2250	2600	36	30	25 to 26
95	7125	1900	2375	2850	38	31 to 32	27
100	7500	2000	2500	3000	40	33	28 to 29

This table is calculated upon the conclusions preceding it, and gives at sight, on the one hand, the quantity of wheat which can be ground by a given effective power, and, on the other, the approximate number of pairs of stones which may be erected when it is desired to fit up a mill with a determined power.

It is easy to see, from this table, that the number of pairs of stones varies in accordance with the three systems adopted. We believe the table will be a sufficient guide for the construction of flour mills, whatever may be the description of prime mover employed. It must be remarked, that it is most frequently upon such data that the number of stones ought to be determined, when an old mill is to be replaced by a new one, rather than upon the power of the mill which previously existed; for there is generally no comparison whatever between the work given out by a mill on the old system, with a pair of French stones of 1·8 or 2·1 m. in diameter, and that of a mill with modern English stones. In fact, we have known it to happen, that in one mill, where there had been two pairs of old stones of 2 m. in diameter, three or four pairs of small stones of 1·3 m. in diameter were erected, whilst, in other mills, six, eight, and even ten were worked to advantage.

These notable differences arise from various causes. Thus it will be understood, that if the prime mover, applied to an old mill, be badly constructed and badly arranged, it will utilize very little of the disposable force, and will, therefore, only give out an amount of work much below what it ought to do. Besides, the large French stones, with large eyes but ungrooved, can be made to grind little or much at pleasure, whilst, on the other hand, the flour is generally of a lower quality. We may say, in fact, that the quantity of wheat ground by a pair of large stones, in a given time, is almost always double that ground by a pair of small stones.

In reference to this subject, there is yet another remark to be made, which will not be without importance. In many localities, without adopting the English system altogether, there have been mills established on a mixed system; that is to say, that the gear, the manner of grinding, and chiefly the hydraulic prime mover, have been improved. Such mills give out sufficiently advantageous results, and, in fact, in some cases, produce more with a given force than they have been capable of producing at a later period, when they have been replaced by apparatus entirely on the English system. This has caused surprise, and the constructor has been blamed for obtaining worse results after than before the re-erection.

It must be recollected, that when the details of a French mill are improved—that is to say, when a good water-wheel is applied to it, and a good system of gearing, but still keeping the large stones, and not encumbering them with much accessory apparatus, since it is, after all, when taken as a whole, considerably less complicated than the English mill which is substituted for it—when worked with the same amount of power, it should produce more than the latter, although this latter is generally preferred, because the machinery is more complete, and better adapted for working in a regular and continuous manner.

We must also remark, that there are millers who prefer stones of from 1·4 to 1·5 m. in diameter, and sometimes even of 1·6 m.; but still adopting the English system in the general details—that is to say, the stones are grooved and dressed in exactly the same manner as those of 1·3 m. in diameter. They are made to produce more in a given time than the latter, although they are not driven at so rapid a rate, this never exceeding 90 or 100 revolutions per minute. These larger dimensions may have the advantage of simplifying the machinery, and diminishing the number of

stones, on the one hand, and perhaps, on the other, utilizing a greater per centage of the whole power of the prime mover. It will, in fact, be easily comprehended, that the power of a mill, comprising several pairs of stones of 1·3 m. in diameter, may at times be too great for them to work well, whilst it might be thoroughly utilized with stones of from 1·5 to 1·6 m. in diameter. Again, it may happen that the power to be disposed of is not sufficient to drive two pairs of small stones, whilst it is too much for one pair; or that it is not desirable to go to the expense of gearing for a second pair of stones; whilst, with a single pair of larger stones, all the power may be profitably employed, and the stones made to work well, with less first cost, and less after expense for repairs, and keeping in order.

We conclude these remarks by a statement of the results derived from mills, of different epochs:—

1830.—*First Statement of Produce, obtained from an old Steam-Mill, belonging to M. Benoit, at St. Denis, now no longer in existence.*

Produced by grinding 100 parts of Wheat, according to the American system.

Wheat flour,..................1st quality,..64 ⎫		
Flour separated from the oatmeal,..1st " ..3 ⎬ All flour,		
" " 2nd " ..6 ⎪ = 75 per 100		
" 3rd and 4th, " ..2 ⎭		
Coarse bran,....20 kilog. to the hectolitre,....6 ⎫		
Fine " 34 " " ....7 ⎬ Various products,		
Coarse meal, 28 to 30 " " ....6 ⎪ = 23		
To be re-ground, 45 to 50 " ....4 ⎭		
Waste and loss,...............................= 2		

General total,..................... 100 kilog.

1837.—*Second Statement of Produce; namely, of 3520 Setiers (42,240 Bushels) of Wheat, weighing 417,452 kilog., obtained from a Mill, on the English system, near Paris.*

Flour, 1st and 2nd quality,......300,579	= 72 per 100		
" 3rd quality,.............1,840 ⎫ = 2·3 "			
" 4th " ....7,586 ⎭			
Siftings,.....................2,856	= ·7 "		
Various products,.............88,016	=21·5 "		
Waste and loss,...............16,575	= 3·5 "		

General total,.......... 417,452 kilog.

1848.—*Third Statement of Produce; namely, of 100 Setiers (1,200 Bushels) of Wheat, weighing 11,800 kilog.*

Flour, 1st quality,..................8,260	= 70 per 100	
" 2nd " 236	= 2 "	
" 3rd and 4th,................472	= 4 "	
Various products,.................2,360	= 20 "	

11,328 kilog.

SAW-MILLS.

447. Saw-mills may be divided into two distinct categories; namely, those in which the saws have a continuous motion, and those in which the motion is reciprocatory.

The first class comprises not only circular saws, but also those which consist of a thin flexible steel-plate, passed round two drums or pulleys, like an ordinary pulley-belt.

The second class comprises straight saws, acting vertically or horizontally, or sometimes slightly inclined.

We shall here give the notes of some experiments upon a sawing-machine, having several saw-plates arranged side by side in a frame, weighing altogether nearly 400 kilog.

The power expended by the prime mover was, for ·161 sq. m. in area, sawn through per minute, in dry oak, 3·7 horses power; and 4·5 horses power for an area of ·131 sq. m. sawn through per minute, in oak that had been cut four years. In these instances, four saw-plates were worked at once, which gives for each saw-plate, in the first instance, ·925 horses power per plate; and, in the second, 1·125 horses power.

The width of the *set* of the saw is ordinarily 3 to 4 millimètres at the outside.

A reciprocating saw, making, on an average, 120 strokes per minute, with a length of stroke equal to ·6 m., the cranks being ·3 m. in radius, passes in a minute through a space equal to

$$120 \times 2 \times ·6 = 144 \text{ mètres};$$
or,
$$2·4 \text{ m. per second.}$$

Now, with such a stroke, we can saw through a thickness of from 50 to 60 centimètres, and even more. In taking the lower of these two dimensions, the work obtained per minute, with an *advance* of 2 millimètres, is

$$120 \times ·002 \times ·5 = ·12 \text{ sq. m.,}$$
for the area sawn through, measured upon one side only.

This, per hour, is

$$·12 \times 60 = 7·8 \text{ sq. m.}$$

WORK GOT THROUGH, WITH A LONG SAW, BY TWO MEN.

448. Two men, giving on an average 50 strokes per minute, can go on, without stopping, for 3 or 4 minutes. Allowing that they stop every 30 seconds, or half minute, the stroke of their saw being ·975 m., the entire length of the plate, 1·3 m., they will saw through a length of ·92 m. in 7 minutes. This gives for the area sawn through—

$$·92 \times ·315 = ·2898 \text{ sq. m.};$$
or, per minute,
$$·2898 \div 7 = ·0414 \text{ sq. m.}$$

Thus, the work of these two men is very nearly equal to that of one of the saw-plates in the sawing-machine first described, which requires a force equal to one horse power. This difference may easily be accounted for, when it is recollected that, in the sawing-machine, a considerable part of the motive power is expended in overcoming the friction of the various moveable parts, through which the motion is communicated to the saw-frame; whilst, in manual sawing, the power is applied directly to the saw, and the frame is always a very light affair, especially as compared with that in the machine.

In a manually-worked saw, such as we have alluded to, the teeth are ·013 m. apart, so that 75 teeth come into action during the stroke of ·975 m. The depth of these teeth is ·0065 m.; that is to say, half their pitch. They are very slightly bent to each

side, and the workmen chamfer off their inner edges, alternately on one side and on the other.

As the saw only acts during its descent, it may be deduced, from the preceding statements, that its mean advance is

$$·92 \text{ m.} \div 7 = ·1314 \text{ m. per 1'};$$
and per stroke of the saw,
$$·1314 \div 50 = ·00263 \text{ m.;}$$
that is to say, a little above 2½ millimètres. This advance is very nearly the same as that ordinarily given to a machine-saw, when sawing oak.

VENEER-SAWING MACHINES.

For veneer saws, which generally work upon hard wood, and which, moreover, produce sheets of peculiar thinness, and perfectly equal and regular throughout, it is obviously impossible to advance through the wood at such a rate as is customary in cutting deal bulks into boards.

The velocity of these saws is, perhaps, greater than for any other purpose. It is not less, in fact, than 280 strokes per minute, and often reaches even 300 strokes, which is more than double the ordinary velocity formerly adopted.

If the saw only advances through mahogany at the rate of ½ millimètre for each revolution, the length sawn through per minute will be

$$300 \times ·0005 = ·15 \text{ m.;}$$
and per hour,
$$·15 \times 60 = 9 \text{ mètres.}$$

If the width of the wood be 40 centimètres, the area sawn through per hour will be

$$9 \times ·4 = 3·6 \text{ square mètres;}$$
and per day's work, of 12 hours, allowing 2 hours for grinding the tools, fixing the wood, arranging the saw, lubricating, &c., the total work done will be

$$3·6 \times 10 = 36 \text{ sq. m., sawn through.}$$

We may remark, that the actual price paid to saw-mill owners for sawing mahogany is, at Paris, generally 28 fr. per 100 kilog., 20 sheets of veneer to the inch, or 27 millimètres, of width being given.

It is scarcely twenty years since the time that 10 francs per kilog., or 1,000 francs per 100 kilog., was paid for this description of sawing; and it was very rarely that so many sheets of veneer were got out of the same thickness of wood. This immense difference will give some idea of the effects of competition, and the improvements continually made in the construction of machinery.

CIRCULAR SAWS.

450. Circular saws are, without question, the simplest, and capable of the greatest number of applications in the industrial arts. They are employed of all dimensions, from those of 2 or 3 centimètres in diameter, to those of 1 mètre, and even more. The smallest and weakest are generally used for cutting very minute articles, in bone, horn, or ivory. In the machines for cutting the flat sides of wheel-teeth, we find circular saws employed, of from 6 or 8 centimètres, up to 14 or 16 centimètres in diameter, according to the power of the machine, and the strength of the teeth to

be cut. In carpentry, cabinet-making, and coach-making, circular saws are employed of from ·12 m. to ·6 m. in diameter. In engineers' workshops, circular saws may be considered indispensable, on account of the rapidity of their action, and also on account of the perfection of their work. The saws used in these workshops are generally from ·2 to ·4 m. in diameter, and they revolve at a rate not less than 400 revolutions per minute, and in some cases 600. and even more.

EXPERIMENTS WITH A CIRCULAR SAW, ·7 M. IN DIAMETER.

FIRST TRIAL.—Kind of wood sawn: oak, one year after being cut, ·222 m. in depth :—

Number of revolutions of the saw per 1',.................. 266
Area sawn per minute,................................. ·18 sq. m.

SECOND TRIAL.—Kind of wood sawn: dry deal, in planks, ·27 m wide, by ·027 m. thick :—

Number of revolutions of the saw per 1',.................. 244
Area sawn in 1',.. ·75 sq. m.

These results show that, for small pieces of wood, one circular saw does as much work as four vertical rectilinear saws in the same time, and with the same motive power.

It must be remarked, that the area sawn, as noted above, is the product of the depth of the piece by the length sawn, and not the sum of the two faces separated by the saw, as is customary in calculating wood.

CHAPTER XIV.

EXAMPLES OF FINISHED DRAWINGS OF MACHINERY.

BALANCE WATER METER.

EXAMPLE PLATE Ⓐ.

In approaching the completion of our labours for the instruction of the Practical Draughtsman in Industrial Design, we now lay before him our promised descriptive details of the finished example plates which have been developed for his guidance. Our Plate Ⓐ, of this series, is given as a specimen of careful and accurate line-drawing on the part of the draughtsman who committed the design to paper, and fidelity on the part of the engraver who retransferred the delineation to the copperplate, and worked up the "effects" on the rounds, and the general lights and shades.

The little instrument here selected as the means of conveying a lesson on "finish," is the full size of a fluid meter, capable of measuring something more than 800 gallons of water, or as much as is necessary for the condenser of a six horse steam-engine, per hour. It is the invention of Mr. Charles William Siemens of Birmingham, a brother of Mr. E. W. Siemens of Berlin, the inventor of the "Prussian State Telegraph," both of which gentlemen must be well known to the readers of these pages, from their many contributions to physical science and the constructive arts.

The "balance meter" is of the rotatory kind, and has been contrived with the view of securing, within the compass of extremely simple details, the power of registering the quantity of water flowing through a pipe, with equal accuracy at all pressures, and without in any way impeding the continuous flow from the supplying head. Fig. 1 is a longitudinal elevation of the meter, a portion of the indicating dial being broken away to show the internal indicating details. Fig. 2 is a corresponding longitudinal section of the meter, exhibiting both the rotatory measuring apparatus, and the index gearing. The whole of the apparatus is contained within the cylindrical cast-iron shell, A, having plain end flanges, B, for bolting it in the line of the water supply-pipe, and a short cylindrical box, C, screwed on the upper side to hold the index gearing. This shell is cast hollow and open throughout, but with three projecting annular ribs for boring out as a seat for a drawn brass lining tube, D, inserted for the purpose of securing a perfectly uniform area throughout the waterway; and within this waterway are placed two hollow metal drums, E, supported on longitudinal spindles, F, set in the axial line of the shell. These spindles are carried at their outer ends in bearings, G, in the centres of the fixed cone pieces, H, one of which is in section, and the opposite or inner spindle bearings are in a single central bracket opposite the rib, I, of the shell. Each longitudinal half, from the centre line, is precisely the same in construction. The cones, H, have each projecting spindle pieces, passing to near each end of the shell, where they are steadied concentrically with the shell's axis, by cross bars, J, in shallow ring pieces recessed into each end of the shell; whilst the cones themselves are steadied by four thin radial blades, K, fitting to the brass lining. The inner surfaces of these cones are concave, and the slightly convex faces of the drums, E, project a little way into these concavities, as shown on the right side of the figure. The drums, E, are the prime motive details, each having a set of screw blades, or twisted vanes, L, set in reverse directions, or right and left-handed. Motion is conveyed from the drum spindles by pinions, M, one on the inner end of each spindle. Each pinion gears into two opposite crown wheels, N, so that the two drums are compelled to revolve at the same rate in opposite directions. The lower crown wheel is simply carried on a short stud-shaft, running in bearings in the centre bracket, being merely used to connect the two pinions on the lower side; whilst the upper wheel is fast on the lower end of a prolonged shaft, supported in the same bracket, and passed through a hole in the side of the shell, to give motion to the counter above. The special object of this application of the second crown wheel, is the neutralizing the lateral pressure upon the drum bearings, in the transmission of motion from one drum to the other; and to reduce the working friction to the highest degree of refinement, the total weight of each drum is calculated to be just equal to that of its bulk of the fluid surrounding it. The water enters the meter, as indicated by the duplex spreading arrow, passing through a coarse grating, P, intended to retain pieces of wood and bulky matters, but permitting the water, with its ordinary impurities, to pass through. After passing this grating, the fluid is collected towards the axis of the shell, by the first internal conical incline, Q, of a duplex cone piece inserted within the shell, and the flow is then directed outwards by the second reverse cone, R, and spread uniformly over the quick external cone of the pieces, H. The object of this direction of the fluid is to prevent *partial currents*, which would otherwise disturb the motion of the working drum; and as water, in passing through pipes, sometimes acquires a rotatory motion, the conical block, H, is armed with the radiating blades, K, to direct the fluid in a line parallel with the axis, prior to its reaching the drums beyond.

The current, thus uniformly spread and directed, now meets the right-handed screw blades of the first drum, E, which is thus caused to revolve, the water at the same time acquiring a certain deflection, in consequence partially from the resistance of the drum to rotation, and partially from the friction of the fluid against the surface of the revolving drum.

The amount of this deflection or "slip" of the water, varies with the velocity of the current, and would, of course, affect the accuracy of the measurement, were it not for the correcting influence of the second or left screw-bladed drum. The blades on this drum are of precisely the same pitch as those on the first; and as they revolve, they meet the water at an angle so much greater than occurs at the first drum, as is due to this angular deflection. Hence the water tends to drive the second drum faster than the first, and the fluid suffers twice that amount of deflection in the reverse direction. Hence the combination of the two drums produces a powerful water-pressure engine, upon which the slight friction of the apparatus exercises no appreciable retarding effect. Moreover, the friction of the water on the drum surface increases in the ratio of its velocity, and the result is, that the combined drums move, under all circumstances, in the exact ratio of the current. The outer edges of the screw blades do not work in absolute contact with the internal surface of the fixed shell, A, but no water can slip through this way without impinging on the vanes, in consequence of a slight contraction of the shell between the two drums. After passing both drums, the water is again directed as in the first instance, and passes off to the service-pipe at the opposite end of the shell.

The counter or indicating apparatus possesses some peculiar features, as regards simplicity of details, and the dispensing with a stuffing-box for the communicating shaft, o, of the drums. It is entirely contained in the cylindrical brass case, c, in the top of which a strong plate-glass cover, s, is screwed in from the under side. A strong brass plate, T, divides the case from the meter,

and has a central hole for the passage through of the vertical spindle, o. A worm, or endless screw, U, upon this spindle, gives motion to the wheel, V, the horizontal spindle of which has a worm, w, cut upon it, and gearing with a horizontal wheel, X. The spindle of this latter wheel carries a broad pinion, Y, which drives both the horizontal spur-wheels, Z, the first of which has 101, and the second 100 teeth.

The wheel with 101 teeth works loose upon its spindle, but carries round with it a dial-plate, a, graduated on its circumference to 100 parts. The lower wheel of 100 teeth is fixed upon the same spindle as the first, and carries an index hand, which works round above the dial, and points to the divisions thereon; and a fixed hand, b, points as well to the same graduations. The train of worm-wheels is so proportioned, that exactly 10 gallons of water must pass through the meter, in order to move the dial-plate under the fixed hand through one division. One entire revolution of the dial, consequently, indicates the passage of 1,000 gallons of water, for which the moving differential hand passes through only a single division on its dial. An entire revolution of the latter, therefore, signifies the passage of 100,000 gallons. The reading of such a dial is extremely simple. If we suppose the fixed hand to point to 47, and the hand on the dial to 89, this will show that 89,470 gallons have passed.

The whole chamber of the counter is filled with purified mineral naphtha, or other non-corrosive liquid, which communicates with the impure liquid passing through the meter, only through the medium of the capillary space round the upright spindle, o, and does not intermingle with it, although both liquids are under the same pressure.

The actual measurements by this meter have been found to agree so perfectly with the calculations, in which the frictional surfaces against the water are taken into account, that Mr. Siemens considers any means of adjustment to be unnecessary. Much, however, depends upon the formation of *perfect* screw vanes upon the drum, to insure uniform results; but all difficulty on this head has been very successfully removed, by casting the drums in metal moulds, using a peculiar composition, which does not shrink in cooling, and runs very fine.

The only parts of this meter where wear and tear is to be expected, are the pivots of the rotatory drums, and these are made of hard steel, and abut against agate plates; but considering that all weight is taken off the bearings, and that the water simply glides over the drum surfaces, these pivots may reasonably be expected to run for years without requiring attention.

An important practical advantage of this form of meter, is its compact form, and the facility which it offers for adjustment in a line of pipes below street pavement, or at any required elevation or direction. The internal working parts are quite self-contained, and inaccessible without unsoldering the ends, so that they may be intrusted to the care of ordinary workmen.

In addition to the employment of the meter for water-works purposes, it may be usefully applied for registering the water supplied to steam-boilers, in order to ascertain the actual evaporation going on, so as to afford a correct estimate of the value of the fuel on the one hand, and the engine and boiler on the other.

ENGINEER'S SHAPING MACHINE.

EXAMPLE PLATE B.

Our second example plate is in a more ambitious style of illustrative finish, and, as a work of higher effort, it forms a most appropriate subject for the advanced stage of our instructions. It goes further than Plate A, in as far as, in addition to its value as a drawing worth copying, it presents some most important features of symmetry in its abstract design, and carries up the mechanical disciple into an elevated range of workmanlike contrivance, and the perfection of the minutest details. The credit of so good a design belongs to Mr. G. P. Renshaw, C.E., of Nottingham.

When Watt was laying the foundation of our present magnificent mechanical achievements, he was met at every turn by practical difficulties, in the want of constructive tools for working out his ideas; and many of his great conceptions were doomed, for this reason, to remain mere suggestive designs. For the same reason, numberless works, which the growth of mechanical contrivances has turned into every-day operations, were treated and put down as simple impossibilities, in the days when long screws were made by the crude process of wrapping a wire round a mandrel, and compressing it between elastic dies. But things are now very different with us. Even our farm operations have begun to feel the benefits of machinery; and, as a necessary consequence, we now find establishments for making and repairing steam-engines and other intricate mechanism in retired country villages. This substitution of machine tools for hand labour, whilst it has introduced great accuracy of workmanship, has been the great cause of that cheapness of construction which, coupled with the application of new and better-suited materials, has made us the eminent manufacturers we are.

The "finish" of machinery has also latterly met with increased attention, involving, in many respects, a judicious lightness of details, and conducing to attentive management; for the attendant naturally cares more for an elegant machine or steam-engine than for one of ruder construction, and he therefore feels his pride far deeper involved in its performances.

Of the long list of machine tools now in existence, the lathe is by far the most ancient, and it is yet the most important—whether we regard it in reference to the extent and variety of its applications, or the intrinsic beauty of its action. But such a tool would be very far from meeting the requirements of the modern engineer, who has, therefore, gradually accumulated separate machines for planing, slotting, shaping, fluting, nut and wheel cutting and boring machines, with many other specially adapted tools. Each of these is limited in its power, and is restricted to a particular class of work—so that the engineer is compelled to pass his work through many separate tools, before he can complete a single piece of combined mechanism. This system of working is productive of many evils, as the loss of time in transferring and refixing heavy details, and the increase in the chances of error due to repeated readjustment. And in many branches of manufacture, more especially in light work, where good tools would be highly advantageous for occasional use, the expense of the several kinds dis-

courages their adoption. We are, therefore, driven to look for a constructive machine of simple construction, which shall in itself unite the functions and powers of the existing detached tools. Professor Willis, in his late Exhibition Lecture at the Society of Arts, has, indeed, generally alluded to this, in speaking of the want of "machines much more comprehensive, and yet simple in form, by means of which the construction of machinery in general will attain to greater perfection, and machine tools be introduced into workshops of a smaller character than at present, in the same manner as the lathe." It is precisely this that Mr. Renshaw has endeavoured to carry out in his two chief modifications of, or foundations upon, the common lathe and slotting machine.

The essential features of the several plans, arranged by Mr. Renshaw, consist in the combination of the ordinary circular-cutting motions and arrangements of the lathe, with the rectilinear action of the planing or shaping machine, or their derivatives. The composite principle may be applied to most of the machine tools used in the different branches of useful and ornamental manufactures, so as to open out a new field in the arrangement of constructive machinery. Thus, in the case of the lathe, for example, it is applicable not only to the execution of various kinds of plain work, but also to the beautiful, though subservient, branch of complex or geometrical turning. For instance, if the sliding bar carrying the slide-rest be worked by an adjustable crank-pin, working in a slot in the end of the bar, or by changeable cams, the revolutions of the crank being proportioned to those of the lathe mandrel by the interposition of the ordinary change-wheels of the lathe, most of the varieties of work hitherto produced only by complicated and isolated kinds of lathes may be executed—as eccentric, elliptical, swash, rose, cycloidal, and others; the tools, cutters, or drills being applied either to edges or surfaces, or angularly, by the adjustment for the fast headstock, while, to vary the pattern, it is simply necessary to alter the proportions of the wheels.

Comprehensiveness is a prominent feature in this invention; some of the individual parts, like the machines themselves, serving for several uses, and thus favouring simplicity; so that a lathe, embracing the above functions, for instance, may still possess the steadiness and convenience necessary for the ordinary plain work of the amateur. The engineer and mechanist do not require these ornamental curves, but each may introduce the system of change-wheels in conjunction with the composite lathe, or cutting tools for various uses, besides the ordinary ones of sliding, screw-cutting, and boring, as for finishing cams, snails, spirals, and volutes of various kinds, for barrelling and tapering work, whether circular or rectilinear, and for planing dovetails, V's, and other angular work.

To explain this, let fig. 1 represent the principal gearing of a composite lathe, in which A represents the main driving-shaft, actuating the mandrel, B, of the lathe by means of a pinion, C, which can be slid out of gear by a clutch; D, back gearing for slow speed, as usual; E, screw-wheel and tangent-screw, with intermittent ratchet-motion feeding in either direction; G, guide-screw; H, grooved shaft for actuating the transverse slide of the slide-rest by intermediate gearing; I, the same for moving the vertical slide; K, reversing-screw, corresponding to the pitch of the guide-screw; L, grooved shaft, in connection with the dif ferential or barrelling motion, which is attached to the vertical slide, and consists of a segmental screw-wheel, embracing a motion of about 60°, gearing with a tangent-screw on the shaft, L. The

segment has a radial slot, in which an adjustable crank-pin is fixed, the crank-pin being attached to the bearings of the screw for moving the vertical slide, by means of a connecting-rod—the

Fig. 1.

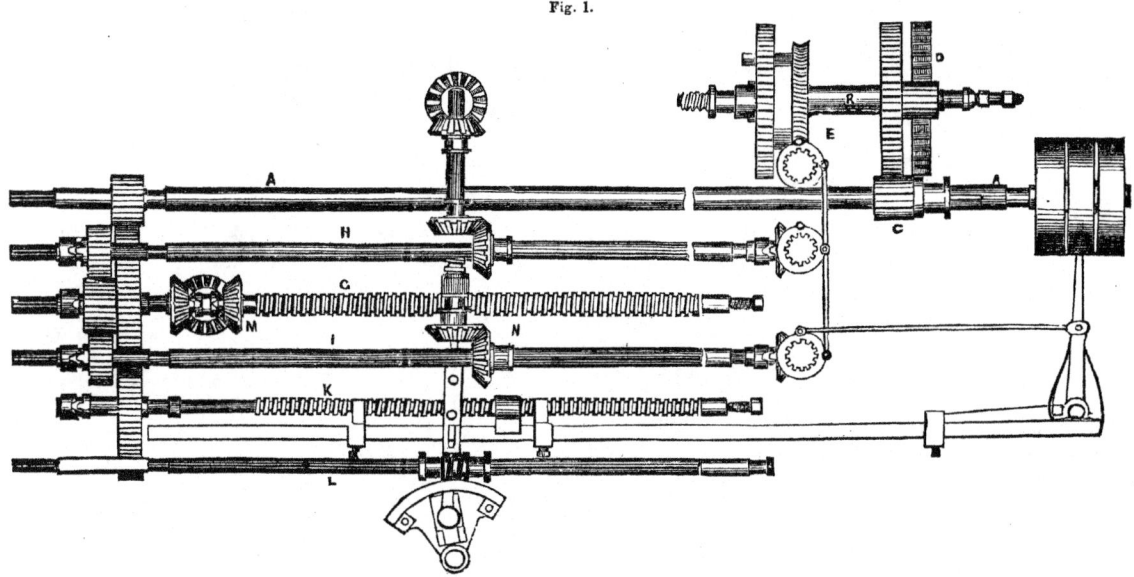

bearings of the screw, which slide in dovetails, and consequently the vertical slide, being thus affected by the eccentricity of the crank-pin. The shafts, A, H, and I, and screws, G and K, are connected by a system of wheels, the arrangement of which is clearly shown in the end view, fig. 2; but G, H, I, and K, may be disconnected from their respective wheels at pleasure by clutches or frictional nuts. A, G, H, I, and L, also project at the end to the right hand of fig. 1, so as to carry change-wheels when necessary, and H and I have intermittent ratchet-feeding movements at the opposite end, similar to that at E, for working the tangent-screw. All these are worked by the reversing bar in connection with the screw, K. An ordinary reversing movement, M, is interposed between the guide-screw, E, and its driving-wheel, for reversing the motion in sliding and screw-cutting. When the lathe is used for surfacing, this reversing motion is better applied on the driving-shaft, A. Hand adjustments, not shown in the figure, are applied to the boxes of the guide-screw, G, and of the screws of the vertical and transverse slides of the slide-rest. A composite lathe, thus geared, may be applied to all the ordinary descriptions of work. For sliding, boring, and screw-cutting, the mandrel is worked by the pinion, C, whilst change-wheels connect A with G. The height of the tool for turning is conveniently adjusted by the vertical slide of the slide-rest. Sup-

Fig. 2.

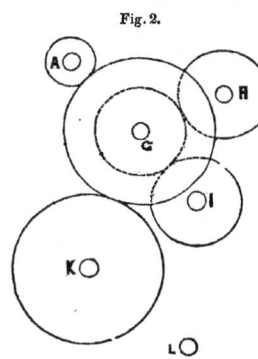

pose it is desired to stop the lathe at any particular point when the attendant is absent, the screw, K, is put in gear by its clutch, and by means of a detent stop-movement, it stops the lathe at the precise point, by throwing the belt off the fast pulley on the end of A, which travels with considerable rapidity. If it be required to turn a long cone of greater taper than can conveniently be done by traversing the following head-stock, the cutting-tool is set over the work by raising the vertical slide by its hand adjustment, whilst G and I are also connected by change-wheels, so that the slide rises or falls with the cut. If a connecting-rod is to be barrelled, the crank-pin of the differential apparatus is adjusted for eccentricity to suit the rise of the sweep, and L is connected with G by the change-wheels, to spread the arc over the required length. The barrelling may be used in conjunction with the taper adjustments, as will be evident to the practical mechanic. The same parts apply equally to rectilinear cutting, whether parallel or taper, in all directions of the cube, and for barrelling in a vertical plane, the pinion, C, being disconnected with the mandrel, and the feed being applied by the intermittent ratchet motions. For cutting the hollows of connecting-rods, &c., an intermittent revolving motion is given to the tool by a tangent-screw movement as usual, but, in addition, applying to cranks and levers held on the face-chuck; or, instead of the latter movement, the work may be set eccentrically, the hollows being then worked by the tangent-screw movement in connection with the mandrel.

Edge-cams, snails, volutes, of spiral curvature, with any number of rises, or compounds of circular and spiral arcs, of which fig. 3 gives examples, may be accurately shaped or planed on the edges, by connecting the tangent-screw with the transverse slide of the slide-rest, during the reciprocating action of the cutting tool, by means of change-wheels. To do this in the present tool, the ratchet-feed movements of E and I are put in gear, I being

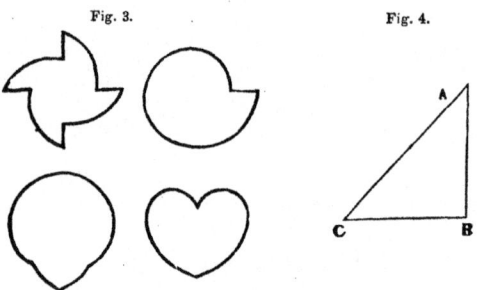

Fig. 3.   Fig. 4.

prevented from moving the vertical slide by sliding the pinion, N, out of gear by means of an eccentric, whilst I and H are connected by change-wheels. In the same way, face-cams and other forms may be shaped by varying the connections.

Angular and diagonal work in any position may also be worked in this lathe without tilting the tool, by means of the same set of change-wheels. To explain this, we may observe that any angle, such as B A C, fig. 4, may be produced, by setting one of the slides to move through the space, B C, or sine of the angle, whilst the

tion in the remaining direction of the cube. To reverse the angle, a subsidiary wheel is introduced into the pair of change-wheels.

In many cases a crank movement is convenient, in addition to the guide-screw planing movement, to work short strokes with rapidity; while the guide-screw serves for longer ranges, and also to adjust the slide-rest. The crank disc is then driven by a bevil pinion on the shaft, A, the connecting-rod being attached to one of the bearings of the guide-screw, which is made to slide similarly to the barrelling movement.

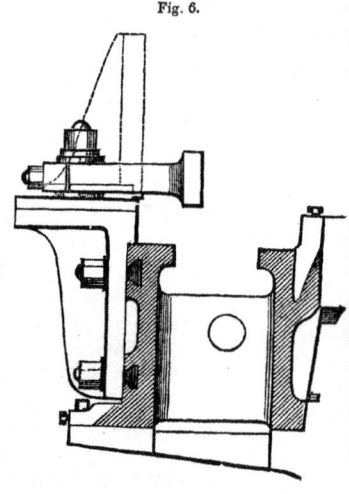

Fig. 6.

Fig. 5 represents a composite lathe, or shaping machine, constructed on the model of the ordinary planing machine, and designed for accurately finishing the pieces forming the framings of marine and other engines at one setting, but also applicable to a variety of other work, as it combines the powers of the lathe with the ordinary drilling, boring, planing, slotting, and shaping machines. The work is placed or traversed between the upright standards, A A, as in the ordinary planing machine, whilst a vertical cutting action may be given to the slide-rest and head-stock, carrying the lathe mandrel, by two connecting-rods, B B, actuated by crank discs beneath the bed, and balanced, if necessary. The connecting-rods are adjustable for length by means of a cross shaft, C, actuating a screw-wheel and screw in each; D is the tangent-screw motion, as usual, and E is a slide to regulate the eccentricity of the tool during turning and planing hollows, which may be automatically fed, when requisite, by an eccentric, not shown in the figure. A screw, F, gives the cross motion, and another at the back of the slide, E, which it actuates, adjusts the mandrel in a vertical plane. By the diagonal principle we described, the octagonal recesses, or seats, for plummer-block brasses, and other angular work, may be executed with precision.

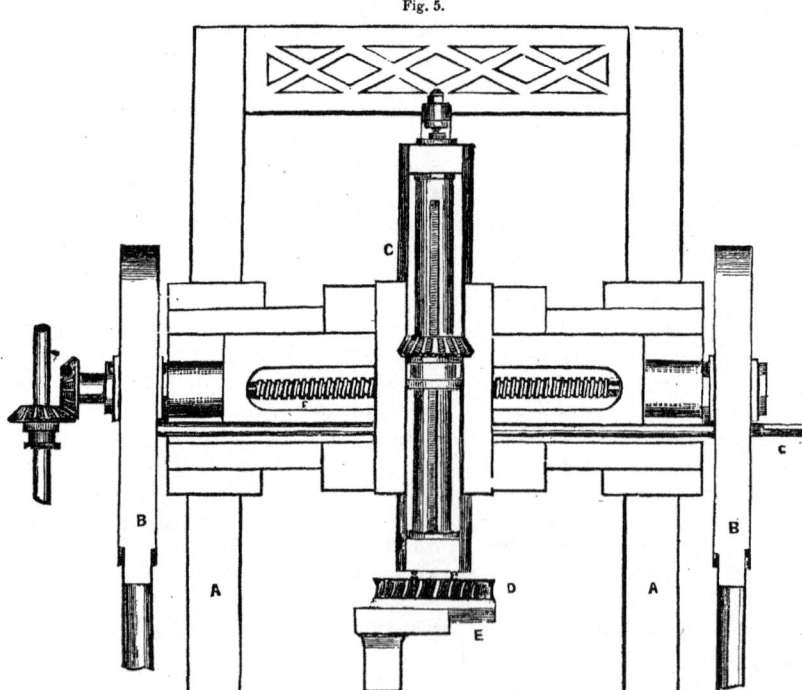

Fig. 5.

other slide traverses the cosine, A B. To apply this practically, any two of the slides, actuated by G, H, and I, are connected by the proportionate wheels, whilst the third gives the cutting mo-

other angular work, may be executed with precision.

Fig. 6 represents a convenient form of bed. The bed-chuck applies to the side, as used for holding plummer-blocks whilst their soles are planed. A second chuck (dotted) may be super-posed for fixing work vertically; and a slide may be added to draw up the work, which may then project between the bearers of the bed. For long works, a bed-chuck is used at each end. Levers, also, may be passed between the bed, by means of a diametric slide on the face-chuck, when requisite.

We now come to Plate ⓑ itself in detail. That plate repre-sents a side elevation of a composite slotting and shaping ma-chine, with self-acting gearing, as adapted for the entire finishing of large cranks, levers, wheels, and other work, ordinarily depend-ent upon the efforts of several tools. The main frame consists of a large and elegant column, with an open rectangular base, and bottom flange for bolting down to the masonry. The upper por-tion has cast upon it, on one side, a pilaster bracket piece, with two horizontal projecting arms, to carry the vertical cutting slide, A; and on the other, a pillar bracket to support one end of the main crank disc shaft; on the front side of the rectangular base is bolted a double-armed bracket, to carry the vertical spindle of the cutting face-chuck, like the mandril and face-plate of a large lathe, as set on end. The cutting slide, A, like that of a common slotting machine, is fitted to traverse in dovetail faces on the overhead bracket arms, being actuated by the revolution of the pin in the disc, B. At c are two pairs of bevil pinions, connected to work simultaneously by an intermediate vertical shaft, D, the two vertical pinions being each on the projecting end of a hori-zontal screw spindle, governing the traverse motions of a pair of horizontal dovetailed slides, on which the vertical slide faces of the slotting bar, A, are carried. This is for adjusting the eccen-tricity of the tool in turning. Viewed from the front, the fram-ing of these slides has the form, I, of which the vertical portion and the two arms to the left are covered by the moving details, the latter being completely thrust in when the cutting tool of the slide, A, exactly coincides with the centre of the revolving work on the face-chuck, as also with the crank disc, B. At E is an-other shaft for giving a continuous feeding motion to the trans-verse slides, by the intervention of a worm and tangent-screw, or worm-wheel. This corresponds to the traverse or surfacing movement in the lathe. A hand-wheel, F, is fitted on the pro-longed end of the shaft, D, for manual adjustment when the worm-wheel gear is disconnected by slackening the screw, G, the bear-ing, H, at the other end of the spindle being constructed with a joint to allow of this disengagement. Another shaft, I, carries a spur pinion to actuate the rack, J, on the cutting slide, this pinion being capable of traversing on the shaft by means of a groove and feather, along with the slides of the cutting bar. In this way a continuous vertical feed motion, for turning or boring, is secured, the shaft, I, being connected with the shaft, K, by a worm and wheel; the hand-wheel, L, on the bottom end of a ver-tical shaft. connected at its upper end to the shaft, K, by a pair of bevil pinions, is the hand adjustment. This motion serves also to adjust the cutting bar, previous to tightening the nut on the stud bolt in front, for the reciprocating action. During the working of the reciprocating cutter slide, however, this adjusting gear is disengaged, and is kept disengaged by an eccentric and slide actuated by the hand-wheel, N, which moves the entire adjustment in one mass. At the back of the cutter slide, near

the upper end, is a nut, O, whereby the crank disc connecting-rod may be detached when wide lateral ranges of the slide are wanted in turning. The general details of the driving gear for the turn-ing and planing actions, are fully delineated in the plate; but it may be explained, that at P is a hand-lever, working over a semi-circular arc, suitably notched and contrived to smft the bearing, Q, of the horizontal shaft, R, by an eccentric, so as to throw either of the opposed or antagonistic bevil wheels on this shaft into gear with its corresponding bevil wheel. This movement enables the workman to connect either the circular action of the face-chuck, through the large bevil wheel beneath it, or the rectilinear action of the cutting slide, by means of the vertical shaft passing up the centre of the main column, and geared to the horizontal crank disc shaft above, by a bevil wheel and pinion, or, by setting this adjustment at an intermediate position, both may be disen-gaged. At s is a foot-break lever to stop the revolution of the work when heavy masses are under operation, a friction strap from this lever being passed over a pulley on the shaft, R, for this purpose.

At T is a cone pulley, working in connection with the cone pul-leys on the two upper or continuous feeding shafts, for the circular cutting action, the respective pulleys being set to coincide verti-cally when connected. The face-chuck can be fixed during the reciprocating action of the cutting slide, by the clamp, U. This clamping movement consists of a worm, with a square spindle for shipping on a handle, driving a worm-wheel on the end of a spin-dle, connected interiorly with a segmental wedge, the sides of which are portions of a right and left screw-thread respectively. The upper part of this segmental piece is flattened, to permit the free revolution of the face-chuck when driven by the screw gear-ing, as indicated by the large worm-wheel, in gear with a worm, fast on the spindle of the main front hand-wheel. Near the base of the tool is a hand-wheel, v, for the angular adjustment of the mandril frame or headstock for taper work. For this purpose the headstock is attached to the main frame by a central tenon and circular dovetails, which afford a support during the slackening of the holding bolts.

An eccentric chuck, having two slides at right angles to each other, and an upper worm-wheel adjustment, is fitted on the face-chuck mandril. The lower slide, for giving the intermittent feed in shaping the rectilinear sides, w, of a crank, has a double-acting ratchet-wheel, temporarily connected by a rod with the correspond-ing feeding disc of the large worm-wheel on the face chuck, when the latter is fixed at U. The intermittent feed is primarily derived from the edge-groove cam on the crank disc, B. This groove works the upper stud-pin of a bell-crank lever, set on a stud centre in the side of the main frame, and from the lower horizontal arm of this lever a rod descends to the worm-wheel mechanism of the face-chuck.

The upper side of the eccentric chuck is limited to the ac-tual adjustment of the work, and, by means of the two slides conjointly, adjustments may be made for shaping the bosses of the cranks, as well as the hollows at x. The obliquity of the straight sides, w, of the crank is adjusted by the upper screw-wheel, which need only be of a diameter equal to the length of the crank; or, instead of this plan, the sides, w, may

z

be worked out differentially by duly proportioning the feeds to suit.

In cutting out a crank on this tool, the wrought-iron mass is first faced. The bosses are then bored out either by an ordinary boring bar fitted into the tool, or by means of the turning tool. After the work has been adjusted as to centre on the truly set face-chuck, it is clamped down, and a bolt, having a T-headed nut entering a groove in the chuck, is then passed through the bore of each boss, and the external clamps being removed, the remaining turning and shaping processes are gone through. The work requires no further shifting or disturbance after being once properly adjusted for position, as the slides of the eccentric chuck, which are graduated, give the true centres.

This shaping machine is more peculiarly fitted for executing very heavy work than the lathe, supported by the mandril only, because the plan of revolution is horizontal, and hence friction is reduced whilst the chucking is facilitated. And when the work has a considerable overhang, as in the case of a crank, its revolution in a vertical plane, as on a lathe, entails some loss of power and liability to vibration. This, of course, applies only to heavy work, as pieces of moderate size, though with a preponderating side, may be readily worked with accuracy in the lathe by means of counterweights attached to the back of the chuck. Exact balance is attainable by an adjustment of the leverage.

Mr. Renshaw has since made a tool of simpler appearance, but of still greater workshop qualifications, being intended for slotting and shaping heavy work of considerable length, and serving, besides, as a complete vertical lathe for boring and turning large wheels, the outsides of cylinders, and other articles, as well as the self-acting shaping out of curved surfaces, which cannot be so turned in the common lathe.

The main frame is, in this instance, a plain stout column, with suitable brackets for the overhead gear cast on it. The crank disc shaft is driven by eccentric oval spur-wheels, for compensation and quick return; and the tool-holding slide in front of the main cutting slide, whilst it serves to give a fine adjustment to the tool for circular cutting, may also be screwed on at right angles and at different heights. It is removed altogether when the tool cuts in right lines. The mandril, or face-chuck spindle, descends into a pit, so as to bring the chuck-face considerably lower than it otherwise would be. When revolving for circular work, it is raised by bevil-wheels below, but it is let down solid for slotting.

For turning round and hollow surfaces, a vertical worm or tangent screw, driven from the main gearing, is put in gear with a worm-wheel on the crank disc shaft behind, and the required arc is obtained by adjusting the crank pin radius to suit, and by suitable change-wheels, borrowed from a screw-cutting lathe, and applied to actuate the worm.

For taper slotting, the table is made to tilt as usual, but the axis of motion is at right angles to the long traversing slide, so as to apply also to boring and turning. The table is also graduated on its edge all round. The mandril is driven by a large inverted bevil-wheel, concealed beneath the chuck, and a cross shaft is so fitted to the face-chuck, that, on traversing it longitudinally, either a worm at the front end may be put into gear to turn the

table for rectilinear cutting, or a bevil-wheel at the opposite end, to drive the mandril for circular cutting.

A particularly elegant plan is also adopted for reversing the continuous self-acting feed. For this purpose the actuating worm shaft carries a right and left-threaded worm, opposed to, or reversed, as regards each other. This compound worm is fitted to a corresponding duplex worm-wheel, so that either the right or the left thread may be put in gear. This ingenious plan is also suitable for other purposes, and particularly as a substitute for the motion commonly used in rack lathes, being cheaper, as doing away with three spur-wheels, and more convenient, as the whole of the hand gear can be thus carried on the rest-saddle. When the work is of very large diameter, and revolves, the turner sits on a cross plank.

EXPRESS LOCOMOTIVE ENGINE.

EXAMPLE PLATES C, D, E.

The three plates constituting this series of views are by far the finest examples of the kind ever executed. As specimens of shading, they are chiefly remarkable for a fine bold depth of lining, where every individual line tells its tale. Plate C is a longitudinal section of the engine; and Plates D and E are transverse sections. The section, Plate D, is taken one half through the barrel of the boiler at the steam dome, showing the sectional area of the innermost expanded portion of the inside fire-box; the other half section is taken at a point above the crank-axle, where the narrow neck of the inside fire-box occurs. Plate E also furnishes two distinct half sections, one through the smoke-box cylinder and blast-pipe, and the other through the fire-box, in the line of the safety-valve.

SPECIFICATION.

The engines to be made with inside cylinders, outside and inside frames, and six wheels; the driving-wheel being seven feet six inches diameter, and arranged in the manner hereinafter described.

The *Cylinders* to be eighteen inches diameter, and the length of stroke two feet, fitted up with pistons made of wrought-iron or steel, to be made by Mr. Goodfellow of Manchester. The cylinders to be of the hardest and best iron, and to be free from all defects; to be bored perfectly parallel, and true when fitted. The cylinder faces to be made accurately to the drawing; also, the ports and passages and the faces to be scraped to a perfect surface for the valves.

The *Boilers* to be eleven feet nine inches long in the cylinder, and four feet three and a quarter inches external diameter, and to be made perfectly circular and straight. The plates, angle-iron, and rivets, to be of the best Lowmoor or Bowling iron, or of equal quality, with the maker's name stamped in a legible manner on each plate. The rivets to be three-fourths of an inch diameter, and to be one and three quarter inches apart from centre to centre of rivet. The plates for the cylindrical part of boiler to be three-eighths of an inch in thickness, and those for the outer shell of fire-box to be of Lowmoor or Bowling iron, or of equal quality, three-eighths of an inch in thickness; and the tube plates of the smoke-box end, also, to be of Lowmoor or Bowling iron, or of equal quality; to be three-fourths of an inch thick. The plates of the smoke-boxes and smoke-box door to be of the best Staffordshire iron, five-sixteenths of an inch in thickness. The chimneys to be made also of Staffordshire iron, one quarter of an inch in thickness; and the whole of the parts of the boilers and smoke-boxes to be made and fitted up in the manner shown in the drawings, which will be supplied.

The *Fire-boxes* to be made as shown in drawing, and introduced as shown in the cylinder part of the boiler, four feet nine inches; to be made of the best copper plate, free from all defects when worked. The tube-plate to be three-fourths of an inch in thickness where the tubes are fixed. The sides and end plates to be three-eighths of an inch thick, and the roof-plates to be seven-sixteenths of an inch thick. The bottom plates to be one-half inch thick. The boxes to be made with a middle partition in them; the plates of these partitions to be of copper, made three-eighths of an inch in thickness, and formed as shown in drawing.

The following are the leading inside dimensions of the fire-box: —Length on fire-bar to be five feet ten inches and one quarter. The length at roof to be ten feet six inches. Depth above fire-bars at front plate, six feet five inches. Depth at door-plate, six feet ten inches. Width on fire-bar, four feet. Length in cylinder of boiler, four feet nine inches. Height at narrowest part, two feet three inches. Height at tube-plate, three feet. Width at tube-plate, three feet nine inches.

The top of the box to be supported by twenty-five wrought-iron bearers, twenty of which to be five inches deep by one inch thick, and the five nearest tube-plate five inches deep by one and a half inches thick. These bearers to rest at their ends on the side plates of the fire-box; and to be screwed to the top plate by bolts one inch diameter, placed four and a half inches from centre to centre, screwed into the top plate. The screw to be of fine thread, next head of bolt, to be one inch and an eighth diameter; the head of the bolt to be inside the fire-box, and a nut on the end of the bolts on the top of the bearers, with one inch screw.

The *Fire-box* to be stayed to the boiler by copper bolts, seven-eighths of an inch diameter, screwed into the plates with a fine-threaded screw, having both ends riveted carefully, and placed four inches apart from centre to centre. This also applies to the mid partition.

The end plates above the fire-box to be stayed to the smoke-box tube-plate, by connecting them together by two stay bolts, each one inch and a quarter diameter.

The *Tubes* to be of brass, and made the very best quality, by the manufacturer who supplies the company at present; or of other equal quality, and to the approval of the company's engineer. There will be three hundred and three tubes in each engine; the size, one and three quarter inches outside diameter, to section furnished; and the thickness of metal to be No. 12 wire-gauge at fire-box end, and No. 14 wire gauge at smoke-box end.

The *Wheels* are to be made entirely of the best scrap wrought-iron, and of the very best workmanship. The driving-wheel, without the tyre, to be seven feet one and a half inches diameter. The tyres to be of the best Lowmoor, Bowling, or of equal

quality; to be finished five and a quarter inches wide, and two and a quarter inches thick on the tread. The sizes of the wheel in all its parts will be furnished by the company's locomotive engineer at Wolverton.

The *Crank Axles* to be made of the very best iron from the Low-moor, Bowling, or the Haigh foundry forges, or of other equal quality, complete and perfect to the sizes given when finished. A full-size drawing of the crank-axle in its parts will be supplied. The outside bearings to be seven inches diameter, and ten inches in length. The inside bearings seven inches diameter, and four and a quarter inches in length. The crank bearings to be seven inches diameter, and four inches in length.

The *Straight Axles* to be tubular, as shown in the drawing, of best quality of iron, seven and a quarter inches external diameter, and one and a half inch thick of metal. The bearings of the leading and trailing axles to be the same size as the crank; viz., seven inches diameter by ten inches long.

The *Axle Boxes* and brass bearings to be made according to the drawing which will be supplied.

The *Springs*, links, and attachments to the axle-boxes, to be supplied by the company, and applied according to the instructions of their engineer at Wolverton.

The *Pumps* to be made of tough brass to the drawing furnished. The clacks and boxes to be accurately finished and fitted. The pump-rams to be made of strong tough brass, with wrought-iron cross-heads, as per drawing.

The *Steam Pipes*, blast and feed pipes, to be made of the best copper, three-sixteenths of an inch thick, with copper flanges, as per drawings to be supplied.

Regulator to be made of brass, on the equilibrium principle, as per drawing.

The *Eccentric Straps* to be made of the best wrought-iron, lined with gun metal of the best quality, according to drawing, accurately fitted, and to have all the oil siphons forged on.

The *Slide Valves* to be made of gun metal, and to have an outside lap of one and a quarter inch. They are to have an oil or grease cup attached on each side of the smoke-box, to lubricate them.

The *Connecting-rods* to be made of the very best quality of wrought-iron, fitted accurately. The straps to be made as per drawing, and the oil siphons to be forged on them.

The *Expansion Gear* to be made as per drawing, all the working and wearing joints and surfaces to be steeled and hardened, or case-hardened. The distance from the centres of the leading wheel axle to the centres of the middle axle, to be exactly eight feet four inches, and from the centre of the middle to the centre of the trailing axle, eight feet six inches.

These *Engines* are to be manufactured of the very best materials and workmanship throughout, and supplied in every respect with water-gauges, steam-taps for heating water in tender, whistle blow-off cocks, cylinder-cocks, pet-cocks, reversing and expansion gear worked from the foot-plate; screw draw-bars (proper and in duplicate), ash-pan, damper, sand-boxes, a full set of tools, lamp-irons, &c.

Detail drawings of all the parts will be supplied by the company's engineer at Wolverton, previous to manufacture.

The *Safety Valves* to be two in number, and to have Salter's balance applied; each valve to be three and a half inches diameter, and the levers to be of such length, that one pound upon the end of the lever shall indicate exactly one pound upon each square inch of the valve.

The range of the spring balance to be graduated up to one hundred and fifty pounds.

All the steam joints to be fitted together by scraping, so as to be iron to iron when the joint is made; and the bolts to be placed not more than three inches apart from centre to centre of bolt.

The *Cylinder* and *Valve-chest Covers* to be of wrought-iron, to drawings furnished.

The *Fire-frame* to be made in two parts, with a drop apparatus, to drawings.

These engines to have brass domes over the steam-pipe and safety-valve, of the best yellow sheet brass; finished and fitted in the best manner, to drawings to be supplied.

The engines and tenders to have four distinct coats of the best paint, to be finished to a specimen colour furnished by the company's engineer. Between each coat of paint, to be rubbed down with ground pumicestone to a level smooth surface, and all imperfections removed; to be lined and finished as required, and to receive four distinct coats of the best carriage varnish, and properly hardened between each coat.

All the axles, bolts, pins, screws, and parts of machinery of these engines, to be made exactly to gauges determined by Mr. M'Connell, so that they may be perfect duplicates of each other throughout; and the company's engineer at Wolverton, or his assistant, shall at all times, when they think proper, visit the work while in progress, to see that the materials and construction are quite according to specification and drawing. Any alteration in the minor details of this specification to be adopted, if considered advisable by Mr. M'Connell.

TENDERS.

The *Frames* are to be entirely of wrought-iron, the framing to be made of the form and dimensions as shown in the drawing; the plates being of the best Staffordshire iron, fitted up in the best manner. The side tank plates to be also of Staffordshire iron, three-sixteenths of an inch thick, with strong angle-irons as shown, and framed with flat plates outside; the floor and top plates throughout are to be one quarter of an inch thick.

The *Wheels* to be three feet nine inches diameter, to be six in number, and to be made entirely of wrought-iron, of the very best quality and workmanship. The tyres of the wheels to be of the best Lowmoor, Bowling, or patent shaft iron, or of equal quality, to be approved by the company's engineer, finished to two inches and a quarter thick on the tread.

Drawings of the wheels, with axles and axle-boxes, in detail, will be supplied.

The *Axles* to be tubular, as per drawing, of quality of iron approved by the company's engineer.

The *Springs*, as in the case of the engines, to be supplied by the company, and applied according to the engineer's instructions.

The apparatus of the *Break* will be according to drawing, and a break is to be applied to each wheel.

The *Tenders* are to be capable of containing two thousand gallons of water, and two tons of coke, and to have spring-buffers on each end; to be supplied by the company, and fixed according to the instructions of their engineer.

The *Draw-rod* of the tender will go through from one buffer-spring to the other. The floor of tender and foot-plate of engine to be exactly a level when properly loaded and roadworthy; with a joint flap-plate fixed to the tender, to overlay between the engine and tender.

WOOD-PLANING MACHINE.

EXAMPLE PLATE F.

The drawing given in our Plate F, introduces the student to increased complexity of details; and whilst it affords him an opportunity of testing his acquirements on minute work, it also well exemplifies the practice of cast shadows.

The machine is the production of Messrs. J. M'Dowall & Sons, of the Walkinshaw Foundry, Johnstone, Renfrewshire. Fig. 1 is a complete longitudinal elevation of the improved planing machine, as in working order, with a board in the act of passing through it to be planed. Fig. 2 is a corresponding plan of the machine. The entire apparatus is carried upon the long main vertical side standards, A, cast in suitable lengths, and bolted down to the foundation by lugs, as at B. These frames are connected together by transverse end-pieces and tie-rods, to form a strong rectangular carrying-frame; and at one end of it is the first motion driving-shaft, C, shown as broken away from its actuating power. This shaft has an inner end-bearing in one of the side standards, and it carries the large first motion-strap pulley, D, giving motion to the whole of the cutting movements. From this pulley, a broad open strap, E, passes to a small pulley, F, on the outer end of a cross shaft, G, running in bearing brackets, H, bolted to the framing at the opposite end of the machine. This shaft also carries an outside pulley, I, from which a crossed strap, J, passes back to a small pulley, K, on the shaft of the compound rotatory planing cutter, L, for planing the upper surface of the board or flooring deal, M. The spindle of this cutter is carried in vertically adjustable end-bearings, N, fitted to the vertical edges of the bracket standards, O, which are bolted down on the upper edges of the main framing pieces. The cross shaft, G, also carries a pair of equal-sized strap pulleys, P, whence twisted straps, Q, pass to the two broad pulleys, R, on the vertical spindles of the two cutter heads, S, which cut the edges of the wood, and, if necessary, tongue and groove them. These two latter cutter spindles are carried in bearings, T, on horizontal dovetail slide-pieces, U, adjustable at different distances on each side the longitudinal centre of the machine, by the action of two screw-spindles, one of which is actuated by the outside hand-wheel, V, whilst the other spindle, which is only to be shifted occasionally, is adjustable by a key, to be shipped on to the square head, W, on the opposite side of the machine. The front spindle carries a fine pitched worm, X, in gear with a horizontal worm-wheel, Y, fast on the spindle of a small index-hand, which points to a graduated arc, Z, and thus indicates the exact "set" of the cutters for the particular breadth of timber under treatment.

As the deal is passed into the machine to be planed, it is first of all entered beneath the nipping feed cams, a, which carry it continuously forward to the cut. Each nipping arrangement consists of a horizontal traversing plate of metal, b, tongued at its opposite ends, to slide freely, but accurately, in corresponding grooves in the top plates, c, of the standards; and upon these plates, c, are attached a pair of vertical parallel standards, d, connected at their upper ends by a light cross bar, e, which answers as well for the bearings of the overhead cross-adjusting spindle, f, for the "set" of the nippers. Each standard, d, is slotted down its centre, to receive and guide the traversing nut bearings, g, of the cross cam-spindle, h, a screw-spindle, i, being passed down from above, and through the nuts, g, so as to enable the cam-spindles, h, to be set up or down by the screw action. This screw action is worked, when necessary, by handles shipped on to the end of the cross-spindle, f, by the workman, who thus works the screws simultaneously through the two pairs of small bevil-wheels, j. Each cam-spindle, h, has an eccentric cam, a, loosely hung upon it by an eye, the cam-eye being entered upon the spindle up against an adjustable collar, k, on the latter; and the cam-spindle, h, is set fast in the standard slots by the outside adjusting nut, l. Thus arranged, the nipper forms a complete traversing frame, capable of free horizontal movement along its guide grooves. Beneath the level of its traverse support, two projecting eye-pieces, m, are cast on the plate, b, each eye carrying a joint-stud, n, whence short links, o, pass to corresponding eyes, p, on the upper ends of the two sides of the vibrating lever frame-piece, q. Each frame is carried on a stud centre, r, in the framing, and each has a bottom joint-eye, s, for connection by a link-rod, t, to the actuating cam-feed mechanism at the front or entering end of the machine. Each frame has also a heavily-weighted bent lever, u, attached to its bottom cross bar, and contrived so as to tend to draw the frame continually backward in the opposite direction to the traverse of the wood.

The primary movement is given to the entire series of these nipping feeders—of which there are six altogether, three being at each end of the machine—by a toothed pinion, v, on the first motion shaft. This pinion gears with a large toothed wheel, w, set on a cross shaft, x, and carrying a second pinion, y, in gear with a second spur-wheel, z, fast on the actuating cam-shaft, 4. On this shaft are keyed the three separate cams, or differential eccentric pieces, 1, 2, 3. Opposite to, and over the periphery of each cam, is set an antifriction pulley, 5, carried on the horizontal arm of a bell-crank lever, 6, the three bell-cranks being carried loosely on a stud shaft, 7. The longer vertical arms of these bell-cranks are connected by eyes, 8, at their lower ends to the respective rods, t, which are severally linked, as already described, by end and intermediate eyes, to the bottom of each of the nipping frames. The three cams are so set at starting, that they shall each act at different periods of the revolution of their carrying shaft, in such manner that a uniform feed action may be given to the board passing through the machine. In other terms, they are set at equal distances asunder in the direction of revolution of their shaft, each cam being linked to and made to actuate

two nippers. Thus, the corresponding nippers of each pair have always the same relative position, as marked 1, 2, and 3. Then, as the planing goes on, and the cams revolve, each pair of nippers is made to traverse forward—say in the direction of the arrows at 1—by the upward revolving action of the corresponding cam. This forward traverse is the positive feed action; for the moment the nipping frame moves in this direction, the prominent eccentric portions of the cams, a 1, are thereby carried down, or jammed hard upon the upper surface of the timber, squeezing it firm down upon the bottom plates, b, so that the timber is carried forward to the cut, as if it were permanently attached to the nipping feed-frame. Whilst this positive feed is being given to the wood, the two pairs, 2, of the nippers are being brought back by the action of their weighted levers, as their corresponding cam is descending in its revolution; these two nippers are consequently slipping over the wood, for, on the instant of the return movement towards the entering end of the machine, the prominences of the nipping cams are drawn out of nipping contact, and the frames go back without interfering with the feed traverse of the wood in the forward direction. As delineated in the plate, the third pair of nippers are still in forward gear, and acting, by reason of the position of their actuating cams, to carry forward the wood in concert with the nippers, 1. By this means, as each cam comes round, it gives its forward feed and back traverse in regular uniform succession, each succeeding nipper gradually relieving the last in feeding action. And although two nippers always thus tend to come into action at the same time, derangement cannot ensue from this cause, inasmuch as the quickest forward feeding nippers at any given moment carry forward the wood free of the other nippers, which give way in their nipping action to the higher rate of motion, by reason of the consequent slip or disengagement of the nipping cam. In this way the feed is constantly uniform, as although it is furnished by three separate actions, yet each only comes into actual feeding play at the moment that it is required to keep up the regularity of movement.

As the board is thus carried forward, it comes first above the three finishing planes in the frame, 9, over which it is held down by the three rollers, 10, which run in adjustable bearings held down by the helical springs, 11, adjustable to any desired tensional pressure by the nuts, 12, on their screwed spindles, 13, carried in the stationary frames, 14. After passing these pressers, the emerging end of the wood, as planed and finished on its under surface, proceeds beneath the duplex pressing pulleys, 15, set on a stud centre on the free end of a lever arm, 16, fast to the horizontal shaft, 17, carried in end bearings, 18, in the end frame, and held down by the lever and weight, 19. Thence it enters beneath the pair of horizontal pressing rollers, 20, similarly held down by adjustable helices, 21; and it is between these two rollers that the planing of the upper surface takes place. At the moment, however, of its passage beneath the duplex pulley, 15, it is first acted upon by the two cutting heads, s. In the present example, these cutters are arranged for tongueing and grooving the opposite edges of the flooring deal, as is usual in laying flooring. Thus, in the elevation, fig. 1, the two square cutters, 22, take off the two angles of one edge of the deal, having the central feather or tongue standing up, whilst the other double angular single cutter, 23, takes off the sharp angles from the tongue. Again, the opposite cutter head, for the other side, carries three plain central grooving cutters, 24, for producing the plain groove, whilst a fourth duplex cutter, 25, is added, to shave off the angular edges in a similar way. This completes the edge finish of the board; and the latter then being held well down by the rollers, 20, is submitted to the action of the rotatory cutter, or "thicknesser," L, for bringing the upper side of the wood to a fair level, and equalizing the thickness of the deal, when the latter is drawn completely through the machine in a finished state.

WASHING MACHINE FOR PIECE GOODS.

EXAMPLE PLATE G.

The three views on this plate illustrate a machine, first in perspective elevation, and then in plain geometrical section, presenting good studies for "effect," and contrasting the working drawing with the perspective picture. Fig. 1 is a perspective elevation of the washer complete, showing the whole of the gearing for actuating the moving details; fig. 2 is a longitudinal section on a larger scale; and fig. 3 is a corresponding transverse section— that is, at right angles to fig. 2. The main body of the machine consists of an open rectangular cistern, A, of cast-iron, which is kept about half full of the cleansing water. A couple of horizontal transverse shafts, B, C, are passed through this cistern, being carried in bearings in the two opposite side plates, and projecting through on one side to carry the spur-wheels, D, E. These shafts are made to revolve in the same direction by the revolution of the intermediate driving shaft, F, carrying a third spur-wheel, G, in gear with the other two. The two shafts, B, C, have each a pair of end discs, H, I, fast upon them, to hold the diametrically opposed parallel rail bars, J, which form the flat winces or revolving frames, for acting upon the goods in the washing movement. These details, indeed, constitute the whole of the action.

The same central wheel, G, also drives an overhead wheel, K, of similar size, for actuating squeezing rollers, L. These rollers are of large diameter and of considerable breadth, and are set in bearings in the pair of vertical standards, M, carried on a cross bar on the top of the cistern, on which also is a low standard, N, for the bearing of the overhanging end of the bottom roller driving shaft. The bearings of this bottom roller are fixed; but those of the upper one are adjustable in the central vertical slots of their standards, by means of screws and hand-wheels at the top, to give any required pressure to the issuing goos.

In erecting the machine for work, the shafts and rails of the washing movement are set in one plane, and the water-level is adjusted to the line of the shaft centres. The fabric to be cleansed is then fed in at one end, O, of the cistern, where two lengths are represented as being entered. Here it descends beneath a fixed guide-roller, P, and thence passes beneath the pair of nipping rollers, Q, set in bearings on the side of a division piece, R, and adjustable by hand-wheels and screws. After leaving these rollers, the course of the goods is again downwards, beneath the fixed guide-roller, S, and thence between the first pair of vertical guide-bars, T. The direction is then round the under side of the flat wince at the opposite end of the cistern, the fabric being turned back over the bars, J. It then returns towards the front end of the cistern, and is similarly passed round the bars, J, of the disc, I, from the upper side—this return course being through the second pair or space of the division bars, T. The fabric finally returns through the third guide-space, and in contact with the wince bars, and is then passed up beneath the guide-roller, U, set at the water-level at the delivering end. From this point, it passes over the top of the external guide-roller, V, and is finally delivered through the squeezing rollers, L. As there are two lines of goods shown under treatment, it is obvious that both follow the same course.

POWER-LOOM.

EXAMPLE PLATE H.

We here illustrate the treatment of a piece of textile machinery in a comparatively plain style. The rounds only are slightly shaded up, whilst relief is given to the drawing merely by flat tinting upon the main framing. The loom is the invention of Mr. William Milligan, of Bradford, who has accomplished in it the desirable objects of putting any number of picks into a given length of warp, whilst the number of picks are capable of variation without the use of change-wheels, or the alteration of the weight on the yard-beam, so that the warp may be kept as tight as its strength will bear, without involving any unevenness in the woven fabric. It has an advantage over all friction motions— that it will neither slip nor fray the cloth, and weaves wet weft as well as dry.

Fig. 1 on our plate is a complete side or end elevation of the loom in working order, looking on the "taking-up motion" side; and fig. 2 is a corresponding longitudinal or front elevation, that is, looking on the cloth-beam side. The cloth-beam is at A, being carried on a spindle supported in a slot in the side standards, on one end of which spindle is a spur-wheel, B, outside the frame, in gear with the pinion, C. This pinion is carried on the fixed stud-shaft of the wheel, D, and moves along with this wheel, which again is in gear with a pinion, E, carried round along with the ratchet-wheel, F. Immediately above the cloth-beam, and resting upon the fabric in the act of being wound thereon, and with its ends supported in vertical slots, G, in the loom side-frames, is a horizontal rod, H. This rod, as it bears freely upon the folds of cloth on the beam, is gradually elevated in its guide-slots by each additional fold of the cloth, as the beam takes up the fabric by its slow revolution. The end of the spindle of the cloth-beam has also upon it a loose bent slotted lever, I, standing up at a slight inclination with the vertical line, and behind the rod, H. This lever has an adjustable pin in its slot, to which pin is jointed one end of the link, J, the other end of which is similarly connected to a slot in the upright lever, K, behind. This lever is connected, as we shall hereafter explain, with the eccentric tappet, L, keyed or one end of the tappet-shaft, M.

When the loom is in action, as the horizontal rod, H, of the cloth-beam gradually rises from the accumulated folds of the cloth beneath it, it presses against the inclined side of the lever, I, raising it by degrees to a vertical position. By this action, with every slight advance of the lever, I, towards the vertical line, it thus pushes back the lever, K, by the intervention of the connecting-rod, J, so as to shorten the extent of the traverse of the lever, K. The latter lever works loose in a fixed stud centre, N, in the side-frame, and, thus suspended, it is connected by its straight pendant end, or lower arm, with the wheel-work which we have just described, and by its back angular arm, with the eccentric tappet, L, on the same shaft as the ratchet-wheel, F; and outside this wheel is set the regulator, O, the lower eye of which turns loosely on the ratchet-shaft as a centre. This regulator is simply a slotted lever, having a sliding-piece, P, set to move up and down in the slot; and at its upper end is a short collar, acting as a bearing for the upper end of a screwed spindle, Q, the lower opposite end of which is passed through a screwed hole in the sliding-piece, P. In this way the sliding-piece, P, answers as a nut for the screw, Q, and the turning of the screw consequently allows of the raising or lowering of the nut or slide-piece at pleasure. To the top of the regulator are hinged three detents, R, each of which takes into the teeth of the ratchet-wheel, F. On first setting the loom to work, the height of the slide-nut, P, of the regulator, is first adjusted to suit the required number of picks to be laid into the fabric per inch, and the regulator and lever, I, are pushed forward by means of the lever, K, as far as the rod, H, will permit. When the loom is put in motion, the eccentric, L, during one-half of its first revolution, presses against the projecting angular end of the lever, K, and pushes it out to an extent equal to its eccentricity, whereby the regulator is drawn back, to a corresponding extent, by the connecting-rod, S, whilst the detents, R, bring round the ratchet-wheel, F. During the remaining half of the revolution of the eccentric, the angular tail of the lever, K, descends as far as the then degree of elevation of the cloth-beam rod, H, will permit, and the detents, R, are raised out of their position, and lifted as many teeth back as is equal to the distance retraversed, the three detents, T, suspended from the centre of the wheel, B, serving to hold the ratchet-wheel fast whilst this change occurs. It will thus be seen, that whilst the detents, R, are always drawn the same distance during one-half revolution of the eccentric, the distance to which they are returned in the other half revolution must be less, as the cloth-beam rod, H, is raised higher by the winding on of the cloth. The lever, I, should be parallel with the slots in which the rod, H, works, when the projecting end of the lever, K, is elevated to the top by the eccentric, L, and it should rest on the rod, H, when the eccentric is down.

At U is a short lever connected with the weft-motion of the loom, which lever raises the detents, T, by means of a chain, off the ratchet-wheel, to stop the movement when the weft breaks. The lever, U, is fast on one end of the horizontal rod, V, on the other end of which is a balanced lever, worked by the weft thread, on the principle of the ordinary well-known weft-stopping apparatus.

DUPLEX STEAM BOILER.

EXAMPLE PLATE 9.

This, our ninth example plate, illustrates a most effective style of treatment of a stationary steam boiler, its seating and mountings. In these views the convex and concave rounds are well brought out, and considerable relief is given to the furnace doors and boiler ends by the judicious employment of shadows. The water in the sectional view, and more especially the brickwork in the elevation, supply materials for the development of the picturesque; and the plate, upon the whole, is a fair type of a class of work

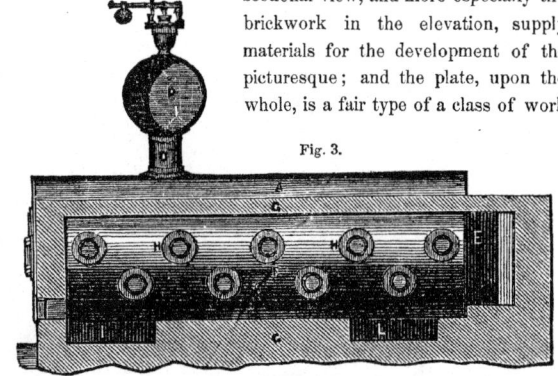

Fig. 3.

in which a good display is made without much elaboration. The boiler, which is the production of Messrs. Bellhouse & Co., of the Eagle Foundry, Manchester, is of the duplex or "twin" kind; that is, two distinct steam generators are combined together, to work as one boiler, the two being placed side by side, with a central tubular chamber between them. It is this intermediate flue which forms the distinguishing feature of the contrivance, the smoke and heated air from the two generators being passed through this chamber, on their way from their respective furnaces, to the chimney.

Fig. 1, on the plate, is a front end elevation of the duplex boiler, as erected in brickwork; fig. 2 is a transverse vertical section corresponding, the section being taken through the two furnaces, the brickwork and flues, and the overhead steam-chest; fig. 3, the wood engraving in the body of the description, is a longitudinal section of the arrangement, taken through the intermediate chamber, the external flues, waterways, and the steam-chest; and fig. 4 is a sectional plan to correspond. Both these latter views are drawn to a scale of one-half the corresponding views in the plate.

The two boilers or generators, A, are of the common cylindrical, tubular class, with internal furnaces and flues, B, running right through them from end to end. They are set in a brick foundation, C, suitable flues being formed in the walls of brickwork, to answer for the special arrangements of the combination. Each boiler is fired separately, through the usual end furnace doors, D, and the gaseous products pass off from each set of furnace bars in the direction of the arrows, the two currents meeting and forming into one, in the main end transverse flue, E, in the brickwork. This combined current then turns again towards the front of the boiler, passing directly through the intermediate chamber of tubes.

F, which chamber is formed on its two walls by the contiguous surfaces of the boilers, A, and on its top and bottom by an overhead arch, G, of brickwork, and the mass of the brickwork base. The short tubes, H, which cross the space between the two boilers, are water-spaces, being open at each end into the respective boilers, beneath the water-line therein; thus, the heated current being intercepted by this arrangement of tubular water-spaces, as it traverses the intermediate chamber, imparts its heat to an extended heating area. The tubes are disposed in two rows, sloping at reversed angles from one boiler to the other, to aid the internal circulation and the passing away of the steam. This central thoroughfare, F, then conveys the current of heat and gaseous products to the front end of the boiler, where it diverges, as at I, descending into a short transverse flue, J, passing

Fig. 4

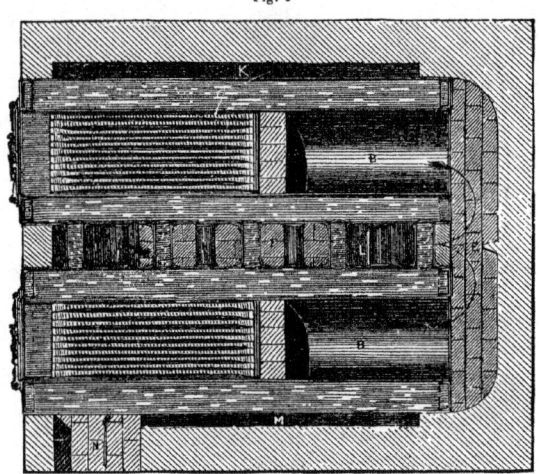

beneath the generator on that side. This conveys the current into the external longitudinal flue, K, surrounding and covering in a great portion of the outer side and bottom of that generator; and this flue, K, then forms the duct for the traverse of the current a second time to the far end of the boilers. Having reached this part, the current next enters another bottom transverse flue, L, beneath the back end of the intermediate chamber or cell, F, and through this short flue the current enters the external longitudinal flue, M, of the opposite generator, precisely similar to the before-mentioned external flue, K. In this way, this latter generator is well heated externally, like the former one; and as the flue runs all the way back to the furnace end of the boiler, the current finally passes off along it, and through the short branch, N, to the chimney. With a boiler so contrived, the whole of the large flue area in the centre of the boiler is well exposed to the direct heat of the furnaces; and the greatest possible portion of the external boiler surface is similarly acted upon, and heated after the current leaves the central passage, whilst the possession of this central chamber admits of the perfect commingling of the gaseous products of combustion, and the obtainment of a greatly increased heating area, from the arrangement of the pipes therein. The two generators, thus equally and uniformly heated, furnish

each its own supply of steam, through the overhead vertical pipes, O, to the horizontal steam-chest, P. Any number of such generators may, of course, be combined together, securing all the advantages of an intermediate flue-cell between each.

DIRECT-ACTING MARINE ENGINES.

EXAMPLE PLATE J.

This plate deserves careful study for its round shading. The development of the right-hand cylinder in the elevation is a beautifully executed piece of work; and the firm, bold, flat tinting of the side view of the deep sole-plate, throws out the pump and small branch pipes very powerfully. It is to be remarked that, in this instance, flat tints are sparingly used, the more minute details being left plain; but tints were absolutely necessary in the plan, for giving a due idea of depth.

The *Duncan Hoyle* paddle steamer, in which these engines are fitted, was built by Messrs. John Scott & Sons, of Greenock, a firm as well and favourably known in connection with the past history and modern practice of naval architecture, as is that of Messrs. Scott, Sinclair & Co., with marine engineering. This vessel measures 200 tons, her length is 145 feet, breadth 18 feet, depth 9 feet; and her engines, to which we are now directing attention, are of 90 nominal horse power. The two steam cylinders are each 37 inches diameter and 3 feet stroke, placed diagonally fore and aft the ship, and nearly at right angles to each other—the amount of divergence from the true right angle being a trifling extent due to the local necessities of the hull. They occupy a space on the vessel's floor of 15 feet fore and aft, by 5 feet 6 inches transversely.

We have ourselves a strong feeling in favour of the oscillating engine for most marine and river purposes; but we admit the existence of some force, in what the designer—Mr. G. W. Jaffrey—of the *Duncan Hoyle's* engines urges on behalf of this fixed-cylinder, direct-action arrangement. He claims an especial feature of superiority, on the ground that the weight is better distributed, covering a large surface of the vessel's bottom; whilst all the parts are firmly and rigidly bound together, so that no one part can yield from another. For this latter reason, the loose-working jingling action, not uncommon in old oscillators, can never arise in the engines now before us. They are obviously applicable either for direct connection with paddles, or as geared screw engines. The *Duncan Hoyle* was built for the Australian coasting trade, to run between Melbourne, Geelong, and Launceston. Her owner, Captain Kincaid, gives a most favourable account of her performances since she left this country; and particularly as a sea-boat, as she went out under canvas only. Besides this, later accounts tell us that her engines have worked admirably, and have not been afflicted with a single hot bearing, although put to work at once, just as they left the Scottish shores. Indeed, we have the best possible proof of her good qualities, in the fact that she has since changed hands at an advance of £10,000 upon her original cost.

CHAPTER XV.

DRAWING INSTRUMENTS.

" A good workman never complains of his tools,"—although a very ancient proverb, and having a poet for its advocate, is, nevertheless, one which is very commonly used in an incorrect sense, if it is not indeed untrue in all its applications. It is certainly a very usual thing for a bad workman to throw the blame of his inefficiency on his tools; but it is quite as certain that a good workman will not work with any but the very best tools. The draughtsman, then, who aims at excellence and accuracy in his mechanical delineations, must not only possess himself of first-rate mathematical instruments, but he must preserve them in perfect order.

The varieties of drawing instruments are extremely numerous. We shall, however, confine our illustrations to such as are of more recent invention, or more improved construction.

A lead pencil needs no description. But the form to be given to its working-point is a very important subject of consideration. For drawing straight lines with the assistance of a straight edge, the point should be flat, and slightly rounded. Such a point produces as fine a line as a conical point, whilst it is much stronger, and preserves its integrity for a longer time. This point may also be used in describing circles of large diameter, but small circles require a conical point.

Messrs. Marion, of Regent street, London, have registered a very ingenious little instrument for sharpening lead pencils and crayons. Our engraving, fig. 1, represents a side elevation of the tool in the act of sharpening a pencil. A projection, A, is formed on the side of a piece of metal, sufficiently large to allow of a conical aperture, B, corresponding with the required cone of a pointed lead pencil. One side of this projection is slotted to receive the cutting edge of the small knife, c, which is attached to the inclined portion, D, of the metal block by the screw, E, passing through a slot in the knife. A short projection, F, is formed upon the knife for the convenience of adjustment, and when set, it is held in position by the two set-screws, G. A small handle is screwed into the block at H, from behind, for the convenience of holding the instrument when in use, and the end of this handle is hollowed to receive the small projection, F, on the knife, c, for the facility of holding it when detached for the purpose of sharpening the edge. An adjustable guide, I, is secured by the pinching-screw, J, by one end, beneath the block, and is furnished with two arms, K, jointed on to the end of the rod of the guide, for embracing the pencil, L, during the cutting operation.

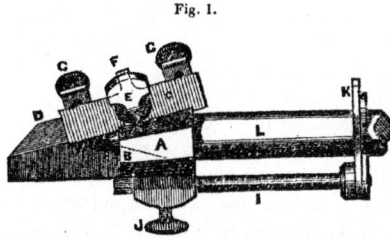

Fig. 1.

In using this instrument, the pencil is simply passed between the two guide-arms, K, and its end is inserted in the conical hole, B. It is then turned round between the finger and thumb, and the knife-edge coming into contact with the end to be sharpened, quickly pares off the material. By this simple apparatus an excellent point is given to the pencil in a very short time, saving the draughtsman from all the troubles and inconveniences of blunt penknives and fractured lead.

A mathematical drawing-pen consists of a pair of flat, tapered steel-blades, fixed to a handle of ivory or ebony. The ink is contained between the blades, and flows out from between the points, the thickness of line produced being dependent on the distance asunder of the points, which distance is regulated by a pinching-screw. In order to maintain a uniform thickness of line, care must be taken to clean the outsides of the points after each fresh supply of ink. It is often necessary to draw a number of lines, of different thicknesses, immediately succeeding each other. In this case, the inconvenience of repeatedly turning the adjusting-screw of the pen may be avoided by using a pen of the construction represented in figs. 2 and 3. This pen is the invention of M. Maubert, a French engineer, and differs from the ordinary drawing-pen in the shape of the points, g, h, of which fig. 3 is an end view. These points are made broad and rounded, and are bent at the sides, so as to present convex surfaces towards each other; in other words, they touch each other at their centres, but are gradually more separate towards each side; and in using the pen, if a fine line is wanted, it is held vertically; if a thick line is needed, it is inclined more or less to either side, so as to bring the more separated portions of the acting edges in contact with the paper. With the exception of the shape of the points, the pen represented in fig. 2 may be taken as an example of the best construction of a mathematical drawing-pen. The blades are formed of a single piece of well-tempered steel, and are fixed upon an ivory handle, by means of a brass socket. In some pens, the tips only of the blades are of steel, the remainder being of German silver, or of brass; and one blade is jointed at its root, so as to be capable of being opened out and cleaned, when necessary. A spring is fixed between the blades, so as to keep them open as far as the regulating screw will admit. Whilst, on the one hand, this facility in cleaning is an advantage; on the other, there is an accompanying liability of the joint getting loose, in which case the points can never be kept opposite to each other, and it is quite impossible to preserve uni

Fig. 2.

Fig. 3.

2 A

formity and cleanness of lining with a pen in such a state. In making mechanical drawings in outline, and with shadow lines, two thicknesses of lining are necessary; and for this purpose, the secondary adjustment drawing-pen will be found very convenient. This modification of the common drawing-pen is the invention of Mr. G P. Renshaw. It is represented in fig. 4. It has a regulating

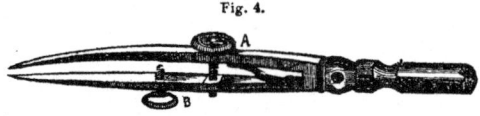

Fig. 4.

screw, A, like an ordinary drawing-pen; and by means of this screw the points are set for the thick or shadow line, whilst a secondary screw, B, is introduced, for regulating the thin or face line. The pen is made with a stronger spring than usual, and when a fine line is wanted, the points are pinched together by the grasp of the fingers, as closely as the screw, B, will permit; whilst a thick line is produced, by allowing the points to stand as far apart as the screw, A, is set for. We may here remark, that in using a drawing pen of any construction, care must be taken not to press it against the straight edge, or ruler, as this will close the points; and if the pressure is not uniform, which is pretty certain to be the case, where any pressure is used, a line of irregular thickness will be the inevitable result.

In fig. 5 is represented a duplex pen, commonly known as the "road-pen." It is a very convenient instrument for drawing lines in couples, parallel to each other. It consists of two pens, fixed upon one handle, their distance apart being regulated by a screw, with a central button, the portions entering the shanks of the pen having the thread in opposite directions, so as to open or shut the shanks according to the direction in which the button is turned. The two pens are of the usual construction, with regulating screws; and they may both be set for the same thickness of line or not, as convenient. Thus, one can be set for the face-line, and the other for the shadow, or back-line, of a hedge, or other parallel-edged prominence. This instrument is mostly used in topographical drawing.

In some cases of instruments is still to be found a pen for drawing dotted lines, resembling the ordinary lining-pen, in shape, with the addition of a small wheel, like a spur-rowel, and pivoted in the rounded points of the pen-blades. The ink is introduced between the blades, and the points of the rowel pass through it, and are intended to transfer to the paper beneath just sufficient ink to produce a line of dots. The action of the instrument, however, is very imperfect, and it is all but discarded by modern draughtsmen, who prefer drawing dotted lines with the ordinary pen. Indeed, the time gained by using the rowel dotting-pen, when in perfect working condition, is lost in bringing it to that condition. Besides, the pitch and depth of the dotted lining are liable to constant variation, according as the work in hand is on a large or small scale; and with the common pen, the operator can easily effect the necessary changes, whilst the dotting-wheel binds him down to one class of line.

We are, however, indebted to the ingenuity of French draughts-

men for a dotting-pen of very elegant action, and capable of producing a great variety of dotted linings. This instrument is represented in figs. 6 and 7, the former being a side elevation, and the latter a transverse vertical section. To a neat ebony or ivory handle is attached a small frame, E, carrying two pulleys, or running-wheels, F, G. The latter wheel is carried upon a steel stud, riveted to the plate, E, and of considerable diameter, for the sake of steadiness. This stud, likewise, carries a disc, b, made to revolve with the wheel, G, by means of a pin, a, entering a socket in the latter. A nut is passed on the screwed end of the stud, to retain the wheel and disc. The disc, b, is of slightly less diameter than the wheel, G, and it is formed with indentations, to act as a rotatory cam. Immediately above the disc is the lever, H, which carries a pencil, or pen, of the ordinary description. The lever, H, vibrates on a screw-pin, securing it to the framing, E, and it is pressed down by a blade-spring, d. It is formed with a projection, c, which enters the indentations on the periphery of the disc, b; so that the rotation causes it, and with it the pen or pencil, to rise and fall. The action of the instrument is obvious. The back of the plate, E, is guided along the edge of a ruler, or square, the wheels being permitted to run on the paper; this motion turns the disc, b, and causes the pen to rise from or touch the paper at intervals, according to the character of the indentations on the disc. The pulley, F, is simply to preserve the level of the instrument, and is carried loose on a pin, screwed into the frame, E. A number of discs are provided with different patterns of indentations, so that any one may be substituted for the disc, b, to correspond to the description of dotted line the draughtsman desires to produce.

A draughtsman requires several descriptions of compasses. The simplest are distinguished as dividers, and are used for transferring measurements from a drawing which is being copied, or from a scale; and also, as the name implies, for dividing lines and circles into equal parts. For this latter purpose, it is on the trial and error system that they are employed, if at all. Dividers consist of a pair of legs, pointed at one end, and jointed together at the other; the points, and a considerable portion of the leg, being of steel, whilst the shanks are of brass, German silver, or composition-metal. German silver or composition-metal is to be preferred to brass, as the latter gets soiled sooner, contracting a species of greasiness from the atmosphere and perspiration of the hand, accompanied by an unpleasant odour. The joint of the dividers, and of all compasses, must be made free from all cross play or lateral looseness. The most ordinary kind are fastened simply by a common screw. We have, indeed, seen some very ordinary

Fig. 5.

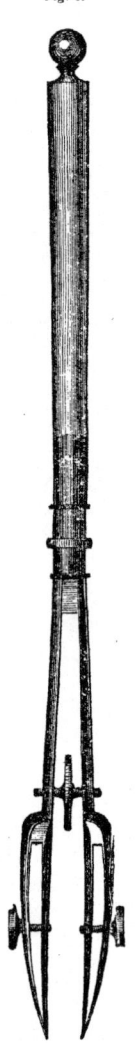

ones riveted together. The better kind have a steel pin passed through the leaves of the joint, upon which a flat brass or other

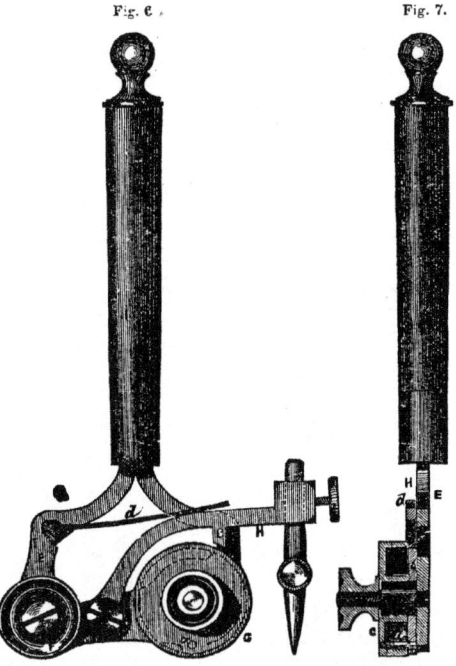

Fig. 6 . Fig. 7.

metal nut is passed, at the further side. This nut has two small holes upon its face, for the introduction of the points of a turn-screw, to be met with in most sets of instruments. The joint-leaf of one leg of a pair of compasses is usually of steel, as this arrangement gives a smoother action than when both sides of the joint are of the same metal. The better kind are also made with two steel leaves on one side, which are introduced between three brass ones on the other; but some have only one leaf on one side, and two on the other. A perfect compass-joint is a thing seldom met with, and draughtsmen are continually subject to annoyance, arising from the inequality of action of the joints of their com-

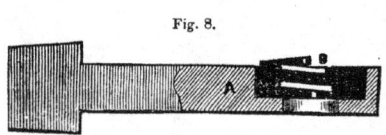

Fig. 8.

passes. After some little usage, these parts invariably im-bibe the bad habit of an alternate tightness and looseness, so that when the screw is adjusted to tighten the joint for one part of its movement, the objectionable slackness is only removed at the expense of an equally provoking stiffness in another part. Messrs. Bentley's "spiral spring compasses" aim at remedying this evil, by the adaptation of a small coiled spring to the joint, in such a manner as to equalize the pressure of the frictional surfaces throughout the entire movement. Our sketch, fig. 8, which re-presents a side view of the end of the centre joint of the compasses, explains the mode of application of the spring. The centre joint, A, which is sectioned to show the spring, has a recess bored out of one side of it, just large enough to receive the short coiled spring,

B. When this centre joint is inserted between the two eyes forming the outer joints, the spring reacts from the bottom of its box against one of the eyes or cheeks of the outside joint, thus keeping up a regular smooth working pressure on the joint surface.

Externally, this little modification in no way affects the appear-ance of the instrument, as the spring, being entirely embedded in its recess, is not seen. At a mere trifle in the increase of the cost, an important objection is here remedied by very simple means.

Some dividers are made with one of the legs so fitted as to be capable of a slight adjustment independently of the main joint. These are called "hair dividers," and are represented in fig. 9. The leg, A, is not, like the other, soldered to the shank, but is formed with a long thin strip of metal, which lies in a groove on the inside of the shank, and is fixed to the latter by a screw, at its upper end, near the compasses joint. This thin strip acts as a spring to bring the point, A, nearer to the point of the other leg. A screw, B, passed through the shank, adjusts the point, A, a slight distance in or outwards, thus affording a means of taking measurements more minutely accurate than with the mere direct action of the hand upon the main joint. Our fig. 9 may be taken as the representation of a very excellent style of dividers. The point should be strong, and not too finely tapered, and they should meet when the in-strument is closed.

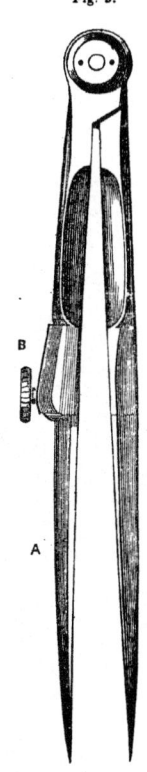

Fig. 9.

All sets of instruments contain a large pair of compasses, in addition to the dividers, which is usually of similar construction, except that one of the legs is made to fit into a socket in the shank, and a pencil or pen may be substi-tuted, as required. The pencil-holder and pen are both jointed, so that, in every case, they may be put in the best position for action. In the better kind, the fixed leg is also jointed; so that in describing circles of large diameter, the centre point may still be entered vertically into the paper. A lengthening bar is also provided, which can be fitted into the shank-socket, whilst the pen or pencil can be placed at the end of the bar, thus giving the compasses a greater range.

In figs. 10 and 11, we have represented a modification of this instrument, of German invention. This tool has no separate pieces, but is so arranged, that a pen, pencil, or point, may be brought into action as desired. The shanks are forked, and the leg pieces are jointed to their extremities. One of the leg pieces is formed with a steel point at one end, and a pen at the other; whilst the other leg has a steel point at one end, and a lead pencil at the other. The legs are jointed to the shanks by their longi-tudinal centres, and can be turned between the forks, so as to bring into action whichever end of the leg is required. A small pinching-screw is passed through one side of the shank, near its extremity, to fix the leg in position.

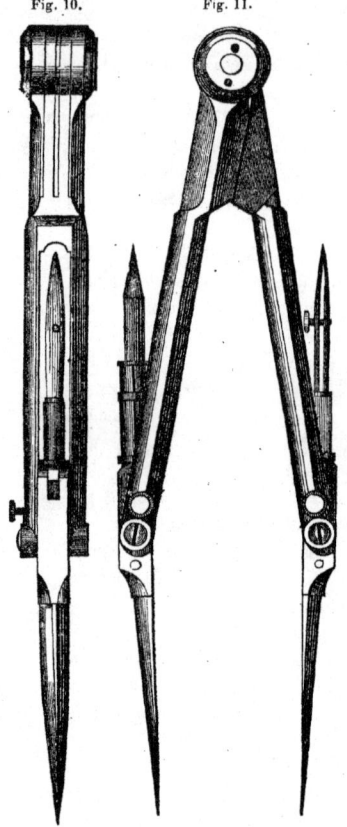

Fig. 10.   Fig. 11.

Fig. 12.

Fig. 12 is the representation of a somewhat smaller pair of compasses, in which the pen is formed in one piece with a steel point, which may be inverted, or a pencil-holder introduced instead. This is a convenient instrument for small work.

Another form of compass is represented in figs. 13, 14, 15, and 16. This is a "pocket," or "turn-in" compass, and takes up a very small space when closed, as in fig. 13. Fig. 14 is a cross section, taken at the line 1—2, in fig. 13. Figs. 15 and 16 are front and side views of the instrument when fully open. These compasses are of French construction, and in some points not unlike the German pair just described. The shanks are each jointed, and their lower portions are forked to receive the swivelling points, which are jointed to them at their extremities. The swivelling points are formed respectively with a pen and pencil at their opposite extremities, and any one of these may be turned round into working position when required. A lateral screw for fixing the points, as in the German instrument, would be an improvement. Grooves are formed in the upper ends of the shanks, as shown in the section, fig. 14, and in these the points lie when the instrument is folded, as in fig. 13. When in this state, the pen and pencil points lie within the forks of the lower joints. This tool is particularly convenient for those who require to carry drawing instruments with them from place to place.

We have next to describe the various forms of compasses of a smaller size, and called "bow compasses." No mechanical draughtsman can be without these, for the larger size are far too heavy and cumbrous

for the smaller and more delicate work which he is constantly called upon to execute. Fig. 17 is a front, and fig. 18 a side elevation of a very neat form of jointed bow compasses with a pen. The main joint is embraced by two eye plates, to which a small handle is attached. A portion of this handle is milled, to give control over the instrument and facility in turning it. It will also be observed that the centre point is a needle, held by a small screw, in a socket formed in the leg of the instrument. This arrangement affords a means of adjustment as to length, whilst the point can easily be replaced if accidentally broken. Compasses of the larger size are sometimes made with similar needles, but this refinement is considered by most draughtsmen as unnecessary in them, if the needle is not indeed inferior to the ordinary point, which, from its greater

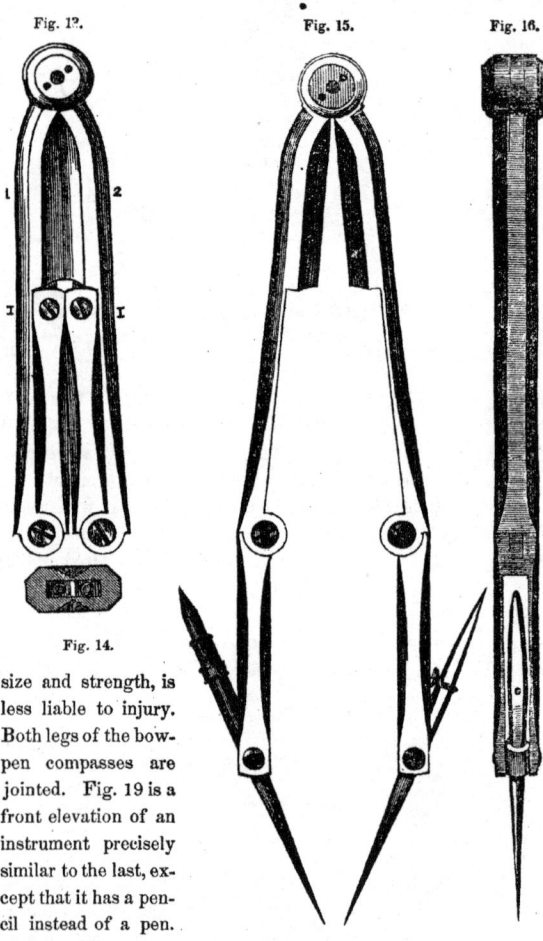

Fig. 12.   Fig. 15.   Fig. 16.

Fig. 14.

size and strength, is less liable to injury. Both legs of the bow-pen compasses are jointed. Fig. 19 is a front elevation of an instrument precisely similar to the last, except that it has a pencil instead of a pen. These compasses require to be adjusted to any desired radius by the direct action of the hand. In work where great accuracy and minuteness is called for, it will often be found a very tedious matter to obtain a true adjustment in this manner, particularly if the joints of the instrument are not in perfect working condition. This difficulty is got over in what are termed "spring," or "screw" bow compasses.

Fig. 20 is a side, and fig. 21 a front view of a pair of pen compasses of this class. The use of such instruments is confined to

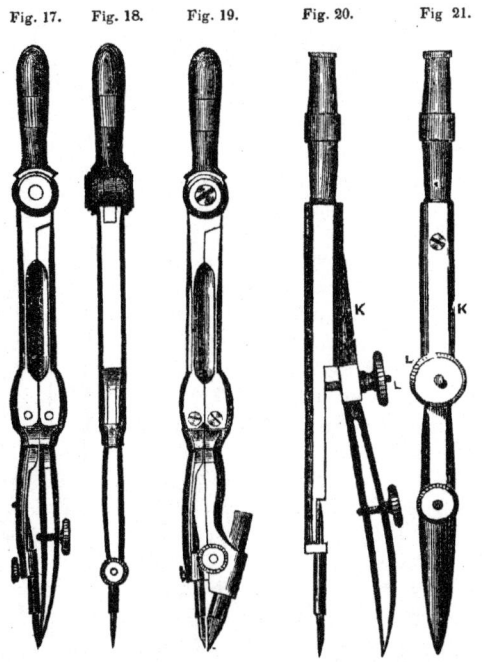

Fig. 17.　Fig. 18.　Fig. 19.　Fig. 20.　Fig 21.

very small circles, of half or three quarters of an inch in radius at the most. In the example we have selected for illustration, the centre leg is of brass, or German silver, and is in one piece with the milled handle. It is also provided with a needle point. The pen is made with a spring-tempered steel shank, K, which lies in a groove cut in the centre leg, or body, and which is fixed to the latter, at its top, by a screw. A small screw spindle, L, is passed through an opening in the pen shank, and is jointed to the centre leg, and a button, or nut, is passed on to the screw spindle outside the shank. This pen shank is so fixed as to have a tendency to stand out from the centre leg to the full extent of the instrument's range, and by turning the button of the screw, L, it may be forced in or allowed to open, so as to give the necessary adjustment. Fig. 22 is a side elevation of a pair of slightly modified spring-and-screw compasses; it is shown with a socket, carrying an engraver's *burin*. An ivory handle is fixed to the centre leg, or body of the instrument; and this arrangement is considered by some artists to give greater control over its action. The commoner kind of spring bow compasses consists of a single piece of steel forming the two legs, and

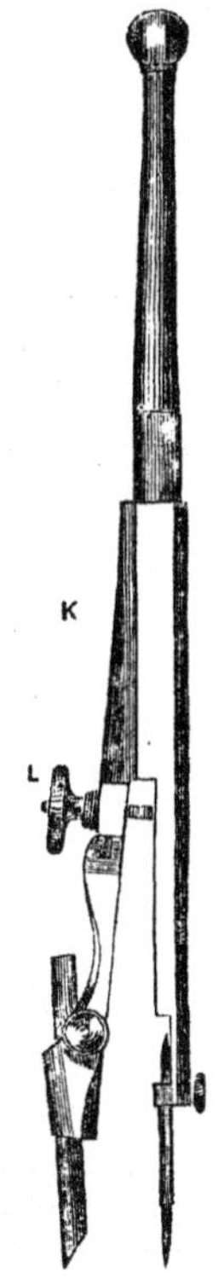

having a small brass handle attached. The steel of the legs is so tempered as to give them a tendency to stand apart, and the radius distance is regulated by a screw in the same manner as in the instruments represented in figs. 20, 21, and 22.

The draughtsman has frequently to delineate circles of a radius far exceeding the range of ordinary compasses, and for this purpose he must provide himself with "beam" compasses. A good form of this instrument is represented in side elevation, in fig. 23, and in transverse vertical section, in fig. 24. It consists of a wooden bar, or ruler, T, of considerable length, and of a T section, being formed of two strips united by a dovetail joint. This construction prevents warping or bending, and is necessary where a scale is cut on the bar, as any deviation from a straight line would render the measurement inaccurate. The compasses are provided with a pen, or pencil leg, and a centre leg, these being fitted upon the bar with socket pieces, M, M'. These socket pieces are fixed at any point along the bar, by pinching screws at the side; but to prevent the point of the screw from injuring the bar, a loose plate of metal is interposed next to the bar, as shown in the section, fig. 24. The socket, M, is in a solid piece with its pen, or pencilholder; but the centre leg, N, is in a separate piece from its socket, M', and is capable of minute adjustment back or forward in the latter. The socket, M, has a cylindrical groove along its under side, in which slides the head of the leg, N. This head is formed with a

Fig. 22.

Fig. 23.　　　　　　　　　　　　　　Fig. 24.

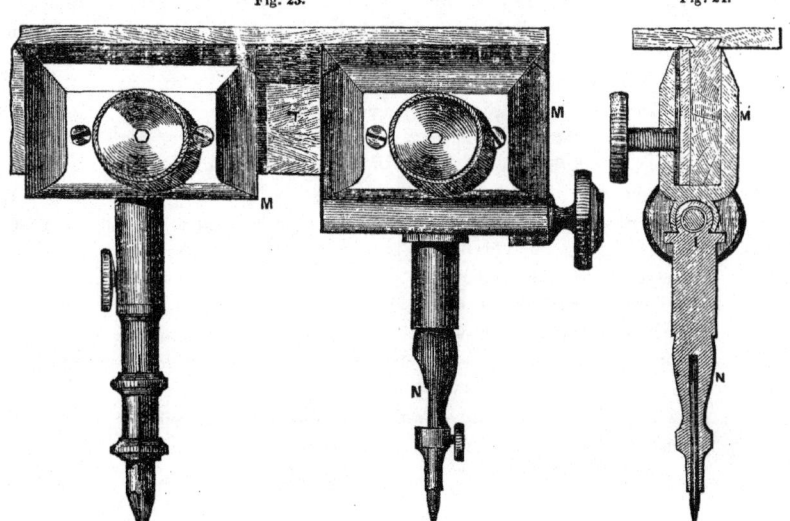

horizontal screw passage, or nut, to receive the screw spindle, I, which is held by an eye at the end of the socket groove, and is actuated by means of a button on the outside. By turning the screw, I, in either direction, the centre leg may be adjusted with great accuracy at any part of the socket. In adjusting the instrument to any measurement, the pencil socket, M, is loosened, and set pretty near the mark, and fixed; the exact length of radius is then obtained by adjusting the centre leg by means of the screw. A pair of beam compasses, or dividers, of somewhat different description, are represented in side elevation in fig. 25. In this instrument, which is entirely of metal, the centre

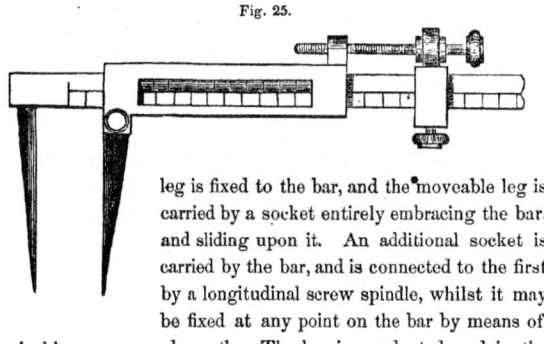

Fig. 25.

leg is fixed to the bar, and the moveable leg is carried by a socket entirely embracing the bar, and sliding upon it. An additional socket is carried by the bar, and is connected to the first by a longitudinal screw spindle, whilst it may be fixed at any point on the bar by means of a pinching screw underneath. The bar is graduated, and in the larger socket an opening is made having a bevilled edge, upon which a vernier scale is cut, so that very minute measurements may be taken. In setting the instrument, the smaller socket is fixed at a convenient point on the bar and then the larger socket, which carries the moveable point, pencil, or pen, is set back or forward, as necessary, by the longitudinal screw connecting it to the smaller socket.

Of the compasses class of drawing-instruments, there now remain to be described the proportional dividers. This instrument is represented, in front and side elevation, in figs. 26 and 27. Its use is to increase or reduce measurements to a different scale to that of the original drawing, of which a copy is being made; and a great deal of time may be saved by employing it, whilst there is much less risk of making mistakes with it, than when the draughtsman, in reducing a measurement, has first to take the distance, on the original drawing, in his common dividers, and, by applying it to the scale of that drawing, ascertain how much it is arithmetically; and then to find the corresponding distance on the reduced scale, which he has again to take in his dividers, so as to apply it to the copy in hand. With the proportional dividers, on the other hand, the action of taking the measurement on the original drawing, at one end of the instrument, adjusts its other end to the measurement, as increased or reduced to the scale of the copy. The instrument consists of a couple of elongated slotted brass plates, connected by an adjustable joint, J, and provided with steel points at both extremities of each plate. It will be obvious that, if the joint, J, is adjusted exactly in the centre between the extreme points, on opening the dividers, the distances between the points, at each end, will be equal: but if the joint, J, is adjusted, as in the figure, so that the length of the legs on one side is only half that on the other, then the distance between the points at one end will be half that between the points at the other end. In the same manner, by shifting the joint, J, still nearer one side of the instrument, a still less distance will be measured

by one end, as compared with the other; but the measurements will always bear the same proportion to each other as that which is, for the time being, between the portions of the instrument on each side of the joint, J. To enable the draughtsman to set the instrument to any desired proportion, the sides of the slot are graduated, and a projection on the joint has an index-line cut upon it, which is to be placed opposite the number corresponding to the desired proportion, in adjusting the instrument. When being adjusted, the points of the instrument should accurately coincide; and to secure this, a pin is fixed in one of the plates or legs, and a notch is cut in the other to receive it. The instrument is made to answer various purposes, in addition to that of reducing drawings. Thus, the joint may be so set, that when one end is applied to the radius of a circle, the other end will give the side of an inscribed polygon. One of the sides of the instrument is usually graduated for this purpose, and there are also divisions for finding the proportions between similar plane figures, and for finding the proportions between cubes or spheres. The proportional dividers require to be very accurately made, and great care must be taken of them; for if the points become injured or bent, or if the joint gets loose, the instrument will be rendered useless.

In copying drawings, where time is a matter of more consideration than the preservation of the original drawing, a great deal of time is frequently saved by laying the original upon the paper for the copy, and pricking the principal points through the former. A convenient instrument for this purpose is represented in partial section, in fig. 28, and consists of a needle point, held by a screw, e, in a brass socket, with an ivory handle. The socket is made to take off by unscrewing, and uncovers a small screw-driver, which

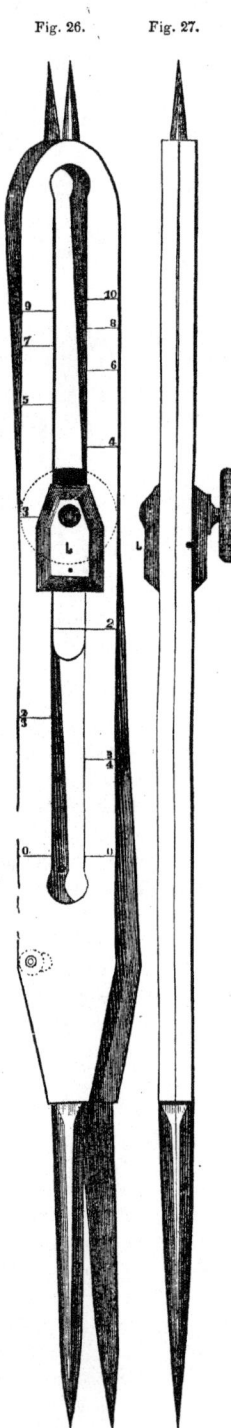

Fig. 26.   Fig. 27.

will serve to turn the screw, e, or any of the smaller screws in the other instruments.

In treating of drawing ellipses,* we have already described one of the many instruments constructed for that purpose. The well-known "trammel" is one of the simplest in construction, but it is very defective in practice. In figs. 29 and 30 we give an elevation and plan of a trammel of the newest and most improved form, in which the practical defects are very much lessened, but the contrivances by which this approximate perfection is attained are of such a nature as to require a more than ordinary excellence and accuracy of workmanship in the construction. The trammel consists of a metal bar, R, on which are fitted three sliding sockets, which can be adjusted at any points on the bar. Two of these sockets carry centre legs, P, O, and the third carries a pen, or pencil, s. In addition to these details, a guide-plate, Q, is required, having a couple of grooves cut in its upper face, at right angles to each other. This guide-plate has two short pin points, on the under side, to prevent it from slipping on the paper upon which it is placed. In ordinary instruments the legs, O and P, terminate in simple points, which are respectively caused to traverse the grooves in the guide-plate, Q, in describing the ellipse. It is, however, found to be almost impossible to obtain a smooth action with this arrangement, as the pressure on the points, being oblique to their line of movement along the guide-grooves, the friction is apt to be irregular, and so cause a varying motion of the pen or pencil point, and produce

Fig. 28

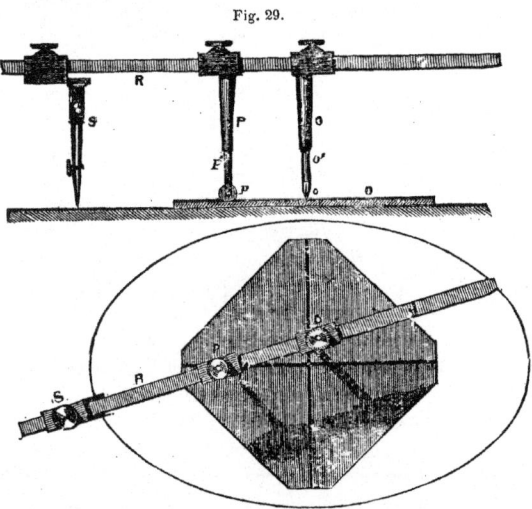

Fig. 29.

Fig. 30.

an uneven outline. In the instrument represented in figs. 29 and 30, the parts which traverse the guide-grooves in the plate, Q, consist of small steel wheels, o, p, carried in the forked ends of the

* See page 17.

steel spindles, o', p', which are entered loose into the socket legs, O, P. Thus, whilst the wheels considerably alleviate the friction arising in traversing the grooves, they always maintain their posi-

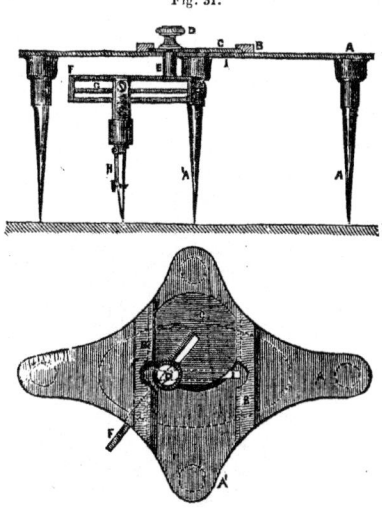

Fig. 31.

Fig. 32.

tion with regard to the grooves, whatever be the position of the bar, R, and pen, s. In adjusting the instrument, it is simply necessary to set the pen and centre legs, so that the distance of the two latter from the former shall correspond respectively with the semi-transverse and semi-conjugate axes of the ellipse to be described. With the instrument represented in the engravings it will not be possible to describe any ellipse which does not lie wholly outside the guide-plate, Q; and where smaller ellipses are required, a smaller guide-plate must be used.

Beyond comparison, the best instrument we have seen for drawing ellipses is that invented by Mr. Webb, and represented in elevation in fig. 31, and in plan in fig. 32. It consists of a lozenge-shaped table, A, of thin metal, supported upon four pointed legs, A'. Two parallel guides, B, are fixed across the top of the table, A, and a disc, C, is fitted between them, in such a manner as to be just capable of turning and sliding between the guides, B. The disc has a slot at one side, extending from the centre to the circumference, and in this is fixed, at any point, by a screw, D, a spindle, E, passing down through the table, A, below which it has fixed to it a slight frame, F, carrying a screw spindle, G. This screw serves to adjust the pen, or pencil, H, back or forward, on the frame, F. The spindle, E, works in a slot, I, in the table, A, which slot is at right angles to the disc guides, B. The instrument is caused to operate by turning the spindle, E, by means of the button, D, which action turns the carrier frame, F, and also the disc, B. It then follows, that if the spindle, E, were fixed in the centre of the disc, B, the point of the pen would describe a circle. If, however, the spindle, E, is fixed eccentrically in the disc, the rotation of the latter, between its guides, B, will cause the spindle to traverse the slot, I, in the table, A, in such a manner that the point of the pen will describe a perfect ellipse. In adjusting the instrument, two lines are drawn on the paper at right angles to each other, and the points of the legs, A', are placed upon these lines, when the slot, I, will be immediately above one of them, which will answer for the transverse axis of the ellipse, whilst the other one will be immediately below a line midway between the two guides, B, and will serve for the conjugate axis. The disc, B, is then set with its slot at right angles to the slot, I, in the table, A, and the semi-conjugate axis being marked upon the paper beneath, the point of the pen, H, is adjusted to it by turning the screw, G. The disc, B, is then turned a quarter round, so that its slot may coincide with the slot, I, and the screw, D, being loosened, the spindle, E, is moved back or forward along the disc slot, until the point of the pen, H, coincides with the end of the transverse axis of the ellipse. When so adjusted, the nut, D, is screwed down to fix the spindle, E, to the disc, B, and the ellipse may then be described. The legs, A', of the table are formed with telescopic socket joints, inside which very delicate springs are placed, of just sufficient strength to lift the pen's point off the paper, when not in the act of describing an ellipse, whilst a slight pressure of the hand, holding the table, A, during the drawing action, will overcome the resistance of the springs, and allow the pen, or pencil, to touch the paper. The legs, A, may be formed with a screw socket joint in addition, so that they may be accurately adjusted as to length, in order to preserve the table, A, perfectly level.

A very convenient instrument for describing ellipses of small eccentricity, or which differ very little from circles, is the elliptical compasses, consisting of two round legs, jointed together like ordinary compasses, upon one of which a pencil-holder is fitted with a tubular socket, so as to move longitudinally and circularly upon the leg. The pencil-holder is jointed, so that the pencil point may be adjusted at any distance from the leg. In using the instrument, the point of the leg carrying the pencil-holder is placed in the centre of the ellipse, and the leg is inclined in the direction of the transverse axis, by stretching out the other leg along the prolongation of the axis. The legs are held steady by one hand, and the pencil is carried round with the other, being kept in contact with the paper, by causing it to move up and down the leg as well as to rotate. In order that the ellipse may be drawn accurately in any desired position, it is necessary that the leg carrying the pencil-holder should be held perpendicular to the conjugate axis. To secure this, one of the legs should have a point branching out on one, or on both sides of the point, which is placed on the transverse axis, and the additional point, or points, should be in such a position as, when touching the paper, to keep the legs of the compasses in the perpendicular position alluded to. It is for want of this important addition that elliptical compasses have hitherto been found to be fallacious, and, in fact, useless. The instrument is not applicable to very oblong ellipses, because the inclination of the pencil becomes too great for the production of a clean line.

It is often necessary, particularly in topographical drawings, to make an estimate of the measurement of a series of curved, undulating, or irregular lines, as the circumference of a field, or the outline of any other irregularly-shaped area; for which purpose an "opisometer," or circumference measurer, is used. This instru-

ment is represented in separate elevations, taken at right angles to each other, in figs. 33 and 34. It consists of a short screw spindle, fixed in a bracket frame, and attached to an ivory handle. Working upon the screw spindle, like a nut, is a small disc, with a tapered and finely-milled edge. This disc is made to roll along the line to be measured, and, in doing so, it necessarily traverses along the screw from end to end. When the end of the line is reached, the instrument is traversed along a graduated rectilinear scale in the reverse direction to that in which it was passed over the line to be measured. This movement brings back the disc to the end of the screw from which it started; and when this point is reached, the distance traversed on the scale is obviously equal to the length of the original line. Care must be taken to keep the handle of the instrument in a vertical position, and to assist in this one of the bracket arms is formed with a pin, projecting down almost to the level of the bottom of the

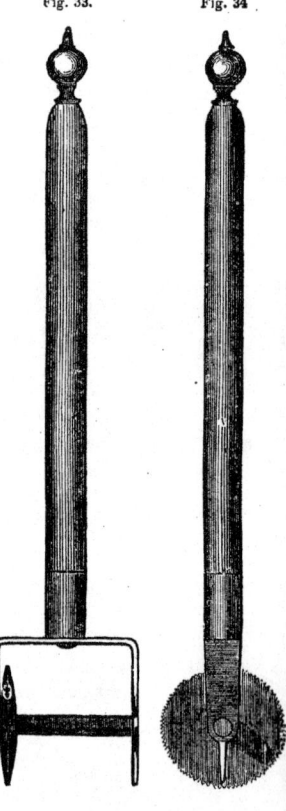

Fig. 33.   Fig. 34.

disc. It is also necessary that the disc should roll with a uniform pressure. This instrument may be used for measuring curved surfaces as well as curved lines.

Several very ingenious instruments have been invented for a purpose similar to that for which the opisometer is used, but presenting more serious difficulties. The usual method of discovering the area of a figure drawn on a plan, is to divide it into a number of triangles or trapeziums—to measure the base and altitude of each, and take the sum of their products. By a careful process of this kind, the area may be discovered with great accuracy; but as it is necessary to revise the calculations several times, both for the purpose of obviating faults in the arithmetical part of the work, and in order, by taking the average of a few independent measurements, to increase the probable accuracy of the result, this method of calculation, especially when the figure is irregular, entails a considerable amount of labour of an irksome kind. Attempts have been made to avoid this by cutting the figure from the sheet of paper, and weighing it in a delicate balance against weights consisting of parts of the same paper, of determinate sizes; but this method—at first sight simple and practical—is rendered of little use by the impossibility of obtaining paper of uniform thickness throughout the sheet, the variation of thickness—and hence of weight—being greater than the amount of error that could be allowed in the results

Several "planimeters," or instruments for mechanically measuring the area of plain surfaces, were exhibited in the Great Exhibition of 1851, and are noticed in Mr. Glaisher's admirable report on Class X., "Philosophical Instruments, and processes depending upon their use." All, or nearly all of these, aimed at the solution of the problem by integrating the differential expression of a curve, traced on a plane surface, being conceived on the old, and now almost forgotten, view of the differential calculus, which regarded the differential of a magnitude as a measure of the velocity of its increase at any instant. Suppose a straight line to be carried, with a uniform motion, along the base line, or abscissa, of any curvilinear area, remaining always parallel to itself, and perpendicular to the base line, and that, during this motion a moveable point in the line, so carried, is always kept on the circumference, or boundary line, of the area. Then it is clear, that the velocity of increase of the area will be proportional to, and therefore measured by, the length of the ordinate, or portion of the moveable line included between the base line and the describing point. Again, a disc, or wheel, can be supposed to revolve with an angular velocity always proportionate to the same ordinate; in which case the total angle of revolution described by it will increase by similar increments with the curvilinear area, and will, consequently, always be proportionate to, and a measure of, that area. The area may therefore be read off, upon its circumference, by any method which keeps account of the number of revolutions made by this wheel, which may be called the integrating wheel, disc, or roller. If the circumferences of two circles be connected by teeth, or by simple contact, so as to work together, their angular velocities will be inversely as their radii; so that, if the radius of one of them be constant, the angular velocity of that one will be directly as the radius of the other. Thus, any mechanical arrangement securing the condition that a roller, or disc, shall be carried round on its centre, by contact with a uniformly revolving circle of a radius always equal to the length of the variable ordinate, will at once be a solution of the problem. The condition alluded to may be obtained by employing a couple of discs at right angles to each other, or by using a cone and a disc, with their axes parallel to each other. The former construction is adopted in one or two instruments, invented by continental mathematicians, the latter by Mr. Sang of Kirkaldy.

Mr. Sang's instrument, which is represented in perspective in fig. 35, indicates the area of any figure, however irregular, on merely carrying the point of a tracer round its boundary; and, besides the advantage of not injuring the drawing, it possesses that of speed and accuracy. A frame, A, carries an axle, which has on it two rollers, B, of equal size, and a cone, C. It is heavy, so that it maintains its parallelism on being pushed along the paper. The sides of the frame are parallel to the edge of the cone, and are fitted to receive the circumference of four friction rollers, R, which move along A, and carry a light frame, F, terminating on the tracing-point, P, to which the handle, H. is attached by a universal joint. The frame, F, also carries a wheel, I, which, by means of a weight, is pressed on the surface of the cone, and receives motion from it as the tracer is carried along the

paper. The index-wheel, I, only touches the cone by a narrow edge, the rest of its circumference being of smaller diameter, and containing a silver ring divided into 200 parts, which are again subdivided by a vernier into 2,000 parts. The value of each of

Fig. 35.

these divisions is the $\frac{1}{100}$th part of a square inch; so that one turn of the wheel represents 20 inches. Another index wheel, T, moved by I, is divided into five parts, each of which represents 20 inches, so that a complete revolution of T values 100 inches. The eye-glass, E, assists in reading the divisions and vernier.

It is apparent, from the construction of this instrument, that if the tracer be moved forward, it will cause the index to revolve, not simply in proportion to that motion, but in proportion to the motion of the tracer, multiplied by the distance of the edge of the index-wheel, from the apex of the cone; and that the revolving motion of the index will be positive or negative, according as the tracer is carried backwards or forwards. Hence, if the tracer be carried completely round the outline of any figure—on arriving at the end of its journey, the index-wheel will show the algebraic sum of the breadth of the figure at every point, multiplied by the increment of the distance of the points from the apex of the cone; that is to say, the area of the figure.

This instrument possesses great simplicity of construction. Both factors of the continuous multiplication are directly transmitted from the motion of the tracing point in the simplest manner. The influence of the elasticity of the parts of the machine on the accuracy of its indications, may be discovered by moving the tracer a second time over the boundary of the figure, after having turned the whole instrument round 180°. The effects of the imperfections in the mechanism will now have changed signs, and one of the results will probably be found to be a little too large, and the other a little too small. The average between the two is the exact area of the figure, and is more to be depended on than the results of measurements made by scale and calculation in the usual way. A careful operator, in using the planimeter, will always take the average of two tracings in this manner; but when he experiences the rapidity with which this may be done, he will find the trouble as nothing in comparison with the harassing labour of calculating by scale and multiplication.

Mr. Miller, of Woolwich, has devised a very useful modification of the common jointed rule. This instrument is termed a "radiator," and our engraving, fig. 36, represents a portion of it in plan, whilst fig. 37 is an end elevation. The inner edges of the legs are used as rulers, and the joint has a transparent

2 B

centre, A, which is placed directly over the point to be drawn to. A graduated arc, B, is supplied, and the brass legs are furnished

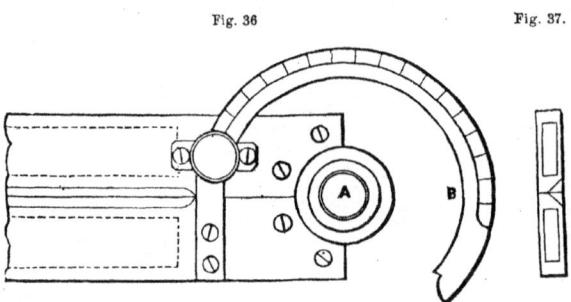

Fig. 36　　　　　　Fig. 37.

with sockets, which admit of any length of ruler being used. The radiator is applicable to the following purposes :—

For drawing lines in perspective, or geometrical drawing, to a point or centre; for setting off angles as a protractor; for a right-angled triangle, or any other angles; and for setting out polygons of different numbers of sides. In using it, the centre of the glass is placed over the centre to be drawn to, and a line is drawn along the inner edge of the ruler from the point required. When many lines are to be drawn to one centre, the hand must be placed upon one leg, to allow the other to be moved to the several points.

Two forms of protractors, or instruments for setting off or measuring angles have already been described;* a third, and much approved form, consists of a circular bar divided to 360°, and having two diametrical arms, one of which carries a vernier adapted to the divided circle. In laying off angles, or in the construction of any general delineations by this instrument, the bearings must first be marked on the original sheet, and thence transferred to the required position by parallel rulers, or some similar adjunct. Thus, two separate instruments are necessary, and the accuracy of the indications suffers correspondingly. These inconveniences are entirely done away with in Mr. Simpson's elegant duplex straight-edge protractor, which is represented in plan in fig. 38. A graduated quadrant, forming an index for angles, is made in one piece with a parallel bar, A, which is connected at each extremity by means of traverse bars, B, with a similar bar, A, the space between the two being of such a width as to admit the straight edge, C, at any part of which it can be fixed by the pinching screw, E. A central transverse piece, D, which is screwed to the two bars, A, carries a pivot, or joint stud, for the eye of a radial straight-edge, F, having its edges bevelled off for ruling close to the paper. A screw, G, and clamping plate are provided to fix the radial straight bar, F, at any angle. Immediately above the centre of the radius bar, F, and fixed to it at both ends, is a smooth rod, H, upon which slides the socket, I. This socket carries the two straight-edges, J, lying in one straight line, and united together by a bridge-piece embracing the socket, I, and adjusted upon it by means

* See page 8 and plate I.

of screws, so as to be capable of being kept at all times accurately at right angles with the radius bar, F. At a short distance from the centre of motion of the radius bar, F, is a segmental opening, graduated to 30°, on each side of the centre, or zero point, forming two verniers, for instruments differently divided, and for the minute subdivision of the graduations of the quadrant on the piece, A. By this apparatus any angles may be measured and laid off by the quadrant, and transferred to any point on the paper without the aid of any additional instrument, as the whole instrument may be moved to any desired point on the straight-edge, C, without any shift of position with reference to the meridian line or starting point. With additional scales on the right angle straight-edges, J, the instrument may be employed, as an offset scale, for plotting surveys and laying down sections.

One of the most economically useful instruments of the draughtsman is the Pentagraph; but it is one which requires such extreme accuracy and truthfulness in its construction, that its consequent cost puts it out of the reach of the majority of those who need it. By means of it, drawings may be copied on an enlarged or reduced scale, by the mere action of carrying a tracing point over the lines of the original drawing. The motion of the tracing point is communicated to the delineating

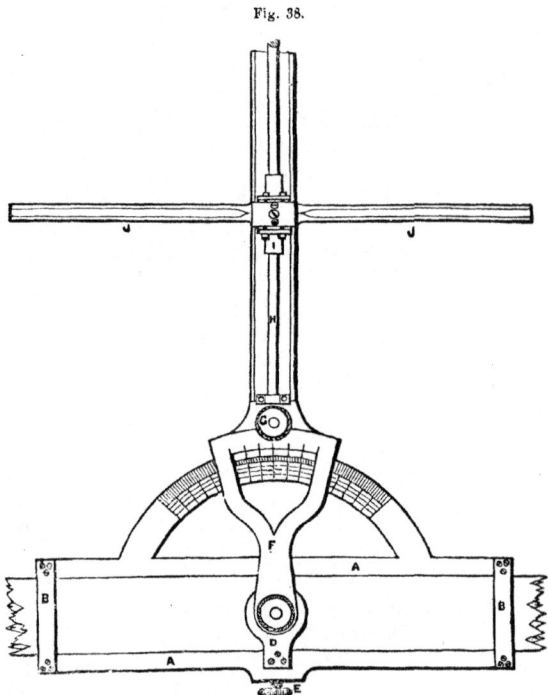

Fig. 38.

pencil by the angular movements of a series of levers oscillating upon a fixed centre. If one arm of a lever is twice as long as the other, the arc described by its extremity will be twice as great, whatever be the extent of the movement. In this case, however the radii of the arcs would be uniform, and an arrangement is required, providing for the increase or decrease in length of the two radii, but in such a manner that they shall continually be in the same proportion to each other. This is effected by making the main lever with joints midway between the ex-

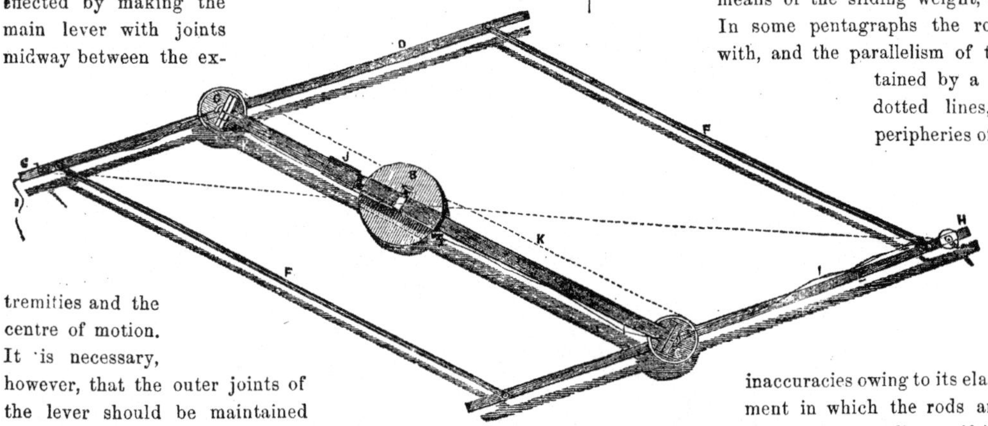

Fig. 40.

tremities and the centre of motion. It is necessary, however, that the outer joints of the lever should be maintained constantly parallel to each other, and it is likewise desirable that the instrument should be capable of adjustment for different proportions, otherwise its scope of usefulness would be sadly narrowed. These several conditions are fulfilled in the instrument represented in our engraving, fig. 40, which is a pentagraph of the most modern and approved design and construction. The main lever, A, turns upon a centre carried by the weight, B, which has fine points upon its under side to prevent its slipping upon the paper. The lever, A, passes through a socket at the centre, and may be fixed by a pinching screw at any point of its length; it is graduated at the side, and the socket is formed with a vernier index for the estimation of minute measurements. To the extremities of the lever, A, are jointed the discs, C, which are formed with sockets on their under sides to receive the bars, D, E. These bars are graduated in a similar manner to the main lever, and vernier indices are formed in the plates, C, to correspond. The parallelism of these bars is maintained by the rods, F; the tracing point is at G, and the delineating pencil at H, or *vice versa*, as the case may be. A string, I, is passed from the tracing point through guide eyes at the joints, C, C, to a small bell-crank lever, at H, by means of which the pencil is raised when it is not wished to mark; this being effected by drawing the string, I, at the tracing point. As represented in the engraving, the instrument is adjusted to copy a drawing upon an enlarged scale. To obtain the correct action of the instrument it is necessary that the tracer, G, pencil, H, and centre of motion, B, be in a straight line. The proportion of reduction or enlargement being determined on, the main lever, A, is so adjusted in its socket, B, that the portions of the lever on each side of the centre may have this proportion to each other; this being indicated by the graduated scale on the side of the lever. The bars, D, E, must then be correspondingly adjusted in their carrying sockets, the

distance between the tracer, or pencil, and joint being always equal to the distance between the joint and turning centre on the respective side of the main lever, A. The instrument, when adjusted, is balanced on its centre by means of the sliding weight, J, upon the lever, A. In some pentagraphs the rods, F, are dispensed with, and the parallelism of the bars, D, E, maintained by a belt, K, indicated in dotted lines, passed round the peripheries of the discs, C, grooved for the purpose. This belt is usually of thin flat steel wire, similar to that used for watch springs—a belt of ordinary material causing inaccuracies owing to its elasticity. The arrangement in which the rods are used is, however, superior, as the belt is apt to slip, or, if it is too tight, it occasions an injurious strain on the joints.

Another form of pentagraph has been suggested by Mr. R. Foster, jun., of Dublin, which seems susceptible of being rendered a very efficient instrument. It is delineated in fig. 41. The small and shallow circular box, A, contains the actuating mechanism, and is arranged to turn at pleasure upon the fixed centre stud, B; and from each side of the box, a rod, C, D, projects, the points of the rods being brought into a horizontal line with the stud centre, B. The box is in horizontal section, to exhibit the

Fig. 41.

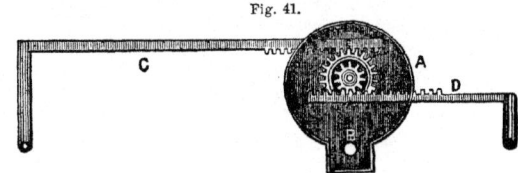

internal gearing. The end of each rod has rack-teeth upon it, the teeth on the rod, C, gearing with a spur-wheel, E, fast on a stud in the centre of the box; whilst the other rod, D, similarly gears, with a pinion, F, on the same centre. These two wheels are, of course, changeable, their relative radii being always determinable by the proportion to be observed between the original and the copy, of any drawing to be reduced or enlarged by the instrument. The same relation is also to be kept up between the lengths of the two rods, in order that both the angular and longitudinal traverse actions may coincide. It is then obvious that whatever figure is traced out by the point on one rod, will be delineated by the pencil on the other, in the proportion determined by the wheels and the leverage of the rods. The rods may be either worked on opposite sides, or both on the same side.

In this practically descriptive account of the draughtsman's tools, we have endeavoured to put the student in possession of the best examples of delineative mechanism which the collective experience of the time, has produced. The subject is a wide one, and would bear indefinite extension in the way of analysing the varieties of design and construction which individual experience or fancy has suggested. But such a mode of treatment would necessarily be digressive; and we have, therefore, steadily adhered to a critical examination of what our own experience warrants us in presenting to the practical draughtsman, as the best and most trustworthy aids in the prosecution of his studies in *Industrial Design*.

With this our task is accomplished. The pages now before the student are given to him in the hope that they may be found to form—

"A volume of detail, where all is orderly set down."

and that they really redeem the promises held out in our prefatory remarks. The English language now, for the first time, possesses a text-book of design in connection with those industrial pursuits which have rendered the sons of the British islands so pre-eminently famous. If it fulfils but a small portion of the purposes for which we have designed it, we shall rest satisfied in having accomplished something towards the spread of that particular education in which the continental industrialist has hitherto left us so far behind.

"Men are universally divided, as regards their artistical qualifications," says the eloquent author of "*Modern Painters*," "into three great classes—a right, a left, and a centre. On the right side are the men of facts; on the left, the men of design; in the centre, the men of both." Let it be our mission to weaken this disunion of the two first, by adding to the weight and number of the centre or composite class. The right and the left may each hold to, and discuss their respective facts and designs, but nothing really good can arise from all this, until the practised experimentalist shall impose that check upon the theoretical designer, which the latter will again return, in opposing the false deductions arising from misapprehended facts. "Art," says Whewell, "is the parent, not the progeny of science; the realization of principles in practice forms part of the prelude, as well as the sequel, of theoretical discovery." But we must guard against the empiricisms of practice by judicious theoretical comparisons. Our men of practice and our men of science have lived too much apart. "The dexterous hand and the thoughtful mind," the labourer who toils with sweated brow, and he who exerts the conceptions of the imaginative brain, find their strength in union alone.

No book, however profoundly it may be designed, or however clearly it may be written, can make a draughtsman. To certain inherent qualifications, the ambitious student must add attentive assiduity and patient toil. The first elements will be useful; the second are absolutely essential. Let each of our readers recall the admirable words of Gibbon:—"Every man who rises above the common level has received two educations—the first from his teachers; the second, more personal and important, from himself." These are words which Bacon would have said must be "chewed and digested." In his "Advice on the Study and Practice of the Law," Mr. Wright has, most happily and effectively, discussed a similar topic. He says, "The student may rest assured that, without industry, and that confidence which an ardent love of fame, and an enthusiastic desire for improvement, never fail to inspire, he will not become eminent; and he must remember that society forms a very different opinion of the man of sound judgment and perseverance, who seldom fails in his attempts, and the fanciful and vain, who, whilst they imagine themselves *more capable* to learn than others, pass their lives in indolent or trifling pursuits, without acquiring that knowledge of their profession which ensures accuracy and success in practice." These are the well-considered ideas of men who have combined both thought and action. Their pithy eloquence embodies whole chapters of matter worthy of sinking deeply into the student's memory, where they must arouse him from any dreamy and deceptive contemplations of comparative excellence; for the superficial thinker is but too apt to be thus led away, forgetting that such comparisons continually lessen the advantages on his side, as the acquisitions which he perhaps superciliously boasts are mouldering away.

With these views, and to further such ends, we have written this book; and with such views do we now commit the venture to the world of industrial readers.

INDEX.

197

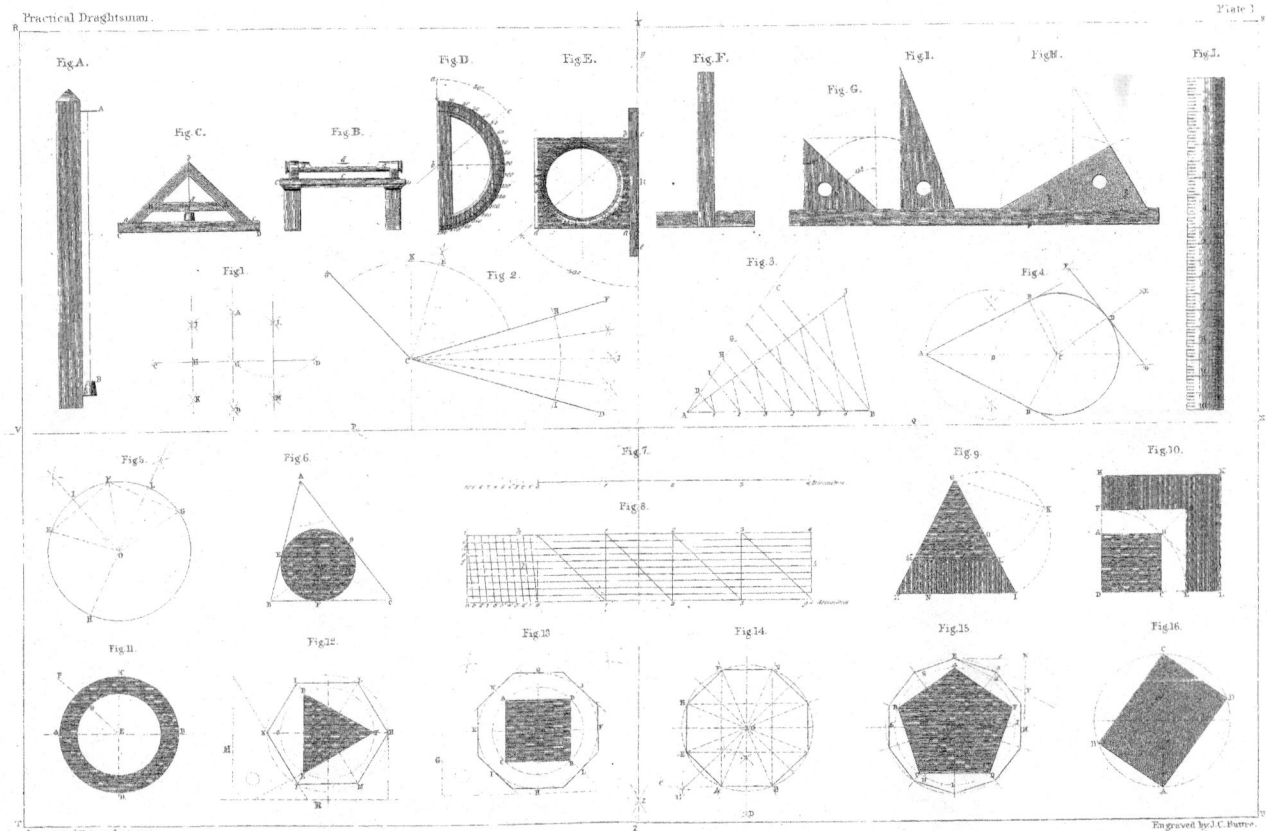

Plate 2.

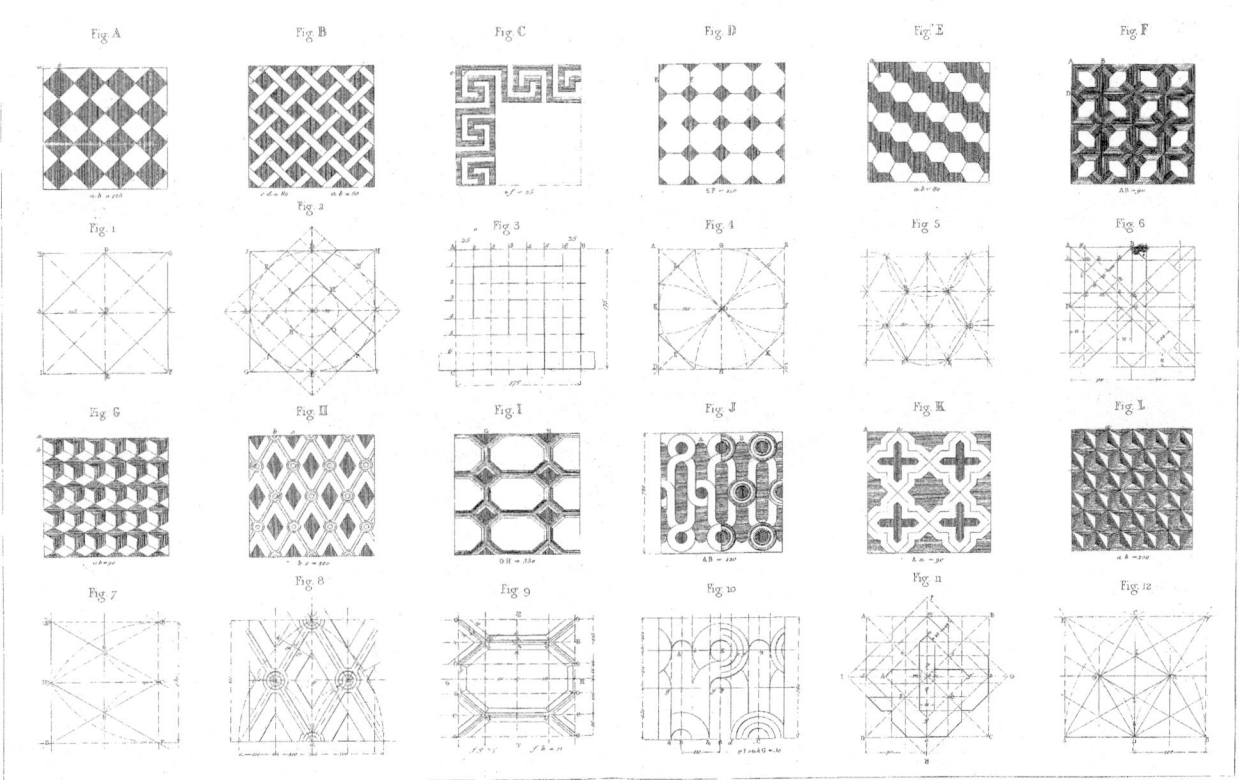

Fig A.   Fig B.   Fig C.   Fig D.   Fig E.   Fig F.

Fig 1.   Fig 2.   Fig 3.   Fig 4.   Fig 5.   Fig 6.

Fig G.   Fig H.   Fig I.   Fig J.   Fig K.   Fig L.

Fig 7.   Fig 8.   Fig 9.   Fig 10.   Fig 11.   Fig 12.

Armengaud Frères et Amouroux.

Engraved by J.C.Buttre.

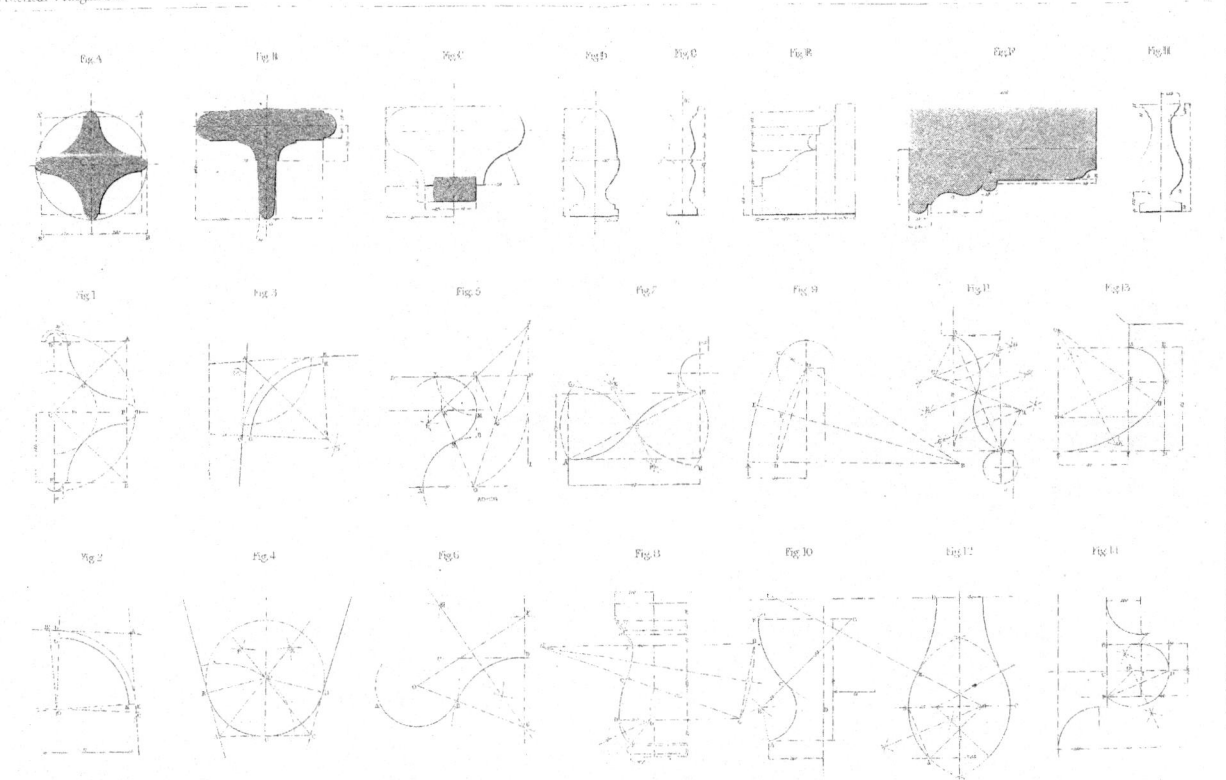

Plate 4

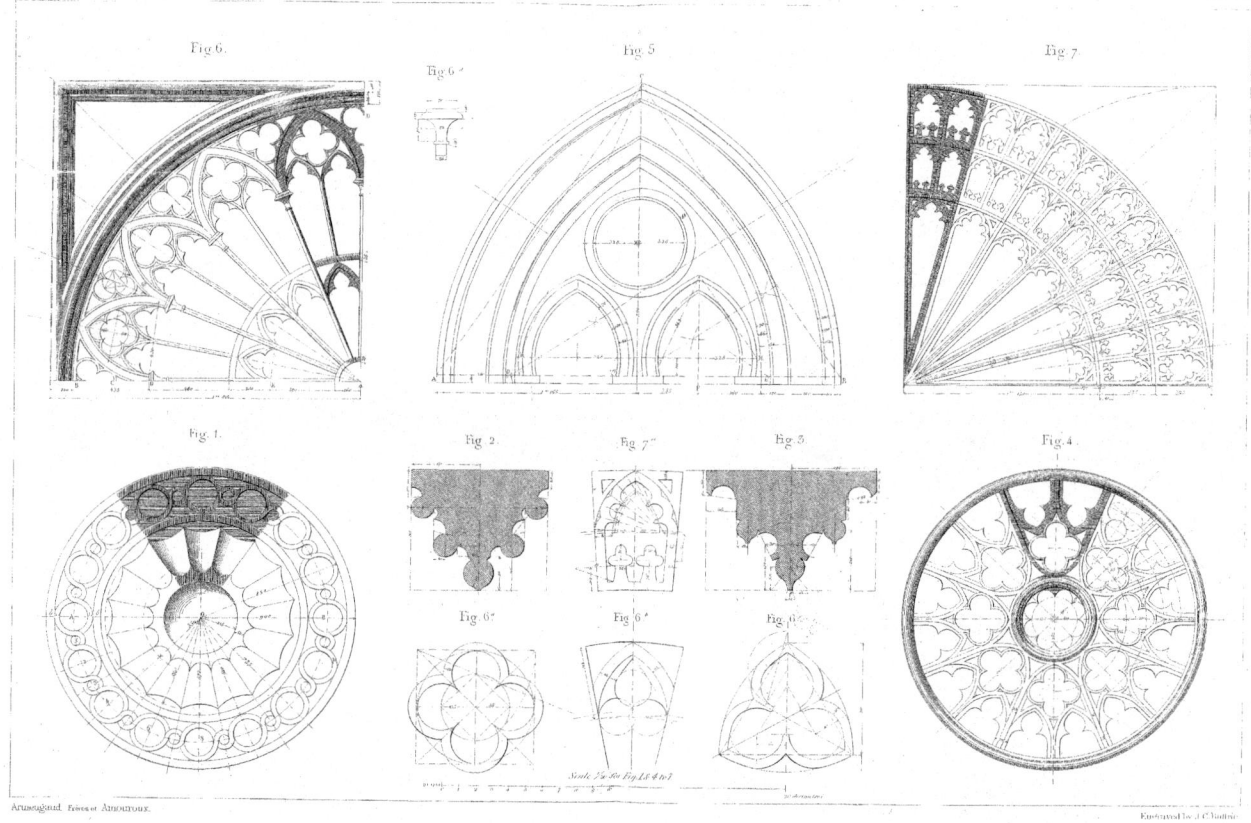

Fig 6.

Fig 6°

Fig 5.

Fig 7.

Fig 1.

Fig 2.

Fig 7″

Fig 3.

Fig 4.

Fig 6″

Fig 6°

Fig 6

Scale 1/4 for Fig 1.8.4 & 5

Plate 5.

Fig. A. Fig. B. Fig. C. Fig. D. Fig. D'.

Fig. 1. Fig. 3. Fig. 5.

Fig. 2. Fig. 7. Fig. 6. Fig. 8. Fig. 4.

Fig. 7bis.

Plate 6.

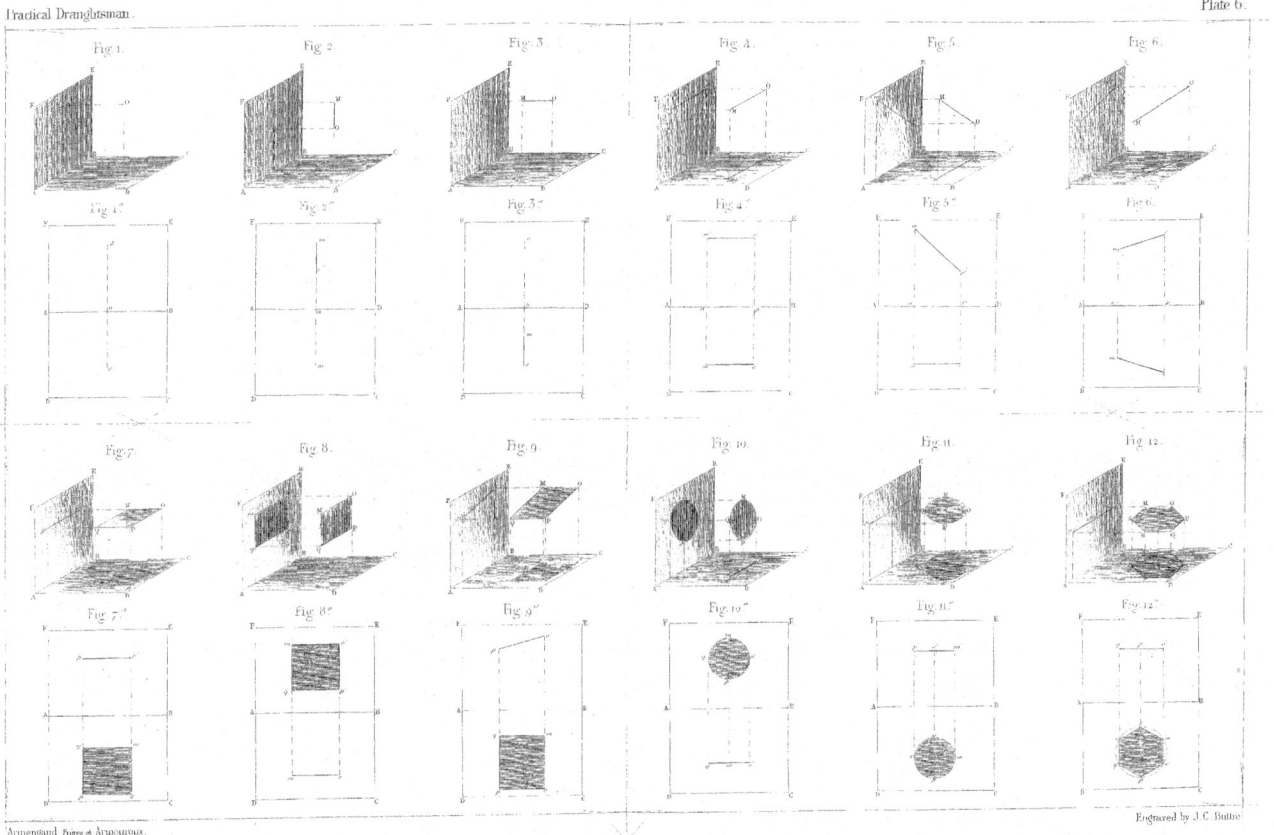

Fig. 1. Fig. 2. Fig. 3. Fig. 4. Fig. 5. Fig. 6.

Fig. 1". Fig. 2". Fig. 3". Fig. 4". Fig. 5". Fig. 6".

Fig. 7. Fig. 8. Fig. 9. Fig. 10. Fig. 11. Fig. 12.

Fig. 7". Fig. 8". Fig. 9". Fig. 10". Fig. 11". Fig. 12".

Armengaud Frères et Armouroux.

Engraved by J.C. Buttre.

Plate 7

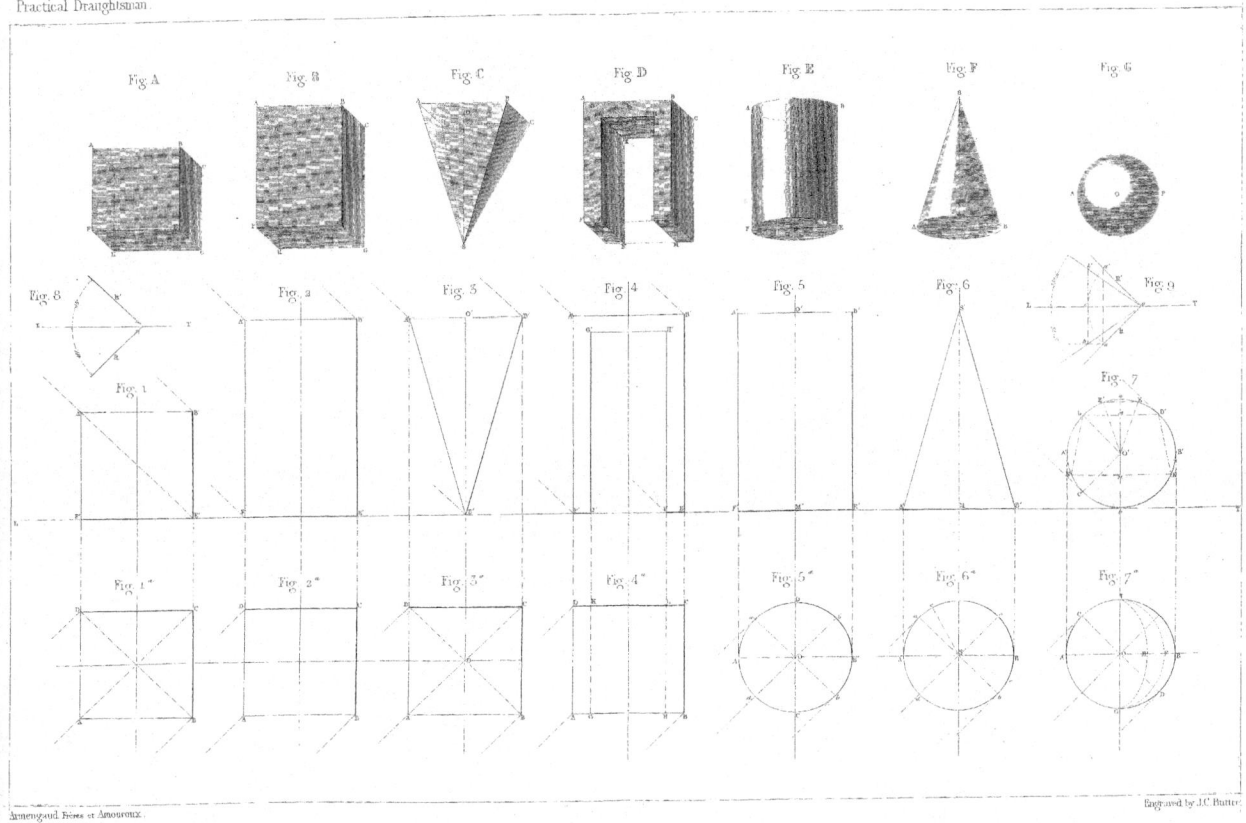

Plate 8

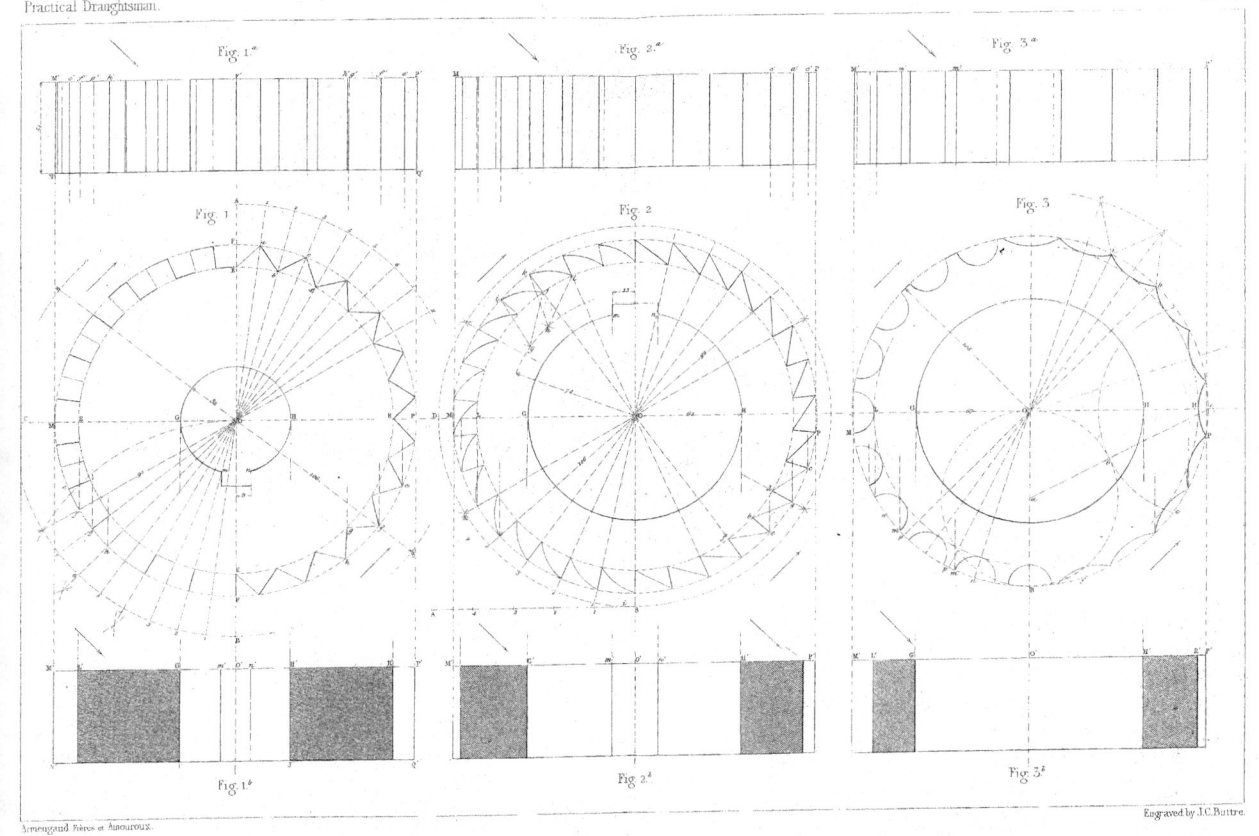

Fig. 1.ª

Fig. 2.ª

Fig. 3.ª

Fig. 1

Fig. 2

Fig. 3

Fig. 1.ᵇ

Fig. 2.ᵇ

Fig. 3.ᵇ

Armengaud Frères et Amouroux.

Engraved by J.C.Buttre.

Plate 9

Fig. 2 Fig. 7 Fig. 1 Fig. 6 Fig. 4

Fig. 3 Fig. 8 Fig. 9 Fig. 5 Fig. 10

Plate II.

Plate 12

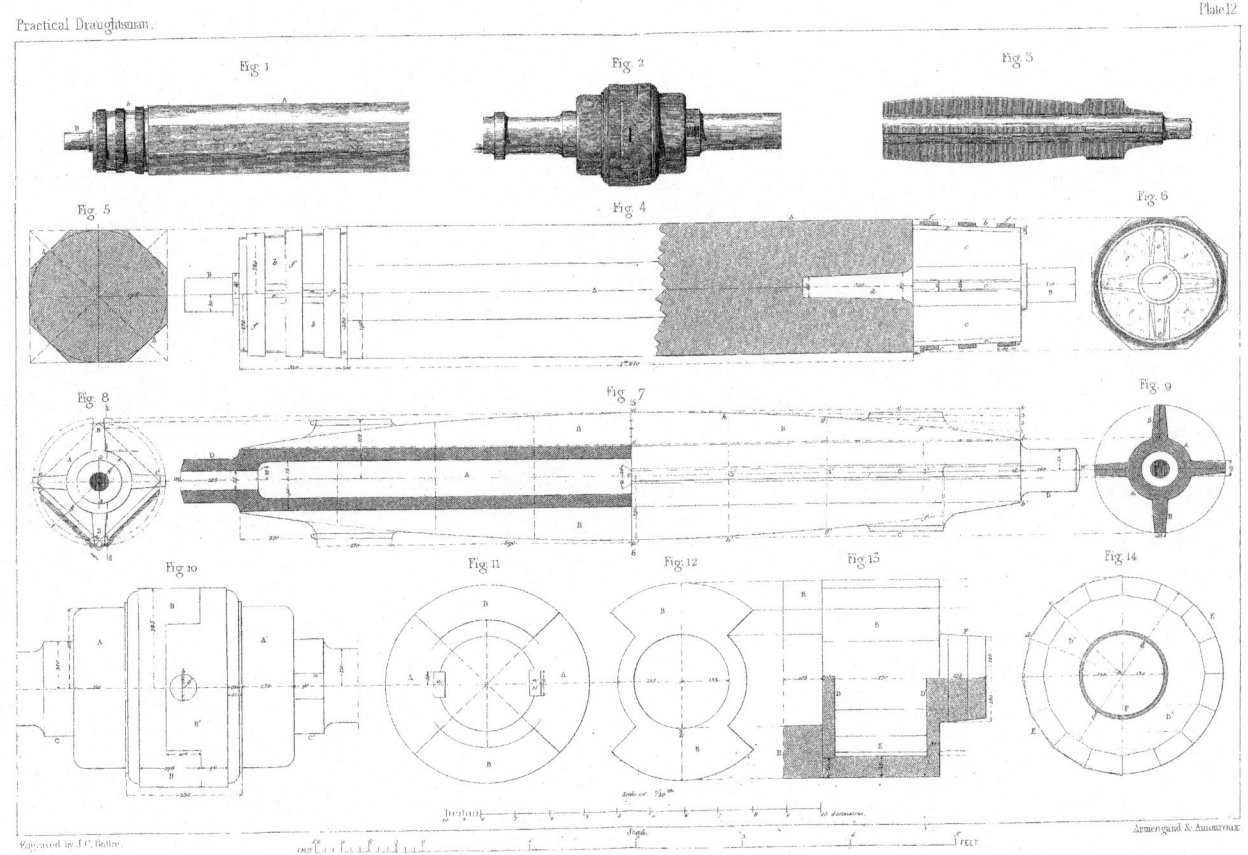

Fig. 1

Fig. 2

Fig. 3

Fig. 5

Fig. 4

Fig. 6

Fig. 8

Fig. 7

Fig. 9

Fig. 10

Fig. 11

Fig. 12

Fig. 13

Fig. 14

Plate 13.

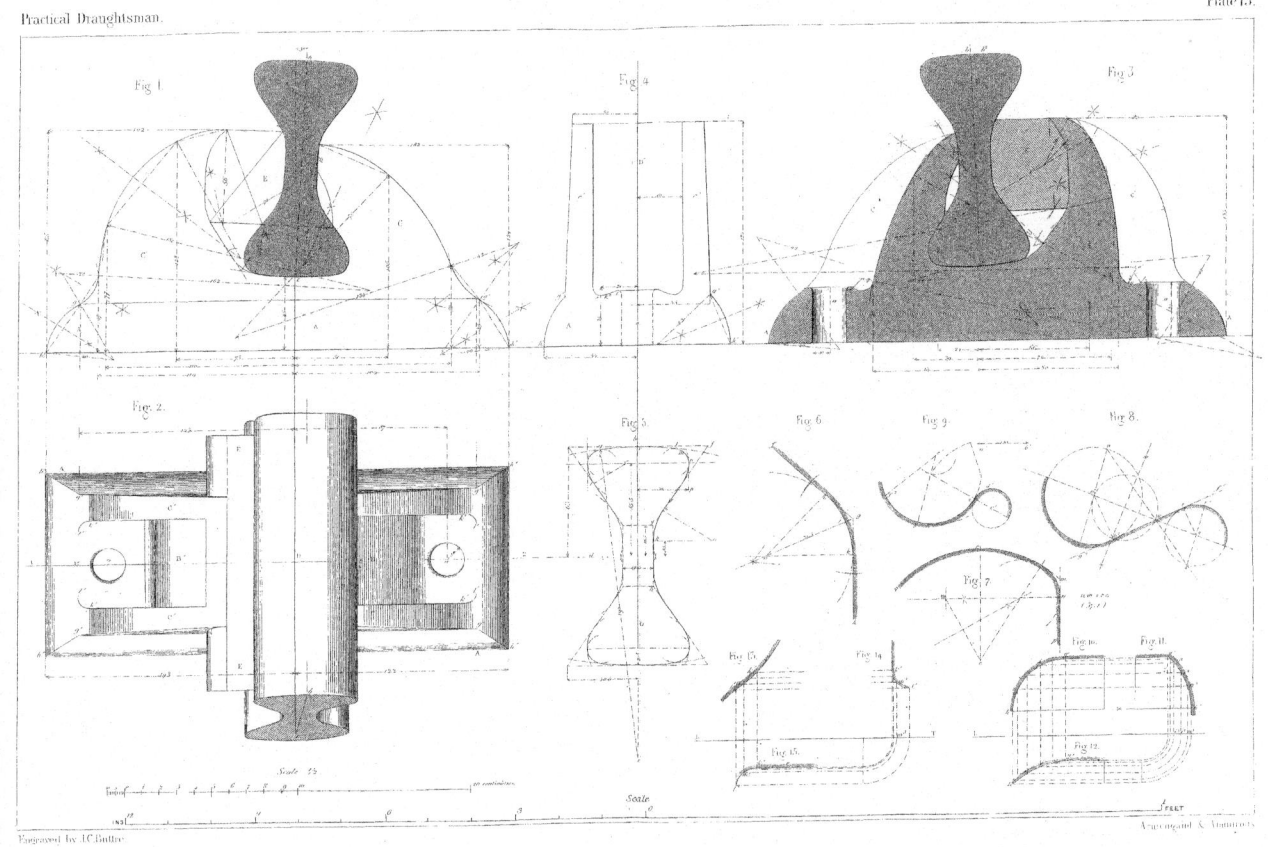

Fig. 1.

Fig. 4.

Fig. 3.

Fig. 2.

Fig. 5.

Fig. 6.

Fig. 9.

Fig. 8.

Fig. 7.

Fig. 15.

Fig. 14.

Fig. 10.

Fig. 11.

Fig. 13.

Fig. 12.

Scale

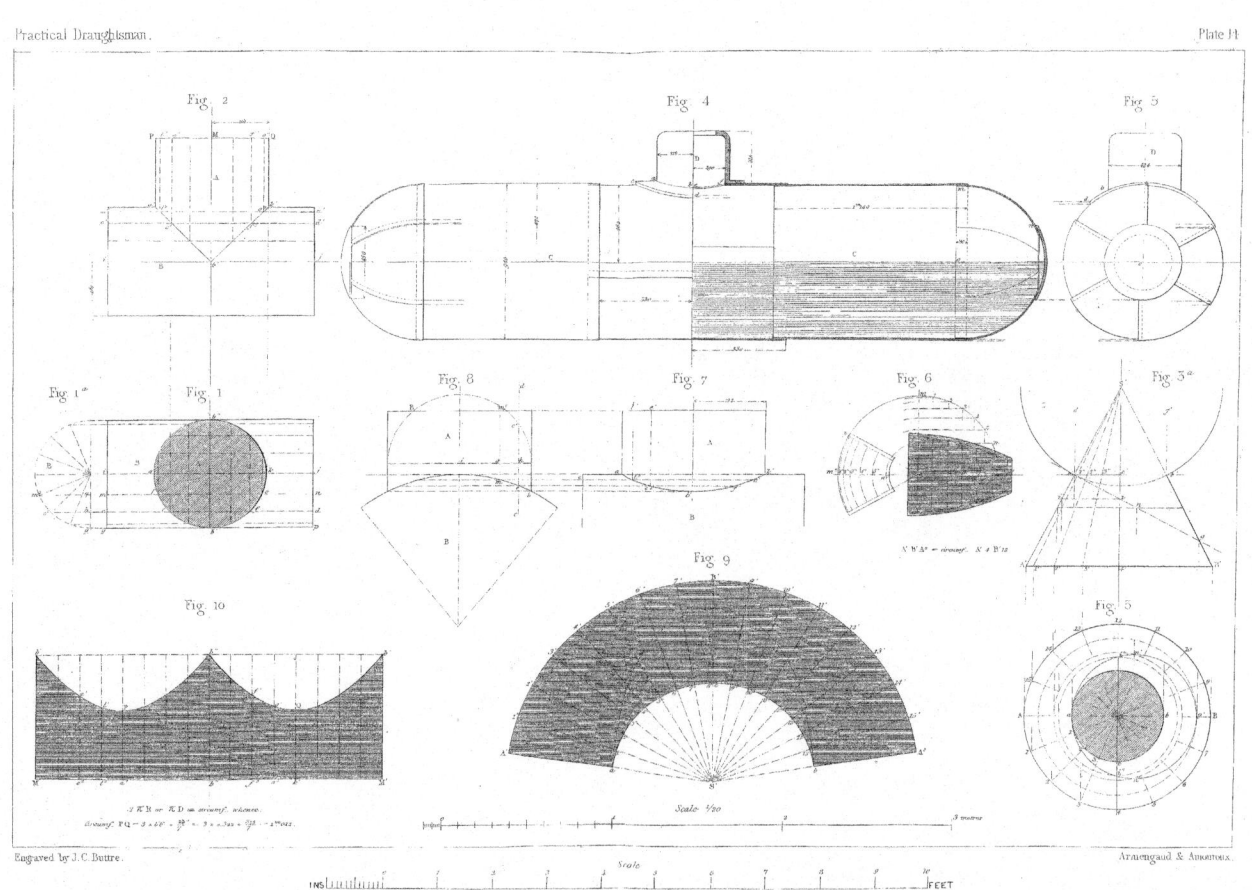

Fig. 2

Fig. 4

Fig. 5

Fig. 1ᵃ   Fig. 1

Fig. 8   Fig. 7   Fig. 6   Fig. 3ᵃ

Fig. 10

Fig. 9

Fig. 5

Scale ⁵⁄₂₀

INS   Scale   FEET

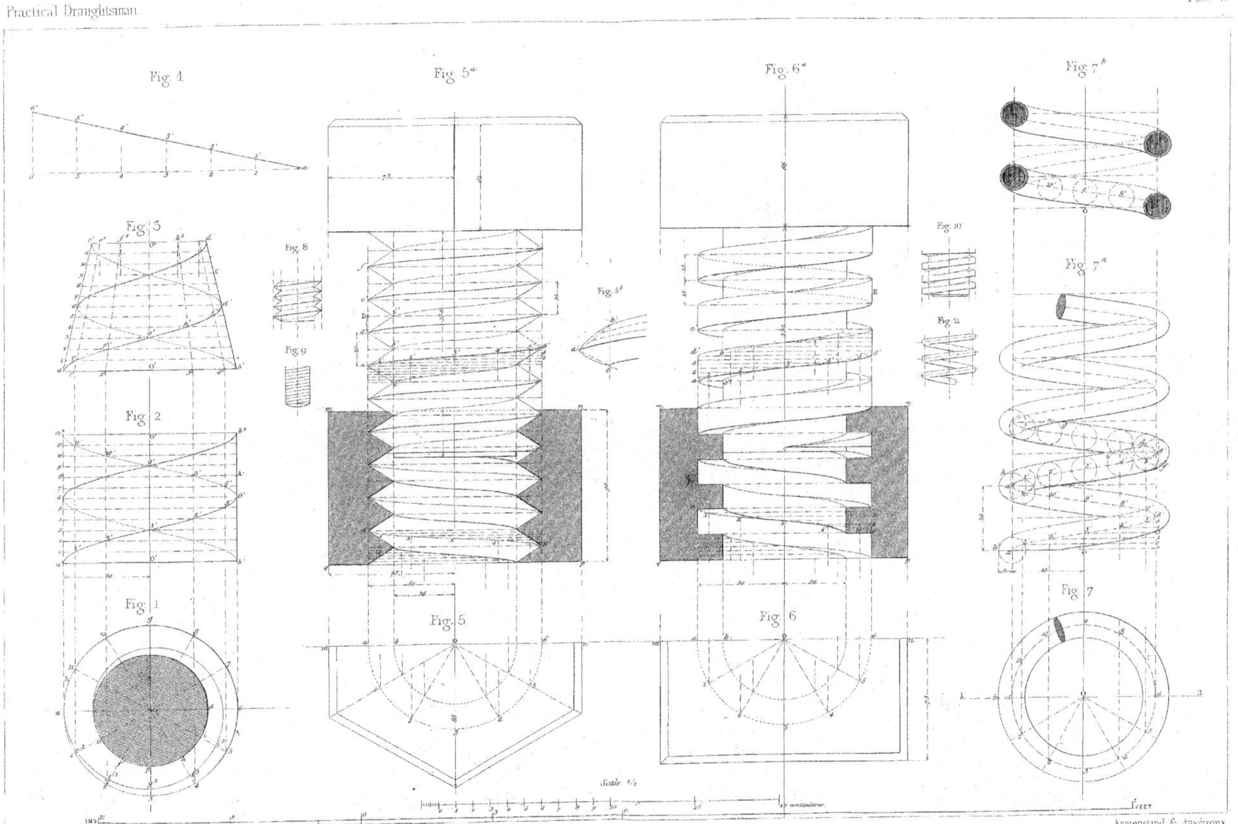
Fig. 4
Fig. 5a
Fig. 6a
Fig. 7b
Fig. 3
Fig. 8
Fig. 9
Fig. 5b
Fig. 10
Fig. 11
Fig. 7a
Fig. 2
Fig. 1
Fig. 5
Fig. 6
Fig. 7
Scale 1/2
centimetres
Feet

Engraved by J.C. Buttre

Armengaud & Amouroux.

Plate 1

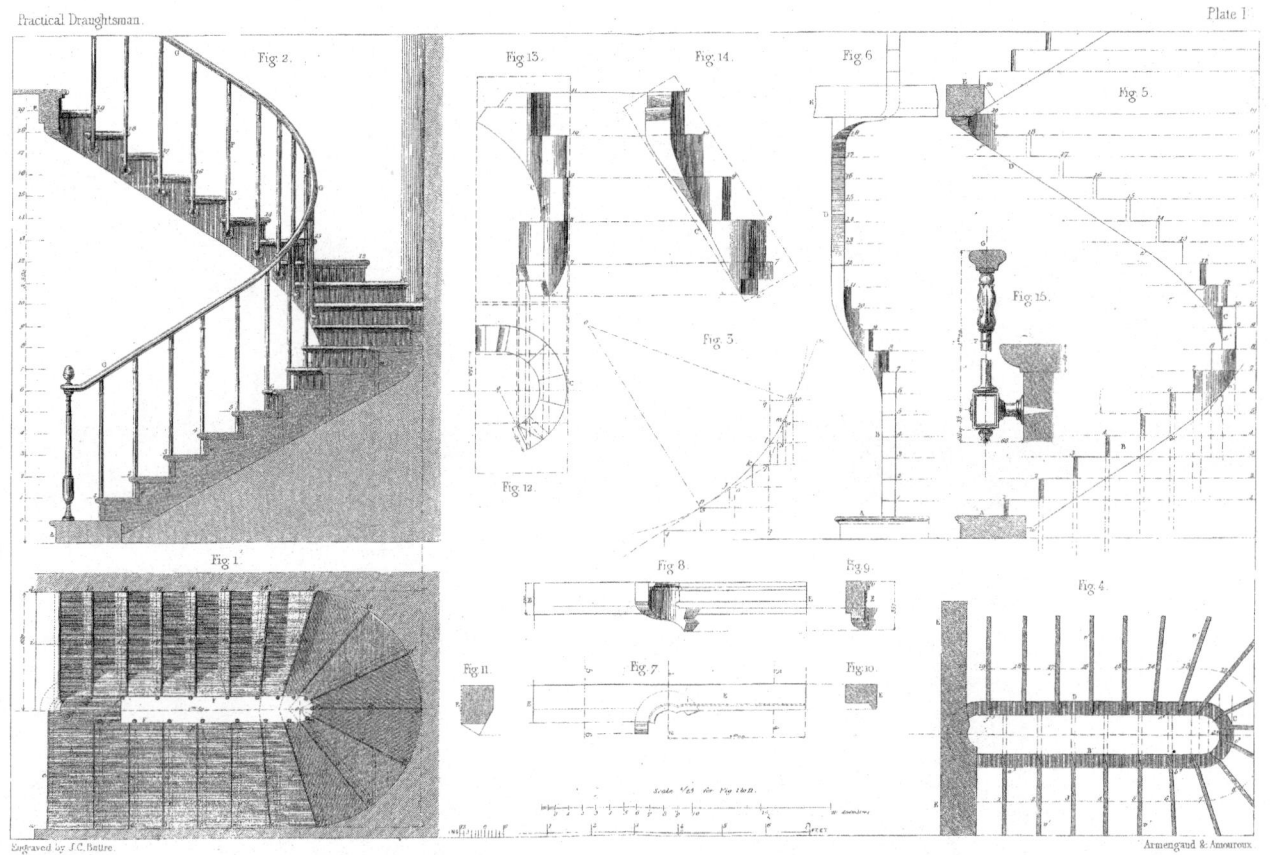

Fig. 2.

Fig. 13.

Fig. 14.

Fig. 6.

Fig. 5.

Fig. 3.

Fig. 15.

Fig. 12.

Fig. 1.

Fig. 8.

Fig. 9.

Fig. 11.

Fig. 7.

Fig. 10.

Fig. 4.

Scale 1/48 for Fig. 1&11.

Plate 17

Fig. 1''

Fig. 1'

Fig. 2'

Fig. 2''

Fig. 1

Fig. 5''

Fig. 5'

Fig. 2'''

Fig. 2''

Fig. 5

Fig. 5'''

Fig. 2'

Fig. 2

Fig. 4

Fig. 6

Fig. 8

Fig. 6''

Fig. 10

Fig. 4''

Fig. 5

Fig. 7

Fig. 9

Fig. 12

Fig. 11

Plate 18

Fig 1.

Fig. 2

Fig 3.

Fig 4.

Fig 5.

Fig 6

Fig 7.

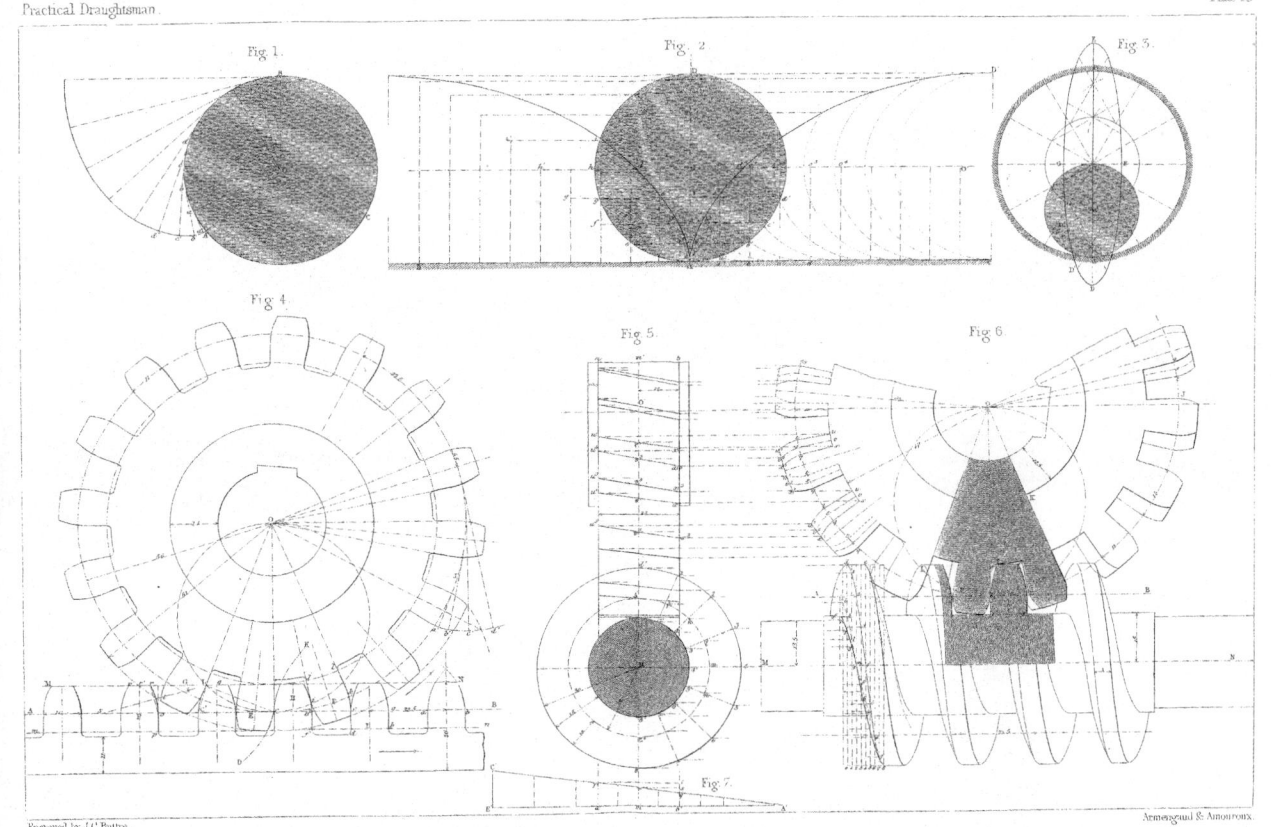

Plate 19

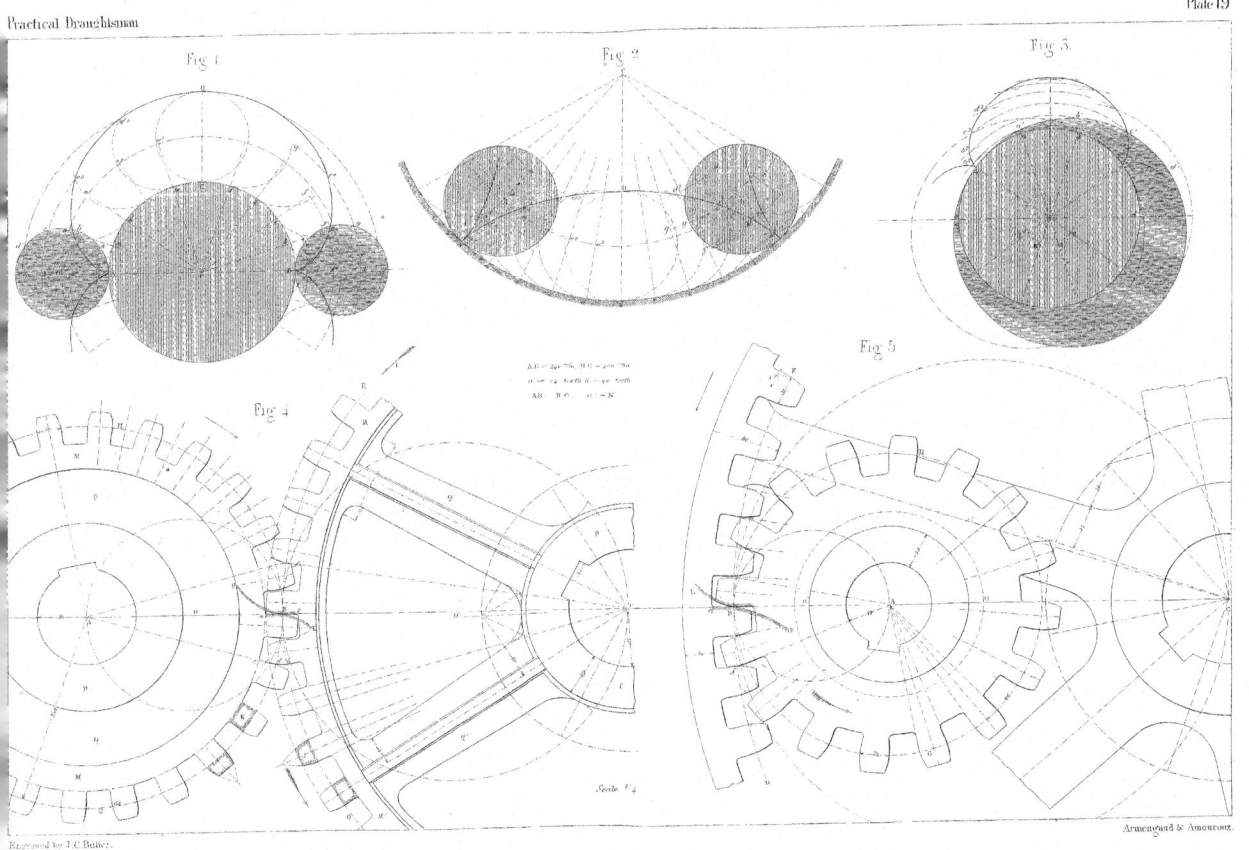

Plate 20

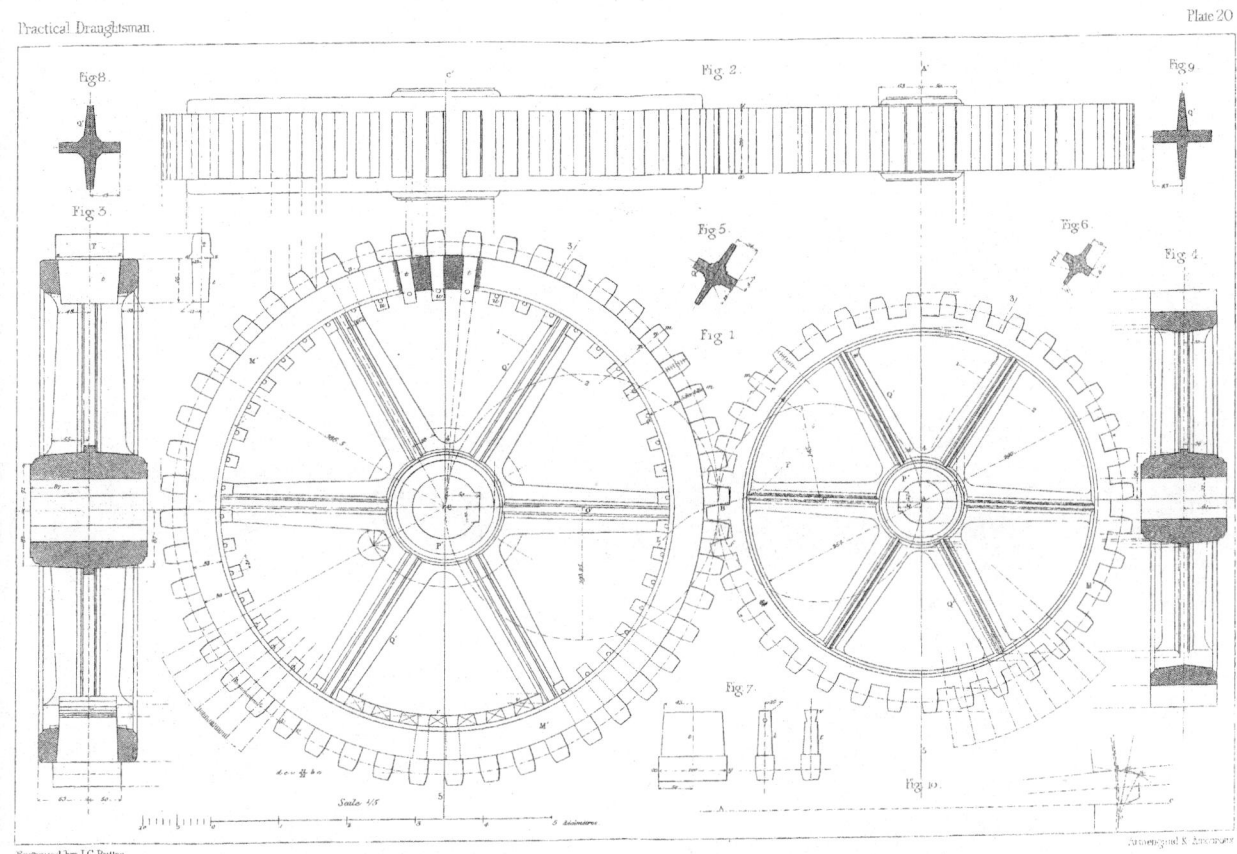

Fig 8.

Fig 2.

Fig 9.

Fig 3.

Fig 5.

Fig 6.

Fig 4.

Fig 1.

Fig 7.

Fig 10.

Scale 4/5.

Plate 29

Fig. 7

Fig. 10.

Fig. 3

Fig. 8.

Fig. 11.

Fig. 1.

Fig. 12

Fig. 13.

Fig. 6.

Fig. 2.

Fig. 5

Fig. 9.

Fig. 14.

Fig. 15.

Fig. 4

Scale ⅕ th

INS.

FEET

Engraved by J.C. Butler

Armengaud & Amoureux.

Plate 22

Fig. 5.   Fig. 5″   Fig. 1.   Fig. 2″   Fig. 2.   Fig. 6.

Fig. 5.

Fig. 3.

Fig. 4.

Fig. 7.

Fig. 8.

Scale

Scale

Plate 23

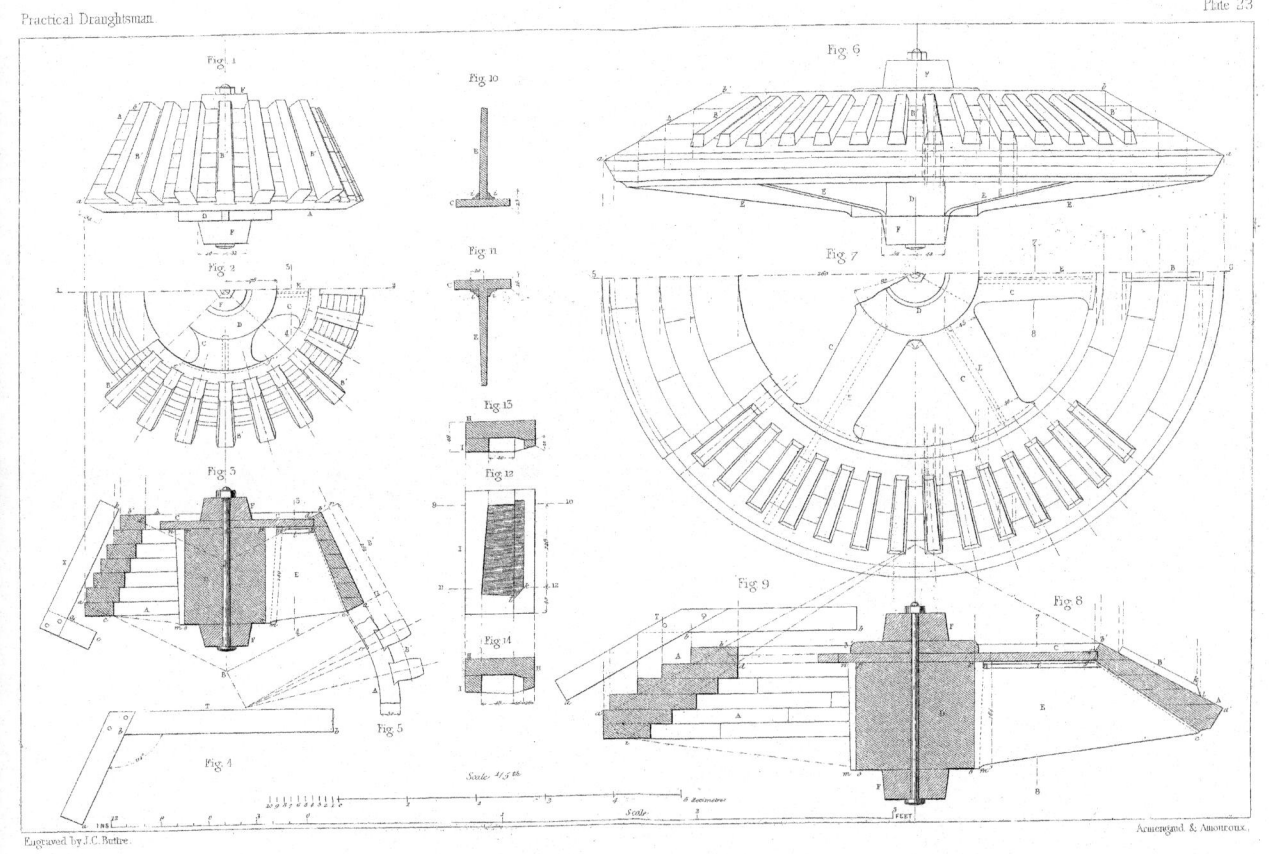

Fig 1

Fig 10

Fig 6

Fig 2

Fig 11

Fig 7

Fig 3

Fig 15

Fig 5

Fig 12

Fig 9

Fig 8

Fig 4

Fig 14

Fig 5

Scale: 1/5 th.

Scale

Plate 24.

Fig. 5

Fig. 4.

Fig. 2.

Fig. 1.

Fig. 3.

Fig. 6.

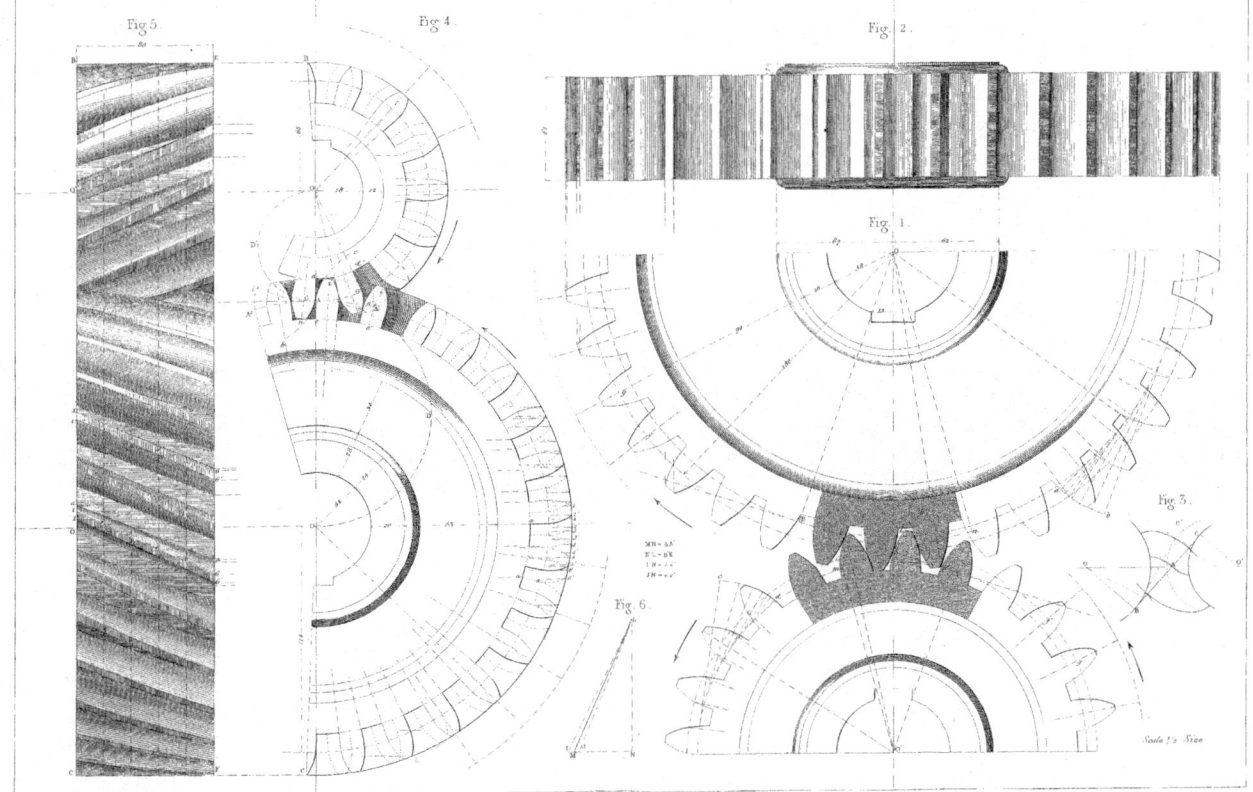

Engraved by J.C.Buttre.

Armengaud & Amoureux.

Plate 25

Fig B   Fig A   Fig 1   Fig D   Fig F   Fig E

Fig C   Fig G   Fig B

Fig 4   Fig 2   Fig 6

Fig 5   Fig 3   Fig 7   Fig 9

Plate 26

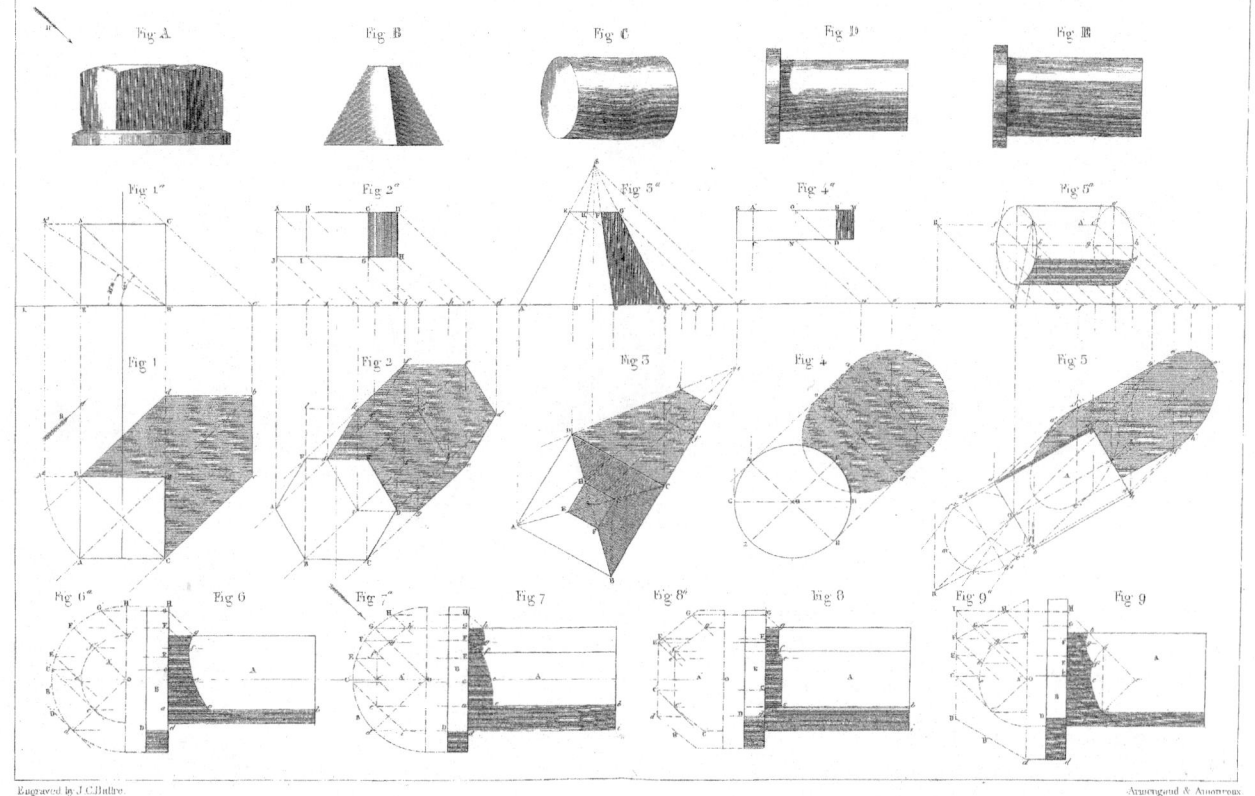

Fig A. Fig B. Fig C. Fig D. Fig E.

Fig 1'' Fig 2'' Fig 3'' Fig 4'' Fig 5''

Fig 1 Fig 2 Fig 3 Fig 4 Fig 5

Fig 6'' Fig 6 Fig 7'' Fig 7 Fig 8'' Fig 8 Fig 9'' Fig 9

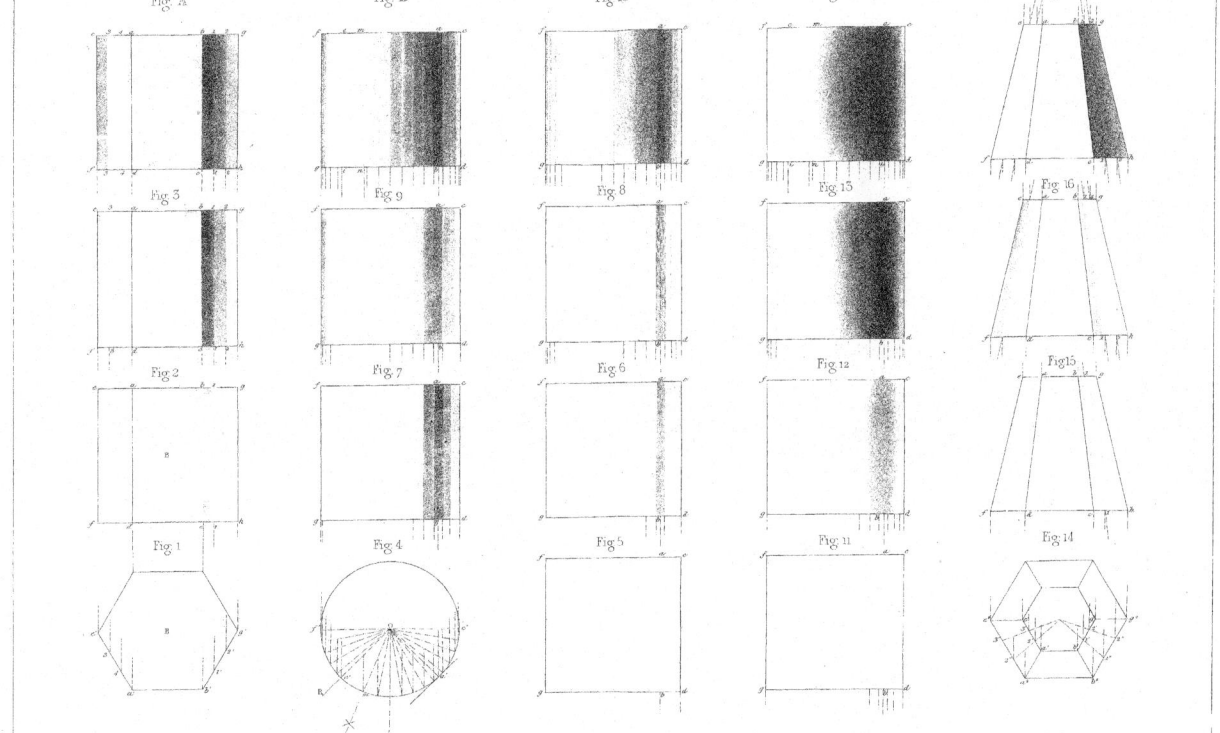

Fig. A   Fig. B   Fig. 10   Fig. C   Fig. D

Fig. 3   Fig. 9   Fig. 8   Fig. 13   Fig. 16

Fig. 2   Fig. 7   Fig. 6   Fig. 12   Fig.15

Fig. 1   Fig. 4   Fig. 5   Fig. 11   Fig. 14

Plate 28

Fig A. Fig B. Fig C. Fig D. Fig E. Fig F.

Fig 1″ Fig 2″ Fig 3″ Fig 4″ Fig 5″

Fig 4

Fig 5

Fig 1 Fig 2 Fig 3

STUDY OF SHADING.

Plate 29

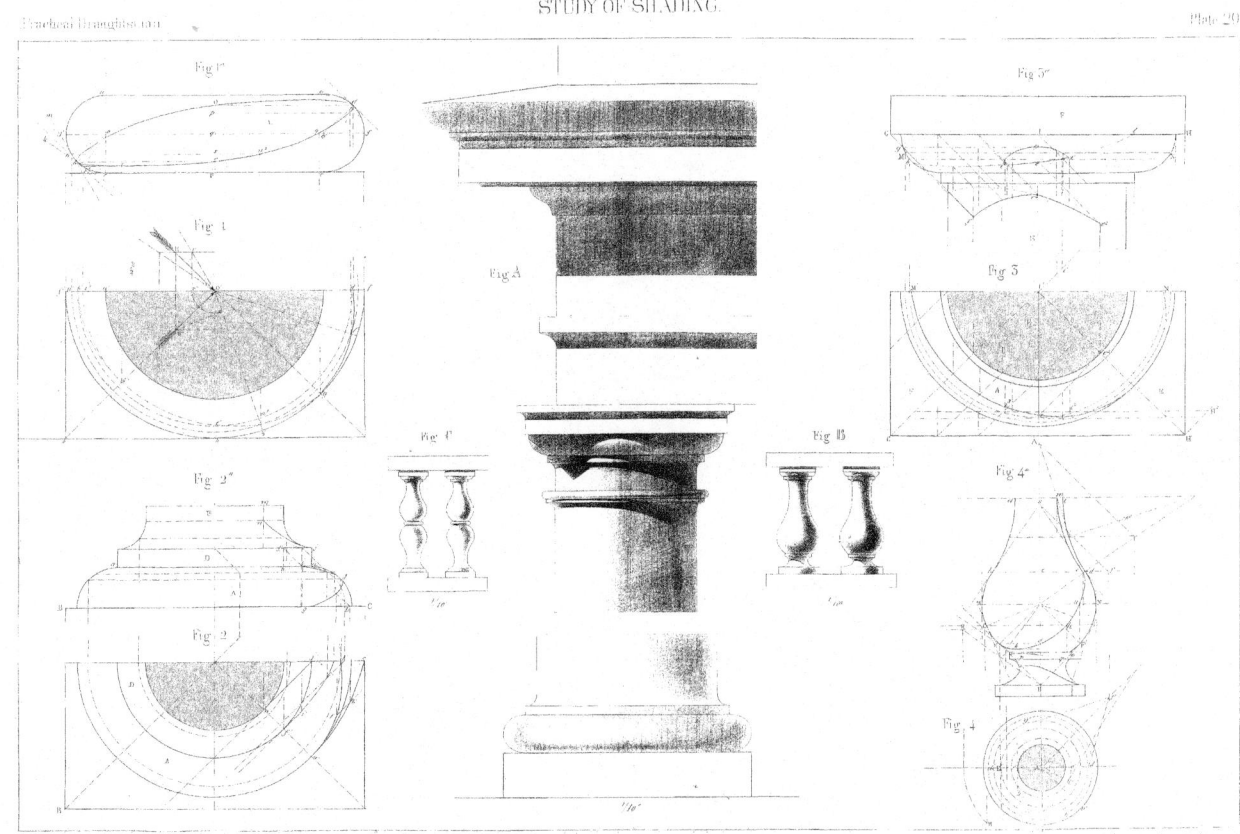

Fig 1"

Fig 1

Fig 2"

Fig 2

Fig C

Fig A

Fig B

Fig 5"

Fig 5

Fig 4"

Fig 4

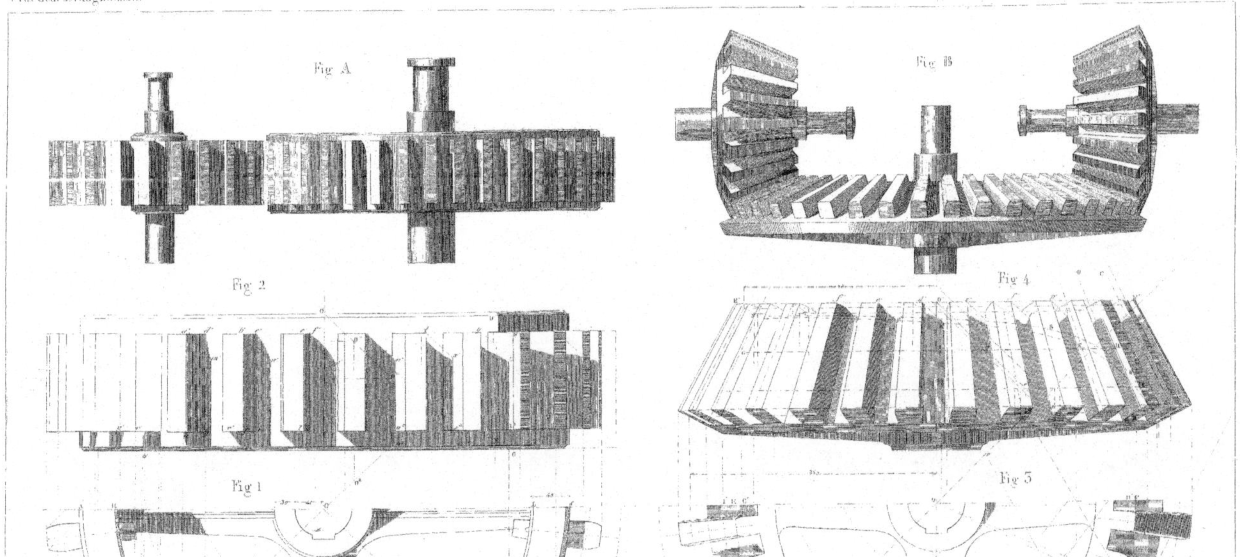
Fig. A
Fig. B
Fig. 2
Fig. 4
Fig. 1
Fig. 3
Scale 1/5
Scale

Engraved by J.C. Buttre. Armengaud & Amouroux

Plate 31

Fig 5

Fig 10

Fig 1

Fig 2

Fig 2″

Fig 3

Fig 10″

Fig 4

Fig 7

Fig 6

Fig 6″

Fig 8

Fig 9

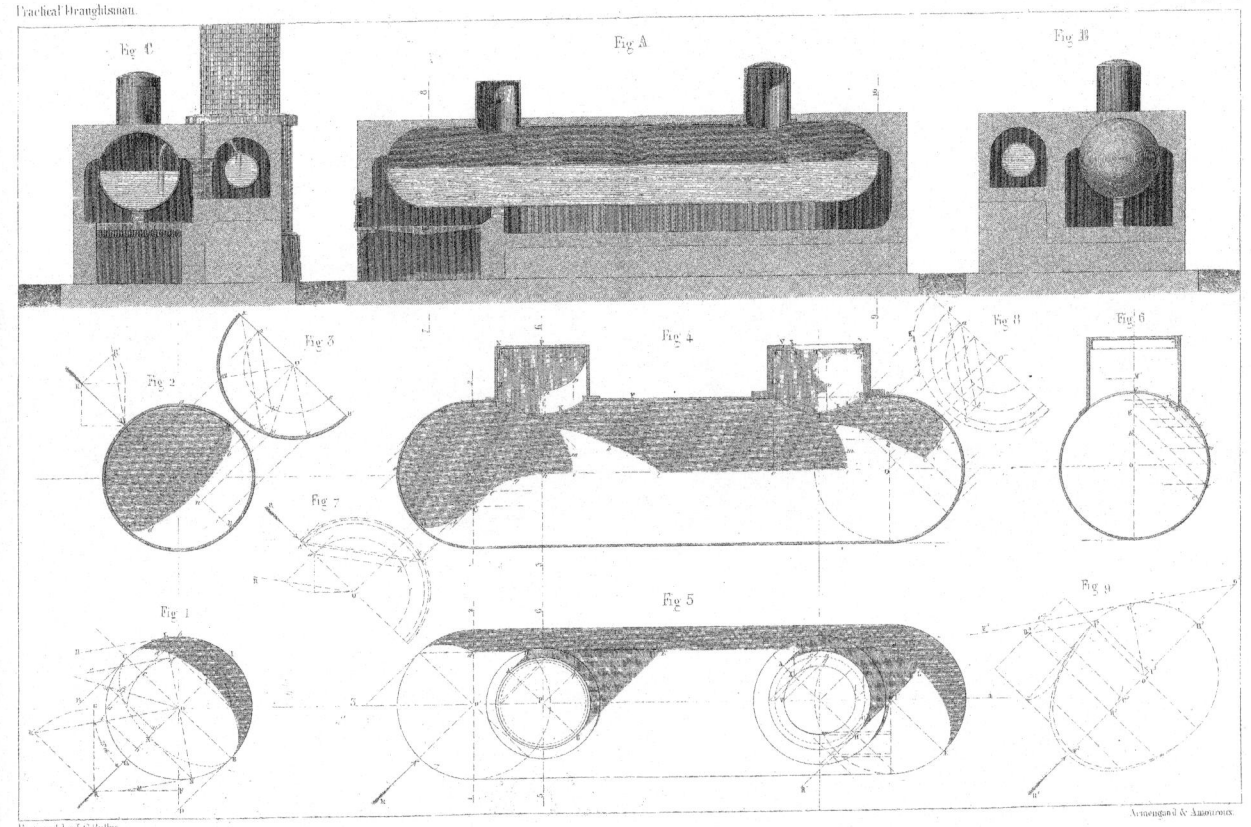

Plate 32

Fig C.

Fig A.

Fig B.

Fig 2.

Fig 3.

Fig 4.

Fig 8.

Fig 6.

Fig 7.

Fig 1.

Fig 5.

Fig 9.

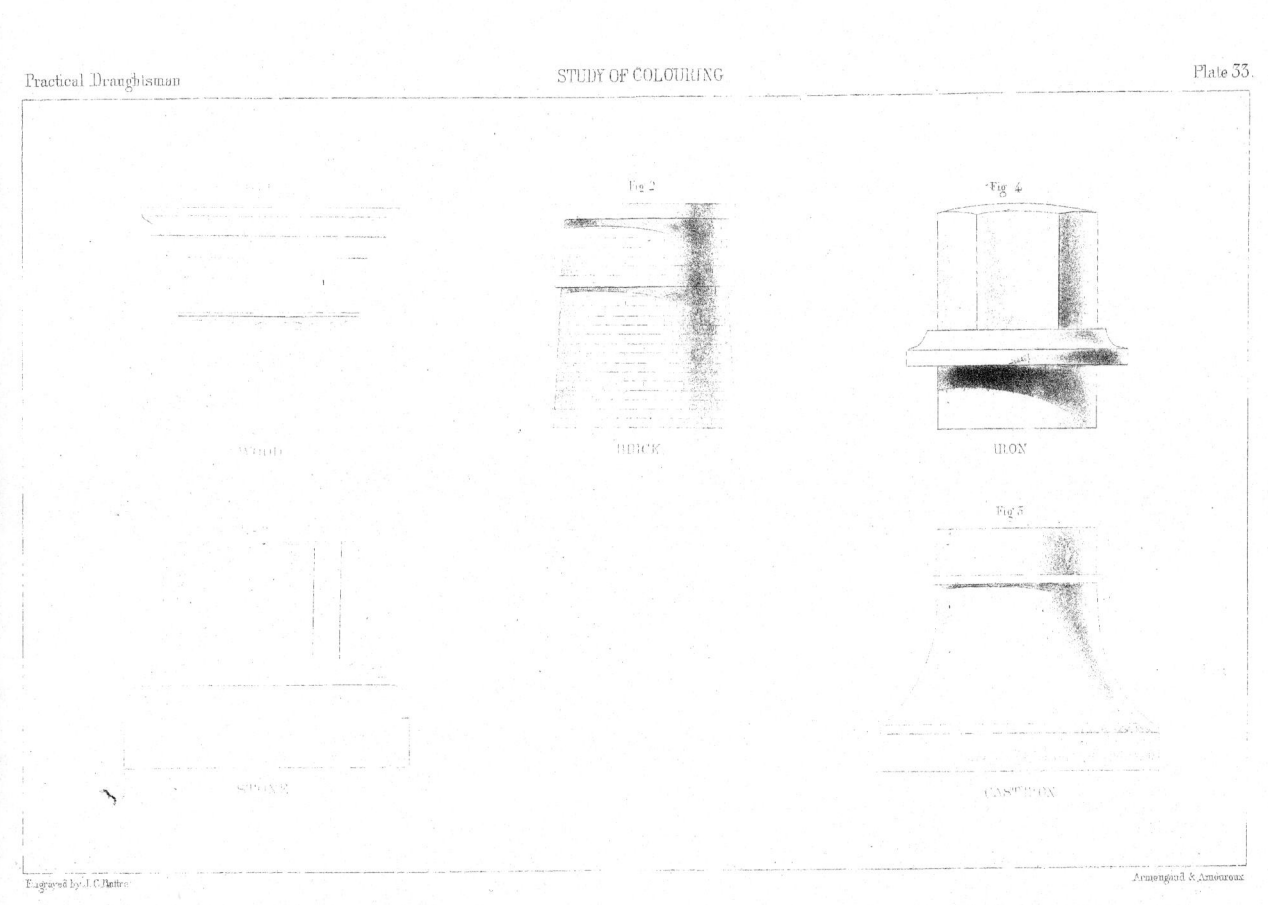

Fig 1

Fig 2

Fig 4

Fig 3

WOOD

BRICK

IRON

STONE

CAST IRON

Plate 34

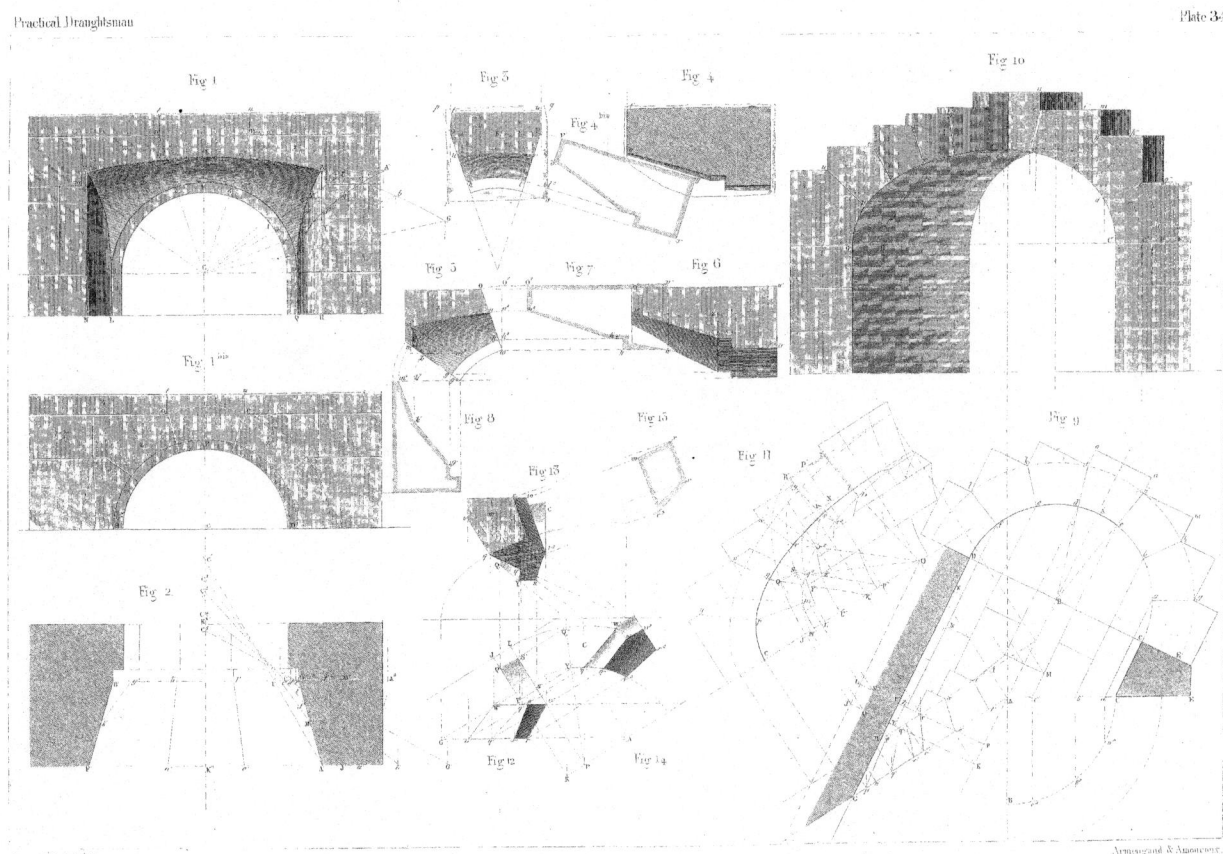

Fig 1

Fig 3

Fig 4

Fig 4 bis

Fig 10

Fig 1 bis

Fig 5

Fig 7

Fig 6

Fig 2

Fig 8

Fig 13

Fig 13

Fig 11

Fig 9

Fig 12

Fig 14

Plate 35

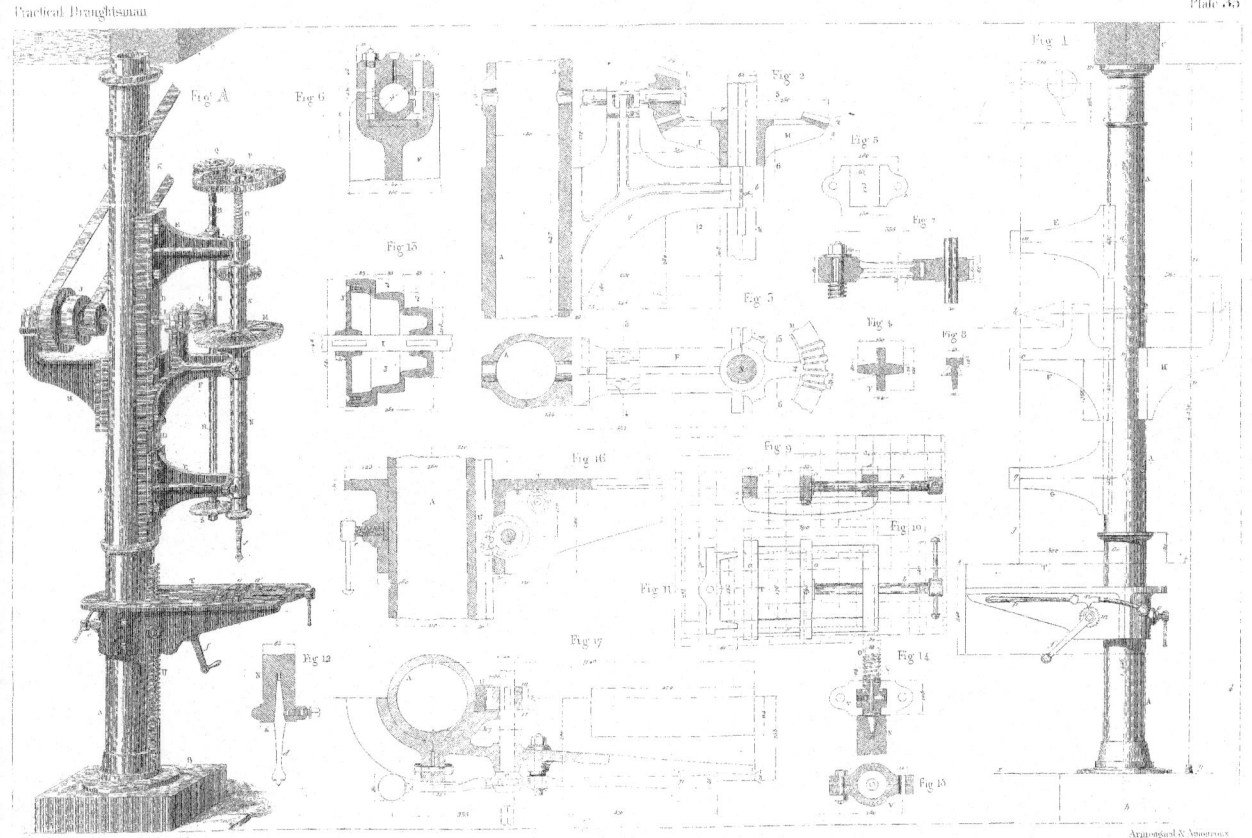

Fig. A
Fig. 6
Fig. 2
Fig. 3
Fig. 5
Fig. 7
Fig. 1
Fig. 13
Fig. 5
Fig. 4
Fig. 8
Fig. 16
Fig. 9
Fig. 10
Fig. 11
Fig. 12
Fig. 17
Fig. 14
Fig. 15

Plate 36

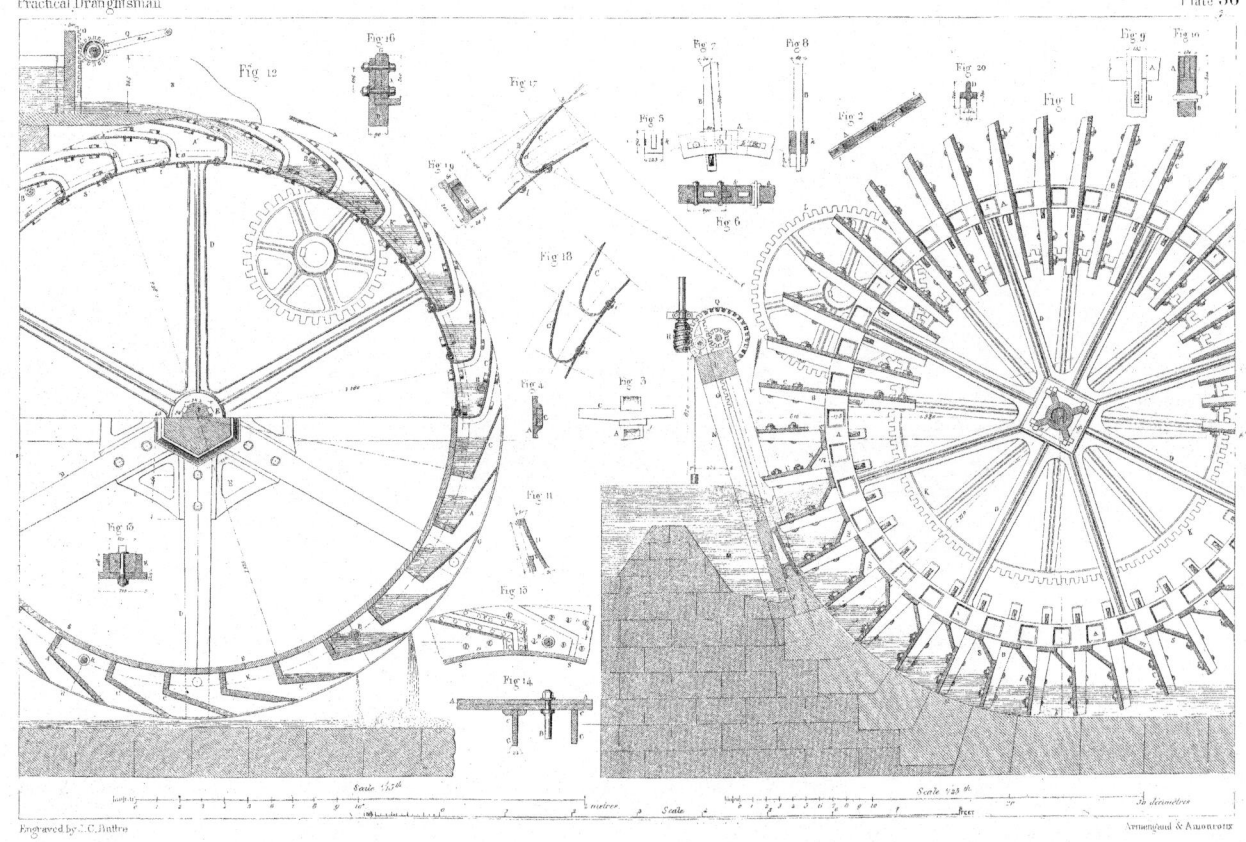

Fig 12

Fig 16

Fig 17

Fig 7

Fig 8

Fig 9

Fig 10

Fig 5

Fig 2

Fig 20

Fig 1

Fig 19

Fig 6

Fig 18

Fig 4

Fig 3

Fig 15

Fig 11

Fig 13

Fig 14

Scale 1/25th

Scale 1/25th

Scale

Plate 37

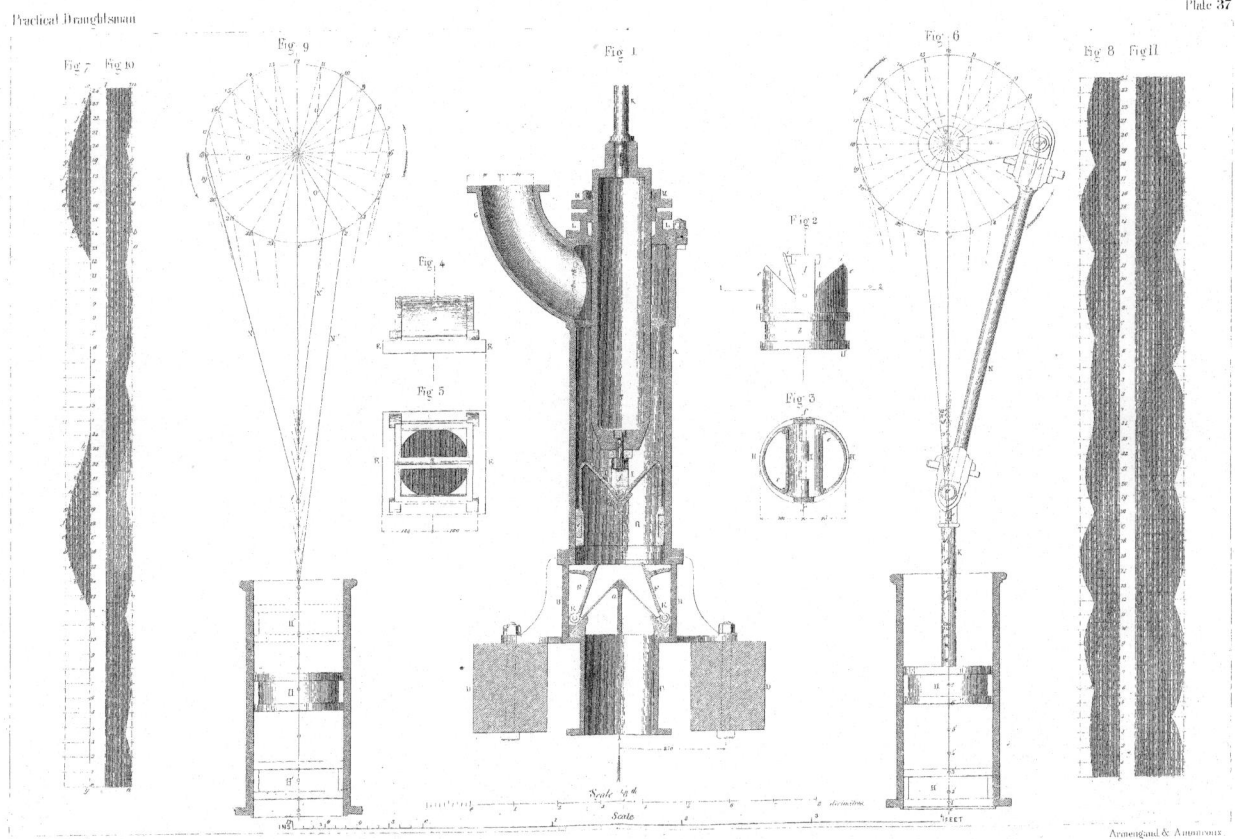

Fig 7   Fig 10   Fig 9   Fig 1   Fig 6   Fig 8   Fig 11

Fig 4

Fig 2

Fig 5

Fig 3

Scale

Scale

FEET

Engraved by J.C. Buttre.

Armengaud & Amoureux.

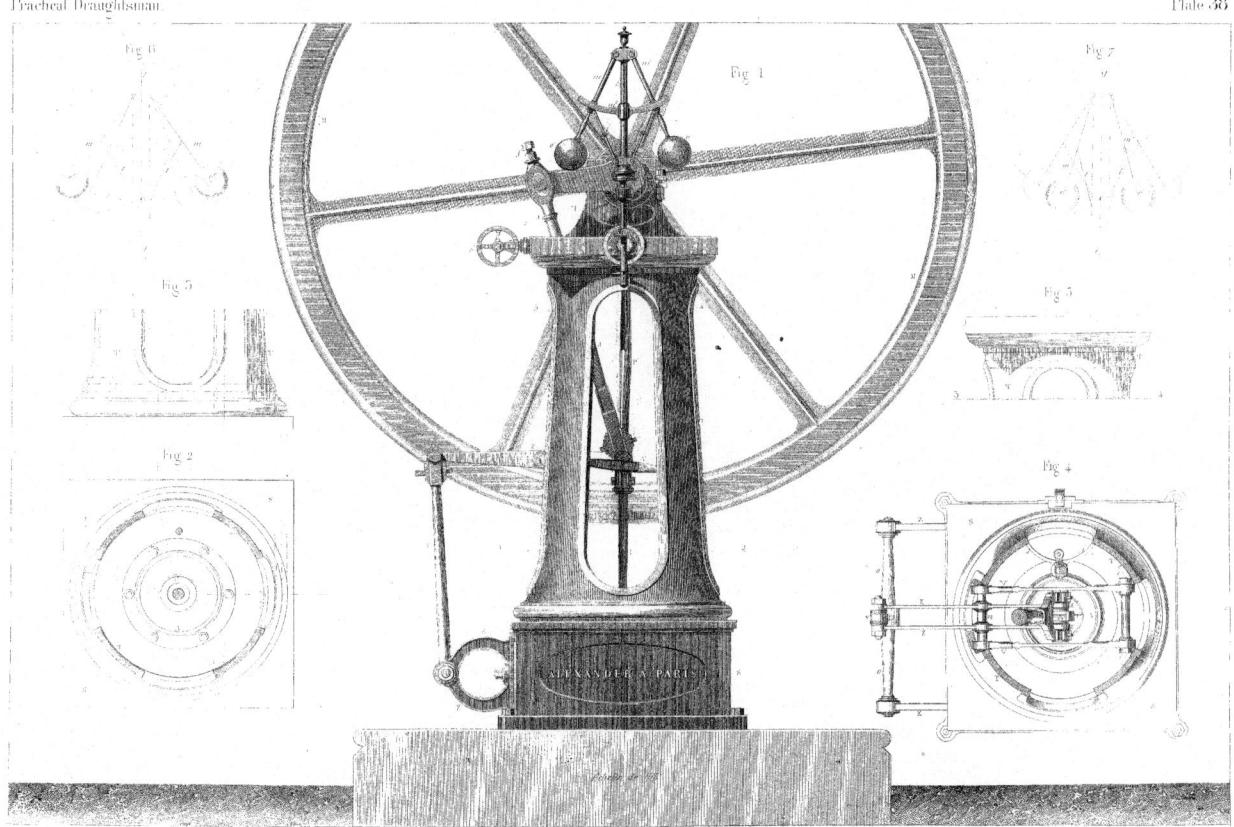

Fig 6

Fig 1

Fig 7

Fig 5

Fig 3

Fig 2

Fig 4

ALEXANDER A PARIS

Plate 39

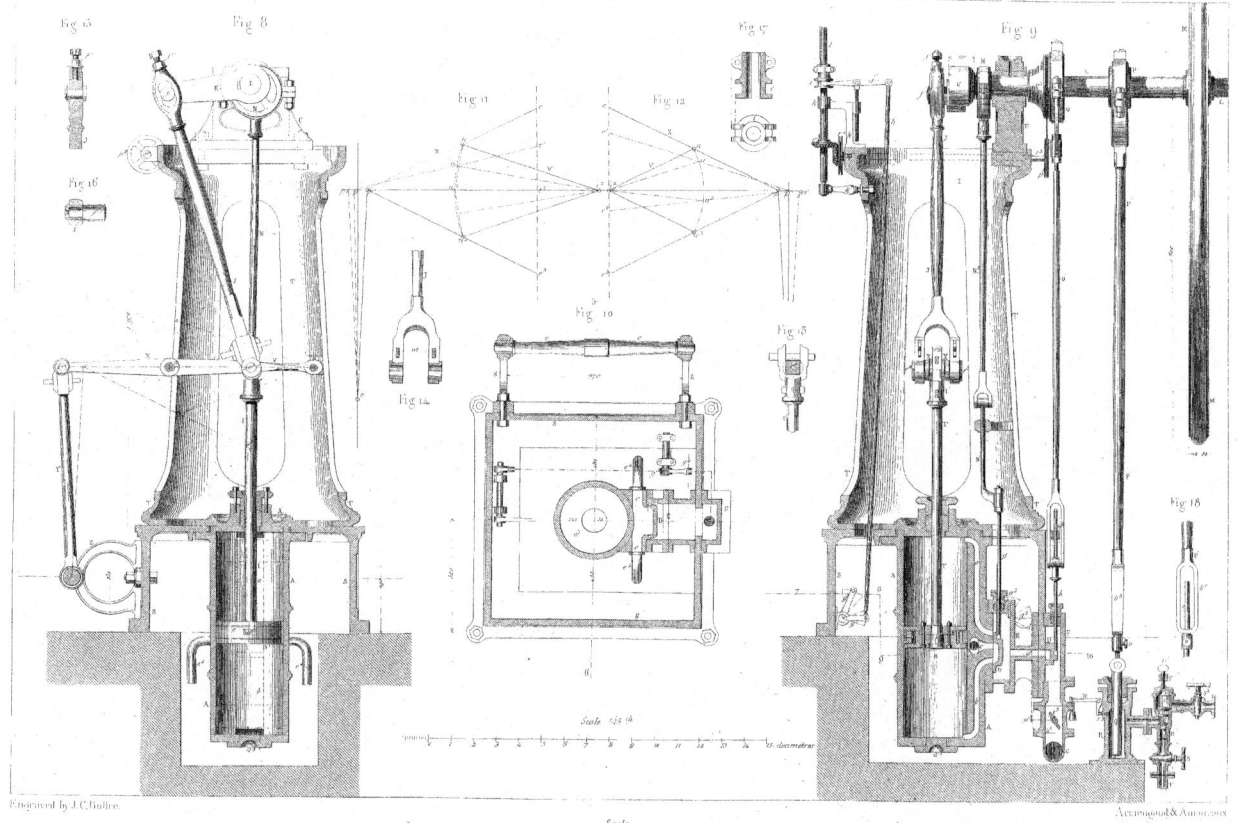

Fig 15.

Fig 8.

Fig 16.

Fig 11.

Fig 12.

Fig 17.

Fig 9.

Fig 10.

Fig 13.

Fig 14.

Fig 18.

Scale

INS FEET

Scale

Plate 40

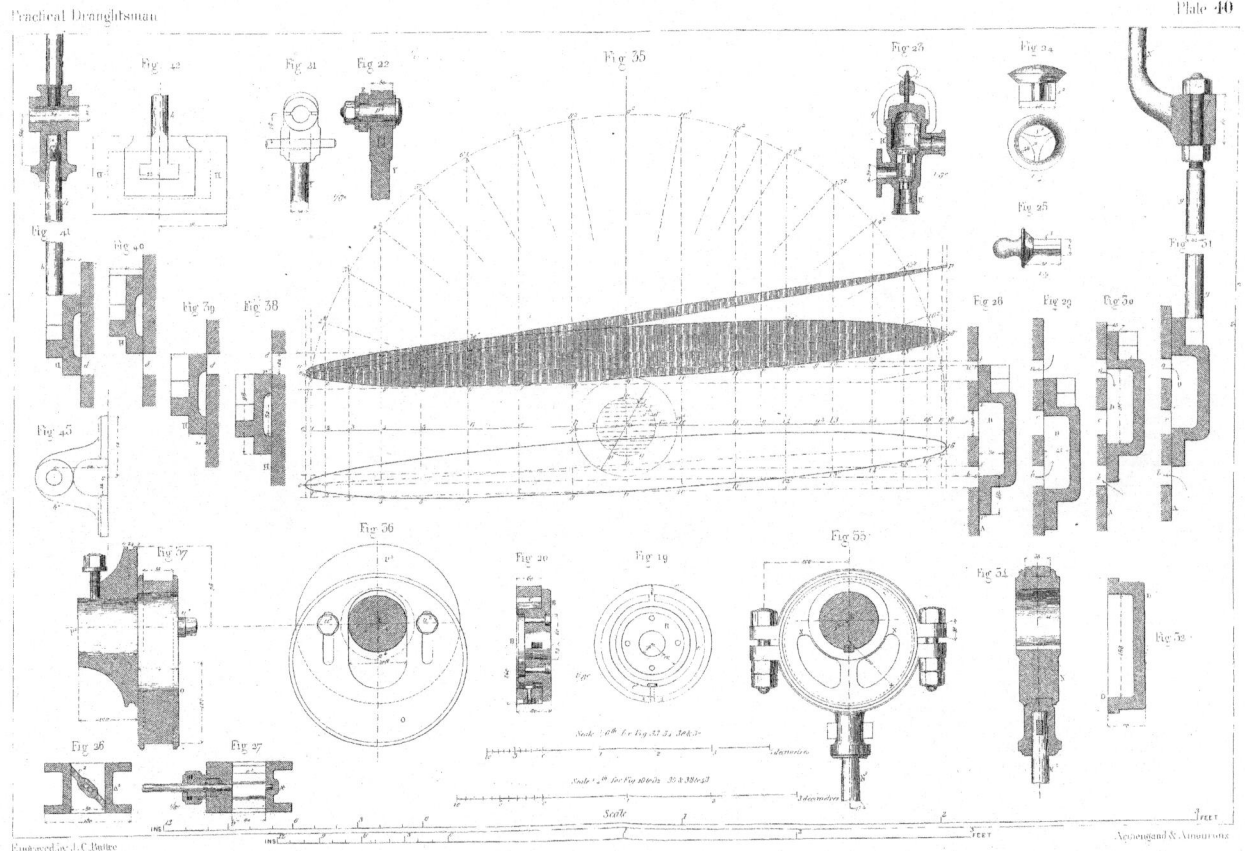

Plate 44

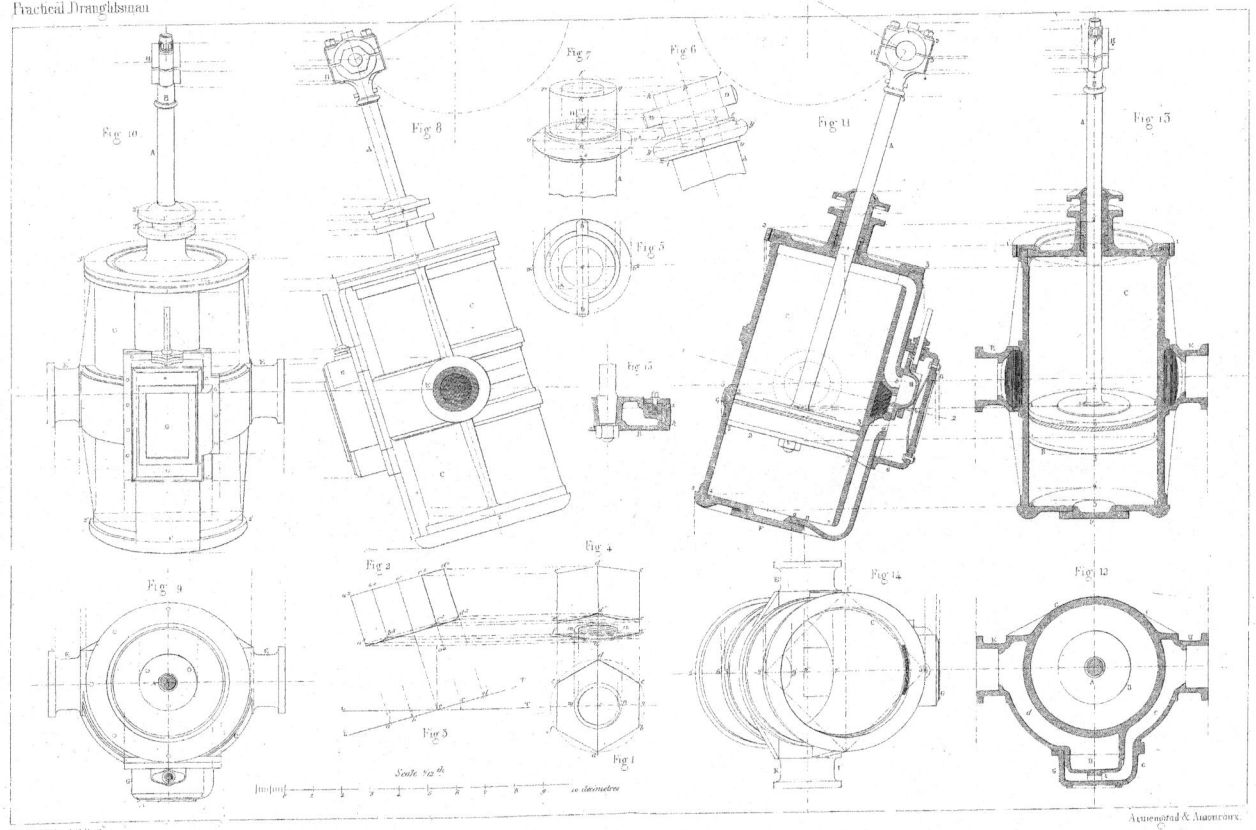

Plate 42

Fig A   Fig B   Fig C   Fig D   Fig E

Fig 4   Fig 6   Fig 7   Fig 9   Fig 11

Fig 5   Fig 5   Fig 1   Fig 12   Fig 13

               Fig 2   Fig 8   Fig 10

Plate 43

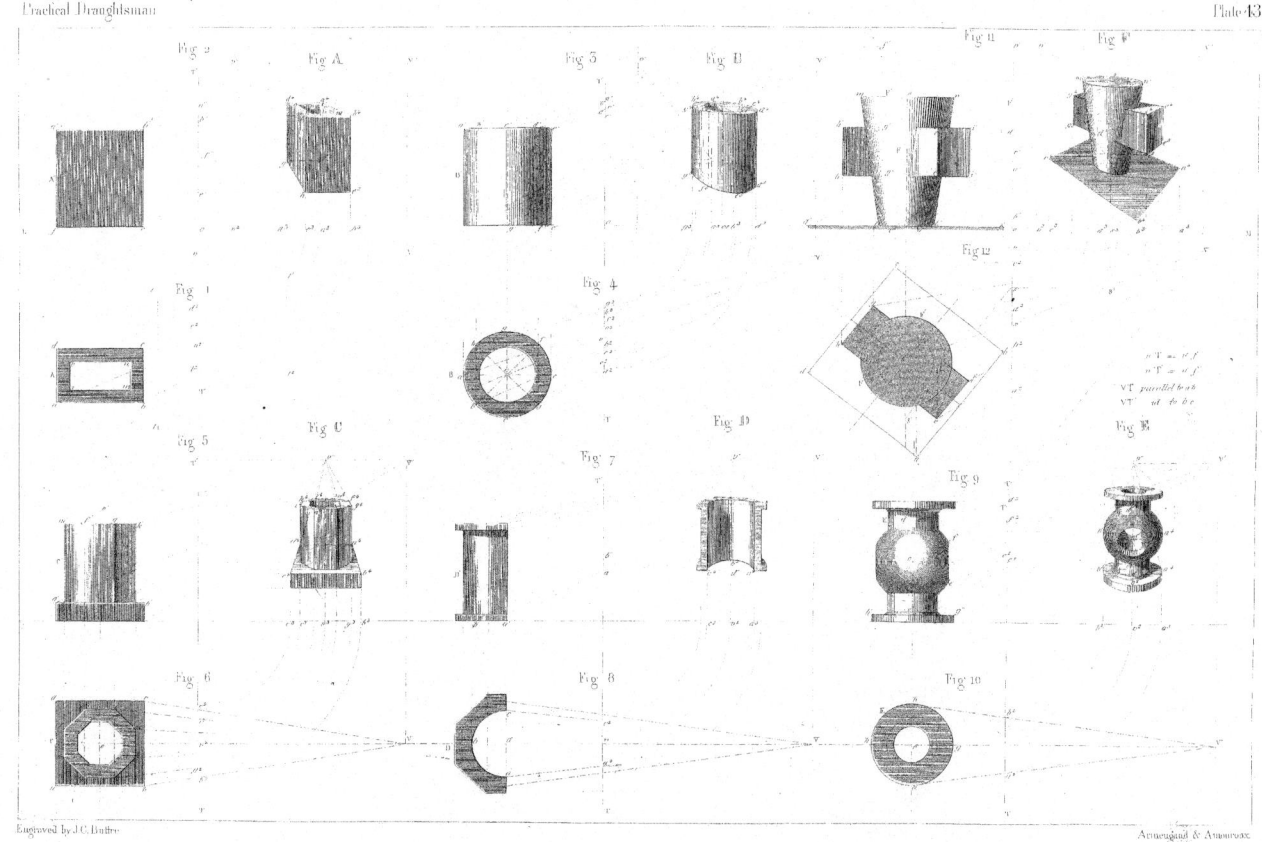

Plate 44

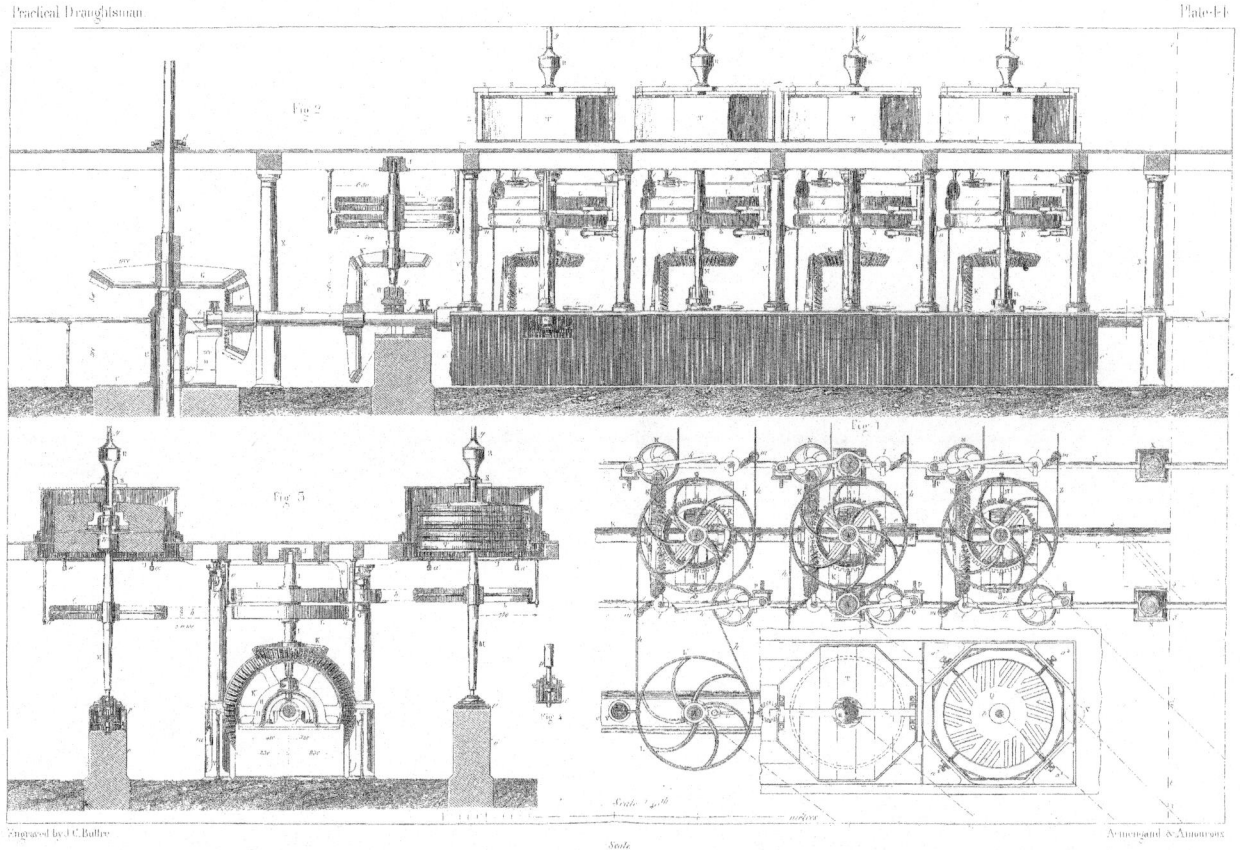

Plate 45

Fig 6

Fig 5

WATER METER.

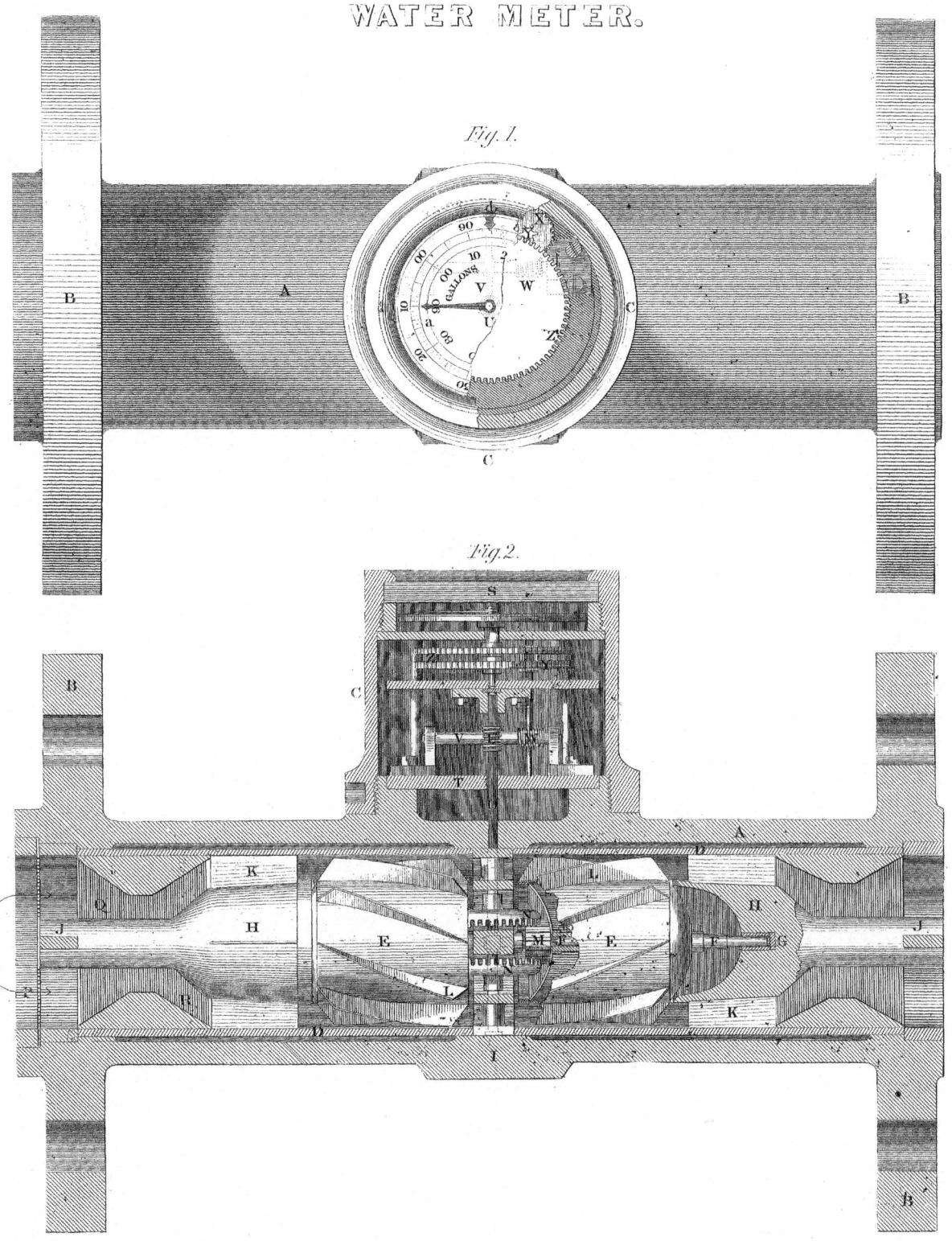

Fig. 1.

Fig. 2.

ENGINEER'S SHAPING MACHINE.

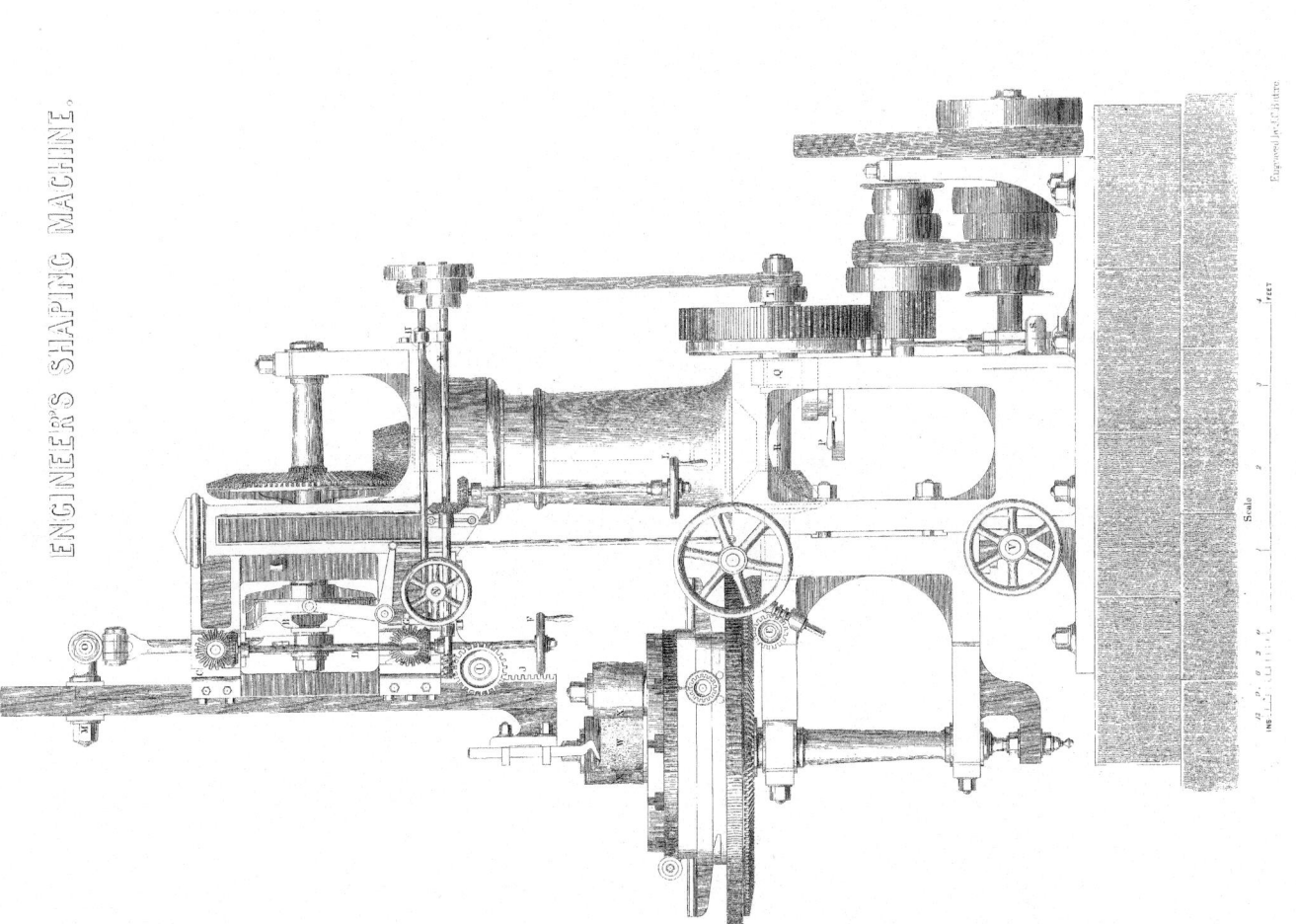

Scale

Engraved by J.C. Buttre

EXPRESS   LOCOMOTIVE.

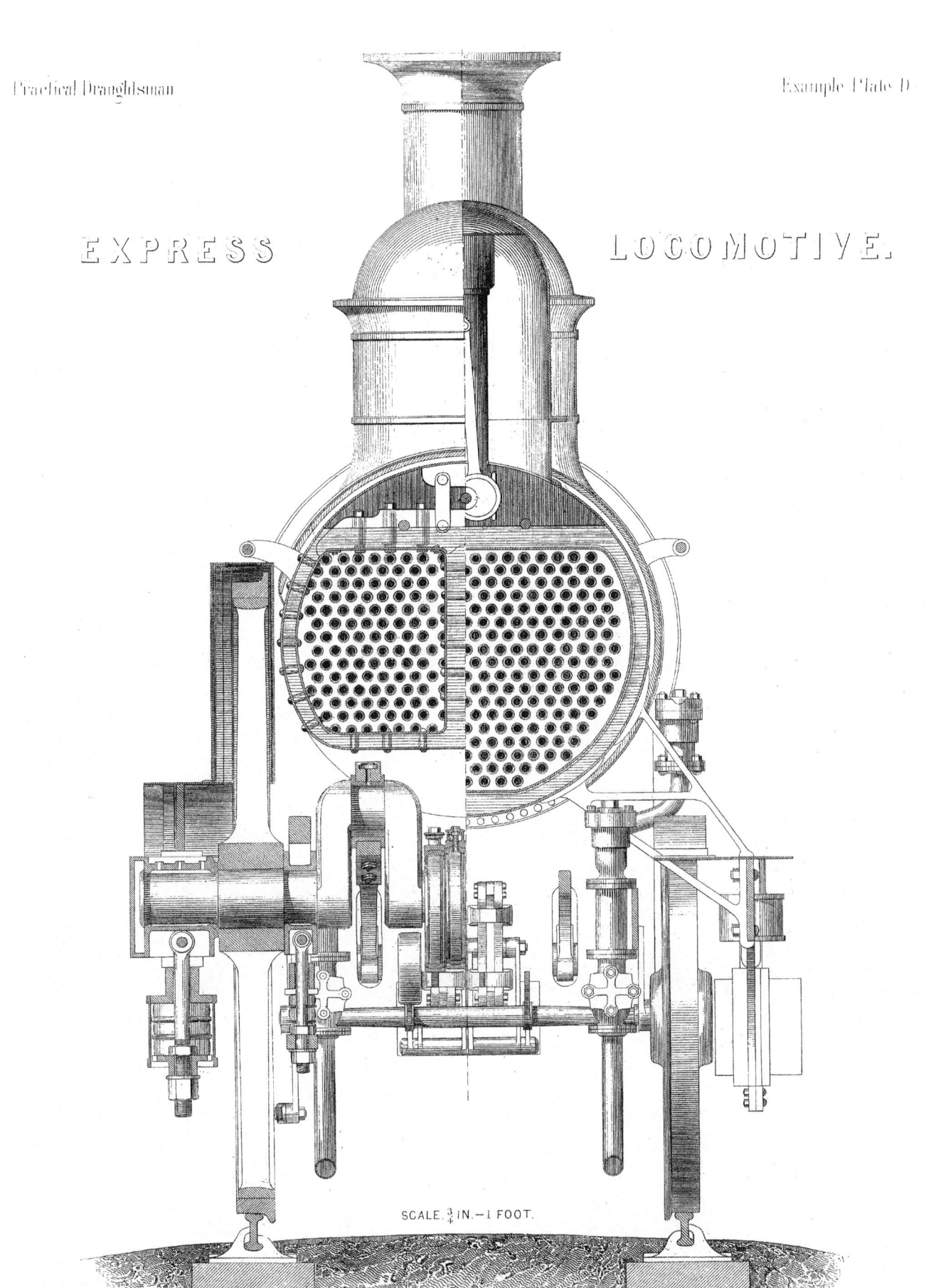

SCALE. $\frac{3}{4}$ IN.—1 FOOT.

Engraved by J.C.Bu

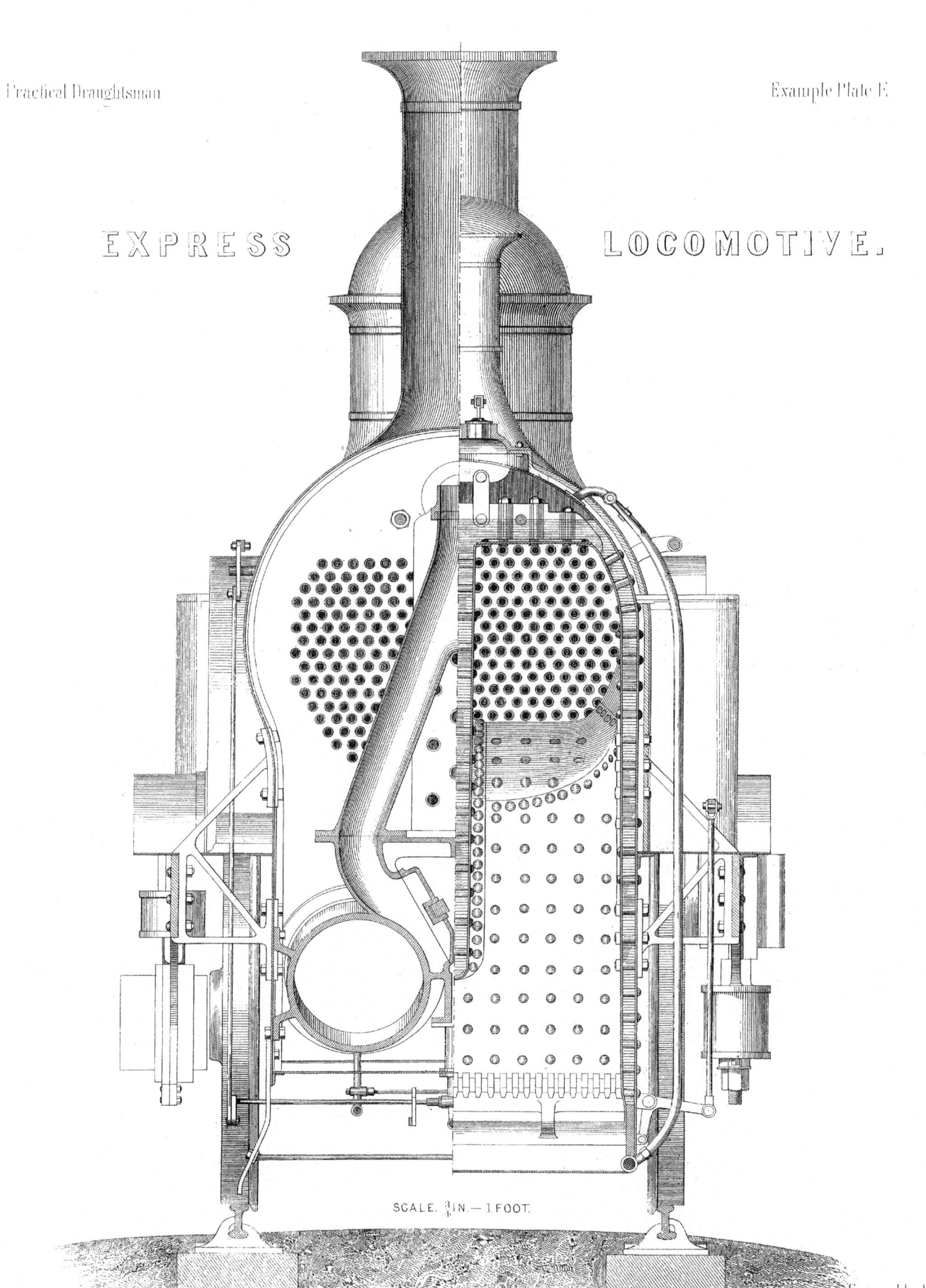

EXPRESS   LOCOMOTIVE.

SCALE. ⅜IN.— 1 FOOT.

Engraved by J.C.Bul

al Draughtsman.

Fig 1

Fig 2

Engraved by J.C.Buller.

Scale

WASHING MACHINE FOR TEXTILE FABRICS.

Fig. 1

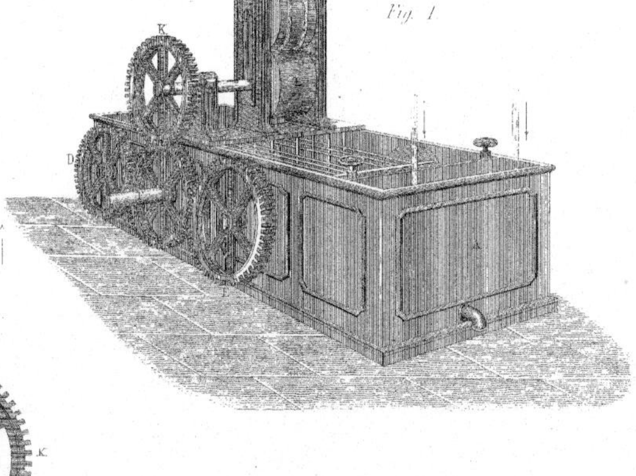

Fig. 2

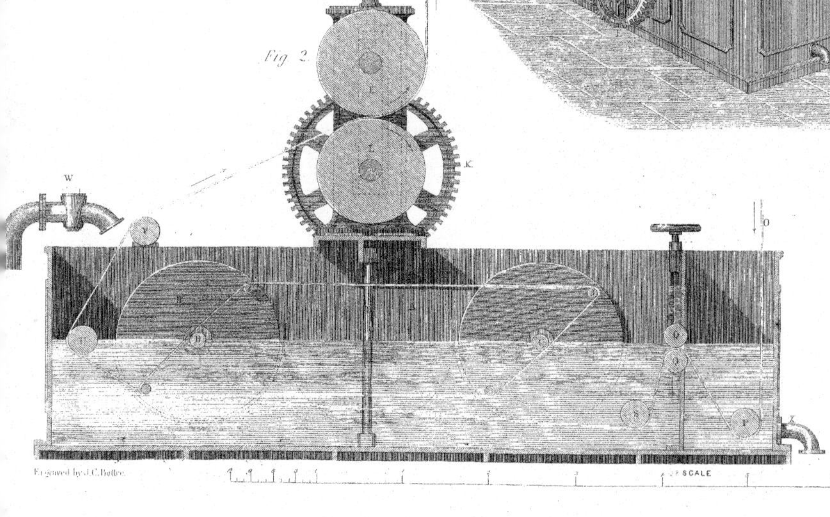

Fig. 3

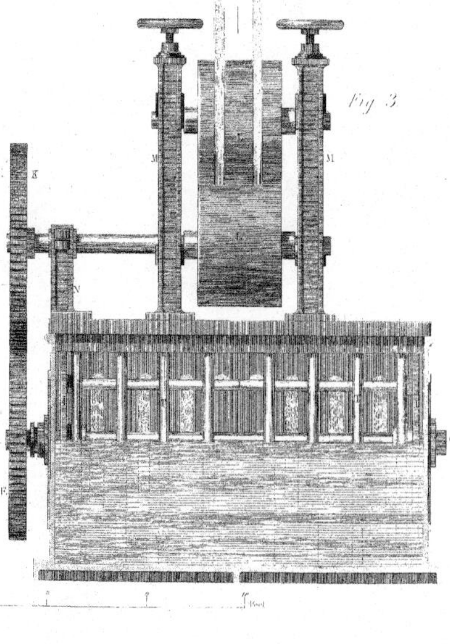

Engraved by J.C. Bellee.

SCALE

Feet

POWER-LOOM.

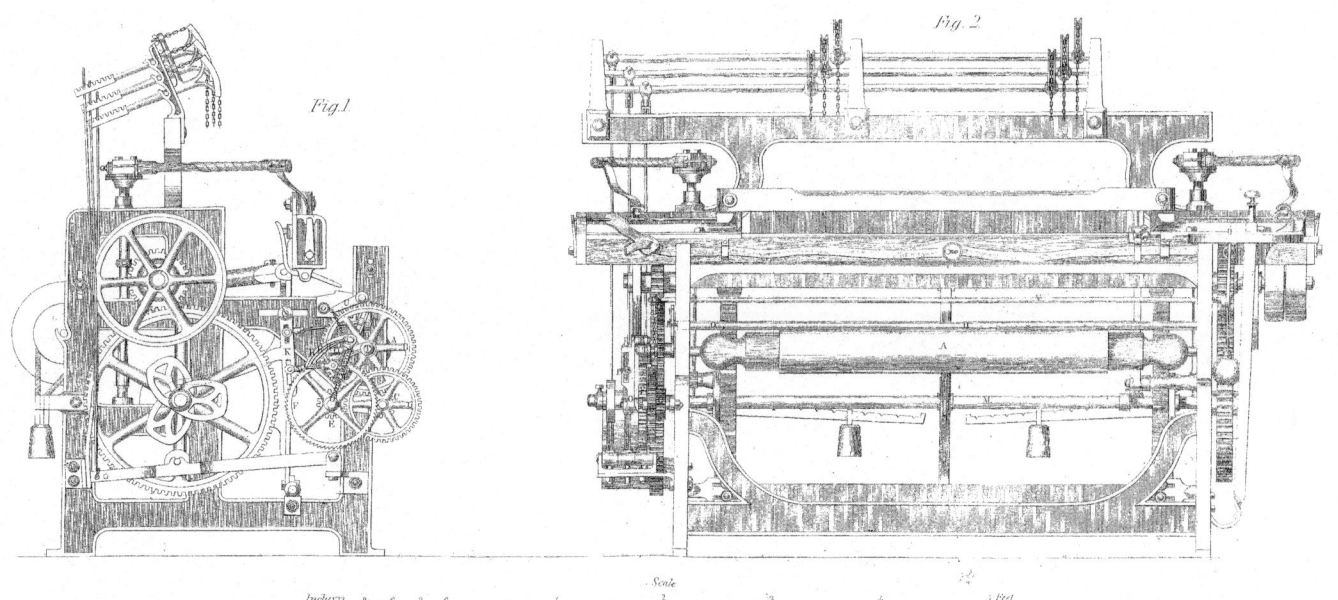

Fig.1.

Fig.2

Inches 12   0   9   6   3   0   Scale   1   2   3   4   5 Feet

DUPLEX STEAM BOILER.

Fig 1.

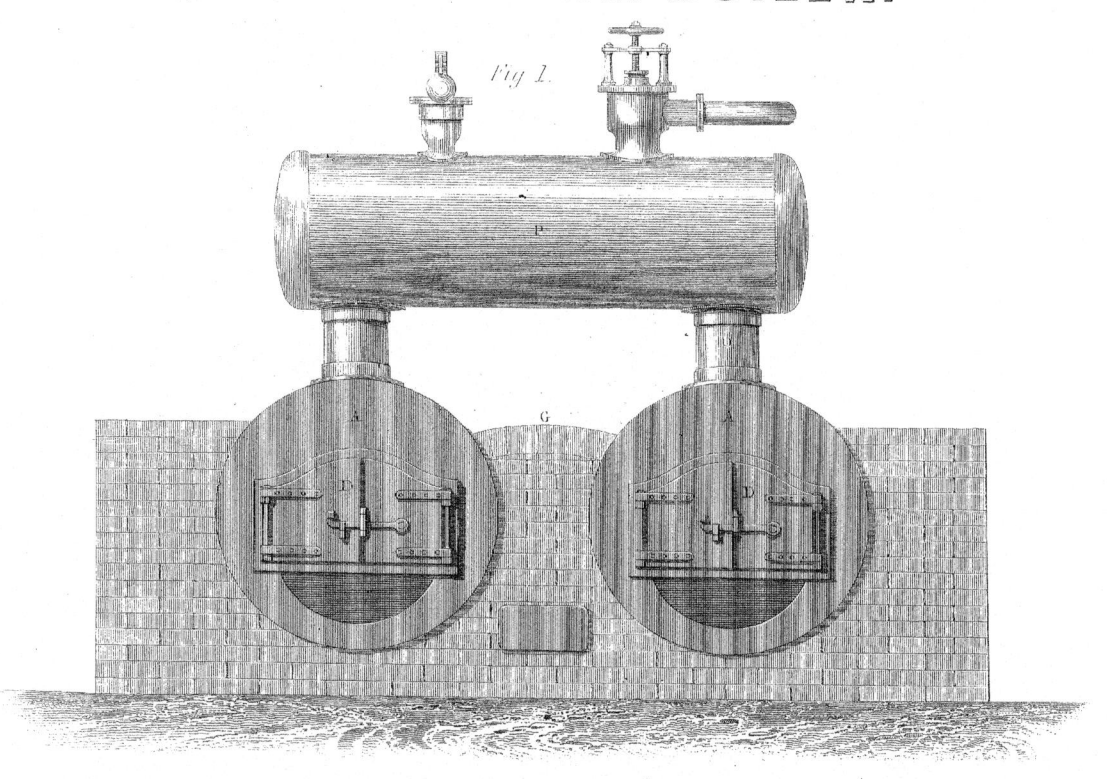

Fig 2.

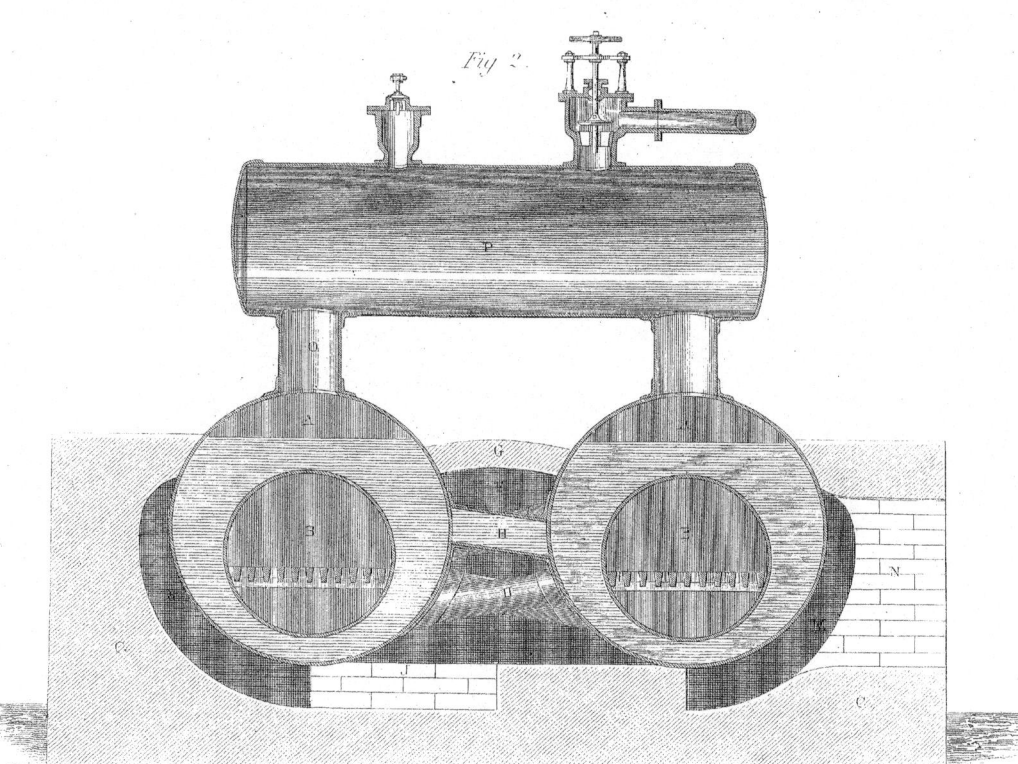

Engraved by J.C.Bultre

SCALE

Ins 12 6 1 5 1 Feet

DIRECT-ACTING MARINE ENGINES.

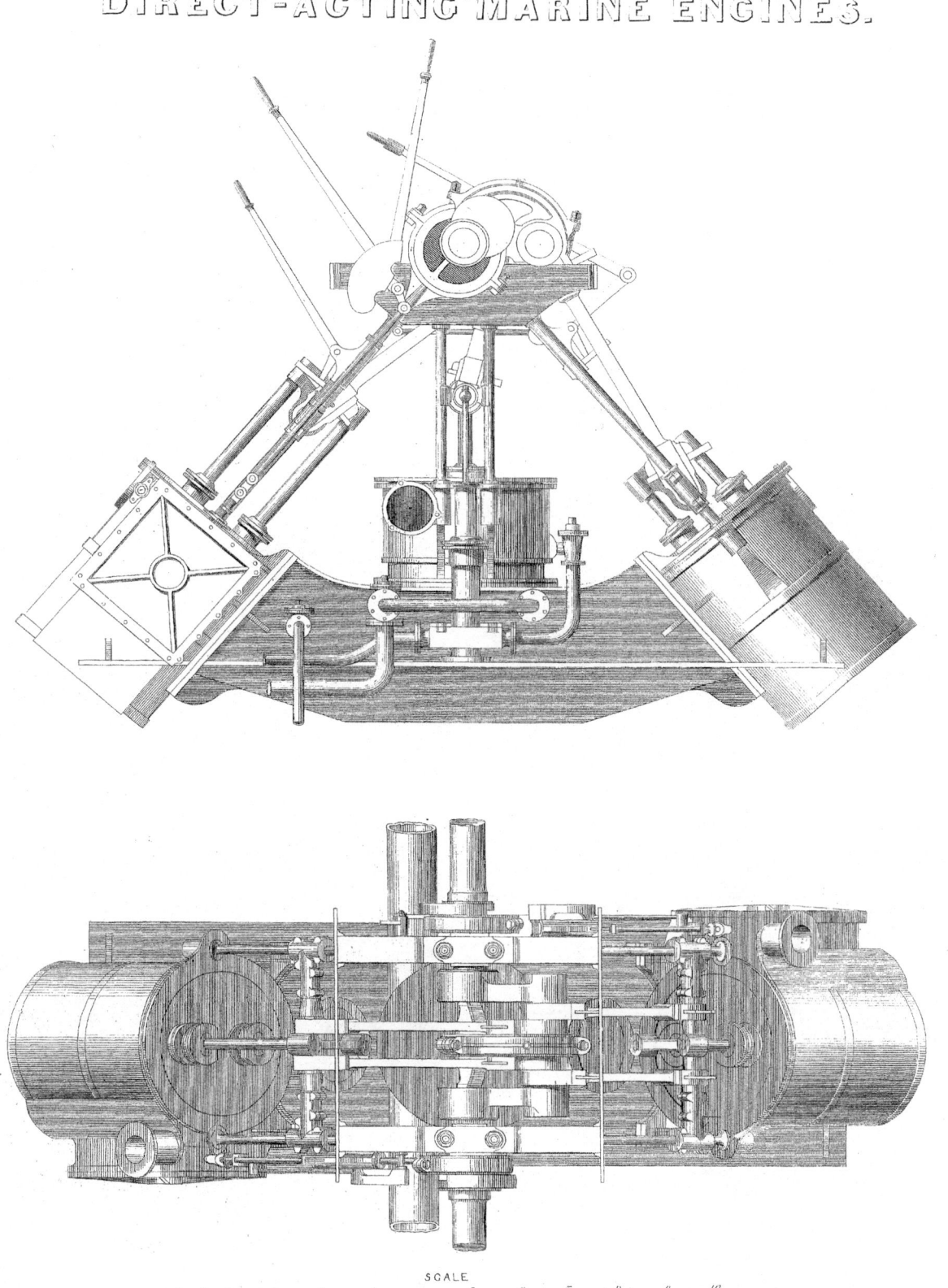

SCALE

Inches |........| 1 2 3 4 5 6 7 8 9 10 Feet

Printed in Dunstable, United Kingdom

82202493R00179